JACK THE RIPPER

=

NEWSPAPERS FROM HULL VOLUME 1

Copyright © 2015 Mike Covell

Layout Copyright © 2015 Creativia

Published 2015 by Creativia

Paperback design by Creativia (http://www.creativia.org)

ISBN: 978-1508554516

Cover art by http://www.thecovercollection.com

All rights reserved. No part of this book may be reproduced or transmitted in any form or by any means, electronic or mechanical, including photocopying, recording, or by any information storage and retrieval system, without the author's permission.

Contents

Introduction – A brief History of Kingston upon Hull

Notes about the Hull Police in 1888

The Hull Newspapers

    The Eastern Morning News and Hull Advertiser,

    The Hull News,

    The Hull Times,

    The Hull Daily News/Evening News,

    The Hull Daily Mail,

Information Gathering and the Hull Press

    News Agencies

    The Central News Agency

    The Press Association

    Correspondents

    Other Newspapers

    The Advent of the Telegraph and the Hull Press

    The Advent of the Telephone and the Hull Press

    The Advent of the Railway and the Hull Press

Stop the Press - An Introduction to the Newspaper Reports

    Notes about collection of the reports

    Notes about transcription of the reports

THE REPORTS 1879 – 1932

Stop the Press - Editors Comments

Appendix I   Currency

Appendix II   Police Districts – London

Appendix III   Hull Ripper Craze's 1888 – 1988

Appendix IV   Newspaper Reports featured

Bibliography and Further Reading

    Jack the Ripper General Reference

    Jack the Ripper – Press Associated

    Hull History

    Maps

    Acknowledgements

Mike Covell

Introduction – A brief History of Kingston upon Hull

I have always had an interest in the series of crimes known as the "Whitechapel Murders," and remember reading book after book on the series of unexplained murders when I was younger, always hungry for more information. In 2006, I was diagnosed with a heart condition and forced from work, with no future, and little to do; I picked up pen and pad, and began writing. I was undecided on my subject, and as fate would have it, I was eventually face to face with the murders once again, when a member of Hull City Council's Museum Staff, jokingly told me "We have Jack the Ripper's paintings." I began researching the links that my home town of Kingston upon Hull had with the murders, looking at known suspects, and their links to the city! During the course of my research I decided to read through all the Hull based newspapers, which were in circulation during 1888, to see how they reported the events and if they shed any light on the people I was researching. I was surprised that although a lot of information was passed via agencies, much of the information was new, as Hull newspapers had correspondents in London. Eventually, after printing off hundreds of snippets, I decided to digitise all the reports, so they would be available in one place, but the more I typed, the more I realised I was onto something special. I spent many hours trawling through other national and international newspaper archives for stories on Hull, including material from America, New Zealand and Australia. At one point I even gained access to newspapers from South Africa, all in the search for articles about Jack the Ripper and Hull.

This book offers no Suspect, nor a theory, or even a final Solution, instead, it offers you, the reader, a chance to take a step back in time, and read the newspaper reports of the most infamous murder series ever committed. Every twist and turn is here, with theories, and suspects, victims and locations, and a plethora of new material to please criminologists, local historians, and even the most seasoned of Ripperologists.

Newspapers from Hull Volume 1

Contemporary Newspapers are of course a mixed blessing, whilst on one hand they contain a useful account of the investigation and how it unfolded, on the other hand more often than not, the reports are riddled with errors, and inaccuracies, helping to create myths that until the official police files were released, were accepted as gospel truth.

In many cases, having the newspaper accounts, helps fill in the gaps in the case, often where the official files are missing or lost, thus giving us a point of reference to research further. The newspapers also offer a regional view of the murders, and how the local populace where affected, from local people claiming to be Jack the Ripper, to local police officers arresting people on "Ripper-like conduct". There was even a local newspaper on the receiving end of a letter purporting to be from Jack the Ripper himself!

There are moments where the imagination soars, and we are left with the fantastic and more often than not fictional creations of an overzealous correspondent. Where these fanciful claims came from and how they crept into the case is a matter that has had Ripperologists and serious students of the case left feeling dismayed, as more and more people attach credence to them, where none should be given. We will see firsthand how some of these myths were created, from the gentleman seen with the Gladstone bag, to the possibility that the victims knew each other.

Here for the first time ever, is the complete collection of available press reports from Hull during the "Autumn of Terror", including reports on the five commonly accepted victims, witnesses, suspects, officials and events during that period.

However, the reports don't stop there!

I have also uncovered reports on victims and events pre and post 1888, including an early "Torso Murder", and reports on suspects such as Maybrick, Tumblety, and several lesser known suspects. The section of reports that took place in 1888 feature every article published in the Hull press during the period that mentioned the murder. It also includes articles on such topics as "The Gateshead Murder," and "Torso Murders," of London that are, from time to time, associated with "Jack the Ripper," and the "Whitechapel Murders."

Mike Covell

Whitechapel, London 1888, an unknown assassin struck terror into the hearts of the thousands who lived in the dark twisting alleys and the slums that lay off them.

No one really knows the identity of the serial killer who killed throughout this small East End district, but to date over 100 suspects have been put forward. [1] These range from Royalty, to Doctors, to Sailors and School Teachers. It is doubtful after so long we will ever truly find out the real identity of this person or persons, but we do have a name, a name that will live on for eternity, that name is Jack the Ripper.

Initially, however, the British press had other names for the murderer, from the "Whitechapel Murderer," to the "Whitechapel Fiend," but the first that really caused a sensation was "Leather Apron."

On September 7th 1888 a report signed by Acting Superintendent W. Davies, was created that was essentially a brief overview of the murder of Mary Ann Nichols. The report stated,

> *A man named "Pizer alias Leather Apron" has been in the habit of ill using prostitutes in various parts of the Metropolis for some time past, and careful inquiries have been made to trace him, but without success. There is no evidence against him at present. Enquiries are being continued.*

The file, Ref. MEPO 3/140, f 238, is a Metropolitan Police file and can be viewed at London's Public Record Office, and despite their being no evidence to link "Leather Apron" to the crimes, it was enough to create a press sensation. Days earlier, on September 4th 1888 The New York Times had featured the story of "Leather Apron" and the story was ran in Britain, mainly by The Star, although reports appeared across the country, that sensationalized "Leather Apron," as a personification of evil in the East End.

There are three schools of thought on were the name came from, one it that it was penned by the murderer himself in a letter addressed to the Central News Agency on 27th September 1888 from London EC. [2]

The second is that the name came from an enterprising journalist, with either Charles Moore or his subordinate Thomas Bulling to blame. Both worked for the Central News Agency, which was a major news gathering and dissemination service during the period. [3]

The third is that the name came from a hoaxer, the most infamous of which was Maria Coroner, who appeared in Bradford Borough Court on the charge of, "written certain letters tending to cause a breach of the peace." [4]

What we do know is that it was a name that would spread fear, not just into the residents of East End London but much further afield, a name now synonymous with evil and a name that has become a part of our heritage. The "Ripper Craze" was sweeping the streets of Whitechapel, and just over 200 miles away, the residents of Kingston upon Hull where also experiencing it, through the contemporary newspaper reports!

Kingston upon Hull during the period of the murders was a busy port, the City itself was surrounded by docks, and strangers from far afield would come and visit the bustling port, seeking both business and pleasure. Old Dock built in 1778[5], Princess Dock built in 1829[6], and Humber Dock built in 1840[7], surrounded the City, built where the moat once stood side by side with the walls, marking the City boundary. Alexander Dock built in 1885[8], and Victoria Dock built in 1850[9], stood to East and Albert Dock built in 1869[10] and William Wright dock stood to the West, which was completed in 1880[11]. Further West along the Humber stood the St Andrews Dock which was completed in 1883[12]. In a way Kingston upon Hull was not unlike the docklands area that stood only a stone's throw from Whitechapel, perhaps this is why the case became so popular here. This coupled with the fact that the City was inundated with strangers, immigrants and criminals, using the docks as transportation hubs to Europe and further afield. Prostitution thrived in the City off the back off the sailors visiting, and several known brothels were in operation. [13] Hull was a popular destination amongst the immigrants of northern Europe, who stayed in Hull, travelled south to London or caught the train across the Pennines to Liverpool and on to either Ireland, or further afield to New York. [14] By the year 1840 the Hull and Selby Railway came to Hull and a station was erected on Kingston-street to the west of Humber Dock. The line brought traffic through to Hull and vice versa but its distance from the town centre proved problematic and another line and new station was put forward. By the year 1847 a new station, named Paragon Station, was erected much closer to the central business district of the newly expanding town. It proved much more popular and by 1851 the new hotel, that adjoined the station, would open, eventually being named the Royal Station Hotel after the 1854 visit of Queen Victoria. The Paragon terminus would be the major station for passengers and the Kingston-street station demolished in 1858 with a newer larger freight terminus erected on Wellington-street. Other lines to Withernsea, Hornsea, and Bridlington quickly followed bringing people to and from smaller outlying towns and villages and with it crime, and criminals. The City at this time was also a maze of alleys, entry's, yards and passageways, which led from the main streets onto smaller courts and terraces. A mixture of wealthy businessmen in their large houses lived side by side with lower class citizens who resided in cramped and often unsanitary conditions and because of this crime and disease was rife in the lower class areas of the city. Due to the increased population Kingston upon Hull began to expand in all directions and was a major port in both Great Britain and the World. The town, by 1888, had taken over 7,901 acres of land, for a population of 202,400. [15] The fishing industry had also increased to include 487 fishing smacks, and 22 steam cutters, bringing in an average of 30,000 tons of fish per annum! [16] A search of the census for males working in the fishing industry at this point reveals that numerous fishermen came from southern coastal towns in Devon and Cornwall, with numerous Hull fishermen citing Brixham as their place of birth. It was a boiling pot of mixed races, different classes, and a constant battle of good against evil with an understaffed over stretched police force. By 1888 trade in Hull was also on an international scale, with trade incoming and outgoing to and from destinations such as Russia, Sweden, Norway, Germany, Denmark, Holland, Belgium, France, Portugal, Spain, the Mediterranean, the Black Sea, India, Australasia, North and South America, and a national coasting trade via our own waters. [17] At the end of 1888 and the beginning of 1889 John W. Mason wrote a report for the Health of the Borough of Kingston upon Hull. [18] In his report he stated that in the year 1888 within the boundaries of Hull there was a staggering 6,230 births recorded, with an equally staggering 3,297 deaths recorded. Thus giving a birth rate equal to 30.8 per 1,000 of a population of 202, 359, residing in 47,088 houses, giving an average of 4.7 people per house. [19]

The report goes further and breaks births down via the male and female sex, and deaths down by sex and age. Progressing even further the report states that in Hull in 1888 88 lives were lost due to accident and negligence, and 95 deaths recorded in Hull were due to violence, including homicide and suicide. [20] In terms of the social conditions in Hull, the report stated that 57 lodging houses existed in Hull, with a capacity for a staggering 1509 lodgers! [21]

With this in mind it made sense that when the Whitechapel Murders began, the city of Hull would be on high alert for anyone visiting the city via sea, road, or rail, and with newspaper men in place in London, it wasn't long before the exploits in Whitechapel were spread across the newspapers in Hull.

Mike Covell

Notes about the Hull Police

During the year of 1888 the Hull Police Force had its main headquarters at number 20 Parliament-street, Hull, which was known as Central/Command/Control. The station had stood on this site since the 1850's when the Hull Corporation and the Hull Watch Committee deemed it necessary to build something new and clean as opposed to the old damp run down houses they were using at that time. In the early years of the Hull Watch the watchmen had to use their own houses, or a number of houses set up around the city as bases for their watch. There was a central prison, and there had been from 1299 when Edward I established the first legalised system of capital punishment in Hull, and up until the year 1778 public executions were a common occurrences on the streets of Hull. In 1785 local builders, and brothers, Edward and Thomas Riddle were charged with creating a gaol on what is now Castle-street, and currently the site of a hotel. The establishment of the Gaol Act of 1823 meant that Hull needed a new gaol and in 1829 a five wing building was created south of the Castle-street gaol on the east of the junction of Kingston-street and Manor House-street. Despite the new gaol Hull still needed a police station that would centralise its operations and create a place that would be cleaner and better suited to the needs of the growing Hull police force. The police station was discussed as early as November 15th 1850, when The Hull Packet and East Riding Times, featured a report and letter calling for a new police station that would be more suitable for its role in the town. Then, on January 7th 1853 in The Hull Packet and East Riding Times, it was announced that the station would get the go ahead. By January 21st 1853, The Hull Packet and East Riding Times, featured an advertisement for building tenders for the project, and a further article, in The Hull Packet and East Riding Times, December 9th 1853, later stated that the land had been acquired for £7,250, and building would commence on the new central police station. With a new police station, and several smaller police stations established around Hull, a new gaol was built. Hull Borough Gaol and House of Correction, was built on Hedon-road and about 2 miles from the town of Hull. The building was commenced in 1865 and completed in 1869, based in the new model principle to designs by David Thorp, the Borough Surveyor, and his successor R.G. Smith. David Thorp was also responsible for the Parliament-street Police Station as well as the Borough Gaol, and held the post of the first Borough Surveyor of Hull from 1851 until he died in 1865. Curiously, he passed away eight days before the foundation stone was laid for the gaol. The Borough Gaol was constructed of brick, and consisting of a body and three main annexes with residence for the Governor, Chaplain, and other officials. The main body of the site consists of 12 acres of land and in 1878 was handed to the over to the Government as part of the Prisons Act. Both Frederick Bailey Deeming and John Rennard had spent time here under the watchful eye of then Governor Harold Webster and in more recent years the prison has played host to members of the I.R.A., members of the Kray firm, members of the Richardson's, and Hull's most notorious prisoner Charles Bronson, although at the time of writing (March 2013) there is talk of closing several wings.

The Chief Constable, during the period covered in this book, was Captain Gurney, his Deputy Chief was a C. Jones and both men were well known officers, in fact, in later years they would be associated with a murder case that filled countless newspaper columns in 1891 when Mary Jane Langley was murdered at Marfleet. The Hull police, in 1888, had two Superintendents, seven Inspectors, thirty two Sergeants, twelve Detectives, and two hundred and twenty two Constables. [1]

During the year of 1888 the following Officers were sworn in, [2]

Name	Badge Number	Date Badge Issued
George William Marshall	267	January 4th 1888
Arthur Edward Anderson	63	January 12th 1888
James William Burton	145	February 2nd 1888

Mike Covell

Abraham Thomas Leonard	111	February 9th 1888
Thomas Blackburn	216	May 3rd 1888
John Cooper	257	May 24th 1888
Thomas Bratton	41	June 7th 1888
George Sprigg	99	June 22nd 1888
William Stephenson	193	July 3rd 1888
William Ambrose Hall	71	July 18th 1888
A. Haigh	267	July 18th 1888
A. Maple	250	July 18th 1888
Charles Jones	184	September 20th 1888

The City was covered by five smaller stations which were situated at the following locations throughout the city at that time, Gordon-street, which was A Division, Norfolk-street, which was BDW, Worship-street, which was B Division, Church-street, which was C Division, and Crowle-street, which was C-Sub Division. [3] Although each division was responsible for policing their own patch, there was inevitable areas where patches overlapped and the force, not unlike the Metropolitan Police of London, were considered a team with officers from other divisions often called from one area of the city to provide cover in another area. It wasn't all plain sailing though, and on occasion the Hull police would often fall foul of the Hull Watch Committee, who were officials bound to keep an eye on the police force. The Hull Watch Committee would hold regular meetings to discuss, debate, and decide on funding, subscriptions, uniforms, punishments and rewards to the police officers that worked under them. Whilst many police officers worked hard to maintain safety and security on their patch, there were inevitably a small number of police officers that fell foul of the Watch Committee and in turn ended up in the press with sordid details of their actions. Drinking, gambling, and even visits to prostitutes were a common event and in the 1870's the Hull Packet was full of stories about the Hull Watch Committee and the Hull Police Force failing at what they were tasked to do.

The boundary of Hull was surrounded on all sides by the East Riding Police Force. The East Riding area covered a greater area than Hull, but with a much smaller population, because of this only parish constables were responsible, as early as 1839, as policing their own parishes. Most of the ground under the jurisdiction of the East Riding Police force was either small villages, towns such as Beverley, and a vast expanse of rural ground. The modern East Riding Constabulary came into force on October 14th 1856 when the magistrates and clerk came to the conclusion that 48 ordinary and 12 mounted or superintending constables were required at a cost of £4,200 per annum. During the third week of September in the year 1872 Colonel Layard, Chief Constable of the East Riding Police, died. It was an event that would mean a new police Chief Constable required and on November 1st of that year Major Henry J. Bower became the second Chief Constable of the East Riding Police. It was a post that he would keep until 1899 and was therefore present during the Autumn of Terror and several other subsequent "Ripper Scares" that would occur in the district during those years. [4]

Meanwhile Kingston upon Hull's population was rising, and between 1801 and 1901 the population rose from 22,000 to 239,000, a leap of 217,000! During the period of 1888 the population of Hull was said to be at 202,400 residents dwelling within the city boundaries, meaning that 277 officers had to police a staggering number of people, and this figure was rapidly rising with the real possibility that "Jack the Ripper" might be on his, or her, or their, way to Hull! [5]

Mike Covell

The Hull Newspapers

Over the years Hull has had numerous newspapers with the earliest being mentioned on July 31st 1750 when The York Courant, mentioned both The Hull Journal and The Hull Courant. On May 29th 1787, The Hull Packet and Humbrian Gazette started publication, with the earlier editions being used as a vehicle to spread the word on slavery by William Wilberforce. From July 5th 1794 The Hull Advertiser and Exchange Gazette was printed by Mr. William Bell. The Hull Rockingham was published between the years 1808 and 1840. The Hull and Eastern Counties Herald commenced printing in 1838, and The Hull News in 1852. Between the years 1830 and 1840 The Hull Observer was printed on Tuesdays and The Hull Saturday Journal printed on Saturdays. The Hull Free Press commenced publication just prior to 1860. The Hull Morning Telegraph printed between 1855 and ceased in 1880 when it was embodied in The Hull Express. The year 1862 saw the rise and fall of The Hull Morning Star. On January 1st 1859 The Hull Daily Express commenced publication, and later became The Hull Evening News, and later The Hull Express. Other newspapers published in Hull include such titles as The Talisman, The Kingston Literary Wreath, The Hull Quarterly Magazine, The Portfolio, The Immortal, The Whitefriargate Papers, The Third Port, The Bellman, The Hull and Lincolnshire Bellman, The Jester, and The Critic. In 1865 The Hull Advertiser amalgamated with The Eastern Morning News. From 1867, and for just 14 weeks, The Hull Morning Paper was published by Messrs. Wallis.

The Hull newspapers that cover the year 1888 that are available for perusal at the Hull History Centre are;

The Eastern Morning News and Hull Advertiser,

The Hull News,

The Hull Times,

Newspapers from Hull Volume 1

The Hull Daily News/Evening News,

The Hull Daily Mail,

The Eastern Morning News

The Eastern Morning News ran from 1864 until 1929, and was a morning newspaper, with Liberal views. It had benefited immensely from a Palmerston Governments abolition of the "Paper Duty" and was the most popular newspaper from the period. Within its first year The Eastern Morning News had incorporated the Hull Advertiser, a publication which began in 1794! By February 5th 1884 the newspaper changed its format from a weekly published piece to a daily selling paper, covering the news six days a week. [1] The Eastern Morning News was a daily newspaper and was published by William Hunt, of 42, Whitefriargate, with offices on 29 Hutt Street, Spring Bank. The newspaper was one of the few to have a telephone line to ensure speedier news coverage.[2] The Eastern Morning News also had offices in London, at 47, Fleet-street., E.C, in Goole at Ouse-street, and at Grimsby on Cleethorpes-road. Priced at one penny per issue, the company was also responsible for The Hull Express, Hull Weekly Express and Grimsby Express. [3] In the 1880's the Hull Daily Mail and Eastern Morning News had a strong dislike of each other and a war of words broke out that lasted for some years between the newspapers.

Hull News

The Hull News ran from 1852 until 1929. The newspaper was a Liberal Evening publication and published by James Alfred Cooke, of 58, Whitefriargate. [4] The newspaper was one of the few based in Hull to have a telephone line installed within their Whitefriargate offices. [5] The newspaper advertised that it had a circulation of 30 thousand, 10 thousand in the villages around Hull, and 20 thousand in Hull itself. The newspaper was priced at two pence and published on Saturday evenings. [6]

Hull Times

The Hull Times was created in 1857 and ran until 1984. [7] It was a popular weekly newspaper and published by Richard Simmons, at 22,

Mike Covell

Whitefriargate. [8] Through the years the newspaper changed to cover local news and became known as The Hull and East Yorkshire and Lincolnshire Times, The Hull and Lincolnshire Times, and as The Hull Times. It remained a popular newspaper until it was amalgamated into The Hull Daily Mail.

Hull Daily News/Evening News

Hull Daily News began on the 5th February 1884, and was an extremely popular newspaper. By 1923 it had changed its name to the Hull Evening News and eventually ceased publication in 1930. [9] The Hull Daily News was a Liberal newspaper and also published by James Alfred Cooke, of 58, Whitefriargate. The newspaper was one of the few based in Hull to have a telephone line installed. [10] Priced at one penny, the advertisements during the period described the newspaper as "The most popular evening paper for Hull, and is to be found in nearly every family in the town" [11]

Hull Daily Mail

The Hull Daily Mail was founded in September 1885 by political Conservative activists, including Sir Albert Rollitt M.P. and future M.P., F.B. Grotian. The newspaper was founded to counter argue the views presented in The Hull News and The Eastern Morning News. The first edition of the newspaper hit the shelves of Hull newspaper vendors and street sellers on September 29th 1885 and became an instant hit. By 1886 The Hull Daily Mail had incorporated the weekly newspapers, The Hull Packet and The Hull and Yorkshire Times. [12] With the purchase of several local newspaper titles the aim was to publish a newspaper at least once a day with a move away from the stuffy newspapers of old to a more modern bright newspaper. The Conservative Evening newspaper was published by Richard Simmons, at 22, Whitefriargate. [13] The Hull Daily Mail was still publishing reports on the case many years after the initial scare in London, with the reports featured here together for the first time. The Hull Daily Mail is still going strong today and is Hull's only newspaper, with the same company responsible for The Hull Advertiser, a weekly free newspaper, and Flashback, a monthly newspaper that features local history items and photographs from the archives of The Hull Daily Mail.

Other Hull Based Newspapers During 1888

There were other publications in Hull during the year 1888 but sadly, none of these exist.

The Hull Arrow was a weekly newspaper, published by Abraham Johnson and Frederick William Guy, on Bowlalley lane. [14] The Hull Globe was published by M. Waller and H.J. Corlyon, from their offices at 56, Lowgate. [15] Atkinson's Trade Directory of Hull lists the following newspapers during the period,

Eastern Morning News, Daily, 42 Whitefriargate, William Hunt,

Hull Arrow, Weekly, Bowlalley-lane, Abraham Johnson and Frederick William Guy

Hull Bill of Entry and Daily Shipping List, Daily, 162 High-street, Thomas Grassam

Hull News, Liberal Evening, Daily, and Weekly editions, 58 Whitefriargate, James Alfred Cooke

Hull Daily Mail, Conservative Evening, 22 Whitefriargate, Richard Simmons,

Hull and East Riding Critic,

Hull Express, Evening, 42 Whitefriargate, William Hunt,

Hull Globe, 56 Lowgate, M. Waller and H. J. Corlyon,

Hull Times, Weekly, 22 Whitefriargate, Richard Simmons

The Hull Packet and East Riding Times

The Hull Packet and East Riding Times began on May 29th 1787 as a four page newspaper with just eight columns. It sold for 7d, which was considered quiet expensive at the time, and as such was not a widely

Mike Covell

circulated newspaper. In 1790 the newspaper was published by Ann Price, one of the earliest examples of a woman working on a newspaper in Hull, with Robert Peck taking over publishing and moving operations to 22 Scale-lane, Hull. By November 1827 the newspaper was bought by Mr. Allanson and was increased in size and renamed The Hull Packet and Humber Mercury. It was, during this period, published by T. Topping, who was based on Lowgate. In the year 1830 the newspaper was sold from Topping to Goddard and Brown who published the newspaper until 1839. Eventually Mr. Goddard relinquished his position and Brown teamed up with Mr. Andrew Clarke Wardale, and with Mr. Quinn, sometimes referred to as Queen, as the editor. Mr. Quinn later left to work with Mr. Goddard at Goddard's opposition newspaper, The Hull and East Riding Times, which ceased printing in 1841. By the year 1842 the newspaper was sold to a Mr. Thomas Freebody who was acting on behalf of a consortium of Hull based Conservatives. The editor at this point was Mr. T. Ramsey, who would later be sacked on account of his religious convictions. By 1886 the newspaper was bought by The Hull Daily Mail.

The newspaper was full of stories on local crime, shipping intelligence, science, police, foreign intelligence, literary notices, and many other topics that concerned daily life in Hull and with a superior print quality to other local titles of the period.

Publishing history with alternate titles:

The Hull Packet (1787-30 June 1807)

The Hull Packet and Original Weekly Commercial, Literary and General Advertiser (7 July 1807-6 November 1827)

The Hull Packet and Humber Mercury, or Yorkshire and Lincolnshire General Advertiser (13 November 1827-5 April 1833)

The Hull Packet (12 April 1833-18 November 1842)

The Hull Packet and East Riding Times (25 November 1842-26 February 1886)

Information Gathering and the Hull Press

The newspapers published in Hull during the 19th Century all had to get their news stories for publishing, be it from agencies or correspondents. This chapter looks at just how the newspapers managed to get their story.

News Agencies

During the 1870's there was an upsurge in news agencies, both in the metropolitan area, and internationally. These agencies were clearing houses for the news, and via telegraph, disseminated stories to other newspapers both nationally and internationally. The Hull based newspapers utilised these agencies to gather news for publishing. The news agencies were not without their problems however, as the Times, in 1895, accused the Central News Agency of distributing sensational and imaginative stories, reports and telegrams. One such report featured in The Times, dated May 15th 1895, and accused the agency of taking events in Japan and elaborating upon them so much that even those in Japan knew nothing of the reported claims made. Other similar accusations followed in The Times, notably their February 8th 1895 and June 15th 1895 editions.

The Central News Agency

The most popular news agency that features in the articles is by far the Central News Agency, an organisation that was set up by the Central Press in 1863 by William Saunders and his brother in law, Edward Spencer. It wasn't until 1870-1871 that the organisation became the Central News Agency and competition came from its competitors The Press Association and Reuters, which it managed to undercut.

The Central News Agency was a Conservative dominated news agency, which was involved in the process of disseminating news stories, via telegraph. The agency was formed in 1870, two years after The Press Association, by philanthropist, M.P. and Social Reformer, William

Mike Covell

Saunders. By 1880 the agency was a Limited Liability Company, and was directed by Bennet Burleigh. [16]

The Press Association

The Press Association or Press Agency was a Liberal organization, which was involved in the process of disseminating news stories, via telegraph. The organisation was set up in 1868 by a group of regional newspaper owners with an aim to provide a London based service that would collect and report news from around the British Isles. The launch of the organisation made headlines in numerous British newspapers in September 1868 when it was announced that a central newspaper/telegraph operation was to be soon available to the British press.

Correspondents

All of the Hull based newspapers had correspondents in the capitol from as early as June 9th 1823, when The Hull Packet and Original Weekly Commercial, Literary and General Advertiser, published a report on a meeting held in London for the relief of Spain. More and more correspondents would travel to London over the next few years, and many flocked en masse mainly to cover the Parnell Commission, an investigation that looked into allegations made against Irish parliamentarian Charles Stewart Parnell. It all centred around the murder of two leading members of the British Government in Ireland, Chief Secretary for Ireland Lord Frederick Cavendish, and the Permanent Under-Secretary for Ireland, T.H. Burke, who were murdered in Dublin at the Phoenix Park, on May the 6th 1882. In March 1887, The Times newspaper ran a series of articles entitled "Parnellism and Crime", and looked at a collection of letters which seemed to bear the signature of Charles Stewart Parnell. One such letter, bearing Parnell's signature, appears to excuse and condone the murder. Parnell denied any wrong doing, and claimed the letters a forgery, but after debate and argument, an investigation was ordered. The investigation began in 1887 and ran until 1889, finally finding Parnell not guilty. [17] During this period several Hull newspaper men where in the Capitol and several of the Hull newspapers even had regional offices in the capital.

Other Newspapers

You will notice throughout the book that a small fraction of reports reference other newspapers, which include, The Daily Telegraph, The Echo, The Evening News (London), The Independence Belge, The London Star, New York Herald, Pall Mall Gazette, The Standard, The Star, St James's Gazette, The Times. A full list of newspaper reports will feature at the end of this work.

The Advent of the Telegraph and the Hull Press

The advent of the Electronic Telegraph speeded news from elsewhere in the British Isles. The telegraph basically sent electronic signals via cables from location to location; these would then be deciphered by the receiver and turned into a readable message. Atkinson's 1888 Trade Directory of Hull states that inland telegrams came to Hull throughout the day, with most offices opening from 8:00 in the morning until 8:00 at night. The telegram offices at this point in time were based throughout the city at Fish Market, Pier-street, Alexandra Dock, Anlaby-road, Beverley-road, Cumberland-street, Hessle-road, Myton-place, Stepney, and Witham, as well as a central office that was open constantly. The same publication, also informs us that the city was covered by no fewer than 32 post offices, which had a staggering 10 collections a day, from as early as 4:45 a.m. until the last collection as late as 8:30 p.m. all six days a week with three collections on Sundays. Mail from London to Hull arrived at 7:00, 8:45, 11:10, 1:30, 2:15, 3:00, 4:35, 6:30, and 7:00. Post was either sent via postman, or via private boxes throughout the day.

The Advent of the Telephone and the Hull Press

Up until 1877 the electronic telegraph was a much relied on piece of technology with all long distance communications relying on it, but by 1877 many companies began commutating via a new invention, the telephone, and on November 30th 1877, The Hull Packet and East Riding Times, featured a lengthy article heralding the invention and its possible uses. Telephone exchanges were soon a common site with subscriptions paid to communication companies; subscribers could call other subscribers, usually through a switchboard. Initially boys were chosen to relay messages between subscribers, but after several instances of mischievous behaviour, girls were chosen for the job. It wasn't long before subscribers could be connected direct, and allows an even speedier conversation, cutting out the middle man or in this case girl! [18] The first ever exchange was opened in London on the 21st August 1879, known as the Telephone Company Ltd. By the 6th of September 1879, the Edison Telephone Company of London opened its first exchange. By 1880, the High Court ruled that no public telephone system could be operated without a licence from the Postmaster General. A private company provided a telephone service in Hull at this time but it later amalgamated with others and became the National Telephone Company. The National Telephone Company (NTC) operated from 1881 until 1911, when it was taken over by the General Post Office, in 1912, under the Telephone Transfer Act of 1911. By this time, Hull had set up its own exchange, in 1904 Kingston Communications was launched, and remains to this day, being the only exchange in the UK not under control by British Telecom. [19]

It is clear that in Atkinson's Trade Directory of Hull, several of the local newspapers were operating at least one line, with The Hull Daily Mail and The Hull News, each having one telephone line installed. The Eastern Morning News had two lines, one at its Whitefriargate Office, and one at its Spring Bank office at 29 Hutt-street. This would have been beneficial to The Eastern Morning News as it covered a wider area than any of the other newspapers at this time, taking in both Yorkshire and Lincolnshire. It would have made communication between the offices much easier, even though the office was only a mile away, and could be walked in under thirty minutes! [20] The Hull Police also had a telephone line installed at their Parliament-street Police Station.

The Advent of the Railway and the Hull Press

Near completion of the railway ensured powerful channels of news collection and distribution. Hull during the period was a well-connected town and the third largest port after London and Liverpool. Prior to the railway links Hull had a long history of coaches that travelled to and from the city. The earliest known example of the Hull Coaches dates back to the 1670's, when a coach bound for London left the Land of Green Ginger.

The unusually named street was once the location of a hostelry named "The Reindeer", which housed the local Post Office. [21] By 1815 Steam Packets were being run from the town to neighbouring Selby, and York, and further afield to London. Another successful route was that between Hull and Grimsby, enabling travellers to cross the Humber, leaving their coaches on the south bank. [22]

By 1825 Robert Stephenson had outline plans to create a railway system to the town of Hull, for the benefit of local merchants and others concerned in the prosperity of Hull. The plan involved creating a network between Hull and the already existing Leeds and Selby railway, by widening the bridge over the River Ouse. The plan hit several barriers, the worst of which was finding public subscription for such a scheme. [23] By 1834, a plan was submitted to subscribers to inform them of the measures that needed to be undertaken to bring the railway to Hull. The amount of money needed, it was estimated, would exceed £340,000, but this would ensure that wagons, coaches, and engines, as well as providing for any contingency that might appear along the way. [24] By 1835 shares were offered in the railway at £50, needing a deposit of a £ to raise the estimated £350,000 needed. [25] By 1st of July 1840, the railway was opened for the first time for traffic, and a grand opening ceremony was held, involving marching bands, Councillors, the Officers of the Garrison, Police and many more of the town's notables. [26] From that point on "Railway Fever", as it was dubbed in Hull's press, had taken over and several other lines were planned and later opened.

Mike Covell

Introduction to the Newspaper Reports

Kingston upon Hull was a thriving port and town, with trade links to Europe which was established as early as the 1600's. The town was a popular destination for sailors, foreigners and criminals and as such, a vast network of news reporting covered the whole of Hull and covered just about every aspect of life in and around Hull and even further away.

Notes about the collection of newspaper reports:

In all cases the newspaper reports featured have been collected from the above named Hull based newspapers by myself. These reports have been gathered via spending many hours in the Hull's Central Library, when the local studies was situated there, to the multi million pound Hull History Centre. Many hours were logged on the microfilm readers, as the reports are on microfilms, and in many cases between the poor print quality and the printing process some reports are illegible and dark in colour. This enabled me to carry out the collection of each month from each newspaper to enable a chronological picture to emerge but also to ensure that the material I was collecting was not disturbed by a third party. In some cases, however, I have been unable to match a date with a report, due to this unforeseen circumstance; I have searched other online newspapers for similar stories, to give a time frame of when the newspaper carried the story. Further re-visits were carried out as some reports where badly damaged during the removal from screen to hard copy. During these re-visits I have also endeavoured to find the date and newspaper which carried the articles which bore no date. After spending hours printing off the reports, they were filed on card, in waterproof files chronologically and in order of each newspaper. An endeavour which almost took as much time as the transcription process! Whilst this took some time, it enabled me to collect, catalogue and read the newspapers as they appear in this book. In some cases digital collections were consulted, these included the 19th Century British Newspaper's online, the British Library's newspapers online, the Times digital archive, Ripper Casebook Press Project, and jtrforums.com for content that sheds further light on the reports featured within. In all cases, every single source is noted.

Notes about the transcription process:

In all cases the transcriptions are letter for letter inscriptions, including any names or locations which have been spelt phonetically. This included incorporating the same grammar, punctuation, and spelling mistakes. Several of the articles have the same name or location spelt differently with up to three variations offered per name. In these cases I have added notes in thus, [Notes: ....]. These notes will include points on spelling, biographical detail, where required, and other significant points. Dates and newspaper titles are at the top of each article, in some cases, several sub articles appear under the main headline, these are separated sub headings that are written in capital letters. If several articles appear in the same newspaper on different pages, or on the same page but in other areas, they will be dated individually.

Census Entries bear, for example, the following digits, [RG, HO, P, F, P, GSU] which refers to,

- Class RG Registration District Number
- HO Registration District Number
- Piece is a collection of individual enumerator's books for a given district
- Folio is a sheet within the individual enumerator's book
- Page refers to the page within the individual enumerator's book
- GSU Roll – Only Ancestry UK uses this catalogue reference, and so if one is using other digital census collections it is not required.

Mike Covell

The Rise of the Newspaper

Although newspapers where printed as far back as the late 1700's, it wasn't until the first steam press printed The Times in 1814 [1] a year later, stamp duty would increase to 4d per newspaper, putting heavy burden on the printer and purchaser. [2] Between 1815 and 1837 newspapers were established in major cities across Britain including The Manchester Guardian (1821,) The Sunday Times (1822,) and The Standard (1827.) [3] By 1837, British Newspaper's where thrown a lifeline, when the Newspaper Tax was reduced from 4d per copy to just 1d per copy, thus enabling higher print runs, and cheaper newspapers, but this still wasn't enough. [4] By the second half of the nineteenth century the emergence of mass produced, mass circulated, and mass read newspapers. Newspapers were no longer available to just the upper classes, but available to the working and to some extent lower classes. By 1851 Reuters was formed in London, becoming the first News Agency in Britain, and paving the way for similar news collection and dissemination services. [5] It wasn't until between the 1850's and 1860's that newspaper's really took off after the abolition of the "Taxes on Knowledge", which was a stamp duty on newspapers, and customs and excise papers. [6] During this period both daily and weekend newspapers grew at an alarming rate, more so in the counties, and offered the reader differing views to the traditional liberal newspapers of the period. [7] By 1863 the national count showed that over 1,000 newspapers existed in Britain, many of which were published two or three times throughout the day. [8] It was estimated that by the year 1850 the circulation of the daily press was around 60,000 whilst Sunday newspapers sold an estimated 275,000 copies. [9]

Massive moves in education were also playing a part, with illiteracy a major problem in early Victorian Britain. The Elementary Education Act 1870, often referred to as Forster's Education Act, was a guide to schooling all children between the ages of 5 and 12 in both England and Wales. The act was created by William Forster, who was a Liberal MP, and was introduced on February 17th 1870. The Elementary Education Act of 1873, Elementary Education Act of 1876, Elementary Education Act of 1879 (Industrial Schools) and the Elementary Education Act of 1880 soon followed and education in England and Wales improved greatly. It also meant that more people could read and write, regardless of their social standing, and as such more people could understand what was going on in their local and national newspapers.

All that was left was for something massive to occur, something that might help not only to sell newspapers, but something so big it would even help launch new newspapers. That something, would be a series of murders known as The Whitechapel Murders, and involved an unnamed suspect known as Jack the Ripper.

Brief Notes on the London Press

During 1888 there were thirteen morning and nine evening national dailies, covering the whole of London, and covering every aspect of the news. [1] These included, The Star, which was an evening paper, founded in January 1888. [2] The newspaper called for sweeping social and political reform, an overhaul of Scotland Yard, and Irish Home Rule. [3] The newspaper was run by T.P. O'Connor, a radical and Irish Nationalist MP, who eventually jumped on the murders, and used them to further his cause, and attack the Met Police. [4] During the murders The Star's circulated almost monthly, from 261,000 copies sold during the aftermath of the Annie Chapman murder, 190,000 by September, 217,000 during the first week of October, and 300,000 by the time Mary Kelly was found murdered in Millers-court. [5] The popularity of The Star was in part due to the fact that T.P. O'Connor had decided to shorten long stories, and favoured shorter, sharper stories instead, maintaining the interest of the reader. [6] In terms of the number of reports available out there for anyone wishing to research further, the following reports are available:

- A search of the 19th Century British Newspaper's online for the term "Jack the Ripper" revealed a staggering 3559 hits.

- A search of the British Library's Newspaper's online for the term "Jack the Ripper" revealed a staggering 6505 hits.

Internationally the case would also fill thousands of newspaper columns.

- A search of the Australian Newspaper Archive for the term "Jack the Ripper" revealed a staggering 3226 hits

Mike Covell

- A search of the New Zealand Newspaper Archive for the term "Jack the Ripper" revealed a staggering 4612.hits
- The Casebook Press Project has a staggering 5449 reports from 298 different countries.
- JTRForums.Com has thousands of images of newspaper reports from numerous countries and archives across the world.

Despite these staggering numbers, the picture is still missing pieces, and as we shall see, there are still many reports awaiting discovery.

The Murders

Many have argued over the years the true number of poor unfortunates who were murdered in Whitechapel during the last few months of 1888. The majority argue that there were only five real Ripper victims,

- Mary Ann "Polly" Nichols
- Annie Chapman
- Elizabeth Stride
- Catherine Eddowes
- Mary Jane Kelly

Many have argued that Martha Tabram was an early victim of Jack the Ripper, whilst other Ripperologists have stated that there could have been many more.

There have been numerous books on the victims of Jack the Ripper, including Jack the Ripper and the Whitechapel Murders, amongst some of the most respected titles are The Complete Jack the Ripper A – Z, Paul Begg, Martin Fido, and Keith Skinner, and Jack the Ripper – An Encyclopaedia, John J. Eddleston, and The Ultimate Jack the Ripper Sourcebook, Stewart P. Evans and Keith Skinner, Robinson, 2001, so to avoid going over old ground I will briefly outline their deaths in the text

25

under the dates on which their bodies were either discovered or the date on which they died.

To give clarity and be fair to everyone I will cover the press reports in all the Hull Newspapers registered in Kingston upon Hull during the period that cover these murders.

Mike Covell

The Reports

Pre – 1888 Newspaper reports,

> *Prior to the series of murders believed, by some, to have been of the hand of "Jack the Ripper," and the even larger cannon of murders known as the Whitechapel Murders, there was another odd crime that some theorists have investigated and mentioned in relation to the case, more so because a similar crime occurred in 1888 during the period when "Jack the Ripper" was at work in Whitechapel and surrounding environs. These cases were also given a name and linked together by the cruel nature in which the bodies were found. They were known as "The Thames Torso Murders" and the Hull press were quiet eager to cover them in 1873 when the first "body" was discovered.*

The Hull Packet and East Riding Times, September 12th 1873,

> *HORRIBLE DISCOVERY IN THE THAMES. The greater part of the limbs and body of a woman have lately been found in the Thames under circumstances that leave scarcely any doubt as to the committal of an almost unparalleled horrible murder. About half past six o'clock on Friday morning the attention of a policeman named Fan[illegible] was called to the upper left part of a woman on the short of the river near the waterworks at Battersea. About four hours afterwards, Fieury, one of the South Western Railway police, found the corresponding upper quarter of the same body at Burnswick Wharf, Nine Elms. Inspector Marley found the lungs under the second arch of Battersea Bridge. The skin of a woman's face was subsequently found near Limehouse, and it had evidently been purposely stripped off to prevent identification. The portions of the body were removed to the Wandsworth Union Workhouse to await identification. The remains had the appearance of not having been long in the water and the trunk showed that the lower limbs had been forcibly torn away. On Monday further portions of the murdered woman were found. At half past ten o'clock on that morning the right leg was picked up by the Thames police off Woolwich and was taken to the dead house. Shortly before the inquest (held before Mr. W. Carter, the coroner for East Surrey) part of the right thigh was brought to the workhouse from Woolwich, and before the Jury were sworn the upper part of the left arm was brought in, having been found at Greenwich.*

Evidence was taken at the inquest as to the finding of the remains; and Dr. W. Kempster said: I am a divisional surgeon of police of the V Division. On Friday last I was called to go to the police station at Battersea, and there had shown to me a portion of a human body. It was the left side and thorax of a female perfectly fresh, and in my opinion death had not occurred many hours. The remains were those of a woman of about 48 years. They were uninjured, and there was no wound. The body was separated below the second and third vertebra above the spinal column, and divided from the lower part immediately below the fourth rib. The ribs had been cut through at the back partially through the spinal column. The arm had been removed. A knife and fine saw had been used, and, in my opinion, no other instrument. The collar bone had been divided. I am of the opinion the body was cut up immediately after death. About two p.m. on the same day I saw the right side of the same body exactly matching. When I put them together they formed parts of the same body. I noticed a wart or mole about an inch on the inner side of the right nipple that had been there during the whole of life. There was also on the chest a large white soar, the result of a burn, probably in the childhood. It was very distinctly perceptible. There was a very small mole on the right side of the neck. To all appearances the body was that of a perfectly healthy woman. On the following day I was shown the scalp on the whole of a human face, with the exception of the chin and the right side portion of the mouth. The scalp had been divided with a knife down to eye, and the rest of the integuments pulled off, the lower part of the nose being cut off, but not detached. It had decidedly been cut with a sharp knife. It had been taken from the skull within 36 hours of death; one eyebrow and a portion of the other was there. There was a slight quantity of dark hair on the upper lip. The hair was very dark, thin, and short, but it would be impossible to say whether it was cut off before or after death. The skin was between dark and fair, and the face coarse, but not in the least pockmarked. The skin of the face corresponds with the body. The ears were pierced, and the aperture not closed up at all. She was apparently of mature age. I carefully examined the scalp, and on the right temple is a very large bruise, about three or four inches in diameter, and there was blood in the skin, which to my mind indicates a blow inflicted immediately before death. There were three divisions of the bruise, one evidently a cut caused in separating the scalp from the skull, but the two anterior were contused, the result of two severe blows with a blunt weapon. I am of the opinion they were given during life. There were no further marks of violence. There has also been an arm and a leg found. The inquiry was adjourned until Monday, when important evidence will be forthcoming. Further portions of the murdered woman were found on Tuesday. Tue right forearm was found off Battersea, the pelvis off the Royal Arsenal at Woolwich, the other thigh at Battersea late in the

Mike Covell

> *afternoon. On Wednesday morning a human foot, supposed to belong to the other mutilated remains, were picked up off the shore of the Surrey Canal, near Rotherithe, and was taken to Clapham Workhouse. It was supposed that the murder had been committed on a barge, the body having been cut up and thrown into the Thames, but up to Wednesday night no trace of the murderer could be found, although the police had been untiring in their inquiries, and excitement and gossip had spread for miles up the river. The remains, too, had not been identified, although they had been seen by some hundreds of persons.*

The Hull Packet and East Riding Times, September 12th 1873,

> *THE HORRIBLE DISCOVERY IN THE THAMES. LATEST PARTICULARS. The police have so far obtained no clue to the perpetrator of the horrible murder of a woman, nor as to the woman's identity. It is curious to observe that the majority of the ghastly remains have been found near the connexions with the Thames, and this puzzling fact has naturally led to the belief that the pieces have been dropped at different parts of the river, or at different conditions of the tide. The strongest suspicion, therefore, attaches the perpetration of the deed to the hands of some waterside character. The whole of the pieces are in the custody of Mr. Hayden, the resident medical officer of the Clapham and Wandsworth Union Workhouse, and they have been officially seen by the most competent medical authorities, who support the views so unhesitatingly given in the evidence of Dr. Kempster – that the remains are those of a murdered woman. Mr. Hayden regards the sawing through the pelvis, apart from the revolting character, as a heavy piece of manual work for one man. The portion of the pelvis found on Tuesday at Woolwich Arsenal forms the left side of the lower portion of the trunk, and must have weighed when first committed to the water about 30lbs. The large bone in the lower part of the back had been sawn through, and the stomach roughly cut away. The thigh part found has some marks on it which are like scalds in life, while others are like post mortem burns – the latter as if the joint had been placed on something burning. The foot has been cut off at the joint. The suspected barge has been found and the woman alive on board. This disposes of what was supposed to be a strong clue. It was rumoured last night that one of the feet found is larger than the other; and the possibility of two women having been murdered is discussed.*

The Hull Packet and East Riding Times, September 12th 1873,

We have had a fresh horror during the past week, which recalls the Greenacre story of many moons ago. The mutilated remains of a woman have been discovered in the Thames. The body of the unfortunate victim was hacked to pieces, and the parts distributed over the river; and when they were discovered, on Saturday, they were not to have been in the river more than twelve hours. Some portions of the body were found in Battersea, others near the Nine Elms Station, and the scalp was discovered at Limehouse, the portions of the body having thus been scattered over many miles of the river. This horrible occurrence reminds us how constantly such crimes are committed in London, and also how often they escape detection. It would be premature to express an opinion with regard to this particular case, but we have recently had so many failures of the police to detect the perpetrators of murders that we cannot be sanguine in the present instance. The recent instances of the Eltham murder, the Regent Canal murder, the late outrage in Richmond Park, and many others will at once recur to the mind, and show how utterly defective in our system of detection of crimes at least against persons. Perhaps if a hundred thousand pounds were involved, there would be as much energy and skill manifested in the search for the murderer as was so creditably displayed in the capture and conviction of the American forgers. There is a great public scandal involved in the fact, which it were vain to deny, that offences against the property are punished much more surely and swiftly than offences against persons. Money is accounted more valuable than life.

The Hull Packet and East Riding Times, September 19th 1873,

THE THAMES TRAGEDY. Up to the beginning of the present week the police had learnt nothing positive as to the perpetrator of the supposed murder of a woman on or near the Thames, whose remains were at different parts taken out of the water. Nor had the police been much more fortunate in learning the poor woman's real identity. She had been two or three times recognised by persons who had a relative or a friend missing, but they seem to have been mistaken in their impressions. The strongest and most positive attempt at identification was that made by a Mrs. Christian, whose lodger a woman named Cailey had been missing. It however remains to be seen whether Mrs. Cailey will turn out to be the murdered woman, the police think not. On Monday the adjourned inquest on the remains was held, and very little further evidence was taken. On the opening of the court evidence was taken as to the finding of the various portions of the body, and the jury then for a second time viewed the remains, which since the commencement of the inquiry had been carefully joined together by Dr. Haden, the medical officer of the workhouse. On returning to the court the medical

Mike Covell

evidence was gone into, and Drs. Kempster and Haden were examined, both agreeing that all the parts found were portions of the same individual, and that the head was severed from the body after death through their opinions as to the bruise on the scalp were different. Dr. Kempster believed that the blow which caused the bruise would have been fatal, Dr. Haden held the opinion that such a blow would not have been fatal. Then came the evidence of Mrs. Christian, who had identified the body. She deposed that her late lodger Mrs. Cailey had represented herself as a person possessed of property, and that the object of her visit to London was to get her affairs settled by her solicitors. The witness declared that had it not been for the difference in height she should have been certain as to her identity. It will be remembered that nothing was said of this difference when Mrs. Christian first saw the body, and according to the most undeniable testimony, said on seeing the body, "Yes, those are the dear cheeks." She added when before the Coroner that the points of resemblance between the deceased and Mrs. Cailey consisted in the short black hair, the slight moustache and upper lip, and the shape of the lower part of the nose. Mrs. Cailey's brother was called into court, but was not sworn. He declined to state positively that the deceased was his sister. It may be stated that Mr. Bere, the brother of Mrs. Cailey, is firmly convinced that the remains are those of his "dear sister." He states also that though he knew little of his sister's husband, he was aware that after his death she was in receipt of adjacent income, but from what source he is ignorant. A sister of Mrs. Cailey has also identified the body of Mrs. Cailey's, but she was not brought forward as a witness. The police appear to discredit the idea that the remains are those of Mrs. Cailey, and it was stated that certain information had been received leading to the hope that she would be discovered are long alive and well. The jury returned a verdict of "murder against some person or persons unknown." At twenty minutes to eight o'clock on Monday morning another portion of the body was found off Hungerford Bridge, so that the authorities are now in possession of fourteen pieces. The last piece discovered formed part of the right arm from the elbow to within a few inches of the shoulder. On Monday night, Abel Beer, another brother of Mrs. Cailey, examined the new connected body lying at the workhouse, and expressed himself strongly of the opinion that it is that of his sister. It will be remembered that one prominent mark on the body is that if a severe scald or burn. He stated that he remembered the accident which caused this, she having spilt some boiling water over herself in childhood. This evidence is contrary to the views of the Scotland Yard detectives. The brother who was spoken to at the inquest has, it is said, got less inclined to doubt that the parts belong to his sister. The Government late on Tuesday night offered a reward of £200 for information as to the murder. The supposition that the murdered woman was Mrs. Cailey is exploded by the discovery of the veritable lady herself, who was found in the flesh at Chelsea on Wednesday. She was confronted with her landlady and some of her relatives, by whom she was identified. It is again repeated that the police are on the eve of making some important discovery, and that they have received information to which they attach more than usual interest.

The Hull Packet and East Riding Times, September 19th 1873,

ANOTHER EXTRAORDINARY DISCOVERY. On Tuesday an extraordinary discovery was made in the parish of Whitechapel. For some years past Mr. Robert Bell occupied the house situated at No. 3, Mill-yard, Whitechapel. On Tuesday morning, finding the heavy rain of the past few days had come through the ceiling in the top front room, he went upon the roof of the house and removed the tiles, when he was horrified by finding a basket, which on being opened contained a human skull. He at once went to the Leman-street police-station, when Inspector Pound sent Police officer Cooper, 99, H, to accompany Mr. Bell to the house, where he discovered in a fish basket, between the roof and the ceiling, the skull of a male adult, with half the scalp attached, and in such a condition that leaves little doubt that's rats must for some time past have been eating away the flesh. Mr. Bell states that he has not the slightest idea how it came there, no one to his knowledge having been missed since he occupied the house. The last time he was on the roof was in 1871. The skull was at once, by the inspector's instructions, removed to the police station.

The Hull and North Lincolnshire Times, September 20th 1873,

THE THAMES TRAGEDY. Up to the beginning of the present week the police had learnt nothing positive as to the perpetrator of the supposed murder of a woman on or near the Thames, whose remains were at different parts taken out of the water. Nor had the police been much more fortunate in learning the poor woman's real identity. She had been two or three times recognised by persons who had a relative or a friend missing, but they seem to have been mistaken in their impressions. The strongest and most positive attempt at identification was that made by a Mrs. Christian, whose lodger a woman named Cailey had been missing. It however remains to be seen whether Mrs. Cailey will turn out to be the murdered woman, the police think not. On Monday the adjourned inquest on the remains was held, and very little further evidence was taken. On the opening of the court evidence was taken as to the finding of the various portions of the body, and the jury then for a second time viewed the remains, which since the commencement of the inquiry had been carefully joined together by Dr. Haden, the medical officer of the workhouse. On returning to the court the medical evidence was gone into, and Drs. Kempster and Haden were examined, both agreeing that all the parts found were portions of the same individual, and that the head was severed from the body after death through their opinions as to the bruise on the scalp were different. Dr. Kempster believed that the blow which caused the bruise would have been fatal, Dr. Haden held the opinion that such a blow would not have been fatal. Then came the evidence of Mrs. Christian, who had identified the body. She deposed that her late lodger Mrs. Cailey had represented herself as a person possessed of property, and that the object of her visit to London was to get her affairs settled by her solicitors. The witness declared that had it not been for the difference in height she should have been certain as to her identity. It will be remembered that nothing was said of this difference when Mrs. Christian first saw the body, and according to the most undeniable testimony, said on seeing the body, "Yes, those are the dear cheeks." She added when before the Coroner that the points of resemblance between the deceased and Mrs. Cailey consisted in the short black hair, the slight moustache and upper lip, and the shape of the lower part of the nose. Mrs. Cailey's brother was called into court, but was not sworn. He declined to state positively that the deceased was his sister. It may be stated that Mr. Bere, the brother of Mrs. Cailey, is firmly convinced that the remains are those of his "dear sister." He states also that though he knew little of his sister's husband, he was aware that after his death she was in receipt of adjacent income, but from what source he is ignorant. A sister of Mrs. Cailey has also identified the body of Mrs. Cailey's, but she was not brought forward as a witness. The police appear to discredit the idea that the remains are those of Mrs. Cailey, and it was stated that certain information had been received leading to the hope that she would be discovered are long alive and well. The jury returned a verdict of "murder against some person or persons unknown." At twenty minutes to eight o'clock on Monday morning another portion of the body was found off Hungerford Bridge, so that the authorities are now in possession of fourteen pieces. The last piece discovered formed part of the right arm from the elbow to within a few inches of the shoulder. On Monday night, Abel Beer, another brother of Mrs. Cailey, examined the new connected body lying at the workhouse, and expressed himself strongly of the opinion that it is that of his sister. It will be remembered that one prominent mark on the body is that if a severe scald or burn. He stated that he remembered the accident which caused this, she having spilt some boiling water over herself in childhood. This evidence is contrary to the views of the Scotland Yard detectives. The brother who was spoken to at the inquest has, it is said, got less inclined to doubt that the parts belong to his sister. The Government late on Tuesday night offered a reward of £200 for information as to the murder. The *supposition that the murdered woman was Mrs. Cailey is exploded by the discovery of the veritable lady herself, who was found in the flesh at Chelsea on Wednesday. She was confronted with her landlady and some of her relatives, by whom she was identified. It is again repeated that the police are on the eve of making some important discovery, and that they have received information to which they attach more than usual interest.*

The Hull and North Lincolnshire Times, September 20th 1873,

ANOTHER EXTRAORDINARY DISCOVERY. On Tuesday an extraordinary discovery was made in the parish of Whitechapel. For some years past Mr. Robert Bell occupied the house situated at No. 3, Mill-yard, Whitechapel. On Tuesday morning, finding the heavy rain of the past few days had come through the ceiling in the top front room, he went upon the roof of the house and removed the tiles, when he was horrified by finding a basket, which on being opened contained a human skull. He at once went to the Leman-street police-station, when Inspector Pound sent Police officer Cooper, 99, H, to accompany Mr. Bell to the house, where he discovered in a fish basket, between the roof and the ceiling, the skull of a male adult, with half the scalp attached, and in such a condition that leaves little doubt that's rats must for some time past have been eating away the flesh. Mr. Bell states that he has not the slightest idea how it came there, no one to his knowledge having been missed since he occupied the house. The last time he was on the roof was in 1871. The skull was at once, by the inspector's instructions, removed to the police station.

The Hull Times, September 30th 1873,

THE THAMES MYSTERY. The reward of £200 offered by the Government has not yet succeeded in bringing in any clue to the perpetrator of the murder of the woman, parts of whose body were found in the Thames. The Lancet considers it absurd, in the highest degree to suppose that the recent mutilation was a hoax of medical student's, and remarks:- "There is very strong evidence that the woman met with a violent death, and that the in the first instance severe blows were dealt on the right side of the head with some heavy blunt instrument; But, in the absence of the skull, it is impossible to determine positively the extent of the injury. It would appear that the victim had thus been stunned, the body was immediately deprived of all its blood by a section of the carotid arteries in the neck, since there were no clots in any of the veins in the body. Contrary to the popular opinion, the body has not been hacked, but dexterously cut up; the joints have been opened, and the bones neatly disarticulated, even the complicated

Mike Covell

> joints at the ankle and elbow, and it is only at the articulations of the hip joint and shoulder that the bones have been sawn through. In the trunk the sectors have all been made in the most favourable parts.

The Hull and North Lincolnshire Times, September 30th 1873,

> *THE THAMES MYSTERY. The reward of £200 offered by the Government has not yet succeeded in bringing in any clue to the perpetrator of the murder of the woman, parts of whose body were found in the Thames. The Lancet considers it absurd, in the highest degree to suppose that the recent mutilation was a hoax of medical student's, and remarks:- "There is very strong evidence that the woman met with a violent death, and that the in the first instance severe blows were dealt on the right side of the head with some heavy blunt instrument; But, in the absence of the skull, it is impossible to determine positively the extent of the injury. It would appear that the victim had thus been stunned; the body was immediately deprived of all its blood by a section of the carotid arteries in the neck, since there were no clots in any of the veins in the body. Contrary to the popular opinion, the body has not been hacked, but dexterously cut up; the joints have been opened, and the bones neatly disarticulated, even the complicated joints at the ankle and elbow, and it is only at the articulations of the hip joint and shoulder that the bones have been sawn through. In the trunk the sectors have all been made in the most favourable parts.*

The Hull Packet and East Riding Times, October 24th 1873,

> *No new light has yet been cast on the Thames tragedy. The mutilated remains, which have hitherto been kept steeped in methylated spirits at the Clapham Union Workhouse, have been interred, so that identification can be proceeded with through the photograph alone.*

The Hull Packet and East Riding Times, November 7th 1873,

> *Some renewal of excitement, in regard to the Thames mystery, has been caused at Clapham by the declaration of a Mrs. Carter that the description of marks on the mutilated remains coincides with peculiarities that distinguished her daughter, who is missing. The matter is being carefully investigated.*

Further reading on the Thames Torso Mystery

The Thames Torso Murders of Victorian London, R. Michael Gordon, McFarland & Company, 2002
The Thames Torso Murders, M. J. Trow, Wharncliffe Books, 2011

26th December 1887 Fairy Fay is allegedly killed.

To date the victim remains a mystery. As early as September 10th and 11th 1888 when The Daily Telegraph published that a murder had occurred on December 26th 1887, but no names were given, it was believed that she was the first victim. It appears, however, that the writer of the article was mistaken as it was claimed that Fairy Fay had been killed by a blunt stick. She was first named as a victim in an article by Terence Robertson in Reynolds News on October 29th 1950. He claimed that she had been found murdered on a backstreet running parallel to Commercial-road on Boxing Night 1887. It is claimed that Inspector Reid was in charge of the case, however, despite these claims no newspaper articles, entry into the death index, death certificate, or mention in the official files has ever been discovered. Fairy Fay remains a mystery, and even searching for death entry's in the district bearing any female name fails to turn up any clues on the case.

Further Reading:
The Complete Jack the Ripper A to Z, Paul Begg, Martin Fido, and Keith Skinner, John Blake, 2010
Jack the Ripper – An Encyclopaedia, John J. Eddleston, Metro Publishing, 2010

25th February 1888 Annie Millwood is attacked.

Annie Millwood, sometimes referred to as Fanny, was proposed as a possible victim in The Complete History of Jack the Ripper. Millwood was the widow of a soldier and resided at number 8 White's Row which was a lodging house. On February 25th 1888 she was treated at the Whitechapel Workhouse Infirmary after receiving stab wound to her legs and lower parts of her body. It was claimed that the attack was carried out by a strange man who brandished a clasp knife.

Mike Covell

> *Millwood recovered from her injuries and was discharged from the South Grove Workhouse on March 21st 1888. By March 31st Millwood was around the rear of her building when she collapsed and ultimately died of natural causes. Her death was registered as "a sudden effusion into the pericardium from the rupture of the left pulmonary artery through ulceration."*
>
> *Annie Millwood's death is registered thus,*
> *Name: Annie Millwood, Estimated Birth Year: abt 1850, Date of Registration: Apr- May- Jun- 1888, Age at Death: 38, Registration District: Mile End Old Town, Inferred County: London, Vol: 1c, Page: 293*
>
> *Further Reading:*
> *The Complete Jack the Ripper A to Z, Paul Begg, Martin Fido, and Keith Skinner, John Blake, 2010*

> *The Complete History of Jack the Ripper, Phillip Sugden, Constable and Robinson, 2002, P. 359*
> *Jack the Ripper – An Encyclopaedia, John J. Eddleston, Metro Publishing, 2010*

28th March 1888 Ada Wilson is assaulted.

> *At 2.30am on March 28th 1888 Ada Wilson was returning home at number 9 Maidman-street, Burdett-road, Mile End, London, when she opened the door and discovered an unknown man in her house. The man, described as being about 30 years old, with a sun burnt face, fair moustache and about 5ft 6in in height. He wore a wideawake hat, light coloured trousers and a dark coat. The man demanded money, which Ada refused, when the man produced a clasp knife and stabbed her twice in the throat. Her neighbours heard her screams and came to her aid, leaving her attacker to escape, whilst medical attention was sought. On April 27th, to everyone's surprise Ada was discharged from hospital. As the press of the period hungered for other possible victims Ada was added to the list despite the obvious motive in this case being theft.*

Newspapers from Hull Volume 1

1871 Census, Class RG10, P556, F116, P8, GSU823398
54 Sidney-street, Mile End Old Town, London

Robert C. Wilson	35	Head	Ships Chandler / Shop foreman
Charlotte Wilson	33	Wife	[illegible] Maker
Charlotte E. Wilson	6	Dau	Scholar
Ada R. Wilson		3	Dau
Robert R. Wilson		1	Son

1881 Census, Class RG11, P468, F88, P20, GSU1341102
56 Gill-street, Stepney, Limehouse, London

Robert Wilson	45	Head	Labourer
Charlotte Wilson	40	Wife	
Ada Wilson	17	Dau	Scholar
Roland Wilson	9	Son	Scholar
James Wilson	7	Son	Scholar
John Wilson	5	Son	Scholar
William Wilson	3	Son	Scholar

The murder was featured in several newspapers, including, The Birmingham Daily Post, March 29th 1888
The Bristol Mercury and Daily Post, March 29th 1888, The North Eastern Daily Gazette, March 29th 1888, The Huddersfield Daily Chronicle, March 29th 1888, The Leeds Mercury, March 29th 1888, The Liverpool Mercury etc, March 29th 1888, The Morning Post, March 29th 1888, The Huddersfield Chronicle and West Yorkshire Advertiser, March 31st 1888, The Jackson's Oxford Journal, March 31st 1888, The Lancaster Gazette and General Advertiser for

Mike Covell

Lancashire, Westmoreland, and Yorkshire, March 31st 1888, The Manchester Times, March 31st 1888, The Eastern Post, March 31st 1888, The East London Observer, March 31st 1888, The East London Advertiser, March 31st 1888, and The Wrexham Advertiser, and North Wales News, March 31st 1888, with the following featuring in depth reports on the case, The Lloyd's Weekly Newspaper, April 1st 1888, Reynolds's Newspaper, April 1st 1888, and The Illustrated Police News, April 7th 1888 (in depth report and illustration)

1891 Census, Class RG12, P296, F91, P26, GSU6095406
20 Salter-street, Limehouse, London

Robert Wilson	54	Head	
Charlotte Wilson	53	Wife	
Robert Wilson	20	Son	Carman
John Wilson	16	Son	Green Grocers Assistant
William Wilson	14	Son	Wine/Twine/Wire Worker
Ada Wilson	22	Dau	Twine Spinner Rope

1901 Census, Class RG13, P322, F73, P31
6 Salter-street, Limehouse, London

Robert O. Wilson	64	Head	
Charlotte Wilson	62	Wife	
Ada Wilson	32	Dau	Packer Jam Factory
Robert R. Wilson	30	Son	Carman
William Wilson	25	Son	Blacksmith Labourer

| Lilly Wilson | 6 | Dau | | |

| 1911 Census, Class RG14, P27 |
| 42 Carlton Vale, Kilburne, N. W., Paddington |

Christopher James Hewitson	34		
Ellen Maud Hewitson	28		
Emily Maud Hewitson	2		
Doris Ellen Hewitson	0		
William Thomas Wardle	14		
John Harold Hobday	23		
Ada Wilson	42	Widower	Temporary House Work

The 1911 Census also states, Total Years Marriage Lasted: 4, Total Children Born Alive: 1, Children Still Alive: 1

Further Reading:
The Complete Jack the Ripper A to Z, Paul Begg, Martin Fido, and Keith Skinner, John Blake, 2010
Jack the Ripper – An Encyclopaedia, John J. Eddleston, Metro Publishing, 2010

3rd April 1888 Emma Elizabeth Smith is attacked.

Mike Covell

> *At around 1.30am on the morning of April 3rd 1888 Emma Elizabeth Smith was walking past St. Mary's Church when she noticed 3 men coming towards her. Concerned for her safety she crossed the road but they followed her and at Osborne-street she was attacked, robbed and raped. Depending upon which source you consult she reached the lodging house between either 2am and 3am or 4am and 5am, with the Inspector Edmund Reid stating that it was the latter, despite being assaulted only 300 yards from her lodging house. Mary Russell, the deputy lodging house keeper, and Annie Lee took Smith to the London Hospital. Dr. George Haslip, the House surgeon ascertained that Smith had been raped using a blunt object, possibly a stick, inserted into her vagina which in turn caused a tear to the perineum. She didn't respond to her treatment and subsequently fell into a coma. Again depending upon whatever source you consult she either died pf peritonitis at 9am on April 4th 1888 or on April 5th 1888. As the motive appeared to be robbery, and three men were involved, the case was not linked to the Jack the Ripper murders, with only a few, including Walter Dew, believing her case was linked. One of the enduring mysteries of the Emma Smith case was not the murder but the aftermath itself. On the way to the hospital they passed a number of police officers on their rounds yet not one was informed of the incident and none asked for assistance.*
>
> *Emma Elizabeth Smith's death is registered thus:*
> *Name: Emma Elizabeth Smith, Estimated Birth Year: abt 1843, Date of Registration: Apr- May-Jun- 1888, Age at Death: 45, Registration District: Whitechapel, Inferred County: London, Vol: 1c, Page: 190*
>
> **Further Reading:**
> *The Complete Jack the Ripper A to Z, Paul Begg, Martin Fido, and Keith Skinner, John Blake, 2010*
> *Jack the Ripper – An Encyclopaedia, John J. Eddleston, Metro Publishing, 2010*
> *The Ultimate Jack the Ripper Sourcebook, Stewart P. Evans, and Keith Skinner, Robinson, 2001*

The Hull Daily Mail, April 6th 1888,

> *SHOCKING OUTRAGE ON A WOMAN. A widow named Emma Elizabeth Smith, aged 45, of Spitalfields, was returning home late on Easter Monday, and when in Whitechapel-road, she was set upon and brutally maltreated by some men, at present unknown. She was taken to the London Hospital, where she died this morning from injuries she received.*

The Hull Daily Mail, April 9th 1888,

> HORRIBLE AND FATAL OUTRAGE ON A WIDOW. At the inquest, at the London Hospital on Saturday, on Emma Elizabeth Smith, aged 45, a widow, who was waylaid, robbed, and barbarously murdered in Whitechapel, while returning home late on Easter Monday evening, a verdict of wilful murder against some persons unknown was returned. The evidence of the deceased and a medical witness showed that deceased was set upon by a number of young ruffians, who first robbed her, then outraged her, and ruptured the perineum by means of a blunt instrument, causing fatal inflammation.

The Hull Daily News, April 9th 1888,

> HORRIBLE AND FATAL OUTRAGE ON A WIDOW. At the inquest, at the London Hospital on Saturday, on Emma Elizabeth Smith, aged 45, a widow, who was waylaid, robbed, and barbarously murdered in Whitechapel, while returning home late on Easter Monday evening, a verdict of wilful murder against some persons unknown was returned. The evidence of the deceased and a medical witness showed that deceased was set upon by a number of young ruffians, who first robbed her, then outraged her, and ruptured the perineum by means of a blunt instrument, causing fatal inflammation.

> ***7th August 1888 Martha Tabram***
> For many Ripperologist's Martha Tabram was Jack the Ripper's first victim mainly because her murder appeared to be the start of what is commonly referred to as escalation. The modus operandi of the murderer was evolving and it was almost as if the killer was trying to see what worked best. To other theorists the murder of Martha Tabram was unrelated to Jack the Ripper and was a random attack that was purely coincidental in the usage of a knife, and the location of the murder in relation to the other later victims.
> On the morning of August 7th 1888 at the early time of 4.50 am, John Reeves, who resided at 37 George Yard Buildings, George Yard, Whitechapel, was descending the stairs of that building when he came across a woman lying on the floor. It was not uncommon for unfortunates to find places to rest away from common lodging houses, but a pool of blood made Reeves draw attention of the discovery to Police Constable Thomas Barrett, (226H), who in turn called for a doctor. Doctor Timothy Robert Killeen attended and declared that life was extinct and had been for three hours. This was interesting as earlier in the

Mike Covell

> *morning, at 3.30 am, Alfred George Crow, a cabman, who resided at 35 George Yard Buildings, passed the body at that time but assumed that the body was nothing more than an unfortunate sleeping and ignored it. Dr. Killeen testified at the inquest that Tabram had suffered a staggering 39 stab wounds on her body.*
>
> *Among the wounds were the left lung, stabbed in 5 places, the right lung, stabbed in 2 places, the heart, stabbed in 1 place, the liver, stabbed in 5 places, the spleen, stabbed in 2 places, and the stomach, stabbed in 6 places. Dr. Killeen testified that he believed, based on the wounds, that at least two sharp objects were used, a knife and possibly a dagger or bayonet.*
>
> *Martha Tabram's death is registered thus:*
> *Name: Martha Tabram, Estimated Birth Year: abt 1849, Date of Registration: Jul- Aug- Sep- 1888, Age at Death: 39, Registration District: Whitechapel, Inferred County, London, Vol: 1c, Page: 210*
>
> ***Further Reading:***
> *The Complete Jack the Ripper A to Z, Paul Begg, Martin Fido, and Keith Skinner, John Blake, 2010*
> *Jack the Ripper – An Encyclopaedia, John J. Eddleston, Metro Publishing, 2010*
> *The Ultimate Jack the Ripper Sourcebook, Stewart P. Evans, and Keith Skinner, Robinson, 2001*

The Hull Daily News, August 10th 1888,

> THE SUPPOSED MURDER AT WHITECHAPEL. At an inquest yesterday afternoon on a woman found dead on Tuesday morning in George Yard Buildings, Whitechapel, her name was stated to be Martha Turner, and it was proved no fewer than 39 knife wounds had been inflicted on the deceased. The inquest was adjourned.

The Hull Daily Mail, August 15th 1888,

> THE WHITECHAPEL MYSTERY. SUPPOSED CLUE. Up to the present all attempts on the part of the police to dispel the mystery surrounding the death of the woman Turner, who was found in George Yard, Whitechapel, under circumstances previously reported, have failed. Inquiries have brought to light the fact that on the night preceding the murder the deceased and a woman giving the name of Connolly were in company with two soldiers, and that something was said as to the deceased accompanying one of the men to George

Yard. As bearing on this incident, the statement of Police constable Barrett is important. That officer was on duty in the neighbourhood of George Yard about two o'clock on the morning of the tragedy, and noticed a soldier loitering. Barrett remarked that it was quiet time he was in barracks, and the soldier replied that he was waiting for a comrade who had accompanied a woman to one of the buildings close at hand. At a parade of soldiers which took place at the Tower on Monday, Barrett identified the man whom he had accosted as described, but the soldier refused to give any account of himself. A parade will take place at Wellington Barracks, probably to day, and Barrett will then be accompanied by a woman Connolly. The police state that the mortal wound which the woman received in the left breast presented the appearance of having been inflicted by a bayonet, whereas the other wounds were knife wounds. The deceased, who had been known as Martha Turner, is said to have lived apart from her husband for some years, and to have latterly got her living as a hawker. Yesterday morning the police received from a man at Guildford a letter of inquiry. The man gives the name of Thomas Hunt, and states that illness had prevented his coming to ascertain if the woman Turner was his wife.

31st August 1888 Mary Ann Nichols

Name: Mary Ann Nichols, Estimated Birth Year: abt 1846, Date of Registration: Jul- Aug- Sep- 1888, Age at Death: 42, Registration District: Whitechapel, Inferred County, London, Vol: 1c, Page: 219

September 1st 1888

The Eastern Morning News, September 1st 1888,

ANOTHER WHITECHAPEL TRAGEDY. BRUTAL MURDER OF A WOMAN. The Central News says: - Following close upon the recent ghastly tragedy in Whitechapel, Londoners were yesterday horrified to hear of a similar outrage perpetrated in a manner which has seldom been equalled for brutality. At a very early hour in the morning a constable on beat duty found lying in Bucks-row, a narrow thoroughfare abutting on Thomas-street, Whitechapel, the dead body of a woman about 40 years of age. The throat was gashed with two cuts, penetrating from the front of the neck to the vertebrae. The body was at once taken to the Whitechapel mortuary, where it was found that the unfortunate victim's abdomen had been ripped up from thighs to breast in a most revolting manner, the intestines protruding from three deep gashes. The clothes were cut and torn in several places, and the face was bruised and much discoloured. The

Mike Covell

> *woman's dress seems to shows that she was in poor circumstances and marks upon some of the under garments indicate that she had been an inmate of the Lambeth Workhouse. This summarises the facts of the case. All besides, is in profound mystery. The police have no clue to the perpetrator of the foul deed, and the neighbours can give no information, or make only such statements as rather add to than diminish the mysteriousness of the affair. Circumstances, however, point pretty clearly to the fact that the crime was not committed at the spot where the victim was found where the victim was found. The doctor who examined the body calls attention to the fact that hardly half a pint of blood was on the ground at the spot, yet the wound is, especially that in the throat, must have bled profusely. Blood marks have been found leading to a place some three hundred yards distance, but yet they have not enabled anyone to establish the scene of the murder. A woman living in Brady-street, an adjoining thoroughfare, heard screams of "police!" and "Murder!" in the small hours, the cries dying away towards Bucks-row, but the information can add nothing else. Up to a late hour last night the matter remained as unsolved as at the hour when the body was found. Telegraphing at midnight the Central News says: - The body of the deceased has been identified as that of a married woman named Mary Ann Nichols, who has been living apart from her husband for some years. She has been an inmate of the Lambeth Workhouse on and off for seven years. She was discharged from the workhouse a few months ago, and went into domestic service at Wandsworth, suddenly leaving her situation under suspicious circumstances seven weeks ago. Since that time she has frequented the locality of Whitechapel-road on the night of the murder under the influence of drink.*

September 3rd 1888

The Hull Daily Mail, September 3rd 1888,

> THE BRUTAL MURDER AT WHITECHAPEL The inquest was resumed at Whitechapel this morning on the body of Mary Ann Nicholls, who was found murdered on Friday morning in Buck's Row, no arrest has yet been made.- Inspector Spratling, J Division, said that at half past four o'clock on Friday morning, when in Hackney Road, he received information of the findings of the body. He went to the mortuary in company with a constable. Witness described the nature of the injuries. The Inspector was unable to describe the precise condition of the clothes at the time the body was found.- It was stated to the Coroner that another officer, Inspector Helson, would give evidence on this point.- Witness proceeding, said between eleven o'clock and noon he examined Buck's Row but found no blood stains. Afterwards he examined the London

> District Railway embankments of the Great Eastern Railway without discovering any traces of blood or any weapon. Henry Tomkin, horse slaughterer, who was working in Winthrop Street, adjoining Bucks Row, with two companions, said they heard no suspicious noises during the night, though the gate of the slaughter house was open. They left at about 12 [illegible]. On hearing of the murder, he and the other two men went to the spot. Witness was of the opinion that the woman was murdered in her clothes, and at the place where the body was found,- Inspector Helson (J Division) described the condition of the deceased's clothing, and said there were no cuts on any part of the apparel. There was no cut under the stays.- Charles Cross, cartman, in the employ of Messrs Pickford, stated when he first discovered the body on the way to work, the clothes were above the knees. From the position of the body he formed the impression that the woman had been outraged.- The inquest was adjourned for the night.

September 4th 1888

The Eastern Morning News, September 4th 1888,

> THE WHITECHAPEL TRAGEDY. The inquest on the body of Mary Ann Nichols, who was found murdered in Whitechapel on Friday morning last, was resumed yesterday morning before Mr. Wynne Baxter, the coroner for East Middlesex. Inspectors Sparklin and Helson gave evidence, describing the wounds and the clothing worn by the deceased. Inspector Helson stated that all the wounds could have been inflicted while the deceased wore her stays. He was of the opinion that the murder was committed on the spot. William Nichols said that deceased was his wife. She left him about seven years ago, and was given to drink. He believed she had been living with various men. Ellen Holland stated that she knew the deceased for about six weeks. She last saw her about half past two on Friday morning last, when she was the worse for drink. She was alone. She did not know any of the deceased's acquaintances. The inquiry was then adjourned for a fortnight. The Central News says another desperate assault, which stopped only short of murder, was committed upon a woman in Whitechapel on Saturday night. The victim was leaving the Foresters Music Hall, Cambridge Heath-road, where she had been spending the evening with a sea captain, when she was accosted by a well-dressed man, who asked her to accompany him. She invited him to go to her apartments, and he acquiesced, requesting her in the meantime to walk a short distance with him, as he wanted to meet a friend. They had reached a point near to the scene of the murder of the woman Nicholls, when the man violently seized his companion by the throat and

Mike Covell

> *dragged her down a court. He was immediately joined by a gang of women and bullies, who stripped the unfortunate woman of her necklace, earrings, and brooch. Her purse was also taken, and she was brutally assaulted. Upon attempting to shout for aid, one of the gang laid a large knife across her throat, remarking, "We will serve you as we did the others." She was eventually released. The police have been informed, and are prosecuting inquiries into the matter, it being regarded as a probable clue to the previous tragedies.*

September 6th 1888

The Eastern Morning News, September 6th 1888,

> THE WHITECHAPEL MYSTERY. *The authorities now investigating this mysterious case assert that they have a clue, but in what direction they are not permitted to make the faintest allusion. "If we did", remarked one of the officers, "Justice would be undoubtedly frustrated" but the chain of evidence is, it is alleged, being fast drawn round the persons implicated- for it is believed there are more than one concerned- though the persons watched will not at present be arrested unless they make an effort to leave the district. The reason of this is sworn evidence which might be lost by precipitate action is likely to reveal the criminal at the forthcoming coroner's inquiry. It is not improbable that one man, not immediately concerned in the crime, but who has a knowledge of the circumstances, may make a confession, and thus shield himself from serious consequences which might otherwise ensue.*

September 8th 1888

> **September 8th 1888 Annie Chapman is murdered.**
>
> *Name: Annie Chapman, Estimated Birth Year: abt 1841, Date of Registration: Jul- Aug- Sep- 1888, Age at Death: 47, Registration District: Whitechapel, Inferred County, London, Vol: 1c, Page: 175*

The Hull Daily News, September 8th 1888,

> THE WHITECHAPEL MURDER. *The inquest was resumed at Whitechapel, on Monday on the body of Mary Ann Nichols, who was found murdered on Friday morning in Buck's Row. No arrest has yet been made. Inspector Spratling, J. Division said at half past four o'clock on Friday morning, when in the Hackney road, he received information of the finding of the body. He went to the*

mortuary in company with a constable. Witness described the nature of the injuries. The inspector was unable to describe the precise condition of the clothes at the time the body was found. It was stated to the coroner that another officer, Inspector Helson, would give evidence on this point. Witness proceeding, said; between eleven o'clock and noon he examined Buck's Row but found no blood stains. Afterwards he examined the London District Railway embankments of the Great Eastern Railway without discovering any traces of blood or any weapon. Henry Tomkin, horse slaughterer, who was working in Winthrop Street, adjoining Bucks Row, with two companions, said they heard no suspicious noises during the night, though the gate of the slaughter house was open. They left at about 12 [illegible]. On hearing of the murder, he and the other two men went to the spot. Witness was of the opinion that the woman was murdered in her clothes, and at the place where the body was found,- Inspector Helson (J Division) described the condition of the deceased's clothing, and said there were no cuts on any part of the apparel. There was no cut under the stays.- Charles Cross, cartman, in the employ of Messrs Pickford, stated when he first discovered the body on the way to work, the clothes were above the knees. From the position of the body he formed the impression that the woman had been outraged. The Court adjourned for luncheon, and subsequently the inquest was adjourned for a fortnight.

The Hull and East Yorkshire and Lincolnshire Times, September 8th 1888,

THE BRUTAL MURDER AT WHITECHAPEL. *The inquest was resumed at Whitechapel, on Monday on the body of Mary Ann Nichols, who was found murdered on Friday morning in Buck's Row. No arrest has yet been made. Inspector Spratling, J. Division said at half past four o'clock on Friday morning, when in the Hackney road, he received information of the finding of the body. He went to the mortuary in company with a constable. Witness described the nature of the injuries. The inspector was unable to describe the precise condition of the clothes at the time the body was found. It was stated to the coroner that another officer, Inspector Helson, would give evidence on this point. Witness proceeding, said; between eleven o'clock and noon he examined Buck's Row but found no blood stains. Afterwards he examined the London District Railway embankments of the Great Eastern Railway without discovering any traces of blood or any weapon. Henry Tomkin, horse slaughterer, who was working in Winthrop Street, adjoining Bucks Row, with two companions, said they heard no suspicious noises during the night, though the gate of the slaughter house was open. They left at about 12 [illegible]. On hearing of the murder, he and the other two men went to the spot. Witness was of the opinion that the woman was*

Mike Covell

> *murdered in her clothes, and at the place where the body was found,- Inspector Helson (J Division) described the condition of the deceased's clothing, and said there were no cuts on any part of the apparel. There was no cut under the stays.- Charles Cross, cartman, in the employ of Messrs Pickford, stated when he first discovered the body on the way to work, the clothes were above the knees. From the position of the body he formed the impression that the woman had been outraged. The Court adjourned for luncheon, and subsequently the inquest was adjourned for a fortnight. ANOTHER WHITECHAPEL OUTRAGE. Another desperate assault, which stopped only short of murder, was committed upon a woman in Whitechapel on Saturday night. The victim was leaving the Foresters Music Hall, Cambridge Heath-road, where she had been spending the evening with a sea captain, when she was accosted by a well-dressed man, who asked her to accompany him. She invited him to go to her apartments, and he acquiesced, requesting her in the meantime to walk a short distance with him, as he wanted to meet a friend. They had reached a point near to the scene of the murder of the woman Nicholls, when the man violently seized his companion by the throat and dragged her down a court. He was immediately joined by a gang of women and bullies, who stripped the unfortunate woman of her necklace, earrings, and brooch. Her purse was also taken, and she was brutally assaulted. Upon attempting to shout for aid, one of the gang laid a large knife across her throat, remarking, "We will serve you as we did the others." She was eventually released. The police have been informed, and are prosecuting inquiries into the matter, it being regarded as a probable clue to the previous tragedies.*

September 10th 1888

The Hull News, September 10th 1888,

> THE LONDON MURDERS. ANOTHER SUPPOSED CLUE. IMPORTANT ARREST. *An important charge was made at the Thames Police court yesterday which the police believe may throw some light upon the recent tragedies in Whitechapel. Charles Ludwig, aged 40, a decently dressed German, of 1 The Minories, was charged with being drunk and threatening to stab Alexander Finlay, of Leman Street, Whitechapel, when the accused came up drunk, and in consequence was refused to be served. He then said to prosecutor, "What are you looking at?" and then pulled out a knife and tried to stab the witness. Ludwig followed him round the stall, and made several attempts to stab him. A constable came up, and he was given into custody. Constable 221 H said the prisoner was in a very excited condition, and witness had previously received information that prisoner was wanted in the city for attempting to cut a woman's*

throat with a razor. On the way to the station he dropped a long bladed open knife, and on him was found a razor and a long bladed pair of scissors. Inspector Pimley asked the magistrate to remand the prisoner, as they had not had sufficient time to make the necessary inquiries concerning him. A city constable, John Johnson, stated that early that morning he was on duty in the Minories when he heard the screams of "Murder" proceeding from a dark court in which there was no lights. The court led to some railway arches and was well known as a dangerous locality. On going into the court he found the prisoner with a prostitute. The former appeared to be under the influence of drink. Witness asked what he was doing there, when he replied "Nothing." The woman, who appeared to be in a very frightened and agitated condition, said, "Oh! Policeman, do take me out of this." The woman was so frightened that she could then make no further statement. He sent the man off and walked with the woman to the end of his beat, when she said, "He frightened me very much when he pulled a big knife out," and witness said, "Why didn't you tell me that at the time? She replied "I was too much frightened." He then went and looked for the prisoner, but could not find him, and therefore warned several other constables of the occurrence, Witness had been out all morning trying to find the woman, but up to the present time without success. He should know her again. He believed the prisoner worked in the neighbourhood. The magistrate thereupon remanded the prisoner. The arrest has caused intense excitement in the neighbourhood. Prisoner professes not to be able to speak English. He has been in this country about three months. He accounts for his time for about three weeks but nothing is known of his doings before that time. Yesterday the Press Association reporter visited the City Newsrooms, Ludgate Circus, and made enquiries of the proprietor as to the circumstances under which the wearing apparel was left there by a strange man on the morning of the 8th inst. Mr. Walker attached no importance to the incident at the time, nor does he now believe that the discovery will have the slightest connection with the crimes now under investigation. Another representative of the Press Association had an interview yesterday afternoon with Alexander Fireberg, of 51 Leman Street, who states that he was assaulted by the man Ludwig, or Ludwig Wetzel, now in custody, and into whose antecedents the police are now inquiring. Fireberg, who is a youth about eighteen years old, stated that he was standing at a coffee stall, at the corner of Commercial Road, about 3-45 yesterday morning, when he noticed a man go by in the company with a woman. His attention was directed to the man by the fact that he was respectably dressed, and in company with a poorly dressed woman. The man and woman were going in the direction of the Minories. The man was about 5ft, 6in, high, and wore a silk hat, came to the coffee stall a quarter of an hour after, and an altercation ensued because he

Mike Covell

> *would not pay a halfpenny for a cup of coffee. He then pulled out a long bladed knife, and chased Fireberg round the stall. A constable arrived on the scene, and the man was taken into custody for attempting to stab Fireberg, who describes his assailant as being about 40 years of age, and as walking with a stiff leg. He had a brown grey beard.*

The Hull Daily News, September 10th 1888,

> *ANOTHER TRAGEDY IN WHITECHAPEL. FRIGHTFUL DISCOVERY. A WOMAN HORRIBLY MUTILATED. HEART AND LIVER TORN OUT. SICKENING DETAILS. At six on Saturday the body of a woman was found in Brown's-lane, late Hambro-street, Spitalfields, in a back lane, with her throat cut and otherwise shockingly mutilated. LATEST PARTICULARS Another telegram says:- Early on Saturday a discovery was made in Hanbury-street, Whitechapel, of the body of a woman shockingly mutilated and murdered. The scene of the crime is not far from Buck's-row, where the woman Nicholls was recently murdered. The discovery was made by John Davies, living at 29, Hambro'-street, in the yard of which the body was found. Mr. Davis was crossing the yard at a quarter to six when he saw a horrible looking ass lying in the corner. While he was gone to give information to the police, Mrs. Richardson, an old lady, sleeping on the first floor, was aroused by her grandson, and looking out of the back window saw the body lying in the yard. The throat was cut from ear to ear, and the deceased was lying on her back with legs outstretched, her clothes were pushed up above the knees, and the body was ripped up from groin to breast bone, the heart and liver where torn out, and the remains were lying in a pool of blood. Chief Inspector West, who was soon called to the spot, states that the woman's name is believed to be Annie Siffey, aged 45, and for the last few months she has been sleeping at a common lodging-house at 35, Dorset-street, Spitalfields, where she was seen at two o'clock that morning. Like Mary Ann Nicholls, who is supposed to have been murdered by the same hands, she was a prostitute, and was known in the neighbourhood of Brick-lane as "Dark Annie." She was five feet high, fair brown wavy hair, blue eyes, and had one or two teeth missing. Soon after the discovery became known the scene of the crime was visited by large crowds, and great consternation prevailed at the succession of the horrible murders in this part of London, this being the fourth case within a comparatively short period. The barmaid of the Bell Inn, Birch-lane, where the murdered woman is said to have been drinking in company with a man, said she opened the house at five o'clock and was very busy on account of Spitalfields Market being held on Saturday. She could not say whether she had served the deceased or not. The*

> body was removed in a rough coffin and placed in the mortuary at Old Montagu-street, where an excited crowd gathered. The universal opinion in the locality is that the murderer is the same man who killed Mrs. Nicholls, and possibly also two other woman who were murdered earlier in the year. On the wall of the yard where the body was discovered the words were found to be written, "Five! Fifteen more, and then I give myself up." The deputy of the lodging-house, Timothy Donovan, last saw the deceased alive shortly before two o'clock, when he refused to admit her, as she was somewhat the worse for drink, and had not the requisite for 8d. Several persons are being examined at the police-station. It is stated that two men have identified the deceased as a woman named Ellen Clarke with whom they were drinking on Friday. In explanation of her being known by the name of Siffey, it is said she lived for some time with a man who worked at sieve making. The police hold the opinion that the murderer is a semi-maniac, and has perpetrated other murders in the East End. Up to half-past two the police had not obtained a clue to the murderer. The report that an arrest had been made arose from the fact that a man was taken to the police station for assault.

The Hull Daily News, September 10th 1888,

> LATEST NEWS. THE HORRIBLE TRAGEDY IN WHITECHAPEL. LATEST PARTICULARS. A Press Association telegram. Despatched at 9-45 a.m. states there is practically nothing new up to this hour in regard to the shocking crime of Saturday morning. Although two or three men have been apprehended on suspicion they have given satisfactory accounts of their movements and, and have been liberated. A MAN IN CUSTODY IN DEPTFORD Inspector Chandler, at Commercial-road police-station, received information after midnight on Sunday that a person was detained at Deptford on suspicion. He proved to be a young man apprehended in Old Kent-road, and his answers to interrogations being considered satisfactory, he was shortly afterwards released. CONTINUED EXCITEMENT At the time of this despatch a group of people stand around the Police-station in Commercial-street, in expectation of anything transpiring in connection with the inquiries of the police. THE INQUEST The inquest opens at ten o'clock at the Boys' Institute, Whitechapel-road. AN ARREST AT GRAVESEND The Press Association's Gravesend correspondent telegraphs at ten o'clock that a man has been arrested at Gravesend on suspicion of being the perpetrator of the Whitechapel murder. Mr. Superintendent Berry, between eight and nine o'clock last night, had a communication that there was a suspicious looking individual at the Pope's Head public-house, West-street, and at once despatched a sergeant to the house and had the man apprehended. It was

Mike Covell

> noticed that his hand was bad, and on examining it the superintendent found it had evidently been bitten. REPORTED APPREHENSION OF "LEATHER APRON" A later message from Whitechapel-road states that it is reported that a man known as "Leather Apron" has been apprehended and taken to Leman-street Police Station, but at present no positive information can be obtained, but that someone is in custody there is no doubt. THE ARREST OF "LEATHER APRON" The Press Association telegraphs that about one o'clock this morning a detective arrested a man known as "Leather Apron," who was wanted in connection with the Whitechapel murder, at 22 Mulberry-street, Commercial-street. The real name of the man is John Piser, but his friends deny that he has ever been known by the nickname of "Leather Apron." When the detective called at the house the door was opened by the prisoner himself. "Just the man I want," said the detective, who charged him on suspicion of being connected with the murder of the woman Liffey. The detective searched the house and took away some finishing tools which prisoner was in the habit of using in his work. By trade he is a boot finisher, and for some time has been living at Mulberry-street, with his stepmother, Mrs Piser, and a married brother who works at cabinet making. When he was arrested by the detective this morning his brother was at work, and the only inmates of the house was his stepmother, his sister-in-law, and a Mr. Nathan, for whom he has worked. His stepmother and his sister-in-law declare positively to a representative of the Press Association that Piser came home at half-past ten on Thursday night, and had not left the house since. They further stated that prisoner was unable to do much work on account of ill health, and that he is by no means strong. Sometime since he was seriously injured in a vital part. About six weeks ago he left the Convalescent Home on account of a carbuncle in the stomach. He is about 35 years of age, and since he was three years old has been brought up by Mrs Piser. He lost his father some sixteen years ago. At the Leman-street Police Station, where Piser was taken, a large force of police was kept in readiness with drawn staves. Only a few people amongst the crowd seemed aware that an arrest had been made, so quietly did the police act in Mulberry-street that few even in the neighbourhood connected the arrest with murder. RETICENCE OF THE POLICE The Police at Leman-street refused to give any information. It was stated from Scotland-yard that such an arrest had been made. This however is in direct contradiction to the statement made by one of Piser's own relatives. ANOTHER ACCOUNT. Another account received by the Press Association states that a large number of long bladed knives and several hats were found in Piser's possession. The arrest was made by Detective-sergeant Thicke.

The Hull Daily Mail, September 10th 1888,

THE WHITECHAPEL MURDER. SEVERAL ARRESTS. The Press Association's Gravesend correspondent telegraphs that at ten o'clock a man arrested at Gravesend on suspicion of being the perpetrator of the Whitechapel murders. Mr. Superintendent Berry, who between eight and nine o'clock on Sunday night had a communication that there was a suspicious looking individual at the Pope's Head public house, West-street, and at once despatched a sergeant to the house, and had the man apprehended. It was noticed that his hand was bad, and on examining it, the superintendent found that it had evidently been bitten. In answer to the inspector, the prisoner stated that he was going down Brick-lane, Spitalfields, at 4.30 on Saturday morning, when a woman fell down in a fit. He stopped to pick her up, whereupon she bit him through the hand. Two policemen then came up, and he ran away.- Dr Whitcome, the police surgeon, having examined the man's clothing, discovered blood spots on two shirts the man was carrying in a bundle. He was also of opinion that blood had been wiped off his boots. The woman was in the street, and not at the back of a lodging house. Prisoner added that on Friday he was walking about Whitechapel all night. Detective sergeant Abberley, from Scotland Yard, has arrived to further examine the man in custody. A later telegram from Gravesend states that the man arrested there is named Pigott, and the circumstances of suspicion are on strong that Detective inspector Abberline has conveyed him to London by the South Eastern train. Prisoner was not handcuffed, and was smoking a clay pipe and carrying a white handle. His arrival created no stir, and he was conveyed in a four wheeled cab to Commercial-street Police Station. He will be detained there pending the arrival of a witness to identify him. He answers the description of "Leather Apron," and when apprehended had no vest on. His clothes are spotted in several places with blood and his hands are cut. He also has a black beard, and is apparently recovering from a severe attack of delirium tremens. He stated that the wounds on his hands were caused by the bite of a woman. Great excitement still prevails. On being examined by the police at Commercial-street Piggott was found to be bespattered with blood from head to foot, even his boots bearing traces of a sanguinary struggle. In his pockets were found a few coppers and a piece of a lead pencil. He sits in a cell in a state of deep lethargy, taking no notice of anything. His whole demeanour [illegible] a recent bout of excessive drinking. He adheres to the original statement. Pigott, the man arrested at Gravesend, has been examined by Dr. Phillips, divisional surgeon, and pronounced insane. In due course he will be removed to the Infirmary. The Press Association telegraphs at 10.30 a.m.:- "Leather Apron" was arrested at nine o'clock, this morning, at 22, Mulberry-street, Commercial-street, His name is John Pizer." The Press Association telegraphs:- About one o'clock this morning a detective arrested a man known as "Leather Apron," who was

Mike Covell

wanted in connection with the Whitechapel murder, at 22, Mulberry-street, Commercial-street. The real name of the man is John Pizer, but his friends deny that he has ever been known as "Leather Apron." When the detective called at the house the door was opened by the prisoner himself. "Just the man I want," said the detective, who charged him on suspicion of being connected with the murder of the woman Liffey- The Detective searched the house and took away some finishing tools which the prisoner was in the habit of using in his work by trade. He is a boot finisher, and has for some time been living at Mulberry-street with his stepmother, Mrs Pizer, and a married brother, who works at cabinet making. When he was arrested by the detective this morning his brother was at work, and the only inmates of the house were the prisoner's step mother, his sister-in-law, and a Mr. Nathan, for whom he has work. His step mother and his sister-in-law declare positively to a representative of the Press "Association that Piser came home at half-past ten on Thursday night and had not left the house since. They further stated that the prisoner was unable to do much work on account of ill health, and that he is by no means strong. Some time since he was seriously injured in a vital part. About six weeks ago he left the Convalescent Home on account of a carbuncle in the stomach. He is about 35 years of age, and since he was three years old, has been brought up by Mrs Piser. He lost his father some 16 years ago. At the Leman-street police station, where Piser was taken, a large force of police kept in readiness with drawn staves. Only a few people amongst the crowd out seemed aware that an arrest had been made. So quietly did the police act in Mulberry-street that few even in the neighbourhood connected the arrest with the murder. The police at Leman-street refused to give any information. It was stated from Scotland yard that such an arrest had been made. This, however, is in the direct contradiction made by the prisoner's own relatives. Another account received by the Press Association states that a large number of long bladed knives and several hats were found in prisoner's possession. The arrest was made by Detective sergeant Thicke. The Press Association in a later despatch says the excitement upon the arrest of the man said to be "Leather Apron" was intense, large crowds surrounding the police station and discussing the affair. The police however, refuse to give details. At present the prisoner has evidently not been specifically charged with any offence. Several residents in Mulberry-street in an interview with the Press Association's representative, stated that the prisoner was harmless sort of person, and unlikely to commit the crime alleged. Nothing further can be ascertained about Piser. He has not yet been charged with any offence, and is merely detained pending further inquiries. The detectives do not appear to be very clear as to his being the man known as "Leather Apron." THE INQUEST. The inquest on the body of Annie Chapman, who was found murdered in

Hanbury-street, Whitechapel, on Saturday was opened at ten o'clock by Mr Wynne Baxter, District Coroner, at the Working Lads Institute, Whitechapel Road.- Inspector Nelson, J Division, represented the police.- Mr Collier deputy coroner, accompanied Mr Wynne Baxter. The jury having been sworn in went to view the body at the mortuary. On their return John Davies deposed: I live at 29, Hanbury-street, Spitalfields. I am a carman, and occupy a front room with my wife and three sons. On Friday night I went to bed at eight o'clock. My sons came in at different times, the last at about quarter to 11. I was awake between three and five o'clock, but fell to sleep for about half an hour, and got up at about quarter to six. I went across to the yard. On the ground floor there is a front door leading into a passage through the basement. There is a back door in the passage. Sometimes the doors are left open during the night. I have never known either of them to be locked. Anyone can open the front door by the latch, and enter the yard by the passage, I cannot say whether the back door was latched when I got down, but the front door was wide open, which was not an unusual circumstance.- Witness being asked to describe the general appearance of the yard, was not very clear in his statements.- The Coroner said the police in country places had generally prepared a plan of the locality which was the subject of investigation. Certainly this was of sufficient importance for such a plan .- Inspector Chandler promised that a plan should be drawn up.- The Coroner said that delay might prove fatal.- Witness resuming said: When I opened the back door of the yard I found a woman lying on her back. I called two men in the employ of Mr Bayley, packing case maker in Hanbury-street, three down from no. 29. They came and looked at the body. I do not know them personally.- In reply to the Coroner, Inspector Chandler said the men referred to were not known to the police.- The Coroner expressed surprise at this. He said the men must be found, if they had not already been seen and identified. Davis (continuing) said: I informed the inspector at Commercial-street what I had seen in the yard. I heard no voice on Saturday evening. - Amelia Palmer, living at 30, Dorset-street, lodging house, was next examined. She said her husband was an army pensioner. She knew the deceased for five years, and identified the body as that of Annie Chapman, a widow. Her husband died at Windsor 18 months ago. Prior to that she received 10s a week from him. Deceased was called Mrs Liffey, because she lived with a man who was a sieve maker. She had been staying at 35, Dorset-street. Witness had seen her several times the worse for drink, and she was frequently out in the streets late at night. On Friday afternoon witness saw her in Dorset-street about five o'clock. She said she had no money, and had been in the casual ward, and she could not pay for her lodging. - Timothy Donovan (35), Dorset-street, deputy of a common lodging house, identified the body at the Mortuary as the woman who had

Mike Covell

> *lodged at his house occasionally. She was not at No. 35 last week until Friday afternoon, about three o'clock. She went into the kitchen, and he did not see her again till Saturday morning at 1.45. She afterwards left the house, and said she should come back again for a bed. She was somewhat the worst for liquor, and when she left in the morning the witness said, "You can find money for your bed." He did not see her with any man that night. Sometimes she came to the house with a man said to be a pensioner, and sometimes with other men, and witness had refused to allow her a bed. Replying to the Coroner, witness added that, the pensioner had told him not to admit her with any other man. - Inspector Chandler, in answer to the Coroner, said nothing was known of the man called the pensioner.- Donavan (resuming) said on August 29th deceased had a row with another woman in the kitchen, and sustained a bruise over her eye.- John Evans, night watchman, 35, Dorset-street, said he saw the deceased go out on Saturday morning, she never returned. She was worse for drink. Witness knew she was on the streets at night, but only knew of the man with whom she associated. He used to come to her on Saturdays. He called about half past two on Saturday last, and when he was told of the murder went away without saying anything. He did not know this man's name or address. The inquest was adjourned until Wednesday.*

John Pizer:
Born in Poland and known as "Leather Apron." Pizer Died of Gastro-enteritis at the London Hospital in July 1897. He is also known as Piser, and Piza.

1851 Census, Class HO107, P1532, F403, P7, GSU174762, St James, Duke's Place, London

Israel Piza	Head	38	General Dealer	B. Poland
Abigail Piza	Wife	40		B. Surrey
John Piza	Son	7 mo		B. London St James, Duke's Place
Elizabeth Moss		63	Servant	
Ann Salter		59	General	

			Servant	

1861 Census, Class RG9, P294, F62, P28, GSU542608, German Jews Hospital, Mile End Old Town, London

John Piser	Inmate	10	Scholar	B. 1851

1871 Census, Class RG10, P556, F23, P45, GSU823398

Israel Pizer	Head	58	Town Traveller	B. Poland
Augusta Pizer	Wife	50		B. Stepney, Middlesex
Samuel G Pizer	Son	10		B. Poland
Leah Cohen	Mother in Law	76		

John Pizer's death:
Name: John Pizer, Estimated Birth Year: abt 1850, Date of Registration: Jul- Aug- Sep- 1897, Age at Death: 47, Registration District: Whitechapel, Inferred County: London, Vol: 1c, Page: 205

The Hull Daily News, September 10th 1888,

THE WHITECHAPEL TRAGEDY. SEARCH FOR THE MURDERER. NUMEROUS ARRESTS. Although the police have made most diligent inquiry after the murderer of the woman, whose real name is Chapman, they had up to last night failed to find the slightest clue to his whereabouts. As a matter of fact, they are in the dark as to the personal appearance of the man for whom they are looking. It is true that they possess the description of a man who is known as "Leather Apron," and will arrest him if he can be found, but their theory is that "Leather Apron" is more or less a mythical personage, and that he is not responsible for the terrible crimes with which his name has been associated. All the same the details of his appearance have been widely circulated, with a view to his early apprehension. All the police in the vicinity are on the look-out for him. On Saturday night a large force of police constables and detectives closely watched the neighbourhood. Men were posted at all the entrances and exits of

Mike Covell

the numerous alleys and passages in the neighbourhood, who every few minutes made a thorough examination of the places under their surveillance, and from time to time these were visited by the Inspectors on duty, with a view to ascertaining whether any suspicious character had been observed. From ten o'clock at night until late in the morning a large crowd occupied Hanbury street, in the vicinity of the notorious house, No. 29. When the public houses emptied the occupants swarmed into the street, causing a good deal of trouble to the police by their behaviour. The people living in the adjoining houses obtained no rest until between four and five o'clock, when the crowd gradually melted away, only, however, to reassemble again in greater force as soon as daylight appeared. In the course of Saturday night and Sunday morning the police arrested two men on suspicion of being concerned in the crime. One man, whose appearance left little doubt in the minds of his captors that he was the Hanbury street murder, was found by an officer in Buck's row shortly after 1 o'clock on Sunday morning. A murder was, it will be remembered, committed in the neighbourhood but a short time since, and the police have since been constantly pursuing their investigation in that quarter. The man upon whom suspicion rested presented a most forbidding appearance. He appeared to be hiding in the street, and when accosted by the officer, rushed off at the top of his speed. An alarm was raised, and after a short race he was arrested. He was a villainous-looking fellow with long hair and shaggy beard, dressed only in a pair of ragged blue serge trousers and an old dirty shirt. He resisted his captors, but was eventually secured and conveyed to Bethnal Green Police Station. It was said at the time that he was carrying a long knife concealed in the sleeve of his shirt, but on examination no weapon was found upon him. He gave an account of himself which was, in the first instance, considered unsatisfactory, but inquiries were immediately set on foot, and in the result the man, who appears to be a common vagrant, was released from custody. The second arrest was effected in Gloucester street, where a man aged about 40, having the look of a seafarer, was arrested. It was pretty obvious, however, from the replies which he gave, and his general appearance that he was not the man sought for, and after he had spent some time in Commercial street Station he was also set at liberty. It is suggested that the first mentioned man is the person who has been spoken of by Mrs. Fiddymont, wife of the proprietor of the Prince Albert public-house, situate at the corner of Brushfield street and Stewart street. Mrs. Fiddymont has stated to the police that at seven o'clock on Saturday morning a rough-looking man came into the place and got some ale. He presented an excited appearance, and some blood-spots were said to have been observed on his right hand. This man, however, had a coat and hat on. The police, however, who gave information very unwillingly, and who do not accept the theory that the crime has been committed by the man designated "Leather Apron," are indisposed to believe that the person seen by Mrs. Fiddymont has any connection with the crime. They are unwilling, indeed, to accept assistance or suggestion from any private source and work upon a plan of their own, which consists of frequent visits to the common lodging-houses of the neighbourhood and a strict watch at night on all the streets in the vicinity. All day to-day five policemen have guarded the scene of the crime in Hanbury street. No one was admitted unless he lived in the house. In the street half a dozen costermongers took up their stand and did brisk business in fruit and refreshments. Thousands of respectably dressed persons visited the scene, and occasionally the road became so crowded that the constables had to clear it by making a series of raids upon the spectators. The windows of the adjoining houses were full of persons watching the crowd below. A number of people also visited the house in Dorset street where the murdered woman lodged. It may be mentioned here that the soldier who had frequently visited the woman at this place did not return to the house on Saturday night. The police, however, attach no importance to this circumstance. Inquiries have been made at Vauxhall and at Windsor where Chapman or "Sievy," as she was more generally called, is said to have relatives, but so far without any fresh information obtained as to her antecedents. The deceased has been identified by persons who have known her since she has lived in London, but her relatives, if she possesses any, have not yet communicated with the police. The small portion of writing on the envelope found upon the body, bearing the stamp of the Sussex Regiment, has not yet been identified or traced. The authorities of St Bartholemew's Hospital, where the woman spent some time, have been communicated with, but they have not been able to afford any information of a useful character. The usually lively condition of Whitechapel and Spitalfields on a Sunday was considerably augmented to-day by reason of the excitement aroused by the murder. In the course of the day nearly a dozen persons were arrested, and conveyed to the Commercial street Police Station. In the afternoon a vast crowd had collected about the streets. As each apprehension was made they rushed pell mell towards the station, obviously under the idea that the murderer of the woman had been caught. Shortly before five o'clock a man was arrested in Dal street after a long chase on a charge of assault. The officer who arrested him proceeded with his prisoner by way of Hanbury street to the police station and so was obliged to make his way through the crowd. Outside the house his prisoner stood in some danger of being mobbed, but the crowd eventually gave way, and the prisoner was safely lodged in the station. A few minutes later two men were arrested in Wentworth street. As soon as the crowd saw them in the hands of the police there were loud cries of "Leather Apron," and thereupon hundreds of persons turned out from the side streets and followed

Mike Covell

the officers in a tumultuous throng to the station. Not five minutes afterwards a woman was apprehended on some small charge, and the excitement became so intense that a posse of officers was sent out from the building to preserve order. These marched three and four abreast up and down the pavement, and while they were so engaged yet another prisoner was brought in. There was a good deal of shouting in the mob, which surged about in a dangerous fashion, but by-and-bye a diversion was caused by the rapid passage along Banbury street of three men who were supposed to be two detectives and their prisoner. The centre man bore a striking resemblance to "Leather Apron," and the cry of "That's him," having been raised, a rush was made at him, but the little party immediately turned down a side street, and the police prevented the crowd from proceeding further. In the neighbourhood of the mortuary, which is situated in Eagle place, at the Whitechapel end of Hanbury street, all was quiet during the day. The green doors opened now and again to admit some inspectors of police and several medical gentlemen, but all others were rigidly excluded. The inquest on the body will be held to-morrow (Monday) by Dr MacDonald, the coroner for the district. Dr Phillips, the surgeon, and the witnesses who first discovered the body, will be called, and the police will also give certain evidence. Dr Phillips believes that the woman had been dead for two hours or more when she was discovered. It is a remarkable fact, however, that the man Richardson, who first went into the yard where the corpse was discovered says that he actually sat down on the step of the passage to cut a piece of leather off his shoe and yet did not see the body. This, however, may be explained by the circumstances that the passage door opens outward and toward the left, and so would conceal the body behind it. It is the custom to leave both of the passage doors open at night, and although they were found shut on the morning of the murder no suspicion was excited on that account. The advisability of employing bloodhounds to trace the perpetrator of the crime has been eagerly discussed by the inhabitants of the district. It is considered by experts that the time has gone by for such an experiment, and it is pointed out also that in the case of the Blackburn murderer, who was discovered by this means, the circumstances were different, and that the present case does not admit of the test. LEATHER APRON Reference is made in the above report to a mysterious being bearing the name of "Leather Apron," concerning whom a number of stories have for a week or more been current in Whitechapel. A reporter of the Star, who has been making some inquiries among a number of women in the East-end gives the following description of the man:- He is five feet four or five inches in height, and wears a dark close fitting cap. He is thickset and has an unusually thick neck. His hair is black, and closely clipped, his age being about 39 or 40. He has a small black moustache. The distinguishing feature of his costume is a leather apron, which he always wears, and from which he gets his nickname. His expression is sinister, and seems full of terror for the women who describe it. His eyes are small and glittering. His lips are usually parted in a grin which is not only not reassuring, but excessively repellent. He is a slipper-maker by trade, but does not work. His business is blackmailing women late at night. A number of men in Whitechapel follow this interesting profession. He has never cut anybody, so far as is known, but always carries a leather knife, presumably as sharp as leather knifes are wont to be. This knife a number of the women have seen. His name nobody knows, but all are united in the belief that he is a Jew or of Jewish parentage, his face being of a marked Hebrew type. But the most singular characteristic of the man is the universal statement that in moving about he never makes any noise. What he wears on his feet the women do not know, but they agree that he moves noiselessly. His uncanny peculiarity to them is that they never see him or know of his presence until he is close by them. "Leather Apron" never by any chance attacks a man. He runs away on the slightest appearance of rescue. One woman whom he assailed some time ago boldly prosecuted him for it, and he was sent up for seven days. He has no settled place of residence, but has slept oftenest in a fourpenny lodging-house of the lowest kind in a disreputable lane leading from Brick-lane. The people at this lodging-house denied that he had been there and appeared disposed to shield him. "Leather Apron's" pal "Mickeldy Joe," was in the house at the time, and his presence doubtless had something to do with the unwillingness to give information. "Leather Apron" was last at this house some weeks ago, though this account may be untrue. He ranges all over London, and rarely assails the same woman twice. He has lately been seen in Leather-lane, which is in the Holborn district. ANOTHER WOMAN STABBED. At five minutes after 11 o'clock a man suddenly attacked a woman in the Spitalfields Market, while she was passing through. After felling her to the ground with a blow, he began kicking her, and pulled out a knife. Some women who had collected, having the terrible tragedy that brought them there still fresh in their minds, on seeing the knife, raised such piercing shrieks of "Murderer," &c that they reached the enormous crowds in the busy street. There was at once a rush for Commercial street, where the markets are situate, as it was shouted out by some that there was another murder, and by others that the murderer had been arrested. Seeing the immense crowd swarming round him, the man who was the cause of the alarm made more furious efforts to reach the woman, from whom he had been separated by some persons who interfered on her behalf. He, however, threw them on one side, fell upon the woman knife in hand, and inflicted various stabs on her head, and cut her forehead, neck and fingers before he was again got away from her. The woman then lay motionless. The crowd then took up the shout of "Murder!" and

Mike Covell

> the people who were on the skirts raised cries of "Lynch him." At this juncture the police arrived, arrested the man, and after a while had the woman conveyed on a stretcher to the police station in Commercial street where she was examined by the divisional surgeon. She was found to be suffering from several wounds, but none of them considered dangerous. She was subsequently removed to the London Hospital where she was detained as an in patient. The blind man is described as having a most ungovernable temper, and he was seen whilst the woman was leading him along to stab her several times in the neck. Blood flowed quickly, and it was at first thought that another terrible murder had been committed. The affair occurred midway between Buck's row and Hanbury Street, where the last two horrible murders have been committed.

The Eastern Morning News, September 10th 1888,

> ANOTHER BRUTAL MURDER IN WHITECHAPEL. HORRIBLE MUTILATION OF THE VICTIM. A PANIC STRICKEN POPULACE. ARRESTS ON SUSPICION. FULL DETAILS. On Saturday morning, at a quarter past six, the neighbourhood of Whitechapel was horrified to a degree bordering on panic by the discovery of another barbarous murder of a woman at 29, Hanbury-street (late Brown-lane), Spitalfields. Hanbury-street is a thoroughfare running between Commercial-street and Whitechapel Road, the occupants of which are poor and for the most part of Jewish extraction. The circumstances of the murder are of such a revolting character as to point to the conclusion that it had been perpetrated by the hand which committed that in Buck's Row and the two previous murders, all of which have occurred within a stone's throw of each other. The murdered woman, who appears to have been respectably connected, was known in the neighbourhood by women of the unfortunate class as Annie Sivvy, but her real name was Annie Chapman. She is described by those who knew her best as a decent, although poor, looking woman, about 5ft. 2in. or 5ft. 3in. high, with fair brown wavy hair, blue eyes, large flat nose; and, strange to say, she had two of her front teeth missing, as had Mary Ann Nicholls, who was murdered in Buck's Row. When her body was found it was respectably clad. She wore no head covering, but simply a skirt and bodice and two light petticoats. A search being made in her pockets nothing was found but an envelope stamped "The Sussex Regiment." The house in Hanbury-street in the yard of which the crime was committed is occupied by a woman named Richardson, who employs several men in the rough packing line. There is a small shop in front at the basement of the house, which is utilised for the purposes of a cat's meat shop. From the upper end of the house there is a passage at either end leading to a small yard, some 13ft. or 14ft. square, separated from the adjoining houses by a

slight wooden fence. There is no outlet at the back, and any person who gains access must of necessity make his exit from the same end as his entry. In the yard there were recently some packing cases, which had been sent up from the basement of the dwelling, but just behind the lower door there was a clear space left, wherein the murder was undoubtedly committed. The theory primarily formed was that the unfortunate victims had been first murdered and afterwards dragged through the entry into the back yard, but from an inspection made later in the day it appears that the murder was actually committed in the corner of the yard, which the back door when open places in obscurity. There were some marks of blood observable in the passage, but it is now known that these were caused during the work of removal of some packing-cases, the edges of which accidentally came in contact with the blood upon the spot from which the unhappy victim was removed.

The discovery of the murder appears to have been made by John Davis, a porter in Spitalfields Market, and one of the occupants of 29, Hanbury-street, but at 5.25, about three-quarters of an hour before the body was found, Albert Cadosch, who lodges next door, had occasion to go into the adjoining yard at the back, and states that he heard a conversation on the other side of the palings as if between two people. He caught the word "No,' and fancied he subsequently heard a slight scuffle, with the noise of a falling against the palings, but thinking that his neighbours might probably be out in the yard he took no further notice and went to his work. It is stated, however, that in the house the back premises of which happened to become the scene of this hideous crime no fewer than six separate families reside, and some people who live on the ground floor and are credited with being "light sleepers" assert emphatically that during the night and morning they heard no sound of a suspicious nature, which is likely enough in view of the pact that the passage from the front to the back of the house has been invariably left open for the convenience of dwellers in the building, the traffic being constant. When the man Davis made his discovery he made no attempt to ascertain the condition of deceased, but immediately alarmed the other inmates of the house, and then proceeded to acquaint the police at the Commercial-street station with what had occurred. In the meantime Mrs. Richardson, the principal occupier of the premises (sic), together with a young woman named Eliza Cooksly, sleeping on the second floor, were aroused, and under the notion that the building was on fire ran to the back bedroom window, whence they were enabled to see the murdered woman lying on the paved yard. When the police arrived they found that the woman had been murdered in a terribly brutal fashion. Her clothes were disarranged, her throat cut, and her body mutilated in a manner too horrible for description. With as little delay as possible the officers

Mike Covell

removed the body to the nearest mortuary. Among other statements bearing upon the finding of the body is one by Mrs. Richardson, the landlady at 29, Hanbury-street, who says: "I have lived at this house fifteen years, and my lodgers are poor but hard-working people. Some have lodged with me as long as twelve years. They mostly work at the fish market or the Spitalfields Market. Some of the carmen in the fish market go out to work as early as 1 a.m., while others go out at four and five, so that the place is open all night and anyone can get in. It is certain that the deceased came voluntarily into the yard, as if there had been any struggle it must have been heard, several lodgers sleep at the back of the house, and some had their windows open, but no noise was heard from the yard. One of my lodgers, a carman, named Thompson, employed at Goodson's, in Brick Lane, went out at four o'clock in the morning. He did not go into the yard, but he did not notice anything particular in the passage as he went out. My son John came in at ten minutes to five, and he gave a look round before he went to market. He went through to the yard, but no one was there then, and everything was right. Just before six o'clock, when Mr. Davis, another of my lodgers, came down, he found the deceased lying in the corner of the yard, close to the house, and by the side of the step. There was not the slightest sign of a struggle, and the pool of blood which flowed from the throat after it was cut was close to the step where she lay. She does not appear to have moved an inch after the fiend struck her with the knife. She must have died instantly. The murderer must have gone away from the spot covered in blood. There was an earthenware pan containing water in the yard; but this was not discoloured, and could not, therefore, have been used by the murderer. The only possible clue that I can think of is that Mr. Thompsons's wife met a man about a month ago lying on the stairs. This was about four o'clock in the morning. He looked like a Jew, and spoke with a foreign accent. When asked what he was doing there, he replied he was wanting to do a 'doss' before the market opened. He slept on the stairs that night, and I believe he has slept on the stairs on other nights. Mrs. Thompson is certain she could recognise the man again both by his personal appearance and peculiar voice." With regard to the history and recent movements of the victim a woman named Amelia Farmer has given important information. She states that the deceased, whom she had known for a considerable time, had been a fellow-lodger with her. The name of the deceased was Annie Chapman, and she was the wife of a veterinary surgeon, who died at Windsor about 18 months ago. Annie Chapman had for a long time been separated from her husband by mutual agreement, and had been allowed 10s. a week by him for her maintenance. The money had been sent by Post-office order, and had always come regularly. About 18 months ago the instalments suddenly ceased, and, upon inquiry being made, it was found that the husband had died. Annie Chapman had two children, but where they were she could not say. The deceased had a mother and sister, who were living in the neighbourhood of Brompton or Fulham. Farmer had been in the habit of writing letters for her friend, but could not remember the exact address of the mother or sister, but thought it was near the Brompton Hospital. Last Monday, Chapman had intimated her intention of communicating with her sister, saying-- "If I can get a pair of boots from my sister I shall go hop picking." Another relation, a brother-in-law of the deceased, lived somewhere in or near Oxford-street. Farmer asserted that her murdered friend was apparently a sober, steady-going sort of woman, and one who seldom took any drink. For some time past she had been living occasionally with a man who had been in the militia, but was now working at some neighbouring brewery. He was a good-tempered man, rather tall, about 5ft. 10in., fair, and of florid complexion. He was the last man in the world to have quarrelled with Chapman, nor would he have injured her in any way. At the beginning of the week, the deceased had been rather severely knocked about in the breast and face by another woman of the locality through jealousy, and had been obliged to go to the casual ward. As a regular means of livelihood she had not been in the habit of frequenting the streets, but had made antimacassars for sale. Sometimes she would buy flowers or matches with which to pick up a living. Farmer was perfectly certain that on Friday night the murdered woman had worn three rings, which were not genuine, but were imitations, otherwise she would not have troubled to go out and find money for her lodgings, as a lodging-house keeper said she did on Friday night. The deputy of a lodging-house at 30, Dorset-street, states that Annie Chapman used to lodge there about two years ago with a man called Jack Sivvy, a sieve maker; hence her nickname was Annie Sivvy. She appeared to be a quiet woman, and not given to drinking; in fact, he was quite surprised to hear that she had been seen drinking the night before her murder. The woman had two children to his knowledge--a boy who was a cripple, and who he believed was at some charitable school, and a daughter who was somewhere in France. Timothy Donovan, the deputy at the lodging-house, 35 Dorset- street, stated that the deceased had been in the habit of coming there for the past four months. She was a quiet woman, and gave no trouble. He had heard her say she wished she was as well off as her relations, but she never told him who her relations were or where they lived. A pensioner or a soldier usually came to the lodging-house with her on Saturday nights and generally he stayed until the Monday morning. He would be able to identify the man instantly if he saw him. After the man left on Monday deceased would usually keep in the room for some days longer, the charge being eightpence per night. This man stayed at the house from Saturday to Monday last, and when he went the deceased went with him. She was not seen

Mike Covell

at the house again until Friday night about half-past eleven o'clock, when she passed the doorway, and Donovan, calling out, asked her where she had been since Monday, and why she had not slept there, and she replied, "I have been in the Infirmary." Then she went on her way in the direction of Bishopsgate-street. About 1.40 a.m. on Saturday morning she came again to the lodging-house, and asked for a bed. The message was brought upstairs to him, and he sent downstairs to ask for the money. The woman replied, "I haven't enough now, but keep my bed for me. I shan't be long." She was the worse for drink at the time, and was eating some baked potatoes. He saw nothing of her again until he was called to the mortuary yesterday morning, when he identified the deceased by her features and her wavy hair, which was turning gray. After deceased left on Monday last he found two large bottles in the room, one containing medicine, and labelled in a manner which confirmed her statement that she had been under medical treatment. On being asked whether he knew a man called "Leather Apron," Donovan said he knew him well. He came to the lodging-house about twelve months ago, a woman being his companion. In the early hours of the morning the woman commenced screaming murder, and it seems that "Leather Apron" had knocked her down and tore her hair and clothes. "Leather Apron" said the woman was trying to rob him, but he (Donovan) did not believe him, and turned him out of the house. The man had come there several times since for a lodging, but they would not admit him. No definite clue has as yet been obtained of the perpetrator of the fiendish crime, but the populace is in a state of excitement, which is prolific in rumours which may or may not lead to results. For instance, it was ascertained on Saturday night that a pawnbroker in Mile End Road had detained rings which had been presented to him for pledge, but which on being tested had not been found genuine. Should these rings prove to be those taken from Annie Chapman, and should Amelia Farmer be able to identify them, a solid trace of the bloodthirsty and cruel murderer will be obtained which may lead to his capture. Another clue was furnished by Mrs. Fiddymont, wife of the proprietor of the Prince Albert public-house, better known as the "Clean House," at the corner of Brushfield and Stewart Streets, half a mile from the scene of the murder. Mrs. Fiddymont states that at seven o'clock on Saturday morning she was standing in the bar talking with another woman, a friend, in the first compartment. Suddenly there came into the middle compartment whose rough appearance frightened her. He had on a brown stilt hat, a dark coat, and no waistcoat. He came in with his hat down over his eyes, and with his face partly concealed, and asked for half pint of four ale. She drew the ale, and meanwhile looked at him through the mirror at the back of the bar. As soon as he saw the woman in the other compartment watching him he turned his back, and got the partition between himself and her. The thing that struck

Mrs. Fiddymont particularly was the fact that there were blood spots on the back of his right hand. This, taken in connection with his appearance, caused her uneasiness. She also noticed that his shirt was torn. As soon as he had drunk the ale, which he swallowed at a gulp, he went out. Her friend went out also to watch him. The story is corroborated by the friend alluded to, whose name is Mrs. Mary Chappell, living in Stewart-street. Mrs. Chappell says that when the man came in, the expression of his eyes caught her attention--his look was so startling and terrifying. It frightened Mrs. Fiddymont so that she requested her to stay. He wore a light blue check shirt, which was torn badly, into rags in fact, on the right shoulder. There was a narrow streak of blood under the right ear, parallel with the edge of his shirt. There was also dried blood between the fingers of his hand. When he went out she slipped out at the other door, and watched him as he went towards Bishopsgate-street. She called Joseph Taylor's attention to him, and Joseph Taylor followed him. Joseph Taylor is a builder at 22, Stewart-street. He states that as soon as his attention was attracted to the man he followed him. He walked rapidly, and came alongside him, but did not speak to him. The man was rather thin, about 5ft. 8in. high, and apparently between forty and fifty years of age. He had a shabby genteel look, pepper and salt trousers which fitted badly, and dark coat. When Taylor came alongside him the man glanced at him, and Taylor's description of the look was, "His eyes were as wild as a hawk's." Taylor is a perfectly reliable man, well known throughout the neighbourhood. The man walked, he says, holding his coat together at the top. He had a nervous and frightened way about him. He had a ginger-coloured moustache and had short sandy hair. Taylor ceased to follow him, but watched him as far as "Dirty Dick's," in Halfmoon-street, where he became lost to view. On the wall of the yard near where the body was found there was written, "Five. 15 more and then I give myself up." Reference is made in the above report to a mysterious being bearing the name of "Leather Apron," concerning whom a number of stories have for a week or more been current in Whitechapel. Of this individual the following description is given:-- He is 5ft. 4in. or 5ft. 5in. in height, and wears a dark close-fitting cap. He is thickset, and has an unusually thick neck. His hair is black, and closely clipped, his age being about 38 or 40. He has a small black moustache. The distinguishing feature of his costume is a leather apron, which he always wears, and from which he gets his nickname. His expression is sinister, and seems to be full of terror for the women who describe it. His eyes are small and glittering. His lips are usually parted in a grin, which is not only not reassuring, but excessively repellent. He is a slippermaker by trade, but does not work. His business is blackmailing women late at night. A number of men in Whitechapel follow this interesting profession. He has never cut anybody, so far as is known, but always carries a leather knife, presumably

Mike Covell

as sharp as leather knives are wont to be. This knife a number of the women have seen. His name nobody knows, but all are united in the belief that he is a Jew or of Jewish parentage, his face being of a marked Hebrew type. But the most singular characteristic of the man is the universal statement that in moving about he never makes any noise. What he wears on his feet the women do not know, but they agree that he moves noiselessly. His uncanny peculiarity to them is that they never see him or know of his presence until he is close by them. "Leather Apron" never by any chance attacks a man. He runs away on the slightest appearance of rescue. One woman whom he assailed some time ago boldly prosecuted him for it, and he was sent up for seven days. He has no settled place of residence, but has slept oftenest in a four penny lodging-house of the lowest kind in a disreputable lane leading from Brick Lane. The people at this lodging house denied that he had been there, and appeared disposed to shield him. "Leather Apron's" pal, "Mickeldy Joe," was in the house at the time, and his presence doubtless had something to do with the unwillingness to give information. "Leather Apron" was last at this house some weeks ago, though this account may be untrue. He ranges all over London, and rarely assails the same woman twice. He has lately been seen in Leather Lane, which is in the Helborn district. The whole of the East End up till a late hour on Saturday night was in a state of consternation, at the latest and what undoubtedly is the most horrible of a series of murders which have taken place within so small an area and during so short a period. All day nothing else was talked of, even by men who are hardened to seeing a great deal that is brutal. Strong, buxom, muscular women seemed to move in fear and trembling, declaring that they would not dare to venture in the streets unaccompanied by their husbands. What has added to the frantic state of the inhabitants of Whitechapel is the fact that the murder was committed in broad daylight and in a street sufficiently near to the Spitalfields Market as to be, at the time in question, a busy thoroughfare. LATEST PARTICULARS. Although the police have made most diligent inquiry after the murderer of the woman, whose real name is Chapman, they had up to last night failed to find the slightest clue to his whereabouts. The police are unwilling to accept assistance or suggestion from any private source, and work upon a plan of their own, which consists of frequent visits to the common lodging houses of the neighbourhood, and a strict watch at night in all the streets in the vicinity. In the street yesterday half a dozen costermongers took up their stand and did brisk business in fruit and refreshments. Thousands of respectably dressed persons visited the scene, and occasionally the road became so crowded that the constables had to clear it by making a series of raids upon the spectators. In the course of yesterday nearly a dozen persons were arrested, and conveyed to the Commercial street Police Station. In the afternoon a vast crowd had collected about the streets. As each apprehension was made they rushed pell mell towards the station, obviously under the idea that the murderer of the woman had been caught. Last night police were posted in strong force throughout the neighbourhood. Their precautions are such they consider it impossible that any further outrage can be perpetrated. ANOTHER WOMAN STABBED. At five minutes after eleven o'clock on Saturday forenoon a man suddenly attacked a woman in Spitalfields-market while she was passing through. After felling her to the ground with a blow, he began kicking her and pulled out a knife. Some women who had collected, having the terrible tragedy that brought them there still fresh in their minds, on seeing the knife, raised such piercing shrieks of "Murder" that they reached the enormous crowds in Hanbury-street. Seeing the immense crowd swarming around him, the man who was the cause of the alarm made more furious efforts to reach the woman, from whom he had been separated by some persons who interfered on her behalf. He, however, threw these on one side, fell upon the woman, knife in hand, and inflicted various stabs on her head, cutting her forehead, neck and fingers before he was again pulled off. When he was again pulled off the woman lay motionless - the immense crowd took up the cry of "Murder", and the people who were on the streets raised cries of "Lynch him." At this juncture the police arrived, arrested the man, and after a while had the woman conveyed on a stretcher to the police-station in Commercial-street, where she was examined by the divisional surgeon.

The Hull Daily News, September 10th 1888,

Although the police have made most diligent inquiry after the murderer of the woman, whose real name is Chapman, they had up to last night failed to find the slightest clue to his whereabouts. As a matter of fact, they are in the dark as to the personal appearance of the man for whom they are looking. It is true that they possess the description of a man who is known as "Leather Apron," and will arrest him if he can be found, but their theory is that "Leather Apron" is more or less a mythical personage, and that he is not responsible for the terrible crimes with which his name has been associated. All the same the details of his appearance have been widely circulated, with a view to his early apprehension. All the police in the vicinity are on the look-out for him. On Saturday night a large force of police constables and detectives closely watched the neighbourhood. Men were posted at all the entrances and exits of the numerous alleys and passages in the neighbourhood, who every few minutes made a thorough examination of the places under their surveillance, and from time to time these were visited by the Inspectors on duty, with a view to ascertaining

Mike Covell

whether any suspicious character had been observed. From ten o'clock at night until late in the morning a large crowd occupied Hanbury street, in the vicinity of the notorious house, No. 29. When the public houses emptied the occupants swarmed into the street, causing a good deal of trouble to the police by their behaviour. The people living in the adjoining houses obtained no rest until between four and five o'clock, when the crowd gradually melted away, only, however, to reassemble again in greater force as soon as daylight appeared. In the course of Saturday night and Sunday morning the police arrested two men on suspicion of being concerned in the crime. One man, whose appearance left little doubt in the minds of his captors that he was the Hanbury street murder, was found by an officer in Buck's row shortly after 1 o'clock on Sunday morning. A murder was, it will be remembered, committed in the neighbourhood but a short time since, and the police have since been constantly pursuing their investigation in that quarter. The man upon whom suspicion rested presented a most forbidding appearance. He appeared to be hiding in the street, and when accosted by the officer, rushed off at the top of his speed. An alarm was raised, and after a short race he was arrested. He was a villainous-looking fellow with long hair and shaggy beard, dressed only in a pair of ragged blue serge trousers and an old dirty shirt. He resisted his captors, but was eventually secured and conveyed to Bethnal Green Police Station. It was said at the time that he was carrying a long knife concealed in the sleeve of his shirt, but on examination no weapon was found upon him. He gave an account of himself which was, in the first instance, considered unsatisfactory, but inquiries were immediately set on foot, and in the result the man, who appears to be a common vagrant, was released from custody. The second arrest was effected in Gloucester street, where a man aged about 40, having the look of a seafarer, was arrested. It was pretty obvious, however, from the replies which he gave, and his general appearance that he was not the man sought for, and after he had spent some time in Commercial street Station he was also set at liberty. It is suggested that the first mentioned man is the person who has been spoken of by Mrs. Fiddymont, wife of the proprietor of the Prince Albert public-house, situate at the corner of Brushfield street and Stewart street. Mrs. Fiddymont has stated to the police that at seven o'clock on Saturday morning a rough-looking man came into the place and got some ale. He presented an excited appearance, and some blood-spots were said to have been observed on his right hand. This man, however, had a coat and hat on. The police, however, who gave information very unwillingly, and who do not accept the theory that the crime has been committed by the man designated "Leather Apron," are indisposed to believe that the person seen by Mrs. Fiddymont has any connection with the crime. They are unwilling, indeed, to accept assistance or suggestion from any private source and work upon a plan of their own, which consists of frequent visits to the common lodging-houses of the neighbourhood and a strict watch at night on all the streets in the vicinity. All day to-day five policemen have guarded the scene of the crime in Hanbury street. No one was admitted unless he lived in the house. In the street half a dozen costermongers took up their stand and did brisk business in fruit and refreshments. Thousands of respectably dressed persons visited the scene, and occasionally the road became so crowded that the constables had to clear it by making a series of raids upon the spectators. The windows of the adjoining houses were full of persons watching the crowd below. A number of people also visited the house in Dorset street where the murdered woman lodged. It may be mentioned here that the soldier who had frequently visited the woman at this place did not return to the house on Saturday night. The police, however, attach no importance to this circumstance. Inquiries have been made at Vauxhall and at Windsor where Chapman or "Sievy," as she was more generally called, is said to have relatives, but so far without any fresh information obtained as to her antecedents. The deceased has been identified by persons who have known her since she has lived in London, but her relatives, if she possesses any, have not yet communicated with the police. The small portion of writing on the envelope found upon the body, bearing the stamp of the Sussex Regiment, has not yet been identified or traced. The authorities of St Bartholemew's Hospital, where the woman spent some time, have been communicated with, but they have not been able to afford any information of a useful character. The usually lively condition of Whitechapel and Spitalfields on a Sunday was considerably augmented to-day by reason of the excitement aroused by the murder. In the course of the day nearly a dozen persons were arrested, and conveyed to the Commercial street Police Station. In the afternoon a vast crowd had collected about the streets. As each apprehension was made they rushed pell mell towards the station, obviously under the idea that the murderer of the woman had been caught. Shortly before five o'clock a man was arrested in Dal street after a long chase on a charge of assault. The officer who arrested him proceeded with his prisoner by way of Hanbury street to the police station and so was obliged to make his way through the crowd. Outside the house his prisoner stood in some danger of being mobbed, but the crowd eventually gave way, and the prisoner was safely lodged in the station. A few minutes later two men were arrested in Wentworth street. As soon as the crowd saw them in the hands of the police there were loud cries of "Leather Apron," and thereupon hundreds of persons turned out from the side streets and followed the officers in a tumultuous throng to the station. Not five minutes afterwards a woman was apprehended on some small charge, and the excitement became so intense that a posse of officers was sent out from the building to preserve order.

Mike Covell

These marched three and four abreast up and down the pavement, and while they were so engaged yet another prisoner was brought in. There was a good deal of shouting in the mob, which surged about in a dangerous fashion, but by-and-bye a diversion was caused by the rapid passage along Banbury street of three men who were supposed to be two detectives and their prisoner. The centre man bore a striking resemblance to "Leather Apron," and the cry of "That's him," having been raised, a rush was made at him, but the little party immediately turned down a side street, and the police prevented the crowd from proceeding further. In the neighbourhood of the mortuary, which is situated in Eagle place, at the Whitechapel end of Hanbury street, all was quiet during the day. The green doors opened now and again to admit some inspectors of police and several medical gentlemen, but all others were rigidly excluded. The inquest on the body will be held to-morrow (Monday) by Dr MacDonald, the coroner for the district. Dr Phillips, the surgeon, and the witnesses who first discovered the body, will be called, and the police will also give certain evidence. Dr Phillips believes that the woman had been dead for two hours or more when she was discovered. It is a remarkable fact, however, that the man Richardson, who first went into the yard where the corpse was discovered says that he actually sat down on the step of the passage to cut a piece of leather off his shoe and yet did not see the body. This, however, may be explained by the circumstances that the passage door opens outward and toward the left, and so would conceal the body behind it. It is the custom to leave both of the passage doors open at night, and although they were found shut on the morning of the murder no suspicion was excited on that account. The advisability of employing bloodhounds to trace the perpetrator of the crime has been eagerly discussed by the inhabitants of the district. It is considered by experts that the time has gone by for such an experiment, and it is pointed out also that in the case of the Blackburn murderer, who was discovered by this means, the circumstances were different, and that the present case does not admit of the test. LEATHER APRON Reference is made in the above report to a mysterious being bearing the name of "Leather Apron," concerning whom a number of stories have for a week or more been current in Whitechapel. A reporter of the Star, who has been making some inquiries among a number of women in the East-end gives the following description of the man:- He is five feet four or five inches in height, and wears a dark close fitting cap. He is thickset and has an unusually thick neck. His hair is black, and closely clipped, his age being about 39 or 40. He has a small black moustache. The distinguishing feature of his costume is a leather apron, which he always wears, and from which he gets his nickname. His expression is sinister, and seems full of terror for the women who describe it. His eyes are small and glittering. His lips are usually parted in a grin which is not only not reassuring, but excessively repellent. He is a slipper-maker by trade, but does not work. His business is blackmailing women late at night. A number of men in Whitechapel follow this interesting profession. He has never cut anybody, so far as is known, but always carries a leather knife, presumably as sharp as leather knifes are wont to be. This knife a number of the women have seen. His name nobody knows, but all are united in the belief that he is a Jew or of Jewish parentage, his face being of a marked Hebrew type. But the most singular characteristic of the man is the universal statement that in moving about he never makes any noise. What he wears on his feet the women do not know, but they agree that he moves noiselessly. His uncanny peculiarity to them is that they never see him or know of his presence until he is close by them. "Leather Apron" never by any chance attacks a man. He runs away on the slightest appearance of rescue. One woman whom he assailed some time ago boldly prosecuted him for it, and he was sent up for seven days. He has no settled place of residence, but has slept oftenest in a fourpenny lodging-house of the lowest kind in a disreputable lane leading from Brick-lane. The people at this lodging-house denied that he had been there and appeared disposed to shield him. "Leather Apron's" pal "Mickeldy Joe," was in the house at the time, and his presence doubtless had something to do with the unwillingness to give information. "Leather Apron" was last at this house some weeks ago, though this account may be untrue. He ranges all over London, and rarely assails the same woman twice. He has lately been seen in Leather-lane, which is in the Holborn district. ANOTHER WOMAN STABBED. At five minutes after 11 o'clock a man suddenly attacked a woman in the Spitalfields Market, while she was passing through. After felling her to the ground with a blow, he began kicking her, and pulled out a knife. Some women who had collected, having the terrible tragedy that brought them there still fresh in their minds, on seeing the knife, raised such piercing shrieks of "Murderer," &c that they reached the enormous crowds in the busy street. There was at once a rush for Commercial street, where the markets are situate, as it was shouted out by some that there was another murder, and by others that the murderer had been arrested. Seeing the immense crowd swarming round him, the man who was the cause of the alarm made more furious efforts to reach the woman, from whom he had been separated by some persons who interfered on her behalf. He, however, threw them on one side, fell upon the woman knife in hand, and inflicted various stabs on her head, and cut her forehead, neck and fingers before he was again got away from her. The woman then lay motionless. The crowd then took up the shout of "Murder!" and the people who were on the skirts raised cries of "Lynch him." At this juncture the police arrived, arrested the man, and after a while had the woman conveyed on a stretcher to the police station in Commercial street where she was

Mike Covell

> *examined by the divisional surgeon. She was found to be suffering from several wounds, but none of them considered dangerous. She was subsequently removed to the London Hospital where she was detained as an in patient. The blind man is described as having a most ungovernable temper, and he was seen whilst the woman was leading him along to stab her several times in the neck. Blood flowed quickly, and it was at first thought that another terrible murder had been committed. The affair occurred midway between Buck's row and Hanbury Street, where the last two horrible murders have been committed.*

The Hull Daily Mail, September 10th 1888,

> *THE HORRIBLE TRAGEDY IN WHITECHAPEL. LATEST PARTICULARS. A Press Association telegram, despatched at 9:45 this morning, states that there is practically nothing new up to this hour in regard to the shocking crime of Saturday morning. Although two or three men have been apprehended on suspicion, they have given satisfactory accounts and have been liberated. Inspector chandler, at Commercial-road Police Station, received information after midnight on Sunday that a person was detained at Deptford on suspicion. He proved to be a young man apprehended in Old Kent-road, and his answers to interrogations being considered satisfactory he was shortly afterwards released. At the time of this despatch a group of people were standing around the police station in Commercial-street in expectation of anything transpiring in connection with the enquiries of the police. Although the police have made the most diligent inquiries after the murderer of the woman Chapman, they had up to Sunday night failed to secure a clue to his whereabouts. As a matter of fact they are in the dark as to the personal appearance of the man for whom they are looking. It is [illegible] the description of a man who is known as "Leather Apron," and will arrest him if he can be found, but their theory is that "Leather Apron" is more or less a mythical personage, and that he is not responsible for the terrible crimes with which his name has been associated. All the same the details of his appearance have been widely circulated, with a view to his early apprehension. All the police in the vicinity are on the look-out for him. From ten o'clock at night until late in the morning a large crowd occupied Hanbury-street, in the vicinity of the notorious house, No. 29. When the public houses emptied the occupants swarmed into the street, causing a good deal of trouble to the police by their behavior. The people living in the adjoining houses obtained no rest until between four and five o'clock, when the crowd gradually melted away, only, however, to reassemble again in greater force as soon as daylight appeared. In the course of Saturday night and Sunday morning the police arrested two men on suspicion of being concerned in the crime. One man, whose*

appearance left little doubt in the minds of his captors that he was the Hanbury-street murder, was found by an officer in Buck's row shortly after 1 o'clock on Sunday morning. A murder was, it will be remembered, committed in the neighbourhood but a short time since, and the police have since been constantly pursuing their investigation in that quarter. The man upon whom suspicion rested presented a most forbidding appearance. He appeared to be hiding in the street, and when accosted by the officer, rushed off at the top of his speed. An alarm was raised, and after a short race he was arrested. He was a villainous-looking fellow with long hair and shaggy beard, dressed only in a pair of ragged blue serge trousers and an old dirty shirt. He resisted his captors, but was eventually secured and conveyed to Bethnal Green Police Station. It was said at the time that he was carrying a long knife concealed in the sleeve of his shirt, but on examination no weapon was found upon him. He gave an account of himself which was, in the first instance, considered unsatisfactory, but inquiries were immediately set on foot, and in the result the man, who appears to be a common vagrant, was released from custody. The second arrest was effected in Gloucester street, where a man aged about 40, having the look of a seafarer, was arrested. It was pretty obvious, however, from the replies which he gave, and his general appearance that he was not the man sought for, and after he had spent some time in Commercial street Station he was also set at liberty. It is suggested that the first mentioned man is the person who has been spoken of by Mrs. Fiddymont, wife of the proprietor of the Prince Albert public-house, situate at the corner of Brushfield-street and Stewart-street. Mrs. Fiddymont has stated to the police that at seven o'clock on Saturday morning a rough-looking man came into the place and got some ale. He presented an excited appearance, and some blood-spots were said to have been observed on his right hand. This man, however, had a coat and hat on. The police, however, who gave information very unwillingly, and who do not accept the theory that the crime has been committed by the man designated "Leather Apron," are indisposed to believe that the person seen by Mrs. Fiddymont has any connection with the crime. They are unwilling, indeed, to accept assistance or suggestion from any private source and work upon a plan of their own, which consists of frequent visits to the common lodging-houses of the neighbourhood and a strict watch at night on all the streets in the vicinity. All day to-day five policemen have guarded the scene of the crime in Hanbury-street. No one was admitted unless he lived in the house. In the street half a dozen costermongers took up their stand and did brisk business in fruit and refreshments. Thousands of respectably dressed persons visited the scene, and occasionally the road became so crowded that the constables had to clear it by making a series of raids upon the spectators. The windows of the adjoining houses were full of persons watching the crowd below.

Mike Covell

A number of people also visited the house in Dorset-street where the murdered woman lodged. It may be mentioned here that the soldier who had frequently visited the woman at this place did not return to the house on Saturday night. The police, however, attach no importance to this circumstance. Inquiries have been made at Vauxhall and at Windsor where Chapman or "Sievy," as she was more generally called, is said to have relatives, but so far without any fresh information obtained as to her antecedents. The deceased has been identified by persons who have known her since she has lived in London, but her relatives, if she possesses any, have not yet communicated with the police. The small portion of writing on the envelope found upon the body, bearing the stamp of the Sussex Regiment, has not yet been identified or traced. The authorities of St Bartholemew's Hospital, where the woman spent some time, have been communicated with, but they have not been able to afford any information of a useful character. The usually lively condition of Whitechapel and Spitalfields on a Sunday was considerably augmented to-day by reason of the excitement aroused by the murder. In the course of the day nearly a dozen persons were arrested, and conveyed to the Commercial street Police Station. In the afternoon a vast crowd had collected about the streets. As each apprehension was made they rushed pell mell towards the station, obviously under the idea that the murderer of the woman had been caught. Shortly before five o'clock a man was arrested in Dal-street after a long chase on a charge of assault. The officer who arrested him proceeded with his prisoner by way of Hanbury-street to the police station and so was obliged to make his way through the crowd. Outside the house his prisoner stood in some danger of being mobbed, but the crowd eventually gave way, and the prisoner was safely lodged in the station. A few minutes' later two men were arrested in Wentworth-street. As soon as the crowd saw them in the hands of the police there were loud cries of "Leather Apron," and thereupon hundreds of persons turned out from the side streets and followed the officers in a tumultuous throng to the station. Not five minutes afterwards a woman was apprehended on some small charge, and the excitement became so intense that a posse of officers was sent out from the building to preserve order. These marched three and four abreast up and down the pavement, and while they were so engaged yet another prisoner was brought in. There was a good deal of shouting in the mob, which surged about in a dangerous fashion, but by-and-bye a diversion was caused by the rapid passage along Banbury street of three men who were supposed to be two detectives and their prisoner. The centre man bore a striking resemblance to "Leather Apron," and the cry of "That's him," having been raised, a rush was made at him, but the little party immediately turned down a side street, and the police prevented the crowd from proceeding further. In the neighbourhood of the mortuary, which is situated in

Eagle place, at the Whitechapel end of Hanbury-street, all was quiet during the day. The green doors opened now and again to admit some inspectors of police and several medical gentlemen, but all others were rigidly excluded. The inquest on the body will be held to-morrow (Monday) by Dr MacDonald, the coroner for the district. Dr Phillips, the surgeon, and the witnesses who first discovered the body, will be called, and the police will also give certain evidence. Dr Phillips believes that the woman had been dead for two hours or more when she was discovered. It is a remarkable fact, however, that the man Richardson, who first went into the yard where the corpse was discovered says that he actually sat down on the step of the passage to cut a piece of leather off his shoe and yet did not see the body. This, however, may be explained by the circumstances that the passage door opens outward and toward the left, and so would conceal the body behind it. It is the custom to leave both of the passage doors open at night, and although they were found shut on the morning of the murder no suspicion was excited on that account. The advisability of employing bloodhounds to trace the perpetrator of the crime has been eagerly discussed by the inhabitants of the district. It is considered by experts that the time has gone by for such an experiment, and it is pointed out also that in the case of the Blackburn murderer, who was discovered by this means, the circumstances were different, and that the present case does not admit of that. To-night the police are posted in strong force throughout the neighbourhood. Their precautions are such that they consider it impossible that any further outrage can be perpetrated. The inhabitants of the place, however, although by day regarding the matter as one for discussion and excitement rather than serious regard, profess to fear that the miscreant will soon be at his dark work again, and that if he be captured at all he will be taken red handed in the commission of another horrible crime. A correspondent supplies the following: - Last night the Scotland-yard authorities had come to a definite conclusion as to the real description of the murderer of two at least of the hapless women found dead at the East End, and the following is the official telegram wired to every station throughout the metropolis and suburbs: "Commercial-street, 8.20 p.m. - Description of a man wanted, who entered the passage of a house at which the murder was committed with a prostitute at 2 a.m., the 8th - Age 37; height, 5ft. 7in.; rather dark beard and moustache; dress, short dark jacket, dark vest and trousers, black scarf, and black felt hat; spoke with a foreign accent.

September 11th 1888

The Hull Daily News, September 11th 1888,

Mike Covell

THE HORRIBLE TRAGEDY IN WHITECHAPEL. London, Monday. MORE ARRESTS.-THE POLICE AND THE PRESS. The Press Association, telegraphing at noon, says:- Reports are constantly arriving at headquarters, and men who supposed resemble that of the supposed murderer being arrested. At present, no fewer than seven persons are in custody in different parts of the East End on suspicion. The police at various centres have, however, received strict instructions from Scotland Yard, not to communicate details to the press, and it has not yet transpired whether either of the arrests is likely to lead to the identification of the culprit. The Press Association has been informed that in more than one case a brief investigation has proved that the person suspected would have no connection with the outrage, and he has accordingly been released immediately. "LEATHER APRON" UNLIKELY TO COMMIT THE CRIME. The Press Association, in a later despatch, says the excitement upon the arrest of the man said to be "Leather Apron" was intense, large crowds surrounding the police station, and discussing the affair. The police however, refuse to give details. At present the prisoner has evidently not been specifically charged with any offence. Several residents in Mulberry street, in an interview with the Press Association representative stated that prisoner was a harmless sort of person and unlikely to commit the crime alleged. ARRIVAL OF PIGOTT IN LONDON. Pigott, the man arrested at Gravesend, arrived at London Bridge by train this afternoon, in charge of Detective Abberline, who was met at the railway station by Detective Stacey, from Scotland Yard. Prisoner was not handcuffed, and was smoking a clay pipe and carrying a white bundle. His arrival created no stir and he was conveyed in a four wheeled cab to Commercial street police station. He will be detained there, pending arrival of witnesses sent to identify him. He answers the description of "Leather Apron," and will when apprehended had no vest on. His clothes are spotted in several places with blood, and his hands are cut. He has a black beard, and is apparently recovering from a severe attack of Delirium Tremens. He stated that the wounds on his hands were caused by the bite of a woman. Great excitement still prevails. BLOOD BESPATTERED FROM HEAD TO FOOT. On being examined by the police at Commercial-street Station, Pigott was found to be bespattered with blood from head to foot, even his boots bearing traces of a sanguinary struggle. In his pockets were found a few coppers and a piece of lead pencil. He sits in a cell in a state of deep lethargy, taking no notice of anything. His whole demeanour betokens a recent bout of excessive drinking. He adheres to his original statement. THE IDENTITY OF PIGOTT. Two woman who know "Leather Apron," have seen Pigott at Commercial Station, but neither can identify him. Prisoner, however, is detained until he recovers his normal state. The police surgeon is of the opinion that it will be some hours before he is in a

> *rational state of mind. The two women have meanwhile been taken to Bethnal Green Station to see whether they can identify the man in custody there. PIGOTT PRONOUNCED INSANE. Pigott, the man arrested at Gravesend, has been examined by Dr. Phillips, Divisional Surgeon, and pronounced insane. In due course he will be removed to the infirmary. Nothing further can be ascertained about Piser. He has not yet been charged with any offence, and is merely detained pending further enquiries. Detectives do not appear to be very clear as to his being the man known as "Leather Apron."*

The Hull Daily News, September 11th 1888,

> *THE WHITECHAPEL MURDER. Mr S. Montague M.P, has given £100 as a reward for the capture of the perpetrator of the Whitechapel murder. The Press Association says although the two men, Pigott and Piser, arrested on Monday of suspicion of being implicated in the murder in Hanbury Street, are still in charge of the police, it has not yet transpired that there is any evidence against either of them connecting them with the actual commission of the crime. Pigott has not yet recovered from the effects of delirium with which he was affected at the time of his arrest, and a close watch is kept upon him at the infirmary, as there is some doubt as to how far his symptoms may be assumed. The fact that he was, on his own admission, in Brick Lane on the night murder, suggests the desirability of further enquiries before he is finally released. The prisoner was still in the cell at Leman Street station this morning, though no formal charge had been made against him.*

The Hull Daily Mail, September 11th 1888,

> *THE WHITECHAPEL MURDER. LATEST PARTICULARS. Mr S. Montague M.P, has given £100 as a reward for the capture of the perpetrator of the Whitechapel murder. The Press Association says although the two men, Pigott and Piser, arrested on Monday of suspicion of being implicated in the murder in Hanbury Street, are still in charge of the police, it has not yet transpired that there is any evidence against either of them connecting them with the actual commission of the crime. Pigott has not yet recovered from the effects of delirium with which he was affected at the time of his arrest, and a close watch is kept upon him at the infirmary, as there is some doubt as to how far his symptoms may be assumed. The fact that he was, on his own admission, in Brick Lane on the night murder, suggests the desirability of further enquiries before he is finally released. The prisoner was still in the cell at Leman Street station this morning, though no formal charge had been made against him. No further*

Mike Covell

> *arrests have been made up to one o'clock today. Inquiries are being made by Detective Inspector Thicke and other officers into the antecedents of the two men still in custody, but so far no direct evidence has been obtained. Piser will probably be charged on suspicion in order to allow the police time to complete their investigations. A crowd of people wait outside Leman Street Police station in the expectation of witnessing the release of the man, but the excitement now has subsided. Piser's lodgings have been visited again by the detectives, but nothing further has been discovered. A number of men outside Leman Street Station this afternoon were admitted into the station yard, and Piser was brought out and placed among them. A man of dark complexion was asked if he "could identify the man," and hi picked out Piser. This is supposed to imply that Piser was seen in the morning in Hanbury Street with the deceased.*

The Eastern Morning News, September 11th 1888,

> *THE WHITECHAPEL TRAGEDY. SEARCH FOR THE MANIAC MURDER. THE POLICE BAFFLED. About none o'clock yesterday morning, Detective Sergeant Thicke, H Division, who has had charge of the case, and been most energetic in making inquiries, succeeded in capturing the man known as "Leather Apron," in Whitechapel. A large number of long bladed knives and several hats were found in his possession. He denied that he was "Leather Apron." A man giving his name as William Henry Pigott, aged about forty, was arrested late on Sunday night by P.C. Vellensworth, of the borough police, in the Pope's Head Tavern, West Street, Gravesend. The man's hand was badly bitten, and there were blood marks on his clothes. He answered somewhat to the description published by the man wanted. He admitted having been in Whitechapel on the Saturday morning, about the place where the murdered woman's body was found, and said he had an altercation with a woman, who bit his hand, and that he struck her on the head, knocked her down, and ran away. He declared he knew nothing more. He was then handed over to the charge of Inspector Abberline, of Scotland Yard police, who arrived with his prisoner at Commercial-street Police Station at a quarter to one in the afternoon, in a four wheel cab. Pigott was lodged in the Commercial-street Police Station, but witnesses (among them Mrs Fiddymont, who is supposed to have a distinct recollection of the man wanted) failed to identify him. Dr Phillips subsequently saw Pigott, and pronounced him insane. THE INQUEST. Mr Wynne Baxter, Coroner for East London, yesterday opened an inquest at the Boys' Institute, in Whitechapel, on the body. The absorbing interest taken in the case was evidenced by the large attendance of the police at the inquiry and by the crown which had gathered outside. The services of a number of constables were*

requisitioned for the maintenance of order. The police authorities were represented by Inspector Halson, of the I Division. The jury having visited the mortuary for the purpose of viewing the body. John Davis, by whom the corpse was discovered, was sworn. He deposed that he was a carman, living in Hanbury-street, Spitalfields, where he occupied one front room. He heard nothing unusual during Friday night, though he was awake during a considerable part of the night. When he got up just before six on Saturday morning the front door was open, but this was of frequent occurrence, and did not surprise him. He went into the yard, which was separated by high rails from those on either side. There was a small recess between the backdoor steps and the left hand fence, and in that recess he found the body of a woman lying on her back, with her head towards the house, her feet towards the woodshed, and her clothes above her thighs. He at once went out into the street, and called in two men whom he knew by sight, but not by name. The police said that these men had not been found, and the Coroner stated that they must be produced. He added that the inquiry would be materially helped if a plan of the yard were constructed, and the police authorities promised that one should be forthcoming on the next occasion. Witness resumed: The men, after looking into the yard, ran off to find a policeman, while he himself proceeded to report the case at Commercial-street Police Station, whence constables were sent on to Hanbury-street. He had never previously seen the woman. He was not the first out of bed in the house on Saturday morning, since a man named Thompson was called at half-past three to go to his work. He had never seen in the passage of the house women who did not live there. Amelia Farmer, the wife of an army pensioner, stated that on Saturday she saw the body lying at the mortuary, and identified it as that of Annie Chapman, whom she had known or four or five years. She was the widow of Frederick Chapman, who died about 18 months ago. Up to that time he had resided at Windsor, where he was a veterinary surgeon, but deceased had been parted from him for the last four or five years, and had during that time lived in various places, but usually in common lodging houses. Two years ago she lived in Dorset-street with a man who made wire sieves, and from that fact was nicknamed "Sievey." Witness last saw the sieve-maker, whose name she did not know, about eighteen months since. During her husband's life deceased received money from him from time to time. Witness saw her in Dorset-street on Monday last. She then had a black eye, and also showed witness a bruise on her chest, saying that the injuries had been caused by a woman who sold books. Deceased explained that on the previous Saturday (September 1st) she was in a beerhouse in Dorset-street with a man named Ted Stanley, a very respectable man. Another man named "Harry, the Hawker," and the book-selling woman were also there, and a quarrel arose, in consequence of

Mike Covell

a dispute as to some money taken from the counter. Thus quarrel brought about later on the struggle in which the injuries were inflicted. On the following day, Tuesday, witness again saw deceased, who said she was no better, and had had nothing to eat that day, and intimated that she meant to go into the casual ward. Chapman did crotchet work and sold flowers for a living, but also, she believed, went on the streets at night. They again met about five o'clock on Friday afternoon, when she once more complained of illness, and said she had been in a casual ward. Deceased was an industrious woman when sober, but was often the worse for drink, and had led a very irregular life. She had a mother and sister in London, but they were not on good terms, and she never stayed with them. Witness knew no one likely to have injured deceased. Timothy Donovan, "deputy" of a lodging house in Spitalfields, identified the body as that of a woman who had lived there during the past four months. She was not there last week, except on Friday, when she came in at two o'clock in the afternoon. She then told him that she had been in the Workhouse Infirmary. About 1.45 on Saturday morning she went out, saying she had not money to engage the bed she usually occupied, but asking that it might not be let to anyone else, as she would soon be back. She had had drink at this time, but could walk straight. He did not see her with any man on Friday night. She had slept on other occasions with an army pensioner, and she had come to the house with other men, but he had refused her admission. The Coroner asked whether anything was known of the pensioner referred to, and the inspector replied in the negative. Witness went on to say that when deceased left early on Saturday morning he did not see which way she went, but he believed the watchman did. He did not see her again alive. She was usually on good terms with the other lodgers, but about a week before her death she received a black eye from another woman who hawked laces, &c. John Evans, night watchman at the same lodging house, said he last saw the deceased shortly before two o'clock on Saturday morning, when she left the house, saying she had no money for her lodgings, but would soon be back with some. He watched her go to Paternoster-row, and turn to the right, but she never returned. When she first entered the kitchen that night she said she had been to her sister's in Vauxhall. Witness knew that she lived a rough life, but had only seen her with the pensioner who had been spoken of. This man came to the lodging house after the murder on Saturday to make some inquiries about deceased. At this stage the inquiry was adjourned until two o'clock today. LATEST PARTICULARS. A very widespread belief prevailed in Whitechapel last evening that "Leather Apron" was actually in custody, and the supposed fact had a curiously tranquillising effect upon the lower orders in the district. Unfortunately the popular faith is not warranted by the facts. All the men arrested on suspicion, as already stated, have been released, save one who was at a late hour still in the cells at Leman-street Police Station. This man is detained as a matter of precaution while the inquiries are being made into the truth of certain statements made by him. It is evident that the police have not much faith in the report that he is the man named, because they have not thought it necessary for the purpose of identification to call in Donovan, the lodging house "deputy," and other persons who knew "Leather Apron," well. It may be stated here that the police do not share the popular dread and suspicion of "Leather Apron," whose criminal record is simply that of a street bully and sneak of the ordinary type, and he is in their opinion utterly incapable, physically and morally, of the crimes imputed to him, the committal of which required, after all, an amount of coolness and nerve with which no one who knows "Leather Apron" will credit him, and involve risks which a man of his character would be the last to incur. Most of the arrests made yesterday have been connected, presumably, with which the police theory that the murderer and the agitated man with bloodstained fingers and the matted hair who entered the Prince Albert Tavern shortly before six o'clock on the morning of the murder are one and the same person. Mrs. Fiddymont, who served this man with refreshments, and took particular notice of him, is confident that she would recognise him even in a crowd, and some persons who were drinking in the tavern at the time are equally confident. Mrs. Fiddymont was twice called upon by the police yesterday to test her memory. At the Commercial-street Police Station 17 men were paraded before her, but she failed to recognise any of them, and at Leman-street Police Station she was unable to identify any one of the nine men who stood up before her. It appears that a man answering the description of "Leather Apron" was recently an in-patient Jewish Convalescent Home at Norwood, recovering from a severe carbunels in the neck. The man stated that he had previously been treated at Paddington Infirmary. The man Pigott, who was arrested at Gravesend, and certified by Dr. Phillips to be insane, was removed last evening to the Whitechapel Infirmary. Sir Charles Warren resumed his duties at Scotland Yard yesterday morning, and during the day conferred with some of the chief officials respecting the murders. It is rumoured that he had under consideration the advisability of offering a reward for the apprehension of the murderer. The statement lacks confirmation, but it is certain that great indignation prevails in the East End that this obvious means of eliciting information has not been resorted to. So strong did this feeling become that a meeting of the chief of the local tradesmen was held yesterday, at which an influential committee was appointed, consisting of sixteen well known gentlemen, with Mr. J. Aarons as the Secretary. The committee issued last evening a notice stating that they will give a substantial reward for the capture of the murderer, or for information leading thereto. The movement has been

Mike Covell

warmly taken up by the inhabitants, and it is certain that a large sum will be subscribed within the next few days. The proposal to form district Vigilance Committees also meets with great popular favour and is assuming practical form. Meetings have been held at various working men's clubs and other organisations, political and social, in the district, at most of which the proposed scheme was heartily approved and volunteers enrolled. We learn that Dr. Forbes Winslow is in communication with the Criminal Investigation Department with reference to the murders. He is of opinion that they are the work of one person, who is either a discharged lunatic from some asylum or one who has escaped from such an institution. He has suggested to Scotland Yard authorities that all the asylums should be communicated with, and particulars requested respecting the recent discharge of homicidal lunatics or of persons who may have effected their escape from such institutions. The present whereabouts of such lunatics should, in Dr. Winslow's opinion, be at once ascertained. This advice will probably be immediately followed out. From inquiries which have been made at Windsor, it seems that the deceased was the widow of a coachman in service at Clewer, and not a veterinary surgeon, as stated by Amelia Palmer in her evidence at the inquest yesterday. While deceased lived at Clewer she was known to the police for her drinking propensities, and had been in the custody of Superintendent Hayes for the offence, but had not been charged before the magistrates. Her husband was obliged to separate from her owing to her dissolute habits, but, as the witness Palmer stated, he spent her post office order, payable at Commercial-road, each week for 10s. There were two children of the marriage – a boy and a girl. The former lay ill for some time in a London hospital, while the latter lived at Windsor, but the police have no knowledge of their whereabouts. The husband of the deceased woman was obliged to resign his situation owing to ill-health, and he died in Grove-road, Windsor, about Christmas, 1886. These particulars have been forwarded by Supt. Hayes, at Windsor, to Supt. Shore, of the Scotland-yard police. In response to telegraphic inquiries, and one of the constables at Windsor was sent to London yesterday afternoon to identify the remains. A statement made by a young woman named Lyons, of the class commonly known as "unfortunates," may be worth mentioning. She says that at three o'clock on Sunday afternoon she met a strange man in Flower and Dean-street, one of the worst streets in the East End of London. He asked her to go to the Queen's Head, public house at half-past six and drink with him. Having promised that she would do so, he disappeared, but was at the house at the appointed time. While they were conversing Lyons noticed a large knife in the man's right hand trouser pocket, and called another woman's attention to the fact. A moment later Lyons was startled by the remark which the stranger addressed to her: - "You

> are about the same style of woman as the one that's murdered," he said. "What do you know about her?" asked the woman, to which the man replied, "You are beginning to smell a rat. Foxes hunt geese, but they don't always find 'em." Having uttered these words, the man hurriedly left. Lyons followed until near Spitalfields Church, and turning round at this spot and noticing that the woman was behind him the stranger ran at a swift pace into Church-street, and was at once lost to view.

The Hull Daily News, September 11th 1888,

> THE WHITECHAPEL MURDERS. ARRESTS ON SUSPICION. DISCHARGE OF PISER. LATEST PARTICULARS. Every available detective who could be spared from other districts of London has been drafted into Whitechapel, and altogether the police authorities have been working with exceptional vigour in the hope of capturing the murderous monster whom, within only a few months, has done to death no fewer than four miserable women. It cannot be said that any considerable measure of success has rewarded this official zeal. A number of arrests have been made, and the police have taken their prisoners to the station houses, attended by clamouring crowds, only to find in most instances that the captives were decent people, totally unconnected with the crimes of which they were suspected, and able to give satisfactory accounts of themselves. Very early in the day the popular excitement in Whitechapel was suddenly sent up to fever heat by the announcement that the man "Leather Apron," accused everywhere directly and by implication of the whole series of murders, had been arrested. There was no improbability in the report, for "Leather Apron" has a strongly marked individuality. His haunts are well known to hundreds of persons, and the detective energy of the Metropolitan police has been concentrated for days past upon his capture. Nevertheless, "Leather Apron" is still at large. An arrest was made, as stated in our columns yesterday, but the suspect proved to be one John Piser, a boot finisher by trade, living at 22, Mulberry-street, and described and known as an inoffensive and fairly industrious working man. It is said that Piser bears some resemblance to "Leather Apron," and that appears to be the only ground for his arrest. Piser took his arrest very quietly, and accompanied the detectives without saying a word to Leman-street Police-station, where he was detained for several hours. Several persons personally acquainted with "Leather Apron" were afforded the opportunity of carefully examining the missing desperado. Meanwhile the police had examined the inmates of 22, Mulberry-street, and had searched the premises from top to bottom, but the only instruments found capable of being used as lethal weapons were some finishing tools used by Piser in his business. Piser

had given at Leman-street an account of his recent movements, which, confirmed by independent testimony, and corroborated by the evidence collected by the police themselves, left the authorities no option but to release their captive, which was done as quietly as possible in the course of the afternoon. The unhappy man, however, was unable to return to his humble home, the whole of Mulberry-street being occupied by an excited and dangerously exasperated crowd of men and women, attracted thither by the report that the dreaded "Leather Apron" had been arrested in that locality. Piser therefore wisely waited until dusk before rejoining the family circle from which he had been so unceremoniously separated. In addition to the arrest of the man Pigott, at Gravesend, described yesterday during the day several other arrests were made, and Mrs. Fiddymont and other witnesses were driven from one police station to another, in the hope that they might identify the prisoners, but in almost every case the arrest was made simply on suspicion, and inquiry only resulted in the release of the prisoners. It cannot be said that the methods pursued by the police are above criticism. It was complained yesterday that they have been paying too much attention to common lodging houses and such like places, and that the area of their activity is needlessly limited. They are constantly in receipt of suggestions, anonymous and otherwise, but such gratuitous counsel is not effusively received, the detective department preferring to work upon the lines laid down by themselves. It has been ascertained practically beyond doubt that in the Whitechapel district no knives have been sold recently at all resembling the keen, strong weapon with which the last two crimes were almost certainly committed. It had been hoped that the two rings which the murderer tore from the finger of his victims would afford a valuable clue. On the assumption that the murderer was poor and ignorant this hope was not without justification, but whether it be that he is in no immediate want, or that he has ascertained that the rings were of base metal, the missing jewellery has not been offered for sale or pledge. Every pawnbroker in the Metropolis has been warned, and should the murderer's needs or his lack of knowledge induce him to produce his plunder in a London pawnshop, his immediate capture is assured. The scene of the murder was again visited yesterday by crowds of morbid sight seers, and there was a good deal of excitement throughout the squalid district, due chiefly to the arrests and the many rumours to the arrest. Intelligent observers who have visited the locality express the utmost astonishment that the murderer could have reached a hiding place after committing such a crime. He must have left the yard in Hanbury-street reeking like a slaughterman, and yet if the theory that the murder took place between five and six be accepted, he must have walked in almost broad daylight along the streets comparatively well frequented, even at that early hour, without his startling appearance attracting the slightest *attention. Consideration of this point has led many thinking people to the conclusion that the murderer came not from the wretched class from which the inmates of common lodging houses are drawn. More probably, it is argued, he is a man lodging in a comparatively decent house in the district, in which case he would be able to retire quickly to his home, which, once reached, he would be able at his leisure to remove from his person all traces of his hideous crime. It is, at any rate, practically certain that the murderer, if in the habit of using common lodging houses, would not have ventured to return to such lodgings smeared with blood, which he must have done, and with every one suspicious and alert in the consequence of the crime committed only the previous week. Nor is it likely, for similar reasons, that he could have cleaned himself in any tavern horse troughs or public fountains to be found in the Whitechapel-road and other thoroughfares in the district. The police are therefore exhorted not to confine their investigations, as they accused of doing, to common lodging houses and other resorts of criminal and outcasts, but to extend their inquiries to the class of householders exceedingly numerous in the East End of London, who are in the habit of letting furnished lodgings without particular inquiry into the character or antecedents of those who apply for them. From this direction it is not improbable that, as in the case of LeFroy, will come the first trustworthy clue to the murderer. As an evidence to the effect which the murders have had upon the public mind, several drunken men have professed to be connected with the outrages, and in one surrounded by an excited crowd with the result only of wasting the time of the police and adding to the panic which prevails in some parts of London. Inquiries made in Windsor yesterday make it highly probable that Mrs. Chapman was the same woman who had been in Superintendent Haves custody for drunkenness though she was never brought before the magistrates. It was stated at the inquest yesterday that the murdered woman was the wife of a veterinary surgeon, but it would appear from information received from Windsor that in her happier days Mrs. Chapman was the wife of a respectable coachman in the service of a gentleman at Clower, near Windsor, but who was compelled to retire from his service through ill health. His illness lasted for some time, and he died at Grove-road, Windsor, at Christmas, 1886. Chapman had been forced to separate from his wife in consequence of her habits. During her residence in the East End and until his death she received an allowance of ten shillings a week from her husband. There were two children, a boy and a girl. The boy was admitted to the London Hospital, and the girl was for some time at Grove-road, Windsor, but nothing is known about her present whereabouts. It is stated that Supt. Hayes sent one of his men to London yesterday afternoon, and that the policeman identified the body at Whitechapel Mortuary as that of Mrs. Chapman formerly of Windsor. A very widespread belief prevailed in Whitechapel last* evening that "Leather Apron" was actually in custody, and the supposed fact had a curiously tranquillising effect upon the lower orders in the district. Unfortunately the popular faith is not warranted by the facts. All the men arrested on suspicion, as already stated, have been released, save one who was at a late hour still in the cells at Leman-street Police Station. This man is detained as a matter of precaution while the inquiries are being made into the truth of certain statements made by him. It is evident that the police have not much faith in the report that he is the man named, because they have not thought it necessary for the purpose of identification to call in Donovan, the lodging house "deputy," and other persons who knew "Leather Apron," well. It may be stated here that the police do not share the popular dread and suspicion of "Leather Apron," whose criminal record is simply that of a street bully and sneak of the ordinary type, and he is in their opinion utterly incapable, physically and morally, of the crimes imputed to him, the committal of which required, after all, an amount of coolness and nerve with which no one who knows "Leather Apron" will credit him, and involve risks which a man of his character would be the last to incur. Most of the arrests made yesterday have been connected, presumably, with which the police theory that the murderer and the agitated man with bloodstained fingers and the matted hair who entered the Prince Albert Tavern shortly before six o'clock on the morning of the murder are one and the same person. Mrs. Fiddymont, who served this man with refreshments, and took particular notice of him, is confident that she would recognise him even in a crowd, and some persons who were drinking in the tavern at the time are equally confident. Mrs. Fiddymont was twice called upon by the police yesterday to test her memory. At the Commercial-street Police Station 17 men were paraded before her, but she failed to recognise any of them, and at Leman-street Police Station she was unable to identify any one of the nine men who stood up before her. It appears that a man answering the description of "Leather Apron" was recently an in-patient Jewish Convalescent Home at Norwood, recovering from a severe carbunels in the neck. The man stated that he had previously been treated at Paddington Infirmary. The man Pigott, who was arrested at Gravesend, and certified by Dr. Phillips to be insane, was removed last evening to the Whitechapel Infirmary. Sir Charles Warren resumed his duties at Scotland Yard yesterday morning, and during the day conferred with some of the chief officials respecting the murders. It is rumoured that he had under consideration the advisability of offering a reward for the apprehension of the murderer. The statement lacks confirmation, but it is certain that great indignation prevails in the East End that this obvious means of eliciting information has not been resorted to. So strong did this feeling become that a meeting of the chief of the local tradesmen was held yesterday, at which *an influential committee was appointed, consisting of sixteen well known gentlemen, with Mr. J. Aarons as the Secretary. The committee issued last evening a notice stating that they will give a substantial reward for the capture of the murderer, or for information leading thereto. The movement has been warmly taken up by the inhabitants, and it is certain that a large sum will be subscribed within the next few days. The proposal to form district Vigilance Committees also meets with great popular favour and is assuming practical form. Meetings have been held at various working men's clubs and other organisations, political and social, in the district, at most of which the proposed scheme was heartily approved and volunteers enrolled. We learn that Dr. Forbes Winslow is in communication with the Criminal Investigation Department with reference to the murders. He is of opinion that they are the work of one person, who is either a discharged lunatic from some asylum or one who has escaped from such an institution. He has suggested to Scotland Yard authorities that all the asylums should be communicated with, and particulars requested respecting the recent discharge of homicidal lunatics or of persons who may have effected their escape from such institutions. The present whereabouts of such lunatics should, in Dr. Winslow's opinion, be at once ascertained. This advice will probably be immediately followed.*

Percy LeFroy:
The case of Percy LeFroy, aka Percy Lefroy Mapleton, and Percy Mapleton Lefroy dominated the British press in June and July 1881 and was referred to as "The Brighton Railway Murder." On June 27th 1881 Isaac Frederick Gold, who was a coin dealer, was brutally murdered on the train from London Bridge Station to Brighton. Gold had boarded the train and gone into a first class compartment in the third carriage, and was later joined by LeFroy, who was aged just 21 at the time. When the train arrived at Preston Park Station LeFroy was seen exiting the carriage in a distressed state. The case made headline news when the police examined the carriage and found blood and bullet holes, and LeFroy's story of being mugged didn't add up. His wounds were superficial at best, the volume of blood didn't seem to match the wounds, and LeFroy was found with medals in his possession that he could not account for. Eventually the body of Mr. Gold was discovered in Balcombe Tunnel, which was on the route, and he had been shot, stabbed, robbed, and dumped. The search was on for LeFroy, and eventually the British press joined the hunt. The Daily Telegraph published a description, on July 1st 1881, and a wanted poster, featuring the first ever artists impression to be featured in the British press, by July 2nd 1881

Mike Covell

> *the national press featured the image, and on July 8th 1881 LeFroy was located and arrested. A short trial followed, and LeFroy was eventually found guilty, on November 29th 1881 LeFroy was hanged at Lewes prison.*
>
> *Coincidentally, several people involved in this case also became involved in the Whitechapel Murders:*
>
> *The coroner at the inquest was Wynne Edwin Baxter, the coroner on several Whitechapel victims. He conducted the inquests into the deaths of Annie Millwood, Emma Elizabeth Smith, Martha Tabram, Mary Ann Nichols, Annie Chapman, Elizabeth Stride, Rose Mylett, Alice McKenzie, the "Pinchin-street Torso" and Frances Coles.*
>
> *Lyttelton Forbes Winslow was present during the trial on behalf of the Mapleton family. Winslow was a psychiatrist and very vocal during the Jack the Ripper murders, writing to the police and the press. He claimed that he knew who the murderer was, and could catch him with the aid of 6 police constables.*
>
> ***Further Reading:***
> *All Stations to Murder, Barry Herbert, Silver Link Publishing, 1994*
> *The Complete Jack the Ripper A – Z, Paul Begg, Martin Fido, Keith Skinner, John Blake Publishing, 2010*
> *The Murderers' Who's Who, J. H. H. Gaute, Robin Odell, Pan Books, 1980*
> *The Scotland Yard Files, Paul Begg and Keith Skinner, Headline Publishing, 1993*

September 12th 1888

The Hull Daily Mail, September 12th 1888,

> THE WHITECHAPEL TRAGEDY. A FRESH CLUE. FURTHER PARTICULARS. Although no fresh arrests were made on Tuesday in connection with the Whitechapel murders, the police have obtained a clue which, although at present of a very slender character, may, they think, develop into a very important piece of evidence. It appears that on the morning of the murder of the woman Chapman, a man whose name if for the present withheld was in Hanbury-street, and noticed a woman in the company of two men. They appeared to be quarrelling, and he heard the men make some threats. Such an incident is, however, very common in the district, and the man, after taking a good look at the disputants, passed on his way. It is not known whether the man

made a statement to the police as soon as he heard of the murder. If he did so, no action has been taken upon it until yesterday when it seems to have struck the police that Pizer might have been one of the men in Hanbury-street at the time in question. The man was re-quested to attend at Leman-street Police station, and on his arrival, about one o'clock, some twenty men, mostly brought in from the adjacent thoroughfare, were paraded before him. The result somewhat startled the police, for the man, without a moment's hesitation, pointed to John Pizer as the man he heard threatening a woman in Hanbury-street on the morning of the murder. Pizer calmly protested that the man was entirely mistaken, but he was put back to the cells. The authorities do not express much confidence in their ability to establish a case against Pizer. Pizer's friends and relatives are not seriously alarmed at the alleged identification, for they are confident they will be able to prove an alibi without difficulty. Beyond the alleged identification, there is practically no evidence against Pizer. His lodgings have been thoroughly searched more than once, and nothing of a suspicious character has been found. Serious efforts have been made to find the rings torn from Chapman's fingers by the murderer, but not a trace of them has been found. It is probable that they have been destroyed, and with them it is feared disappears the most hopeful means of bringing the murderer to justice. The police during the afternoon and evening made careful enquiries into the statements made by the man who professed to identify Pizer. The manner of this man, who is apparently of Spanish blood and displays a blue ribbon on his coat, did not inspire much confidence in his veracity, and he was severely cross examined by a sort of informal tribunal consisting of experienced detective officers. The witness added to his first statement that he not only saw the prisoner in Hanbury-street on the morning of the murder, but that he actually took him by the collar when he was about to strike the woman. The man, it appears, first volunteered his statement on Monday, and he has since displayed anxiety to view the remains of the murdered woman Chapman. The curiosity, which was really believed to have been the inspiring motive of the voluntary testimony, was not gratified. Pizer is physically a very weak man and for that reason does not keep at work very closely. He is ruptured and in other ways infirm, and has been under hospital treatment on and off for a long time past. Each time the police searched Pizer's lodging they found no trace of blood stained clothing, or induced anything of suspicious character; but they carried off five knives, which were at once subjected to chemical analysis. All are of the class used in the leather currying trade, having blades about six inches in length, with stout handles sometimes notched in a peculiar way. There was to all appearances no blood either on the blades or the handles. Meanwhile the police continued their inquiries into witness statements, with the results that about eight o'clock they arrived at the

Mike Covell

> *conclusion that the man had not stated the truth, and there were no grounds for keeping Pizer any longer in custody. He was accordingly set at liberty, and at once proceeded to Mulberry-street, where he received the congratulations of his relatives and friends. The conduct of the man who professed to identify Pizer caused much indignation. The man Pigott is still under surveillance at the Whitechapel Infirmary. It has been suggested that he is feigning insanity, but the physicians who have examined him are of a contrary opinion. Another communication says: An important discovery, which throws some considerable light upon the movements of the murderer immediately after the committal of the crime, was made yesterday afternoon. A little girl happened to be walking in the back garden or yard of the house, 25, Hanbury-street, the next house but one to the scene of the murder, when her attention was attracted to peculiar marks on the wall and on the garden path. She communicated the discovery to Detective Inspector Chandler, who had just called at the house in order to make a plan of the back premises and the three houses for the use of the coroner at the inquest, which will be resumed to-day. The whole of the yard was then carefully examined, with the result that a bloody trail was found distinctly marked for a distance of five or six feet in the direction of the back door of the house. Further investigation left no doubt that the trail was that of the murderer, who it was evident, after finishing his sanguinary work, had passed through or over the dividing fence between Numbers 29 and 27, and thence into the garden of No. 25. On the wall of the last house there was found a curious smear which had probably been made by the murderer, who, alarmed by the blood soaked state of his coat, took off that garment and knocked it against the wall. Abutting on the end of the yard at 25 are the works of Mr. Bailey, a packing case maker. In the yard of this establishment in an out of way corner the police found some crumpled paper stained, almost saturated, with blood. It was evident that the murderer had found the paper in the yard of 25, and had wiped his hands with it, afterwards throwing it over the wall into Bailey's premises.*

The Hull Daily Mail, September 12th 1888,

> *THE WHITECHAPEL MURDER. INTERVIEW WITH "LEATHER APRON." The Press Association's representative had an interview this morning with John Piser, at 22, Mulberry-street. He was released from Leman-street Police Station about 8.30 p.m. on Tuesday. In reply to questions, the ex-prisoner said: - "Whatever particulars the world at large and the police authorities wish to know as to where I was staying when these atrocious and horrible crimes were committed, I am quite willing to give. I came into this house at a quarter to 11 on Thursday night. I knocked, and my sister opened the door. My sister's young*

man was present. We had some conversation about work. My sister first went to bed, and put the bolt in the latch so that anyone going out could not get back in again. From Thursday until I was arrested I never left the house except to go into the yard. I was seen several times in the yard by a neighbour. On Monday morning Sergeant Thicke came, I opened the door. He said I was "wanted" and I asked "What for?" He replied "You know what for you will have to come with me." I said, "Very well, I will go with you with the greatest of pleasure." The officer said, "You know you are Leather Apron," or words to that effect. Up to that moment I did not know I was called by that name. I have been in the habit of wearing an apron from my employment but not recently. When I arrived at the police station I was searched. They took everything from me according to custom. As I suppose they could find nothing that could incriminate me, thank God, or connect me with the crime I have been unfortunately suspected me of. I know of no crime, and my character will bear the strictest investigation. I am generally here, but occasionally stay at a lodging house, but not in Dorset-street. Before coming here on Thursday, I was at Holloway. Last Sunday week I was accosted in Church-street by two females unknown to me. One of them asked if I was the man, referring presumably to the Buck's-row murder? I said, "God forbid my good woman." A man then came and asked to treat him to a beer. I walked on. I do not know Mrs Tiddyman's public house, and was ignorant of such a name as Mrs Siffy until it was published. I do not know the woman. On Tuesday a man came to Leman-street Station, and at the request of the police I went out into the yard. A stalwart man, of a negro cast, whom I know to be a boot finisher placed his hand upon my shoulder. I said "I don't know you; you are mistaken." His statement that he saw me threaten a woman in Hanbury-street is false. I can give a full account of my whereabouts. I shall see if I can not legally proceed against those that have made statements about me. The charges against me have quite broken my spirits, and I fear I shall have to place myself under medical treatment." The Press Association's representative adds that Pizer is a man of medium height, with a moustache and whiskers. For a man of his class he displays more than an ordinary amount of intelligence. He was perfectly at ease when making his statement, and more than once appealed to his farther for confirmation of his story. The Press Association telegraphs this morning that at the inquest this morning on the murdered woman it is understood that Pizer will probably called as a witness. Meanwhile, the police have advised him to refuse to be interviewed. Pizer's brother states that John was treated well while in custody. The release of the prisoner took place shortly before nine o'clock last evening, when he left the prison in company with his brother Samuel, for his house in Mulberry-street, where is return was hailed with much rejoicing by his relatives and friends. The reported traces of blood on

Mike Covell

> the dividing wall of Nos. 29 and 27, Hanbury-street, is not confirmed this morning on inquiry of the police authorities. A later telegram from the Press Association states, with regard to the alleged funding of pieces of paper smeared with blood in the back premises of Bailey's packing case shop in Hanbury-street, investigation has proved that the stains are not those of blood but of some sewage matter. The police attach no importance to this supposed clue, or to the marks on the wall of the yard. Piggott still remains under police supervision in the Infirmary.

The Hull Daily Mail, September 12th 1888,

> THE PIMLICO MYSTERY. The Press Association says that although the river is in the immediate neighbourhood of the spot where the arm of the young woman was discovered has been dragged, no further portions of the body have been found. The Thames police are assisting in the search. Close to the place where the arm was discovered is a sluice under the embankment wall, from which flows a stream of water from a brewery in Grosvenor Road.

The Hull Daily Mail, September 12th 1888,

> ANOTHER SUPPOSED MURDER AND MUTILATION. The London Star, in a late edition yesterday published the following account of a supposed murder and mutilation:- A discovery, which is said to afford incontestable proof of a murder and mutilation was made in Pimlico on Monday, in the canal near Ebury Bridge and Grosvenor Road. A policeman's attention was attracted to something at which a number of boys were pelting stones. He had the object of the boys amusement extracted from the planks of timber amongst which it was entangled, and on examining it he found it to be a woman's arm. He had it at once removed to the station, where it was inspected by Dr Neville, of Pimlico Road, the police surgeon. The arm had been removed from the shoulder, and had evidently been done by an unskilful person. It must have been removed from the body of a person murdered but a day or two, as when touched the blood began to trickle freely from it. The instrument must have been exceedingly sharp, the joint cut into, and the limb removed at the shoulder socket. There was a cord tied round the arm above the elbow. The person murdered must have been a very fine young woman, as the arm was fully as long as that of a man 5ft, 10in, or 5ft, 11in.

The Hull Daily Mail, September 12th 1888,

THE INQUEST. The adjourned inquest on the body of Annie Chapman, who was murdered in Hanbury-street on Saturday morning, was resumed this afternoon at the Boys Institute, Whitechapel, by Mr Wynne Baxter.- Inspectors Abberline and Helson attended to represent the police. A plan of the locality was prepared for the information of the jury. There was a large attendance of the public.- Fontain Smith, printing warehouseman, deposed that he recognised the deceased as his sister. She was the widow of a head coachman, who formerly lived at Windsor, and had lived apart from him for three or four years. He last saw her alive a fortnight ago. She did not tell him where she was living.- James Kemp, packing case maker, Shadwell, said he worked at 23, Hanbury-street for Mrs Bailey, his usual time for going to work was six o'clock. On Saturday he got there at ten minutes or a quarter past six. His employer's gate was open. While he was there he was waiting for the other man to come, an elderly man named Davis, living near, ran into the road, and called him. Witness went, accompanied by James Green and others. He saw a woman lying in the yard of No. 29, near the door steps. Her clothes were disarranged. Nobody entered the yard until the arrival of Inspector Chandler. The woman's face and hands were smeared with blood, and the position of the hands indicated that a struggle had taken place. The woman's internal organs had been torn out and were lying over her shoulders. Witness went to fetch a piece of canvas to throw over the body, and when he returned the inspector was in possession of the yard.- James Green, another of Mr Bailey's workmen, corroborated.- Amelia Richardson, 29, Hanbury-street, said she and her son occupied separate parts of the house. Francis Tyler carried on the work of packing case maker there. He came at eight o'clock on the Saturday morning instead of six, the usual hour. Her son lived in John-street, and was occasionally late. About six o'clock on Saturday morning her grandson, Thomas Richardson, hearing a commotion in the passage, he went out, and on returning said there was a woman murdered in the yard. Witness went down and saw other people in the passage. The Inspector was the first person who entered the yard. She was awake part of Friday night, but heard no noise. Witness proceeded to describe the number of lodgers in the house and the apartments they occupied.

The Hull Daily News, September 12th 1888,

THE POLICE AND THE PRESS. We commend to the notice of the police authorities elsewhere than in London the following from the Star: The police, justly or unjustly, come in for a large share of the blame of these undiscovered crimes. It is true that Whitechapel is densely populated and difficult to cover, but it is also true that under anything like intelligent police management such a

Mike Covell

> *quartette of openly committed murders could hardly have occurred. One thing is absolutely certain, and that is the murderers will always escape with the ease that now characterises their escape in London until the police authorities adopt a different attitude towards the Press. They treat the reporters of the newspapers, who are simply news gatherers for the great mass of the people, with a snobbery that would be beneath contempt were it not senseless to an almost criminal degree. On Saturday they shut the reporters out of the mortuary; they shut them out of the house where the murder was done; the constable at the mortuary door lied to them; some of the inspectors at the offices seemed to wilfully mislead them; they denied information which would have done no harm to make public, and the withholding of which only tended to increase public uneasiness over the affair. Now if the people of London wish murderers detected they must have all this changed. In New York, where the escape of a murderer is as rare as it is common here, the reporters are far more active agents in ferreting out crime than detectives. There are no more numerous or more intelligent than the reporters of London, but they are given every facility and opportunity to get all the facts, and no part of any case is hidden from them unless the detectives' plan makes it necessary to keep it a secret. The consequence is a large number of sharp and experienced eyes are focussed upon every point of a case, a number of different theories develop which the reporters themselves follow up, and instances in which the detection of a criminal is due to a newspaper reporter are simply too common to create any particular comment. Reporters are not prying individuals simply endeavouring to gratify their own curiosity. They are direct agents of the people who have a right to the news and a right to know what their paid servants the police and detectives are doing to earn the bread and butter for which people are taxed. No properly accredited reporter ever wishes to know or print anything that will thwart the ends of justice, but he does desire and is fully entitled to the fullest scope in examining all the details of the case. The sooner the police authorities appreciate the act on this the sooner the Whitechapel fiend will be captured and human life in London rendered a little more safe.*

The Hull Daily News, September 12th 1888,

> *THE WHITECHAPEL MURDERS. PISER STILL IN CUSTODY. SUPPOSED CLUE. – A TRAIL OF BLOOD. Although no fresh arrests were made yesterday in connection with the Whitechapel murders, the police have obtained a clue which, although at present of a very slender character, may, they think, develop into an important piece of evidence. It appears that on the morning of the murder of the woman Chapman, a man, whose name is for the present withheld,*

was in Hanbury-street, and noticed a woman in the company of two men. They appeared to be quarrelling, and he heard the men make use of threats. Such an incident is, however, very common in the district, and the man, after taking a good look at the disputants, passed on his way. It is not known whether the man made a statement to the police as soon as he heard of the murder. If he did so, no action was taken upon it until yesterday, when it seems to have struck the police that Piser might have been one of the men seen in Hanbury-street at the time in question. The man was requested to attend, at Leman-street Police Station, and on his arrival about one o'clock some twenty men, mostly brought in from the adjacent thoroughfare, were paraded before him. The result somewhat startled the police, for the man, without a moment's hesitation, pointed to John Piser as the man whom he heard threatening a woman in Hanbury-street on the morning of the murder. Piser calmly protested that the man was entirely mistaken, but he was put back to the cells. The authorities do not express much confidence in their ability to establish a case against Piser. Piser's friends and relatives are not seriously alarmed at the alleged identification, for they are confident they will be able to prove an alibi without difficulty. Beyond the alleged identification, there is practically no evidence against Piser. His lodgings have been thoroughly searched more than once, and nothing of a suspicious character has been found. Strenuous efforts have been made to find the rings torn from Chapman's fingers by the murderer, but not a trace of them has been found. It is probable that they have been destroyed, and with them it is feared disappears the most hopeful means of bringing the murderer to justice. The police during the afternoon and evening made (illegible) inquiries into the statements made by the man who professed to identify Piser. The manner of this man, who is apparently of Spanish blood and displays a blue ribbon on his coat, did not inspire much confidence in his veracity, and he was severely cross-examined by a sort of informal tribunal consisting of experienced detective officers. The witness added to his first statement that he not only saw the prisoner in Hanbury-street on the morning of the murder, but that he actually took him by the collar when he was about to strike the woman. The man, it appears, first volunteered his statement on Monday, and he has since displayed anxiety to view the remains of the murdered woman Chapman. This curiosity, which was really believed to have been the inspiring motive of his voluntary testimony, was not gratified. Piser is physically a very weak man, and for that reason does not keep at work very closely. He is ruptured and in other ways infirm, and has been under hospital treatment on and off for a long time past. Each time the police searched Piser's lodgings they found no trace of blood-stained clothing, or indeed anything of a suspicious character; but they carried off five knives, which were at once subjected to chemical analysis. All are of the

Mike Covell

class used in the leather currying trade, having blades about six inches in length, with stout handles sometimes notched in a peculiar way. There was to all appearance no blood either on the blades or the handles. Meanwhile the police continued their inquiries into the witnesses statements, with the result that about eight o'clock they arrived at the conclusion that the man had not stated the truth, and that there were no grounds for keeping Piser any longer in custody. He was accordingly set at liberty, and at once proceeded to Mulberry-street, where he received the congratulations of his relatives and friends. The conduct of the man who professed to identify Piser has caused much indignation, it having kept several experienced officers from prosecuting inquiries in other directions. His statement, clear enough at first, utterly failed to stand the test even of ordinary questioning. In the course of a three hours examination to which he was subjected yesterday afternoon he contradicted himself over and over again. In the result he was not allowed to view the body at the mortuary and was sharply sent about his business. It should be clearly understood that the police have never made a charge against Piser, and that he was taken into custody purely as a matter of precaution to allow the allegations affecting him to be sifted. The man Pigott is still under surveillance at the Whitechapel Infirmary. It has been suggested that he is feigning insanity, but the physicians who have examined him state that he could not be held responsible for his actions. AN IMPORTANT DISCOVERY. An important discovery, which throws some considerable light upon the movements of the murderer immediately after the committal of the crime, was made yesterday afternoon. A little girl happened to be walking in the back garden or yard of the house, 25, Hanbury-street, the next house but one to the scene of the murder, when her attention was attracted to peculiar marks on the wall and on the garden path. She communicated the discovery to Detective-Inspector Chandler, who had just called at the house in order to make a plan of the back premises and the three houses for the use of the coroner at the inquest, which will be (illegible) The whole of the yard was then care (illegible) with the result that a bloody trail was (illegible) marked for a distance of five or six (illegible) in the direction of the back door of the house. Further investigation left no doubt that the trail was that of the murderer, who it was evident after finishing his sanguinary work had passed through or over the dividing fence between Numbers 29 and 27, and thence into the garden of No. 25. On the wall of the last house there was found a curious smear which had probably been made by the murderer, who, alarmed by the blood-soaked state of his coat, took off that garment and knocked it against the wall. Abutting on the end of the yard at 25 are the works of Mr. Bailey, a packing-case maker. In the yard of this establishment in an out of the way corner the police found some crumpled paper stained, almost saturated, with blood. It was evident that the murderer had found *the paper in the yard of 25, and had wiped his hands with it, afterwards throwing it over the wall into Bailey's premises.* ANOTHER SUPPOSED MURDER AND MUTILATION. *The London Star, in a late edition, publishes the following account of a supposed murder and mutilation. - "A discovery, which is held to afford incontestable proof of a murder and mutilation, was made in Pimlico to-day. In the canal near Ebury Bridge and Grosvenor road a policeman's attention was attracted to something at which a number of boys were pelting stones. He had the object of the boys amusement extricated from the planks of timber amongst which it was entangled, and on examination he found it to be a woman's arm. He had it at once removed to the station where it was inspected by Dr. Neville, of Pimlico road, the Police Surgeon. The arm had been removed from the shoulder, and had evidently been done by an unskilful person. It must have been removed from the body of a person murdered but a day or two ago, as when touched the blood began to trickle freshly from it. The instrument must have been exceedingly sharp, the joint being cut into and the limb removed at the shoulder socket. There was a cord tied round the arm above the elbow. The person murdered must have been a very fine young woman, as the arm was fully as long as that of a man of 5 ft. 10 in. or 5 ft. 11 in. There were a few abrasions on portions of the skin, but these might be caused by knocking against timber in the water. The police deny all knowledge of the suspect. A representative of the Press Association had an interview to-night with Dr Neville, of Pimlico, who examined the arm of a young woman found yesterday. He stated that the limb was but cleanly, but not apparently with a scientific object, so that it is supposed a murder has been committed. The police are making careful search for other portions of the body to-day.* THE POLICE AND THE PRESS. *We commend to the notice of the police authorities elsewhere than in London the following from The Star: The police, justly or unjustly, come in for a large share of the blame of these undiscovered crimes. It is true that Whitechapel is densely populated and difficult to cover, but it is also true that under anything like intelligent police management such a quartette of openly committed murders could hardly have occurred. One thing is absolutely certain, and that is that murderers will always escape with the ease that now characterises their escape in London until the police authorities adopt a different attitude towards the Press. They treat the reporters of the newspapers, who are simply news-gatherers for the great mass of the people, with a snobbery that would be beneath contempt were it not senseless to an almost criminal degree. On Saturday they shut the reporters out of the mortuary; they shut them out of the house where the murder was done; the constable at the mortuary door lied to them; some of the inspectors at the offices seemed to wilfully mislead them; they denied information which would have done no harm to make public,*

Mike Covell

> *and the withholding of which only tended to increase the public uneasiness over the affair. Now if the people of London wish murderers detected they must have all this changed. In New York, where the escape of a murderer is as rare as it is common here, the reporters are far more active agents in ferreting out crime than the detectives. They are no more numerous or more intelligent than the reporters of London, but they are given every facility and opportunity to get all the facts, and no part of any case is hidden from them unless the detectives' plan makes it necessary to keep it a secret. The consequence is that a large number of sharp and experienced eyes are focussed upon every point of a case, a number of different theories develop which the reporters themselves follow up, and instances in which the detection of a criminal is due to a newspaper reporter are simply too common to create any particular comment. Reporters are not prying individuals simply endeavouring to gratify their own curiosity. They are direct agents of the people who have a right to the news and a right to know what their paid servants the police and detectives are doing to earn the bread and butter for which the people are taxed. No properly accredited reporter ever wishes to know or print anything that will thwart the ends of justice, but he does desire and is fully entitled to the fullest scope in examining all the details of the case. The sooner the police authorities appreciate and act on this the sooner the Whitechapel fiend will be captured and human life in London rendered a little more safe.*

The Eastern Morning News, September 12th 1888,

> THE WHITECHAPEL TRAGEDIES. SCENES IN THE NEIGHBOURHOOD. RELEASE OF "LEATHER APRON." ANOTHER CLUE. A TRAIL OF BLOOD.
> A representative of the Central News, who patrolled the streets and alleys of Whitechapel on Monday night and the early hours of yesterday morning, writes as follows: - The scare, which the disclosure of the fourth and most horrible of the murders occasioned in the district, has considerably subsided. People having become familiar with the details of the tragedy, and being calmed by the knowledge of the active measures adopted for their protection by the police, are returning to their normal condition of mind. This is plainly evidenced by the aspect which Whitechapel road presented on Monday night, and up to an early hour of the morning - a very different one from that of the corresponding period of the previous day. On Sunday night the pavements were almost deserted, but 24 hours later groups of men and women chatted, joked, and boisterously laughed upon the flagstones until long after St. Mary's clock struck one. In passing through the groups of people, the words most frequently heard in their conversation were "Leather Apron." The term has become a byword of the

pavement and gutter, and one oftener hears it accompanied by a laugh than whispered in a tone which would indicate any fear of the mysterious individual who is supposed to live under that nickname. Whilst a large number of persons, including many members of the police force, believe in the guilt of "Leather Apron," the talk of the footways convinces the passer-by that a large number of other inhabitants of the East end are skeptical as to his personality. So it may be said with truth that the thoroughfares on Monday night presented their customary appearance. There was the usual percentage of gaudily dressed, loud, and vulgar women at the brightly lighted cross ways; and the still larger proportion of miserable, half fed, dejected creatures of the same sex upon whom hard life, unhealthy habits, and bad spirits have too plainly set their stamp. Soon after one o'clock the better dressed members of the motley company disappeared; but the poor wretches crawled about from lamp to lamp, or from one dark alley's mouth to another, until faint signs of dawn appeared. Off the main road - in such thoroughfares as Commercial street and Brick lane - there was little to attract attention. Constables passed silently by the knots of homeless vagabonds huddled in the recess of some big door way; other constables, whose plain clothes could not prevent their stalwart, well drilled figures from betraying their calling, paraded in couples, now and again emerging from some dimly lighted lane and passing their uniformed comrades with an air of profound ignorance. The streets referred to by the constables in the main thoroughfare, as "round at the back," presented a dismal appearance, the dim yellow flames of the not too numerous public lamps only rendering the darkness of the night more gloomy. Such passages as Edward street, connecting Hanbury and Prince's streets, Flower and Dean street, between Brick lane and Commercial street, which, in daylight, only strike one as very unwholesome and dirty thoroughfares, appear unutterably forlorn and dismal in the darkness of the night. In almost any one of these dark and filthy passages a human being's life might be every night sacrificed were the blow dealt with the terrible suddenness and precision which evidently characterised the last two homicides; and a police force of double the strength of that now employed, and organised under the best possible conditions, might well be baffled in its efforts to capture the murderers. In the immediate neighbourhood of St. Mary's Church a wide entry presented a deep cavern of intense blackness, into which no lamp shone, and where such an occurrence as that of Saturday morning might easily take place unobserved. In a squalid thoroughfare between Hanbury street and Whitechapel road some houses have been pulled down, the space being now waste ground enclosed by wooden palings. This unilluminated spot is separated by a house or two from an alley which, at a point some yards from the street, turns at right angles apparently towards the unoccupied space mentioned. Into the mouth of this passage a slatternly woman, her face half hidden in a shawl, which formed her only headdress, thrust her head, and in a shrill and angry voice shrieked, "Tuppy!" The cry was answered by the appearance of an evil looking man, with a ragged black beard, who in reply to an impatient question "Where is she?" muttered in a surly tone, "Round there," at the same time jerking his thumb backwards towards the alley. "Well, come 'long 'ome, then. I ain't agoin' to wait for she," replied the woman, who, with the dark man limping after, soon disappeared round the corner of the street. There was no subsequent indication of the presence of a third person. The light from the street was so dim that there was no possibility of recognising the features of the man and women, and certainly if either had borne traces of crime they would have attracted no attention. Such occurrences as the above are, the police say, quite usual, and they neither have, nor wish to have, authority to question any individual whose conduct may attract attention without exciting suspicion.

"The scare which the disclosure of the fourth and most horrible of the murders occasioned

LATEST PARTICULARS. LONDON, TUESDAY NIGHT. No fresh arrests have been made in connection with the Whitechapel murders, the police obtained information which at one time promised to develop into important evidence. It had been intended to liberate John Piser on Monday evening, but at the last moment it was decided to keep him in custody, the police not being quite satisfied upon one or two points in respect to him. Yesterday morning information was received, which, if well founded, would have made out a case of some strength against Piser. On the morning of the murder of Mrs. Chapman a man in Hanbury street noticed a woman in the company of two men. They appeared to be quarrelling, and the heard the men make use of threats. Such an incident is, however, very common in the district, and the man, after taking a good look at the disputants, passed on his way. Yesterday the police resolved to inquire if Piser was one of the men seen in Hanbury street at the time in question. The man who saw the quarrel was requested to attend at Leman street Police station. On his arrival about one o o'clock, some twenty men, mostly brought in from the adjacent thoroughfare, were paraded before him. The man, without a moment's hesitation, pointed to Piser as the man whom he heard threatening the woman in Hanbury street on the morning of the murder. Piser protested that the man was entirely mistaken, but he was put back in the cells, and more closely watched. The police, during the afternoon and evening, made careful inquiries into the statements made by the man who professed to identify Piser. The manner of this man, who is, apparently, of Spanish blood, and displays a blue ribbon on his coat, did not inspire much confidence in his veracity, and he was severely cross examined by a sort of informal tribunal, consisting of experienced detective officers. The witness added to his first statement that he not only saw the prisoner in Hanbury street on the day of the murder, but that he actually took him by the collar when he was about to strike the woman. The man first volunteered his statement on Monday, and he subsequently displayed anxiety to view the remains of Mrs. Chapman, which, however, was not permitted. Piser's brother declares that he did not leave the house between Thursday and the day of his apprehension, because he had been subjected to annoyance at being followed by people, who called him Leather Apron. Piser is physically a very weak man, and for that reason does not work very closely. He suffers from hernia, is in other ways infirm, and has been under hospital treatment for a long time. From his lodgings the police have carried off five knives, which have been subjected to careful examination. All of them are of the class used in the leather currying trade, having blades about six inches in length, with stout handles, sometimes notched in a peculiar way. There is apparently, no blood either on the blades or the handles, but on some of the blades are marks apparently caused by rust. The examination of the knives led to the conclusion that none of the marks was a blood stain. About eight o'clock last evening the police arrived at the conclusion that the man referred to above had not stated the truth, and that there were no grounds for keeping Piser any longer in custody. He was accordingly set at liberty, and at once proceeded to Mulberry street, where he received the congratulations of his relatives and friends. The conduct of the man who professed to identify Piser has caused much indignation, it having kept several experienced officers from prosecuting inquiries in other directions. His statement, clear enough at first, utterly failed to stand the test even of ordinary questioning. In the course of a three hours examination to which he was subjected yesterday afternoon he contradicted himself over and over again. In the result he was not allowed to view the body at the mortuary and was sharply sent about his business. It should be clearly understood that the police have never made a charge against Piser, and that he was taken into custody purely as a matter of precaution to allow the allegations affecting him to be sifted.

An important discovery which throws considerable light upon the movement of the murderer immediately after the committal of the crime was made. This afternoon a little girl happened to be walking in the back garden, or yard, of the house, 25 Hanbury-street, the next house but one to the scene of the murder, when her attention was attracted to peculiar marks on the wall and on the garden path. She communicated her discovery to Detective Inspector Chandler, who had just called at the house to make a plan of the back premises of the three houses, for the use of the Coroner. The yard was then carefully examined, with the result that a bloody trail was found distinctly marked for a distance of five or six feet in the direction of the back door of the house. The appearances suggested that the murderer, after his crime, had passed through or over the dividing fence between Nos. 29 and 27, and thence into the garden of No. 25. On the wall of the last house was a curious mark, between a smear and a sprinkle, as if the murderer, alarmed by the blood soaked state of his coat, had taken it off, and knocked it against the wall. Abutting on the end of the yard of No. 25 are the works of Mr. Bailey, a packing case maker. In the yard of this establishment, on an out of the way corner, the police yesterday afternoon found some crumpled paper, stained, almost saturated, with blood. It is supposed that the murderer found the paper in the yard of No. 25, wiped his hands with it, and threw it over the wall into Mr. Bailey's premises. The house No. 25, like most of the dwellings in the street, is let out in tenements direct from the owner, who does not live on the premises, and has no direct representative therein. The back and front doors are always left either on the latch or wide open, the tenant of each room looking after the safety of his own apartment. The general appearance of the trail of blood and other indications seem to show that the murderer intended to make his way into the street through the house next door but one, being frightened by some noise or light in No. 29 from retreating by the way which he came. On reaching the yard of No. 25, he made for the back door, and then suddenly remembering his blood stained appearance, he must have stopped, and, catching sight of the pieces of paper lying about, he doubtless retraced his steps to the end of the yard, and then performed his gruesome toilet. He might have had some thought of retreating by way of Bailey's premises, but the height of the walls made such a course somewhat perilous, and he finally made his way into Hanbury-street through the house. He could have met with no difficulty, as both back and front doors were open, and he could wait in the passage if anyone was passing down the street. These matters suggest that the murderer was alive to the risk of detection, and acted with so much circumspection as to dispel the idea that he was a reckless maniac. Strenuous efforts have been made to find the rings torn from Chapman's fingers by the murderer, but not a trace of them has been found. It is probable that they have been destroyed, and with them it is feared disappears the most hopeful means of bringing the murderer to justice. The man Pigott is still under surveillance at the Whitechapel Infirmary. Mr. S. Montagu, M.P. for the Whitechapel Division of the Tower Hamlets, has offered £100 as a reward for the capture of the Whitechapel murderer. SINGULAR DISCOVERY IN LONDON. SUPPOSED MURDER. A discovery which is held to afford incontestable proof of a murder

> *and mutilation was made in Pimlico to-day. In the canal near Ebury Bridge and Grosvenor-road a policeman's attention was attracted to something at which a number of boys were pelting stones. He had the object of the boy's amusement extricated from planks of timber amongst which it was entangled, and on examination he found it to be a woman's arm. He had it at one removed to the station, where it was inspected by Dr Neville, of Pimlico-road, the police surgeon. The arm had been removed from the shoulder, and had evidently been done by an unskillful person. It must have been removed from the body of a person murdered but a day or two, as when touched the blood began to trickle freshly from it. The instrument must have been exceedingly sharp, the joint being cut into, and the limb removed at the shoulder socket. There was a cord tied round the arm above the elbow. The person murdered must have been a very fine young woman, as the arm as fully as long as that of a man of five feet ten or five feet eleven. There were a few abrasions on portions of the skin, but these might be caused by knocking against the timber in the water. As soon as the medical examination had been concluded, Inspector Adams had the arm removed to the mortuary in Milibank-street, and then proceeded with his investigations. His first care was to have the whole of the river in the immediate neighbourhood dragged. The work was continued until a late hour last evening but no more human remains were found. The police records of missing persons were also carefully searched, but they yielded nothing that could be described as a clue. As already stated, the limb found yesterday was comparatively fresh; at any rate, it formed part of a living body not more than four days ago. It is possible that the arm may have been placed where found by some medical student or other practical joker, but this view is not shared by the authorities. Inquiries are being made at the various hospitals and private medical schools.*

September 13th 1888

The Hull Daily News, September 13th 1888,

> *THE PIMLICO MYSTERY. The Press Association says that although the river is in the immediate neighbourhood of the spot where the arm of the young woman was discovered has been dragged, no further portions of the body have been found. The Thames police are assisting in the search. Close to the place where the arm was discovered is a sluice under the embankment wall, from which flows a stream of water from a brewery in Grosvenor Road.*

The Hull Daily News, September 13th 1888,

Mike Covell

> THE LATEST LONDON HORROR. *Yesterday afternoon Dr. Thomas Neville, divisional surgeon, visited the mortuary at Ebury Bridge, Pimlico, for the purpose of minutely examining the arm found in the Thames on Tuesday. The limb will for the present remain at the mortuary, awaiting orders of Mr. Troutbeck, the district coroner, who has been officially informed of the discovery, but it is improbable an inquest will be held. The Thames police are making every endeavour to find other portions of the body, if there are any, in the river, and officers of the Criminal Investigations Department are making inquiries. The authorities still believe that a murder has been committed.*

The Eastern Morning News, September 13th 1888,

> THE SINGULAR DISCOVERY IN LONDON. *The Thames police were engaged for several hours yesterday afternoon in dragging the river between Pimlico Steam-boat Pier and the London, Brighton and South Coast Railway Bridge, between which points the arm of the woman was found on Tuesday. A careful examination was also made of the timber rafts floating in the river, but no discovery of human remains was made. It is the opinion of the river police that the arm was dropped over the embankment. In regard to the theory that the arm might have been thrown on to the river bank by a medical student with a view to create a scare, a representative of the Central News called at one of the chief London hospitals yesterday, where he was assured that the arm could not possibly have been removed by a student from any hospital dissecting room.*

The Hull Daily News, September 13th 1888,

> THE WHITECHAPEL MURDERS. *The Press Association telegraphs on Wednesday;- At the inquest to-day on the murdered woman it is understood that Piser will probably be called as witness. Meanwhile the police have advised him to refuse to be interviewed. Piser's brother states that John was treated well in custody. The release of the prisoner took place shortly before nine o'clock last evening, when he left prison in company with his brother Samuel for his house in Mulberry-street, where his return was hailed with much rejoicing by his relatives and friends. The reported discovery of traces of blood on the dividing walls of number 29 and 27, Hanbury street is not confirmed to-day. A later telegram from the Press Association states:- With regard to the alleged finding of pieces of paper smeared with blood, in the back premises of Bailey's packing case shop, in Hanbury street, investigations have proved the stains are not those of blood, but of some sewage matter. The police attach no importance either to*

> this supposed clue or the marks on the wall in the yard. Piggott still remains under police observation in the infirmary.

The Eastern Morning News, September 13th 1888,

> THE WHITECHAPEL TRAGEDIES. POLICE STILL AT FAULT. THE ADJOURNED INQUEST. The police continued their inquiries and investigations yesterday, but their labours were entirely without reward, and it is now beginning to be admitted, even in official circles, that the detectives are once more at fault. The slender clue afforded by the blood trail in the yard of No. 25 Hanbury-street was eagerly taken up, but so far it has not resulted in anything that can be described as important evidence. The man Pigott is still an inmate of the Workhouse Infirmary, and it is stated that his mental condition has not materially improved. The idea that he was connected in some way with the recent terrible crimes has not been entirely abandoned, and he is still kept under surveillance, while diligent inquiries are being made into his antecedents. Another arrest on suspicion was made yesterday, this time at Holloway, but it was speedily ascertained that the man was a harmless lunatic, and he was sent to the Workhouse Infirmary. It is not considered possible that another murder can be committed in Whitechapel district with impunity, for the whole neighbourhood is thoroughly roused. Woman of the class from which the late victim was taken are suspicious of every stranger, and the streets are nightly patrolled by large numbers of plain clothes constables. Meanwhile careful inquiries are being made in the directions suggested by Dr. Forbes Winslow, who adheres strenuously to his opinion that the murderer at large is a maniac. The relatives of the murdered woman Chapman, who occupy respectable positions in life, have taken charge of the remains, which will be interred privately. The woman Durrell has identified the body of the woman whom she saw talking with a man outside the scene of the tragedy about half-past five on Saturday morning. This corroborates other witnesses, and leaves little doubt that the murder was committed between half-past five and six o'clock, in almost broad daylight. --- The inquest on the body of Annie Chapman, the victim in the last of the East End tragedies, was continued yesterday, before Mr. Wynne Baxter, coroner for the district, at the Working Lads' Institute, Whitechapel. The interest taken in the case appeared if anything to have increased, the crowd outside the building being larger than on the former occasion. Fontaine Smith, who had his address inaudibly, deposed that he was brother to the deceased, who was the widow of John Chapman, and was 47 years of age. It was some

Mike Covell

> *time since he last saw her, and she did not then tell him anything as to what she was doing, or who where her associates. James Kent, packing-case maker, living at Shadwell, deposed to having been called into the yard of 39, Hanbury-street, by the man who discovered the body. This he described as lying between the steps and the fence. The clothes which the woman was wearing were thrown back as far as the knees, and round her neck was a handkerchief, which seemed to be almost concealed in the wound in the throat. The face and hands were smeared with blood. The appearances led him to believe that the woman had struggled while on her back. There were also bloodstains on the legs, some of the entrails were lying across the left shoulder, and appeared to have been dragged out and then thrown at the body. A piece of canvas was thrown over the corpse, and the police were summoned. James Green, who was in company with Kent, gave similar evidence, and Amelia Richardson, occupier of No. 29, Hanbury-street, was then called. She said she carried on a packing case making business, for which she used the workshop in the yard. Her son and a man named Tyler helped her in the business, but lived away. She first heard of it from her grandson, who went downstairs at six o'clock in consequence of the commotion in the passage. She slept badly during Friday night, but heard no disturbance. The first floor back was occupied by an old man and his imbecile son, but the latter was quiet inoffensive. There were a number of other lodgers in the house. The front and back doors were always left open, as were those of all the other houses in the neighbourhood. People often went through the passage into the backyard, but she heard no one do so on Saturday morning, and anyone who did must have walked very stealthily. Ellen Hardman, another occupier having been examined. John Richardson, Mrs. Richardson's son, said he went to 29, Hanbury-street at a quarter to five on Saturday, as he always did on market mornings. He went through the passage, opened the back door, and sat on the steps to cut a piece of loose leather from his shoe, using an old table-knife, which he did not usually carry, but which on this occasion he had put into his pocket by mistake. He could not have failed to see the body if it had been in the yard then. John Piser, the man who was taken into custody on Monday morning, but released on Tuesday night, was then called. He is a small dark man of the ordinary Jewish type, with black moustache and side whiskers. His desire, he said, was to clear his character and the Coroner remarked that he had been called for that purpose. Piser then made a statement relative to his whereabouts and proceedings before, during, and after the time of the murder was supposed to have been committed, the Coroner observing that these statements could be corroborated. The inquiry was then again adjourned.*

The Hull Daily News, September 13th 1888,

THE WHITECHAPEL MURDERS. THE POLICE BAFFLED. The police continued their inquiries and investigations yesterday, but their labours were entirely without reward, and it is now beginning to be admitted, even in official circles, that the detectives are once more at fault. The slender clue afforded by the blood trail in the yard of No. 25 Hanbury-street was eagerly taken up, but so far it has not resulted in anything that can be described as important evidence. Some persons who have examined the marks have expressed some doubt as to their being bloodstains, but on the whole there is good reason to believe that they are really the tracks of the assassin. In regard to the blood stained paper found in Bailey's packing case yard adjoining No. 25 Hanbury-street, there is practically no room for doubt that it was used by the murderer to cleanse his hands and thrown by him where it was found. The little girl, Laura Sickings, and other inmates of numbers 29, 27, and 25, have been questioned by the police, and the paper has been handed over to the police doctors for more scientific examination. A woman named Mrs. Durrell made a statement on Tuesday to the effect that about half past five o'clock on the morning of the murder of Mrs. Chapman she saw a man and a woman conversing outside No. 29, Hanbury-street, the scene of the murder, and that they disappeared very sufficiently. Mrs. Durrell was taken to the mortuary on Wednesday, and identified the body of Chapman as that of a woman whom she saw in Hanbury-street. If this identification can be relied upon it is obviously an important piece of evidence, as it fixed with precision the time at which the murder was committed, and corroborated the statement of John Richardson, who went into the yard at a quarter to five and has consistently and persistently declared that the body was not then on the premises. Davis, the man who first saw the corpse, went into the yard shortly after six o'clock. Assuming, therefore, that the various witnesses had spoken the truth, which there is not the slightest reason to doubt, the murder must have been committed between half past five and six o'clock, and the murderer must have walked through the streets in almost broad daylight without attracting attention, although he must have been at the time more or less stained with blood. This seems incredible, and it has certainly strengthened the belief of many of those engaged in the case that the murderer had not so far to go to reach his lodgings in a private house. Among the many suggestions made to the police is one urging that the pupils of the murdered woman's eyes should be photographed, on the chance of the retina retaining an image of the murderer capable of reproduction. DR. FORBES WINSLOW'S THEORY. Dr. Forbes Winslow writes as follows in The Times of yesterday: - My theory having been circulated far and wide with reference to an opinion given to the authorities of the Criminal Investigation Department, I would like to qualify such statements in your columns. That the murderer of the three victims in Whitechapel is one and

Mike Covell

the same person I have no doubt. The whole affair is that of a lunatic, and as there is "method in madness," so there was method shown in the crime and in the gradual dissection of the body of the latest victim. It is not the work of a responsible person. It is a well-known and accepted fact that homicidal mania is incurable, but difficult of detection, as it frequently lies latent. It is incurable, and those who have been the subject of it should never be let loose on society. I think that the murderer is not of the class of which "Leather Apron" belongs, but is of the upper class of society, and I still think that my opinion given to the authorities is the correct one - viz., that the murders have been committed by a lunatic lately discharged from some asylum, or by one who has escaped. If the former, doubtless one who, though suffering from the effects of homicidal mania, is apparently sane on the surface, and consequently has been liberated, and is following out the inclinations of his morbid imaginations by wholesale homicide. I think the advice given by me a sound one - to apply for an immediate return from all asylums who have discharged such individuals, with a view of ascertaining their whereabouts. INTERVIEW WITH "LEATHER APRON." The Press Association's representative had an interview on Wednesday with John Piser, at 22, Mulberry-street. He was released from Leman-street Police Station about 8.30 p.m. on Tuesday. In reply to questions, the ex-prisoner said:- "Whatever particulars the world at large and the police authorities wish to know as to where I was staying when these atrocious and horrible crimes were committed, I am quite willing to give. I came into this house at a quarter to 11 on Thursday night. I knocked, and my sister opened the door. My sister's young man was present. We had some conversation about work. My sister first went to bed , and put the bolt in the latch so that anyone going out could not get back in again. From Thursday until I was arrested I never left the house except to go into the yard. I was seen several times in the yard by a neighbour. On Monday morning Sergeant Thicke came, I opened the door. He said I was "wanted" and I asked "What for?" He replied "You know what for, you will have to come with me." I said, "Very well, I will go with you with the greatest of pleasure." The officer said, "You know you are Leather Apron," or words to that effect. Up to that moment I did not know I was called by that name. I have been in the habit of wearing an apron from my employment but not recently. When I arrived at the police station I was searched. They took everything from me according to custom. As I suppose they could find nothing that could incriminate me, thank God, or connect me with the crime I have been unfortunately suspected me of. I know of no crime, and my character will bear the strictest investigation. I am generally here, but occasionally stay at a lodging house, but not in Dorset-street. Before coming here on Thursday, I was at Holloway. Last Sunday week I was accosted in Church-street by two females unknown to me. One of them asked if I was the man, referring presumably to the Buck's-row murder? I said, "God forbid my good woman." A man then came and asked to treat him to a beer. I walked on. I do not know Mrs Tiddyman's public house, and was ignorant of such a name as Mrs Siffy until it was published. I do not know the woman. On Tuesday a man came to Leman-street Station, and at the request of the police I went out into the yard. A stalwart man, of a negro cast, whom I know to be a boot finisher placed his hand upon my shoulder. I said "I don't know you; you are mistaken." His statement that he saw me threaten a woman in Hanbury-street is false. I can give a full account of my whereabouts. I shall see if I can not legally proceed against those that have made statements about me. The charges against me have quite broken my spirits, and I fear I shall have to place myself under medical treatment." The Press Association's representative adds: Piser is a man of medium height, with a moustache and whiskers. For a man of his class, he displays more than an ordinary amount of intelligence. He was perfectly at ease making his statement, and more than once appealed to his father for confirmation of his story. INQUEST OF THE MURDERED WOMAN. The adjourned inquest on the body of Annie Chapman, who was found murdered in Hanbury-street, Whitechapel, on Saturday was resumed on Wednesday at the Working Lads Institute, Whitechapel, by Mr Wynne Baxter. Inspectors Abberline and Helson attended to represent the police. A plan of the locality was prepared for the information of the jury. There was a large attendance of the public. Fountain Smith, printing warehouseman, deposed that he recognised deceased as his sister. She was the widow of a head coachman, who formerly lived at Windsor, and had lived apart from him for three or four years. He last saw her alive a fortnight ago. He gave her 2s. She did not tell him where she was living. James Kemp, packing case maker, Shadwell, said he worked at 23, Hanbury-street, for Mr. Bailey. His usual time for going to work was six o'clock. On Saturday he got there at ten minutes or a quarter past six. His employers gate was open. While he was waiting for the other men to come an elderly man named Davis, living near, ran into the road and called him. Witness went, accompanied by James Green and others. He saw a woman lying in the yard of No. 29, near the doorsteps. Her clothes were disarranged. Nobody entered the yard until the arrival of Inspector Chandler. The woman's hands and face were smeared with blood, and the position of the hands indicated that a struggle had taken place. The woman's internal organs had been torn out, and were lying over her shoulder. Witness went to fetch a piece of canvas to throw over the body, and when he returned the inspector was in possession of the yard. James Green, another of Mr. Bailey's workmen, corroborated. Amelia Richardson, 29, Hanbury-street, said she and her son occupied separate parts of the house. Francis Tyler carried on the work of a packing case maker there. He came at

Mike Covell

> *eight o'clock on Saturday morning, instead of six, the usual hour. Her son lived in John-street, and was occasionally late. About six o'clock on Saturday morning, her grandson, Thomas Richardson, hearing a commotion in the passage, went out, and on returning said there was a woman murdered in the yard. Witness went down and saw people in the passage. The inspector was the first person who entered the yard. She was awake part of Friday night, but heard no noise. Witness proceeded to describe the number of lodgers in the house, and the apartments they occupied. John Piser said he lived at 22, Mulberry-street, and was a shoemaker. He was known by the name of "Leather Apron." On Thursday night he arrived at the house from the West End shortly before eleven o'clock. He remained indoors until he was arrested by the police on Monday, the 10th inst, at nine o'clock. – By the Coroner: He never left the house till then. He remained indoors because his brother advised him. – You were the subject of suspicion? – I was the object of unjust suspicion. – where were you on the 30th August. – I was staying at the Crossingham's common lodging house, Holloway-road. The jury did not question the witness and the inquiry was adjourned until today.*

September 14th 1888

The Hull Daily Mail, September 14th 1888,

> *THE HORRIBLE DISCOVERY IN A CANAL. Mrs. Potter living in Spencer Buildings, Westminster, applied to the magistrate at Westminster yesterday, in great distress, for advice. She said she feared the arm found the other day belonged to her daughter, aged 17, who left home last Saturday, and had not since been heard of. She had described her daughter to Dr Neville, who expressed the opinion that from her description the arm very probably was her daughters. The magistrate referred Mrs. Potter to the police.*

The Eastern Morning News, September 14th 1888,

> *THE WHITECHAPEL TRAGEDIES. ACTIVITY OF SCOTLAND YARD CHIEFS. No fresh facts of importance transpired yesterday in connection with the Whitechapel murder beyond the evidence given at the inquest. Dr. Phillips' positive opinion that the woman had been dead quiet two hours when he first saw the body at half past six throws serious doubt upon the accuracy of at least two important witnesses, and considerably adds to the prevailing confusion. There have been no further arrests, but some important information respecting the two lunatics under surveillance has been obtained. The man arrested at*

Holloway has for some reason been removed to the asylum at Bow. His own friends give him an indifferent character. He has been missing from home for nearly two months, and it is known that he has been in the habit of carrying several large butchers' knives about his person. Inquiries are now being made with a view to tracing his movements during the past two months. The Central News, telegraphing late last night, says: - The principle officers engaged in investigating the Whitechapel murders were summoned to Scotland Yard yesterday, and conferred with the chief officer. Later in the day Mr. Bruce, Assistant Commissioner, and Colonel Monsell, Chief Constable, paid a private visit to the Whitechapel district without notifying the local officers of their intention to do so. They visited the scene of the Buck's-row murder, as well as Hanbury-street, and made many inquiries. They spent nearly a quarter of an hour at No. 29, Hanbury-street, and minutely inspected the house and the yard in which were found the mutilated body of Mrs. Chapman. The police have satisfied themselves that the man Pigott could have had nothing to do with the murders, his movements having been fully accounted for, and he is no longer under surveillance. Most of the street doors in Hanbury-street and the neighbourhood heretofore left on the latch all night have now been fitted with locks, and the lodgers supplied with keys.

September 15th 1888

The Eastern Morning News, September 15th 1888,

THE WHITECHAPEL TRAGEDY. ANOTHER ARREST. The bloodstained newspaper, which were found in Bailey's Yard, close to Hanbury Street, and upon which it is conjectured the Spitalfields murderer wiped his hands after committing his fearful crime, have been subjected to analysis, and the stains are certified to be those of human blood. The police who made the search state distinctly that the paper was not there when they made the search last Saturday, and though they have been closely examined at this point, they adhere to their statement. It is not clear, moreover, that the murderer could have thrown the newspapers in the spot where they were found from the backyard in Hanbury Street, but if he threw the paper, which was rolled up into a round mass, over the wall, it might easily have been blown or kicked into the corner in which it was found. The police precautions are even stronger than before the murderer hitherto having selected Friday or Saturday for the commission for his crimes. Our Maidstone correspondent states that a Scotland Yard Detective has arrived there and interviewed the commander of the Sussex Regiment, with a view to identifying the writing on the envelope found on the murdered woman. A

Mike Covell

> statement has been made by a woman named Lloyd, living in Heath Street, Commercial Road, which may possibly prove of some importance. While standing outside a neighbours door on Monday night she heard her daughter, who was sitting on the doorstep, scream, and on looking round saw a man walk hurriedly away. The daughter states that the man peered into her face, and she perceived a large knife at his side. A lady living opposite stated that a similar incident took place outside her house. The man was short of stature, with a sandy beard, and wore a cloth cap. The woman drew the attention of some men, and they pursued him at some distance. He turned up a bye street and was eventually lost sight of. The Central News telegraphing last night, says:- The police have today been in communication with the pensioner who is said to have been seen in the company of the murderer woman Chapman. He has voluntarily explained his connection to the deceased and his antecedents. His statements are, it is understood, entirely satisfactory, and he will be produced as a witness when the inquest is resumed. In the course of today's investigations, the police have become possessed of some further information, from which it is hoped important results will follow. All ranks are working in the most indefatigable spirit, and a complete sense of security seems to be entertained by the inhabitants. LONDON, Friday Midnight. A man has been arrested on a charge of threatening to stab people in the neighbourhood of the Tower. A roughly sharpened knife was found upon him. He is a short, stout man, with a sandy beard and wears a dark cap. The police offer no opinion as to the value of the latest arrest. It is pointed out as a fact which cannot be too clearly emphasised, that any one harbouring a person who may be a murderer is liable to be arrested as an accessory after the fact.

The Hull and East Yorkshire and Lincolnshire Times, September 15th 1888

> THE WHITECHAPEL TRAGEDY. THE INQUEST. The inquest on the body of Annie Chapman, who was found murdered in Hanbury-street, Whitechapel, on Saturday, was opened at ten o'clock on Monday by Mr. Baxter, District Coroner, at the working lads' Institute, Whitechapel-road. – Inspector Nelson, J Division, represented the police. – The court and vicinity were crowded, and the latest newspapers were eagerly scanned by those in waiting for the commencement of the proceedings. – Mr. Collier, deputy coroner, accompanied Mr. Wynne Baxter. The jury having been sworn went to view the body at the mortuary. On their return John Davies deposed: I live at 29, Hanbury-street, Spitalfields. I am a carman, and occupy a front room with my wife, and three sons. On Friday night I went to bed at eight o'clock. My sons came in at

different times, the last at about a quarter to 11. I was awake between three and five o'clock, but fell to sleep for about half an hour, and got up at a quarter to six. I went across the yard. When I opened the back door of the yard I found a woman lying on her back. I called two men in the employ of Mr Bayley, packing case maker, in Hanbury-street, three doors from No, 29. They came and looked at the body. I do not know them personally. – In reply to the Coroner, Inspector Chandler said the men referred to were not known to the police. – The Coroner expressed surprise at this. He said the man must be found, if they had not already been seen and identified. – Davis (continuing) said: I informed the inspector at Commercial-street what I had seen in the yard. I heard no voice on Saturday evening. - Amelia Palmer, living at 30, Dorset-street, lodging house, was next examined. She said her husband was an army pensioner. She knew the deceased for five years, and identified the body as that of Annie Chapman, a widow. Her husband died at Windsor 18 months ago. Prior to that she received 10s a week from him. Deceased was called Mrs Liffey, because she lived with a man who was a sieve maker. She had been staying at 35, Dorset-street. Witness had seen her several times the worse for drink, and she was frequently out in the streets late at night. On Friday afternoon witness saw her in Dorset-street about five o'clock. She said she had no money, and had been in the casual ward, and she could not pay for her lodging. - Timothy Donovan (35), Dorset-street, deputy of a common lodging house, identified the body at the Mortuary as the woman who had lodged at his house occasionally. She was not at No. 35 last week until Friday afternoon, about three o'clock. She went into the kitchen, and he did not see her again till Saturday morning at 1.45. She afterwards left the house, and said she should come back again for a bed. She was somewhat the worst for liquor, and when she left in the morning the witness said, "You can find money for your bed." He did not see her with any man that night. Sometimes she came to the house with a man said to be a pensioner, and sometimes with other men, and witness had refused to allow her a bed. Replying to the Coroner, witness added that, the pensioner had told him not to admit her with any other man. - Inspector Chandler, in answer to the Coroner, said nothing was known of the man called the pensioner.- Donavan (resuming) said on August 29th deceased had a row with another woman in the kitchen, and sustained a bruise over her eye.- John Evans, night watchman, 35, Dorset-street, said he saw the deceased go out on Saturday morning, she never returned. She was worse for drink. Witness knew she was on the streets at night, but only knew of the man with whom she associated. He used to come to her on Saturdays. He called about half past two on Saturday last, and when he was told of the murder went away without saying anything. He did not know this man's name or address. The inquest was adjourned until Wednesday. The inquest was resumed on

Mike Covell

Wednesday, at the Boys' Institute, Whitechapel, by Mr Wynne Baxter. – Inspectors Abberline and Helson attended to represent the police. A plan of the locality was prepared for the information of the jury. There was a large attendance of the public. Fontain Smith, printing warehouseman, deposed that he recognised deceased as his sister. She was the widow of a head coachman, who formerly lived at Windsor, and had lived apart from him for three or four years. He last saw her alive a fortnight ago. He gave her 2s. She did not tell him where she was living. James Kemp, packing case maker, Shadwell, said he worked at 23, Hanbury-street, for Mr. Bailey. His usual time for going to work was six o'clock. On Saturday he got there at ten minutes or a quarter past six. His employers gate was open. While he was waiting for the other men to come an elderly man named Davis, living near, ran into the road and called him. Witness went, accompanied by James Green and others. He saw a woman lying in the yard of No. 29, near the doorsteps. Her clothes were disarranged. Nobody entered the yard until the arrival of Inspector Chandler. The woman's hands and face were smeared with blood, and the position of the hands indicated that a struggle had taken place. The woman's internal organs had been torn out, and were lying over her shoulder. Witness went to fetch a piece of canvas to throw over the body, and when he returned the inspector was in possession of the yard. James Green, another of Mr. Bailey's workmen, corroborated. Amelia Richardson, 29, Hanbury-street, said she and her son occupied separate parts of the house. Francis Tyler carried on the work of a packing case maker there. He came at eight o'clock on Saturday morning, instead of six, the usual hour. Her son lived in John-street, and was occasionally late. About six o'clock on Saturday morning, her grandson, Thomas Richardson, hearing a commotion in the passage, went out, and on returning said there was a woman murdered in the yard. Witness went down and saw people in the passage. The inspector was the first person who entered the yard. She was awake part of Friday night, but heard no noise. Witness proceeded to describe the number of lodgers in the house, and the apartments they occupied. The inquest was resumed on Thursday by Mr Wynne Baxter, at the Lads' Institute, Whitechapel. – Inspector Chandler, H. Division, Metropolitan Police, deposed he was on duty on Saturday morning a few minutes after six, at the corner of Hanbury-street. He saw several men running, one of whom said another woman had been murdered. Witness accompanied him to 29, Hanbury-street, Whitechapel. About two yards from a water-tap was a leather apron, which was afterwards shown to the police surgeon. There was also a nail box and a piece of steel in the yard. There was no evidence of any person having climbed over the fence dividing the yard from the next yard. Marks were found on the wall of No. 25 on Tuesday last. There were no traces of blood outside of the yard where the body was found. Inspector

Chandler proceeded to describe the clothing on the body, and said the underclothing was not torn at all. The Foreman asked with reference to the envelope that had been found and the mention of a pensioner named Stanley, did the police promise to produce that man? Inspector Chandler replied that he had been unable to find him. The Foreman said it was very important, as the pensioner had been staying with the deceased night after night. The inspector replied that nobody knew who he was. The lodging house keeper had been requested to inform the police if the man came there. The Coroner – The pensioner knows his own business, but I should have thought he would come forward himself. The inquiry was again adjourned. FUNERAL OF THE VICTIM. The funeral of Annie Chapman, the victim of the Hanbury-street murder, took place early this morning. Strict secrecy was observed in the arrangements, and the removal of the body from the mortuary attracted little attention. Several relative s of the deceased met the hearse at the Manor Park Cemetery, where the interment took place and a service was duly performed. The body was enclosed in a black covered coffin of elm.

From inquiries which have been made in Windsor, it seems that the deceased was the widow of a coachman in service at Clewer. While the deceased lived at Clewer she was in custody for drunkenness, but had not been charged before the magistrates. Another fresh point was elicited in the form of a statement made by a woman named Darrell, who minds carts on market mornings in Spitalfields Market. She asserts that about half-past five on Saturday morning she was passing the front door of No. 29, Hanbury-street, when she saw a man and a woman standing on the pavement. She heard the man say "Will you?" and the woman replied "Yes," and they then disappeared. Mrs. Darrell does not think she could identify the couple. A meeting of the chief local tradesmen was held yesterday, at which an influential committee was appointed, consisting of sixteen well-known gentlemen, with Mr. J. Aarons as the secretary. The committee issued last evening a notice stating that they will give a substantial reward for the capture of the murderer or for information leading thereto. The movement has been warmly taken up by the inhabitants, and it is thought certain that a large sum will be subscribed within the next few days. The proposal to form a district vigilance committee also meets with greater popular favour and is assuming practical form. Meetings were held at the various working men's clubs and other organizations, political and social, in the districts, at most of which the proposed scheme was heartily approved. The Press Association says a statement was made on Thursday night to a reporter by a person named Lloyd, living in Heath-street, Commercial-road, which may possibly prove of some importance. While standing outside a neighbour's door on Monday night she

Mike Covell

heard her daughter, who was sitting on the door step, scream, and on looking round saw a man walk hurriedly away. The daughter states that the man stared into her face, and she perceived a large knife at his side. A lady living opposite stated that a similar incident took place outside her house. The man was short of stature, with a sandy beard, and wore a cloth cap. The woman drew the attention of some men who were passing to the strange man, and they pursued him some distance. He turned up a bye-street, and was eventually lost sight of. A Press Association's representative had an interview on Wednesday with John Piser at 22 Mulberry-street. He was released from Leman-street Police Station about 8.30 last night. In reply to questions the ex-prisoner said:- Whatever particulars the world at large and the police authorities wish to know as to where I was staying when these atrocious and horrible crimes were committed I am quite willing to give. I came into this house at a quarter to eleven on Thursday night. I knocked and my sister opened the door. My sister's young man was present, and we had a conversation about work. My sister first went to bed and put the belt in the latch, so that anyone going out afterwards would not get in again. From Thursday until I was arrested I never left the house except to go into the yard I was seen several times I the yard by a neighbour. On Monday morning Sergeant Thicke came. I opened the door. He said I was wanted and I asked what for. He replied, "You know what for; you will have to come with me." I said, "Very well; I will go with the greatest pleasure." The officer said, "You know you are 'Leather Apron,'" or words to that effect. Up to that moment I did not know I was called by that name. I have been in the habit of wearing an apron from my employment, but not recently. When I arrived at the police station I was searched. They took everything from me, according to custom, as I suppose. They found nothing that could incriminate me, thank God, or connects me with the crime that I have been unfortunately suspected of. I know of no crime, and my character will bear the strictest investigation. I am generally here, but occasionally at a lodging house, but not in Dorset-street. Before coming here on Thursday I was at Holloway. Last Sunday week I was accosted in Church street by two females, unknown to me. One of them asked me if I was the man, referring presumably to the Buck's row murder. I said "God forbid, my good woman." A man then asked me to treat him to beer. I walked on. I do not known Mrs. Fiddyman's public house, and was ignorant of such a name as Mrs. Siffy until it was published. I don't know the woman. Yesterday a man came to Leman-street station, and at the request of the police I went out into the yard. A stalwart man, of Negro cast, whom I know to be a boot finisher, placed his hands upon my shoulder. I said, "I don't know you, you are mistaken." His statements that he saw me threaten a woman in Hanbury-street is false. I can give a full account of my whereabouts. I shall see if I cannot legally proceed against those who have made statements about me. The charges against me have quite broken my spirits, and I fear I shall have to place myself under medical treatment. The Press Association representative adds that Piser is a man of medium height, with a moustache and whiskers. For a man of his class he displays more than an ordinary amount of intelligence. He was perfectly at ease when making his statement, and more than once appealed to his father for confirmation of his story.

The Hull Daily News, September 15th 1888,

THE HORRIBLE TRAGEDY IN WHITECHAPEL. SEARCH FOR THE MURDERER. During the week London has been greatly agitated concerning the murders committed in the neighbourhood of Whitechapel, the last being that of a woman named Chapman, who was found on Saturday morning so horribly mutilated in a yard in Hanbury-street. The police have been very active, and numerous arrests have been made, but up to the present time no evidence has been forthcoming to connect any of the prisoners with the tragedies, and with one exception all have been released. The principle interest attached to the apprehension of a man named Piser, who was believed to be a character known as "Leather Apron," and who is alleged to have been frequenting the streets under suspicious circumstances. But the police have failed to in any way associate him with the deeds of blood which have been committed. Another arrest was that of a man named Piggott, at Gravesend, who was found to be in a blood spattered condition. In this case the man was afterwards pronounced insane, and was detained in custody. All day on Sunday five policeman guarded the scene of the crime in Hanbury-street. No one was admitted unless he resided in the house. In the street half a dozen costermongers took up their stand and did a brisk business in fruit and refreshments. Thousands of respectably dressed persons visited the scene, and occasionally the road became so crowded that the constables had to clear it by making a series of raids upon the spectators. The windows of the adjoining houses were full of persons watching the crowds below. A number of people also visited the house in Dorset-street, where the murdered woman lodged. The usually busy condition of Whitechapel and Spitalfields on a Sunday was considerably augmented on Sunday by reason of the excitement aroused by the murderer, in the course of the day nearly a dozen persons were arrested and conveyed to the Commercial-street Police Station. In the afternoon a vast crowd had collected about the streets, and as each apprehension was made they rushed pell-mell towards the station, obviously under the idea that the murderer of the woman had been caught. Shortly before five o'clock a man was arrested in Dale-street after a long phase on a charge of

Mike Covell

assault. The officer who took him proceeded with his prisoner by the way of Hanbury-street to the police station, and so was obliged to make his way through the crowd outside the house. His prisoner stood in some danger of being mobbed, but the crowd eventually gave way, and the prisoner was safely lodged in the station. A few minutes later two men were arrested in Wentworth-street. So soon as the crowd saw them in the hands of the police there were loud cries of "Leather Apron," and thereupon hundreds of persons turned out from the side streets and followed the officers in a tumultuous throng to the station. Not five minutes afterwards a woman was arrested on some trifling charge, and the excitement became so intense that a posse of officers were sent out from the building to preserve order. These marched three and four abreast up and down the pavement, and while they were so engaged yet another prisoner was brought in. There was a good deal of shouting by the mob, which surged about in a dangerous fashion, but by and by a diversion was caused by the rapid passage along Hanbury-street of three men who was supposed to be two detectives and the prisoner. The centre man bore a striking resemblance to "Leather Apron," and the cry of "That's him" having been raised, a rush was made at him, but the little party immediately turned down a side street and the police prevented the crowd from proceeding further. The scene of the murder was again visited on Monday by crowds of morbid sight seers, and there was a good deal of excitement throughout the squalid district, due briefly to the arrests and the many rumours of arrest. Intelligent observers who have visited the locality express the utmost astonishment that the murderer could have reached a hiding place after committing such a crime. He must have left the yard in Hanbury-street reeking like a slaughterman, and yet if the theory that the murder took place between five and six he accepted, he must have walked almost in broad daylight along streets comparatively well frequented, even at an early hour, without his startling appearance attracting the slightest attention. Sir Charles Warren resumed his duties at Scotland Yard on Monday morning, and during the day conferred with some of the chief officials respecting the murders. A meeting of the chief local tradesmen was held on Monday, at which an influential committee was appointed, consisting of sixteen well known gentlemen, with Mr. J. Aarons as the Secretary. The committee issued on Monday a notice stating that they will give a substantial reward for the capture of the murderer, or for information leading thereto. The movement has been warmly taken up by the inhabitants, and it is certain that a large sum will be subscribed within the next few days. The proposal to form district Vigilance Committees also meets with great popular favour and is assuming practical form. Meetings have been held at the various working men's clubs and other organisations, political and social, in the district, at most of which the proposed scheme was heartily approved and volunteers enrolled. AN IMPORTANT DISCOVERY. An important discovery, which throws considerable light upon the movements of the murderer immediately after the committal of the crime, was made on Tuesday afternoon. A little girl happened to be walking in the back garden of the yard of the house 25, Hanbury-street, the next house but one to the scene of the murder, when her attention was attracted to peculiar marks on the wall, and on the garden path. She communicated the discovery to Detective Inspector Chandler, who had just called at the house in order to make a plan of the back premises of the three houses for the use of the coroner at the inquest, which was resumed on Wednesday. The whole of the yard was then carefully examined, with the result that a trail of blood was found distinctly marked for a distance of five or six feet in the direction of the back door of the house. Further investigation left no doubt that the trail was that of the murderer, who it was evident after finishing his sanguinary work, had passed through or over the dividing fence between numbers 29 and 27, and thence into the garden of 25. On the wall of the last house there was found a curious mark between a smear and a sprinkle, which had probably been made by the murderer, who, alarmed by the blood soaked state of his coat, took off that garment and knocked it against the wall. Abutting on the end of the yard at 25 are the works of Mr. Bailey, a packing case maker. In the yard of this establishment is an out of the way corner the police on Tuesday afternoon found some crumpled papers stained, almost saturated with blood. It was evident that the murderer had found the paper in the yard of number 25, and had it wiped his hands with it, afterwards throwing it over the wall into Bailey's premises. The house, No. 25, like most of the dwellings in the street, is let out in tenements direct from the owner, who does not live on the premises, and has no direct representative therein. The back and front doors are therefore always left either on the latch or wide open, the tenant of each room looking after the safety of his own particular premises. The general appearance of the trail and other indications seem to show that the murderer intended to make his way as rapidly as possible into the street through the house next door, but being frightened by some noise or light in No. 29, retreated by the way which he came. On reaching the yard of No. 26, he made for the back door, and then suddenly remembering his bloodstained appearance, he must have hesitated a moment, and then catching sight of the places of paper lying about he doubtless retraced his steps to the end of the yard, and there performed his toilet. He might have had some thoughts of retreating by way of Bailey's premises, but the height of the walls made such a course somewhat perilous, and he finally elected to make his way into Hanbury-street by way of the house. He could have met with no difficulty, so both back and front doors were open, and he could, if needful, wait in the passage while anyone might be passing down the street. It will be seen that the discoveries made on Tuesday afternoon prove that the murderer was fully alive to the danger of detection, but such cunning is not of course incompatible with the theory of his insanity. It, however, somewhat lessens the chances of his capture and unfortunately, dispels the idea of his being an utterly reckless maniac. The St. Jude's Vigilance Association has only been in existence about four weeks. It is largely composed of working men, assisted by some of the members belonging to Toynbee Hall, its operations being confined to this neighbourhood. No action has yet been taken as to the result of the watching which has been done by the association. In an interview with a newspaper representative, a member of the committee stated that rows are constantly occurring in the district and that the police force is too small to deal with the disturbers of the peace. The night after the murder in Buck's-row a man and a woman disturbed Wentworth-street for more than half an hour. Two members of the committee were present, but no policeman could be found. Another brawl took place only on Tuesday in the same thoroughfare, and one of the committee who became aware of it looked for a constable for twenty minutes before one was found. The inhabitants of a certain fixed point, and it was only after two years endeavour that they obtained their object. Inquiries last night failed to discover that any similar associations have been started. THE POLICE BAFFLED. The police continued their inquiries and investigations on Wednesday, but their labours were entirely without reward, and it is now beginning to be admitted, even in official circles, that the detectives are once more at fault. The slender clue afforded by the blood trail in the yard of No. 25 Hanbury-street was eagerly taken up, but so far it has not resulted in anything that can be described as important evidence. Some persons who have examined the marks have expressed some doubt as to their being bloodstains, but on the whole there is good reason to believe that they are really the tracks of the assassin. In regard to the blood stained paper found in Bailey's packing case yard adjoining No. 25 Hanbury-street, there is practically no room for doubt that it was used by the murderer to cleanse his hands and thrown by him where it was found. The little girl, Laura Sickings, and other inmates of numbers 29, 27, and 25, have been questioned by the police, and the paper has been handed over to the police doctors for more scientific examination. A woman named Mrs. Durrell made a statement on Tuesday to the effect that about half past five o'clock on the morning of the murder of Mrs. Chapman she saw a man and a woman conversing outside No. 29, Hanbury-street, the scene of the murder, and that they disappeared very sufficiently. Mrs. Durrell was taken to the mortuary on Wednesday, and identified the body of Chapman as that of a woman whom she saw in Hanbury-street. If this identification can be relied upon it is obviously an important piece of evidence, as it fixed with precision the time at which the murder was committed, and corroborated the statement of John Richardson, who went into the yard at a quarter to five and has consistently and persistently declared that the body was not then on the premises. Davis, the man who first saw the corpse, went into the yard shortly after six o'clock. Assuming, therefore, that the various witnesses had spoken the truth, which there is not the slightest reason to doubt, the murder must have been committed between half past five and six o'clock, and the murderer must have walked through the streets in almost broad daylight without attracting attention, although he must have been at the time more or less stained with blood. This seems incredible, and it has certainly strengthened the belief of many of those engaged in the case that the murderer had not so far to go to reach his lodgings in a private house. POLICE DESCRIPTION OF THE SUPPOSED MURDERER. An official description of the supposed murderer has been circulated by the police in London and the provinces as follows:- Description of a man who entered a passage of a house at which the murder was committed of a prostitute, at 2-0 a.m. on the 8th:- Age, 37; height, 5feet 7 inches; rather dark beard and moustache; dress, shirt, dark jacket, dark vest, and trousers, black scarf, black felt hat, spoke with a foreign accent. AN INTERVIEW WITH "LEATHER APRON" The Press Association's representative had an interview this morning with John Piser, at 22, Mulberry-street. He was released from Leman-street Police Station about 8.30 p.m. on Tuesday. In reply to questions, the ex-prisoner said:- "Whatever particulars the world at large and the police authorities wish to know as to where I was staying when these atrocious and horrible crimes were committed, I am quite willing to give. I came into this house at a quarter to 11 on Thursday night. I knocked, and my sister opened the door. My sister's young man was present. We had some conversation about work. My sister first went to bed, and put the bolt in the latch so that anyone going out could not get back in again. From Thursday until I was arrested I never left the house except to go into the yard. I was seen several times in the yard by a neighbour. On Monday morning Sergeant Thicke came, I opened the door. He said I was "wanted" and I asked "What for?" He replied "You know what for, you will have to come with me." I said, "Very well, I will go with you with the greatest of pleasure." The officer said, "You know you are Leather Apron," or words to that effect. Up to that moment I did not know I was called by that name. I have been in the habit of wearing an apron from my employment but not recently. When I arrived at the police station I was searched. They took everything from me according to custom. As I suppose they could find nothing that could incriminate me, thank God, or connect me with the crime I have been unfortunately suspected me of. I know of no crime, and my character will bear the strictest investigation. I am generally here, but occasionally stay at a lodging house, but not in Dorset-street. Before coming

Mike Covell

here on Thursday, I was at Holloway. Last Sunday week I was accosted in Church-street by two females unknown to me. One of them asked if I was the man, referring presumably to the Buck's-row murder? I said, "God forbid my good woman." A man then came and asked to treat him to a beer. I walked on. I do not know Mrs. Tiddyman's public house, and was ignorant of such a name as Mrs Siffy until it was published. I do not know the woman. On Tuesday a man came to Leman-street Station, and at the request of the police I went out into the yard. A stalwart man, of a negro cast, whom I know to be a boot finisher placed his hand upon my shoulder. I said "I don't know you; you are mistaken." His statement that he saw me threaten a woman in Hanbury-street is false. I can give a full account of my whereabouts. I shall see if I can not legally proceed against those that have made statements about me. The charges against me have quite broken my spirits, and I fear I shall have to place myself under medical treatment." The Press Association's representative adds: Piser is a man of medium height, with a moustache and whiskers. For a man of his class, he displays more than an ordinary amount of intelligence. He was perfectly at ease making his statement, and more than once appealed to his father for confirmation of his story. THE INQUEST. The inquest on the body of Annie Chapman, who was found murdered in Hanbury-street, Whitechapel, on Saturday was opened at ten o'clock by Mr Wynne Baxter, District Coroner, at the Working Lads Institute, Whitechapel Road.- Inspector Nelson, J Division, represented the police.- Mr Collier deputy coroner, accompanied Mr Wynne Baxter. The jury having been sworn in went to view the body at the mortuary. On their return John Davies deposed: I live at 29, Hanbury-street, Spitalfields. I am a carman, and occupy a front room with my wife and three sons. On Friday night I went to bed at eight o'clock. My sons came in at different times, the last at about quarter to 11. I was awake between three and five o'clock, but fell to sleep for about half an hour, and got up at about quarter to six. I went across to the yard. On the ground floor there is a front door leading into a passage through the basement. There is a back door in the passage. Sometimes the doors are left open during the night. I have never known either of them to be locked. Anyone can open the front door by the latch, and enter the yard by the passage, I cannot say whether the back door was latched when I got down, but the front door was wide open, which was not an unusual circumstance.- Witness being asked to describe the general appearance of the yard, was not very clear in his statements.- The Coroner said the police in country places had generally prepared a plan of the locality which was the subject of investigation. Certainly this was of sufficient importance for such a plan.- Inspector Chandler promised that a plan should be drawn up.- The Coroner said that delay might prove fatal.- Witness resuming said: When I opened the back door of the yard I found a woman lying on her back. I called two men in the employ of Mr Bayley, packing case maker in Hanbury-street, three down from no. 29. They came and looked at the body. I do not know them personally.- In reply to the Coroner, Inspector Chandler said the men referred to were not known to the police.- The Coroner expressed surprise at this. He said the men must be found, if they had not already been seen and identified. Davis (continuing) said: I informed the inspector at Commercial-street what I had seen in the yard. I heard no voice on Saturday evening.- Amelia Palmer, living at 30, Dorset-street, lodging house, was next examined. She said her husband was an army pensioner. She knew the deceased for five years, and identified the body as that of Annie Chapman, a widow. Her husband died at Windsor 18 months ago. Prior to that she received 10s a week from him. Deceased was called Mrs Liffey, because she lived with a man who was a sieve maker. She had been staying at 35, Dorset-street. Witness had seen her several times the worse for drink, and she was frequently out in the streets late at night. On Friday afternoon witness saw her in Dorset-street about five o'clock. She said she had no money, and had been in the casual ward, and she could not pay for her lodging.- Timothy Donovan (35), Dorset-street, deputy of a common lodging house, identified the body at the Mortuary as the woman who had lodged at his house occasionally. She was not at No. 35 last week until Friday afternoon, about three o'clock. She went into the kitchen, and he did not see her again till Saturday morning at 1.45. She afterwards left the house, and said she should come back again for a bed. She was somewhat the worst for liquor, and when she left in the morning the witness said, "You can find money for your bed." He did not see her with any man that night. Sometimes she came to the house with a man said to be a pensioner, and sometimes with other men, and witness had refused to allow her a bed. Replying to the Coroner, witness added that, the pensioner had told him not to admit her with any other man.- Inspector Chandler, in answer to the Coroner, said nothing was known of the man called the pensioner.- Donavan (returning) said on August 29th deceased had a row with another woman in the kitchen, and sustained a bruise over her eye.- John Evans, night watchman, 35, Dorset-street, said he saw the deceased go out on Saturday morning, she never returned. She was worse for drink. Witness knew she was on the streets at night, but only knew of the man with whom she associated. He used to come to her on Saturdays. He called about half past two on Saturday last, and when he was told of the murder went away without saying anything. He did not know this man's name or address. The inquest was adjourned till Wednesday afternoon. The inquest was resumed on Wednesday. Fountain Smith, printing warehouseman, deposed that he recognised deceased as his sister. She was the widow of a head coachman, who formerly lived at Windsor, and had lived apart from him for three or four years.

Mike Covell

He last saw her alive a fortnight ago. He gave her 2s. She did not tell him where she was living. James Kemp, packing case maker, Shadwell, said he worked at 23, Hanbury-street, for Mr. Bailey. His usual time for going to work was six o'clock. On Saturday he got there at ten minutes or a quarter past six. His employers gate was open. While he was waiting for the other men to come an elderly man named Davis, living near, ran into the road and called him. Witness went, accompanied by James Green and others. He saw a woman lying in the yard of No. 29, near the doorsteps. Her clothes were disarranged. Nobody entered the yard until the arrival of Inspector Chandler. The woman's hands and face were smeared with blood, and the position of the hands indicated that a struggle had taken place. The woman's internal organs had been torn out, and were lying over her shoulder. Witness went to fetch a piece of canvas to throw over the body, and when he returned the inspector was in possession of the yard. James Green, another of Mr. Bailey's workmen, corroborated. Amelia Richardson, 29, Hanbury-street, said she and her son occupied separate parts of the house. Francis Tyler carried on the work of a packing case maker there. He came at eight o'clock on Saturday morning, instead of six, the usual hour. Her son lived in John-street, and was occasionally late. About six o'clock on Saturday morning, her grandson, Thomas Richardson, hearing a commotion in the passage, went out, and on returning said there was a woman murdered in the yard. Witness went down and saw people in the passage. The inspector was the first person who entered the yard. She was awake part of Friday night, but heard no noise. Witness proceeded to describe the number of lodgers in the house, and the apartments they occupied. John Piser said he lived at 22, Mulberry-street, and was a shoemaker. He was known by the name of "Leather Apron." On Thursday night he arrived at the house from the West End shortly before eleven o'clock. He remained indoors until he was arrested by the police on Monday, the 10th inst, at nine o'clock. – By the Coroner: He never left the house till then. He remained indoors because his brother advised him. – You were the subject of suspicion? – I was the object of unjust suspicion. – where were you on the 30th August. – I was staying at the Crossingham's common lodging house, Holloway-road. The jury did not question the witness and the inquiry was adjourned. The inquest on the body was resumed on Thursday, by Mr. Wynne Baxter, at the Lads' Institute, Whitechapel. Inspector chandler, H Division, Metropolitan Police, deposed that he was on duty on Saturday morning a few minutes after six, at the corner of Hanbury-street. He saw several men running, one of whom said another woman had been murdered. Witness accompanied to 29, Hanbury-street. About two yards from a water tap was a leather apron, which was afterwards shown to the police surgeon. There was also a nail box and a piece of steel in the yard. There was no evidence of any person having climbed over the fence dividing the yard from the next yard. Marks were found on the wall of No. 25 on Tuesday last. There were no traces of blood outside of the yard where the body was found. Inspector Chandler proceeded to describe the clothing on the body, and said the underclothing was not torn at all. The Foreman asked with reference to the envelope that had been found and the mention of a pensioner named Stanley, did the police promise to produce that man? Inspector Chandler replied that he had been unable to find him. The Foreman said it was very important, as the pensioner had been staying with the deceased night after night. The inspector replied that nobody knew who he was. The lodging house keeper had been requested to inform the police if the man came there. The Coroner – The pensioner knows his own business, but I should have thought he would come forward himself. Dr. George Phillips, divisional police surgeon, said he examined the body of the deceased in the yard when it was discovered on Saturday morning. He described the injuries, which were of a frightful nature, and must have been inflicted with a long thin, sharp knife, such as slaughtermen use. The inquest was adjourned until Wednesday next. ANOTHER WOMAN STABBED. At five minutes after eleven o'clock on Saturday forenoon a man suddenly attacked a woman in Spitalfields Market while she was passing through. After felling her to the ground with a blow, he began kicking her and pulled out a knife. Some women who had collected, having the terrible tragedy that brought them there still fresh in their minds, on seeing the knife, raised such piercing shrieks of "Murder!" that they reached the enormous crowds in Hanbury-street. There was at once a rush for Commercial-street, where the markets are situate, as it was declared by some that there was another murder, and by others that the murderer had been arrested. Seeing the immense crowd swarming around him, the man who was the cause of the alarm made more furious efforts to reach the woman, from whom he had been separated by some persons who interfered on her behalf. He, however, threw these on one side, fell upon the woman, knife in hand, and inflicted various stabs on her head, cut her forehead, neck, and fingers before he was again pulled off. When he was again pulled off the woman lay motionless – the immense crowd took up the cry of "Murder," and the people who were on the streets raised cries of "Lynch him!" At this juncture the police arrived, arrested the man and after a while had the woman conveyed on a stretcher to the police station in Commercial-street where she was examined by the divisional surgeon. She was found to be suffering from several wounds, but none of them were considered dangerous. She was subsequently removed to the London Hospital, where she was detained as an in-patient. Her assailant is described as a blind man, who sells laces in the streets, and whom she led about from place to place. The blind man is described as having a most ungovernable temper, and he was seen whilst the woman was

Mike Covell

leading him along to stab her several times in the neck. Blood flowed quickly, and it was at first thought that another terrible murder had been committed. The affair occurred midway between Buck's Row and Hanbury-street, where the last two horrible murders have been committed. STARTLING INCIDENTS. The Press Association says a statement was made on Thursday to a reported by a person named Lloyd, living in Heath-street, Commercial-road, which possibly prove of some importance. While standing outside a neighbour's door on Monday night she heard her daughter, who was sitting on the door step, scream, and on looking round saw a man walk hurriedly away. The daughter states that the man peered into her face, and she perceived a large knife at his side. A lady living opposite stated that a similar incident took place outside her house. The man was short of stature, with a sandy beard, and wore a cloth cap. The woman drew the attention of some men who were passing to the strange man, and they pursued him some distance. He turned up a bye street, and was eventually lost sight of. No further arrest has been made up to the last evening. On the question of the hour at which the crime was committed, concerning which there was a difference between the evidence of the man Richardson and the opinion of Dr. Phillips, a Press Association reporter yesterday elicited that Mr. Cadoche, who lives in the next house to number 29, Hanbury-street, where the murder was committed, went to the back of the premises at half past five a.m., and as he passed the wooden partition he heard a scuffle and then someone fell heavily against the fence. He heard no cry for help, and so he went into his house. Some surprise is felt that this statement was not made in evidence in the inquest. Inquiry reveals the circumstance that some of the four murdered women were known to one another, but there is great reticence amongst the women of the locality to give information, partly because of shame at making public the life they are leading, also from fear of being subjected to rough usage. Although there is not so much surface excitement as earlier in the week, there is a very strong feeling in the district, and a large number of people continue to visit the locality. The rumour was prevalent yesterday that inquiries were being made by a detective at Maidstone, with a view to the identification of the handwriting on the envelope found near the body, but the Press Association correspondent states that this is incorrect. FUNERAL FOR THE WOMAN CHAPMAN. The funeral of Annie Chapman, the victim of the Hanbury-street murder, took place early yesterday. Strict secrecy was observed in the arrangements, and the removal of the body from the mortuary attracted little attention. Several relatives of the deceased met the hearse at the Manor Park Cemetery, where the interment took place and the service was duly performed. The body was enclosed in a black covered coffin of elm. THE LATEST LONDON HORROR. On Wednesday afternoon Dr. Thos. Neville, divisional surgeon, visited the mortuary

> at Ebury Bridge, Pimlico, for the purpose of minutely examining the arm found in the Thames on Tuesday. The limb will for the present remain at the mortuary, awaiting the orders of Mr. Troutbeck, the district coroner, who has been officially informed of the discovery, but it is improbable that an inquest will be held. The Thames police are making every endeavour to find other portions of the body, if there are any in the river, and the officers of the Criminal Investigations Department are making enquiries. The authorities still believe that a murder has been committed. THE MYSTERIOUS DEATH OF A LADY IN LONDON. The mysterious death of a well-dressed female in Blackfriars-road, London, late on Saturday night, has caused great excitement. The deceased was seen about eleven on Saturday night lying on the pavement. Two well-dressed men were standing over her, and one, who had a parcel in his hand, informed the police officer who came up that the lady was his wife. He offered to go for medical aid, and handed the parcel to the police officer. Both men then went away, and nothing has been seen of them. The parcel was found to contain boots and other items of some value. The female was removed to St. Thomas's Hospital, were life was found to be extinct. There were superficial bruises on both shoulders, indicating that she had been roughly used. On the parcel was the name of a tradesman residing at Sun-street, Canterbury. On Sunday morning the police telegraphed to this address, and subsequently received a reply that the deceased was a married woman named Byrne, the wife of a military man residing in that city. She had property of considerable value upon her, and it is supposed that the object of the two men was robbery. Dr. Luard, of St. Thomas's Hospital, has been instructed to make a post mortem examination to ascertain the precise cause of death.

September 17th 1888

The Hull Daily Mail, September 17th 1888,

> THE LONDON HORROR. The attention of the police is being directed to the elucidation of a very suspicious incident which occurred on Friday. At about 10.30 p.m., a man passed through Tower subway from the Surrey to the Middlesex side, and said to the caretaker, "Have you caught any of the Whitechapel murderers yet?" He then produced a knife about a foot long with a curved blade, and remarked "This will do for them." He was followed, but ran and was lost sight of near Tooley Street. The man is described as about 80 years of age, 5ft, 3in, in height, complexion and hair dark, with moustache and false whiskers, which he pulled of whilst running away, dressed in new black diagonal suit, light dust overcoat and dark cloth double peak cap. Some of the detective

Mike Covell

> *officers who have been engaged in investigating the East End murders returned to headquarters shortly before midnight on Saturday, having just received some important information. What those information's were they said they were not at liberty to disclose, but expressed themselves hopeful of being able to elucidate the mystery. The detective officers continued their investigation yesterday, but up to a late hour last night no arrest had been made, neither is there any immediate prospect of arrest being made. The public of the neighbourhood continue to make their statements, which are committed to writing at Commercial Street station, and in several instances the police have been cognisant of what the informants consider to be suspicious movements of individuals whose appearance is thought to resemble the man wanted. The lapse of time, it is feared, will lessen the chance of the perpetrator being discovered.*

The Eastern Morning News, September 17th 1888,

> *THE WHITECHAPEL TRAGEDIES. No further arrest has been made in connection with the murder of Annie Chapman, and the police practically have no substantial clue to work upon. The report that in their anxiety to bring the criminal to justice the members of H Division of Police have subscribed £50 to supplement the reward of £100 offered by Mr Samuel Montagu, M.P., is unfounded. The police of this division entertain hopes that the private offer of a reward of £100 may lead many of those who are frequenters of common lodging houses in the neighbourhood to have hitherto been rather reluctant to give information, to come forward and give evidence which may materially facilitate the work of the officers engaged in the unravelling the mystery. A large number of extra police and detectives are still engaged in patrolling the neighbourhood, and the increased surveillance has tended to abate the alarm in the East End.*

The Hull Daily News, September 17th 1888,

> *THE WHITECHAPEL MURDER. ANOTHER MAN IN CUSTODY. The man who is detained at Commercial Street, and answers the description communicated by several persons, was handed over to the police officer on Friday, near Flower and Dean street, Spitalfields, his movements having created since on Friday grave suspicions. The man is about 5 feet 7 inches in height, with hair, beard and moustache inclined to be sandy, shabbily dressed, with cloth skull cap. On being searched one of the most odd accumulations of articles were found, including two purses usually carried by females, and several pocket handkerchiefs. The man has no fixed abode. Detectives are investigating his recent movements. A SINGULAR INCIDENT. The attention of the police is being*

directed to the elucidation of a very suspicious incident which occurred on Friday. About 10-30p.m. a man passed through the Tower subway from the Surrey to Middlesex side, and said to the caretaker- "Have you caught any of the Whitechapel murderers yet?" He then produced a knife about a foot long with a curved blade, and remarked- "This will do for them." He was followed, but ran away, and was lost sight of in Tooley Street. The man is described as about thirty years of age, 5 feet 3in. in height, complexion and hair dark, with moustache and false whiskers, which he pulled off while running away. Dressed in new black diagonal suit, light dust overcoat, and dark cloth double peak cap. THE PENSIONER DISCOVERS HIMSELF. The pensioner Stanley, who has been referred to as associating with the murdered woman, has given the police an account of his movements since he last saw the deceased, which was on the Sunday preceding the murder. He has since been following his usual employment, without attempt at concealment. Stanley is said to be superior to the class frequenting lodging houses in Spitalfields, and has known Chapman some two years.

September 18th 1888

The Hull Daily Mail, September 18th 1888,

THE WHITECHAPEL MURDERS. It has transpired that on the day of the Hanbury Street murder a man went into the lavatory at the City Newarcome, Ludgate Circus, and there changed his clothes, hurriedly departing and leaving behind a pair of trousers, a shirt, and socks. Nobody connected with the establishment saw him at the time, and when the clothes were found they were thrown into a dust box, and, being placed therein in the street, were carried away by scavengers. They do not appear to have attracted special attention at the time. On the following Tuesday a police officer visited the house and made inquiries of the proprietor. The matter is being followed up by the police. The inquest on the body of Mary Ann Nicholls, who was murdered in Buck's Row, Whitechapel, on 31st August, was resumed yesterday.- Thomas Eade, employed on the East London Line, deposed that on the 8th inst, he saw a man of a suspicious appearance in Cambridge Heath Road. The man had a large knife partly concealed in his pocket. The witness called on some other men to assist in arresting him, but they refused, and the man got away.- Several other witnesses were called, but although they slept in the street where the body was found they heard no noise. The police had no new evidence. The inquiry was adjourned until Saturday.

Mike Covell

September 19th 1888

The Eastern Morning News, September 19th 1888,

> THE LONDON MURDERS. ANOTHER SUPPOSED CLUE. IMPORTANT ARREST. An important charge was made at the Thames Police court yesterday which the police believe may throw some light upon the recent tragedies in Whitechapel. Charles Ludwig, aged 40, a decently dressed German, of 1 The Minories, was charged with being drunk and threatening to stab Alexander Finlay, of Leman Street, Whitechapel, when the accused came up drunk, and in consequence was refused to be served. He then said to prosecutor, "What are you looking at?" and then pulled out a knife and tried to stab the witness. Ludwig followed him round the stall, and made several attempts to stab him. A constable came up, and he was given into custody. Constable 221 H said the prisoner was in a very excited condition, and witness had previously received information that prisoner was wanted in the city for attempting to cut a woman's throat with a razor. On the way to the station he dropped a long bladed open knife, and on him was found a razor and a long bladed pair of scissors. Inspector Pimley asked the magistrate to remand the prisoner, as they had not had sufficient time to make the necessary inquiries concerning him. A city constable, John Johnson, stated that early that morning he was on duty in the Minories when he heard the screams of "Murder" proceeding from a dark court in which there was no lights. The court led to some railway arches and was well known as a dangerous locality. On going into the court he found the prisoner with a prostitute. The former appeared to be under the influence of drink. Witness asked what he was doing there, when he replied "Nothing." The woman, who appeared to be in a very frightened and agitated condition, said, "Oh! Policeman, do take me out of this." The woman was so frightened that she could then make no further statement. He sent the man off and walked with the woman to the end of his beat, when she said, "He frightened me very much when he pulled a big knife out," and witness said, "Why didn't you tell me that at the time? She replied "I was too much frightened." He then went and looked for the prisoner, but could not find him, and therefore warned several other constables of the occurrence, Witness had been out all morning trying to find the woman, but up to the present time without success. He should know her again. He believed the prisoner worked in the neighbourhood. The magistrate thereupon remanded the prisoner. The arrest has caused intense excitement in the neighbourhood. Prisoner professes not to be able to speak English. He has been

> *in this country about three months. He accounts for his time for about three weeks but nothing is known of his doings before that time. The Central News has ascertained that the real name of the man Charles Ludwig is Wetzel. He came to this country from Hamburg about 15 months ago, and is a hairdresser by trade. He bears an indifferent character, being described as cowardly and quarrelsome and given to drink. The woman who complained that Wetzel threatened to murder her has not yet been found, but there should be little difficulty in tracing her, as she only has one arm.*

September 20th 1888

The Hull Daily News, September 20th 1888,

> *THE WHITECHAPEL MURDER. IMPORTANT STATEMENT. The landlord of the hotel in Finsbury, where the prisoner Weitzel, charged on Tuesday with stabbing a youth in Whitechapel, stayed sometimes, stated to a representative of the Press Association that since the last Whitechapel murder he had been very suspicious of Weitzel. On the Sunday after the murder he called about nine o'clock in a very dirty condition, saying he had been out all night, and began talking about the Spitalfields affair. He brought with him a case of razors and a large pair of scissors, and after a time wanted to shave the landlord. Previous to this visit he had not been there for eighteen months and his accounts of his movements was contradictory. He was an extraordinary man, always in bad temper, and frequently grinding his teeth when enraged. The landlord believed he had some knowledge of anatomy having been a doctors assistant in the German army. He always carried razors and scissors with him. On Monday night, when the landlord refused to let him sleep there, he threw down the razors in a passion. He had changed his dress since his last appearance. The landlord knew that he associated with low women. LETTER FROM THE HOME SECRETARY. In reply to a communication from a committee of gentlemen in Mile-end-road, as to the offer of a reward for the apprehension of the Whitechapel murderers, the Home Secretary has written through his private secretary stating that if he had considered the case a proper one for the offer of a reward, the Secretary of State would at once have offered one on behalf of the Government; but the practice of offering rewards for the discovery of criminals was discontinued some years ago because experience showed that such offers tended to produce more harm than good, and the Secretary of State was satisfied that there was nothing in the circumstances of the recent case to justify a departure from this rule. RESUMED INQUEST. The inquest on the body of Annie Chapman, who was murdered in Hanbury street, on the morning of the*

Mike Covell

8th inst., was resumed by Mr. Wynne Baxter, at Whitechapel, on Wednesday. Chief Inspector West, Inspectors Abberline, Helson and Chandler attended. Eliza Cooper, of 25 Dorset street, deposed that she was a hawker, and lodged at that address for five months. She knew deceased. Witness had a quarrel with her on Tuesday before her death. Afterwards she noticed deceased's face was marked. The last time witness saw her alive was on Wednesday, the 5th inst., in the Ringers public house. Deceased had three brass rings on her left hand. The deceased associated with a man named Ted Stanley, and others. She used to bring them to the public house. Dr. G. Baxter Phillips, re-called, proceeded to give additional details of the result of his examination of the body. Certain incisions and bruises led him to the conclusion that the woman was seized by the chin while the incisions in the throat were inflicted. He thought that if he gave any further details of the results of his examination it would be thwarting justice. The coroner intimated that at this point ladies and boys should leave the court, and the foreman of the jury said the jury were of the opinion that the evidence which the doctors desired to keep back should be given. Dr. Phillips: The evidence will not elucidate the cause of death. The Coroner: That is a matter of opinion. Dr. Phillips: Death took place before the injury was inflicted. The Coroner: That is a matter of opinion, doctor, and it might be [illegible] by other medical evidence. The evidence of the doctor on the first day was read over. Proceeding, Dr. Phillips said the abdominal walls had been removed. There was a greater portion of skin removed on the right side than on the left, a portion constituting the navel was wanting, He removed the intestines in the same manner as he found them in the yard. The witness proceeding to give further details of the condition of the internal organs. The weapon used was probably five or six inches or more in length. The manner of cutting the body indicated a certain amount of anatomical knowledge. In reply to the coroner, witness added that he himself could not have inflicted the injuries under a quarter of an hour, even in a hurried manner. Elizabeth Young, living at No. 3 Church-row, deposed to seeing deceased with a tall dark man like a foreigner about half past five on the morning of the 8th in Hanbury street. They were talking. The man said, "will you?" and the woman replied "Yes." Witness left them standing together.- Edward Stanley, known as "the pensioner," was then called and said he knew deceased for some time, and last saw her alive on Sunday, the 2nd instant, about half past two. Witness never slept from Saturday to Monday, at 35 Dorset street. In reply to the coroner, he said he was never in the Royal Sussex Regiment.- Timothy Donovan, deputy at 35, Dorset street (re-called), said last witness was called "the pensioner," and Hay had stayed with the deceased at the lodging house several times from Saturday to Monday.- The inquest was adjourned to Wednesday next.

Newspapers from Hull Volume 1

The Eastern Morning News, September 20th 1888,

THE WHITECHAPEL TRAGEDIES. RESUMED INQUEST. THE MEDICAL EVIDENCE. The inquest on the body of Annie Chapman, the victim in the last of the Whitechapel tragedies, was resumed yesterday before Mr Wynne Baxter, the District Coroner. Some unimportant evidence having been given by a woman with whom deceased had a quarrel in a public house, Dr Phillips, the police surgeon, was re-called, and had his previously given testimony read over to him. In answer to a suggestion that he should lay before the jury certain facts which he had expressed his unwillingness to state openly, Dr Phillips again said that the publication of the further facts could throw no light on the cause of death, and such publication was, therefore, to be deprecated. The coroner, however, insisted that Dr Phillips should proceed with his testimony, saying that the press might be trusted to use discretion in reporting it, and witness accordingly went on to detail further facts as to the gross and bestial manner in which the body had been mutilated after death. He gave reasons for believing that the knife used by the murderer was long and extremely sharp, and again expressed the conviction, based on the manner in which the abdomen had been opened, and the missing portions of the body excised, that the outrage was committed by someone possessed of anatomical knowledge. All the injuries could not have been inflicted in less than quarter of an hour, and would probably take longer. The organs removed from the abdomen would not occupy such space, and might easily be concealed. The Coroner observed that the doctor who examined the body of Nicholls, the other murdered woman, was of opinion that in that case the injuries to the abdomen were inflicted first. Elizabeth Long identified the dead woman as one whom she saw talking in Hanbury-street, at half past five on the morning of the murder, to a man whom she would not be able to recognise, and as to whom she could only say that he was dark, rather tall, over 40, apparently a foreigner, and shabby genteel as to his dress. Both were talking loudly, but she only heard the man ask "Will you?" and the woman reply "Yes." Edward Stanley, otherwise known as "the pensioner," to whom frequent references has been made as a person who from time to time stayed with the deceased at the lodging house in Dorset-street, was then called. He deposed that he last saw her, as far as he remembered, on Sunday, the 2nd inst. He was not really in receipt of a pension, and had never belonged to the Sussex Regiment. He was a bricklayers' labourer by trade. Donovan, the lodging house deputy, was recalled, and identified "the pensioner" as the man who had repeatedly stayed with deceased from Saturday till Monday, an allegation strongly denied by Stanley. Albert Cadosch, a carpenter, living at 27, Albert-street, said that on the morning of the murder he was in the back yard, when he heard first a voice in the yard next door, and then a fall against the fence. This he fixed as having taken at twenty minutes past five. William Stephens, a youth, living at the Dorset-street lodging house, said that early on the morning of the murder he saw deceased pick up in the kitchen part of an envelope resembling that found in the yard, with the words "Sussex Regiment" upon it. This was all the evidence in the possession of the police at present, and the inquiry was again adjourned. WEITZEL, THE MAN IN CUSTODY. The landlord of the hotel in Finsbury, where the prisoner Weitzel, charged on Tuesday with stabbing a youth in Whitechapel, stayed sometimes, stated to a representative of the Press Association that since the last Whitechapel murder he had been very suspicious of Weitzel. On the Sunday after the murder he called about nine o'clock in a very dirty condition, saying he had been out all night, and began talking about the Spitalfields affair. He brought with him a case of razors and a large pair of scissors, and after a time wanted to shave the landlord. Previous to this visit he had not been there for eighteen months and his accounts of his movements was contradictory. He was an extraordinary man, always in bad temper, and frequently grinding his teeth when enraged. The landlord believed he had some knowledge of anatomy having been a doctors assistant in the German army. He always carried razors and scissors with him. On Monday night, when the landlord refused to let him sleep there, he threw down the razors in a passion. He had changed his dress since his last appearance. The landlord knew that he associated with low women. THE QUESTION OF A GOVERNMENT REWARD. In reply to a communication from a committee of gentlemen in Mile-end-road, as to the offer of a reward for the apprehension of the Whitechapel murderers, the Home Secretary has written through his private secretary stating that if he had considered the case a proper one for the offer of a reward, the Secretary of State would at once have offered one on behalf of the Government; but the practice of offering rewards for the discovery of criminals was discontinued some years ago because experience showed that such offers tended to produce more harm than good, and the Secretary of State was satisfied that there was nothing in the circumstances of the recent case to justify a departure from this rule. A PICCADILLY SENSATION. What at first was supposed to be another dreadful outrage – one to be added to the catalogue which has so excited London and the country – was committed in Piccadilly yesterday morning. The wildest rumours were circulated, but the real facts almost bring the case down into the category of common assaults. It seems that a woman, named Adelaide Rodgers, of 21, Stangate, Westminster Bridge-road, ran out of Down-street between two and three o'clock yesterday morning, and informed a policeman stationed in Piccadilly that she had been stabbed. She was bleeding profusely from a serious wound on the right cheek, and had already become faint from loss of blood. She *was at once conveyed to St. George's Hospital, nearby, where her injuries were attended to by Dr Ward, who is uncertain whether the wound was inflicted by a thrust with a blunt knife, or by a blow from a stick. The police incline to believe the latter view, and are not disposed to attach much importance to the case. They are in possession of Mrs Rogers' description of the man by whom she was attacked, but decline to communicate it to the press on the ground that her accounts are contradictory. It is stated, however, that the man is tall, dark, and respectably dressed. The unsatisfactory nature of Mrs Rogers' statements may be due to the condition in which she was found to be when the hospital was reached, but in any case there seems to be little chance that her assailant will be discovered.*

September 22nd 1888

The Eastern Morning News, September 22nd 1888,

THE WHITECHAPEL TRAGEDIES. The man who was arrested at Holloway on suspicion of being the concerned in the Whitechapel murders, and subsequently removed and detained at Bow Asylum, will shortly be released. His brother has given a satisfactory explanation as to his whereabouts on the morning of the murder. It has transpired that the authorities of the asylum would not allow the police to interrogate the patient whilst there, as it is against the rules laid down by the lunacy commissioners.

The Hull and East Yorkshire and Lincolnshire Times, September 22nd 1888,

THE OUTRAGES IN LONDON. THE WHITECHAPEL MURDER. The inquest on the body of Annie Chapman, who was murdered in Hanbury street, on the morning of the 8th inst., was resumed by Mr. Wynne Baxter, at Whitechapel, on Wednesday. Chief Inspector West, Inspectors Abberline, Helson and Chandler attended. Eliza Cooper, of 25 Dorset street, deposed that she was a hawker, and lodged at that address for five months. She knew deceased. Witness had a quarrel with her on Tuesday before her death. Afterwards she noticed deceased's face was marked. The last time witness saw her alive was on Wednesday, the 5th inst., in the Ringers public house. Deceased had three brass rings on her left hand. The deceased associated with a man named Ted Stanley, and others. She used to bring them to the public house. Dr. G. Baxter Phillips, re-called, proceeded to give additional details of the result of his examination of the body. Certain incisions and bruises led him to the conclusion that the woman was seized by the chin while the incisions in the throat were inflicted. He thought that if he gave any further details of the results of his examination it would be thwarting justice. The coroner intimated that at this point ladies and boys should leave the court, and the foreman of the jury said the jury were of the opinion that the evidence which the doctors desired to keep back should be given. Dr. Phillips: The evidence will not elucidate the cause of death. The Coroner: That is a matter of opinion. Dr. Phillips: Death took place before the injury was inflicted. The Coroner: That is a matter of opinion, doctor, and it might be [illegible] by other medical evidence. The evidence of the doctor on the first day was read over. Proceeding, Dr. Phillips said the abdominal walls had been removed. There was a greater portion of skin removed on the right side than on the left, a portion constituting the navel was wanting, He removed the intestines in the same manner as he found them in the yard. The witness proceeding to give further details of the condition of the internal organs. The weapon used was probably five or six inches or more in length. The manner of cutting the body indicated a certain amount of anatomical knowledge. In reply to the coroner, witness added that he himself could not have inflicted the injuries under a quarter of an hour, even in a hurried manner. Elizabeth Young, living at No. 3 Church-row, deposed to seeing deceased with a tall dark man like a foreigner about half past five on the morning of the 8th in Hanbury street. They were talking. The man said, "will you?" and the woman replied "Yes." Witness left them standing together.- Edward Stanley, known as "the pensioner," was then called and said he knew deceased for some time, and last saw her alive on Sunday, the 2nd instant, about half past two. Witness never slept from Saturday to Monday, at 35 Dorset street. In reply to the coroner, he said he was never in the Royal Sussex Regiment.- Timothy Donovan, deputy at 35, Dorset street (re-called), said last witness was called "the pensioner," and Hay had stayed with the deceased at the lodging house several times from Saturday to Monday.- The inquest was adjourned to Wednesday next. In reply to a communication from a committee of gentlemen in Mile-end-road, as to the offer of a reward for the apprehension of the Whitechapel murderers, the Home Secretary has written through his private secretary stating that if he had considered the case a proper one for the offer of a reward, the Secretary of State would at once have offered one on behalf of the Government; but the practice of offering rewards for the discovery of criminals was discontinued some years ago because experience showed that such offers tended to produce more harm than good, and the Secretary of State was satisfied that there was nothing in the circumstances of the recent case to justify a departure from this rule. The landlord of the hotel in Finsbury, where the prisoner Weitzel, charged on Tuesday with stabbing a youth in Whitechapel, stayed sometimes, stated to a representative of the Press

Association that since the last Whitechapel murder he had been very suspicious of Weitzel. On the Sunday after the murder he called about nine o'clock in a very dirty condition, saying he had been out all night, and began talking about the Spitalfields affair. He brought with him a case of razors and a large pair of scissors, and after a time wanted to shave the landlord. Previous to this visit he had not been there for eighteen months and his accounts of his movements was contradictory. He was an extraordinary man, always in bad temper, and frequently grinding his teeth when enraged. The landlord believed he had some knowledge of anatomy having been a doctors assistant in the German army. He always carried razors and scissors with him. On Monday night, when the landlord refused to let him sleep there, he threw down the razors in a passion. He had changed his dress since his last appearance. The landlord knew that he associated with low women. At half past two o'clock on Wednesday a woman was found lying on the ground in Down-street, Piccadilly, with her face bleeding from cuts. She was in a very exhausted condition, and was removed to St. George's Hospital. Although no serious results are anticipated from the injuries, the woman was severely bruised and cut. From inquiry at the hospital, the Press Association's representative learned that the woman's name was Adelaide Rutter, or Rogers, of 21 Stangate-street, Westminster. The principal wound was on the left temple. It was thought at first that she had been stabbed, but on examination the medical gentleman came to the conclusion that the injury had been inflicted by a blow from a walking stick. The woman remains in hospital, but no serious consequences are apprehended. At the Thames Police Court on Tuesday, C. Ludwig, 40, a German, living in the Minories, was charged with threatening to stab Alexander Finlay, of Leman-street, Whitechapel. Prosecutor was standing at a coffee stall when the accused came up, and being drunk was refused to be served. After some remark to the prosecutor Ludwig pulled out a knife and tried to stab him, following him several times round the stall. The constable who apprehended the prisoner said he had previously received information that he was wanted in the city for attempting to cut a woman's throat. On the way to the station he dropped a long bladed knife, and in his possession were found a razor, and a long bladed pair of scissors. – Inspector Fimley asked for a remand pending inquiries. – John Johnson, 866 City police, stated that early that morning he heard screams in a court in the Minories. He found the prisoner there with a woman who was very frightened, and asked to be taken away. After prisoner had disappeared she told witness he threatened to stab her. – Prisoner was remanded.

Mike Covell

September 24th 1888

The Hull Daily Mail, September 24th 1888,

FIENDISH MURDER OF A YOUNG WOMAN NEAR GATESHEAD. A PARALLEL TO THE WHITECHAPEL TRAGEDIES. A young woman named Beatmore, 28 years of age, was the victim of a horrible murder at Birtley, near Gateshead, on Saturday night or yesterday morning. It appears that the deceased, who was in delicate health, had been at Gateshead Dispensary on Saturday for medicine, and on returning home she went out to purchase some sweets, with which to take her medicine. She called at several farms while she was out, and at half past seven at night left the house of an acquaintance named Mrs Newall, evidently with the intention of returning home. She had not arrived at eleven o'clock and her mother and stepfather went to look for her, without success, and concluded that she must have spent the night with some neighbour. Early in the morning a miner named John Fish going to work found the body of the deceased at the bottom of the railway embankment in a horribly mutilated condition. The county police were communicated with, and Superintendent Harrison and Sergeant Hutchinson, of Birtley were soon on the spot. A closer inspection revealed the fact that the lower part of the deceased's body had been cut open and the entrails torn out. She was also cut about the face. The body was conveyed home, and a doctor sent for, who expressed the opinion that the cuts had been made with a knife. The affair has caused quite a panic in the district, the resemblance to the Whitechapel tragedy encouraging the idea that the maniac who has been at work in London has travelled down to the North of England to pursue his fiendish vocation. No arrests have been made. Telegraphing at eleven o'clock on Sunday night, a Newcastle correspondent says: Further inquiries made at the scene of the murder do not diminish the shocking brutality of the crime. The unfortunate woman was stabbed in three places, once in the bowels and twice in the face. The wound in the stomach is very deep, the knife having knocked off a piece of the vertebrae. The body was found only a few hundred yards from the girl's home by the side of the colliery railway. Beatmoor was last seen at eight o'clock on Saturday night, and the man Fish found her on Sunday morning. There were no marks of a struggle and no trace of footsteps. The police are completely baffled, as the murderer has left not the slightest clue. During Sunday thousands of persons visited the spot where the body was found, and the affair has caused the utmost consternation.

September 25th 1888

The Hull Daily Mail, September 25th 1888,

THE TRAGEDY NEAR GATESHEAD. THE MURDERER STILL AT LARGE. OPENING OF INQUEST. The inquest on the body of Jane Beatmoor, or Savage, as she was better known, was opened yesterday morning, before Mr. Coroner Graham. The inquiry took place at the house of Mr. Charles Robson, the Three Tuns Hotel, about a mile from Birtley Railway Station, and a like distance from the place where the tragedy occurred. It is a wayside inn, right upon the main road, and, except for a house or two round it, there is no habitation nearer to it than the house in which the dead woman lived, more than half a mile away. The opening of the inquiry was fixed for half past ten o'clock. Having viewed the body, the jury proceeded to the place where the body was found. At the very top of the field, only a few yards behind the house, runs the waggon way which the Birtley Coal Company use to convey their produce to Pelaw Mais. Here it was assuming the woman was murdered where her body was found and the tragedy occurred. The waggon way runs parallel to the main road, and consists of a single line of rails of a six feet gauge. On each side of the rails there is a footway, which is commonly used by the people living round about. On the further side, there is a gutter, or ditch, some eight or nine feet deep, at the place where the jurymen got upon the waggon way, but gradually shallowing towards Eighton Banks, the nearest village upon the waggon way. It is hardly a village, but merely a cluster of red tiled houses, like others scattered along this countryside. About 200 yards from Eighton Banks, at a place where the gutter was some two feet deep, the body was found. There was little for the jury to do except to have described to them how the deceased was lying partly on her left side, with her head in the hollow, and her feet pointing towards the rails. The ground was wet and sodden by the drizzling rain, and the grass was made black by the trampling of many feet. There was nobody about now, but there were ample signs of the crowds of people who had flocked to the place after the horrible discovery. The place was right at the bottom of a fence that separates a field of hay from a field of oats. P.C. Dodds told how, about half past ten o'clock on Saturday night, he passed along the other side of the waggon way, within a half a dozen yards of the place where the body must have been lying, but suspected nothing. He had, he said, gone again on Sunday night, to see whether it would have been possible to see the body from where he passed, and he satisfied himself that the darkness, and the fact that the body was lying half concealed behind the embankment, would have prevented him from seeing anything of the occurrence. The waggon way is somewhat elevated above the surrounding

Mike Covell

country and, where the jurymen stood, they had pointed out to them the road which the woman took on Saturday night, and as they might be going over the same road, reach the Three Tuns Inn again, they determined to inspect it for themselves. A hundred yards or so beyond the spot where the body was found, a road runs to the left down to Hall's High Farm, where the deceased had been visiting a friend before she was met upon the road that led to her own home. Further on, upon a road that runs parallel to the waggon way, and between that and the highway, the jury visited Mr Morris public house at West Moor, in which the deceased is said to have purchased some sweets to make palatable the medicine which she was to take. The distance from the house up to Birtley North Side, Hall's High Farm, the waggon way and back to the house again would be scarcely more than a mile. Crossing the field again, the jurors returned to the Three Tuns Hotel, and having heard the evidence the police had produced, adjourned the inquiry. OLD PIT SHAFTS TO BE EXPLORED. The result of inquiries made showed that so far as the medical authorities know at Newcastle and Gateshead Dispensaries the unfortunate woman was not a patient at either of these institutions. At least from a cursory examination of the books, her name does not appear, but she might have been a casual patient, without her name transpiring. The police have decided to search the unused pit shafts in the locality, in order to ascertain whether the supposition that the murder has committed suicide by throwing himself down one of these shafts has any foundation. SCOTLAND YARD AND THE MURDER. Dr. Phillips, who made the post mortem examination of the body of Annie Chapman, the victim of the last Whitechapel murder, has been sent to Durham in connection with the terrible crime committed in that district. Dr. Phillips, who left London on Monday evening, will examine the body of the young woman with a view to ascertain whether the injuries inflicted on her resemble those on the Whitechapel victim. Inspector Roots, of the Criminal Investigation Department, also left London for Durham, with the object of ascertaining whether any of the facts connected with the murder are likely to be serviceable in eliciting the Whitechapel mysteries. ACTION BY THE POLICE. In their efforts to trace the history of the crime the police of the district have worked nobly and indefatigably. They have left no effort untried to elucidate the mystery which still surrounds the affair. P.C. Dodds had up to Monday been on duty for about 29 consecutive hours. Sergeant Hutchinson, of Birtley, had performed similar duty. When he first heard of the crime on Sunday morning, this officer got about making all the inquiries in his power, and he has not relaxed a single effort that was unlikely to throw any light on the matter. Superintendent Harrison, who has from the first devoted much of his time and experience to the investigation, was again on the spot during the whole of Monday, and his instructions and advice have been implicitly followed by several other officers in addition to those already mentioned. SEARCH FOR THE KNIFE. While most of the officers named were engaged in other duties connected with the case, P.C. Reynolds and others made a diligent search in the field of oats that stands in close proximity to the spot where the murder was committed. There was an impression that the perpetrator of the deed, after the commission of the act, must have concealed the instrument with which it was committed somewhere, and it was thought extremely likely that the knife, or whatever ever sharp weapon it may have been, might have been flung by him amongst the oats, where it was likely to remain hidden for a considerable time. This theory at any rate found acceptance with the police, and the search of Monday was decided on and very diligently made. Nothing, however, in the way of discovery rewarded the efforts of the officers. Only a portion of the field was got through, and the search for the weapon will be resumed today. FEELING IN THE DISTRICT. The consternation which the tragedy had caused in the district had but little abated on Monday. The opening of the inquest, indeed tended to still further stir up public feeling, and on all sides there where expressions of horror and detestation of the crime which had been committed. It is by far the worst that has ever taken place in that portion of the country, and a general wish is expressed that if the murderer, whoever he may be, is still alive he may speedily be brought to justice. "We have never had anything so fearful as this," remarked a Birtley man, on Monday. "We have had quarrels and fights, and occasionally bloodshed, but the quarrels have generally been amicably settled, and no life has been taken." The affair, in short, is regarded as a blot on the character of the district, and the police, in their efforts to trace the crime to its proper source, are likely to receive all the aid that the inhabitants of the locality can give them. The deceased young woman was a native to the village. She was very well known to most of the residents, and while deep regret is expressed at her lamentable fate, a very wide sympathy is evinced towards the members of the family to which she belonged. Her aged mother has been completely prostrated with grief at the awful calamity which has befallen her daughter, and all her relatives are, as might be expected, stricken with grief at the occurrence. A PERSON "WANTED" The following description of the person "wanted" on suspicion in connection with the Birtley Fell tragedy has been issued from the County Police Station at Gateshead:- "Durham C. Constabulary, "Chester Division. "Wanted, in the above division, on suspicion of murdering a young woman, near Birtley, on the night of Saturday, the 22nd September, 1888. He was gone immediately after, and has not been seen since. He had in his possession a large knife, with the letters "J.F." scratched on the handle. "William Waddle or Twaddle, about 27 years of age, height 5 feet 9 or 10 inches, fresh complexion, blue eyes, which are small and sunken, brown hair,

Mike Covell

figure proportionate, very bad walker, has tender and walks with toes out, and leans well forward, a labourer, gas worked as a farm servant. Single. Dressed, when last seen, in a black and grey striped tweed suit, hard felt hat, yellow and black striped silk handkerchief round his neck, yellow and white striped union shirt, which is faded, laced black boots, with toe caps, recently repaired with old leather, (his own mending). "It is earnestly requested that diligent search and inquiry be made for this man, and should he be found, detain him, and wire to the undersigned. "John Harrison, Superintendent. "County Police Station, Gateshead."

Jane Beadmore:

In the 1871 and 1881 Censuses, Jane Beadmore, aka Jane Savage, has a birth date of around 1861 for the area of Northumberland. Searching the British Birth Records, 1837 – 1915, I found only one Jane Savage close to that date in that district. The entry states,

Name: Jane Savage, Date of Registration: Oct- Nov- Dec- 1862, Registration District: Newcastle upon Tyne, Inferred County: Northumberland, Vol: 10b, Page: 98

1871 Census, Class RG10, P4993, F35, P20, GSU847375
Northside, Birtley, Chester Le Street

Joseph Savage	35	Head	Coal Miner
Isabella Savage	42	Wife	
Jane B Savage	10	Dau	B. Walker, Northumberland, England, abt 1861
William Savage	4	Son	

1881 Census, Class RG11, P4983, F38, P23, GSU1342198
Northside, Birtley, Chester Le Street

| Joseph Savage | 45 | Head | Coal Miner |

Isabella Savage	52	Wife	
Jane Beadmore	20	Dau	B. Walker, Northumberland, England, abt 1861
William Savage	16	Son	Coal Miner

1891 Census, Class RG12, P4125, F46, P29, GSU6099235
Lamesley, Eighton Banks, Durham

Joseph Savage	54	Head	Coal Miner
Isabella Savage	51	Wife	
William Savage	24	Son	Coal Miner

Thomas Roots:

His birth is registered thus,
Name: Thomas Roots, Date: 1849, Quarter: Jan, Feb, March, District: Malling, County: Kent, Vol: 5, Page: 397.

The 1861 Census shows him as a 12 year old boy, thus, [Class RG9, F95, P34, GSU542703]

Henry Roots	37	Head	Officer Police Officer
Mary Roots	34	Wife	
Thomas Roots	12	Son	Scholar
Hellen Roots	9	Dau	
William Roots	7	Son	
George J Roots	4	Son	
Henry Roots	1	Son	

Mike Covell

1871 April 2nd Census RG10, P616, F11, P16.
141 Beresford Street, Newington, London

Thomas Roots,	*22, Head, Police Sergeant, born West Malling, Kent -*
Eliza Roots,	*26, Wife, born Hertford*

1881 April 3rd Census, 25 Carter Street, Newington, London, RG11, P538, F49, P12

Thomas Roots	*32, Head, Inspector Met. Police, born West Malling, Kent*
Eliza Ann Roots,	*35, Wife born Hertford*
Henry,	*9, Son, born Newington*
Helen M,	*8, Daughter, born Newington*
Ethel,	*6, Daughter, born Newington*
Ella,	*2, Daughter, born Lambeth*
Thomas,	*4 months, Son born Newington*
George Robson,	*37, Boarder, Inspector of Met Police, born Scotland*
Henry M Willson,	*28, Boarder, Inspector of Met Police, born Greenwich*
Mary Ann Ward	*15, General Servant (Domestic)*

Thomas Roots Marriage is registered thus,
Name: Eliza Ann Ratty, Gender: Female, Birth: 1844, Age: 26, Father: William Petty, Spouse: Thomas Roots, Age: 21, Father: Henry Roots, Date: 18th August 1870

Thomas Roots death is registered thus,
Name: Thomas Roots, Date of Birth: 1849, Death: 1890, Quarter: Oct, Nov, Dec, Age: 41,

District: Fulham, County: Greater London, London, Middlesex, Vol: 1A, Page: 212,

The probate entry for Thomas Roots, reads,
Thomas Roots, Died November 9th 1890, Probate December 9th 1890, Middlesex,
Personal Estate £141. 15s. 2d., The Will of Thomas Roots, late of Stanhope Villa, Molesford-road, Parsons Green, in the County of Middlesex who died 3 November 1890 at Stanhope Villa, was proved at the Principle Registry by Eliza Ann Roots of Stanhope Villa, Widow the Relict, the sole Executrix.

The Eastern Morning News, September 25th 1888,

THE MYSTERIOUS MURDERS. WHITECHAPEL AND GATESHEAD. The Central News is enabled to state that Dr. Phillips, who made the post-mortem examination of the body of Annie Chapman, the victim of the last Whitechapel murder, has been sent to Durham in connection with the terrible crime committed in that district. Dr. Phillips, who left London last evening, will examine the body of the young woman who was murdered and mutilated at Birtley, with a view to ascertain whether the injuries inflicted on her resemble those inflicted on the Whitechapel victim. It is further stated that Inspector Roots, of the Criminal Investigation Department, also left London last evening for Durham with the object off ascertaining whither any of the facts connected with the murder of Jane Beetmoor on Saturday night are likely to be serviceable in elucidating the Whitechapel mysteries. Up till a late hour last evening the local police had obtained no clue to the murderer, and the fact that several hours must have elapsed between the committal of the crime and the discovery of the body greatly increases their difficulty. The whole neighbourhood has been scoured, and the people have everywhere shown the greatest zeal to assist the police in the search, but, as stated, their efforts have been so far without reward. The methods and success of the murderer so closely resemble those of the Whitechapel fiend that the local authorities are strongly inclined to connect the two crimes. As in the last two London cases, the murder was effected without any violent struggling on the part of the victim, the actual cause of death being the cutting of the throat, and the same parts of the body mutilated, and in a very similar manner. Even the pitiful detail of the manner in which the victim's hands were upheld, as though in the vain endeavour to save her throat from the murderer's knife, agree in the three crimes. For the present, however, the police suspend final judgment until the results of Dr. Phillip's examination have been made known. In London the detectives continue their inquiries into the recent

Mike Covell

> crimes. Some hope of a clue was received by the discovery in Devonshire-street of a parcel of blood-stained clothes. The garments were submitted without delay to a medical expert, who expressed the opinion that they had not been connected with any crime, but had been thrown away by some person suffering from skin disease.

September 26th 1888

The Eastern Morning News, September 26th 1888,

> THE GATESHEAD MURDER. *The murderer of Jane Savage is still at large and no fresh facts of consequence in connection with the Durham tragedy have transpired to-day. The body of the murdered woman was examined by Dr Phillips, of Whitechapel, this morning, but that gentleman will report direct to Scotland Yard, and meanwhile he declines to make any statement. Inspector Rootes, of the Criminal Investigation Department, has given the local detectives the benefit of his large experience, but so far their united efforts have been without result. The continued absence of the man with whom the deceased kept company has increased the popular suspicion against him. The police have issued handbills minutely describing the man, and they have been distributed very widely. It has been ascertained that he left home on Saturday evening, and said nothing about not returning to sleep as usual. He has disappeared without leaving any trace by which he could be followed. The disused shafts in the neighbourhood will be searched to-morrow in the hope of finding the weapon with which the crime was committed, and possibly the body of the murderer who, it is thought, may have committed suicide. The victim of the foul murder was a young woman named Jane Beetmore, more commonly known in the district as Jane Savage. Her mother, with whom she lived, married a second time, her present husband being one Joseph Savage. Savage follows the calling of a miner, and is a sober, industrious workman, who is respected by all his neighbours. His stepdaughter also was of a quiet, inoffensive nature, and was generally liked. She appears to have been last seen alive while on her way from Moor Inn to Mr. Newall's farm. This must have been about eight o'clock, although several persons state that they saw her between these two places about nine o'clock. After this she does not appear to have been again seen alive. As the night wore on Mr and Mrs. Savage began to feel anxious about the young woman, and as eleven o'clock drew nigh their anxiety gave place to serious misgivings as to her safety. At eleven o'clock they decided to go out in search of her. They did so, and, after walking a considerable distance and making many inquiries, they returned to their home without eliciting any information as to her*

whereabouts. About seven o'clock on Sunday morning, a blacksmith named John Fish was proceeding along the wagon way from Pit Houses, Black Fell, when, at a point known as Sandy Cut, he suddenly came upon the body of the missing woman. The place at which the body was discovered is a dreary looking spot, and one in which a foul deed might be perpetrated with little fear of detection or interruption. The inquest was held on Monday afternoon, when evidence of identification was given by the deceased's stepbrother and by John Fish, blacksmith, who found the body, after which the inquiry was adjourned for a fortnight.

September 27th 1888

The Hull Daily Mail, September 27th 1888,

THE WHITECHAPEL MURDERS. A CONFESSION. The Central News understands that a man, giving the name of John Fitzgerald, gave himself up at the Wandsworth Police station last night, and made a statement to the inspector on duty to the effect that he committed the murder in Hanbury Street. He was afterwards conveyed to the Leman Street Police Station, where he is now detained. The Press Association says, as a consequence of the startling statement made by the Coroner yesterday public interest in the fate of the unfortunate Annie Chapman has been stimulated afresh and this morning the subject again disrupted the foremost place in conversation. The clue afforded by the Coroner is, of course, being followed up by the police, who have now had the information in their possession for a week, but it has not transpired whether they have yet led to any tangible results. The inquiries of the police would necessarily extend to America, and on that account it may be some time before fresh facts could be in the hands of the public. An important point yet to be made clear is as to whether the object of the murderer was the same in the case of the woman Nicholls and of Annie Chapman. - The Coroner in the former case, when he summed up last Saturday, appeared to take that it was, and at the time expressing the opinion that he must have been in receipt of an important commission from the sub-curator of the Pathological Museum attached to one of the Metropolitan hospitals to which he referred in his summing up on the body of Annie Chapman. The opinion he expressed last Saturday regarding Nichol's case thus carries weight. The "shabby genteel" who was seen in Chapman's company shortly before her murder is being sought for, but up to the present it would appear without success. Inquiries at some of the Metropolitan medical institutions show that similar requests have been made for anatomical specimens, but the conditions could not possibly be complied with.

Mike Covell

> *ANOTHER CONFESSOR. A bricklayer, who had evidently been drinking, stated to the Wandsworth police last night he committed the Whitechapel murder. He is detained, but his statement is not credited. The name of the man who made the confession is John Fitzgerald. A companion of his, named John Lucas has made a statement to the effect that Fitzgerald had entered a public house in Wandsworth last evening, and commenced talking about the Whitechapel murder, and produced a knife, with which he illustrated a theory as to how the murder was committed. He then left saying he had no home. He will be charged at the Thames police court.*

The Hull Daily Mail, September 27th 1888,

> *THE WHITECHAPEL MURDERS. A CONFESSION. The Central News understands that a man, giving the name of John Fitzgerald, gave himself up at Wandsworth Police-station last night, and made a statement to the inspector on duty to the effect that he committed the murder in Hanbury-street. He was afterwards conveyed to the Leman-street Police-station, where he is now detained. The Press Association says, as a consequence of the startling statement made by the coroner, yesterday, public interest in the fate of the unfortunate Annie Chapman has been stimulated afresh, and, to-day, the subject again occupies the foremost place in conversation. The clue afforded by the coroner is, of course, being followed up by the police, who have now had the information in their possession for a week, but it has not transpired whether it has yet led to any tangible result. The inquires of the police would necessarily extend to America, and on that account it may be some time before fresh facts could be in the hands of the public. An important point yet to be made clear is as to whether the object of the murderer was the same in the cases of the women Nichols and of Annie Chapman. The coroner, in the former case, when he summed up last Saturday, appeared to think that it was, and at the time of expressing that opinion he must have been in receipt of an important communication from the sub-curator of the Pathological Museum attached to one of the metropolitan hospitals, to which he referred in his summing-up on the body of Annie Chapman. The opinion he expressed last Saturday regarding Nichols' case thus carries weight. The "shabby genteel" man who was seen in Chapman's company shortly before her murder is being sought for, but up to the present it would appear without success. Inquiries at some of the Metropolitan medical institutions show that similar requests have been made for anatomical specimens, but the conditions could not possibly be complied with. ANOTHER "CONFESSOR" A bricklayer, who had evidently been drinking, stated to the*

> *Wandsworth police last night that he committed the Whitechapel murder. He is detained, but his statement is not credited. The name of the man who made the confession is John Fitzgerald. A companion of his named John Locas has made a statement to the effect that Fitzgerald had entered a public house in Wandsworth last evening and commenced talking about the Whitechapel murder, and produced a knife with which he illustrated a theory as to how the murder was committed. He then left, saying he had no home. He will be charged at the Thames Police Court.*

The Eastern Morning News, September 27th 1888,

> *THE WHITECHAPEL TRAGEDY. ADJOURNED INQUEST. VERDICT. SUPPOSED DREADFUL MOTIVE FOR THE CRIME. Yesterday afternoon Mr Wynne Baxter, Coroner for South-East Middlesex, resumed the inquiry into the circumstances attending the death of Annie Chapman, the last victim of the Whitechapel murderer. No further witnesses were called, and the coroner commenced summing up at twenty minutes to three. He pointed out that the evidence of various witnesses seemed to prove that the murder was committed between half past five and six o'clock, notwithstanding that the doctor who examined the body at half past six occurred not less than two hours previously. The woman, although she had been drinking, was fairly sober, but there had been no struggle. Her rings were wrenched from the fingers, but it was probably only a blind, the real object of the murder being to obtain possession of the missing organ of the body. There were no meaningless cuts. The organ had been removed by someone who knew where to find it, and how to remove it without injury to it. No mere slaughterer of animals could have carried out these operations; it must have been some one accustomed to the post-mortem room. It was not necessary to assume that the murderer was a lunatic, "it is clear that there is a market for the missing organ. To show you this, gentlemen of the jury, I must mentioned a fact, which at the same time proves the assistance which publicity in the newspaper press affords in the detection of crime. Within a few hours of the issue of the morning papers, containing a report of the medical evidence given at the last sitting of the court, I received a communication from an officer of one of our great medical schools that they had information which might, or might not, have a distinct bearing on our inquiry. I attended at the first opportunity, and was informed by the sub-curator of the Pathological Museum that some months ago an American had called on him and asked him to procure a number of specimens of the organ that was missing in the deceased. He stated his willingness to give £20 apiece for each specimen with each copy of a publication on which he was then engaged. He was told that his request was*

Mike Covell

> *impossible to be complied with, but he still urged his request. He wished them preserved, not in spirits of wine (the usual medium), but in glycerine, in order to preserve them in a flaccid condition, and he wished them to be sent to America directly. It is known that this request was repeated to another institution of a similar character. Now, is it not possible that the knowledge of this demand may have incited some abandoned wretch to possess himself of a specimen? It seems beyond belief that such inhuman wickedness could enter into the mind of any man, but, unfortunately, our criminal annals prove that every crime is possible. I need hardly say that I at once conveyed my information to the Detective Department at Scotland Yard. Of course I do not what use has been made of it, but I believe that publicity may possibly further elucidate this fact, and therefore have not withheld from you the information. By means of the press some further explanation may be forthcoming from America, if not from here." The Coroner concluded his summing up at three minutes to three, and the jury immediately returned a verdict of "Wilful murder against some person or persons unknown." The Coroner's remarks respecting the motive for the crime caused a profound sensation.*

September 28th 1888

The Hull Daily Mail, September 28th 1888,

> *ANOTHER LONDON MYSTERY. A lad walking along Lambeth Road southward, found a parcel lying in a garden of the Blind School. It was found to contain the decomposed arm of a woman which had lain in lime. An inquiry into the matter is being held. Doubt is this afternoon thrown on the statement that a woman's arm had been found in Lambeth Road, London. THE WHITECHAPEL MURDER. ANOTHER SUSPECT. ANOTHER ATTACK ON A WOMAN. The Press Association learns that a matter that is thought to have a bearing on the Whitechapel murder is being investigated by the Metropolitan Police. Early on Wednesday morning a man, apparently of about 33 years of age, accosted a woman in Whitechapel. At his request she accompanied him for a short distance, when he suddenly caught her by the throat and knocked her down. The woman states that her screams alarmed the man, who then ran away. The description she gave of her assailant was as follows:- About 5ft. 6in. Or 8in. In height; small dark moustache, dressed in light coat and dark trousers, black felt hat and scarf around the neck. The Press Association says that although the police attach no value to the statement made by the man Fitzgerald, who gave himself up at Wandsworth, they are still pursuing their enquiries into his recent movements. He is detained at Leman Street police station. AN AMERICAN CHARGED*

WITH THREATENING TO STAB A WOMAN. At Dalston Police Court, London, this morning Joe Johnson, aged 35, a well set, pale complexioned man, clean shaven, and with a strong American accent, giving his address as 19, Birdhurst Road, St John's Hill, Wandsworth, describing himself as a waiter, was charged with assaulting Elizabeth Hudson in Kingsland early this morning. Prosecutrix, who is described as an unfortunate, stated that at about 2 o'clock this morning, the prisoner accosted her in Hudson Road, put his arm round her waist, and threw her to the pavement. He then produced a long knife and attempted to stab her. She screamed "Murder" and "Police" and the prisoner ran away. The knife was long and had a sharp point.- Alice Anderson, calling herself a feather curler, a friend of Hudson, deposed that between one and two o'clock this morning she was in Kingsland Road, when the prisoner accosted her, and asked to walk home with her. She said "She did not mind" and the prisoner accompanied her. At a dark spot, however he put his arm round her and tried to throw her, but she succeeded in knocking at a door and screamed "Murder." Prisoner then ran off, and a quarter of an hour later she heard screaming and, running along, she met Hunter, who told her a man had thrown her down and attempted to stab her. The prisoner denied that he had a knife, and both the woman ran after him and tried to steal from his pocket. A constable deposed to hearing cries and to stopping the prisoner, who was running away. No knife was found on the prisoner. The accused, in answer to the magistrate, again denied the woman's story. The magistrate said he had better do so, and postponed the case till the afternoon. A later telegraph stated that it was ascertained that the man had given the correct address, but evidence as to his character is still being sought for.

The Hull and East Yorkshire and Lincolnshire Times, September 28th 1888,

THE WHITECHAPEL MURDERS. A CONFESSION. The Central News understands that a man, giving the name of John Fitzgerald, gave himself up at the Wandsworth Police Station on Wednesday, and made a statement to the inspector on duty to the effect that he committed the murder in Hanbury-street. He was afterwards conveyed to Leman-street Police Station. This John Fitzgerald is a plasterer or bricklayers labourer. He says he has been wandering from place to place, and he is believed to have been more or less under the influence of drink lately. He has not yet been formally charged with the crime, but is merely detained pending further inquiries. His description does not tally with that given at the inquest by witnesses of a certain man seen on the morning of the murder. It seems that Fitzgerald first communicated the intelligence to a

Mike Covell

> private individual, who subsequently gave its purport to the police. A search was made, and the man was discovered in a common lodging house at Wandsworth. He is known to have been living recently at Hammersmith. His self-accusation is said to be not altogether clear, and it is even reported that he cannot give the date of the murder, so that the authorities are disinclined to place much reliance on his statement. The police are nevertheless pursuing vigilant inquiries, and if the confession be found to contain any semblance of truth the prisoner will be formally charged before a magistrate at Worship-street.

The Eastern Morning News, September 28th 1888,

> THE GATESHEAD MURDER. FUNERAL OF THE VICTIM. A touching incident at Birtley on Wednesday was the burial of the remains of poor Jane Beetmoor, the murdered woman. When the body was found on Sunday it was immediately conveyed to the lonely cottage occupied by her stepfather (John Savage), her mother, and half brother. The occupants were transferred to the adjoining cottage, and the corpse left in the home which the poor girl, apparently in her usual health, left on Saturday night never to return again alive. The police took possession of the key, and guarded the house and mutilated body locked therein until the "view" of the jury on Monday and the post mortem examination. After the completion of the post mortem examination, the key of the cottage was given up to the deceased's family, and a different state of things prevailed. Friends and relatives, and other persons actuated by feelings of mere curiosity, were allowed to enter and gaze on the features of the dead girl. There was a continuous flow of people from the valley below and the hills above, and the mother and stepfather were too much overcome by the great sorrow which had fallen on them to do anything to prevent their entering their house as they choose. Matters were allowed to continue until the situation became intolerable, and, ultimately, the Rev Arthur Watts, of Durham, who was on a visit of consolation to the grief-stricken parents, in absence of the rector of the parish, prevailed upon the police to take measures to stop a state of things which was so undesirable. The police acted upon his request, and none who was not a friend or relative was permitted afterwards to enter. The funeral procession was of great length, extending at least half a mile. As the streets of Birtley were reached, all the inhabitants came outside to witness the procession pass, and when the churchyard was reached it was found that a large concourse of people had assembled both outside the gates and in the ground itself. The body was taken into the church, where a portion of the burial service of the Church of England, of which the deceased girl was a member, was read by the Rev Arthur Watts, Durham. At the grave, in consequence of the solemnity of the

> *occasion, Mr Watts departed from the usual course, and made a few deeply touching and appropriate remarks. He said: Mourners, sympathisers, pause a moment besides this open grave. A terrible deed has been done in our midst; doubtless began in anger at baffled lust, finished in most malignant spite. Oh! The down slide is a swift slide. What lesson has to-day for each of us? Burn these two lessons of to-day into your memories that they never die out. The down slide is a swift slide. In us, whose manhood is disgraced, pity for the wretched murder has a hard struggle with shame at his crime. We will try to say, "For our sister, who poor mangled body lies there, we fear not; she died rather than sin; she has borne her cross; her soul is with God. Her message to us to-day is – "Die rather than sin." The scene at the grave side was exceedingly affecting, and long after the service had been concluded people lingered, patiently awaiting their turn to look for the last time into the grave. A reporter has held an interview with Dr Phillips, the divisional police surgeon for Whitechapel, who has been making inquiries into the murder near Gateshead. Dr Phillips on Wednesday attended the inquest at Whitechapel for the purpose of answering any further questions which might be put to him with a view of elucidating the mystery, but he arrived while the coroner was summing up, and thus had no opportunity. When told by the reporter of the startling statement in the coroner's summing up, he said he considered it a very important communication, and the public would now see his reason for not wishing in the first place to give a description of the injuries. He attached great importance to the applications which had been made to the pathological museums, and to the advisability of following this information up as a probable clue. With reference to the murder and mutilation near Gateshead, he stated that it was evidently not done by the same hand as the Whitechapel murder, that at Gateshead being simply a clumsy piece of butchery.*

September 29th 1888

The Hull Daily News, September 29th 1888,

> *TELEGRAPH. It is said that "Leather Apron" has entered an action for libel against the Daily Telegraph and The Star for the rather hasty manner in which these two papers assumed that he was the murderer of Mrs. Annie Chapman. The damages are laid, it is said at £5000. "There's nothing like leather!"*

The Hull Daily News, September 29th 1888,

Mike Covell

THE WHITECHAPEL MURDERS. The inquest into the circumstances connected with the death of Annie Chapman was concluded on Wednesday at Whitechapel, before Mr. Baxter. The evidence having been closed at the last sitting, the Coroner proceeded to sum up. He came to the conclusion that no unskilled person could have carried out the operations, and that someone accustomed to the post mortem room must have committed the deed. The desire to possess the missing abdominal organ seemed overwhelming. It was abhorrent to their feelings to conclude that a life should be taken for so slight an object, but he quoted evidence to show that there was a market for that particular part of the anatomy, as stated by an official of the Pathological Museum. He doubted the theory of lunacy, and was of the opinion that the country was confronted with the murder of no ordinary character, committed not from jealousy, revenge or robbery, but from motives less adequate than the many which still disgraced our civilisation. -The jury, without retiring, returned a verdict of wilful murder against some person or persons unknown. The Coroner further stated that he had been informed by the curator of the Pathological Museum that an American had asked him to procure a number of specimens of the organ that was missing in the deceased, saying he wished to issue an actual specimen with each copy of the book on which he was then engaged. He wished them sent to America. The coroner added that he had informed the police, and some explanation might be forthcoming from America. NO CONNECTION WITH THE GATESHEAD TRAGEDY. The Press Association reporter had an interview with Dr. Phillips, the divisional police surgeon for Whitechapel, who has been making inquiries into the murder near Gateshead. Dr. Phillips attended the inquest at Whitechapel for the purpose of answering any further questions which might be put to him with a view to elucidating the mystery, but he arrived while the Coroner was summing up, and thus no opportunity. When told by the reporter of the startling statement in the Coroner's summing up, and he considered it a very important communication, and the public would now see his reason for not wishing, in the first place, to give a description of the injuries. He attached great importance to applications which had been made to the pathological museums, and to the advisability of the following this the murder and mutilation near Gateshead being simply a clumsy piece of butchery. A telegram from the district states that the same opinion is entertained there, the idea being that the mutilation of the body was suggested to the murderer by reading the accounts of the murders in the East end of London. The Press Association says- As a consequence of the startling statement made by the Coroner on Wednesday, public interest in the fate of the unfortunate Annie Chapman has been stimulated afresh, and the subject again occupies the foremost place in conversation. The clue afforded by the Coroner is of course being followed up by the police, who have now had the information in their possession for a week, but it has not transpired whether they have yet led to any tangible result. The inquiries of the police would necessarily extend to America, and on that account, it may be some time before fresh facts could be in the hands of the public. An important point yet to be made clear is as to whether the object of the murderer was the same in the case of the woman Nicholls and of Annie Chapman. The Coroner in the former case, when he summed up last Saturday, appeared to think that it was, and at that time of expressing that opinion, he must have been in receipt of important communications from the sub-curator of the Pathological Museum attached to one of the metropolitan hospitals, to which he referred in his summing up on the body of Annie Chapman. The opinion he expressed last Saturday regarding Nicholls' case, thus carries weight. The "shabby genteel" man who was seen in Chapman's company shortly before her murder is being sought for, but up to present, it would seem without success. Inquiries at some of the metropolitan medical institutes show that similar requests to that made to the curator of the Pathological Museum have been made for anatomical specimens, but the conditions could not possibly be compared with. FIENDISH MURDER OF A YOUNG WOMAN NEAR GATESHEAD. A PARALLEL TO THE WHITECHAPEL TRAGEDIES. A young woman named Jane Beatmoor, 28 years of age, was a victim of a horrible murder at Birtley, near Gateshead, on Saturday night or Sunday morning. It appears that the deceased, who was in delicate health, had been at Gateshead Dispensary on Saturday for medicine, and on returning home she went out to purchase some sweets with which to take her medicine. She called at several farms while she was out, and at half past seven at night left the house of an acquaintance named Mrs Newall, evidently with the intention of returning home. She had not arrived at eleven o'clock and her mother and stepfather went to look for her, without success, and concluded that she must have spent the night with some neighbour. Early in the morning a miner named John Fish going to work found the body of the deceased at the bottom of the railway embankment in a horribly mutilated condition. The county police were communicated with, and Superintendent Harrison and Sergeant Hutchinson, of Birtley were soon on the spot. A closer inspection revealed the fact that the lower part of the deceased's body had been cut open and the entrails torn out. She was also cut about the face. The body was conveyed home, and a doctor sent for, who expressed the opinion that the cuts had been made with a knife. The affair has caused quite a panic in the district, the resemblance to the Whitechapel tragedy encouraging the idea that the maniac who has been at work in London has travelled down to the North of England to pursue his fiendish vocation. No arrests have been made. Telegraphing at eleven o'clock on Sunday night, a Newcastle correspondent says: Further inquiries made at the

Mike Covell

scene of the murder do not diminish the shocking brutality of the crime. The unfortunate woman was stabbed in three places, once in the bowels and twice in the face. The wound in the stomach is very deep, the knife having knocked off a piece of the vertebrae. The body was found only a few hundred yards from the girl's home by the side of the colliery railway. Beatmoor was last seen at eight o'clock on Saturday night, and the man Fish found her on Sunday morning. There were no marks of a struggle and no trace of footsteps. The police are completely baffled, as the murderer has left not the slightest clue. During Sunday thousands of persons visited the spot where the body was found, and the affair has caused the utmost consternation. The inquest was opened on Monday morning, before Mr. Coroner Graham. Evidence of identification was given by the deceased's step-brother, William Savage, and John Fish, blacksmith, spoke to finding the body in a mutilated condition on the Ouston Colliery railway on Sunday morning. The inquest was adjourned for a fortnight. The post mortem examination on Monday showed that on the right side of the face there is a deep cut about an inch wide, which has laid the lower jaw open to the bone. On the left side of the neck below the ear there is a horrible gash about 2 inches in length and extending right down to the top of the spine. This wound alone, in the opinion of the medical men, would have caused instant death. The third and most shocking of the cuts received by the poor woman is in the abdomen. The murderer in the first place plunged the knife, which was evidently a big one, right into the body, and appears to have endeavoured to rip up the abdomen. Failing to do this, he drove the knife into the lower part of the stomach, inflicting a horrible wound, from which the entrails protruded. It is assumed that the unfortunate woman was killed by the blow on her neck, and that subsequently her murderer was endeavouring to hack the body to pieces. The unhappy victim was a girl highly respected in the neighbourhood. She had been in very delicate health for a long time, and on Saturday had been at the Gateshead Dispensary for medicine. Further particulars state that the victim of the foul murder was more commonly known in the district as Jane Savage. Her mother, with whom she lived, was married a second time, her present husband being one Joseph Savage. Savage follows the calling of a miner, and is a sober, industrious workman, who is respected by all his neighbours. His step-daughter also was of quiet, inoffensive nature, and was generally liked. She appears to have been last seen alive while on her way from the Moor Inn to Mr. Newall's farm. This must have been about eight o'clock, although several persons state that they saw her between these two places about nine o'clock, in the company of a young man. After this she does not appear to have been again seen alive. As the night wore on Mr. and Mrs. Savage began to feel anxious about the young woman, and as eleven o'clock drew nigh their anxiety gave place to serious misgivings as to her safety. At 11 o'clock they decided to go out and search for her. They did so, and after walking a considerable distance and making enquiries, they returned to their home without eliciting any information as to her whereabouts. About seven o'clock on Sunday morning, a blacksmith named John Fish was proceeding along the waggon way, from Pit Houses, Black Fell, when at a point known as Sandy Cut, he suddenly came upon the body of the missing woman. The place at which the body was discovered is a dreary looking spot, and one in which a foul deed might be perpetrated with little fear of detection or interruption. The body lay about three or four feet from the line, the head being in the gutter about nine or ten inches deep. After the body had been removed home, Dr. Gallagher was sent for, but he found life was quite extinct, as it must have been for several hours. When the body was discovered it was lying face upwards, and the dress had been pulled up over the face. There were a few coppers found in the pockets, and a small packet of sweets. It is not thought that the deceased was in any way under the influence of drink on Saturday night. When she was in the public house she had only a glass of lemonade, and was quite sober when she left. Dr. Gallagher gives it as his opinion that a sharp instrument had been used, and that after the wounds had been inflicted the deceased could have walked a short distance, which must have been the case, from the fact that no marks of a struggle were found at the place where the body was discovered. Nothing fresh has been elicited concerning the murder of Jane Beetmoor at Birtley on Saturday. The police have not yet arrested Waddel, the suspected murderer, but they have traced the movements of the man whose description exactly corresponds with Waddel's and all the evidence is in favour of their being on the right scent. There need hardly be the slightest doubt that Waddel is somewhere in Scotland. A man answering the published description was seen at Spennymoor on Sunday after the murder. The same man was observed in the afternoon, striking out from Newcastle into the middle of Northumberland. At eight o'clock on Sunday night he was seen at Capheaton, travelling through the loneliest and wildest district of the country. Here the man said he came from Spennymoor, and he inquired the way to Jedburgh. Two days afterwards he was observed at Glen Douglas, about two and half miles from Jodburgh, and there the clue appears to have been lost. The Durham police, however, are in Scotland looking for him, and they are convinced that they will apprehend either Waddel or the man whose resemblance to him is so remarkable, before very long. In the meantime testimony is accumulating connecting Waddel with the crime, one of the latest discoveries being that he was seen in Beetmoor's company at nine o'clock on Saturday evening. On the other hand, those who know Waddel best say that he was in the habit of leaving the district for long periods, and that his sudden disappearance may only be another instance of his characteristic

Mike Covell

> *eccentricity. Everybody is agreed that the suspected man was of a moody, morose temper, shunning contact with his fellows, and there was a mystery about his manners and actions that puzzled all who knew him.*

The Hull Daily Mail, September 29th 1888,

> FIENDISH MURDER OF A YOUNG WOMAN NEAR GATESHEAD. A PARALLEL TO THE WHITECHAPEL TRAGEDIES. *A young woman named Beatmore, 28 years of age, was the victim of a horrible murder at Birtley, near Gateshead, on Saturday night or yesterday morning. It appears that the deceased, who was in delicate health, had been at Gateshead Dispensary on Saturday for medicine, and on returning home she went out to purchase some sweets, with which to take her medicine. She called at several farms while she was out, and at half past seven at night left the house of an acquaintance named Mrs Newall, evidently with the intention of returning home. She had not arrived at eleven o'clock and her mother and stepfather went to look for her, without success, and concluded that she must have spent the night with some neighbour. Early in the morning a miner named John Fish going to work found the body of the deceased at the bottom of the railway embankment in a horribly mutilated condition. The county police were communicated with, and Superintendent Harrison and Sergeant Hutchinson, of Birtley were soon on the spot. A closer inspection revealed the fact that the lower part of the deceased's body had been cut open and the entrails torn out. She was also cut about the face. The body was conveyed home, and a doctor sent for, who expressed the opinion that the cuts had been made with a knife. The affair has caused quite a panic in the district, the resemblance to the Whitechapel tragedy encouraging the idea that the maniac who has been at work in London has travelled down to the North of England to pursue his fiendish vocation. No arrests have been made. Telegraphing at eleven o'clock on Sunday night, a Newcastle correspondent says: Further inquiries made at the scene of the murder do not diminish the shocking brutality of the crime. The unfortunate woman was stabbed in three places, once in the bowels and twice in the face. The wound in the stomach is very deep, the knife having knocked off a piece of the vertebrae. The body was found only a few hundred yards from the girl's home by the side of the colliery railway. Beatmoor was last seen at eight o'clock on Saturday night, and the man Fish found her on Sunday morning. There were no marks of a struggle and no trace of footsteps. The police are completely baffled, as the murderer has left not the slightest clue. During Sunday thousands of persons visited the spot where the body was found, and the affair has caused the utmost consternation.*

The inquest was opened on Monday morning, before Mr. Coroner Graham. Evidence of identification was given by the deceased's step-brother, William Savage, and John Fish, blacksmith, spoke to finding the body in a mutilated condition on the Ouston Colliery railway on Sunday morning. The inquest was adjourned for a fortnight. The post mortem examination on Monday showed that on the right side of the face there is a deep cut about an inch wide, which has laid the lower jaw open to the bone. On the left side of the neck below the ear there is a horrible gash about 2 inches in length and extending right down to the top of the spine. This wound alone, in the opinion of the medical men, would have caused instant death. The third and most shocking of the cuts received by the poor woman is in the abdomen. The murderer in the first place plunged the knife, which was evidently a big one, right into the body, and appears to have endeavoured to rip up the abdomen. Failing to do this, he drove the knife into the lower part of the stomach, inflicting a horrible wound, from which the entrails protruded. It is assumed that the unfortunate woman was killed by the blow on her neck, and that subsequently her murderer was endeavouring to hack the body to pieces. The unhappy victim was a girl highly respected in the neighbourhood. She had been in very delicate health for a long time, and on Saturday had been at the Gateshead Dispensary for medicine. Further particulars state that the victim of the foul murder was more commonly known in the district as Jane Savage. Her mother, with whom she lived, was married a second time, her present husband being one Joseph Savage. Savage follows the calling of a miner, and is a sober, industrious workman, who is respected by all his neighbours. His step-daughter also was of quiet, inoffensive nature, and was generally liked. She appears to have been last seen alive while on her way from the Moor Inn to Mr. Newall's farm. This must have been about eight o'clock, although several persons state that they saw her between these two places about nine o'clock, in the company of a young man. After this she does not appear to have been again seen alive. As the night wore on Mr. and Mrs. Savage began to feel anxious about the young woman, and as eleven o'clock drew nigh their anxiety gave place to serious misgivings as to her safety. At 11 o'clock they decided to go out and search for her. They did so, and after walking a considerable distance and making enquiries, they returned to their home without eliciting any information as to her whereabouts. About seven o'clock on Sunday morning, a blacksmith named John Fish was proceeding along the waggon way, from Pit Houses, Black Fell, when at a point known as Sandy Cut, he suddenly came upon the body of the missing woman. The place at which the body was discovered is a dreary looking spot, and one in which a foul deed might be perpetrated with little fear of detection or interruption. The body lay about three or four feet from the line, the head being in the gutter about nine or ten inches

Mike Covell

> deep. After the body had been removed home, Dr. Gallagher was sent for, but he found life was quite extinct, as it must have been for several hours. When the body was discovered it was lying face upwards, and the dress had been pulled up over the face. There were a few coppers found in the pockets, and a small packet of sweets. It is not thought that the deceased was in any way under the influence of drink on Saturday night. When she was in the public house she had only a glass of lemonade, and was quite sober when she left. Dr. Gallagher gives it as his opinion that a sharp instrument had been used, and that after the wounds had been inflicted the deceased could have walked a short distance, which must have been the case, from the fact that no marks of a struggle were found at the place where the body was discovered. Nothing fresh has been elicited concerning the murder of Jane Beetmoor at Birtley on Saturday. The police have not yet arrested Waddel, the suspected murderer, but they have traced the movements of the man whose description exactly corresponds with Waddel's and all the evidence is in favour of their being on the right scent. There need hardly be the slightest doubt that Waddel is somewhere in Scotland. A man answering the published description was seen at Spennymoor on Sunday after the murder. The same man was observed in the afternoon, striking out from Newcastle into the middle of Northumberland. At eight o'clock on Sunday night he was seen at Capheaton, travelling through the loneliest and wildest district of the country. Here the man said he came from Spennymoor, and he inquired the way to Jedburgh. Two days afterwards he was observed at Glen Douglas, about two and half miles from Jodburgh, and there the clue appears to have been lost. The Durham police, however, are in Scotland looking for him, and they are convinced that they will apprehend either Waddel or the man whose resemblance to him is so remarkable, before very long. In the meantime testimony is accumulating connecting Waddel with the crime, one of the latest discoveries being that he was seen in Beetmoor's company at nine o'clock on Saturday evening. On the other hand, those who know Waddel best say that he was in the habit of leaving the district for long periods, and that his sudden disappearance may only be another instance of his characteristic eccentricity. Everybody is agreed that the suspected man was of a moody, morose temper, shunning contact with his fellows, and there was a mystery about his manners and actions that puzzled all who knew him.

The Hull Daily News, September 29th 1888,

> THE WHITECHAPEL MURDER. A SUPPOSED DISCOVERY. The Press Association learns that a matter, which is thought to have some bearing on the Whitechapel murder, is being investigated by the Metropolitan Police. Early on

Wednesday morning a man apparently about thirty three years of age, accosted a woman and at his request, she accompanied him for a short distance when he suddenly caught her by the throat and knocked her down. The woman states that her screams alarmed the man who then ran away. The description she gave of her assailant was as follows;- About 5ft, 7in, or 8in, in height; small dark moustache, dressed in light coat and dark trousers, black felt hat, and wore a scarf around neck. The Press Association states that, although the police attach no value to the statement made by the man Fitzgerald, who gave himself up at Wandsworth, they are still pursuing their enquiries into his recent movements. He is detained at Leman street police station. SINGULAR AFFAIR IN LONDON. At the Dalston street Police court, London, yesterday, James Johnson, aged 31, a well set, pale complexioned man, clean shaven, and with strong American accent, giving his address as 19, Birdhurst Road, St John's Hill, Wandsworth, describing himself as a waiter, was charged with assaulting Elizabeth Hudson in Kingsland early this morning. Prosecutrix, who is described as an unfortunate, stated that at about 2 o'clock this morning, the prisoner accosted her in Hudson Road, put his arm round her waist, and threw her to the pavement. He then produced a long knife and attempted to stab her. She screamed "Murder" and "Police" and the prisoner ran away. The knife was long and had a sharp point.- Alice Anderson, calling herself a feather curler, a friend of Hudson, deposed that between one and two o'clock this morning she was in Kingsland Road, when the prisoner accosted her, and asked to walk home with her. She said "She did not mind" and the prisoner accompanied her. At a dark spot, however he put his arm round her and tried to throw her, but she succeeded in knocking at a door and screamed "Murder." Prisoner then ran off, and a quarter of an hour later she heard screaming and, running along, she met Hunter, who told her a man had thrown her down and attempted to stab her. The prisoner denied that he had a knife, and both the woman ran after him and tried to steal from his pocket. A constable deposed to hearing cries and to stopping the prisoner, who was running away. No knife was found on the prisoner. The accused, in answer to the magistrate, again denied the woman's story. The magistrate said he had better do so, and postponed the case till the afternoon. A later telegraph stated that it was ascertained that the man had given the correct address, but evidence as to his character is still being sought. Johnson was again brought up at the police court in the afternoon, when his landlady gave him a good character, and said she had known his family for some years. He worked at [illegible]. A police constable described Prosecutrix and her companion as two very bad characters, and there being no further evidence against prisoner, he was discharged.

Mike Covell

The Hull and East Yorkshire and Lincolnshire Times, September 29th 1888,

> FURTHER ALLEGED OUTRAGES IN LONDON. AN AMERICAN CHARGED WITH THREATENING TO STAB A WOMAN. At Dalston Police Court, London, yesterday, Jas. Johnson, aged 35, a well set, pale complexioned man clean shaven, and with a strong American accent, giving his address as 18 Birdhurst-road, St. John's Hill, Wandsworth, describing himself as a waiter, was charged with assaulting Elizabeth Hudson, in Kingsland early this morning. Prosecutrix, who is described as an unfortunate, states that about two o'clock this morning, the prisoner accosted her in Hudson-road, put his arm round her waist, and threw her on the pavement. He then produced a long knife and attempted to stab her. She screamed "Murder" and "Police," and the prisoner then ran away. The knife was long, and had a sharp point. – Alice Anderson, calling herself a feather curler, a friend of Hudson, deposed that between one and two o'clock this morning she was in Kingsland-road when the prisoner accosted her, and asked to walk home with her. She said "She did not mind," and the prisoner accompanied her. At a dark spot, however, he put his arm around her and tried to throw her, but she succeeded in knocking at a door and screamed "Murder." Prisoner then ran off, and a quarter of an hour later she heard screaming, and, running along, she met Hunter, who told her a man had thrown her down and attempted to stab her. The prisoner denied that he had a knife, and both the woman ran after him and tried to steal from his pockets. – A constable deposed to hearing cries and to stopping the prisoner, who was running away. No knife was found on the prisoner. – The accused, in answer to the magistrate, again denied the woman's story, and said he could produce his friends if necessary. The magistrate said he had better do so, and postponed the case till the afternoon. Johnson was again brought up at the Police Court yesterday afternoon, when his landlady gave him a good character, and said she had known his family for some years. He worked at Spiers and Pond's. A police constable described prosecutrix and her companion as two very bad characters, and there being no further evidence against the prisoner he was discharged.

The Hull and East Yorkshire and Lincolnshire Times, September 29th 1888,

> A CHAPTER OF HORRORS. FIENDISH MURDER OF A YOUNG WOMAN NEAR GATESHEAD. A PARALLEL TO THE WHITECHAPEL TRAGEDIES. A young woman named Beetmoor, 28 years of age, was the victim of a horrible murder at Birtley, near Gateshead, on Saturday night or Sunday morning. It

appears that the deceased, who was in delicate health, had been at Gateshead Dispensary on Saturday for medicine, and on returning home she went out to purchase some sweets with which to take her medicine. She called at several farms while she was out, and at half past seven at night left the house of an acquaintance named Mrs. Newall, evidently with the intention of returning home. She had not arrive at eleven o'clock, and her mother and stepfather went to look for her, without success, and concluding that she must have spent the night with some neighbour. Early in the morning a miner named John Fish going to work found the body of the deceased at the bottom of the railway embankment in a horribly mutilated condition. The county police were communicated with, and Superintendent Harrison and Sergeant Hutchinson, of Birtley, were soon on the spot. A closer inspection revealed the fact that the lower part of the deceased's body had been cut open and the entrails torn out. She was also cut about the face. The body was conveyed home, and a doctor sent for, who expressed the opinion that the cuts had been made with a knife. The affair had caused quite a panic in the district, the resemblance to the Whitechapel tragedy encouraging the idea that the maniac who had been at work in London has travelled down to the North of England to pursue his fiendish vocation. The inquest on the body of Jane Beetmoor, or Savage, as she was better known, was opened on Monday morning, before Mr. Coroner Graham. The inquiry took place at the home of Mr. Charles Robson, the Three Tuns Hotel, about a mile from Birtley Railway Station, and a like distance from the place where the tragedy occurred. It is a wayside inn, right upon the main road, and except for a house or two round about it there is no habitation nearer to it than the house in which the dead woman lived, more than half a mile away. The opening of the inquiry was fixed for half past ten o'clock. Having viewed the body, the jury proceeded to the place where the body was found. At the very top of the field, only a few yards beyond the house, runs the wagon way which the Birtley Coal Company use to convey their produce to Pelaw Main. Here it was assuming that the woman was murdered where her body was found, that the tragedy occurred. The wagon way runs parallel to the main road, and consists of a single line of rails of a six feet gauge. On each side of the rails there is a footway, which is commonly used by the people living round about. On the further side, there is a gutter, or ditch, some eight or nine feet deep, at the place where the jurymen got upon the wagon way, but gradually shallowing towards Eighton Banks, the nearest village upon the wagon way. It is hardly a village, but merely a cluster of red tiled houses, like others scattered along this country side. About 200 from Eighton Banks, at a place where the gutter was some two feet deep, the body was found. There was little for the jury to do except to have described to them how the deceased was lying partly on her left side, with her

Mike Covell

head in the hollow, and her feet pointed towards the rails. The ground was wet and sodden by the drizzling rain, and the grass was made black by the trampling of many feet. There was nobody about now, but there was ample signs of the crowds of people who had flocked to the place after the horrible discovery. The place was right at the bottom of a fence that separates a field of hay from a field of oats. P.C. Dodds told how, about half past ten on Saturday night, he passed along the other side of the waggon way, within half a dozen yards of the place where the body must have then been lying, but saw nothing, and suspected nothing. He had, he said, gone again on Sunday night, to see whether it would have been possible to see the body from where he passed, and he satisfied himself that the darkness, and the fact that the body was lying half concealed behind the embankment, would have prevented him from seeing anything of the occurrence. The waggon way is somewhat elevated above the surrounding country, and, where the jurymen stood, they had pointed out to them the road which the woman took on Saturday night, and as they might, by going over the same road, reach the Three Tuns Inn again, they determined to inspect it for themselves. A hundred yards or so beyond the spot where the body was found, a road runs to the left, down to Hall's High Farm, where the deceased had been visiting a friend before she was met upon the road that led to her own home. Further on, upon a road that runs parallel to the waggon way, and between that and the highway, the jury visited Mr. Morris's public house at West Moor, in which the deceased is said to have purchased some sweets to make palatable the medicine which she was to take. The distance from the house, up to Birtley North Side, Hall's High Farm, the waggon way, and back to the house again would be scarcely more than a mile. Crossing the field again, the jurors returned to the Three Tuns Hotel, and having heard what evidence the police had to produce, adjourned the inquiry, EXAMINATION OF THE BODY BY DR PHILLIPS. The Press Association's Newcastle-on-Tyne correspondent says Dr. Phillips, of Scotland Yard, on Tuesday met Colonel W. White, Chief Constable of the County of Durham, and Superintendent Harrison, of the Birtley District, and visited the scene of the murder of the young woman Jane Beetmoor, or Savage, near Gateshead. The body of the deceased was examined by Dr. Phillips, but the result of his examination has not transpired. The work of exploring the old pit shafts in the neighbourhood continues, the police being assisted by several miners. The impression is that Waddle, or Tweddle, the supposed murderer, may have committed suicide. The search for the knife or other weapons is also being continued. A PERSON "WANTED." The following description of the person "wanted" on suspicion in connection with the Birtley Fell tragedy has been issued from the County Police Station at Gateshead:- "Durham C. Constabulary, "Chester Division. "Wanted, in the above division, on suspicion of murdering a young woman, near Birtley, on the night of Saturday, the 22nd September, 1888. He was gone immediately after, and has not been seen since. He had in his possession a large knife, with the letters "J.F." scratched on the handle. "William Waddle or Twaddle, about 27 years of age, height 5 feet 9 or 10 inches, fresh complexion, blue eyes, which are small and sunken, brown hair, figure proportionate, very bad walker, has tender and walks with toes out, and leans well forward, a labourer, gas worked as a farm servant. Single. Dressed, when last seen, in a black and grey striped tweed suit, hard felt hat, yellow and black striped silk handkerchief round his neck, yellow and white striped union shirt, which is faded, laced black boots, with toe caps, recently repaired with old leather, (his own mending). "It is earnestly requested that diligent search and inquiry be made for this man, and should he be found, detain him, and wire to the undersigned. John Harrison, Superintendent, County Police Station, Gateshead. THE WHITECHAPEL MURDER. ADJOURNED INQUEST – VERDICT. A CONFESSION. The Central News understands that a man, giving the name of John Fitzgerald, gave himself up at the Wandsworth Police station on Wednesday, and made a statement to the inspector on duty to the effect that he committed the murder in Hanbury-street. He was afterwards conveyed to Leman-street Police Station. Shortly after the latest murder, the following official telegram was despatched to every police station throughout the metropolis and suburbs: - Description of a man wanted on entering a passage of a house at which the murder was committed with a prostitute. Aged 37 height 5 feet 7 inches; rather dark beard and moustache; dress, short dark jacket, dark vest and trousers, black scarf, and black felt hat; spoke with a foreign accent. ANOTHER ATTACK ON A WOMAN. The Press Association learns that a matter that is thought to have a bearing on the Whitechapel murder is being investigated by the Metropolitan Police. Early on Wednesday morning a man, apparently of about 33 years of age, accosted a woman in Whitechapel. At this first request she accompanied him for a short distance, when he suddenly caught her by the throat and knocked her down. The woman states that her screams alarmed the man, who then ran away. The description she gave of her assailant was as follows: - About 5ft 6in, or 8in, in height; small dark moustache; dressed in light coat and dark trousers, black felt hat, and wore a scarf round the neck. ANOTHER WHITECHAPEL AFFAIR. At the Thames Police Court on Tuesday Charles Ludwig was charged on remand with threatening to stab Alexander Finlay in Whitechapel-road. The evidence of two constables that he was wanted on a charge of attempting to stab a prostitute in the Minories was repeated, and the accused was further remanded. MAKING A "WHITECHAPEL JOB" OF HER. A verdict of wilful murder was returned on Tuesday, at the inquest, against George Nicholson, a journeyman baker, of Aston, Birmingham, for the

Mike Covell

> brutal murder of his wife. The prisoner deliberately smashed the woman's head in with an axe, took her watch and chain, pawned it, and with the proceeds made off to the Walshall, where he was arrested on Sunday. The prisoner was heard to say "I'll make a Whitechapel job of her."

William Waddle:

William Waddle's trial entry is registered thus, [HO27, P209, P166]

Name: William Waddle, Date of Trial: 27 Nov 1888, Trial Year: 1888, Location of Trial: Durham, England, Sentence: Death, Crime: Wilful Murder

The National Archives feature the case in their criminal files, [Ref: HO140/103]

First name: William, Last name: Waddle, Age: 22, Year of birth: 1866, Occupation: Labourer, Date the court session started: 27 Nov 1888, Court: Durham, Area of court: Durham, Victims: Jane Beadmore Or Savage, Record source: A Calendar Of Prisoners Tried At The Assizes

A more detailed record in the same file states:

No: 22, Name: William Waddle, Age: 22, Trade: Labourer, Degree of Instruction: Imp., Name and Address of committing magistrate: Lt. Col. F. F. Sheppee, Pietree House, Chester-le-Street, Date of warrant: 25th Oct, When received into custody: 10th Oct, Offence as charged in the indictment: Feloniously, wilfully and of his malice afterthought did kill and murder one Jane Beadmore commonly known as Jane Savage, at the Township of Birtley, 22nd September 1888, When tried: 29th Nov, Before whom tried: Ditto, Verdict of the jury: Guilty of Wilful Murder, Particulars of previous conviction: [blank], Sentence or order of the court: To be hanged, No: 22.

William Waddle's Death is registered thus,
Name: William Waddle, Est Birth Year: abt 1866, Date of Registration: Oct- Nov- Dec- 1888, Age at Death: 22, Registration District: Durham, Inferred County: Durham, Vol: 10a, Page: 199

George Nicholson:

The Birmingham Daily Post, dated December 18th 1888 featured transcripts of the trial at the Warwickshire Assizes.

England and Wales Criminal Registers, [HO 27, P211, P188]
Name: George Nicholson, Date of Trial: Dec 13th 1888, Trial Year: 1888, Location of Trial: Warwickshire, England, Sentence: Death, Charge: Murder

The North Eastern Daily Gazette, dated January 8th 1889, reported that George Nicholson had been hanged at Warwick Gaol on the morning of that day by notable Victorian hangman, William Berry. It was written that prior to the hanging, Nicholson had confessed his guilt to the gaol governor.

The National Archives features the following entry for the case, [Ref: HO140/109]

First name: George, Last name: Nicholson, Age: 54, Year of birth: 1834, Occupation: Baker, Date the court session started: 13 Dec 1888, Court: Warwick, Area of court: Warwickshire, Victims: Mary Ann Nicholson, Record source: A Calendar Of Prisoners Tried At The Assizes

A more detailed entry in the same file reads:

No: 5, Name: George Nicholson, Age: 54, Trade: Baker, Degree of Instruction: Imp, Name and Address of committing magistrate: A, Hill, Esq, Aston, Daniel Robert Wynter, Esq. Coroner, County of Warwickshire,
Date of warrant: 2nd Oct/25th Sept, When received into custody: 2nd Oct/Ditto, Offence as charged in the indictment: On the 22nd September, 1888, at Aston, feloniously, wilfully and of his malice afterthought, killing and murdering Mary Ann Nicholson./Murder of Mary Ann Nicholson, When tried: 17th Dec, Before whom tried: Ditto, Verdict of the jury: Guilty, Particulars of previous conviction: [Blank], Sentence or order of the court: Death: No: 5.

Death:
Name: George Nicholson, Estimated Birth Year: abt 1835, Date of Registration: Jan- Feb- Mar- 1889, Age at Death: 54, Registration District: Warwick, Inferred County: Warwickshire, Vol: 6D, Page: 357

Mike Covell

> **Mary Ann Nicholson:**
> Death:
> Name: Mary Ann Nicholson, Estimated Birth Year: abt 1835, Date of Registration: Jul- Aug- Sept- 1888, Age at Death: 53, Registration District: Aston, Inferred County: Warwickshire, Vol: 6d, Page: 203

The Hull News, September 29th 1888,

> It is said that "Leather Apron" has entered an action for libel against the Daily Telegraph and the Star for the rather hasty manner in which these two papers assumed that he was the murderer of Mrs. Annie Chapman. The damages are laid, it is said, at £5000. "There's nothing like leather!"

The Hull Daily Mail, September 29th 1888,

> NO CONNECTION WITH THE GATESHEAD TRAGEDY. The Press Association reporter had an interview with Dr Phillips, the divisional police surgeon for Whitechapel, who has been making inquiries into the murder near Gateshead, attended the inquest at Whitechapel for the purpose of answering any further questions which might be put to him with a view to elucidating the mystery, but he arrived when the coroner was summing up, and thus had no opportunity. When told by a reporter of the startling statement in the coroner's summing up he said he considered it a very important communication, and the public would now see his reason for not wishing in the first place to give a description of the injuries. He attached great importance to the applications which had been made to the pathological museums, and to the advisability of following this information up as a probable clue. With reference to the murder and mutilation near Gateshead, he stated that it was evidently not done by the same hand as the Whitechapel murder, that at Gateshead being simply a clumsy piece of butchery. A telegram from the district states that the same opinion is entertained there, the idea being that the mutilation of the body was suggested to the murderer by reading the accounts of the murders in the east end of London. The Press Association says, as a consequence of the startling statement made by the Coroner yesterday public interest in the fate of the unfortunate Annie Chapman has been stimulated afresh and this morning the subject again disrupted the foremost place in conversation. The clue afforded by the Coroner is, of course, being followed up by the police, who have now had the information in their possession for a week, but it has not transpired whether they have yet led to any tangible results. The inquiries of the police would necessarily extend to America, and on that account it may be some time before fresh facts could be in

the hands of the public. An important point yet to be made clear is as to whether the object of the murderer was the same in the case of the woman Nicholls and of Annie Chapman. - The Coroner in the former case, when he summed up last Saturday, appeared to take that it was, and at the time expressing the opinion that he must have been in receipt of an important commission from the sub-curator of the Pathological Museum attached to one of the Metropolitan hospitals to which he referred in his summing up on the body of Annie Chapman. The opinion he expressed last Saturday regarding Nichol's case thus carries weight. The "shabby genteel" who was seen in Chapman's company shortly before her murder is being sought for, but up to the present it would appear without success. Inquiries at some of the Metropolitan medical institutions show that similar requests have been made for anatomical specimens, but the conditions could not possibly be complied with.

September 30th 1888

September 30th 1888 Elizabeth Stride

Name: Elizabeth Stride, Estimated Birth Year: abt 1843, Date of Registration: Oct- Nov- Dec- 1888, Age at Death: 45, Registration District: St George in the East, Inferred County, London, Vol: 1c, Page: 268

September 30th 1888 Catherine Eddowes

Name: Catherine Eddowes, Estimated Birth Year: abt 1845, Date of Registration: Oct- Nov- Dec- 1888, Age at Death: 43, Registration District: London City, Inferred County, London, Vol: 1c, Page: 37

October 1st 1888

The Hull Daily Mail, October 1st 1888,

THE LONDON HORRORS. THE BERNER STREET TRAGEDY. A representative of the Press Association this morning visited a lodging house in Flower and Dean Street, Spitalfields, where the murdered woman, Elizabeth Stride, passed the day before her death. The street is turning off Commercial Street, and one side consists mainly of modern buildings intended for artisans, but occupied almost exclusively by a colony of middle class Jews. On the other

Mike Covell

side are very poor sad and wretched houses, mostly registered lodging houses of which "Long Liz," as she was familiarly known by her associates, lived. A complete of terror prevailed in the street. The watchman of the house, Thomas Bates, said, "Long Liz" had lived with them many years but her real name was never known. She was a Swede by birth, whose husband was drowned at sea many years ago. She was a charwoman, but at times was driven by extremes to walk the streets. She frequently absented for days or months at a time, and she returned last Tuesday, after a prolonged absence, remaining until Saturday night, when she went out about seven o'clock. She appeared quite cheerful. They did not see her alive again,- Mrs Ann Mile, the bed maker at the house, corroborated this, and said a better hearted, good mannered cleaner woman never lived. Though a poor "unfortunate" she worked when she could get work. The Press Association learns that the police have received a statement that a man, aged between 35 and 40 years, and of fair complexion, was seen to throw Stride to the ground, but that it was thought that the parties were man and wife quarrelling, no later inference was made. The police have also been told that about half past ten on Saturday night a man aged about 33, entered a public house in Bailey Street, Whitechapel, and whilst customers in the bar were talking of the Whitechapel murders, he said he knew the Whitechapel murderer, and they would hear about it in the morning, after which he left. OPENING OF THE INQUEST. The inquest on the body of Elizabeth Stride was opened at eleven o'clock this morning by Mr Wynne Baxter at the Vestry Hall, Cable Street, Commercial road. The body was being viewed by the jury presented a dreadful night, the head being almost severed from the body by one awful gash.- William West was the first witness examined. He said that he lived at the International Working Men's Institute and Club, Berner Street, at the side of which is a passage leading to the yard. Two large wooden gates protected the entrance to the yard, and they were sometimes open at night. In the yard there were two or three small tenements. The club was a Socialist Club, and persons of all nationalities were eligible. Witness was at the club on Saturday night from half past ten or eleven when the members were discussing. The bulk of the members left the club by the front door before twelve. Witness's business was at 40, Berner Street; but he lived at 2 William Street, Commercial Road, wither he went past at half past twelve. Before leaving he noticed the gates were open, but there was nothing on the ground.- Norris Eagle, travelling jeweller, and member of the club, said he was at the club on Saturday, and left about quarter to 12. He returned about 20 minutes to one, and as the front door was closed he went through the gateway and side door. He saw nothing in the yard, but about 20 minutes later another member announced the discovery of the body.- Louis Diemschitz, steward of the club, deposed that he returned to his home at the club at one o'clock, riding in a kind of barrow drawn by a pony. He drove through the open gates of the yard, when his pony shied at something on the ground. He felt it with his whip handle, and tried to move it but failed, and jumping down at once he struck a light. He then saw it was a woman. He called his wife, and got a candle. When he saw blood he sent for the police, and just before they arrived a man who he did not know took hold of the deceased's head and showed the wound in the throat. All people in the club were searched before they left, and their names and addresses taken.- In reply to the coroner, Inspector Reid said the body had not yet been identified,- The Foreman of the jury: But we have been told her name is Stride, How is that? The Coroner: Something is known of her. She has been partially identified,- Inspector Reid said he would be prepared with further evidence tomorrow, and the inquiry was accordingly adjourned. THE MITRE COURT TRAGEDY. Up to ten o'clock this morning the body of the Mitre Court victim had not been identified. No arrests have been made in connection with the crime, and with regard to the reported arrest of an American in the borough the city police state they have no official intimation of it. DISCOVERY OF A KNIFE. Early this morning a police constable found in Whitechapel Road a black handled knife, sharp and pointed like a carving knife. The blade was about ten inches long.- At a quarter past three this morning a second man was taken to Leman Street and detained, but the police are reserved as to the extent of the information afforded by the arrests. There is, however, reason to believe that no tangible clue has yet been obtained. THE ARRESTS. The man who was arrested by the Whitechapel police and taken to Leman Street is a short thick set fellow of about 30, close shaven. Upon him was found 1s 1 ½d in money and a razor, and round his throat was a woollen scarf of a violet colour, upon which were several long hairs, evidently of a woman. He said he walked from Southampton and belonged to the Royal Sussex Regiment. Another man is still in custody at Commercial Street station on suspicion. He has given the name of Frank Rape, and was apprehended about 10 o'clock on Sunday night at a public house known as "Dirty Dicks" near Liverpool Street. He was in a drunken condition in one of the bars, and made some wandering statements that he had committed the murders. The police were sent for and removed him. No importance is attached to his drunken boast. RELEASE OF A SUSPECT. The man arrested on Sunday night was released from Leman Street police station this afternoon. The other man is still detained, but the police admit they have discovered little to aid them in finding the murderer. It was this afternoon rumoured that the victim of the Mitre Square murder had been identified as a woman called May, but the police do not confirm this. It is proposed to hold an indignation meeting in Whitechapel on the subject of the murders. THE VIGILANCE COMMITTEE. Another meeting of the Whitechapel Vigilance

Mike Covell

> Committee was held at 74, Mile End Road, this morning, when a resolution was passed that a further letter should be sent to the Home Secretary insisting upon the offer of a large Government reward immediately. A letter was despatched. REWARD BY THE CORPORATION OF LONDON. A member of the London Common Council has given notice of motion for their meeting on Thursday next that the Corporation should offer £250 reward for the detention of murder of the woman in Mitre Court. The Lord Mayor of London, acting on the advice of the City Commissioner of Police, has in the name of the Corporation, offered a reward of £500 for the detection of the Whitechapel murderer. The proprietors of the Financial News have written to the Home Secretary, offering, as instigation of several subscribers to offer through the Government a reward of £500 for the detection of the murders. PRESS OPINION. PROPOSED EMPLOYMENT OF MARINES. The St James Gazette this evening suggests that Marines in plain clothes might be employed to watch for the Whitechapel murderer as they were employed in Dublin, and calls upon the Home Office to revoke its recent decisions, and offer a reward for information leading to the arrest of the criminal. The Pall Mall Gazette says the only practical thing to be done is keep a sharp look out and to dismiss once and for all the coroners theory as to the motive of the murders. The Coroner seems to have been made an innocent victim of a somewhat stupid hoax.- The Gazette sets forth the prices paid by the Pathological Museums for subjects which include 8s 5d as price of a complete course. The organ removed by Chapman's murderer could be had for the asking at any post-mortem room 12 hours after death.

The Hull Daily News, October 1st 1888,

> LATEST NEWS. THE WHITECHAPEL HORRORS. PEOPLE IN FEAR OF THEIR LIVES. POLICE ACTIVITY. LATEST PARTICULARS. A Press Association reporter, who has passed the night near the scene of Saturday night's atrocities in Whitechapel, says one topic seemed to absorb the attention of all, and wherever the cabmen, coffee stall keepers, and the whole class of tramps and prostitutes congregated the dreaded word Whitechapel seemed to exercise a spell. Not only women and children, but men seemed to go in fear of their lives. The police not only parade their beats with measured thread, but with an anxiety which betokens a determination to bring the culprit to justice. Hitherto, the murderer, assuming that there is but one, confined his operations to the Metropolitan police district, but by pursuing his career near the city, he has brought upon has track some 900 additional officers. Both the Metropolitan and the City authorities have greatly augmented the force on duty, and there can be no doubt that the augmentation was absolutely necessary. The force indeed

deserves credit for the sturdiness with which they apply themselves to their terrible task. Since Sunday, a remarkable change has come over the attitude of the police authorities, and information hitherto denied is now cheerfully imparted. It would seem that both Sir Charles Warren and Colonel Fraser are tending to the conviction that publicity is the best detective. Sir Charles Warren has ordered constables to Commercial street station from the A and B Divisions, while Colonel Fraser has drawn men from every available district in the City to that portion of the area nearest Whitechapel, which is considered dangerous. The neighbourhood of Mitre square, where the mutilated remains of the victim not yet identified were found is respectable. The is only one occupied house in it, which is tenanted by Constable Pearce. The square has three entrances, the main one being by Mitre street, and others by Church court and Mitre passage respectively. It was in the south east corner, on the right of the entrance from Mitre street, where the body was found by Watkins. He says: I passed the spot at half past one, and there was nothing in the corner then. I came round at a quarter to two, and on entering the square from Mitre street on the right hand side, turned sharp round to the right, and flashing my light, I saw the body in front of me. Her clothes were pushed right up to her breast, and the stomach was laid bare, with a dreadful gash up to the breast. The throat had an awful gash from ear to ear, the head being nearly severed from the body. It was difficult to ascertain the injuries to the face, owing to the quantity of blood which covered it. I could not say whether one of the ears was cut off. The murderer had inserted the knife under the left eye, and cut the nose completely off, and inflicting a frightful gash down the right cheek to the angle of the jaw bone. I went and asked for the assistance of the watchman Morris, at Hazeitine, Kearney, and Tonge's, and he went for other officers while I sent for Dr. Seguira, of 34, Old Jewry, and Dr. Brown, and the body was removed to the mortuary. The constable adds that it is decidedly probable that the murderer was disturbed by his approach, and left his ghastly work unfinished, escaping by either of the narrow courtways alluded to. It is also believed that the same hand perpetrated the murder of the other woman in Berner street, and that mutilation was intended, but in this case, too, he was disturbed in his work. The theory favoured by the police is, that being disturbed with his first victim, he left her and induced the second woman to go with him. They imagine he decoys them by means of gold, which after the murder, he abstracted from their pockets. It is also suspected that he wears gloves whilst performing his ghastly work. The body of the woman murdered in Berner street, has been identified as that of Elizabeth Stride, better known as "Lizzie Long," lately living at 32, Flower and Dean street, Soho. The other woman is so dreadfully mutilated that it is feared she cannot be recognised, except by her clothes, and the two pawn tickets found lying by her, and the initials "D.C." or "T.C." in blue ink on her left forearm. She is five feet high, has light hazel eyes, auburn hair, a dark chintz dress with three flounces of dark linsey, very old dark green alpacca petticoat, white chemise, brown ribbed stockings, white straw hat trimmed with beads and green and black velvet, large white handkerchief round the neck, and a pair of men's lace up boots. DESCRIPTION OF THE SUPPOSED MURDERER. The description of the man wanted by the police is- Aged 30, height 5 feet 5 inches, complexion far, hair dark, full face, small moustache, stout build and broad shoulders. TWO MEN ARRESTED. Two arrests were made at two o'clock this morning, one man being detained at Leman street, the other at Commercial street station, but nothing has yet been discovered to implicate them. AN IMPORTANT DISCOVERY. The police have also made an important discovery, throwing light on the direction in which the murderer made his escape. A portion of an apron was found in Goulston street, and when the body of the woman found in Mitre Square was examined, it was found that she was wearing a portion of the same apron. It is, therefore, inferred that the murderer escaped through Whitechapel. A man who passed through Church lane, Aldgate, at a half past one yesterday morning says he saw a man seated on a doorstep, wiping his hands. The man, who is described as wearing a short jacket and sailors hat, tried to conceal his face. Mr. Wynne E. Baxter, coroner for East Middlesex, holds an inquest at Vestry hall, Cable street, St George's at eleven o'clock this morning, on the woman Elizabeth Stride, murdered in Berner street. Up to ten o'clock this morning the victim of the Mitre court victim had not been identified. No arrests have been made in connection with the crime, and with regard to reported arrest of an American in the Borough, the City police state they have no official information of it. THE BERNER STREET TRAGEDY. A representative of the Press Association this morning visited the lodging house in Flower and Dean street, Spitalfields, where the murdered woman Elizabeth Stride passed the day before her death. The street is turning off Commercial street, and one side consists mainly of modern buildings, intended for artisans, but occupied almost exclusively by a colony of middle class Jews. On the other side are very poor and wretched houses, mostly registered lodging houses, in one of which "Long Liz" as she was familiarly known by her associates, lived. A complete reign of terror prevailed on the streets. THE VICTIM'S ANTECEDENTS. The watchman of the house, Thomas Bates, said, "Long Liz" had lived with them many years but her real name was never known. She was a Swede by birth, whose husband was drowned at sea many years ago. She was a charwoman, but at times was driven by extremes to walk the streets. She frequently absented for days or months at a time, and she returned last Tuesday, after a prolonged absence, remaining until Saturday night, when she went out *about seven o'clock. She appeared quite cheerful. They did not see her alive again,- Mrs Ann Mile, the bed maker at the house, corroborated this, and said a better hearted, good mannered cleaner woman never lived. Though a poor "unfortunate" she worked when she could get work. The Press Association learns that the police have received a statement that a man, aged between 35 and 40 years, and of fair complexion, was seen to throw Stride to the ground, but that it was thought that the parties were man and wife quarrelling, no later inference was made. The police have also been told that about half past ten on Saturday night a man aged about 33, entered a public house in Bailey Street, Whitechapel, and whilst customers in the bar were talking of the Whitechapel murders, he said he knew the Whitechapel murderer, and they would hear about it in the morning, after which he left. DARING POST OFFICE ROBBERY IN LONDON. The Press Association says that the Aldgate Post Office, a few yards from the scene of the Mitre Court murder, was found this morning to have been entered, and the safe forced. The thieves must have entered the premises during Saturday night from the unoccupied house adjoining. A hole was made in the safe, and the thieves obtained £50 in money, and £350 worth of stamps. The robbery was a most daring one, as the police were patrolling the immediate neighbourhood all night long.*

The Hull Daily Mail, October 1st 1888,

DARING POST OFFICE ROBBERY IN LONDON. EXTRAORDINARY ROBBERY. The Press Association says that the Aldgate Post Office, a few yards from the scene of the Mitre Court murder, was found this morning to have been entered, and the safe forced. The thieves must have entered the premises during Saturday night from the unoccupied house adjoining. A hole was made in the safe, and the thieves obtained £50 in money, and £350 worth of stamps. The robbery was a most daring one, as the police were patrolling the immediate neighbourhood all night long. THE WIFE MURDER IN LONDON. John Brown, 45, was charged at Westminster Police Court this morning with the wilful murder of his wife at Regent Gardens, Westminster. It appears that prisoner returned home on Saturday night, quarrelled with his wife, and cut her throat with a knife, almost severing her head from her body. He then gave himself up to the police. It was stated that the woman had previously sought police protection, the prisoner having been strange in his behaviour, - Prisoner made no remark, and was remanded.

Mike Covell

> **John Brown:**
>
> England and Wales Criminal Registers, [HO 27, P211, P188]
> Name: John Brown, Date of Trial: Oct 22nd 1888, Trial Year: 1888, Location of Trial: Middlesex, England, Sentence: Imprisonment, Charge: Murder, Notes: Guilty of Act done but insane at time of commission of offence. To be kept in custody as a criminal lunatic at Holloway
>
> John Brown's murdered wife was called, according to The Standard, dated October 1st 1888, Sarah, but searches for a Sarah Brown who died in the district at that time have turned up a blank.

The Hull Daily Mail, October 1st 1888,

> THE BIRTLEY MURDER. ALLEGED CAPTURE OF WADDLES. The Press Association's Berwick correspondent says a man matching the description of Waddle, the iron worker, who is wanted in connection with the Birtley murder, was in Berwick on Sunday, and sold his clothes, buying another suit. The clothes which had blood marks on them, have been identified, have been identified by the police, Waddle has decamped. A later telegram from a Newcastle correspondent says:- This afternoon information has been received in Newcastle that William Waddle, the supposed murderer of young Beetmore, near Gateshead, was captured this morning at Yetholm, Roxburghshire.

The Hull Daily Mail, October 1st 1888,

> MORE ATROCITIES IN LONDON. TWO WOMEN MURDERED. HORRIBLE MUTILATION. DESCRIPTION OF SUPPOSED CULPRIT. The Metropolis was yesterday (Sunday) morning thrown into a state of renewed consternation by the announcement that the bodies of two more murdered women had been discovered in the East End. The first of the series of murders was committed so far back as last Christmas, when a woman, whose identity was never discovered, was found murdered in, or consiguous to, the district known as Whitechapel. There were circumstances of peculiar barbarity about the mode in which the body was treated. This fact did not attract so much notice at the time as it did when, on August 7 last, a woman, named Martha Turner, aged 35, was found dead on the first floor landing of some model dwellings in Spitalfields, with 39 bayonet or dagger wounds on the body. On the 31st of the same month the woman Nichols, an unfortunate, was found dead in Buck's-row, Whitechapel. With this probably begins the series of crimes which have lately horrified and

terrified the public, for the mutilation of the body was done with so much technical skill and audacity as to suggest a definite but extraordinary, and at that time unexplained, purpose. What that object was the Coroner recently suggested in the summing up at the inquest of the woman Chapman, who was murdered in the same district, and under similar circumstances, on September 8th. That crime created almost a panic, which had scarcely died away when it became known yesterday that two more murders of apparently the same kind had been committed under circumstances detailed hereunder. THE BERNER-STREET MURDER. The scene of the first of the present outrages is a narrow court in Berner-street, a quite thoroughfare running from Commercial-road down to the London, Tilbury, and Southend Railway. At the entrance to the court are a pair of large wooden gates, in one of which is a small wicket for use when the gates are closed. At the hour when the murderer accomplished his purpose these gates were open. Indeed, according to the testimony of those living near the entrance, the court is seldom closed. For a distance of 18 or 20 feet from the street there is a dead wall on each side of the court the effect of which is to enshroud the intervening space in absolute darkness after sunset. Further back some light is thrown into the court from the windows of a Workingmen's Club, which occupies the whole length of the court on the right, and from a number of cottages occupied mainly by tailors and cigarette makers on the left. At the time when the murder was committed, however the lights in all of the dwelling houses in question had been extinguished, whilst other illumination as came from the club, being from the upper storey, would fall on the cottages opposite, and would only serve to intensify the gloom in the rest of the court. From the position in which the body was found it is believed that the moment the murderer has got his victim in the dark shadow near the entrance to the court he threw her to the ground and with one gash cut her throat from ear to ear. The hypothesis that the wound was inflicted after, and not before the woman fell, is supported by the fact that there are severe bruises on her left temple and left cheek, thus showing that force must have been used to prostrate her, which would not have been necessary had her throat been already cut. When discovered, the body was lying as if the woman had fallen forward, her feet being about a couple of yards from the street, and her head in the gutter, which runs down the right hand side of the court. The woman lay on her left side face downwards, her position being such that although the court at that part is only nine feet wide a person walking up the middle might have passed the recumbent body without notice. MURDERER NEARLY DISCOVERED IN THE ACT. The condition of the corpse, however, and several other circumstances which have come to light during the day, prove pretty conclusively that no considerable period elapsed between the committal of the murder and discovery of the body. In fact, it is pretty generally conjectured

Mike Covell

that the assassin was disturbed at his ghastly work, and made off before he had completed his designs. All the features of the case go to connect the tragedy with that which took place three-quarters of an hour later, a few streets distant. The obvious poverty of the woman, her total lack of jewellery or ornaments, and the soiled condition of her clothing, are entirely opposed to the theory that robbery could have been the motive. The secrecy and despatch of which the crime was effected are equally good evidence that the murder was not the result of an ordinary street brawl. At the club referred to above- the International Workmen's Club- which is an offshoot of the Socialist League, and a rendezvous of a number of foreign residents, Poles, and Continental Jews of various nationalities, it is customary on Saturday nights to have friendly discussion on topics of mutual interests, and to wind the up the evening's entertainment with songs, &c. The proceedings commenced on Saturday about 8.30 with a discussion on the necessity for Socialism amongst Jews. This was kept up until about eleven o'clock, when a considerable portion of the company left for their respective homes. Between 20 and 30 remained behind, and the usual concert which followed was not concluded when the intelligence was brought in by the steward of the club that a woman had been DONE TO DEATH. Within a few yards of them, and within earshot of their jovial songs. The people residing in the cottages on the other side of the court were all indoors and most of them in bed by midnight. Several of these persons remember laying awake and listening to the singing, and they also remember the concert coming to an abrupt termination. But during the whole of the time, from retiring to rest until the body was discovered, no one heard anything in the nature of a scream or woman's cry of distress. It was Louis Diemshitz, the steward of the club, who found the body. Diemshitz, who is a traveller in cheap jewellery, had spent the day at Westow Hill market, near the Crystal Palace, in pursuance of his avocation, and had driven home at this unusual hour, reaching Berner-street at one o'clock. On turning into the gateway he had some difficulty with his pony, the animal being apparently determined to avoid the right hand wall. For the moment Diemshitz did not think much of this occurrence, because he knew the pony was given to shying. He thought perhaps some mud or refuse was in the way. Failing to discern anything in the darkness, Diemshitz poked about with the handle of the whip, and immediately discovered that some large obstacle was in the path. To jump down and STRIKE A MATCH Was the work of a second, and then it became at once apparent that something serious had taken place. Without waiting to see whether the woman, whose body he saw was drunk or dead, Diemshitz entered the club by the side door higher up the court, and informed those in the concert room upstairs that something had happened in the yard. A member of the club named Kozebrodski, but familiarly known as "Isaacs," returned with Diemshitz into the court, and the former struck a match while the latter lifted the body up. It was at once apparent that the woman was dead. The body was still warm, and the clothes wet from the recent rain. But the heart had ceased to beat, and the stream of blood in the gutter, terminating in a hideous pool near the club door, showed but too plainly what had happened. Both men ran off without delay to find a policeman, and about the same time other members of the club, who had by this time found their way into the court, went off with the same object, in different directions. The search was for some time fruitless. At last, however, after considerable delay, a constable was found in Commercial-road. With the aid of the policeman's whistle more constables were quickly on the spot, and the gates at the entrance to the court having been closed, and a guard set on all the exits of the club and the cottages, the superintendent of the district, and divisional surgeon were sent for. In a few minutes Dr Phillips was at once at the scene of the murder, and a brief examination sufficed to show that life had been extinct some minutes. Careful notes having being taken of the body, it was removed to the parish mortuary of St Georges in the East, Cable-street, to await identification. DESCRIPTION OF THE BODY. A representative of the Press Association, who has seen the corpse, states that the woman appears to be about 30 years of age. Her hair is very dark, with a tendency to curl, and her complexion is also dark. Her features are sharp and somewhat pinched, as though she has endured considerable privations recently, an impression confirmed by the entire absence of the kind of ornaments commonly affected by women of her station. She wore a rusty black dress of a cheap kind, of sateen, with a velveteen bodice, over which was a black diagonal [illegible] jacket, with fur trimming. Her bonnet, which had fallen from her head when she was found in the yard, was of black crape, and inside, apparently with the object of making the article fit closer to the head, was folded a copy of the Star newspaper. In her right hand were tightly clasped some grapes, and in her left she held a number of sweetmeats. Both the jacket and the bodice were open towards the top. But in other respects the clothes were not disarranged. The linen was clean and is tolerably good repair. But some articles were missing. The cut in the woman's throat, which was the cause of death, was evidently affected with a very sharp instrument, and was made with one rapid incision. The weapon was apparently drawn across the throat rather obliquely from left to right, the gash being about three inches long and nearly the same depth. In the pocket of the woman's dress were discovered two pocket handkerchiefs (a gentleman's and a lady's), a brass thimble, and a skein of black darning worsted. In addition to Dr Phillips the body was examined both before and after removal to the mortuary, by Dr Kaye and Dr Blackwell, both of whom reside in the vicinity of Berner-street. On the arrival of the Superintendent

Mike Covell

from leman-street Police Station, which took place almost simultaneously with that of the divisional surgeon, steps were immediately taken to ascertain whether the members of the club were in any way connected with the murder. The names and addresses of all the men present were taken, and a vigorous search of persons and premises was instituted, much to the annoyance of the members. The residents in the court had to submit to a similar scrutiny. In neither case, however, was any incriminating evidence discovered. It was five o'clock before the police had finished the investigations at the club, for, in addition to the search referred to above, inquiries were made which resulted in a number of written statements which had to be signed by members. The fact that another murder had been committed soon became known in the neighbourhood, and long before daybreak the usually quite thoroughfare was the scene of great excitement. Extra police had to be posted along the street, and even with this precaution, commotion from an early hour was a matter of extreme difficulty. A large crowd followed the body to the mortuary and here again it was found necessary to take unusual precautions to KEEP BACK THE CROWDS. As the news circulated further afield immense numbers of people flocked to Whitechapel, and before noon the neighbourhood of Aldgate and Commercial road was literally invaded by persons curious to see the spots selected for this and the other murders in the series. Several matters have transpired which tend to fix precisely the time at which the unfortunate woman was murdered. Morris Eagle, one of the members of the club, left Berner street about twelve o'clock, and after taking his sweetheart home returned to the club at about twenty minutes to one, with the intention of having supper. He walked up the yard and entered the club by the side entrance, but neither saw nor heard anything to make him suspect foul play was going on. He might have passed the body in the darkness, but the probability is that he would have stumbled over it if the murder had been committed before that time. Another member of the club - A Russian named Joseph Lave - feeling oppressed by the smoke in the large room, went down into the court about twenty minutes before the body was discovered, and walked about in the open air for five minutes or more. He strolled into the street, which was very quiet at the time, and returned to the concert room without having encountered anything unusual. During the day there were many persons at the mortuary, but nobody succeeded in identifying the body. Several policemen on duty in the district declare that they have seen the deceased about the locality, and it is believed that she belonged to the "unfortunate" class. Mr. Wynne Baxter, the coroner of the district, was communicated with as soon as the details were ascertained, and he has fixes the inquest for today at 11 o'clock at the Vestry hall, Cable street. It is believed in police circles that the murderer was disturbed at his work by the arrival of Diemshitz, and that he made off as soon as he heard the cart at the top of the street. Sir Charles Warren and Major Smith, of the City Police, visited the scene of the murder in the course of the morning. A SUSPECTED MAN. The following description has been circulated by the police of a man said to have been seen in the company of deceased during Saturday:- "Age 23, slight, height, 5ft, 8in, complexion dark, no whiskers, black diagonal coat, hard felt hat, collar and vie, carried a newspaper parcel, respectable appearance." THE STEWARDS STATEMENT. Lewis Diemshitz, the steward of the International Working Men's Club, in the yard of which the murder was committed, made the following statement to a Central News reporter:- "I am a traveller in the common jewellery trade, working for myself alone. I have been a steward of this club for six or seven years, and I live on the premises. It has been my habit for some time past to go on Saturday to Westow Hill Crystal Palace, where there is a market at which I sell my wares. This (Sunday) morning I got back from Westow market as usual, about one o'clock. I drove up to the gate of the clubhouse in my little cart, drawn by a pony, after being all day at the market. The pony is inclined to shy a little, and it struck me when I was passing through the double gates into the yard that he wanted to keep too much to the left side, against the wall. I could not make out what was the matter, so I bent my head to see if there was anything to frighten him. Then I noticed that there was something unusual about the ground, but I could not tell what it was except that it was not level. I mean that there was something like a little heap, but I thought it was only mud or something of the kind, and did not take much notice of it. However, I touched it with my whip handle, and then I was able to tell that it was not mud. I wanted to see what it was, so jumped out of the trap and struck a match. Then I saw that there was a woman lying there. At that time I took no further notice, and did not know whether she was drunk or dead. All I did was to run indoors and ask where my misses was, because she is of weak constitution, and I did not want to frighten her. I found that my wife was sitting downstairs, and I then told some of the members in the club, that something had happened in the yard, but I did not say whether the woman was murdered or only drunk. One of the members, who is known as Isaacs, went out with me. We struck a match and saw blood running from the gate all the way down to the side door of the club. We had the police sent for at once, but I believe it was several minutes before a constable could be found. There was another member of the club named Eagle, who also ran out to get a policeman. He went in a different direction to the other, and managed to find two officers somewhere in Commercial-road. One of them was 252H. An officer blew his whistle and several more policemen came. One of them was sent for a doctor, Dr Phillips the police surgeon, of Spital-square, and Dr Kaye, of Blackwall, both came. The police afterwards took names of all the members of the club, and they

Mike Covell

say that all of us have to give evidence about it. Having been asked to describe the body as well as he could, Diemshitz said: I should think the woman was about 27 or 28 years old. I fancy she was of a light complexion. (This turns out to be incorrect description but the man was too frightened to make a careful examination) It seemed to me that her clothes were in perfect order. I could see that her throat was fearfully cut. There was a great gash in it over two inches wide. She had dark clothes on, and wore a black crape bonnet. Her hands were clenched, and when the doctor opened them I saw that she had been holding grapes in one hand and sweetmeats in the other. I could not say whether or not she was an unfortunate, but if she was I should judge her to be of a rather better class than the woman we usually see about this neighbourhood. I don't think anybody in this district, and certainly none of our members, had ever seen her before. The police removed the body to Cable-street Mortuary. When I first saw the woman she was lying on her left side. Her left hand was on the ground, and the right was crossed over her breast. Her head was down the yard, her feet towards the entrance, and more than about a yard or so inside the gates, I keep my pony and trap inside the gates. But I went down to the club first to deposit my goods there. The man Diemshitz is a Russian Jew, but he is an intelligent person, and speaks English fairly well. STATEMENT OF A RUSSIAN JEW. A man named Morris Eagle, also a Russian Jew, says "I frequent this club, and I was passing into it so late as twenty minutes to one on Sunday morning, which was just 20 minutes before the body was discovered. I had been there early on the evening, but left about 12 o'clock in order to take home my young lady. When I returned, I came along the small streets in the district, but noticed nothing unusual. There were a number of men and women about, as there are about that time, but the streets were more lively than usual, and I saw nothing suspicious when I got back to the club in Berner-street, the front door was closed, and so I passed through the gate on the left hand side of the house to get in by the side door. I went over the same ground as Diemshitz did later on, but I saw nothing on the ground. The gates were thrown wide back. In fact, it is very seldom that they are closed. It is customary for members of the club to go in by the side door to prevent knocking at the front. There is no light in the yard, but of course there are lamps in the streets. After I got into the club there was some singing, and after I had been in some 20 minutes a man came in, and said something about a woman being in the yard. I went and struck a match, and then I could see there was blood on the ground. I heard someone calling for the police, and I ran into Commercial-road. I found two officers at the corner of Christian-street, and told them what was the matter. When one of the policemen saw the blood, he sent his companion for a doctor. In the meantime I went straight to Leman-street, and called out an inspector. I did not notice the appearance of the woman because the sight of the blood upset me, and I could not look at it. STATEMENT OF A RUSSIAN POLE. A young Russian Pole, named Isaac M. Kozebrodski, born in Warsaw, and who spoke the English language imperfectly, gave the following information:- I was in the club last night, I came in about half past six in the evening, and I had not been away since about twenty minutes to one on Sunday morning. Mr Diemshitz called me out into the yard, and told me to come and see what it was. When we got outside he struck a match, and when we looked down on the ground we could see a long stream of blood. It was running down the gutter from the direction of the gate, and reached to the back door of the club, I should think there was blood in the gutter for a distance of five or six yards. I went to look for a policeman at the request of Diemshitz, or some member of the club, but I took the direction towards the Grove-street, and could not find one. I afterwards went into the Commercial-road, and there, along with Eagle, found two officers. The officers did not touch the body, but sent for a doctor. A doctor came, and an inspector arrived just afterwards. While the doctor was examining the body, I noticed she had some grapes in her right hand and some sweets in her left. I think she wore a dark and black dress. I saw a little bunch of flowers stuck above her right bosom. Joseph Lave, a man just arrived in England from the United States, and who was living temporarily at the club until he could find lodgings, says: "I was in the club card this morning about 20 minutes to one. I came out first at half past 12 to get a breath of fresh air. I passed out into the street, but did not see anything unusual. The district appeared to me to be quite. I remained out until 20 minutes to one, and during that time no one came into the yard. I should have seen anybody moving about there, Several members of the club, including the steward, stated that the yard adjoining the building has never been used for immoral purposes. The traffic there is constant and continuous almost all the night through. AN EVIL NEIGHBOURHOOD. The yard in which the body was found is about 10 feet wide. This width is continued for a distance of eight or ten yards, at which point there occurs on the left hand side a small row of houses, which are set back a little, so that the width is increased by two feet or more. The extreme length of the court is 30 yards, and it terminates in a workshop, which is at present being used as a dwelling house. The spot where the murder was committed, therefore, is overlooked on three sides, and insomuch as the gates were open last night, any casual pedestrian might easily have seen the commission of the crime. The windows of the club room are within 10 feet of the spot, while the cottages stand almost opposite and command a complete view of it. None of the occupants of these houses, however, heard the faintest noise in the course of Saturday night or Sunday morning. The residents in the yard are tailors and cigarette makers, and they are not in the habit of retiring very early. A reporter who made inquiry amongst them,

Mike Covell

however, was unable to find any person who had either seen or heard anything suspicious. The club spoken of is occupied by what is known as the National Workmen's Educational Society, and is affiliated to the Socialist League, of which it is a foreign league. Its members seem to be largely composed of Russian Jews, and Jews of other nationalities also find a welcome there. Many of them live on the premises, which, however, are not extensive. At the back there is a fair sized hall, made by demolishing partition between two rooms, and here on Saturday night the numbers gather for the purpose of debate and amusement. On Saturday night the debate was largely attended by Germans, nearly a hundred being at one time in the room. The subject of discussion was- "Is it necessary that a Jew should be a Socialist?" It is proved so interesting that it was carried on to a late hour. After it had terminated there was a concert, at which 60 persons remained. There was considerable singing, and there is no doubt that the noise would have drowned any outcry which might have been made by the wretched creature who was being murdered in the yard beneath. Berner-street is in a very notorious part of Whitechapel. It is close to a district which was formerly known as Tigers Bay, because of the ferocious character of the desperados who frequented it. A few yards distant is the house wherein Lipsky murdered Miriam Angel, and the neighbourhood generally has an evil repute. During the course of yesterday thousands of persons congregated in the vicinity of the scene of the crime, and it was with the greatest of difficulty that the police could keep the street clear. The bulk of the residents are Jews. At the back of the Workingmen's Club there is a Jewish paper published called the Workmen's Friend, which is printed in Hebrew. Shops and lodging homes kept by Jews are very frequently met with A DREADFUL SPECTACLE. The body of the murdered woman, which now lies in St George's mortuary, close to St George's Parish Church, presents a dreadful spectacle, it is the corpse of a woman about 40 years of age, and lies on a slab, exhibits prominently a fearful wound on the throat. The head is slightly thrown to the right, and the gaping orifice is so clearly scooped out that the divisions of the jugular vein and the windpipe can be easily seen. The knife or other implement with which the deed was committed must have been of large size, and very keen. The wound is so wide that there is room for supposition that after the blade was inserted it was partially turned, then drawn with great force from the left to the right. The vertebrae of the neck was scraped, owing to the great force with which the weapon was wielded, and it is obvious that if the murderer had not been interrupted the poor creature would have been hideously mangled, for the savagery of her assailant is evidenced not alone by the terrible wound in the throat, but also by two severe contusions on the head, one on the temple, the other cheek, which seems to point to the conclusion that he was proceeding to further outrage when some chance incident alarmed him and caused him to desist from his infamous work. With the exception of the injuries mentioned, the body bore no sign of ill usage. The woman has the appearance of an unfortunate, but not one of the worst class. Her black curly hair had been well combed, and tied up. Her underclothing was clean, and her two petticoats and black frock were good, although old. She had a black alpacca frock, a black jacket, trimmed with fur, an old velveteen body, once black, but now brown, and a crape bonnet, with some rare space which had been filled up by a current copy of a London evening newspaper, white stockings, white stays, and side spring boots. The bodice of the woman was open, exposing her chest, and the theory built upon this circumstance is the assassin was intending to HACK HER STOMACH but could not carry out his purpose. In the pockets were found two handkerchiefs- one a man's, the other a woman's- and a thimble and a skein of black worsted. There were no rings on the fingers. In her jacket was pinned a small bunch of roses and ferns. Her hair was matted with wet dirt, showing that a struggle had taken place on the ground. It is not believed, however, that the woman was in a recumbent position when attacked, the theory being that her murderer was standing with his left arm around her neck, and that while so placed he drew a knife and inflicted a mortal wound. The position of the body, when found, favours this view, insomuch as no attempt had been made to disarrange the clothing. The woman was lying in an almost natural attitude, with her head towards the bottom of the yard at 40, Berner-street and the legs towards the gate. After the police authorities had been notified of the murder the case was given into the hands of Chief Inspector Swanson and Inspector Abberline, of Scotland yard. In the first instance the police turned their attention to the Working Men's Club. The doors were guarded and no person was allowed egress. After the body had been removed to St George's Mortuary the detectives entered the club, and made careful examination of the inmates. Their pockets were searched, their hands and clothing particularly scrutinized. Some of them allege that they were made to take off their boots. All knives had to be produced, and each man had to give an account of himself before he was allowed to depart. Some of the members say that the detective treated them badly, swearing at them, and shouting "You're no foreigners, or else where's your knives." As a matter of fact, however, the police found nothing suspicious in the club or upon its members, and in the late morning surveillance was withdrawn. Some of the neighbours were also subjected to investigation, but NO CLUE was found. It may be mentioned here that the police discovered no blood splashes upon the wall in the yard. They caused the blood which had flown down the gutter to be removed at an early hour. The information of the crime reached Leman-street Police Station at 10 minutes past one o'clock, and Dr Philips, of 2, Spital-grove,

Mike Covell

the divisional police surgeon, was immediately communicated with. After he had made an external examination of the body it was removed to St, George's Mortuary, where the post mortem will be made to-day. In the course of yesterday Sir Charles Warren, the Chief Commissioner of Police visited the scene of the murder. The police have no clue to the murderer, nor do they profess any hope of discovering one. Dr Blackwell and Dr Simmonds submitted the body to a careful investigation. They discovered, it is understood, no marks except the wound, four or five inches long, in the throat, and no sign that there had been any attempt to further mutilate the body in the horrible manner which added so much inexplicable horror to the Hanbury-street case, and, it seems, to one of yesterday morning's tragedies also. After undergoing preliminary investigation here the body was removed to the Cable-street mortuary, where it will undergo further examination, and where subsequently opportunities will be given for identification. In the course of an interview with Central news reporters, shortly after six o'clock yesterday morning, Abraham Heshbury, a young fellow living at 23 Berner-street, said:- I was one of those who first saw the murdered woman. It was about a quarter to one o'clock I should think when I heard a policeman's whistle blow, and came down to see what was the matter in the gateway. Two or three people had collected, and when I got there I saw a short, dark young woman lying on the ground, with a gash between four and five inches long in her throat. I should think she was from 25 to 28 years of age. Her head was towards the north wall, against which she was lying. She had a black dress on, with a bunch of flowers pinned on the breast. In her hand there was a little piece of paper, containing five or six cachous. The body was not found by Koster, but by a man whose name I do not know. A man who goes out with a pony and barrow, and lives up the archway, where he was going, I believe, so put up his barrow on coming home from market. He thought it was his wife at first, but when he found her safe at home he got a candle, and found this woman. He never touched it till the doctors had been sent for. The little gate is always open, or at all events, always unfastened. But I don't think the yard is one used by loose women. There are some stables there- Messrs Duncan, Woollett and Co's, I believe- and there is a place to which a lot of girls take home sacks which they have been engaged in making. None of them would be there after about one o'clock on Saturday afternoon. None of us recognised the woman, and I don't think she belongs to this neighbourhood. She was dressed very respectably. There seems to be no wounds on the body. There was a row at the club last Sunday night. It went on until about two in the morning, and in the end two people were arrested. The house which adjoins the yard on the south side, No, 38, is tenanted by Bernost Kentorich, who, interrogated as to whether he heard any disturbance during the night, said, "I went to bed early and slept till about three o'clock, during which time I heard NO UNUSUAL SOUNDS Of any description. At three o'clock some people were talking loudly outside my door, so I went out to see what was the matter, and learned that a woman had been murdered. I did not stay out long, though, and know nothing more about it. I do not think the yard bears a very good character at night, but I do not interfere with any of the people about here. I know that the gate is not kept fastened. The club is a nasty place. In this view Mrs Kentorrich, who had come up from the underground kitchen to take part in the colloquy, thoroughly agreed, and both she and her husband, in reply to further questions, corroborated Heshburg's statement as to woman and girls being taken to the club, and as to the disorders which sometimes took place there. In order to inquire further into these matters the Central News representative next visited the club referred to, rather low class little building covered with posters, most of them in the Hebrew language. Mrs Lewis, life of the steward, as she explains I, was standing at the door, the centre of a knot of people. But she declined to call her up her husband, who had been up all night, and had only just gone to bed. Pressed to speak as to the character of the club, Mrs Lewis was inclined to be reticent, but a young man in the crowd volunteered an explanation of ill feeling which existed in the district as to the "Institution." "You see." he explained, "The members are "bad" Jews- Jews who don't hold their religion- and they annoy those who do in order to show their contempt for the religion. At the "Black fast" a week or two ago, for instance, they had a banquet, and ostentatiously ate and drank while we might do neither. They have conceits there till early in the morning, and the woman and girls are brought here. THE ALDGATE MURDER. The Press Association says that shortly before two o'clock yesterday morning, or three quarters of an hour after the crime described above was discovered, a second woman was horribly murdered and mutilated, this being in Mitre-square, Aldgate, within the city boundaries, but on the confines of the now notorious district. It appears that Police constable Watkins (No. 881) of the City Police was going round his beat, when turning his lantern upon the darkest corner of Mitre-square he saw the body of a woman, apparently lifeless, in a pool of blood. He at once blew his whistle, and several persons being attracted to the spot, he despatched messengers for medical and police aid. Inspector Collard, who was in Command of Bishopsgate Police Station, but a short distance off, quickly arrived, followed a few moments after by Mr G. W. Sequeira, surgeon, of 34, Jewry-street, and Dr Gordon Brown, the divisional police doctor, of Finsbury Circus. The scene then disclosed was a MOST HORRIBLE ONE. The woman, who was apparently about 40 years of age, was lying on her back, quite dead, although still warm. Her head was inclined to the left side, her left leg being extended, whilst the right was flexible. Both arms were extended. The throat was cut half way round, revealing a dreadful wound, from which blood flowed in [illegible] quantity, staining the pavement for some distance round. Across the right cheek to the nose was another gash, and a part of the right ear had been cut off. Following the plan in the Whitechapel murders, the miscreant was not content with merely killing his victims. The poor woman's clothes had been pulled over her chest, the abdomen ripped completely open, and part of the intestines laid on her neck. After careful notice had been taken of the position of the body when found, it was conveyed to the City Mortuary in Golden-lane. Here a more extended examination was made. The murdered woman was apparently about forty years of age, about 5ft in height, and evidently belonged to the unfortunate class of which the woman done to death in Whitechapel were members. Indeed, one of the policemen who saw the body expressed his confident opinion that he had seen the woman several times walking in the neighbourhood of Aldgate High-street. She was of dark complexion, with auburn hair, and hazel eyes, and was dressed in shabby dark clothes. She wore a black cloth jacket with imitation fur collar, and three large metal buttons. Her dress was made of green chintz the pattern consisting of Michaelmas daisies. In addition she had on a thin white vest, light drab linsey skirt, a very old dark green alpacca petticoat, white chemise, brown ribbed stockings (mended at the feet with white material), black straw bonnet (trimmed with black beads and green and black velvet), and a large white handkerchief round her neck. In the pockets of the dress a peculiar collection of articles was found, besides a small packet containing tea and other articles, which people who frequent the common lodging houses are accustomed to carry. The police found upon the body a white pocket handkerchief, a blunt bone handled tableknife, a short clay pipe, and a red cigarette case with white metal fittings. The knife bore no traces of blood, so could have no connection with the crime. When the news of this additional murder became known the excitement in the crowded district of Aldgate was intense. Usually a busy place for a Sunday morning, Houndsditch and connecting thoroughfares presented a particularly animated appearance. Men with barrows vending fruit and eatables were doing a brisk trade. Crowds flocked to the entrances of the square where the body had been discovered. But the police refused admittance to all but a privileged few. Sir Charles Warren visited the spot at a particularly early hour, and made himself thoroughly conversant with the neighbourhood and the details of the affair, Major Smith (acting superintendent of the City police), Superintendent Foster, Detective Inspector McWilliams (chief of the City detective department), Detective Sergeants Bownes and Outram, also attended during the morning. A little while after finding of the body all traces of blood had been washed away by the directions of the authorities, and there was little to indicate the terrible crime which had taken place. THE POLICE THEORY. is that the man and woman, who had met in Aldgate, watched the policeman pass round the square, and they entered it for an immoral purpose. Whilst the woman lay on the ground her throat was cu, as described above, causing instant death. The murderer then hurriedly proceeded to mutilate the body, for the wounds, though so ghastly, do not appear to have been caused so skilfully and deliberately as in the case of the murder of Annie Chapman in Hanbury-street. Five minutes, some of the doctors think, would have sufficed for the completion of the murderers work, and he was thus enabled to leave the ground before the return of the policeman on duty. None of the police on duty early yesterday morning appear to have had particular attention drawn to the man and woman together, and this appears strange at first, when it is remarked that within the last few weeks the police have been keeping a particularly keen watch upon suspicious couples. The murderer probably avoided much blood stains, on account of the woman being on her back at the time of the outrage, and, leaving the square by either of the courts, he would have been able to pass quickly away through the many narrow thoroughfares without exciting observation. But one of the most EXTRAORDINARY INCIDENTS. in connection with the affair is that not the slightest scream or noise was heard. A watchman is employed at one of the warehouses in the square, and in a direct line. But a few yards away on the other side of the square a city policeman was sleeping. Many people would be about in the neighbourhood, even at this early hour, making preparations for the market, which takes place every Sunday in what was formerly Petticoat-lane and the adjacent thoroughfare. Taking everything into account, therefore the murder must be pronounced one of the extraordinary daring and brutality. The effect it has had upon the residents in the east of London is extraordinary. All day crowds thronged the streets leading to Mitre-square discussing the crime, and the police in the neighbourhood of the square, under Inspector Izzard and Sergeants Dudman and Phelps and other officers, were fully occupied in keeping back the excited and curious people. The woman, up to the time of writing had not been identified, and the police admit that they have no information which can possibly be termed a clue. SUSPICIOUS INCIDENT. A man named Albert Barker has made the following statement:- I was in the Three Nuns Hotel, Aldgate, on Saturday night when a man got into conversation with me. He asked me questions which now appear to me to have some bearing upon the recent murders. He wanted to know whether I knew what sort of loose women used the public bar at the house, when they usually left the street outside, and where they were in the habit of going. He asked further questions, and from his manner seemed up to no good purpose. He appeared to be a "Shabby Genteel" sort of man, and was dressed in black clothes. He wore a black felt hat, and carried a black bag. We came out together at closing time (twelve o'clock), and I left him

Mike Covell

outside Aldgate Railway Station. LATEST DETAILS. A Press Association reporter, who passed the night near the scene of Saturday night's atrocities in Whitechapel, says one topic seemed to absorb the attention of all, and wherever cabmen, coffee stall keepers, and the whole class and tramps and prostitutes congregated, the dreaded word Whitechapel seemed to exercise a spell. Not only women and children, but men seemed to go in fear of their lives. The policeman only parade their beats with measured tread, but wish an anxiety which betokens a determination to bring the culprit to justice. Hitherto the murderer, assuming that there is but one, confined his operations to the Metropolitan police district, but by pursuing his career near the City he has brought upon his track some 900 additional officers. Both the Metropolitan and the City authorities have greatly augmented the men on duty, and there can be no doubt that the augmentation was absolutely necessary. The force, indeed deserve credit for the sturdiness with which they apply themselves to their terrible task. Since Sunday a remarkable change has come over the attitude of the police, and the information, which was hitherto denied in now cheerfully imparted. It would seem that both Sir Charles Warren and Colonel Fraser are tending to the conviction that publicity is the best detective. Sir Charles Warren has ordered the constables to Commercial-street Station from the A and B Divisions, while Colonel Fraser has drawn men from every available district in the city to the portion of the area nearest Whitechapel which is considered dangerous. A friendly constable, who acted as guide, remarked, "With that man might be the murderer. We can't arrest him." The neighbourhood of Mitre-square, where the mutilated remains of the victim not yet identified were found, is respectable. There is only one house in it, which is tenanted by Constable Pearce. The square has three entrances, the main one being by Mitre-street, and the others by Church-court and Mitre-passage respectively. It was in the south east corner on the right of the entrance from Mitre-street where the body was found by Watkins. STATEMENT BY CONSTABLE WATKINS. He says:- "I passed the spot at half past one, and there was nothing in the corner then. I came round at a quarter to two, and, entering the square from Mitre-street on the right hand side, turned sharp round to the right, and flashing my light, I saw the body in front of me. Her clothes were pushed right up to her breast, and the stomach was laid bare with a dreadful gash up to the breast. The throat had an awful gash from ear to ear, the head nearly being severed from the body. It was difficult to ascertain the injuries to the face owing to the quantity of blood which covered it. I could not say whether one of the ears was cut off. The murderer had inserted the knife under the left eye, and cut the nose completely off, inflicting a frightful gash down the right cheek to the angle of the jawbone. I went and asked for the assistance of the watchman Morris, at Hazeltine, Kearney, and Tonge's, and he went for other officers, while I went for Dr Sequira, or 34, Old Jewry, and Dr Brown, and the body was removed to the mortuary."- The constable adds that it is decidedly probable that the murderer was disturbed by his approach and left his ghastly work unfinished, escaping by the narrow court alluded to. It is also believed that the same hand perpetrated the murder of the other woman in Berner-street, and that mutilation was intended but that in this case, too, he was disturbed in his work. THE POLICE THEORY OF THE CRIMES. The theory favoured by the police is that, being disturbed with his first victim, he left her and induced the second woman to go with him. They imagine he decoys them by means of gold, which after the murder, he abstracted from their pockets. It is also suspected that he wears gloves while performing his ghastly work. THE BERNER-STREET MURDER. THE BODY IDENTIFIED. The body of the woman murdered in Berner-street has been identified as that of Elizabeth Stride, best known as Elizabeth Long, lately living at 32, Flower and Dean-street, Soho. The other woman is so dreadfully mutilated that it is feared she cannot be recognised except by her clothes and the two pawn tickets found lying by her, and the initials D.C., or T.C., in blue ink on her left forearm. She is 5ft high, has light hazel eyes, auburn hair, a dark chintz dress with three flounces, drab Lindsey skirt, very old dark green alpaca petticoat, white chemise, brown ribbed stockings, white straw bonnet trimmed with beads and green and black velvet, large white handkerchief round neck, and a pair of men's lace up boots. THE MAN "WANTED". The description of the man wanted by the police is aged 30, height 5 feet 5 inches, complexion fair, hair dark, full face, small moustache, stout build and broad shoulders.- Two arrests were made about two o'clock this morning, one man being detained at Leman-street, the other at Commercial-street Station, but nothing has yet being discovered to implicate them. IMPORTANT DISCOVERY. The police have also made an important discovery throwing light on which way the murderer made his escape. A portion of an apron was found in Goulston-street, and when the body of the woman found in Mitre-square was examined it was found that she was wearing a portion of the same apron. It was therefore, inferred that the murderer escaped through Whitechapel. A man who passed through Church-lane, Aldgate, at half-past one on Sunday morning, says he saw a man sitting on a doorstep wiping his hands. The man, who is described as wearing a short jacket and sailor's hat, tried to conceal his face. HORRIBLE WIFE MURDER IN LONDON. A pensioner named Brown, employed as a labourer in St. James Park, residing in Regent Gardens, Westminster, murdered his wife about midnight on Saturday, nearly cutting off her head with a knife. The woman had that day applied at the Westminster Police Court for protection, the parties have been living unhappily for some time. Immediately after committing the crime Brown gave himself up to

Mike Covell

> the police, and will be charged with murder. The woman is stated to have been enceinte and Brown's mind is said to have been affected for some time recently, and to have thought his wife was unfaithful.

The Hull Daily News, October 1st 1888,

> TWO MORE WHITECHAPEL MURDERS. WOMEN HORRIBLY BUTCHERED. SHOCKING DISCOVERIES. MURDER IN BERNER-STREET, COMMERCIAL-ROAD. It was sincerely hoped throughout the whole kingdom that the murder and mutilation of the poor wretch Annie Chapman in Hanbury street about three weeks ago would close the ghastly record of mysterious and diabolical atrocities which have been perpetrated on women in the Whitechapel district of London; but this morning we are confronted with a crime which, as far as can be ascertained at present, leaves little doubt as to its having been done by the same assassin or assassins who committed the others. The scene of this, the latest, murder is Berner street, Commercial road, on the St. George's-in-the-East side, and within about 200 yards of Buck's row, or Hanbury street, where the last two murders took place. About five minutes to one o'clock this morning a youth about twenty years of age named Joseph Koster was accosted by a little boy who came running up to him as he was passing on the opposite side of 40 Berner street, used by the International Socialist Club, and told him that a woman was lying in the gateway next to the club, with her throat cut. Koster immediately ran across the road and saw a woman lying on her side in the gateway leading into Dutfield's stabling and van premises. The gate which is a large wooden one, was partly opened, and the woman lying partly in the opening and on the street. He immediately roused the neighbours, and by the aid of a candle it was seen that the woman's throat was cut open very nearly from one ear to the other, and her lips were drawn up as if she had suffered sharp pain. She was dressed in black and appeared to be in mourning. She wore a black bonnet, elastic sided boots, and dark stockings. To her breast was a small bouquet of flowers, and in her left hand she had a small packet of scented cachous. Constable Lamb, 252 East Division, soon afterwards, with the assistance of two other constables had the body, which was quite warm, removed to 40 Berner street, where it was placed in a back room. To all appearances the woman seems to have been taken into the stabling yard, and after having been treated like the former victims, carried out and laid openly in the street. The case, in fact, resembles in many points the Buck's row tragedy. She appears to have been about 26 years of age, and it is not thought that she belonged to the locality in which she was found. The wound must have been inflicted with a very sharp instrument, no trace of which has yet been found, as it

is very deep, and she was lying in a pool of blood with which her clothes were saturated. The news of the tragedy spread with great rapidity, and a large number of detectives from Scotland Yard, together with superintendents and inspectors of police, were soon on the spot. All those who were near the place at the time were detained, taken into the house, and closely examined as to the discovery, but nothing has as yet been obtained which can afford a clue to the murderer and the police have nothing whatever to go on. They seem completely at their wits end, and have taken great precautions up to the present to exclude all representatives of the Press from the house where the body lies. None of the women in the district who have seen her know the murdered woman, and it may be some time before she is identified. She is described as being of a dark complexion and rather slim, and about 4 feet 10 inches in height. Her hair is dark and wavy, with a large fringe in front, and the features somewhat delicate and refined. Dr. Blackhall and his assistant have both examined the corpse, and pronounced that the woman must have been murdered, as she could not have taken her own life. Dr. Phillips, who examined the woman found in Hanbury street, has also been called in, and made an examination of the woman, but he has been ordered to keep the result secret at present. The affair has caused a great sensation throughout London, and the only surmise which can be given at present is that the woman for some reason or another was taken from a respectable district to Whitechapel and there murdered by the author of the former atrocities. A man named Lewis, who, it is said, first made the discovery of the Berner-street murder, resides in Berner-street near the club at No. 40. He travels with some drapery goods, the purchase of which, according to his friends, necessitated his attending Saturday night's late market. He seems to have returned home about a quarter to one, to have proceeded up the entry, which though not narrow, is a very dark one. While proceeding along the wall of No. 40, which is to the north of the entry, he stumbled against something which he presently discovered to be the body of a woman, and at first feared was that of his wife. On entering his door however, he found Mrs Lewis waiting for him, and explaining that a woman was lying outside, he asked a man who was in the house to come outside with him. A match was struck, and the men were horrified to see a great quantity of blood on the ground. The alarm of "murder" was at once given and some neighbours assembled, and lifting the body on one side exposed the wound in the throat. The police were quickly on the spot and took possession of the yard, which was thenceforth closed to the public. The body was, however, suffered to lie where it was found till 4 o'clock. Dr. Blackwell, and subsequently Dr. Simmonds being sent for during the time, and submitting the body to a careful investigation, they discovered, it is understood, no marks of violence except the wound four or five inches long in the throat, and no sign that

Mike Covell

there had been any attempt to further violate the body in the horrible manner which added so much inexplicable horror to the Hanbury street and, as it seems, to one of this morning's murders also. After undergoing preliminary investigation here the body was removed to Cable street mortuary. The house which adjoins the yard on the south side, No. 38, is tenanted by Barnett Kentorrich, who, interrogated as to whether he heard any disturbance during the night, said: I went to bed early, and slept till about three o'clock, during which time I heard no unusual sound of any description. At three o'clock some people were talking loudly outside my door, so I went out to see what was the matter, and learned that a woman had been murdered. I did not stay out long though, and know nothing more about it. I do not think the yard bears a very good character at night, but I do not interfere with any of the people about here. I know that the gate is not kept fastened. The Socialist Club held there is a nasty place. In this view Mrs. Kentorrich, who had come up from the underground kitchen to take part in the colloquy, thoroughly agreed, and both she and her husband, in reply to further questions, corroborated Heshburg's statement as to women and girls being taken to the Club, and as to disorders which sometimes took place there. In order to inquire further into these matters, the reporter next visited the club referred to , a rather low class little building covered with posters, most of them in the Hebrew language. Mrs Lewis, wife of the steward, as she explained, was standing at the door in the centre of a host of people, but she declined to call on her husband, who had been up all night, and had only just gone to bed. Pressed to speak as to the character of the club, Mrs Lewis was inclined to be retired, but a young man in the crowd volunteered an explanation of the institution. "You see," he explained, "the members are bad Jews - Jews who do not heed their religion, and they annoy those who do in order to show contempt for the religion. In the Black Fast a week or two ago, for instance, they had a banquet, and ostentatiously ate and drank, while we might do neither. They hold concerts there till early in the morning, and women and girls are brought there." "Were they here last night?" asked the reporter. "No" said Mrs Lewis, "there was only a concert and discussion on last night." The young fellow who had previously spoken gave some further details at some length on the finding of the body by Lewis, but he could give no further facts that those given in the above statements. The authorities at Leman street Police Station are very reticent, and stated in reply to an inquiry late this evening that they had no further information to report. The Press Association has ascertained from inquiries that the woman murdered in Berner-street has been identified. There appears to be very little doubt as to this as the belief was current in all parts of the neighbourhood., and a woman who is known as "One Armed Liz," living in a common lodging house in Flower and Dean street, stated to a reporter that she had accompanied Sergeant Thicke to St George's mortuary, and had identified the body as that of Annie Stride, an unfortunate, living in a common lodging house in the neighbourhood of Flower and Dean street. "One Armed Liz" refused to give further information, as she said she had been instructed to keep the matter to herself. ANOTHER ACCOUNT. DESCRIPTION OF THE SUPPOSED CULPRIT. The scene of the first of Saturday night's outrages is a narrow court in Berner street E., a quiet thoroughfare, running from Commercial road down to the London, Tilbury, and Southend Railway. At the entrance to the court are a pair of large wooden gates, in one of which is a small wicket for use when the gates are closed. At the hour when the murderer accomplished his purpose these gates were open; indeed, according to the testimony of those living near, the entrance to the court is seldom closed. For a distance of 18 to 20 feet from the street there is a dead wall on each side of the court, the effect of which is to enshroud the intervening space in absolute darkness after sunset. Further back some light is thrown into the court from the windows of a workmen's club, which occupies the whole length of the court on the right, and from a number of cottages occupied mainly by tailors and cigarette makers on the left. At the time when the murder was committed, however, the lights in all of the dwelling houses in question had been extinguished, whilst such illumination as came from the club, being from the upper storey, would fall on the cottages opposite, and would serve only to intensify the gloom of the rest of the court. From the position in which the body was found it is believed that as soon as the murderer had got his victim in the dark shadow near the entrance to the court he threw her to the ground, and with one gash cut her throat from ear to ear. It is thought that the wound was inflicted after and not before the woman fell, as there are sever bruises on her left temple and left cheek, suggesting that she must have been forcibly thrown to the ground. When discovered the body was lying as if the woman has fallen forward, her feet being about a couple of yards from the street, and her head in a gutter which runs down the right hand side of the court, close to the wall. She lay on her left side, face downwards, her position being such that although the court at that part is only nine feet wide, a person walking up the middle might have passed the recumbent body without noticing it. The condition of the corpse, however, and several other circumstances which came to light in the course of yesterday prove pretty conclusively that no considerable period elapsed between the committal of the murder and the discovery of the body. In fact, it is conjectured that the assassin was disturbed while at his ghastly work, and made off before he had completed his designs. All the features of the case connect the tragedy with that which took place three quarters of an hour later a few streets distant. The obvious poverty of the woman, her total lack of jewellery, and the

Mike Covell

soiled condition of her clothing are entirely opposed to the theory that robbery could have been the motive, and the secrecy and despatch with which the crime was effected are equally good evidence that the murder was not the result of an ordinary street brawl. At the club referred to above - the International Workmen's Educational Club - which is an offshoot of the Socialist League, and the rendezvous of a number of foreign residents, chiefly Russians, Poles, and continental Jews of various nationalities, it is customary on Saturday nights to have friendly discussions on topics of mutual interest, and to wind up the evening's entertainment with songs &c. The proceedings commenced on Saturday about 8.30 with a discussion on the necessity of Socialism amongst Jews. This was kept up until about eleven o'clock, when a considerable portion of the company left for their respective homes. Between twenty and thirty remained behind, and the usual concert which followed had not concluded when the intelligence was brought in by the steward of the club that a woman had been murdered within a few yards of them, and within earshot of their jovial songs. The people residing in the cottages on the other side of the court were all indoors, and most of them in bed by midnight. Several of these persons remember lying awake and listening to the singing, and they also remember the concert coming to an abrupt termination; but during the whole of the time from retiring to rest until the body was discovered no one heard anything like a scream or a cry of distress. It was Lewis Diemshitz, the steward of the club, who found the body. Diemshitz, who is a traveller in cheap jewellery, had spent the day at Westow hill Marker, near the Crystal Palace, in pursuance of his avocation, and had driven home at his usual hour, reaching Berner street at one o'clock. On turning into the gateway he had some difficulty with his pony, the animal being apparently determined to avoid the right hand wall. For the moment Diemshitz did not think much of the occurrence, because he knew the pony was given to shying, and he thought perhaps some mud or refuse was in the way. The pony, however, obstinately refused to go straight; so the driver pulled him up to see what was in the way. Failing to distinguish anything in the darkness, Diemshitz poked about with the handle of the whip, and immediately discovered that some large obstacle was in his path. To jump down and strike a match was the work of a second, and then it became apparent that something serious had taken place. Without waiting to see whether the woman whose body he saw was insensible or dead, Diemshitz entered the club by the side door higher up the court, and informed those in the concert room upstairs that something had happened in the yard. A member of the club named Kozebrodski, but familiarly known as Isaacs, returned with Diemshitz into the court, and the former struck a match while the latter lifted the body up. It was at once apparent that the woman was dead. The body was still warm, and the clothes were wet from the recent rain, but the heart had ceased to beat, and the stream of blood on the gutter, terminating in a hideous pool near the club door, showed but too plainly what had happened. Both ran off without delay to find a policeman, and at the same time other members of the club, who had by this found their way into the court, went off with the same object in different directions. The search was for some time fruitless. At last, however, after a considerable delay, a constable, 252 H, was found in Commercial road. With the aid of a policeman's whistle more constables were quickly on the spot, and the gates at the entrance to the court having been closed, and a guard set on all the exits of the club and the cottages, the superintendent of the district and the divisional surgeon were sent for. In a few minutes Dr. Phillips was at the scene of the murder, and a brief examination showed that life had been extinct for some minutes only. Careful note having been taken of the position of the body, it was removed to the parish mortuary of St. George's in the East, Cable street, to await identification. A representative, who has seen the corpse, states that the woman appears to be about 30 years of age. Her hair is very dark, with a tendency to curl, and her complexion is also dark. Her features are sharp and somewhat pinched, as though she had endured considerable privations recently, an impression confirmed by the entire absence of the kind of ornaments commonly affected by women of her station. She wore a rusty black dress of the cheap kind of sateen, with a velveteen bodice, over which was a black diagonal worsted jacket with fur trimming. Her bonnet, which had fallen from her head, was of black crape, and inside, apparently with the object of making the article fir more closely to the head, was folded a copy of an evening newspaper. In her right hand were tightly clasped some grapes, and in her left hand she held a number of sweetmeats. Both the jacket and the bodice were open near the top, but in other respects the clothes were not disarranged. The linen was clean, and in tolerably good repair, but some articles were missing. The cut in the woman's throat, which was the cause of death, was evidently effected with a very sharp instrument, and was made with one rapid movement of the knife, which was apparently drawn across the throat rather obliquely from left to right. In its passage it severed the windpipe, the carotid arteries, and the jugular veins. As the body lies in the mortuary the head seems to be almost severed, the gash being about three inches long and of nearly the same depth. In the pocket of the woman's dress were discovered two handkerchiefs (a gentleman's and a lady's), a brass thimble, and a skein of black darning worsted. In addition to Dr. Phillips, the body was examined both before and after removal to the mortuary by Dr. Kaye and Dr. Blackwell, both of whom reside in the vicinity of Berner street. On the arrival of the superintendent from Leman street police station, which took place almost simultaneously with that of the divisional surgeon, steps

Mike Covell

were immediately taken to ascertain whether the members of the club were in any way connected with the murder. The names and addresses of all the men present were taken, and a rigorous search of persons and premises was instituted, much to the annoyance of the members. The residents in the court had to submit to a similar scrutiny. In neither case, however, was any incriminating evidence discovered. The fact that another murder had been committed soon became known in the neighbourhood, and long before daybreak the usually quiet thoroughfare was the scene of great excitement. Extra police had to be posted right along the street, and even with this precaution locomotion from an early hour was a matter of extreme difficulty. A large crowd followed the body to the mortuary, and here again it was found necessary to take unusual precautions to keep back the crowd. As the news circulated further afield immense numbers of people flocked to Whitechapel, and before noon the neighbourhood of Aldgate and Commercial road was literally invaded by persons curious to see the spots selected for this and the other murders in the series. Several matters have transpired which tend to fix precisely the time at which the unfortunate woman was murdered. Morris Eagle, one of the members of the club, left Berner street about twelve o'clock, and after taking his sweetheart home returned to the club at about twenty minutes to one, with the intention of having supper. He walked up the yard and entered the club by the side entrance, but neither saw nor heard anything to make him suspect foul play was going on. He might have passed the body in the darkness, but the probability is that he would have stumbled over it if the murder had been committed before that time. Joseph Lave - feeling oppressed by the smoke in the large room, went down into the court about twenty minutes before the body was discovered, and walked about in the open air for five minutes or more. He strolled into the street, which was very quiet at the time, and returned to the concert room without having encountered anything unusual. Mr. Wynne Baxter, the coroner of the district, was communicated with as soon as the details were ascertained, and he has fixes the inquest for today at 11 o'clock at the Vestry hall, Cable street. It is believed in police circles that the murderer was disturbed at his work by the arrival of Diemshitz, and that he made off as soon as he heard the cart at the top of the street. The following description has been circulated by the police of a man said to have been seen in the company of deceased during Saturday evening:- "Age 28. Slight. Height 5ft 8in. Complexion dark. No whiskers. Black diagonal coat, hard felt hat, collar and tie. Carried newspaper parcel. Respectable appearance." Charles Letchford, living at 30 Berner street, says:- "I passed through the street at half past 12, and everything seemed to me to be going on as usual, and my sister was standing at the door at ten minutes to one, but did not see anyone pass by. I heard the commotion when the body was found, and heard the policemen's whistles, but did not take any notice of the matter." In an interview with a representative of the Press, Dr. Blackwell made a statement in which he said that about ten minutes past one he was called by a policeman to 40 Berner street, where he found the body of the murdered woman. Her head had been almost severed from her body. The body was perfectly warm, and life could not have been extinct more than 20 minutes. It did not appear to him that the woman was Jewess. She was more like an Irish woman. He roughly examined her, and found no other injuries; but this he could not definitely state until he had made a further examination. The deceased had on a black velvet jacket and a black dress; in her hand she held a box of cachous, whilst pinned in her dress was a flower. Altogether, judging from her appearance, he considered that she belonged to the "unfortunate" class. He had no doubt that the same man committed both murders. In his opinion the man is a maniac, but one at least accustomed to use a heavy knife. His belief was that as the woman held the sweets in her left hand her head was dragged back by means of a silk handkerchief, which she wore round her neck, and that her throat was then cut. One of the woman's hands was smeared with blood, and this was evidently done in the struggle. He had, however, no doubt that the woman's windpipe being completely cut through, she was thus rendered unable to make any sound. Dr. Blackwell added that it did not follow that the murderer would be bespattered with blood, for as he was sufficiently cunning in other things, he could contrive to avoid coming in contact with the blood by reaching well forward. A later telegram says: - The woman murdered in Berner-street has been identified as Elizabeth Stride, who, it seems, had been leading an immoral life, and had resided latterly in Flower and Dean-streets. She was identified by a sister living in Holborn. Her husband, who resides at Bath, has lived apart from her for nearly five years. Up to a late hour last night Stride's murderer had not been discovered. MURDER IN MITRE-SQUARE, ALDGATE. A HORRIBLE SCENE. Great indignation was expressed in all parts of the London last evening at the inability of the police to prevent a recurrence of these outrages. With each fresh murder in the Whitechapel series public alarm has been more accentuated, and unless something can soon be done to restore confidence in the detective powers of the police a panic will be the result. Nothing but the murder is talked of, and the question is being frequently asked, why do not the police resort to more drastic measures? Attention is drawn to the success which attended the use of bloodhounds in connection with the Blackburn murder, and it is seriously suggested that similar methods should be adopted in the East end of London. That both the metropolitan and the city police recognise the gravity of the present crisis is proved by the fact that Major Smith, of the latter force, has had long interviews with Sir Charles Warren at Scotland Yard to-day. Amongst the

Mike Covell

force there is a strong feeling that the old practice of offering Government rewards should be revived, and a large section of the public endorse this view. Since the discontinuance of Government rewards in cases of murder, it is understood that it has been customary to reward the officer or officers making the capture, but it is usually so small that it affords no encouragement to members of the force who do not get any remuneration for working on hours off time. Berner street is within a stone's throw of Hanbury street where the woman Annie Chapman was recently murdered, and adjacent also to Buck's row, where Mary Anne Nichols met her death, and to Osborne street, wherein still another of the unfortunates was shamefully mutilated. It lies to the right of Commercial road going east, and is about eight minutes' walk from Mitre square. Therefore it is seen that the murderer has confined his operations to a radius of about a quarter of a mile. AN EXTRAORDINARY LETTER. The Central News says:- On Thursday week the following letter, bearing the E.C. postmark, and directed in red ink, was delivered to this agency:-

Dear Boss, I keep on hearing the police have caught me but they won't fix me just yet. I have laughed when they look so clever and talk about being on the right track. That joke about Leather Apron gave me real fits. I am down on ------ and I shan't quit ripping them till I do get buckled. Grand work the last job was. I gave the lady no time to squeal. How can they catch me now. I love my work and want to start again. You will soon hear of me with my funny little games. I saved some of the proper red stuff in a ginger beer bottle over the last job to write with but it went thick like glue and I can't use it. Red ink is fit enough I hope ha. ha. The next job I do I shall clip the lady's ears off and send to the police officers just for jolly wouldn't you. Keep this letter back till I do a bit more work, then give it out straight. My knife's so nice and sharp I want to get to work right away if I get a chance. Good Luck. Yours truly, Jack the Ripper

Don't mind me giving the trade name, PS Wasn't good enough to post this before I got all the red ink off my hands curse it No luck yet. They say I'm a doctor now. Ha! Ha!

The whole of this extraordinary epistle is written in red ink, in a free, bold, clerkly hand. It was, of course, treated as the work of practical joker, but it is singular to note that the latest murders have been committed within a few days of the receipt of the letter, and that apparently in the case of his last victim the murderer made an attempt to cut off the ears, and that he actually did mutilate the face in a manner which he has never before attempted. The letter is now in the hands of the Scotland Yard authorities.

Newspapers from Hull Volume 1

The Eastern Morning News, October 1st 1888,

AN ARREST. Shortly before midnight a man, whose name has not yet become known, was arrested in the Borough on suspicion of being the perpetrator of the murders in the East-end yesterday morning. A tall, dark man, wearing an American hat, entered a lodging-house in Union-street, known as Albert Chambers. He stayed there throughout the day, and his peculiar manner riveted the attention of his fellow-lodgers. He displayed great willingness to converse with them, and certain observations he made regarding the topic of the day aroused their suspicions. Last night this mysterious individual attracted the notice of the deputy-keeper of the lodging-house, whose suspicions became so strong that he sent for a policeman. On the arrival of the officer the stranger was questioned as to his recent wanderings, but he could give no intelligible account of them, though he said he had spent the previous night on Blackfriars Bridge. He was conveyed to Stones'-end Police-station, Blackman-street, Borough. A RELEASE. John Fitzgerald, who was arrested at Wandsworth, charged on his own confession with the Whitechapel murder, has been liberated.

October 2nd 1888

October 2nd 1888 The Whitehall Mystery:

Whilst the gaze of London, and the world, was fixed firmly on the East End, the discovery of various pieces of human anatomy which were being discovered across London with one such piece of the puzzle discovered at Whitehall. The location would be the site of the building that would become New Scotland Yard, and it was believed that someone had climbed over the hoardings and dumped the limbless, headless torso in the basement of the building works. The police, however, did not believe the torso to be connected in any way to the murders in Whitechapel but press speculation was rife.

Further reading on the Thames Torso Mystery

The Complete Jack the Ripper A – Z, Paul Begg, Martin Fido, and Keith Skinner, John Blake, 2010

The Thames Torso Murders of Victorian London, R. Michael Gordon, McFarland & Company, 2002

The Thames Torso Murders, M. J. Trow, Wharncliffe Books, 2011

Mike Covell

The Hull Daily Mail, October 2nd 1888,

> THE WHITECHAPEL MURDERS. REWARDS OFFERED. LATEST PARTICULARS. The Public indignation at the inability of the police by their existing methods to bring to justice the murderer or murderers of the six unfortunate women who have been so foully done to death in the East End of London found a practical shape yesterday in the spontaneous offers of substantial rewards by public bodies and private individuals towards the detection of these desperate crimes. A meeting of the Vigilance Committee which has for some time been formed in Whitechapel was held yesterday at Mile End, and a resolution was passed calling upon the Home Office to issue a substantial Government reward for the capture and conviction of the murderer, and a letter embodying this was at once sent to the Home Secretary. One of the murders of Sunday morning took place within the precincts of the City of London, and this fact led one of the Common Councilmen yesterday to give notice that at the next meeting he would move that a reward of £250 should be offered by the Corporation for the detection of the Mitre Square murderer; but the necessity for this step was removed when, later in the day, the Lord Mayor, Mr. Polydore de Keyser, after consulting with Colonel Sir James Fraser, K.C.B, Chief Commissioner of Police of the City of London, announced that a reward of £500 would be given by the Corporation for the detection of the miscreant. The proprietors of the Financial News, a monetary organ, also came forward on behalf of several readers of that journal with a cheque for £300, which was forwarded by their request to the Home Secretary, who was asked to offer that sum for the same purpose in the name of the Government. The proprietors of the Evening Post, which is also chiefly devoted to the interests of the financial world, has commenced a subscription list with a sum of 50 guineas, and has invited other contributions towards a rewards fund. The Vigilance Committee, formed in Whitechapel after the murder of Annie Chapman in Hanbury street, have also raised £300 to stimulate the search for the murderers. Mr. S, Montagu, M.P., it will be remembered offered £100 reward for the detection of the Whitechapel murderer after the Hanbury street crime. The excitement which was created in London on Sunday by the news of the atrocious crimes of Berner Street and Mitre square was doubly intensified yesterday morning, when the daily newspapers carried the startling news into every household, and there was but one subject of conversation everywhere. Thousands of people visited the localities of the crimes, but there was nothing then to see. The police had removed all traces of the murder from the yard in Berner street, where the unfortunate Elizabeth Stride was found with a terrible gash in her throat, while at Mitre square there was nothing which could recall the horrible spectacle

which met the eyes of Constable Watkins at a quarter to two o'clock on Sunday morning. The remains of the disembowelled victim had been removed to the City mortuary, and the pavement had been cleansed. In connection with the latter place, however, a startling discovery was made during the afternoon. Sergeant Dudman had his attention drawn to, 36, Mitre street, a house a short distance from the spot where the murdered woman was found and there he found what appeared to be bloodstains upon the doorway and underneath the window, as if a person had wiped his fingers on the window ledge and drawn a blood stained knife down part of the doorway. Mr. Hurtig, who lives on the premises, said he had only just before noticed the stains, and then quite by accident. Almost immediately afterwards the same police officer had his attention drawn to similar marks on the plate glass window of Mr. William Smith, at the corner of Mitre square, but Mr. Smith scouted the idea that they could have anything to do with the murders, as the windows were covered at night by shutters. The discovery, notwithstanding, caused increased excitement for a time in the locality. The only other trace left by the murderer was the portion of an apron picked up in Goulston street, which corresponded with a piece left on the body of the victim. THE MAN WITH THE SHINY BAG. The young man Albert Bachert, of 13, Newnham street, Whitechapel, made a further statement this morning to a representative of the press. It will be noticed that the man who spoke to him in the Three Nuns Hotel on Saturday night carried a black shiny bag, and it is remarkable that the only man, Mrs. Mortimer observed in Berner street nearly two hours afterwards also carried a black shiny bag. Mrs. Mortimer said:- "The only man whom I had seen pass through the street previously was a young man who carried a black shiny bag, who walked very fast down the street from Commercial road. He looked at the club, and then went round the corner by the Board School,"- Albert Bachert says: "On Saturday night at about seven minutes to twelve I entered the Three Nuns Hotel, Aldgate. While in there an elderly woman, very shabbily dressed, came in and asked me to buy some matches. I refused, and she went out. A man who had been standing by me remarked that those persons are a nuisance, to which I responded, "Yes." He then asked me to have a glass with him, but I refused, as I had just called for one myself. He then asked me if I knew how old some of the women were who were in the habit of soliciting outside. I replied that I knew or thought that some of them who looked about 25 were over 35, the reason they looked young being on account of the powder and paint. He asked if I could tell him where they usually went with men, and I replied that some went to places in Oxford street, Whitechapel, others to some houses in Whitechapel road, and others to Bishopsgate street. He then asked whether I thought they would go with him down Northumberland Alley- A dark and lonely court in Fenchurch Street. I said

Mike Covell

I did not know, but supposed they would. He then went outside and spoke to the woman who was selling the matches, and gave her something I believe. He returned to me, and I bid him good night at about ten minutes past twelve. I believe the woman was waiting for him. I do not think I could identify the woman, as I did not take particular notice of her, but I should know the man again. He was a dark man, about 38 years of age; height about 5ft, 6in, or 7in. He wore a black felt hat, dark clothes (morning clothes), black tie, and carried a black shiny bag." A STRANGE DISCOVERY. It was ascertained last evening that a singular discovery, which was supposed to afford an important clue to the murderer was being investigated by the police at Kentish Town. It appears that at about nine o'clock yesterday morning the proprietor of the Nelson Tavern, Victoria road, Kentish Town, entered the outhouse adjoining the premises for the purpose of pointing out to a builder some alterations he desired executed, when a paper parcel was noticed behind the door. No particular importance was attached to the discovery until an hour later, when Mr. Chinn, the publican, while reading the newspaper, was struck by the similarity of this bundle to the one of which the police have issued a description as having been seen in the possession of the man last seen in company of the woman Stride. The police at the Kentish Town road Police station were acquainted with the discovery, and a detective officer was at once sent out to prosecute enquiries. It was then discovered that the parcel had not been picked up, but had been kicked into the roadway, where the paper burst, and revealed a pair of dark trousers. The description of the man wanted for the murders gives the colour of the trousers he wore to be dark. The fragments of paper were collected and found to be stained with blood, and it is stated that some hair was found also among some congealed blood attached to the paper. It was subsequently ascertained from some lads who had been dragging the trousers through the Castle road that a poor man picked up the article of clothing and carried it off. The detectives are investigating the strange discovery. MEETING OF THE DISTRICT BOARD OF WORKS. A meeting of the Whitechapel District Board of Works was held last evening, Mr. Robert Gladding presiding.- Mr. Cotmur said he thought that the Board as the local authority, should express their horror and abhorrence at the crimes which had been perpetrated in the district. The result of these tragedies had been loss of trade to the district, and the stoppage of certain trades by reason of woman being afraid to pass through the streets without an escort. The inefficiency of the police was shown by the fact that an hour or two later than the tragedies in Berner street and Mitre square the post office in the vicinity had been broken into and much property stolen. The Rev. Daniel Greatorex said emigrants "houses of call" were feeding the panic to such an extent as emigrants refused to locate themselves in Whitechapel, even temporarily. He ascribed the inefficiency of the police to the frequent changes of the police from one district to another, whereby the men kept ignorant of their beats.- Mr. Teller said he hoped that these recent crimes might result in reversion to the old system by which constables were acquainted with every corner of their beats.- Mr. G. T. Brown suggested that the government should be communicated with rather than the Home Secretary or the Chief Commissioner of Police, who were themselves really only on their trial. ANOTHER MYSTERIOUS COMMUNICATION. The Central News says:- A postcard, bearing the stamp "London E., October 1" was received on Monday morning, addressed to the Central News office; the address and subject matter being written in red; and undoubtedly by the same person from whom the sensational letter already published was received on Thursday week. Like the previous missive, this also has reference to the horrible tragedies in East London, forming, indeed, a sequel to the same letter. It runs as follows:- I was not codding, dear old boss, when I gave you the tip. You'll hear about Saucy Jacky's work tomorrow. Double event this time. Number one squealed a bit; couldn't finish straight off. Had not time to get ears for police. Thanks for keeping last letter back till I got to work again. Jack the Ripper. The card is smeared on both sides with blood, which has evidently been impressed thereon by the thumb or finger of the writer, the corrugated surface of the skin being plainly shown upon the back of the card. Some words are nearly obliterated by a bloody smear. It is not necessarily assumed that this has been the work of the murderer, the idea that naturally occurs being that the whole thing is a practical joke. At the same time the writing of the previous letter immediately before the commission of the murders on Sunday was so singular a coincidence that it does not seem unreasonable to suppose that the cool calculating villain who is responsible for the crimes has chosen to make the post a medium through which to convey to the press his grimly diabolical humour. A REPORTED ARREST. The Dublin Evening Mail's London correspondent telegraphs that among the persons arrested on suspicion of being concerned in the murders, is a reporter who imagined that he might confront the murderer if he walked about at night dressed as a woman. He donned female attire and shaved. The experiment, however, failed, for his eccentric appearance caused his sex to be discovered, and he was arrested. LIST OF THE EAST END MURDERS. Six woman have now been murdered in the East End under mysterious circumstances, five of them within a period of eight weeks. The following are the dates of the crimes and names of the victims so far, as known:-

1, Last Christmas week,- an unknown woman found murdered near Osborne and Wentworth Streets, Whitechapel.

Mike Covell

> 2, August 7th,- Martha Turner found stabbed in thirty nine places on a landing in model dwellings known as George Yard Buildings, Commercial Street, Spitalfields.
>
> 3, August 31st,- Mrs Nicholls, murdered and mutilated in Bucks Row, Whitechapel.
>
> 4, September 7th,- Mrs Chapman, murdered and mutilated, Hanbury Street, Whitechapel.
>
> 5, September 30th,- Elizabeth Stride, found with throat cut in Berner Street, Whitechapel.
>
> 6, September 30th,- Woman unknown, murdered and mutilated in Mitre Square, Aldgate.
>
> A SINGULAR THEORY. The Times' Vienna correspondent, in referring to the Whitechapel murders, recalls the case of the Jew named Riller, who was accused in 1884 of having murdered and mutilated a Christian woman near Cracow. He was undoubtedly innocent, but was three times condemned, and the Court of Appeal eventually quashed the sentence. It was proved that among certain fanatical Jews there existed a superstition that if a Jew became intimate with a Christian woman, he would atone for his offence by killing and mutilating the object of his passion. Passages from the Talmud were quoted in support of the view.

The Hull Daily Mail, October 2nd 1888,

> THE WHITECHAPEL TRAGEDIES. LATEST PARTICULARS. ACTION OF THE POLICE. MEDICAL THEORIES. The Central News says: - The popular excitement in the East End of London was very great yesterday. From time to time it was raised to fever-heat by reports of arrests and the finding of weapons, which on investigation proved to be untrue. The scenes of the murders were thronged from morning till night by crowds of morbid sightseers, whose demeanor was, as a rule, by no means reverent, and whose behaviour taxed to the utmost the good humoured forbearance of the police placed on special duty in Berner's-street and Mitre-square. The police, both Metropolitan and City, were extremely active all day, and both forces, to some extent, worked together – a procedure so obviously desirable that the wonder is it has not been followed previously. The full force of the City Detective Department have been set in

motion, and, as far as the task goes of following up suggestions, or carrying out instructions, the detectives were equal to their duties. It is, however, scarcely to be wondered at that the first day's work resulted in nothing that can be construed into what may be termed a promising clue. The murderer left nothing behind him save the ghastly evidence of his crimes, and it seems certain that he managed to reach his abode unobserved and unsuspected. The only trace of his movements after committing the murder in Mitre-square was that afforded by the discovery of a piece of apron as mentioned yesterday. A theory which finds favour in the highest quarter is to the effect that the murderer has two domiciles – one to which he can retreat without attracting the notice of other persons in the house (if others there be), and there removing traces of his crime; the other his ordinary lodgings, which with these precautions, he could enter at any time without danger of attracting attention. It is considered probable that valuable evidence would be forthcoming if the police would prepare and distribute widely a circular to householders asking for confidential information respecting the position, habits, and movements of their lodgers. The desired information would be, it is believed, given without hesitation in the majority of cases, and where no replies were forthcoming the police themselves could ascertain the reason. Information of this character would be greatly stimulated by a substantial reward, or it could be obtained in other ways by the members of vigilance committees. The authorities are stated to have under consideration the practicability of shortening the time of the patrol beats, which in the Metropolitan district are much too long for effective police duty. If the beats are to be shortened the number of policemen must be considerably increased, or Special Constables sworn in. In view of the probability of further murders also it may be thought worthwhile to borrow or buy a couple of bloodhounds, and keep them stationed in different parts of the city. The Central News understands that the result of inquiries made by the detectives yesterday is the establishment of the fact that two murders were committed on Sunday morning by one man. The evidence at the inquiry into the death of the Berners-street victim proves conclusively that the murder was committed between a quarter to one and one o'clock. The murderer, therefore, would have had ample time to walk as far as Mitre-square, Aldgate, and here, again the evidence is clear that the crime was committed between half-past one and a quarter to two. The identification of the Berners-street victim as Elizabeth Stride is practically complete, but it is feared that more difficulty will be experienced in ascertaining the identity of the woman murdered in Mitre-square. The face is badly mutilated, and it wears an unnatural appearance. The inquest on this woman has, in consequence of the lack of identification, been deferred until Thursday next. The Central News says:- A post-card bearing the stamp "London E., October 1," was received on

Mike Covell

Tuesday morning, addressed to the Central News Office; the address and subject matter being written in red and undoubtedly by the same person from whom the sensational letter, given above, was received. It runs as follows:- I was not codding, dear old boss, when I gave you the tip. You'll hear about Saucy Jack's work tomorrow. Double event this time. Number one squealed a bit; couldn't finish straight off. Had not time to get ears for police. Thanks for keeping last letter back till I got to work again. JACK THE RIPPER. The card is smeared on both sides with blood, which has evidently been impressed thereon by the thumb or finger of the writer, the corrugated surface of the skin being plainly shown upon the back of the card. Some words are nearly obliterated by a bloody smear. It is not necessarily assumed that this has been the work of the murderer, the idea that naturally occurs being that the whole thing is a practical joke. At the same time the writing of the previous letter immediately before the commission of the murders of Sunday was so singular a coincidence that it does not seem unreasonable to suppose that the cool, calculating villain who is responsible for the crimes has chosen to make the post a medium through which to convey to the press his grimly diabolical humour. The feeling of indignation against the Home Secretary for not offering a reward has immensely increased since the discovery of the last two murders. The following letter has been forwarded to the Home Office: - "The Financial News, London, October 1st 1888, The Right Hon. Henry Matthews, Q.C., M.P., Secretary of State for the Home Department, "Sir, - In view of your refusal to offer a reward out of Government funds for the discovery of the perpetrator or perpetrators of the recent murders in the East-end of London, I am instructed on behalf of several readers of the Financial News, whose names and addresses I enclose, to forward you the accompanying cheque for £300, and to request you to offer that sum for this purpose in the name of the Government. "Awaiting the favour of your reply, - I have the honour to be your obedient servant; "HARRY H. MARKS. In response to this letter, the Home Secretary has caused the following to be written: - "1st October 1888. "My dear Sir, - I am directed by Mr. Matthews to acknowledge the receipt of your letter of this date containing a cheque for £300, which you say has been contributed on behalf of several readers of the Financial News, and which you are desirous should be offered as a reward for the discovery of the recent murders in the East-end of London. "If Mr. Matthews had been of opinion that the offer of a reward in these cases would have been attended by any useful result he would himself have at once made such an offer, but he is not of that opinion. "Under these circumstances, I am directed to return you the cheque (which I enclose), and to thank you, and the gentlemen whose names you have forwarded, for the liberality of their offer, which Mr. Matthews much regrets he is unable to accept. "I am, Sir, your obedient servant, "E. LEIGH

PEMBERTON." Mr. Phillips, a member of the City Corporation, representing the ward of Aldgate, has given notice of his intention to move at the next council meeting that the Corporation do offer a reward of £250 for the detection of the murderer of the woman found in Mitre-square, which is within the City precincts. This has, however, been anticipated by the Lord Mayor, who has, on behalf of the Corporation, issued an offer of £500 reward for the apprehension of the criminal. The announcement of this offer caused general satisfaction. Newspapers and private individuals and associations have already offered 3700, so that the total sum at the disposal of anyone who shall give information leading to the arrest of the murderer is now £2,000, as an effort will be made to induce the Lord Mayor to open a Mansion House fund, and there is a disposition on the Stock Exchange to take the matter up. The Central News says: - The following is a copy of bills about to be issued by the City Police offering a reward in connection with the Mitre-square murder. "MURDER! £500 REWARD. "Whereas, at 1:45 a.m. on Sunday, the 30th of September last, a woman, name unknown, was found brutally murdered in Mitre-square, Aldgate, in this City, a reward of £500 will be paid by the Commissioner of Police of the City of London to any person (other than a person belonging to a police force in the United Kingdom), who shall give such information as shall lead to the discovery and conviction of the murderer or murderers. "Information to be given to the Inspector of the Detective Department, 26, Old Jewry, or at any police-station. "JAMES FRASER. Colonel, Commissioner. "City of London Police Office, 26, Old Jewry, October 1, 1888." The Central News says: - All the men taken into custody on suspicion have been released, and no further arrests have been made. Yesterday a representative of the Central News interviewed two eminent London physicians for the purpose of ascertaining whether they could throw any scientific light on the East-end murders. Sir James Risdon Bennett, of Cavendish-square, West, in the course of a conversation with the reporter, said: - "I have no desire to promulgate any theory in reference to these murders. My purpose in writing to the Times the other day was simply to demonstrate the absurdity of the theory that the crimes were being committed for the purpose of supplying an American physiologist with uteri. I cannot believe for a moment that any commission has been given out for the collection of uteri. It would be extremely easy here or in America for a physiologist to secure this portion of the intestines. All he would have to do would be to apply to the public hospitals, where there are always many paupers or unclaimed persons, who are made the subjects of experiment, and his demands would be easily met. Supposing, for instance, that a specialist proposed to lecture in the theatre of his institution upon the uterus, he would communicate with the surgeon, who would have no difficulty in providing him with a sufficient number of specimens for all his

Mike Covell

purposes. The notion that the uteri were wanted in order that they might be sent out along with copies of a medical publication is ridiculous, not only ridiculous indeed, but absolutely impossible of realisation. I attach no importance whatever to that. If one sane man had instructed another sane man to procure a number of specimens of the uterus, the modus operandi would have been very different from that which has been pursued in these cases. The murderer has run a fearful and quiet unnecessary risk. The mutilations, he continued, were to a great extent wanton, and did not assist him in the accomplishment of intention. My impression is that the miscreant is a homicidal maniac. He has a specific delusion, and that delusion is erotic. Of course, we have at those moment very little evidence indeed; in fact, I may say no evidence at all as to the state of the man's mind, except so far as it is suggested by the character of the injuries which he has inflicted upon his victims. I repeat that my impression is that he is suffering under an erotic delusion, but it may be that he is a religious fanatic. It is possible that he is labouring under the delusion that he has a mandate from the Almighty to purge the world of prostitutes, and in the prosecution of his mad theory he has determined upon a crusade against the unfortunates of London, whom he seeks to mutilate by deprivation of the uterus. There are, on the other hand, a number of theories which might be speculated upon as to the particular form that his mania takes, but inasmuch as we have no knowledge of the man himself, but only of the commission of his crimes wherewith to guide us, I came to the conclusion that his decision has reference to the matters of a sexual character. The two crimes which were perpetrated yesterday morning do not lead me to modify my opinion that the assassin is a lunatic. Even if it should transpire that in the case of the Mitre-square victim the uterus is missing, I should not be disposed to favour what I may call the American theory in the slightest degree, and I must confess that it was with considerable surprise that I noticed in certain newspapers a disposition so readily to accept the theory which the Coroner who investigated the circumstances attending the murder of the woman Chapman first suggested. It is my opinion that if any person wanted a number of specimens of the uterus and was himself a man possessed of surgical skill he would himself undertake to acquire them rather than employ an agent. No love of gain could possibly induce a sane man to commit such atrocities as these, and, besides this, there is the circumstance remaining as I have previously said, that they might all be secured at the Medical Institutes either of England or America - that is to say, if they were needed for legitimate purposes - practically without any consideration at all. It has been said, and it is a very natural observation, that if the murderer were a lunatic he could not commit these crimes and escape with impunity. That is a comment which any person not fully acquainted with the peculiarities of lunatic subjects might very well make. In my view, however, the extraordinary cunning which is evinced by the homicide is a convincing proof of his insanity. No sane man could have escaped in just the same fashion as this man seems to have done. He must almost necessarily have betrayed himself. It is a matter of common knowledge, however, amongst "mad doctors" that lunatics display a wonderful intelligence, if it may be called so, in their criminal operations, and I have little doubt that if the murderer were other than a madman he would ere this have been captured by the police. In many instances a madman's delusion is directed to only one subject, and he is mad upon that subject alone. I doubt, however, that the murderer of these women is other than a man suffering from acute mania, and, that being so, his infirmity would be obvious to almost every person with whom he came into contact; that is to say, if he were in the presence of either of us we should probably say, "Oh, he's a madman." There are many instances in which the common test is for the doctor to enter into conversation with the suspect, to touch upon a variety of topics, and then as if by accident to mention the matters in regard to which the patient has a special delusion, Then, the person's madness is manifested, although upon every other point he converses rationally. But here the disease is mental, and I should say that the persons with whom he comes into daily contact cannot regard him as a sane person. Dr. Phillip has stated that the injuries inflicted upon these women have been apparently performed by a person possessing some anatomical knowledge. That is likely enough, but would not a butcher be quite capable of treating the body in this way? Since I wrote my letter to the Times I have received several communications in support of my view. One of these comes from the Bishop of Hertford, who agrees me that the theory of the American physiologist has no claims to credit. I wish to have it understood that my only desire is to remove from the public mind the false impression that has been made by the suggestion that a member of the medical profession is more or less responsible for these murders. I have never believed in that theory, and these two last murders confirm me in the opinion that they are the work of a man suffering from acute mania, to whom the ordinary rules of manner and procedure do not apply. Dr. Forbes Winslow, the eminent specialist in lunacy cases, said to our representative: I am more certain than ever that these murders are committed by a homicidal maniac, and there is no moral doubt in my mind that the assassin in each case is the same man. I have carefully read the reports in the morning papers, and they confirm me in the opinion that I had previously formed, while I am clearly of opinion that the murderer is a homicidal lunatic. I also believe him to be a monomaniac; and I see no reason why he should not - excepting at the periods when the fit is upon him - exhibit a cool and rational exterior. I have here in my book - a work on physiology - a case, in which a man had a lust for blood as in this case; and he was generally a person of bland and

Mike Covell

pleasant exterior. In all probability the whole of the murders have been committed by the same hand, but I may point out that the imitative faculty is very strong in persons of unsound mind, and that is the reason why there has been a sort of epidemic of knives. We shall probably find that a good many knives will be displayed to people within the next few weeks. Still, all the evidence that is forthcoming up to the present moment show clearly enough that the Whitechapel crimes have been perpetrated by the same hand. My idea is that, under the circumstances, the police ought to employ for the protection of the neighbourhood, and with a view of detecting the criminal, a number of officers who have been in the habit of guarding lunatics - that is to say, warders from asylums, and other persons who had charge of the insane. These men, if properly disposed in the neighbourhood, would assuredly note any person of unsound mind. I have sent a letter embodying this suggestion to Sir Charles warren, but I have received only a formal communication acknowledging its receipt. It is not easy to prevail upon the police to accept a suggestion from outside sources. This discovered the other day when a man, in imitation of the Whitechapel murderer, drew a knife and sharpened it in the presence of a relative of mine at Brighton in circumstances which have been published in the newspapers. When I made a statement to the police on that occasion they thought very little of it indeed. I attach not the least importance to the American physiologist story. It is a theory which is utterly untenable, and I should think there were very few medical men who ever entertained it seriously. All that has recently happened appears to me to be strong confirmation of the views which I have previously given upon this subject - that the murderer is a homicidal monomaniac of infinite cunning, and I fear he will not be brought to justice unless he be caught while engaged in the commission of one of his awful crimes. THE INQUEST. Mr. Wynne Baxter opened the inquest on the body of the woman Elizabeth Stride, who was found with her throat cut in Berners-street on Sunday morning, at the Vestry Hall, Cable-street, yesterday morning. William West, of 2 William-street, said he was at the International Working Men's Club on Sunday night, and stated that the wooden gates were not closed until late at night. As a rule witness worked at the printing office during the evening, and went into the Club afterwards where he remained until twenty minutes past twelve. He then went into the yard, and noticed that the gates were open. He did not notice any body lying there but it might have been there without his observing it. There was no lamp in the yard. He then went into the club again, and called his brother and Louis Selso, and they left together by the front door. On only one occasion, about twelve months ago, had he noticed a man and woman in the yard, and they walked away when he went towards them. Maurice Eagle, 4 New-road, Commercial-road, stated that he left the club about 11.30 and returned about

12.40. *He went in through the yard as the front door was closed, but did not notice anything in the yard. He was certain he should have noticed a man and woman if they had been there. He was in the habit of going through the yard occasionally but had never seen any men and women there. He remained in the club about twenty minutes. A man named Gigleman came upstairs and said there was a dead woman lying in the yard. He went down and struck a match, and saw a woman lying in a pool of blood on the ground near the gateway. He did not touch the body and went down towards Commercial road for the police. He found two constables and informed them of the murder, and they returned with him to the yard, where a number of people had assembled. One of the policemen sent him to the station for the inspector. He could not say if the woman's clothes were disturbed. He thought the people in the Club would have heard a cry of murder. Lewis Diemschitz, steward of the International Working Men's Educational Club, was the next witness. He stated that he left the Club about half past eleven on Saturday morning, and returned exactly at one o'clock on Sunday morning. He had a costermonger's barrow and pony, and drove into the yard. Both gates were wide open. It was very dark. His pony shied, and he looked down to the ground and saw something lying there, but he could not see what it was. He jumped down and struck a match, but the night being windy he could only see it was some person lying there. He went into the Club and in the front room he found several members, and told them a woman was lying in the yard. He got a candle, and went out at once and discovered a quantity of blood around the body. He did not touch the body, but at once went for the police. He passed several streets without seeing a policeman and returned without one. A man named Isaacs was with him, and they were both shouting for the police. Another man returned with them into the yard, and took hold of the woman's head. Witness then first saw a wound in the throat. The doctor arrived about ten minutes after the constables. The police searched everywhere, and searched and took the names and addresses of those present. The deceased's clothes were in order. She was lying on her side and with her face towards the wall. The doctor put his hand on her bosom and said she was still quite warm. Witness estimated that about two quarts of blood were round the body. He had never seen men and women in the yard. The inquiry was then adjourned until two o'clock to-day.*
LONDON PRESS COMMENTS. Commenting on the Whitechapel murders, St. James Gazette says: - "What may be called only precautions, the frequency of patrolling and the closeness of the watch, have been taken already, but they have manifestly not been taken effectually enough, and more are wanted. When the murderers of Lord F. Cavendish and Mr Burke were being hunted down, Marines in plain clothes were freely employed to drive them into a corner. The same measures might be taken again. The offer of a reward seems to us

Mike Covell

> *decidedly a step which ought to be taken. We have never thought the reasons given for ceasing to work on the cupidity of the associates of criminals were sufficient." The Pall Mall Gazette says: - "The only practical thing to be done is to keep a sharp look out, and to dismiss once for all the coroner's theory as to the motive of murder." The Globe says: - "We have no doubt the police will do all they can to track and seize the criminal, but it has often been noted that the duties imposed upon the police takes them from their proper business, and that new duties of a really objectionable nature have recently been invented. What, however, the public demands, and mist have, is such a thorough and astute inquiry into these shameful atrocities as shall lead to the arrest and punishment of this superlative delinquent. If it cannot be done by the police it must be done by the people.*

The Hull Daily News, October 2nd 1888,

> *THE MURDER NEAR GATESHEAD. THE ARREST OF WADDLE. Yesterday information was received at the Durham County Police Station at Gateshead to the effect that the man William Waddle, wanted on suspicion in connection with the murder of Jane Beetmore, or Savage, at Birtley Fell near Gateshead, had been apprehended at Yetholm, Roxburghshire, a village largely occupied by border gypsies, and situated about seven miles south-east of the town of Kelso. It had been known for several days past that a man answering the description of Waddle had been seen tramping through the northern parts of Northumberland towards Scotland, and for some few days Superintendent Harrison has had six of his Durham constables stationed in the neighbourhood of Belford, Berwick, and Coldstream acting in concert with the local police in their search for Waddle, who has, it appears, begged his way to the boarder country, asking people for money to assist him on his journey in quest of work, stating that he wanted harvesting as he had been accustomed to farm work. Just previous to the receipt of the telegram Supt. Harrison had prepared and got printed a handbill or placard to be sent to all police stations throughout the country describing Waddle's dress and appearance. Waddle, it is stated, called at a second hand clothes shop in Berwick, on Thursday, and intimated that he wished to change his grey suit for an older one. He was accommodated with other garments, and Superintendent Harrison yesterday received the clothes which it is alleged Waddle wore on the night of the murder. He told the woman at the clothes shop that he was hard up, and had decided to exchange his good suit for a worse one and some money to boot. A bargain was struck and Waddle received an old grey jacket and vest, a pair of fustian trousers, and a peak cap, together with 5s, in place of his grey suit and felt hat. The grey suit had some suspicious marks*

about it, and it will be sent to an analytical chemist for thorough examination. There appears little doubt of the identity of the prisoner with the man wanted for the crime. When apprehended he was going out from Yetholm towards the hill to the south-east. The apprehension was affected by Mr. Stenhouse, wool dealer, Yetholm, who, noticing that the man's appearance corresponded with the published descriptions got into conversation with him. Waddle said he was in search of harvest work. Mr. Stenhouse asked him to go with him, as he might find him a job, and the man assented with apparent [illegible]. Mr. Stenholm succeeded in taking him to Yetholm Police station without resistance. In reply to questions by Mr. Stenhouse the prisoner admitted having recently been at Berwick. He further admitted that his name was Waddle or Twaddle, that he had been at Birtley, and that the woman Savage was his wife. Yesterday afternoon Superintendent Harrison started on a journey from Gateshead to Yetholm, and it is expected that the prisoner will be taken to Gateshead today. It is known that the police have evidence which proves on oath that Waddle was in the deceased woman's company on the night of the tragedy. All around the Birtley district the conviction that he was the assassin is very strong.

The Hull Daily Mail, October 2nd 1888,

THE BIRTLEY MURDER. THE ACCUSED BEFORE THE MAGISTRATES. Wm. Waddle, who was arrested at Yetholm on suspicion of being the murderer of the young woman, Jane Beetmore, at Birtley, near Gateshead, was brought up at Newcastle this morning, and after some formal evidence was remanded. He appeared dazed and dejected.

The Hull Daily Mail, October 2nd 1888,

THE LONDON MURDERS. CONTINUED EXCITEMENT. No further arrests have been made in connection with the two last Whitechapel murders, and the exhaustive inquiries made last night in the neighbourhood of Bow and Stratford failed to elicit any trustworthy information respecting the movements of the unhappy woman "Long Liz." So far as at present known, she was last seen at the lodging house at Flower and Dean Street, about seven o'clock on Saturday evening. The remains of the other woman murdered in Mitre Court still await identification at the Golden Lane mortuary. It is believed, however, today her identity will be established, and if her name can be ascertained it may be more easy to obtain a description of the man who may have been her company. Early this morning there was a rumour that the cries of "Murder" and "Police" in a woman's voice had been distinctly heard in the neighbourhood of the club in

Mike Covell

Berner Street; but this is positively contradicted by the police on duty. Evan last night the rush of spectators to Mitre Square to view the spot was so great that extra police were employed to regulate traffic.

The two men detained at Leman Street this morning have been discharged, and now no one remains in custody. A strong reinforcement of detectives from Scotland Yard and Lambeth arrived in Whitechapel this morning. They are being appointed to various suspected districts, to watch various suspected houses and individuals. TWO ARRESTS TODAY. Two arrests were made this morning on suspicion and the men taken to Leman Street Police Station, but the evidence against them is slight. SUPPOSED NARROW ESCAPE OF THE MURDERER. The police believe that, after murdering the woman Stride, the murderer narrowly escaped being caught. They are of opinion that he was in the yard when Mr Diemschitz drove into it, and that he mingled with the crowd that rushed out of the club, and ultimately made his escape before the police arrived. THE REWARDS. SATISFACTION IN LONDON. The Press Association says general satisfaction is expressed on all hands in the City this morning at the offer of a reward of £500 by the police. The placards announcing the reward are posted in all the prominent positions, and are eagerly read by all the crowd. THE MITRE SQUARE MURDER. Some information has come to light in regard to the Mitre Square murder to which the police attach some importance. Two city constables who saw the body at once recognised it as that of the woman they had in custody some time ago on a charge of drunkenness. This woman, when charged, lived at a lodging house in the neighbourhood of Fashion Street, Whitechapel, and the police are accordingly making inquiries in the district. From all parts of the Metropolis the police are in receipt of descriptions of suspected persons, and inquiries from people who have lost relations and friends. A description has been issued by the police of a man said to have been seen in the company of Stride on Saturday night. He is described as of 28 years of age, about 5ft 7in high, and dark complexioned. He had no whiskers, and wore dark clothes and a black felt hat, which was stained. THE ADJOURNED INQUEST. The inquest on the body of the woman known as Elizabeth Stride was resumed at the Vestry Hall, Cable Street, Whitechapel, this afternoon,- Henry Lamb, a constable, deposed to being called to the scene of the murder by the two men from the workingmen's club. There were about 30 people in the yard, but no one was touching the body. He placed his hand on her face and arm and he found they were quite warm. He then sent for assistance. Dr Blackwell arrived 10 minutes afterwards. Witness examined all the hands of all the persons present, and stationed a constable at the yard gate. It was possible that someone might have escaped from the yard after he entered it. He had passed the street about six or seven minutes before he was called, but he did not see anyone from the yard.- Edward Spooner, horse keeper, said he was standing outside the Beehive public house, about half past twelve when he saw two Jews running for the police. They said that a woman had been murdered. Witness went back with them, and he saw a woman lying inside the yard, with about fifteen people, mostly Jews, standing around. Someone struck a match, and witness lifted the chin and saw blood was still throwing from the throat. There was a piece of paper doubled up in the right hand. He stood beside the body for five minutes before the constable came. He did not see if anyone left the yard. He entered the yard about 25 minutes to one o'clock. Witness was searched afterwards, and then left the club. THE CHARGE OF THREATENING TO STAB At the Thames Police Court this morning, Charles Ludwig was again brought up on a charge of threatening to stab Elizabeth Burns, an unfortunate, 55, Flower and Dean Street, Spitalfields, and threatening to stab a coffee stall keeper. The woman said she accompanied him up Butchers Row a fortnight ago, and that when they reached a gateway, Ludwig pulled out a long bladed knife. She screamed, and the police came up. Ludwig walked off but from her statement he was afterwards arrested. The coffee stall keeper said the prisoner came to him the following morning and threatened to stab him. The accused, who seemed of an excitable disposition, was discharged. LETTER FROM THE HOME SECRETARY The following letter was received last evening by the editor of the Financial News:- "Oct 1, 1888, "My dear sir,- I am directed by Mr Matthews to acknowledge the receipt of your letter of this date containing a cheque for £300, which you say has been contributed on behalf of several readers of the Financial News, and which you are desirous should be offered as a reward for the discovery of the recent murders in the East End of London. If Mr Matthews had been of the opinion that the offer of a reward in these cases would have been attended by any useful result, he would himself have at once made such an offer, but he is not of that opinion. Under these circumstances I am directed to return your cheques (which I enclose), and to thank you and the gentlemen whose names you have forwarded, for the liberality of their offer, which Mr Matthews much regrets he is unable to accept,- I am sir, your very obedient servant,

"E. Leigh Pemberton, "Harry H, Marks, Esq." DR. WINSLOW'S OPINION. Dr Forbes Winslow, the eminent specialist in lunacy cases, states:- "I am more certain than ever that these murders are committed by a homicidal maniac, and there is no moral doubt in my mind that the assassin in each case is the same man. I have carefully read the reports in the morning papers, and they confirm me in the opinion which I had previously formed. While I am clearly of the opinion that the murderer is an homicidal lunatic, I also believe him to be a

monomaniac, and I see no reason why he should not, excepting at periods when he the fit is upon him, exhibit a cool and rational exterior. I have here in my book- a work on Psychology- a case in which a man had a lust for blood as of in this case, and he was generally a person of bland and pleasant exterior. In all probability the whole of the murders have been committed by the same hand, but I may point out that the imitative faculty is very strong in persons of unsound mind, and that is the reason why there has been a sort of epidemic of knives. We shall probably find that a good many knives will be displayed to people within the next few weeks. Still all the evidence that is forthcoming up to the present moment shows clearly enough that the Whitechapel crimes have been perpetrated by the same hand. My idea is that under the circumstances the police ought to employ, for the protection of the neighbourhood and with the view of selecting the criminal, a number of officers who have been in the habit of guarding lunatics- that is to say, warders from asylums and other persons who have had charge of the insane. These men, if properly disposed in the neighbourhood, would assuredly note any person who was of unsound mind. I have sent a letter embodying this suggestion to Sir Charles Warren, but I have received only a formal communication, acknowledging its receipt. It is not easy to prevail upon the police to accept a suggestion for outside service. This I discovered the other day, when a man in emulation of the Whitechapel murderer, drew a knife and sharpened it in the presence of a relative of mine at Brighton, under circumstances which have been published in the newspapers. When I made a statement to the police on the occasion, they thought very little of it indeed. I attach not the least importance to the American physiologist story. It is a theory which is utterly untenable, and I should think there are very few medical men who ever entertained it seriously. All that has recently happened appears to me as strong confirmation of the views which I have previously given expression to upon this subject. The murderer is a homicidal maniac of infinite cunning, and I fear he will not be brought to justice unless he be caught while engaged in the commission of one of his crimes. LIST OF THE EAST END MURDERS. Six woman have now been murdered in the East End under mysterious circumstances, five of them within a period of eight weeks. The following are the dates of the crimes and names of the victims so far, as known:-

1, Last Christmas week,- an unknown woman found murdered near Osborne and Wentworth Streets, Whitechapel.

2, August 7th,- Martha Turner found stabbed in thirty nine places on a landing in model dwellings known as George Yard Buildings, Commercial Street, Spitalfields.

3, August 31st,- Mrs Nicholls, murdered and mutilated in Bucks Row, Whitechapel.

4, September 7th,- Mrs Chapman, murdered and mutilated, Hanbury Street, Whitechapel.

5, September 30th,- Elizabeth Stride, found with throat cut in Berner Street, Whitechapel.

6, September 30th,- Woman unknown, murdered and mutilated in Mitre Square, Aldgate.

The Hull Daily Mail, October 2nd 1888,

THE GATESHEAD MURDER. ARREST OF WADDELL. *Yesterday the man Waddell, who is suspected of being the Birtley murderer, was arrested near the village of Yetholm, about seven miles from Kelso, and is at present in custody there awaiting instruction from Inspector Harrison, of the Gateshead Police. Considerable excitement has prevailed all along the borders of Northumberland and Roxburghshire owing to the frequent rumours current that Waddell was in the neighbourhood. The police were all on the alert; but, though the man wanted was reported as having been seen at one place and then at another, he managed to keep out of their hands. A man answering the description of Waddell was supplied with food at various places, but sometimes he decamped before his wants could be supplied. He professed also to be in quest of harvesting or labouring work; but, in a like manner, he generally disappeared which it was offered to him. The Kelso correspondent of the Central News telegraphs: - The apprehension of the man Waddell at Yetholm has given great satisfaction in this district. It is believed that he has made a complete confession of the crime. The arrest was made by Mr. William Stenhouse, wood dealer, Yetholm who encountered the man on a lonely road leading out of Yetholm, on the hills by the way of Halterburn. On being questioned, he admitted that his name was Waddell, that he came from Birtley, and stated that the woman Savage was his wife. He professed to be looking for harvesting, but Mr. Stenhouse remarked that he would not get what he wanted among the hills, and offered him work if he would return. Quiet willingly, apparently, he retraced his footsteps, and Mr. Stenhouse conveyed him directly and without resistance to the police station, where, in the absence of the policeman who was out on his beat, he was locked up. Weddall confessed to having his clothes changed at Berwick as detailed in*

Mike Covell

> the police information. It is expected that the prisoner will be conveyed to Gateshead to-day or to-morrow.

October 3rd 1888

The Eastern Morning News, October 3rd 1888,

> *THE WHITECHAPEL TRAGEDIES. As an indication of the terror which prevails in the East End of London among all classes of woman, an arrest was made which, though suspicious in itself, has ostensibly no bearing on the murders. A young respectable woman named Amy Delling, was walking in the vicinity of Chambers Street, Goodman's Fields, East, when a man spoke to her in passing. Something in his appearance excited her suspicions, and she gave him in charge. Police Constable 132 H, after questioning him, proceeded to search him, much against the man's will, and found a loaded six chambered revolver in his possession. By this time a small crowd had collected and some excitement prevailed. He was taken to Leman Street Police station, where he gave his name as Arthur Curtis, of 912 Sansbury-street, East India Road, Poplar, and stated he was a sailor. He appeared to be slightly intoxicated and gave no reason for having spoken to the woman. On being further searched nothing otherwise suspicious was found in his possession but a loaded revolver, which he bought in New York, for safety. He was charged and detained and will be brought up before the magistrate today. ANOTHER THEORY. The Times Vienna correspondent, in referring to the Whitechapel murders, recalls the case of a Jew named Riller, who was accused in 1884 of having murdered and mutilated a Christian woman near Cracow. He was undoubtedly innocent, but was three times condemned, and in the Court of Appeal eventually quashed the sentence/ It was proved that among certain fanatical Jews there existed a superstition that if a Jew became intimate with a Christian woman he would atone for his offence by killing and mutilating the object of his passion. Passages of the Talmud were quoted in support of this view.*

The Hull Daily News, October 3rd 1888,

> *ANOTHER LONDON HORROR. MURDER AND DISMEMBERMENT. DISCOVERY OF A WOMAN'S MUTILATED BODY. Another ghastly discovery was made in London yesterday afternoon. About five o'clock a carpenter named Frederick Wildborn, employed by Messrs J. Grover and Sons, builders, of Pimlico, who are contractors for the new Metropolitan Police Head-quarters on the Thames Embankment, was working on the foundation, when he came across*

a neatly done up parcel which was secreted in one of the cellars. Wildborn was in search of timber when he found the parcel, which was tied up in paper and measured about two-and-a-half feet long by about two feet in width. It was opened, and the body of a woman, very much decomposed, was found carefully wrapped in a piece of cloth, which is supposed to be a black petticoat. The trunk was minus the head, both arms, and both legs, and presented a ghastly spectacle. The officials of the works were immediately apprised of the discovery and the police were fetched. Dr. Bond, the divisional surgeon to the A. Division, and several other medical gentlemen were communicated with, and subsequently examined the remains, which were handed over to the care of some police-officers, who were told off to see that the trunk was not disturbed. From what can be ascertained the conclusion has been arrived at by the medical men that these remains are those of the woman whose arms have recently been discovered in different parts of London- one in Pimlico and the other in Lambeth, on the opposite side of the River Thames. Dr. Neville, who examined the arms of a female found a few weeks ago in the Thames, off Ebury Bridge, Pimlico, said on that occasion that he did not think it had been skilfully taken from the body, and this fact would appear to favour the theory that the arm. Together with the one found in the grounds of the Blind Asylum in the Lambeth road last week, belong to the trunk discovered today, for it is stated that the limbs appear to have been taken from the body found this afternoon in anything but a skilful manner. The building, which is in course of erection is the new police depot for London, the present scattered headquarters of the Metropolitan police force and the Criminal Investigation Department in Great Scotland Yard and Whitehall Place have been found too small for the requirements of the London police system. The builders have been working on the site for some considerable time now, but have only just completed the foundation. It was originally the site for the National Opera House, and extends from the Thames Embankment, through to Cannon row, Parliament street, at the back of St Stephen's Club, and the Westminster Bridge Station on the District Railway. The prevailing onion is that to place the body where it was found the person conveying it must have scaled the 8ft. hoarding which encloses the works, and carefully avoided the watchmen who do duty by night, must have dropped it where it was found. There appears to be little doubt that the parcel had been in the cellar for some considerable time. NARRATIVES BY THE DISCOVERERS OF THE BODY. A man employed upon the works, who was one of the first to see the remains, has made the following statement to a newspaper representative:- "I went down into one of the cellars, which is about 20ft. by 15ft. in size to look round, when I saw a parcel lying in a corner as though it had been thrown there carelessly. I might say that the cellar is really part of the half-finished basement of what are to be the new police

Mike Covell

officers. The parcel was a paper one, which could easily be carried under the arm. When the parcel was opened I saw that it contained the trunk of a woman wrapped up in a coarse cloth. In cutting off the legs a portion of the abdomen had been cut away. The head and arms were also cut off close to the trunk. The police have been digging up the rubbish and any place where it seems likely any more remains could be hidden but I don't think they have found anything more. The contents of the parcel were very much decomposed, and looked to have been in the place where they found for three weeks or a month. My opinion is that the person putting the parcel where it was found must have got over the hoarding in Cannon-row, and then thrown the bundle down." Another workman says that the parcel was discovered by a man whom he only knows as "George" who went down to get some timber. In his opinion the parcel had been there quite three weeks, as the contents were terribly decomposed. Another workman who has a thorough knowledge of the facts connected with the finding of the ghastly remains has made the following statements:- *"As one of our carpenters was putting away his tools at about five o'clock last night in one of the vaults which are to form the foundation of the main building of the new offices which are to accommodate the police, he saw what seemed to be a heap of paper. As it is very dark in this particular spot, even during the day, the matter somehow did not appear to strike him as curious or out of the way, his passing thoughts being that it was merely a bundle of canvas which was being used on the works. He consequently mentioned the matter to no one, and having left his tools, came away and went home, thinking no more about the mysterious parcel which was to reveal another dreadful crime, probably perpetrated within 100 yards of the King street police station, about 200 or 300 yards from the present offices of the Criminal Investigation Department, and within 50 yards of the Houses of Parliament. This morning, when he went to fetch his tools, he became aware of a peculiar smell proceeding from the dark corner, but at the time made no attempt ascertain the cause. The matter, however, had taken possession of his mind, and later on in the day he mentioned the circumstances to one or two of his fellow workmen. They at once decided to tell the foreman. This was one and the foreman, accompanied by some of the men, proceeded to the spot. One of the labourers was called to shift the parcel. It was then opened and the onlookers were horrified to find that it contained a human body. The legs, arms, and head were missing, and the body presented a most sickening spectacle. The woman had evidently been dead for many days, as decomposition was far advanced. I never saw such a dreadful sight in my life, and the smell was dreadful. After we had got over the first surprise and nausea we sent for the police, and a doctor was also sent for. We could see that the body was that of a full grown woman, and when the doctor came he said the same thing. Almost immediately after that*

Dr. Bond, of the Middlesex Hospital, came and saw the body. He found that it was very brown, and I believe he said that it was the body from which the arms found in the Thames a few days ago had been cut. The body was wrapped in what looked like part of an old black dress of very common material, and it is a very strange thing that other parts of the same dress have been found in other parts of the yard. The police took possession of the remains, and gave orders that no stranger was to be admitted to the enclosure. How long do I think it possible the body could have been lying there? Well, it could not have been where we found it above two or three days, because men are continually passing the spot. The place is very dark, and it is possible that it might have escaped notice on that account; but, now I come to think of it, I know for a fact that it was not there last Friday because we had occasion to do something at that very spot." Asked for his opinion as to how the parcel got into such a curious place, our informant seemed quite taken aback at the simplicity of the question, but said that the person who put the bundle there could not very well have got into the enclosure from the embankment side, as not only would the risk of detection be very great, but he would stand a good chance of breaking his neck. When the discovery became known some 50 or 60 people assembled round the hoarding which encloses the new works, and at half past seven this evening, when the police arrived with an ambulance, large crowds were on the spot, and followed the corpse on its way to the mortuary. EXAMINATION OF THE REMAINS. MEDICAL THEORIES. Dr. Bond did not make an examination of the body last night. On being asked by a reporter his opinion as to whether the arms above referred to belonged to the body recently discovered, the doctor said that it was impossible for him to make any definite statement until after he had made a careful examination. There was, however, a possibility of the limbs and trunk being those of the same person - a fact which is eagerly anticipated by the police authorities who are prosecuting inquiries in the case now known as the Pimlico mystery. A later account says that there is no doubt now that the discovery is connected with a terrible murder from the way in which the body has been treated, it is impossible that it could have been spirited away from a dissecting room after having answered the purpose of lawful operations. Persons who have seen the trunk have described it as being in a very advanced state of decomposition- so much that it was pronounced dangerous by the medical gentleman present for anyone to touch it with the naked hand. One end was quite black, and upon it being taken to the mortuary disinfectants were freely used, and it was placed in spirit to await the post mortem examination. When the parcel was found and opened there was not a scrap of clothing on the trunk, and it was tied with rope lengthways and crossways, just as one would tie up a parcel. The vault is about 24 feet by 30 in size, and 12 or 13 feet deep, and it is nearly covered over with loose planks, the ground showing only a small space at each end of the place. The trunk must have been carried either from the embankment or from Cannon-row. It certainly could not have been thrown over to where it lay from either roadway. It's general appearance, indeed, indicated rather that it had been carefully placed. It is simply astounding that any man could have carried such an offensive burden through the public street without attracting attention, and it is still more extraordinary how it could have been taken to the vault without discovery. The route from Cannon-row to the vault is a difficult one. To reach the vault one must actually pass through the building in course of erection, about which several policemen are constantly patrolling. It is more reasonable to assume that the vault was gained from Cannon-row, and in that case it seems pretty certain that more than one person was concerned in the disposal of the ghastly parcel. One man probably climbed to the top of the hoarding with the assistance of his accomplice, from whom he received the parcel, dropped it on the inner side and then let himself down after it. The other man presumably kept watch while confederate disposed of the remains. How the men could have known of the existence of the vault is not clear, for strangers are not admitted to the works except on business. Possibly the original intention was to place the remains in some out of the way corner in the works in some out-of-the-way corner in the works, and that they were only taken to the vault after that obviously desirable place of concealment had been accidentally discovered. It is satisfactory to state that in view of the possibility of discovery such as that made last night, the arms found at Westminster and Lambeth a short time ago, of which mention is made below, were not buried , as had been supposed. They have been preserved in the usual way and will be taken to the mortuary, in which the trunk now lies. One of the first things which the surgeons will have to do will be to test by actual experiment whether the discovered severed limbs belong to the trunk, and the result will be awaited with profound interest, and anxiety, for if they do not fit the trunk, we shall be driven to the conclusion that not one, but two more mysterious, and horrible crimes have been committed in London. For the present the police and surgical experts are hopeful that the various ligaments will be found to be part of the same body. The head, the most important part for purposes of identification, and legs, are still missing. As to the remaining limbs, the only thing certain is that two arms have been found. The first arm was found on the afternoon of September the 11th by a man named Moore, who works in a timber yard in Grosvenor roar, Westminster. The arm when seen by Moore was lying on the mud on the foreshore of the Thames near Grosvenor road railway bridge. The arm had been cleanly severed from the shoulder, and it evidently belonged to a well-proportioned young woman. Although it had been in the water for several days it presented a white and *shapely appearance. The woman must have been between 25 and 30 years of age. In the opinions of the surgeons who examined the limb, although a knife had been adroitly used, it was not wielded by a surgical expert, and it had certainly never been inside a dissecting room. Everything, in fact, seemed to point to murder, and with this view, it is understood, the police reluctantly agreed, and orders were issued for the river to be dragged, and every arrangement was made for the detection of the murderer, should he endeavour, as it was reasonable to suppose, to dispose of the other parts of the victims body. Nothing occurred, however, until the 19th ult., when a second arm was found in Southwark. A boy was walking along the Lambeth-road about half past seven o'clock on the morning of that date, when he noticed just within the Blind School Garden a parcel, which curiosity prompted him to inspect more closely. He reached it, opened it, and saw to his horror that it enclosed a human arm. The limb was somewhat decomposed, and lime had been thrown over it, but it was recognisable as that of a woman. It was handed over to the police of L Division, and after that it came into their possession little more was heard of it, the police maintaining the utmost reserve regarding the discovery. Telegraphing at midnight, a correspondent says:- No information has been received by the police, so far as can be ascertained, that would assist them in establishing the identity of the young woman, and this is generally believed to indicate that she must have been a member of that numerous class who have separated themselves from their friends owing to their mode of living. Dr. Neville, the divisional police surgeon for Pimlico, who examined the arm found in the Thames, as above stated on 11th September, has not yet been called to see the trunk of the woman, neither does he expect to be called. He states that in his opinion the time which Dr. Bond allows for the decease of this mutilated victim would agree with his own conclusion. Dr. Neville came to the conclusion when he examined the lime submitted to him that it was that of a big woman. Dr. Bond also avers that the remains submitted to him are those of a woman of no small stature. THE WHITECHAPEL MURDERS. LATER PARTICULARS. Telegraphing last night, a London correspondent says: The police think they have obtained a clue to the identity of the woman murdered in Mitre-square. She is supposed to be a person who was taken to the police station a short time ago for drunkenness. She then gave the name of Kelly, and said she lived at 6, Fashion street. One of the pawn tickets found near the body was made out to Jane Kelly, 6, Dorset street. Up to the present, however, there is no information of anyone being missing from these addresses. The authorities at the chief office of the City police had a man detained there on suspicion to-day, but the explanation he gave was satisfactory, and he has been released. This evening, indeed, no one remained in custody in connection with either murder, although* two men were arrested this morning. Great excitement still prevails in the neighbourhood, where general satisfaction is expressed at the offer of large rewards. The police, it is stated, attach considerable importance to the discovery of a pair of trousers at Nelson Tavern, Kentish Town, on Monday morning. A large number of detectives engaged in following up the information in their possession with a view to tracing the missing article of clothing, and as an illustration of the energy with which they are working, it may be mentioned that on Monday night they called up from their beds several persons whose names are connected with the discovery. They have, however, been unable up to the present to trace the trousers, which are described as being made of blue cloth. The paper in which they were wrapped, and which was stained with blood, was on Monday night handed over to the divisional police surgeon, Dr. Downes, for examination, and it is understood that it has since been conveyed to Scotland Yard to be analysed, as it is thought that the stains are those of human blood. THE INQUEST OF ELIZABETH STRIDE. The inquest on the woman known as Elizabeth Stride, murdered in Berner-street on Sunday morning, was resumed by Mr. Wynne Baxter yesterday afternoon at Whitechapel. Police Constable Lamb, 252H, who said about one o'clock on Sunday morning he was in Commercial street, when two men ran to him and said there had been another murder. Witness followed by another constable, ran in the direction indicated, and entering the gateway of No. 40 found the body of a woman on the ground. Her throat was cut. Witness sent for a doctor and inspector. The woman's face and arms were still warm, and the right arm lay across the breast. Her face was about six inches from the wall. The clothes were not disturbed. Dr. Blackwell arrived about ten minutes afterwards, followed by Inspector Pinhorn. Witness then closed the gates. No one was allowed to leave the club after that. Edward Spooner, housekeeper for Messrs. Meredith, biscuit makers said just before one o'clock he followed two men who were calling out "Police." He went into the yard in Berner street and saw the body inside the gate. About 15 people were standing around. Someone struck a light and witness lifted the chin. Blood was still flowing. A constable came five minutes afterwards. Mary Malcolm, Eagle street, Holborn, wife of a tailor said she recognised the deceased as her sister, Elizabeth Watts. She last saw her alive on Thursday evening at witnesses house, and gave her a jacket and 1s. The deceased never told her where she was living. Her husband was a son of Mr. Watts, wine merchant, Bath. Witness believed he had gone to America because the deceased brought disgrace upon him eight years ago by her misconduct with a porter. She then had two children, one, a girl, was now dead, and the boy was at school under the care of his aunt. The deceased lived with a man who went to sea, and was drowned two or three years ago. Witness knew she was called "Long Liz" and used to meet her every

Saturday afternoon at the corner of Chancery lane. She had never missed a Saturday for three years until last Saturday. Witness felt a presentiment on reading the paper on Sunday morning, and went over to Whitechapel. On seeing her in the mortuary she did not at first recognise her by gaslight, but had done so since. Witness had a presentiment at twenty minutes past one on Sunday morning, when there came "a heavy fall on the bed," and she heard "three distinct kisses." Her husband heard the same. One proof of her identity was a mark on the leg of an adder when she was a child. Dr. Blackwell, of Commercial road, deposed that when he first saw the body the neck and chest were quite warm. The silk neck scarf was tightly drawn, and the throat was cut about two inches below the angle of the jaw. The windpipe was completely severed. There was no blood on the clothing. The dress was undone at the top. The injuries were beyond the possibility of self-infliction. Witness had come to the conclusion that the silk scarf was pulled backwards, but he could not say whether the throat was cut while she was still lying on the ground or while she was standing. It might have been done while she was in the act of falling. The inquiry was at this point adjourned till to-day. THE MITRE SQUARE MURDER. THE INITIALS EXPLAINED. Late last night a man giving the name of John Kelly, of 55, Flower and Dean street, which is a common lodging house, came to Bishopsgate street Police Station, and said he believed the woman murdered in Mitre-square was his wife. Subsequently he identified the body, but admitted he was not married to the deceased. Her real husband's name was Thomas Conway, hence the initials "T.C." He last saw deceased on Saturday afternoon, when she went to see a married daughter. He also referred to the pledging of boots and a flannel shirt.

The Hull Daily News, October 3rd 1888,

THE TEXAS AND WHITECHAPEL MURDERS. The New York correspondent of the Daily News telegraphs:- Not a great many months ago a series of remarkably brutal murders of women occurred in Texas. The matter caused great local excitement, but aroused less interest than would otherwise have been the case because the victims were chiefly negro women. The crimes were characterized by the same brutal methods as those of the Whitechapel murders. The theory has been suggested that the perpetrator of the latter may be the Texas criminal, who was never discovered. The Atlanta Constitution, a leading southern newspaper, thus puts the argument:- "In our recent annals of crime there has been no other man capable of committing such deeds. The mysterious crimes in Texas have ceased. They have just commenced in London. Is the man from Texas at the bottom of them all? If he is the monster or lunatic he may be expected to appear anywhere. The fact that he is no longer at work in Texas

Mike Covell

> argues his presence somewhere else. His peculiar line of work was executed in precisely the same manner as is now going on in London. Why should he not be there? The more one thinks of it the more irresistible becomes the conviction that it is the man from Texas. In these days of steam and cheap travel distance is nothing. The man who would kill a dozen women in Texas would not mind the inconvenience of a trip across the water, and once there he would not have any scruples about killing more women." The Superintendent of the New York police admits the possibility of this theory being correct, but he does not think it probable. "There is," he says, "the same brutality and mutilation, the same suspicion that the criminal is a monster or lunatic who has declared war literally to the knife against all womankind, but I hardly believe it is the same individual." PARIS, MONDAY NIGHT. A surgical theory which is advanced here about the Whitechapel murders is that the murderer is a fanatical vivisectionist and disciple of Hoeckel, the German naturalist, who followed in the steps of Darwin in studying the origins of species and who advanced some startling ideas that have not yet been established. A naturalist's aim is visible in the way in which the knife was applied to the two unfortunate beings at Whitechapel. Perhaps there was not time to operate in an exactly like manner in the second series of murders.

The Hull Daily News, October 3rd 1888,

> LATEST NEWS. THE LONDON TRAGEDIES. THE WESTMINSTER HORROR. FURTHER PARTICULARS. The Press Association says the inhabitants of Westminster appear to have only this morning realised the horrible nature of the crime exposed yesterday in their midst, and details of the ghastly discovery in Whitehall are today being discussed by everyone with horrified eagerness. The official investigation into the cause of the victim's death was a commenced at an early hour. Dr. Bond, divisional police surgeon, and Dr. Hibbert, his assistant, arrived at the mortuary shortly after seven o'clock. The mortuary is temporarily placed in an untenanted shop and house, 20 Hillbank Street, and the body was removed there last night and placed in spirits. The doctors examination of the trunk lasted for about an hour and a half, and proved a most unpleasant task owing to the advanced state of decomposition of the flesh. Dr. Bond would not state what the result of the examination was until after he has made his official report, which would be immediately, but he stated that it was intended to obtain the arm which was found in the Thames on the 11th September, and which has since been preserved at Ebury street mortuary, in order to ascertain whether it had been taken from the same trunk. An inquest will probably be held, but this will depend upon the nature of Dr. Bond's report to the coroner, Dr. Troutbeck.

The detectives were also early on the scene, and resumed their inquiries among the workmen employed at the works where the discovery was made. It has been ascertained that the parcel containing the remains was not in the vault on Saturday, as several workmen had been in the habit of using the cellar to conceal their tools, and it would have been noticed. As it was the parcel was first seen on Monday morning, but none of the workmen had the curiosity to look at what was in it until yesterday, when it was dragged out with the results already known. A search is today being made in the cellars and a disused well for any other portions of the remains. THE MITRE SQUARE MURDER. The identification of the mutilated remains of the woman murdered in Mitre Square, Aldgate, is now complete. She has lived for the past seven years with a man named Kelly, in Flower and Dean street, Spitalfields, who yesterday fully identified the body, partly by the linen and partly by the marks on her flesh. He says she had a husband before she came to live with him, and that his name was Tom Conway, a pensioner from the Royal Artillery. She had several children by Conway and one of them was married to a gun maker in Bermondsey, but having falling out with her husband, they separated. The initials of her husband, T.C., were pricked in her arm. Kelly and she had been tramping about Kent last week, and on Saturday morning, when they had their last meal together at the lodging house in Flower and Dean street, she said she would go to her daughter in Bermondsey. Kelly says he cautioned her to be back early, and not to get into the hands of the Whitechapel murderer, but she assured him she was able to take care of herself. He had no suspicion she had fallen a victim until he read in the paper a description of the pawn tickets found on her and the marks on her arm. He then told the police, and they showed him the body, which he identified. THE BERNER STREET MURDER. The Press Association's Bath correspondent telegraphs corroborating the statement of Mrs Malcolm at the inquest, yesterday, as to the history and habits of the woman Elizabeth Watts. She married, about twenty seven or twenty eight years ago, William Watts, son of a wine merchant in Bath. Her husband being then only about twenty years of age. They only lived together two years, when deceased left her husband who went to America. He returned from the country four years ago.

The Hull Daily Mail, October 3rd 1888,

THE GATESHEAD MURDER. WADDELL BEFORE THE MAGISTRATES. The prisoner Waddell, who is charged with the murder at Birtley which created so great a sensation a week ago on account of its similarity to the Whitechapel murders, arrived in Gateshead shortly before ten yesterday morning, Throughout the night crowds had collected at the railway stations and other

Mike Covell

> places to catch a glimpse of the man, but very few succeeded, as the police got him out at the Manors, a suburban station, and conveyed him by cab to Gateshead. Shortly before twelve he was brought before the magistrates, and Superintendent Harrison gave notice of his arrest, adding to this that when charged with wilful murder the prisoner merely answered, "Yes." As he appeared in court he was really a pitiable object. Of intelligence or spirit his features hardly revealed a spark. – The Magistrates remanded him for eight days, and ordered that he should next be brought up at Chester-le-street.

The Hull Daily Mail, October 3rd 1888,

> THE LONDON MYSTERIES. ANOTHER MUTILATED BODY FOUND. The Central News learns that there was found yesterday afternoon, [illegible of the foundations of the new Police Offices, Thames Embankment, the trunk of a female, without head, arms and legs, tightly bound up by a cord, and wrapped in some kind of cloth. The site of the new police offices in course of erection extends from the Embankment right through Cannon-row, Westminster. It seems that yesterday afternoon a man was induced to go into a vault there by his fellow workmen who had been annoyed by the stench arising from it, and the cause of which it was intended to remove if possible. The vault is on the Cannon-row side of the building, and the man saw the body lying on its back in the basement. It rested upon a piece of black cloth. There was not a scrap of clothing on the trunk, and it was tied with ropes lengthways and crossways, just as one would tie up a parcel. The vault is about 24 feet by 30 feet in size, and 12 or 13 feet deep, and it is nearly covered over with loose planks, the ground showing only a small space at each end of the place. The trunk must have been carried either from the Embankment, or from Cannon-row; it certainly could not have been thrown over to where it lay from either roadway. Its general appearance, indeed, indicated rather that it had been carefully placed where it was subsequently found. It is simply outstanding that any man could have carried such an offensive burden through the public street without attracting attention, and it still more extraordinary how it could have been taken into the vault without discovery. The route from Cannon-row to the vault is a difficult one; a hoarding some seven or eight feet high would have to be climbed, and the ground is of a very broken character. From the Embankment side the hoarding is about the same height and to reach the vault one must actually pass through the building in course of construction and round it, about which several policemen are constantly patrolling. It is more reasonable to assume that the vault was gained from Cannon row and so that it seems pretty certain that more than one person was concerned in the disposal of the ghastly parcel. One man

probably climbed to the top of the hoarding with the assistance of his accomplice from whom he then received the parcel, dropped it on the inner side and then let himself down after it. The other man presumably kept watch while his confederate disposed of the remains. How the man could have known of the existence of the vault is not clear, for strangers are not admitted to the works except on business. Possibly the original intention was to place the remains in some out of the way corner in the works and they were only taken to the vault after the obviously desirable place of concealment had been accidentally discovered. A representative of the Central News called upon Dr Bond, the divisional surgeon, at his residence in the Sanctuary, Westminster, who had made an examination of the remains, but that gentleman stated he could give no information whatever, as he had first to make out his official report to Scotland-yard authorities, and he could not do that until the morrow, when he proposed to make a careful examination of the remains. It is satisfactory to state, says the Central News, that, in view of the possibility of a discovery such as that made yesterday, the arm found at Westminster a short time ago was not buried, as had been supposed. It has been preserved in the usual way, and will be taken to the mortuary in which the trunk now lies. One of the first things which the surgeons will have to do to-day will be to test whether the dissevered limb belongs to the trunk found yesterday, and the result will be awaited with profound interest and anxiety; for, if they do not, we shall be driven to the conclusion that not one but two more mysterious and horrible crimes have been committed. For the present, police and surgical experts are hopeful that the various fragments will be found to be part of the same body. Even then, much will remain to be discovered. The head – the most important part for purposes of identification – and the legs are still missing. As to the remaining limbs, the only thing certain is that two arms have been found. The first arm was found on the afternoon of September the 11th by a man named Moore, who works in a timber yard in Grosvenor-road, Westminster. The arm when seen by Moore was lying on the mud on the foreshore of the Thames, near the Grosvenor-road Railway Bridge. It had been cleanly severed from the shoulder, and it had evidently belonged to a well-proportioned young woman. Although it had been in the water for several days, it presented a white and shapely appearance. The woman must have been between 25 and 30 years of age, and the smoothness of the skin and the tapering fingers indicated that she had belonged to the middle, or possibly, even the upper grade of society. In the opinion of the surgeons, who examined the limbs, although the knife had been adroitly used, it was not wielded by a surgical expert, and it had certainly never been inside a dissecting-room. Everything, in fact, seemed to point to murder, and with this view it is understood the police reluctantly agreed, and orders were issued, for the river to be dragged, and

Mike Covell

every arrangement was made for the detection of the murderer, should he endeavor – as it was reasonable to suppose – to dispose of the other parts of his victim's body. Nothing occurred, however, until the 19th ultimo, when a second arm was found in Southward. A boy was walking along the Lambeth-road about half-past seven o'clock on the morning of that date, when he noticed just within the Blind School garden a parcel, which curiosity prompted him to inspect more closely. He reached it, opened it, and saw to his horror that it enclosed a human arm. The limb was somewhat decomposed, and lime had been thrown over it, but it was recognisable as that of a woman. It was handed over to the police of the L division, and after it came into their possession little more was heard of it. The police maintained the utmost reserve regarding the discovery; in fact, the police at Lambeth, Kennington-lane, Kennington-road, and Blackman-street Stations all denied any knowledge of a human arm having been found, but the boy, who is a shoeblack, adhered to his statement that the limb was removed to Kennington-lane Police-station. Mr Trentbeck, the deputy coroner for the City and Liberty of Westminster, was informed of the discovery of the trunk, and at once decided to hold an inquest. His officer arrived on the spot about half-past seven with authority to remove the remains, which, as already stated, were then taken to the mortuary in Millbank-street. THE EAST END TRAGEDIES. SEVERAL ARRESTS. LATEST PARTICULARS. The Central News says a number of persons have seen the body of the woman murdered in Mite-square, but it has not yet been identified. Inquiries are being made among persons who have given information of missing relatives or friends during the past fortnight, and they will be asked to view the body. The bills offering £500 reward on behalf of the City authorities were yesterday widely circulated. The City police are in receipt of innumerable suggestions, not only from London, but from all parts of the country. Many of these are, of course, of no practical value, but some of the information which has thus come into their hands has led them to prosecute inquiries which would otherwise not have been made, and which may lead to important results. Three arrests were made yesterday, but the three persons were subsequently all released. The Central News says: - The inquest on the unknown woman will open on Thursday. It is probable that some sensational and unexpected evidence will be placed before the coroner's jury. The bloodstained apron found in Gouldston-street is still in the possession of the police but beyond indicating the direction of the murderer's flight it has not proved of much service. It will be remembered that in the case of the Hanbury-street murder the murderer also wiped his blood-stained hands, but in that instance he used an old newspaper, which was found in an adjacent yard. Professor J. Wortley-Axe, principal of the Royal Veterinary College, London, has favoured a representative of the Central News with his views upon the employment of bloodhounds might be a useful police auxiliary, but its successful employment would depend upon the efficient training of the dogs, and the promptitude with which they were put upon the track. All dogs have a neutral instinct for blood-odours, but this instinct requires development by training, and in the case of the bloodhound it is necessary to make it an expert at the business. The dog must, in the first place, be familiarized with the odour of blood. The incriminating element of the murder, so far as the dog is concerned, would, of course, be the blood carried in the clothes or upon the boots of the murderer; it is, in fact, a condition precedent of the hunt that some of the blood of the victim should be upon the person of the fugitive. In the country, where the ground and atmosphere may remain undisturbed for a long period, this system of pursuit would work fairly well, "but" (said Professor Axe) "when you come to deal with the streets of large towns, the ground surface of which must necessarily be impregnated with a number of odours, I apprehend that this fact would materially operate against your success in tracking the murderer with bloodhounds. The pavement of our own city, for instance, may possibly stained with the blood of carcasses, such as sheep in transit, as well indeed as with human blood, the result of natural deposit. This would tend to confuse the scent which you desired to follow up unless it were very fresh and strong. Again, the air in large towns is always shifting, or may have been shifted by the ordinary traffic of the street, so that the odour left by the fugitive would not be suffered to abide long without obliteration: hence it comes to this, that if you resort to bloodhounds for the tracking of bloodhounds for the tracking of bloodstained fugitives, your dogs must be perfectly trained, must be experts at the business, and the condition of the ground must be favourable to the return of the odour forming the clue. In large towns the latter presents a serious difficulty."

The authorities have not yet decided whether they will photograph the letter and post-card received by the Central News, and publish copies, with a view to discover the writer, who, it will be remembered, professes to be the murderer. It is somewhat curious that Mr. Richardson, who lives at the house 29 Hanbury-street, where Annie Chapman was found murdered, received yesterday morning a copy of yesterday's Liverpool Daily Post, with the letter and post-mark referred to marked in blue pencil. The newspaper was wrapped in an ordinary stamped cover, and was addressed to "Jack the Ripper, 29 Hanbury-street, London, E.C." The paper was posted in Liverpool on October 1st, and the post-mark is numbered 466. On the reverse side of the wrapper was written: - "Dear Jack, I send you this paper, and hope you will come to Liverpool as I am an associate of yours. – K. T. Please reply to 39, Pitt-street." Richardson immediately handed the paper over to the police, with whom it remains. THE

Mike Covell

INQUEST. Mr. Wynne Baxter yesterday resumed the inquest on the body of Elizabeth Stride. The proceedings did not commence until 2.25, all the jury did not being present at two o'clock, the time fixed. The first witness called was P. C. Henry Lamb (252H), who said about one o'clock on Sunday morning last he was on duty in Commercial-road, when two men came to him. They were shouting "Come on, there's been another murder." As they got to the corner of Berners-street they pointed down it. He ran down Berners-street, followed by another constable. He went into the gateway of 40, Berners-street, and saw something lying on the right-hand side close to the gate. He turned a light on and found it was a woman with her throat cut. He sent the other constable for a doctor and a man to the station for an inspector. There were about 30 people in the yard when he arrived. He put his hand on the face, which was warm. The woman was lying on the left side with her right arm across her breast. The clothes were not disturbed. Some of the blood was congealed. Dr Blackwell arrived about ten minutes after and examined the body. Other evidence, including that of Mary Malcolm, who recognized the body as that of her sister, having been taken, the inquiry was adjourned until today at one o'clock. LIST OF THE EAST END MURDERS. Six women have now been murdered in the East End under mysterious circumstances, five of them within a period of eight weeks. The following are the dates of the crimes and names of the victims so far as known:-

1. Last Christmas week. - An unknown woman found murdered near Osborne and Wentworth-streets, Whitechapel.

2. August 7. - Martha Turner, found stabbed in 39 places, on a landing in model dwellings, known as George-yard Buildings, Commercial-street, Spitalfields.

3. August 31. - Mrs. Nicholls, murdered and mutilated in Bucks-row, Whitechapel.

4. September 7. - Mrs. Chapman, murdered and mutilated in Hanbury-street, Whitechapel.

5. September 30. - Elizabeth Stride, found with her throat cut in Berners-street, Whitechapel.

6. September 30. - Woman unknown, murdered and mutilated in Mitre-square, Aldgate.

The Hull Daily Mail, October 3rd 1888,

ANOTHER LONDON HORROR. A WOMAN'S MUTILATED BODY. SHOCKING DISCOVERY. Another ghastly discovery was made in London yesterday afternoon. About five o'clock a carpenter named Frederick Wildborn, employed by Messrs J. Grover and Sons, builders, of Pimlico, who are contractors for the new Metropolitan Police Head-quarters on the Thames Embankment, was working on the foundation, when he came across a neatly done up parcel which was secreted in one of the cellars. Wildborn was in search of timber when he found the parcel, which was tied up in paper and measured about two-and-a-half feet long by about two feet in width. It was opened, and the body of a woman, very much decomposed, was found carefully wrapped in a piece of cloth, which is supposed to be a black petticoat. The trunk was minus the head, both arms, and both legs, and presented a ghastly spectacle. The officials of the works were immediately apprised of the discovery and the police were fetched. Dr. Bond, the divisional surgeon to the A. Division, and several other medical gentlemen were communicated with, and subsequently examined the remains, which were handed over to the care of some police-officers, who were told off to see that the trunk was not disturbed. From what can be ascertained the conclusion has been arrived at by the medical men that these remains are those of the woman whose arms have recently been discovered in different parts of London- one in Pimlico and the other in Lambeth, on the opposite side of the River Thames. Dr. Neville, who examined the arms of a female found a few weeks ago in the Thames, off Ebury Bridge, Pimlico, said on that occasion that he did not think it had been skilfully taken from the body, and this fact would appear to favour the theory that the arm. Together with the one found in the grounds of the Blind Asylum in the Lambeth road last week, belong to the trunk discovered today, for it is stated that the limbs appear to have been taken from the body found this afternoon in anything but a skilful manner. The building, which is in course of erection is the new police depot for London, the present scattered headquarters of the Metropolitan police force and the Criminal Investigation Department in Great Scotland Yard and Whitehall Place have been found too small for the requirements of the London police system. The builders have been working on the site for some considerable time now, but have only just completed the foundation. It was originally the site for the National Opera House, and extends from the Thames Embankment, through to Cannon row, Parliament street, at the back of St Stephen's Club, and the Westminster Bridge Station on the District Railway. The prevailing onion is that to place the body where it was found the person conveying it must have scaled the 8ft. hoarding which encloses the works, and carefully avoided the watchmen who do duty by night, must have dropped it where it was found. There appears to be little doubt that the parcel had been in the cellar for some considerable time. A workman employed upon the works, who was one of the first to see the remains, has made the following statement to a newspaper representative:- "I went down into one of the cellars, which is about 20ft. by 15ft. in size to look round, when I saw a parcel lying in a corner as though it had been thrown there carelessly. I might say that the cellar is really part of the half-finished basement of what are to be the new police officers. The parcel was a paper one, which could easily be carried under the arm. When the parcel was opened I saw that it contained the trunk of a woman wrapped up in a coarse cloth. In cutting off the legs a portion of the abdomen had been cut away. The head and arms were also cut off close to the trunk. The police have been digging up the rubbish and any place where it seems likely any more remains could be hidden but I don't think they have found anything more. The contents of the parcel were very much decomposed, and looked to have been in the place where they found for three weeks or a month. My opinion is that the person putting the parcel where it was found must have got over the hoarding in Cannon-row, and then thrown the bundle down." Another workman says that the parcel was discovered by a man whom he only knows as "George" who went down to get some timber. In his opinion the parcel had been there quite three weeks, as the contents were terribly decomposed. Another workman who has a thorough knowledge of the facts connected with the finding of the ghastly remains has made the following statements:- "As one of our carpenters was putting away his tools at about five o'clock last night in one of the vaults which are to form the foundation of the main building of the new offices which are to accommodate the police, he saw what seemed to be a heap of paper. As it is very dark in this particular spot, even during the day, the matter somehow did not appear to strike him as curious or out of the way, his passing thoughts being that it was merely a bundle of canvas which was being used on the works. He consequently mentioned the matter to no one, and having left his tools, came away and went home, thinking no more about the mysterious parcel which was to reveal another dreadful crime, probably perpetrated within 100 yards of the King street police station, about 200 or 300 yards from the present offices of the Criminal Investigation Department, and within 50 yards of the Houses of Parliament. This morning, when he went to fetch his tools, he became aware of a peculiar smell proceeding from the dark corner, but at the time made no attempt ascertain the cause. The matter, however, had taken possession of his mind, and later on in the day he mentioned the circumstances to one or two of his fellow workmen. They at once decided to tell the foreman. This was one and the foreman, accompanied by some of the men, proceeded to the spot. One of the labourers was called to shift the parcel. It was then opened and the onlookers were horrified to find that it contained a human body. The legs, arms, and head were missing, and the body presented a most sickening spectacle. The woman had evidently been dead for many days, as decomposition was far advanced. I never saw such a dreadful sight in my life, and the smell was dreadful. After we had got over the first surprise and nausea we sent for the police, and a doctor was also sent for. We could see that the body was that of a full grown woman, and when the doctor came he said the same thing. Almost immediately after that Dr. Bond, of the Middlesex Hospital, came and saw the body. He found that it was very brown, and I believe he said that it was the body from which the arms found in the Thames a few days ago had been cut. The body was wrapped in what looked like part of an old black dress of very common material, and it is a very strange thing that other parts of the same dress have been found in other parts of the yard. The police took possession of the remains, and gave orders that no stranger was to be admitted to the enclosure. How long do I think it possible the body could have been lying there? Well, it could not have been where we found it above two or three days, because men are continually passing the spot. The place is very dark, and it is possible that it might have escaped notice on that account; but, now I come to think of it, I know for a fact that it was not there last Friday because we had occasion to do something at that very spot." Asked for his opinion as to how the parcel got into such a curious place, our informant seemed quite taken aback at the simplicity of the question, but said that the person who put the bundle there could not very well have got into the enclosure from the embankment side, as not only would the risk of detection be very great, but he would stand a good chance of breaking his neck. A later account says that there is no doubt now that the discovery is connected with a terrible murder from the way in which the body has been treated, it is impossible that it could have been spirited away from a dissecting room after having answered the purpose of lawful operations. Persons who have seen the trunk have described it as being in a very advanced state of decomposition- so much that it was pronounced dangerous by the medical gentleman present for anyone to touch it with the naked hand. One end was quite black, and upon it being taken to the mortuary disinfectants were freely used, and it was placed in spirit to await the post mortem examination. When the parcel was found and opened there was not a scrap of clothing on the trunk, and it was tied with rope lengthways and crossways, just as one would tie up a parcel. The vault is about 24 feet by 30 in size, and 12 or 13 feet deep, and it is nearly covered over with loose planks, the ground showing only a small space at each end of the place. The trunk must have been carried either from the embankment or from Cannon-row. It certainly could not have been thrown over to where it lay from either roadway. It's general appearance, indeed, indicated

Mike Covell

rather that it had been carefully placed. It is simply astounding that any man could have carried such an offensive burden through the public street without attracting attention, and it is still more extraordinary how it could have been taken to the vault without discovery. The route from Cannon-row to the vault is a difficult one. To reach the vault one must actually pass through the building in course of erection, about which several policemen are constantly patrolling. It is more reasonable to assume that the vault was gained from Cannon-row, and in that case it seems pretty certain that more than one person was concerned in the disposal of the ghastly parcel. One man probably climbed to the top of the hoarding with the assistance of his accomplice, from whom he received the parcel, dropped it on the inner side and then let himself down after it. The other man presumably kept watch while confederate disposed of the remains. How the men could have known of the existence of the vault is not clear, for strangers are not admitted to the works except on business. Possibly the original intention was to place the remains in some out of the way corner in the works in some out-of-the-way corner in the works, and that they were only taken to the vault after that obviously desirable place of concealment had been accidentally discovered. It is satisfactory to state that in view of the possibility of discovery such as that made last night, the arms found at Westminster and Lambeth a short time ago, of which mention is made below, were not buried , as had been supposed. They have been preserved in the usual way and will be taken to the mortuary, in which the trunk now lies. One of the first things which the surgeons will have to do will be to test by actual experiment whether the discovered severed limbs belong to the trunk, and the result will be awaited with profound interest, and anxiety, for if they do not fit the trunk, we shall be driven to the conclusion that not one, but two more mysterious, and horrible crimes have been committed in London. For the present the police and surgical experts are hopeful that the various ligaments will be found to be part of the same body. The head, the most important part for purposes of identification, and legs, are still missing. As to the remaining limbs, the only thing certain is that two arms have been found. The first arm was found on the afternoon of September the 11th by a man named Moore, who works in a timber yard in Grosvenor roar, Westminster. The arm when seen by Moore was lying on the mud on the foreshore of the Thames near Grosvenor road railway bridge. The arm had been cleanly severed from the shoulder, and it evidently belonged to a well-proportioned young woman. Although it had been in the water for several days it presented a white and shapely appearance. The woman must have been between 25 and 30 years of age. In the opinions of the surgeons who examined the limb, although a knife had been adroitly used, it was not wielded by a surgical expert, and it had certainly never been inside a dissecting room. Everything, in fact, seemed to point to murder, and with this view, it is understood, the police reluctantly agreed, and orders were issued for the river to be dragged, and every arrangement was made for the detection of the murderer, should he endeavour, as it was reasonable to suppose, to dispose of the other parts of the victims body. Nothing occurred, however, until the 19th ult., when a second arm was found in Southwark. A boy was walking along the Lambeth-road about half past seven o'clock on the morning of that date, when he noticed just within the Blind School Garden a parcel, which curiosity prompted him to inspect more closely. He reached it, opened it, and saw to his horror that it enclosed a human arm. The limb was somewhat decomposed, and lime had been thrown over it, but it was recognisable as that of a woman. It was handed over to the police of L Division, and after that it came into their possession little more was heard of it, the police maintaining the utmost reserve regarding the discovery. In fact, the police at Lambeth, Kennington-lane, Kennington-road, and Blackyn-street stations, all denied any knowledge of a human arm having been found. But the boy above mentioned, who is a shoeblack, adhered to his statement that the limb was removed to Kennington-lane Police Station. The boy's statement was in some measure confirmed by that of Jim Moore, a bricklayer, who stated that he saw the boy pick up the parcel, and that he himself saw the arm. The boy, in being further questioned, said the parcel had attracted the notice of others before he passed, but that he was the first to open it. Mr. Troutbeck, the deputy coroner for the City and Liberty of Westminster was informed of the discovery of the trunk, and at once decided to hold an inquest. The officer arrived on the spot about half past seven, with authority to remove the remains which, as already stated, were taken to the mortuary in Millibank-street. A FAMOUS AUSTRIAN CRIME. "WHITECHAPELING" IN ATONEMENT. A Times telegram from Vienna states: - With reference to the recent atrocious murders in London, attention may be called to a crime of an exactly similar kind, which pre-occupied the public in this country for nearly three years. A Galatian Jew named Ritter was accused in 1884 of having murdered and mutilated a Christian woman in a village near Cracow. The mutilation was like that perpetrated on the body of the woman Chapman, and at the trial numbers of witnesses deposed that among fanatical Jews there existed a superstition to the effect that if a Jew became intimate with A Christian woman he would atone for his offence by slaying and mutilating the object of his passion. Sundry passages of the Talmud were quoted which according to one witness, expressly sanctioned this form of atonement. The trial caused an immense sensation, and Ritter, being found guilty, was sentenced to death. The Judges of the Court of Appeal, however, feeling that the man was the victim of a popular error and anti-Semitic prejudice, ordered a new trial upon some technicality. Again a jury pronounced against Ritter, and once

Mike Covell

> more the Court of Appeal found a flaw in the proceeding. A third trial took place, and for the third time Ritter was condemned to be hanged, but upon this the Court of Appeal quashed sentences altogether, and Ritter was released, after having been in prison 37 months. There is no doubt that the man was innocent, but the evidence touching the superstitions prevailing among some of the ignorant and degraded of his co-religionists remains on record and was never wholly disproved.

The Hull Daily Mail, October 3rd 1888,

> *THE LONDON MYSTERIES. THE MITRE SQUARE TRAGEDY. CONFESSION BY A MEDICAL STUDENT. POLICE COURT PROCEEDINGS. EXTRAORDINARY STATEMENT. At Guildhall, London on Wednesday, William Bull, describing himself as a medical student at a London hospital, and living at Stannard road, Dalston, was charged on his own confession, with having committed the murder at Mitre Square. Inspector Izzard said that at 20 minutes to 11 on Tuesday, the accused came to his room at Bishopsgate-street station, and made the following statement:- "My name is William Bull and I live at Dalston. I am a medical student at the London Hospital. I wish to give myself up for the murder in Aldgate, on Saturday night or Sunday morning about two o'clock. I think I met the woman in Aldgate. I went with her up a narrow street not far from the main road for an immoral purpose. I promised to give her half-a-crown, which I did. While walking along together there was a second man, who came up and took the half-a-crown from her. I cannot endure this any longer. My poor head-(here he put his hand to his head, and cried or pretended to cry)- I shall go mad. I have done it and I must put up with it." The Inspector asked what had become of the clothing he had on when the murder was committed. The accused said, "If you wish to know they are in the Lea, and the knife I threw away." At this point the prisoner declined to say any more. He was drunk. Part if the statement was made in the presence of Major Smith. Prisoner gave correct address, but is not known at the London Hospital. His parents were respectable. The Inspector asked for a remand to make enquiries, and this was granted. Prisoner now said he was drunk when he made the statement. He was remanded. The identification of the mutilated remains of the woman murdered in Mitre Square, Aldgate, is now complete. She has lived for the past seven years with a man named Kelly, in Flower and Dean street, Spitalfields, who yesterday fully identified the body, partly by the linen and partly by the marks on her flesh. He says she had a husband before she came to live with him, and that his name was Tom Conway, a pensioner from the Royal Artillery. She had several children by Conway and one of them was married to a gun maker in*

Bermondsey, but having falling out with her husband, they separated. The initials of her husband, T.C., were pricked in her arm. Kelly and she had been tramping about Kent last week, and on Saturday morning, when they had their last meal together at the lodging house in Flower and Dean street, she said she would go to her daughter in Bermondsey. Kelly says he cautioned her to be back early, and not to get into the hands of the Whitechapel murderer, but she assured him she was able to take care of herself. He had no suspicion she had fallen a victim until he read in the paper a description of the pawn tickets found on her and the marks on her arm. He then told the police, and they showed him the body, which he identified. THE BERNER STREET MURDER. The Press Association's Bath correspondent telegraphs corroborating the statement of Mrs Malcolm at the inquest, yesterday, as to the history and habits of the woman Elizabeth Watts. She married, about twenty seven or twenty eight years ago, William Watts, son of a wine merchant in Bath. Her husband being then only about twenty years of age. They only lived together two years, when deceased left her husband who went to America. He returned from the country four years ago. THE ADJOURNED INQUEST. Mr Wynne E. Baxter resumed his inquiry on Wednesday at the Vestry-hall, Cable street, on the body of the Berner street victim, recognised up to the present as Elizabeth Watts. The interest in the proceedings has in no way abated, an on account of the discovery at Westminster last night public feeling has been greatly excited. Large crowds of people assembled outside the Vestry-hall. The first witness called was Elizabeth Tanner, living at 32, Flower and Dean street, Whitechapel. She recognised deceased as Long Liz. Did not know her nationality. Deceased told witness that her husband and children were lost in Princess Alice disaster. She last saw her alive on Saturday afternoon in Queen's Head public house, Commercial street. Did not see her again until that afternoon in the mortuary. Witness was quite certain as to her identity. Deceased left a male acquaintance on Thursday, to live with witness. Never knew that witness had relatives in Holborn and never heard the name Stride mentioned. Deceased, who was a Swede, worked among the Jews. Catherine Lane, living with the last witness, said she recognised the body as that of Long Liz. Deceased told witness on Saturday she had had a quarrel with the man she left on Thursday. Witness had heard deceased speak to people in her own language. Charles Preston, a barber, living at the same address also identified the body as that of Long Liz, and he saw her alive on Saturday. He understood she was born in Stockholm, and came to England in a foreign gentleman's service. Deceased also gave witness to understand that her name was Elizabeth Stride, and that her mother was still alive in Sweden. Michael Kidney, living at 38 Dorset street, Waterside labourer, said deceased was Elizabeth Stride. He had lived with her for nearly three years. She was a

Mike Covell

Swede, and was born three miles from Stockholm. Her husband was a ship's carpenter at Sheerness, and once kept a coffee house at Crisp street, Poplar. He was drowned in the Princess Alice disaster. Did not see the deceased on Thursday. Saw her last on Tuesday, when they parted friendly. Never saw her again and could not account for her disappearance. She had been away from witness five months since he had known her. He never neglected her, but treated her as a wife. Witness further stated voluntarily that he asked at Leman street police station for the assistance of a young, strange detective, as he had important information. He could not get the assistance. The Coroner pressed witness to divulge his information, but witness only reiterated that he had the information.- Replying to Inspector Reid, he said if the police were under his own control he could catch the murderer red handed.- Witness admitted he was intoxicated when he applied at the police station. Edward Johnstone, assistant to Drs Kay and Blackwell, deposed to being called to see the body. Thomas Coran, a lad of about eighteen, produced a knife which he found on the doorstep of No. 253, Whitechapel road twenty four hours after the murder. The knife produced was about twelve inches long, and the handle was neatly folded in a silk handkerchief which had stains like blood upon it.- Joseph Drage, H, 282, said he saw the boy find the knife. The handle and blade were covered with blood, which had dried on. The knife was not on the step an hour previously. A POSSIBLE CLUE. The Press Association states: - Information has been received that the woman "Long Liz" was seen in company of a man on Saturday evening, and a description of him has been circulated. He is said to be 28 years of age, about 5ft 7in in height, and of dark complexion. The police, it is stated, attach considerable importance to the discovery of a pair of trousers at the Nelson Tavern, Kentish Town, on Monday morning. A large number of detectives are engaged in following up the information is their possession, with a view to tracing the missing article of clothing, and, on an [illegible] of the energy with which they see working. It may be mentioned that on Monday night they called up from their beds several persons whose names are connected with the discovery. They have, however, been unable up to present to trace the trousers, which are described as being made from blue cloth. The paper in which they were wrapped, and which was stained with blood, who on Monday night handed over to Divisional Police Surgeon Dr. Downes for examination, and it is understood that it has been conveyed to Scotland Yard to be analysed, and it is thought the stains are those of human blood. THE GOVERNMENT REWARDS. HOUSE TO HOUSE VISITATION. To-day, , plain clothes constables made a house-to-house visitation, leaving copies of a handbill requesting occupiers to give notice to the nearest police station of any suspicious matters which may come within their knowledge concerning the murders. THE SHOCKING

DISCOVRY AT WESTMINSTER. The Press Association says the inhabitants of Westminster appear to have only this morning realised the horrible nature of the crime exposed yesterday in their midst, and details of the ghastly discovery in Whitehall are today being discussed by everyone with horrified eagerness. The official investigation into the cause of the victim's death was a commenced at an early hour. Dr. Bond, divisional police surgeon, and Dr. Hibbert, his assistant, arrived at the mortuary shortly after seven o'clock. The mortuary is temporarily placed in a untenanted shop and house, 20, Hillbank street, and the body was removed there last night and placed in spirits. The doctors examination of the trunk lasted for about an hour and a half, and proved a most unpleasant task owing to the advanced state of decomposition of the flesh. Dr. Bond would not state what the result of the examination was until after he has made his official report, which would be immediately, but he stated that it was intended to obtain the arm which was found in the Thames on the 11th September, and which has since been preserved at Ebury street mortuary, in order to ascertain whether it had been taken from the same trunk. An inquest will probably be held, but this will depend upon the nature of Dr. Bond's report to the coroner, Dr. Troutbeck. The detectives were also early on the scene, and resumed their inquiries among the workmen employed at the works where the discovery was made. It has been ascertained that the parcel containing the remains was not in the vault on Saturday, as several workmen had been in the habit of using the cellar to conceal their tools, and it would have been noticed. As it was the parcel was first seen on Monday morning, but none of the workmen had the curiosity to look at what was in it until yesterday, when it was dragged out with the results already known. A search is today being made in the cellars and a disused well for any other portions of the remains. The Press Association learns that Mr. Troutbeck has decided to hold an inquest on the remains, but the date is not yet fixed and will not probably be for three days at least. The detectives were still employed searching round the scene of the discovery. There are indications that the hoarding surrounding the works has recently been scaled. The police have since thoroughly inspected the clothing attached to the body with the object of ascertaining if there were any blood stains, but the result of this examination has not transpired. The inquest has been fixed for Monday next. THE SURGEONS OPINION. The Press Association learns this afternoon that the surgeons who examined the remains have come to the conclusion that the arm which was found at Pimlico fitted into the trunk found on Tuesday. THREATING FEMALES. Scares have been created at Wood Green and at Lowestoft by men threatening females with the fate of the victims of the London murders. The police express a determination to bring to punishment persons who perpetrate these mischievous and idle threats. August Nochild, 52, described as a sailor, giving an address at

Mike Covell

Christian-street, Whitechapel, was charged at the Guildhall, on Tuesday, before Mr. Alderman Stone, with assaulting Sarah McFarly, an unfortunate, by attempting to strangle her in Holborn-circus. Prosecutrix stated that she lived with a friend in Upper Rathbone-place. She met the prisoner about half past twelve yesterday morning in New Oxford-street. He asked her to go to his house in Whitechapel. She refused to go, when he seized her by the throat, and said, "I will murder you, if you don't. I have murdered the women in Whitechapel, and I would like to do another." She screamed, and a police sergeant coming up she gave prisoner in custody. Sergeant Perry, 77, deposed that he was in Holborn about one o'clock on Tuesday morning when he noticed Nochild speaking to the woman. He then saw the prisoner suddenly seize prosecutrix by the throat, and heard cries of "Murder" and "Police." Witness ran towards them, and caught hold of the defendant. The woman charged prisoner with assault, and witness took him into custody. Both of them were under the influence of drink. Mr. Alderman Stone did not think there was any foundation for the charge, and dismissed the case. AN ALLEGED LUNATIC AT LARGE. On Tuesday Arthur Williams, whose address was given in Beaconfield-terrace, Leytonstone, was brought before Mr. Curtis Bennett, at Hammersmith, on a charge of having been found wandering in High-road, Chiswick, apparently insane. It appeared that the prisoner went to the Chiswick Police Station and referred to the Whitechapel murders, stating that he knew where to find the man. As he appeared strange in his manner the police detained him. The prisoner said he did not know what he had done. He made no assertion but what he could substantiate. A written statement was handed to the magistrate, who read it. The following are extracts: - "I am Williams. Will you sent to Whitehall-place and tell them that I am going to Feltham. It is of no use to employ men unless they are men of education. You will find an ordinary constable smoking his pipe, not looking after the Whitechapel murderer. Why do they not pay them as they do in France? ....You will make a good pump if you have a good handle....Colonel Warren is no use: Monro is the man to look after them. I know the man well, and will find him out. I do not want the reward, but shall go mad soon, if he is not found out. I am off to Hounslow and Feltham at once." Mr. Curtis Bennett, after reading the whole of the document, said it was an incoherent statement. The daughter of the prisoner came forward and stated that her father had had sunstroke, and drink always affected his mind. The Prisoner: I was not drunk on Tuesday. The daughter said her father left home on Sunday. Mr. Curtis Bennett observed that he appeared to have wandered to Chiswick. He accepted the prisoner's recognisance's for his good behaviour for six months, his friends expressing their willingness to take him home.

October 4th 1888

The Hull Daily News, October 4th 1888,

LATEST NEWS. ANOTHER ALLEGED TRAGEDY IN LONDON. A WATCHMAN MURDERED. ARREST OF THE ASSASSIN. THE MURDERER SUPPOSED TO BE THE WHITECHAPEL MONSTER. The Evening News (London) in a third edition to-day, states that a man was seen to go behind a hoarding in High Street, Shadwell, with a woman at half past four this morning. The watchman on duty followed them and called the police. The man killed the watchman with his knife, but was secured by several constables who had hurried up. The Evening News adds that it is believed the man is the Whitechapel murder. THE RUMOURED MURDER AND ARREST IN SHADWELL. The Press Association was informed upon an inquiry at the chief police station for the Shadwell district, in which it was stated that a watchman had been killed this morning, that no information had been received by the police of the alleged murder, and that certainly no arrest had been made in connection with such occurrence. The rumour created much excitement both in the City and Whitechapel when first circulated. EXCITEMENT IN WHITECHAPEL. LATEST PARTICULARS. The Press Association says the excitement in Whitechapel on the subject of the murders continues to increase, and should the miscreant fall into the clutches of a Whitechapel mob, it will go hard with him. A SENSATIONAL RUMOUR-EXCITING CHASE. Late last night reports came to hand again and again that the murder had been captured. Shortly before midnight a story was circulating that an unknown murderer had been surprised in the act of attempting another outrage on a woman in Union Street, Whitechapel. The story went that the woman was lured by the "Monster" into a side street, but the gleam of a steel blade at once roused her to a sense of her danger, and her screams brought to the spot a man and two women, who were said to have been watching the movements of the couple. The would be murderer, it was stated, was pursued by a ,am who knocked the knife out of his hand. The unknown one, however, jumped into a passing cab, bidding the cabman drive wherever he liked. A howling mob swarmed after the fugitive and the police soon captured the vehicle and took the occupant to Leman Street police station. Investigation, however, soon proved that the romantic story had but a slight foundation. It was ascertained that about ten o'clock a well-dressed man rushed out of the Three Nuns public house, in Aldgate, followed by a woman, who had declared he had "been molesting" her. To escape the crowd, the stranger jumped into a cab, and was pursued and captured as above stated. When he was formally charged, the woman stated positively that the prisoner

Mike Covell

had accosted her first in Whitechapel High Street, and that when she refused his proposals, he threatened her with violence. The woman nevertheless declined to prefer any charge, and left the station. The man was detained, pending inquiries. He is an athletic, determined fellow, about 40 years of age, no weapons were found on him. He gave a name but declined to state his address. When removed to the cell his attitude became defiant, and he kept up a conversation with a slightly American accent. He is stated to have been slightly under the influence of drink. He remains in custody. A Maltese sailor arrested at a late hour was released this morning, as was also a third man arrested near Cable street. ANOTHER DESCRIPTION OF THE SUPPOSED MURDERER. The Evening news (London), this evening states that a greengrocer named Mathew Packer, has been found, who states that at a quarter to twelve on Saturday night a man, aged 35, stout, and wearing a wide awake hat, and dark clothes. He was accompanied by a woman with a white flower in her bosom, came to his stall, two doors from the scene of the Berner-street murder, and purchased some grapes. They left in the direction of the club, about a quarter past twelve o'clock. THE ALDGATE MURDER. This morning Mr. Langham, the city coroner, opened the inquest upon the body of the woman murdered in Mitre Square on Sunday morning, and whose name has been variously given as Eddowes, Conway, and Kelly. Mr. Crawford, the city solicitor, represented the police; Major Smith, acting commissioner, and Mr. Superintendent Foster also being present. Eliza Gold, first witness living at 6, Thrawl-street, identified the body as that of her sister Catherine Eddowes, who was a single woman who had lived with John Kelly for some years. Witness last saw her sister alive about four or five months ago. Deceased was a hawker, of sober habits, and before living with Kelly, deceased lived with a man named Conway for some years and had children by him. Witness did not know whether Conway, who was an army pensioner, was still alive. In reply to Mr. Crawford, witness said, she had not seen Conway for some years. John Kelly, living at a lodging house in Flower and Dean-street, a market labourer, said deceased had lived with him for seven years. Her name was Conway, and he last saw her on Saturday last at two o'clock in the afternoon. They parted on very good terms in Houndsditch, deceased saying that she was going to Bermondsey to find her daughter. She promised to return by four o'clock. He heard she had been locked up in Bishopsgate for drunkenness, but made no enquiries believing she would return on Sunday. Deceased never went out for an immoral purpose. When they parted deceased had no money and she left with the intention of getting some from her daughter. She was on bad terms with nobody, and usually returned home about eight o'clock at night. Witness did not know where deceased had got drink, considering she had no money. Deceased last year got money from her daughter. On Friday last the deceased went to Mile End, and stopped in the casual ward. Early in the week witness and deceased were in Kent together, and on Thursday arrived in London, spending the night together at Shoe Lane casual ward, as they had no money. On Friday they arranged that deceased should go to Mile End workhouse, and witness stay at lodging-house. They pawned a pair of boots on Saturday, and spent a great portion of the half-crown in food and drink. Witness stood outside with bare feet whilst deceased pawned the boots. It might have been Friday, and not Saturday. Frederick Wilkinson, deputy of the lodging house in Flower and Dean Street, corroborated the last witness as to Kelly and deceased living on good terms. Deceased did not walk the streets. She said the name of Conway was bought and paid for, meaning that she was married.

The Hull Daily Mail, October 4th 1888,

THE LONDON MURDERS. ANOTHER ALLEGED OUTRAGE IN WHITECHAPEL. EXCITING CHASE AND CAPTURE. Shortly before midnight a story was circulating that the unknown murderer had been surprised in the act of attempting another outrage on a woman in Union-street, Whitechapel. The story went that the woman was lured by the "Monster" into a side street, but the gleam of a steel blade at once roused her to a sense of her danger, and her screams brought to the spot a man and two women, who were said to have been watching the movements of the couple. The would be murderer, it was stated, was pursued by a ,am who knocked the knife out of his hand. The unknown one, however, jumped into a passing cab, bidding the cabman drive wherever he liked. A howling mob swarmed after the fugitive and the police soon captured the vehicle and took the occupant to Leman Street police station. Investigation, however, soon proved that the romantic story had but a slight foundation. It was ascertained that about ten o'clock a well-dressed man rushed out of the Three Nuns public house, in Aldgate, followed by a woman , who had declared he had "been molesting" her. To escape the crowd, the stranger jumped into a cab, and was pursued and captured as above stated. When he was formally charged, the woman stated positively that the prisoner had accosted her first in Whitechapel High Street, and that when she refused his proposals, he threatened her with violence. The woman nevertheless declined to prefer any charge, and left the station. The man was detained, pending inquiries. He is an athletic, determined fellow, about 40 years of age, no weapons were found on him. He gave a name but declined to state his address. When removed to the cell his attitude became defiant, and he kept up a conversation with a slightly American accent. He is stated to have been slightly under the influence of drink. He remains in custody.

Mike Covell

ARRESTS AND RELEASES. A Maltese sailor, arrested at a late hour, was released this morning, as also was a third man arrested in Cable-street. CONTINUED EXCITEMENT. The Press Association says the excitement in Whitechapel on the subject of the murders continues to increase, and should the miscreant fall into the clutches of a Whitechapel mob it will go hard with him. Late last night reports came to hand again and again that the murderer had been arrested. MORE ARRESTS. An American, who refused to give his name or any account of himself, was arrested last night on suspicion of being the East End Murderer. He accosted a woman in Cable-street, asked her to go with him, and threatened that is she refused he would "Riper her up." The woman screamed, and the man rushed to a cab. The police gave chase, got on the cab, seized the man and took him to Leman-street police station, where he exclaimed to the inspector, "Are you the boss?" He was detained. Three men are at present under detention in Leman-street Police Station, two of whom were arrested last evening, and one gave himself up as the murderer at a late hour last night. To all these the police are inclined to attach no small importance. In addition to the arrest of the American, another man answering the description of the Berner-street murderer was arrested at eleven o'clock last night in Whitechapel-road, but he refused to give his name or address. He appears to be in a very excited state. He was following some woman and boys, who stated he was the Whitechapel murderer. He is of dark complexion, with a black moustache, and respectively dressed, stands about 5ft, 10in, in height, and from his appearance seems about 40. The other man who gave himself up looks a somewhat desperate character and says he comes from the Shadwell District. All three men will be minutely examined, and at present the police are not without hope that the arrests will prove important. "JACK THE RIPPER" Consternation has been caused locally by the report that "Jack the Ripper" has sent a postcard to Barrett's confectionary factory at Wood Green saying that he shall visit the neighbourhood and "do for" six of the girls employed at the factory. It is further said that a man answering the published description of the supposed murderer has been seen in Wood Green. People speak of the intention to carry arms to be prepared for a sudden attack. AN EXCITED CROWD.-TIMELY RESCUE. About six o'clock last evening, a man whose name was subsequently ascertained to be John Lock, a seaman, was rescued by the police from an excited crowd in the neighbourhood of Ratcliffe Highway, who were following him and shouting "Leather Apron" and "Jack the Ripper." The cause was not readily explained. When, however, he was examined at the police station his light tweed suit was found to bear stains which were found to be paint, but which the crowd had mistaken for blood. His explanation was perfectly satisfactory, but it was some considerable time before the crowd dispersed and the man able to depart.

LETTER FROM SIR CHARLES WARREN. Sir Charles Warren, replying to a letter from the Whitechapel District Board of Works, complaining of the inefficiency of the police, writes that the police force cannot possibly do more than guard or take precautions against any repetition of recent atrocities, so long as the victims actually, but unwillingly connive at their own destruction. In this particular class of murderer to some retired spot and place themselves in such a position that they can be slaughtered without a sound being heard. Sir Charles requests the board to do all in their power to dissuade the unfortunate women about Whitechapel from going into lonely places in the dark with any persons, whether acquaintances or strangers. He assures the board that every nerve is being strained to detect the criminal, and to render more difficult further atrocities, and he emphatically denied that any changes affecting the efficiency of the police had been made. VOLUNTEERS AND THE MURDERS. Colonel Sir Alfred Kirkby. J.P., the officer commanding the Tower Hamlets Battalion Royal Engineers has offered, on behalf of his officers, a reward of £100, to be paid to anyone who will give information that would lead to the discovery and conviction of the perpetrator perpetrators of the recent diabolical murders recently committed in the districts in which his regiment is situated. Sir Alfred Kirkby is also willing to place the services of not more than 50 members of his corps at the disposal of the authorities, to be utilised in assisting them in any way they may consider desirable at this juncture, either for the protection of the public or finding out the criminals. Of course the volunteers will have to made us of as citizens, and not in a quasi-military fashion. THE THAMES EMBANKMENT MYSTERY. MEDICAL EXAMINATION. We understand that the surgeons who conducted the autopsy yesterday on the remains found at Westminster came to the conclusion that the arm which was washed up by the Thames near Pimlico, and which had been conveyed to Westminster mortuary from Ebury-street, where it had been preserved, fitted into the trunk found at Whitehall. It is also stated that the cord tied around the limb found in the river and a portion of that which was used to tie up the parcel were similar. At the conclusion of the examination the clothing was disinfected and thoroughly inspected by the police, who state that it was covered with maggots and vermin. Adhering to one portion was found a piece of newspaper saturated with blood. It bore no date, but the date when the paper was published can easily be ascertained. The dress stuff was found to be a rich flowered silk underskirt, which proves that the unfortunate victim was not one of the poorer class of society. Nothing was discovered to indicate the cause of death, but the doctors are of the opinion that the woman had been murdered about three weeks, and the advanced state of decomposition was due to exposure. The doctors are preparing an elaborate report of the whole case, which will be submitted at the

Mike Covell

> *inquest to be held at the sessions house, Westminster, on Monday next. A WEDDING RING FOUND. A wedding ring, but not a gold one, has been found in the enclosed ground where the buildings are in progress in Cannon-row, Westminster. A workman entered the ground yesterday morning on the lookout for a job. While standing near the entrance to the vaults where the trunk was found he noticed what appeared to be a ring embedded in the dirt. He picked it up, and having cleaned it, he found that it was a wedding ring, slightly bent. Whether the ring is in any way connected with the murder, or whether it may lead to the identification of the woman, is not, of course, yet known.*

The Hull Daily Mail, October 4th 1888,

> *THE MURDER AT BIRTLEY FELL. DEMEANOUR OF WADDLE IN PRISON. A PLEA OF INSANITY TO BE MADE. With the capture of Waddle, a great deal of the interest felt in this district concerning the murder of Jane Beetmore at Birtley Fell has, pending the further proceedings before the magistrate, abated. The police are stated to be in possession of a good deal more evidence than has been made public, and their chain of testimony is stated to be very strong from their point of view. One most essential link, however, is wanting. They have been unable to find the instrument with which the murder was committed. Diligent search has been made for it. Several parts of the Fell district have been strictly examined, while in the oat field and clover field near the scene of the crime all possible search has been made without avail. The prisoner, ever since his apprehension, has maintained the same reserved demeanour that characterised his conduct at the Police Court. He has had nothing to say to anyone, and has throughout had the air of a man who scarcely knew the position in which he was placed, and who did all he had to do is a purely mechanical manner. On the completion of the formal proceedings at the court on Tuesday, Waddle, in a dejected state was conveyed back to the cells at the Gateshead County Police Court. There he was kept all night, and the police decline to state when the removal will take place. They desire that the proceedings shall be strictly private, and that no crowd shall assemble to see the man taken away. The brother of Waddle, residing at Birtley, called at Newcastle Central Police Station yesterday, and after some conversation, visited the offices of Messrs Clark and Robinson solicitors, Pilgrim-street, and engaged the services of Mr. E Clark, to defend the accused man. The brother, we are informed gives it his opinion that Waddle is insane. Insanity is stated to already be in the family. It is alleged Waddle has exhibited peculiarities of conduct for some weeks past, and on one occasion his landlady became frightened at his peculiarly wild look. Mr Robinson proceeded yesterday afternoon, to the Gateshead County Police*

Station, and informed the officers, that he and his partner, Mr Edward Clark, had been instructed to appear for the defence of Waddle, and requested to have an interview with the prisoner. His request was at once granted. The prisoner was standing against the wall of his cell, with his arms folded, when Mr Robinson entered and walked up to him. The solicitor informed him that he and Mr Clark had been retained by some friends to appear on his behalf at Chester-le-street Petty Sessions on Wednesday next. The prisoner made no reply, and appeared to be in a state of satisfaction. The statement was repeated and eventually the accused said "Yes." Mr Robinson, we understand, could elicit no further remark from the man, and the interview was brought to a close.

The Hull Daily Mail, October 4th 1888,

THE ATROCITIES IN LONDON. ANOTHER FEARFUL TRAGEDY. A WATCHMAN KILLED. CAPTURE OF THE ASSASSIN. SUPPOSED DISCOVERY OF THE WHITECHAPEL MURDERER. The Evening News (London) in a third edition to-day, states that a man was seen to go behind a hoarding in High Street, Shadwell, with a woman at half past four this morning. The watchman on duty followed them and called the police. The man killed the watchman with his knife, but was secured by several constables who had hurried up. The Evening News adds that it is believed the man is the Whitechapel murder. A later telegraph from The Press Association says that upon an inquiry at the chief police station for the Shadwell district, in which it was stated that a watchman had been killed this morning, that no information had been received by the police of the alleged murder, and that certainly no arrest had been made in connection with such occurrence. The rumour created much excitement both in the City and Whitechapel when first circulated. THE MITRE SQUARE TRAGEDY. TOUCHING SCENE AT THE MORTUARY. The Press Association states that it was between ten and eleven o'clock on Wednesday night that the identification of the victim of the Mitre-square tragedy took place. During the day the man John Kelly, who is a poorly clad labourer, thick set, dark, and of medium height, had been in communication with the City police authorities at Jewry-street, and the information imparted by him resulted in his going in the evening, in company with a detective officer, to the mortuary in Golden-lane, where the remains of the unfortunate woman lay. As is now well known, he had not the slightest difficulty, despite the mutilated condition of the face, in recognising the body as that of Kate Conway, a woman with whom he had been living for some seven years, latterly at 55 Flower and Dean-street. Although Kelly was most positive as to the identity of the body, the police deemed it prudent to obtain corroborative evidence on the point, and the man was *accordingly closely questioned as to the relatives of the dead woman. DISCOVERY OF THE DECEASED'S SISTER. He at once informed them that, to his knowledge, a sister of "Kate's" was living at 6, Thrawl-street, a thoroughfare adjacent to Flower and Dean-street. Inquiries were made early on Wednesday morning established the accuracy of this statement, for Kelly, accompanied by a detective and a little girl went straight to the house, and no difficulty was experienced in finding the sister of the deceased. Mrs Frost to use the name which she first gave to the police, lives on the top floor of the house, and the girl was sent upstairs to see her, found the old lady in bed, from which at first she refused to rise. The lass returned to the detective and Kelly with this message, but was requested by the former again to go upstairs, and this time to tell Mrs Frost that her sister was dead, and that it was necessary she should see the police. Thus appealed to, the woman rose, dressed and was soon ready to accompany Detective Abbott on the mission of identification at Golden-lane. Mrs Frost was accompanied by her son, George Gold, and also a young married woman named Lizzie Griffiths. The mortuary was reached at one o'clock, and the sister on beholding the body of her mutilated relative had no difficulty recognising the features. The poor woman, as might be naturally expected, gave way to a paroxysm of grief after gazing on the dreadful sight, and had to be led from the mortuary. Her son George, who is a woodchopper in Thrawl-street, made the question of identity still more certain at once declaring the body to be that of aunt Kate. STATEMENT OF MRS. FROST. Mrs Frost, on recovering composure, made a brief statement to the police. It was to the effect that she had not previously seen her sister for some two years; that the deceased had at one time lived with a man named Conway, and subsequently with John Kelly; and that there were two children whom she had had by Conway still living, one daughter and the other a son. She further mentioned that the daughter was married to a man named Phillips, who is a gunmaker in the neighbourhood of Bermondsey, but that she did not know her address. As to the whereabouts the boy, she declared that she had not the slightest knowledge. The police, it is understood, are anxious to obtain the address of the daughter, though so far they have been unable to obtain any definite information. News is supposed to spread with amazing rapidity in Flower and Dean-street and that immediate neighbourhood, but strange to relate, the intelligence of the identification of the body by Kelly and the sister of the deceased was not generally known there till the morning. This is all the more singular when the fact is remembered that both Kelly and "Kate," the latter in particular, are both well known in Flower and Dean-street. A representative of the Press Association was in the street as late as half past three in the morning making enquiries, but no one with whom he then came in contact- and they were not a few in number- knew that "Kate" had been identified. MRS. FROST INTERVIEWED. A STRANGE STORY. On Wednesday evening a representative of the Press Association interviewed Mrs Frost at her residence in Thrawl-street, Whitechapel. She is a middle sized, stout and somewhat elderly lady, with a face which, though now clouded with sorrow, still retained a pleasant and agreeable appearance. On being ushered into the dimly-lighted room at the top of the house the reporter was received with the utmost courtesy, and the conversation opened by Mrs. Frost explaining that although she had described herself as Mrs. Frost to the police, yet she was known as Mrs. Gold, which was the name of her first husband. She stated, in reply to questions, that her present husband worked at the waterside in unloading cargoes of fruit. She had lived in that street for seventeen years, but although so near she seldom saw her deceased sister. Although on friendly terms, yet they did not associate much together. The last occasion on which they met was, so far as she could remember, some four or five months ago, and then the dead woman called upon her. The real name of her sister was Catherine Eddowes, for she had never been married. For many years "Kate" as they called her, went by the name of Conway, an army pensioner with whom she lived, and by whom she had children. Years ago they separated, and after that and down to the time of her death the deceased lived with the man Kelly. She (Mrs. Frost) was on speaking terms with Kelly, but did not mix with him. Mrs. Frost proceeded to state that she did not know anything of the murder of her sister until that morning, until Kelly came round to the house accompanied by a police officer and a little girl. The latter was sent upstairs to see her, but she was in bed at the time, and told the child she was too ill to get up. Shortly afterwards the girl returned and told her her sister Kate was dead, and that her body was lying at the Golden-lane mortuary. That was between eleven and twelve, and she then got up, and shortly afterwards accompanied the detective to the mortuary. Her son George and a young married woman named Lizzie Griffiths went with her. Disfigured though the face was, yet she had no difficulty in recognising the features and forms of her sister. Here Mrs. Frost commenced to sob violently, and exclaimed twice, with a broken voice, "Oh, my poor sister! That she should come to such and end as this." Somewhat recovering her composure, the old lady went on to say that she did not see the tattoo marks on the arm, nor was she even aware of their existence. To see the face was quite sufficient to convince her of the identity of the dead woman. Although she could not read, she had of course heard about the Whitechapel murders, but she little thought until that morning that her sister was one of Sunday's victims. So far as she could tell the deceased was about 42 years of age. [Section illegible] As to the son, she knew nothing about him, and should not know him even if she saw him. The daughter was about 18 years of age, but the boy was older. Her sister was very well*

Mike Covell

known in the neighbourhood, and had never, to her knowledge, led the life of a prostitute. Here the poor old lady burst forth once more into tears, and gave way to the most violent grief, mourning again and again, "Oh my poor sister! The Lord save us!" It was with the utmost difficulty that those present were able to console Mrs Frost and to induce her to cease crying. THE BIRTHPLACE OF THE VICTIM. The Press Association's Wolverhampton correspondent says Eddowes was a native of that town, and several of her relations state her father was a tinplate worker. She ran away to London when 20 years of age. THE INQUEST. This morning Mr. Langham, the City Coroner, opened the inquest upon the body of the woman murdered in Mitre-square on Sunday morning, and whose name has been variously given as Eddowes, Conway, and Kelly. Mr. Crawford, City Solicitor, represented the police, Major Smith, Acting Commissioner, and Mr. Superintendent Forster also being present. Eliza Gold, the first witness, living at 6 Thrawl-street, identified the body as that of her sister, Catherine Eddowes, who was a single woman, who lived with John Kelly for some years. Witness last saw her alive about four or five months ago. The deceased was a hawker, of sober habits, and before living with Kelly deceased lived with the man Conway for some years, and had children by him. Witness did not know whether Conway, who was an army pensioner, was still alive. In reply to Mr. Crawford, witness said she had not seen Conway for some years. John Kelly, living at a lodging house in Flower and Dean-street, a market labourer, said deceased had lived with him for seven years. Her name was Conway, and he last saw her on Saturday last at two o'clock in the afternoon. They parted on very good terms in Houndsditch, the deceased saying she was going to Bermondsey to find her daughter. She promised to return by four o'clock. He heard she had been locked up in Bishopsgate for drunkenness, but made no inquiries, believing she would return on Sunday. Deceased never went out for an immoral purpose. When they parted deceased had no money, and she left with the intention of getting some from her daughter. Witness did not know where deceased had got drink on Saturday, considering she had no money. The deceased last year got money from her daughter. On Friday last deceased went to the Mile-end, and stopped in the casual ward. Early in the week witness and deceased were in Kent together, and on Thursday arrived in London, spending the night together at Shoe-lane Casual Ward, as they had no money. On Friday they arranged that deceased would go to the Mile-end Workhouse, and witness stay at a lodging house. They pawned a pair of boots on Saturday, and spent the greater portion of half-crown in food and drink. Witness stood outside with bare feet whilst the deceased pawned the boots. It might have been Friday and not Saturday. Frederick Wilkinson, deputy of the lodging house in Flower and Dean-street, corroborated the last witness as to Kelly and the deceased living *there on good terms. Deceased did not walk the streets. She said the name of Conway was bought and paid for, meaning that she was married. Police-Constable Watkins deposed to finding the murdered woman in Mitre-square on Sunday morning, as already reported, with her throat cut, body ripped open, and in a pool of blood. Witness had not heard any footsteps or a cry whilst near the square. Mr. Frederick Foster produced plans and maps of the locality. Wilkinson, the lodging house deputy, recalled, said he could not tell whether any stranger came there between two and three o'clock that morning. Over one hundred people lodged in the house. After luncheon, Inspector Collett was examined, and deposed to being called to the scene of the murder immediately after the discovery of the body. Three black buttons generally used for women's boots, a small metal button, a metal thimble, and a mustard tin containing two pawn tickets were picked up near the body. There was a piece of apron on the body corresponding with another piece picked up in Goulston street, some little way off. Witness detailed the steps taken by the police, with the object of tracking the murderer. A house to house inquiry had been made in the vicinity with practically no result. DR GORDON BROWN'S EVIDENCE. HORRIBLE DETAILS. Dr Gordon Brown, surgeon to the city police, described the position of the body when he saw it a few minutes after two o'clock on Sunday morning. The way in which the body was mutilated was horrible in the extreme. There was no blood on the front of the clothes. A piece of the ear, cut off, dropped from the body. In describing the injuries to the abdomen, witness said the left kidney was carefully taken out, and in his opinion this must have been done by someone who knew where to find it. The womb was cut through, leaving a lump of about three quarters of an inch. The rest of it was missing. The wounds were inflicted with a sharp knife, which must have been pointed. Judging by the cuts in the abdomen, a good deal of knowledge of the position of organs in the abdominal cavity was displayed. The parts removed would be of no use for professional purposes. The removal of the left kidney was especially difficult. Such knowledge would be likely to be possessed by a slaughterer of animals. Witness thought the infliction of all the injuries could be done in five minutes. Witness could assign no reason for the parts being taken away. He felt sure there was no struggle. He believed the act was that of one man only. He should not expect much blood on the person inflicting the wounds described. The inquiry was then adjourned. THE CITY COMMON COUNCIL AND THE REWARD. At the meeting of the Common Council of the City of London this morning, the Lord Mayor said they were aware of the course he had already taken on behalf of the Corporation in offering a substantial reward for the apprehension of the Whitechapel murderer. He was glad to see public opinion was entirely in favour of such a step, and he*

Mike Covell

> would ask them to endorse his action.- This was done in a most enthusiastic manner.

The Hull Daily Mail, October 4th 1888,

> PRESS RELEASE. The Press Association, telegraphing at one o'clock, says that the man arrested in Aldgate has been released, and there was then no one under detention, and the police have absolutely no clue to the murderer. IMPORTANT STATEMENT BY A GREEN GROCER. The Evening News, London, says that a greengrocer, named Mathew Packer, has been found, who states that at a quarter to 12 on Saturday night a man, aged 35, stout, and wearing a wideawake hat and dark clothes, accompanied by a woman with a white flower in her bosom, came to his stall, two doors from the Berner Street murder, and purchased some grapes. They left in the direction of the club about a quarter past 12 o'clock. THE WESTMINSTER MYSTERY. The Press Association says an inspector and a number of plain clothes officers were again searching the basement of the new Police Offices in Whitehall this morning in search of the remaining members of the body found there on Tuesday. It is believed the person who deposited the remains was familiar with the ground passages leading to the spot, which is dark and full of pitfalls. A SUPPOSED CLUE. A Later report from Westminster states that the police have been informed that on Saturday afternoon a respectable looking man, aged about 35, was seen to get under the boarding at Cannon Row and walk quietly away. A description of this man has been circulated. ANOTHER MYSTERY. A rumour was circulated last night that a box had been discovered in the River Lea at Clapton by a man whose name did not transpire. On an examination being made, the box was found to contain some woman's wearing apparel stained with blood. The box, with its contents, was taken to the Hackney Police Station.

The Hull Daily Mail, October 4th 1888,

> THE LONDON TRAGEDIES. THE BERNER STREET MURDER. A correspondent says:- It was established by yesterday's evidence at the inquiry on the Berner-street victim that the woman murdered is Elizabeth Stride, and that Mrs Malcolm was mistaken on Tuesday in stating the deceased was her sister. The clue afforded by the discovery of the blood stained knife on a doorstep will be followed up, although it seems certain that the knife was not in the place an hour before it was picked up, and the object of the person who put it there is unknown. Michael Kidney will probably be examined again respecting [illegible] pretended special information. A Bath correspondent says:- From

further inquiries made here it appears that conflicting evidence of identification in the Berner Street case could be decided if witnesses were called from Bath. The woman Watts could be identified by several Bath persons and also by members of the police force, as she had been charged by the Bath police with drunkenness, and was well known to some members of the force. ANOTHER POSTCARD. *Consternation has been caused locally by the report that "Jack the Ripper" has sent a postcard to Barrett's confectionary factory at Wood Green saying that he shall visit the neighbourhood and "do for" six of the girls employed at the factory. It is further said that a man answering the published description of the supposed murderer has been seen on Wood Green. People speak of their intention to carry arms to be prepared for sudden attack.* A RING FOUND. *A wedding ring, but not a gold one, has been found in the enclosed grounds where the buildings are in progress in Cannon Row, Westminster. A workman entered the ground yesterday morning on the lookout for a job. While standing near the entrance to the vaults where the trunk was found he noticed what appeared to be a ring embedded in the dirt. He picked it up, and, having cleaned it, he found that it was a wedding ring, slightly bent. Whether the ring is in any way connected with the murder, or whether it may lead to the identification of the woman is not, of course, yet known.* ALMOST ANOTHER VICTIM. *An alarming story was told to a detective on Tuesday and it is understood (the Daily Telegraph says) that the Metropolitan Police have for some time been cognisant of its details. If this statement be true- and there appears to be no reason to question it- then sometime between the date of the Hanbury Street murder and last Sunday the bloodthirsty maniac who is now terrifying Whitechapel unsuccessfully attempted another outrage. The woman, who so narrowly escaped is married, but she admits having entered into conversation with a strange man for an immoral purpose. She alleges that he tripped her up, so that she fell upon the pavement. He made an effort to cut her throat, but she shielded herself with her arm, and in doing so received a cut upon it. Alarmed by his failure and fearing her shrieks, the would be murderer ran off, and the woman, when discovered, was removed to the hospital. She has since been discharged, and the wound upon the arm is still to be seen. The occurrence is alleged to have taken place off Commercial Street. Unfortunately, the woman was so muck in liquor when she was assaulted that she cannot recall the man's fan's face or dress, and has been unable to give a description of him, which may account for the secrecy which has been maintained in regard to the attack.*

The Hull Daily News, October 4th 1888,

Mike Covell

THE LONDON TRAGEDIES. THE WESTMINSTER HORROR. FURTHER PARTICULARS. During the operations the works on Wednesday, and while the search was going on, an alarming accident occurred through a scaffold falling. It was known that many policemen where in the vault beneath, and those underneath were terribly startled, and rushed out into the open air, but, fortunately, not one person was hurt, even the workmen on the scaffold escaping. The accident attracted a great crowd, and much excitement was for a time visible. The search was afterwards resumed under the direction of Superintendent Dunlop, but up to half-past ten there had been no result. The Press Association learns that Mr. Troutbeck has decided to hold an inquest on the remains, but the date is not yet fixed and will not probably be for three days at least. The detectives were still employed searching round the scene of the discovery. There are indications that the hoarding surrounding the works has recently been scaled. The Press Association learns on Wednesday that the surgeons who examined the remains have come to the conclusion that the arm which was found at Pimlico fitted into the trunk found on Thursday. A SELF ACCUSED MEDICAL STUDENT. EXTRAORDINARY STATEMENT. At Guildhall, London on Wednesday, William Bull, describing himself as a medical student at a London hospital, and living at Stannard road, Dalston, was charged on his own confession, with having committed the murder at Mitre Square. Inspector Izzard said that at 20 minutes to 11 on Tuesday, the accused came to his room at Bishopsgate-street station, and made the following statement:- "My name is William Bull and I live at Dalston. I am a medical student at the London Hospital. I wish to give myself up for the murder in Aldgate, on Saturday night or Sunday morning about two o'clock. I think I met the woman in Aldgate. I went with her up a narrow street not far from the main road for an immoral purpose. I promised to give her half-a-crown, which I did. While walking along together there was a second man, who came up and took the half-a-crown from her. I cannot endure this any longer. My poor head-(here he put his hand to his head, and cried or pretended to cry)- I shall go mad. I have done it and I must put up with it." The Inspector asked what had become of the clothing he had on when the murder was committed. The accused said, "If you wish to know they are in the Lea, and the knife I threw away." At this point the prisoner declined to say any more. He was drunk. Part if the statement was made in the presence of Major Smith. Prisoner gave correct address, but is not known at the London Hospital. His parents were respectable. The Inspector asked for a remand to make enquiries, and this was granted. Prisoner now said he was drunk when he made the statement. He was remanded. THE ADJOURNED INQUEST ON THE BERNER STREET VICTIMS. Mr Wynne E. Baxter resumed his inquiry on Wednesday at the Vestry-hall, Cable street, on the body of the Berner street victim, recognised up to the present as Elizabeth Watts. The interest in the proceedings has in no way abated, an on account of the discovery at Westminster last night public feeling has been greatly excited. Large crowds of people assembled outside the Vestry-hall. The first witness called was Elizabeth Tanner, living at 32, Flower and Dean street, Whitechapel. She recognised deceased as Long Liz. Did not know her nationality. Deceased told witness that her husband and children were lost in Princess Alice disaster. She last saw her alive on Saturday afternoon in Queen's Head public house, Commercial street. Did not see her again until that afternoon in the mortuary. Witness was quite certain as to her identity. Deceased left a male acquaintance on Thursday, to live with witness. Never knew that witness had relatives in Holborn and never heard the name Stride mentioned. Deceased, who was a Swede, worked among the Jews. Catherine Lane, living with the last witness, said she recognised the body as that of Long Liz. Deceased told witness on Saturday she had had a quarrel with the man she left on Thursday. Witness had heard deceased speak to people in her own language. Charles Preston, a barber, living at the same address also identified the body as that of Long Liz, and he saw her alive on Saturday. He understood she was born in Stockholm, and came to England in a foreign gentleman's service. Deceased also gave witness to understand that her name was Elizabeth Stride, and that her mother was still alive in Sweden. Michael Kidney, living at 38 Dorset street, Waterside labourer, said deceased was Elizabeth Stride. He had lived with her for nearly three years. She was a Swede, and was born three miles from Stockholm. Her husband was a ship's carpenter at Sheerness, and once kept a coffee house at Crisp street, Poplar. He was drowned in the Princess Alice disaster. Did not see the deceased on Thursday. Saw her last on Tuesday, when they parted friendly. Never saw her again and could not account for her disappearance. She had been away from witness five months since he had known her. He never neglected her, but treated her as a wife. Witness further stated voluntarily that he asked at Leman street police station for the assistance of a young, strange detective, as he had important information. He could not get the assistance. The Coroner pressed witness to divulge his information, but witness only reiterated that he had the information.- Replying to Inspector Reid, he said if the police were under his own control he could catch the murderer red handed.- Witness admitted he was intoxicated when he applied at the police station. Edward Johnstone, assistant to Drs Kay and Blackwell, deposed to being called to see the body. Thomas Coran, a lad of about eighteen, produced a knife which he found on the doorstep of No. 253, Whitechapel road twenty four hours after the murder. The knife produced was about twelve inches long, and the handle was neatly folded in a silk handkerchief which had stains like blood upon it.- Joseph Drage, H, 282, said he

Mike Covell

> *saw the boy find the knife. The handle and blade were covered with blood, which had dried on. The knife was not on the step an hour previously. CONSTABULARY HOUSE-TO-HOUSE VISITATION IN WHITECHAPEL. On Wednesday, plain clothes constables made a house-to-house visitation, leaving copies of a handbill requesting occupiers to give notice to the nearest police station of any suspicious matters which may come within their knowledge concerning the murders.*

The Hull Daily Mail, October 4th 1888,

> *THE LONDON MYSTERIES. LATEST DETAILS. LETTER FROM SIR CHARLES WARREN. The Central News, telegraphing last night, says: - Most of the detectives belonging to the City and Metropolitan forces were busily engaged yesterday in investigating suggestions and information conveyed in letters addressed to the authorities by the general public. The number of these communications, received both at Scotland-yard and Old Jewry, is enormous, and requires at each place almost the exclusive services of one officer, whose duty it is – so to speak – to separate the grain from the chaff. Up to the present moment, the chaff has decidedly predominated, but the work is preserved with in the hope that sooner or later, is may yield valuable information. A communication received this morning, which it is not at present desirable to particularize, was considered of such a promising character that a number of experienced officers were specially told off to investigate the accuracy of the information contained in it, the men were engaged in the work all day. Acting (it is understood) on a suggestion in the public journals, a public notice was widely circulated this morning among householders in the East End, stating that certain murders had been committed, and earnestly requesting that anyone possessing information should communicate it at once to the nearest police-station. It is pretty certain that, though no mention of the rewards is made, the handbill will quicken the latent suspicions of many persons who otherwise would not have paid attention to details apparently trivial, but which may have important bearings upon the matter in hand. The red-ink letter and post-card addressed to the Central News and purporting to come from "Jack the Ripper," have been lithographed by the Scotland-yard authorities, and copies will be supplied to the public journals. The facsimile is complete, even to the colour of the ink. If these extraordinary communications really come from the murderer, their publication in facsimile will, of course, be of immense importance in the work of tracking him. The general opinion, however, still is that they were written by an idiotic practical joker. At a recent meeting of the Whitechapel District Board of Works the following resolution was passed: "That this Board regards with horror and*

alarm the several atrocious murders recently perpetrated within the district of Whitechapel and its vicinity, and calls upon Sir Charles Warren so to regulate and strengthen the police force in the neighbourhood as to guard against any repetition of such atrocities." In reply thereto Sir Charles Warren has sent the following: "Sir - In reply to a letter of the 2nd inst. from the Clerk to the Board of Works for the Whitechapel District, transmitting a resolution of the Board with regard to the recent atrocious murders perpetrated in and about Whitechapel, I have to point out that the carrying out of your proposals as to regulating and strengthening the police force in your district cannot possibly do more than guard or take precautions against any repetition of such atrocities, so long as the victims actually, but unwillingly, connive at their own destruction. Statistics show that London, in comparison to its population, is the safest city in the world to live in. The prevention of murder directly cannot be effected by any strength of the police force, but it is reduced and brought to a minimum by rendering it most difficult to escape detection. In the particular class of murders now confronting us, however, the unfortunate victims appear to take the murderer to some retired spot and place themselves in such a position that they can be slaughtered without a sound being heard. The murder, therefore, takes place without any clue to the criminal being left. "I have to request and call upon your Board, as popular representatives, to do all in your power to dissuade the unfortunate women about Whitechapel from going into lonely places in the dark with any persons, whether acquaintances or strangers. I have also to point out that the purlieus about Whitechapel are most imperfectly lighted, and the darkness is an important assistant to crime. "I can assure you, for the information of your Board, that every nerve has been strained to detect the criminal or criminals, and to render more difficult further atrocities. You will agree with me that it is not desirable that I should enter into particulars as to what the police are doing in the matter. It is most important for good results that our proceedings should not be published, and the very fact that you may be unaware of what the Detective Department is doing is only the stronger proof that it is doing its work with secrecy and efficiency. "A large force of police has been drafted into the Whitechapel District to assist those already there to the full extent necessary to meet the requirements, but I have to observe that the Metropolitan police have not large reserves doing nothing and ready to meet emergencies, but every man has his duty assigned to him, and I can only strengthen the Whitechapel District by drawing men from duty in other parts of the metropolis. You will be aware that the whole of the police work of the metropolis has to be done as usual while this extra work is going on, and that at such times as this extra precautions have to be taken to prevent the commission of other classes of crime being facilitated through the attention of the police

Mike Covell

being diverted to one special place and object. "I trust that your Board will assist the police by persuading the inhabitants to give them every information in their power concerning any suspicious characters in the various dwellings, for which object 10,000 handbills - a copy of which I enclose - have been distributed. "I have read the reported proceedings of your meeting, and I regret to see that the greatest misconceptions appear to have arisen in the public mind as to recent action in the administration of the police. I beg you will dismiss from your minds as utterly fallacious the numerous anonymous statements as to recent changes stated to have been made in the Police Force of a character not conducive to efficiency. "It is stated that the Rev. Daniel Greatrex announced to you that one great cause of police inefficiency was a new system of police, whereby constables were constantly changed from one district to another, keeping them ignorant of their beats. I have seen this statement made frequently in the newspapers lately, but it is entirely without foundation. The system at present in use has existed for the last twenty years, and constables are seldom or never drafted from their districts except for promotion or for some particular cause. "Notwithstanding the many good reasons why constables should be changed on their beats, I have considered the reasons on the other side to be more cogent, and have felt that they should be thoroughly acquainted with the districts in which they serve. "And with regard to our Detective Department, a department relative to which reticence is always most desirable, I may say that a short time ago I made arrangements which still further reduced the necessity for transferring officers from districts which they knew thoroughly. "I have to call attention to the statement of one of your members, that in consequence of the change in the condition of Whitechapel in recent years, a thorough revision of the police arrangements is necessary, and I shall be very glad to ascertain from you what changes your Board consider advisable, and I may assure you that your proposals will receive from me every consideration. - I am, Sir, your obedient servant, "CHARLES WARREN. "Metropolitan Police-office, 4, Whitehall-place, S.W., Oct. 3, 1888." THE MITRE-SQUARE TRAGEDY. IDENTIFICATION OF THE VICTIM. There is now (says the Central News) no question that the victim of the Mitre-square tragedy is Catherine Eddowes, otherwise Conway or Kelly, her sister, Eliza Gold, Kelly, with whom she lived, and Frederick Wilkinson, the deputy of the lodging-house at which she had lived off and on for nearly ten years, having alike seen and identified the corpse at the mortuary in Golden-lane. From their statements, it would appear that Eddowes, though in the poorest circumstances, and living with a man to whom she was not married, bore a generally good character, and was not all events a member of the unhappy class from which the other victims have been selected. Kelly, Wilkinson, and Mrs. Gold agree in saying that she worked hard, charing among the Jews in "the lane" during four or five months in the winter, and throughout the greater part of the summer tramping in the country – always with Kelly, hopping, fruit picking, and hay-making. She was born, it appears, in Wolverhampton, rather more than forty years ago, but soon after her birth her parents moved to London, where she was educated at the Dowgate Charity School, and where she has since lived. When she was about 20 years of age, she became acquainted with a soldier named Thomas Conway, whose initials, "T.C.," are tattooed on her arm, and subsequently went to live with him. No marriage ceremony was gone through, but they continued to live as man and wife about twelve years, during which time she bore him several children. Ten years ago, however, Conway deserted the woman, and neither she nor her relatives have heard of him since that time. On finding herself alone, Eddowes – or Mrs. Conway as she was generally called – went to live at a common lodging house at 55, Flower-and-Dean-street, and there, seven years ago, she got to know John Kelly, with whom she had cohabited ever since. At the lodging house both Kelly, and the woman bore a good character as hard-working and well conducted people. Eddowes was last seen by Kelly on Saturday afternoon, when he told her to go and see her daughter, and get the price of a bed for the night. He felt no alarm when she did not return in the evening, as he had heard a rumour that she had been locked up for drunkenness; neither were his fears excited when later on, he heard of the fresh tragedies in the district. But on Tuesday night he learnt that some pawn tickets, which he knew were in the woman's possession, had been found in Mitre-square, and then he went hastily to the police-station to find that the murdered woman was she with whom he had lived so long. The tattooing on the arm was an important factor in the identification, and neither Kelly, Mrs. Gold, nor the other people who saw the body had the slightest doubt as to its identity. Eddowes leaves several children, and these the police are now endeavouring to find. One of them – a daughter – is married to a gunmaker named Phillips, and lives, it is believed, somewhere in Bermondsey, and a son is thought to live in the same district. At Guildhall this morning, William Bull, describing himself as a medical student in the London Hospital, and living at Stannard-road, Dalston, was charged on his own confession with having committed the murder at Mitre-square. Inspector Izzard said that at twenty to eleven last night the accused came to his room at Bishopsgate-street Station, and made the following statement:-"My name is WM Bull, and I live at Dalston. I am a medical student at the London Hospital. I wish to give myself up for murder in Aldgate, on Saturday night or Sunday morning. About two o'clock, I think I met the woman in Aldgate. I went with her up a narrow street not far from main road, for an immoral purpose. I promised to give her half-a-crown, which I did. While walking along together there was a second man, who came up and took the half-crown from her. I cannot endure this any longer. My poor head. (Here he put his hand to his head and cried, or pretended to cry) I shall go mad. I have done it, and I must put up with it." The inspector asked what had become of the clothing he had on when the murder was committed. The accused said, "If you wish to know, they are in the Lea, and the knife I threw away." At this point the prisoner declined to say any more. He was drunk. Part of the statement was made in the presence of Major Smith. The prisoner gave his correct address, but is no known at the London Hospital. His parents were respectable. The inspector asked for a remand to make inquiries, and this was granted. The prisoner now said he was drunk when he made the statement. He was remanded. THE BERNER'S-STREET TRAGEDY. ANTECEDENTS OF THE VICTIM. SUPPOSED MISTAKEN IDENTIFICATION. The Central News states that it obtained information yesterday afternoon respecting the antecedents of the woman murdered in Berner-street, which throws very grave doubt upon the evidence of Mrs. Malcolm, who at the inquest said that she had seen the body, and identified it as that of her sister. There is, it is urged, every reason to believe that Mrs. Manson, who at first was not at all certain in the identification, is really mistaken, and that her sister will sooner or later be found alive and well. An old artilleryman, who had lived for the past three years with Eliza Stride-otherwise known as "Long Liz"-averred yesterday afternoon that he has identified Stride's body at the mortuary without any difficulty. She was, according to his statement, last seen alive on Saturday night at 32, Flower and Dean-street, between six and seven o'clock, when she was in good health. She was of cleanly habits, and had apparently been well educated in her own language-Swedish. She could cook and keep house well, and was expert in the use of the sewing machine, knitting, and all kinds of needlework. The man first became acquainted with her about three years ago when he met her in Commercial-street, and he had lived with her ever since, except during occasional intervals, when she went away to work for some Jews. He lived with her at 35 Devonshire-street down to five months ago, when they moved to No. 36 in the same street. She was quiet and industrious, but was sometimes the worse for drink. Her manner was peculiar. At times she would say that she was going out for half an hour, and would absent herself for two or three days. Before her marriage she was a domestic servant near Hyde-park, and afterwards she and her husband kept a coffee-shop and boarding-house in Crisp-street, Poplar. She lost her husband in the Princess Alice disaster, as well as two children, one of whom was drowned in the father's arms. She herself escaped by climbing up a rope as the vessel was sinking. A man who had got upon the rope before her slipped and kicked her accidentally in the mouth, knocking out her front teeth. Her husband, who was a ship's carpenter, did a good deal of work in the building of the Great Eastern steamship, and the woman herself put the cushions and fittings in their proper places after the vessel was launched. When she became a widow she sold the coffee-shop and went to live in Cannon-street-road. She used to say that she was the mother of nine children. She frequently attended the Swedish church in Princes-street. The man with whom she afterwards lived believes that her surviving children are being brought up in the country at a school connected with the Swedish church. The woman had no relatives in England, but she said that she had a brother-in-law practicing as a surgeon in Kent. She had spoken of a sister residing about three miles from Stockholm. It is understood that the police are in communication with the brother-in-law. THE RELATIVES OF THE WOMAN INTERVIEWED. The Bath correspondent of the Central News has interviewed the relations of Mr Watts, the husband of the woman identified by Mrs Malcolm as her sister. It seems that deceased was married some 28 years ago at Bath, and at that time she was a domestic servant in the house of Mr Watts' father, who was a Bath wine merchant. After the marriage they only lived together for about two years, when the woman is alleged to have forsaken her husband, who was about twenty-two at the time. He went to America, but is now in England leading a roaming life. THE INQUEST. Mr. Wynne Baxter yesterday resumed the inquiry into the death of Elizabeth Stride, who was found murdered at Berners-street on Sunday last. The proceedings did not commence until 1.25, owing to some jurymen being late. Elizabeth Tanner, 32, Flower and Dean-street, was the first witness called. She deposed that she had seen the body in the mortuary, and recognised deceased as the woman known by the name of "Long Liz." She had lodged there about six years. Witness did not know her right name. Deceased had told her she was a Swedish woman, and was married, and that her husband and children had gone down in the Princess Alice. Witness last saw her alive at 6.30 on Saturday afternoon in the Queen's Head public house, in Commercial-street. She did not see her alive after that time. Witness was quiet sure of the identity of deceased, as, in addition to the features she had lost the roof of her mouth at the time of the Princess Alice disaster. Deceased was on board at the time, and her moth was injured. Deceased had stayed at the lodging house from Thursday night, and had paid for her bed on Saturday night. Witness only knew one male acquaintance of deceased, but did not know his name. She knew deceased lived in Fashion-street, and had never heard of any relatives of deceased. She had never heard deceased say she was afraid of anyone or had been threatened. When she came into the lodging house on Thursday she was wearing a long jacket. Deceased had been away about three months, when she returned last Thursday, but witness had seen her frequently. Deceased told her that she was working among Jews, and living with a man in Fashion-street. She *spoke English as well as Swedish. Catherine Lane, 32, Flower and Dean-street, charwoman, said she had lived at the above place since February last. She had seen the body lying at the mortuary, and had recognised it as that of "Long Liz." She last saw deceased alive on Saturday between seven and eight o'clock, in the kitchen. When deceased left the kitchen she gave witness a piece of velvet to mind until she came back. Deceased had sixpence when she left. She knew of nobody likely to injure the deceased. She was certain that deceased was a foreigner. Charles Preston, 32, Flower and Dean-street, said he had lived there eighteen months. He was quiet sure deceased was "Long Liz." He last saw her alive on Saturday evening, between six and seven o'clock. He had always understood deceased was a Swede, and born in Stockholm. She came to England as a servant in a gentleman's family. He had heard deceased say she had kept a coffee-house at Chrisp-street, Poplar, that her name was Elizabeth Stride, and that her mother was alive in Sweden. Michael Kidney, a Dorset-street labourer, stated that he had lived with deceased, and had no doubt about her identity. Her name was Elizabeth Stride, and witness had lived with her about three years. She was a Swede. Last saw deceased alive that day week, when she left witness. On Monday night he went to Leman-street Police-station and asked for a detective, whom he wished placed under his orders. He was intoxicated at the time, and his request was refused. He believed if the police were placed under his orders he could catch the murderer, but he had no definite information. Edward Johnston, 100, Commercial-road, assistant to Dr Blackwell, stated that on Sunday last, shortly after midnight, he was called to Berners-street, and found the woman lying dead. He found the body warm, except the hands, and it did not appear to have been moved. Thomas Coram, 67, Plumber's-row, stated that on Sunday night he was walking along Whitechapel-road, and when opposite No. 253 he saw a knife lying on the steps. (Knife produced, also handkerchief). The handkerchief was wrapped round the knife. A policeman came along, and witness called his attention to it. The Coroner said that the knife was dagger-shaped, about nine or ten inches long, and was very sharp. Witness said it was about 12.30 on Sunday night, when he found the knife. Police Constable Joseph Drage stated that he saw the last witness stooping down by the door and went to him, when he saw the knife, and handkerchief round the handle, lying on the doorstep. He picked up the knife, and found it was smothered with blood. The blood was dry, and the handkerchief was also blood-stained. He took the articles to the Police-station. Doctor Phillips, divisional surgeon, "H" Division, gave evidence as to the post mortem examination which he made on Monday last. He stated that the body was fairly well nourished. There was a deformity in the right leg. The cause of death was undoubtedly due to a loss of blood from the left carotid artery, and to severance of the wind-pipe.*

The inquest was adjourned until tomorrow at two o'clock. AN AMERICAN ARRESTED. *An American who refused to give his name or any account of himself was arrested last night on suspicion of being the Whitechapel murderer. He accosted a woman in Cable-street, asked her to go with him, and threatened that if she refused he would "rip her up." The woman screamed, and the man rushed to a cab. The police gave chase, got up on the cab, seized the man and took him to Leman street Police Station, where he exclaimed to the Inspector, "Are you the boss?" He is detained there, as well as two others arrested last night. A correspondent describes the condition of the district thus: - There was nothing unusual about the appearance of the streets in Whitechapel and adjoining districts on Tuesday night, unless it be in the fact that there were fewer women parading the footways after a late hour. In the evening, from eight o'clock onwards, there was the usual busy current of foot passengers, some returning from work, others promenading for pleasure. In the course of the evening the rumour spread rapidly that another terrible murder had been committed, the body, too, being horribly mutilated. This caused the liveliest excitement, everyone asking everyone else, "Where was it?" The arrival of evening papers, however, had the effect of subduing the alarm, for on finding that, to use the common pronunciation of the pavement, the tragedy was "down Westminster way," the sting was taken out of the news, and when it was further learnt that there was really nothing to indicate that the Westminster affair was the work of the East end fiend, the matter hardly obtained any attention. An enterprising show proprietor in the Mile end road displayed a highly coloured and sensational picture of a murderous tragedy which was introduced to the public as "The Murder in Berner street." This attracted the attention of vast crowds, many of whom evidently placed implicit reliance upon the accuracy of the representations. As the evening wore on, and closing time for the "houses" came, the streets were more and more deserted, the "ladies of the pavement," most of them, withdrawing earlier than usual. One of those who stayed on till the small hours of the morning was asked, "Aren't you afraid to be out at this time of the morning?" She replied, "No." She said the murders were shocking. "But we have no place to go, so we're compelled to be out looking for our lodgings." Another woman, in reply to a similar question, said, "Afraid? No. I'm armed. Look here," and she drew a knife from her pocket. She further declared, "I'm not the only one armed. There's plenty more carry knives now." The coffee stall keepers are grumbling that their trade has been much injured by the terror in the district, for although the condition of the thoroughfares is as usual up to "closing time," there is a great diminution in the number of their customers after midnight. Indeed, some of them say the trade they get is not worth coming out for. There is no lack of constables in the streets. They are to be met everywhere.*

Mike Covell

> *Detectives parade the alleys and courts in twos and threes. It is impossible to be many minutes out of their sight or hearing. THE THAMES EMBANKMENT MYSTERY. The latest information says: - No news has been received by the police, so far as can be ascertained, that would assist them in establishing the identity of the young woman found on the embankment, and this is generally believed to indicate that she must have been a member of that numerous class who have separated themselves from their friends owing to their mode of living. Dr Neville, the divisional police surgeon for Pimlico, who examined the arm found in the Thames on 11th September, has not yet been called. He states that in his opinion the time which Dr Bond allows for the decease of this mutilated victim would agree with his own conclusions. Dr Neville came to the conclusion when he examined the limb submitted to him that it was that of a big woman. Dr Bond also avers that the remains submitted to him are those of a woman of no small stature. A SUGGESTION. A New York telegram says: - Not a great many months ago a series of remarkable brutal murders of women occurred in Texas. The matter caused great local excitement, but aroused less interest than would otherwise have been the case because the victims were chiefly negro women. The crimes were characterised by the same brutal methods as those of the Whitechapel murders. The theory has been suggested that the perpetrator of the latter may be the Texas criminal, who was never discovered. The Atlanta Constitution, a leading Southern newspaper, thus puts the argument: "In our recent annals of crime there has been no other man capable of committing such deeds. The mysterious crimes in Texas have ceased. They have just commenced in London. Is the man from Texas at the bottom of them all? If he is the monster or lunatic, he may be expected to appear anywhere. The fact that he is no longer at work in Texas argues his presence somewhere else. His peculiar line of work was executed in precisely the same manner as is now going on in London. Why should he not be there? The more one thinks of it the more irresistible becomes the conviction that it is the man from Texas. In these days of steam and cheap travel distance is nothing. The man who would kill a dozen women in Texas would not mind the inconvenience of a trip across the water, and once there he would not have any scruples about killing more women." The Superintendent of the New York police admits the possibility of this theory being correct, but he does not think it probable. "There is," he says, "the same brutality and mutilation, the same suspicion that the criminal is a monster or lunatic who has declared war literally to the knife against all womankind, but I hardly believe it is the same individual."*

October 5th 1888

The Hull Daily Mail, October 5th 1888,

"JACK THE RIPPER" CRAZE IN HULL. EXTRAORDINARY CONDUCT OF A DARKEY. OUTRAGE ON A WOMAN. At the Hull Police Court this forenoon before Mr. T. W. Palmer and Mr. E. Lambert, a man of colour, named Samuel Nobb, was charged by Police Constable Leonard (111) 3 with having been disorderly in Adelaide Street on Saturday night.- The officer stated that the prisoner was about the street shouting he was "Jack the Ripper." He saw Noble get hold of one lady and lift her clothes above her head, after which he took hold of another woman, who fell on the street in a dead faint.- Deputy Chief Constable Jones said it took five constables to get the accused into a waggonnette and conduct him into a Police Station.- Mr. Palmer said the Bench considered this to be a very bad case, and imposed a fine of 40s, and costs with alternative of 30 days imprisonment with hard labour.

The Hull Daily Mail, October 5th 1888,

THE WHITECHAPEL CRAZE IN HULL. The excitement which has been caused throughout the country by the horrible atrocities committed in Whitechapel, London, has been equally great in Hull, and it appears a repetition of those incidents which have been frequent in the Metropolis of late has to some extent taken place in Hull. At Hull Police Court this afternoon, before the Mayor (Alderman Toozes) and Mr. T Stratton, a poorly clad woman, named Jane Feeney, was charged on warrant with having used threats towards a woman named Minnie Kirlew.- The Prosecutrix stated that the prisoner threatened her in Manor Street yesterday and said she would "Whitechapel Murder her". Witness stated that she was afraid of the prisoner. A man who was called as a witness said he heard the prisoner when acting very violently, threaten to Whitechapel murder the Prosecutrix.- The Bench ordered the accused to find one surety in £10 to keep the peace for six months, and also sent her to prison or seven days for having been disorderly.

The Hull Daily News, October 5th 1888,

THE WHITECHAPEL MURDERS. The correspondent telegraphing on Thursday night says: The excitement and indignation which are apparent in East London, have been increased to-day by the startling announcement by Dr Browne at the inquest that the similar organ missing from the body of Annie

Mike Covell

Chapman had been cut away from Kate Eddowes, found in Mitre Square. There had been a suspicion of this fact, which now renders the murderer's object the more mysterious since the doctor is so emphatic in his assertion that the obtaining of these portions of a woman's body could be no use to medical research. Dr. Browne stated that the clever manner in which the left kidney and other organ were removed betokened that the murderer was well versed in anatomy, but not necessarily human anatomy, for he could have gained a certain amount of skill by reason of his being a slaughterer of animals. These remarks conclusively show that the same hand which caused the death of the previous victims is also responsible for killing Kate Eddowes, and in all probability Elizabeth Stride in Berner Street, although in the latter case he may have been disturbed before he had time to complete the mutilation at in the peculiarly horrible manner which characterised his fiendish work. The three men who were arrested late on Wednesday night have been liberated, they having satisfactorily established their identity. The man apprehended under suspicious circumstances when leaving the Three Tuns Tavern in Aldgate was very violent throughout the night and refused to satisfy the police as to his antecedents until Thursday morning, when he was discharged. Since the release of these men on Thursday morning the police have made no other apprehensions in connection with the crimes, but the most extraordinary rumours were flying about throughout the locality on Thursday of the capture of the much sought for criminal, and the effect upon the public, already well nigh goaded into exasperation at the continued non-success of the police to hunt down the murder, was indescribable.

Another correspondent writes:- The announcement of Dr. Browne of his disappearance of the portion of the body revived for a time the theory put forward by Mr. Wynne Baxter, the coroner in the Hanbury Street case. The British Medical Journal, however states that the foreign physician who sought to purchase specimens was a gentleman of the highest respectability, that he did not offer a large price, and that he left London eighteen months ago. ANOTHER LETTER FROM THE SUPPOSED MURDERER. The Central News has received the following letter, bearing the E.C. postmark, written in red ink in a round hand, apparently by a person indifferently educated. At the foot is a rude drawing of a sharp pointed knife blade measuring three inches and the handle one:- "3rd October. - Dear Boss, - Since last, splendid success. Two more and never a squeal. Oh, I am master of the art! I am going to be heavy on the guilded - now, we are. Some duchess will cut up nicely, and the lace will show nicely. You wonder how. Oh, we are masters. No education like a butcher's. No animal like a nice woman - the fat are best. On to Brighton for a holiday, but we shan't idle - splendid high-class women there. My mouth waters - good luck there. If

> *not, you will hear from me in the West End. My pal will keep on at the East for a while yet. When I get a nobility - I will send it on to C. Warren, or perhaps to you for a keepsake. O it is jolly. - GEORGE OF THE HIGH-RIP GANG. - Red ink still, but a drop of the real in it." ANOTHER SUPPOSED CLUE. The Evening News (London) on Thursday stated that a greengrocer named Matthew Packer, who lives at 44, Berner Street, only two doors from the club where the body of the first victim of Saturday's butchery was found, states that a quarter to twelve on Saturday night a man aged 35, stout, wearing a wideawake hat, and dark clothes accompanied by a woman with a white flower in her bosom, came to his shop and purchased some grapes. It will be remembered that the woman murdered in Berner Street was found with a bunch of grapes in her hand. Packer declares that the man (who had a quick, commanding way of speaking) stopped talking to the woman in the rain opposite the fruit shop for a good half hour after the purchase of the grapes, and they were still there when he (Packer) and his wife went to bed at about twenty minutes past twelve. The club and the yard in which the murdered woman's body was found were close at hand, and a grape stalk was picked up close to the woman's body. Packer could identify the man immediately, for he had a tolerably long conversation with him while he was buying half a pound of black grapes for the woman; but, strange to say, no detectives had called upon Packer up to Thursday, nor had any attempt whatever been made to follow up this apparently important clue.*

The Hull Daily Mail, October 5th 1888,

> *THE LONDON MURDERS. ANOTHER HORROR AT GUILDFORD. DISCOVERY OF A WOMAN'S LEGS. The Press Association says that Detective Inspector Marshall, of the Whitehall Police, this morning proceeded to Guildford to obtain some human remains, consisting principally of the leg of a woman, which were picked up on the railway there some time ago. Dr Bond will compare them with the trunk lying at Westminster Mortuary. THE MITRE-SQUARE TRAGEDY. THE CONFESSION BY A MEDICAL STUDENT. William Bull, calling himself a medical student, who was remanded on Tuesday at Guildhall Police Court, London, on his confession of having committed the Aldgate murder (Mitre-square), was brought up again to-day. Inspector Izzard now informed Alderman Stone that inquiries had proved that prisoner could not have been connected with the murder in any way.- The Alderman, after expressing regret that he could not punish the prisoner for the trouble he had given, discharged him from custody.*

Mike Covell

THE BERNER-STREET TRAGEDY. INQUEST OF ELIZABETH STRIDE. EXTRAORDINARY EVIDENCE. In inquest on Elizabeth Stride, the victim of the Berner-street murder, was resumed this afternoon by Mr Wynne E. Baxter. Notwithstanding the positive statement by Mrs Malcolm that the deceased was her sister, Elizabeth Watt, it became known this morning before the commencement of the proceedings, that deceased was named Gustafsdotter. She was born in November 1848, at Foreslander, in Gothenburg, Sweden, and married Thomas Stride, a carpenter. The interest in the proceedings is still maintained. At a quarter past two all present were surprised to hear the coroners clerk inform the jury that they were to resume the inquiry into the death of a person unknown, and immediately after Dr Phillips was recalled and stated that he had again examined the body and could not find any injury to palate.- This is in direct contradiction to the statement made by the man Kidney and others, that deceased had in her life lost the roof of her mouth. He had not been able to find any blood on the handkerchief, the stains being those of fruit. He was convinced that the deceased had not swallowed either the skin or the seeds of grapes within many hours of her death. The knife found could not have produced the injuries, which might have been done in two seconds. In cases of suicide the carotid artery was not generally cut as in the present case, and the murderer displayed a knowledge of where to cut the throat.- Dr Blackwell corroborated the last witness. The case was not one of suicide, as no instrument was found near the body. Sven Olsen, clerk to the Swedish Church, Prince's-square, said he had known the deceased 17 years. He bore out the facts stated above, and produced a register which showed she was married to Stride. He thought this was in 1869. The register did not give the date. He gave the deceased the hymn book found in her lodgings.

IMPORTANT STATEMENT BY A SEWER FOREMAN. It may be mentioned in connection with the Mitre-square murder that the foreman of the sewer hands who are engaged in Aldgate in sweeping the streets and clearing away the refuse, &c., in the early hours of the morning, has stated most positively that at the time when the murder is supposed to have been perpetrated he was standing not more than 20 yards away from the spot where the body was subsequently found by the constable and himself. He states emphatically that he never heard any woman's cries for help, nor did any sounds of a struggle reach his ear. WHO IS "THE RIPPER"? IS THERE A GANG? Several correspondents, says the Daily Telegraph, refer to the calligraphy of the "Ripper." "F.C." says "the writing is a decided Civil Service hand." "M.S." has no doubt "the writer is an American." H.E. Ball sets forth many reasons for thinking that "the man is a fish cleaner in one of the markets or elsewhere." Henry Harrison, on the other hand, thinks the expression "squealed" points to a pig sticker, and "Amateur Detective" emphasises the fact that "there are slaughter houses near the scene of the tragedies, and one is a place where the decayed and "played out" horses are butchered." Among the various "hints to the police" are many which have already been acted upon. "F.T.," however thinks "that of the empty warehouses and factories of the district have not been sufficiently searched"; and Alfred C. Calmour (Arundel Club) "ventures to suggest that the sewers in the neighbourhood of the late murders should be searched, as there is just the possibility of the murderer having escaped by them." "M.H." says, "A man could escape through the sewers to more than one place of safety, and could hide his change of clothing on his way to and from the scenes of his dreadful "work," as the "Ripper" calls it." "Bloodhound," combating the idea that the murderer is a madman says: "I have had a larger practical acquaintance with homicidal maniacs than Dr Forbes Winslow ever had, for I have lived with them, and I emphatically assert that this series of crimes is the work of no lunatic, homicidal or otherwise. There is too much coherence of idea, too much fixity of purpose, too much self-control displayed. Insanity has its saving clauses, and this is one of them. These atrocities are the handiwork of no individual but a confederacy. This explains everything: the amazing audacity, the ease with which detection has been evaded, and the commission of two consecutive murders in one night, obviously by the same agency, but not, possibly by the same hand." AMATEUR DETECTIVES AT WORK. Should the murderer again attempt to give effect to his infamous designs in the Whitechapel district he will require, in the interests of his own personal security, not only to avoid the uniformed and plain-clothed members of the Metropolitan Police Force, but to reckon with a small, enthusiastic body of amateur detectives. Convinced that the regular force affords inadequate protection of life and property in this densely populated neighbourhood, a number of local tradesmen decided a few weeks ago to appoint a Vigilance Committee. The duties of the newly-formed band were twofold. In the first place, they were to publish far and wide their disagreement with the Home Secretary by offering a substantial reward to "anyone - citizen or otherwise," who should give information as would bring the murderer or murderers to justice: and, in the second place, they were themselves to patrol the most secluded parts of the district in the dead of night with a view to running the criminal to earth. So worthy a motive they felt confident would at once command the sympathy and support of "the tradesmen, ratepayers, and inhabitants generally." Unfortunately, however, for the realisation of their hopes, experience had proved that those to whom they appealed were more ready to commend than to co-operate. Excluding one or two subscriptions of considerable amounts they have been compelled to admit that funds have not "rolled" in. Nor has the suggestion to hold a large public meeting in furtherance of the objects of the Vigilantes been responded to with alacrity. Yet, undaunted by these disappointments, the committee have worked persistently on. Night after night, at 9 o'clock, meetings have been held in the upper room of a public-house in the Mile End-road, placed at the disposal of the committee by the landlord, who occupies the post of treasurer. The leaders of the movement are drawn principally from the trading class, and include a builder, a cigar manufacturer, a tailor, and a picture-frame maker, a licensed victualler, and "an actor." Inexperienced in practical police duty, the committee decided to call in professional assistance rather than rely solely upon their own resources. For this purpose they engaged the services of two private detectives - men who, though unattached to either metropolitan or city police forces, hold themselves out as experts in the unravelling of mysteries. At the disposal of these executive officers are placed about a dozen stalwart men possessing an intimate acquaintance with the highways and by-ways of Whitechapel. Only those have been selected who are "physically and morally" equal to the task they may any night be called upon to perform. As they were previously numbered among the unemployed, it became unnecessary to fix a high scale of remuneration. Shortly before 12 o'clock these assassin-hunters are dispatched upon their mission. Their foot-fall is silenced by the use of galoshes, and their own safety is assured by the carrying of police-whistles and stout sticks. The area over which this additional protection is afforded is divided into beats, each man being assigned his respective round. Nor is this all. At half an hour after midnight the committee-rooms close by an Act of Parliament, and thence emerge those members of the committee who happen to be on duty for the night. Like sergeants of police they make their tours of inspection, and while seeing that their men are faithfully performing their onerous duties, themselves visit the most sequestered and ill-lighted spots. The volunteer policemen leave their beats between 4 and 5 o'clock in the morning. It should be added that supervision in this way by members of the committee is not forthcoming every night. The fact that most of them are engaged from early in the morning until late at night in the transaction of their own businesses obviously renders such constant effort physically impossible. If it were practicable there are several who would undoubtedly devote night after night with the utmost willingness to ferreting out the being who has caused terror to prevail in the hearts of thousands of residents in the back streets of the district. Although the work of the committee has not yet been crowned with success, it is claimed on their behalf that they have gained much information that may be of service hereafter. By the regular police, it is satisfactory to add, they have not been thwarted in their endeavour to bring the criminal to justice. Suspicions, surmises, and possible clues are *notified to the nearest police-stations from time to time, and one member of the committee at least honestly believes that he is on the right track. Whether his private opinion is justified by fact, time alone can reveal. Meanwhile, he and his colleagues are determined to leave no stone unturned, and firmly continue to maintain that the dark places of Whitechapel demand a more thorough watchfulness on the part of the police than is at present devoted to them. They further report that the number of women of the class to which the victims have belonged has appreciably diminished in the district within the past week. AN ARREST AND RELEASE. A SUPPOSED DISORDERLY VOLUNTEER. The Press Association says a man was arrested in the Whitechapel district early this morning for disorderly conduct. He carried a rifle and a bayonet, and this gave rise to a widespread rumour that the supposed Whitechapel murderer had been caught. The owner of the rifle, who was presumably a volunteer, was subsequently liberated. ARREST OF AN IRISH LEATHER APRON. AN KNIFE COVERED WITH BLOOD. On Thursday a tramp, whose name is unknown, but who describes himself as "Leather Apron," was arrested at Armagh by the police here on a charge of drunkenness and disorderly conduct. When taken into the police barracks he violently assaulted a constable. In his possession were found thee halfpence, a knife covered with blood, and a letter also stained with blood, addressed to the Roman Catholic Primate. AN ARMY PENSIONER IN FEMALE ATTIRE. A REMARKABLE EXPLAINATION. At the Hampstead Petty Sessions on Thursday, WM Webb, 43, an army pensioner, living at Newend-square, Hampstead, was charged with appearing in Heath-street in female costume, with a carving knife in his possession, supposed for an unlawful purpose, - Mackenzie, 591 S, deposed that on Wednesday night, about a quarter to eight, he was on fixed point duty near the Metropolitan Fire Brigade Station, when he saw a crowd outside the Horse and Groom public house, Heath-street. Witness went to ascertain the cause, and saw prisoner in the midst of the crowd, dressed up in the woman's clothes now produced – a hat, skirt, petticoat, and jacket – and with a handkerchief round his neck. Witness told him he was a man, and bade him go away, but he would not. He drew the knife produced about a foot long, with the blade sharpened, from his sleeve, and, acting about with it, said he was going to Whitechapel to catch the murderer. Witness did not know the prisoner, but was known in Hampstead. He did not seem the worse for drink. Witness took him to the station. – Prisoner said he was drunk in the morning, and had some more drink in the evening. Some of his companions had told him that he had not got the luck to go down to Whitechapel to look after the murderer, and so he went home and put his wife's clothes on, in which he came out, but with no intention of going to Whitechapel. It was only a joke. – Inspector Sly, S Division, said that prisoner had shaved off his moustache.*

Mike Covell

> *Witness now believed that prisoner admitted that he had shaved off his moustache. – The Bench said that the constable had acted properly in taking prisoner into custody, and fined the accused 10s, or in default seven days' imprisonment, for disorderly conduct. – Prisoner was locked up in default.*

The Hull Daily Mail, October 5th 1888,

> THE ATROCITIES IN LONDON. AN ARREST AT TIPTREE THIS MORNING. The Press Association's Bishop Stortford correspondent telegraph is that a man has been arrested at Tiptree Heath, near here, on suspicion of being concerned in the Whitechapel murders. He asked alms of Sergeant Creswell, who arrested him. He objected to be searched, and was taken to Kelvedon, where he was detained for inquiries. He answered the description circulated by the Metropolitan police. ANOTHER LETTER FROM THE SELF ALLEGED MURDERER. The Central News has received the following letter, bearing the E.C. postmark, written in red ink in a round hand, apparently by a person indifferently educated. At the foot is a rude drawing of a sharp pointed knife blade measuring three inches and the handle one: - "3rd October. - Dear Boss, - Since last, splendid success. Two more and never a squeal. Oh, I am master of the art! I am going to be heavy on the guilded – now, we are. Some duchess will cut up nicely, and the lace will show nicely. You wonder how. Oh, we are masters. No education like a butcher's. No animal like a nice woman - the fat are best. On to Brighton for a holiday, but we shan't idle - splendid high-class women there. My mouth waters - good luck there. If not, you will hear from me in the West End. My pal will keep on at the East for a while yet. When I get a nobility – I will send it on to C. Warren, or perhaps to you for a keepsake. O it is jolly. - GEORGE OF THE HIGH-RIP GANG. – Red ink still, but a drop of the real in it."
>
> EXCITEMENT INCREASING. The excitement and indignation which are apparent in East London have been increased to-day by the startling announcement by Dr Browne at the inquest that the similar organ missing from the body of Annie Chapman had been cut away from Kate Eddowes, found in Mitre Square. There had been a suspicion of this fact, which now renders the murderer's object the more mysterious since the doctor is so emphatic in his assertion that the obtaining of these portions of a woman's body could be no use to medical research. Dr. Browne stated that the clever manner in which the left kidney and other organ were removed betokened that the murderer was well versed in anatomy, but not necessarily human anatomy, for he could have gained a certain amount of skill by reason of his being a slaughterer of animals.

These remarks conclusively show that the same hand which caused the death of the previous victims is also responsible for killing Kate Eddowes, and in all probability Elizabeth Stride in Berner Street, although in the latter case he may have been disturbed before he had time to complete the mutilation at in the peculiarly horrible manner which characterised his fiendish work. WHAT THE BISHOP OF LIVERPOOL SAYS. The Bishop of Liverpool last night at a meeting to raise funds for additional curates in that city, said a number of people in East London were living more like beasts than human creatures. He knew the Whitechapel district and the clergymen ministering there, and he could quite understand the tragedies which recently occurred. Such a state of things horrified the whole community and people wanted to be aroused to see what man was capable of if left alone. If such tragedies aroused the people to a sense of what should be done in the way of providing sufficient clergy to go from house to house and room to room, so that no dark place would go unexamined, some good out of evil would come. He agreed with an old divine, who said that man if left to himself was half devil and half beast, and Whitechapel was an illustration of it. INFERENCES TO BE DRAWN. [From the "Newcastle Chronicle"] A dense fog still hangs over the atrocious crimes committed at the East End of London. Nor is the thickness of theories in the least diminished by the amplified details of doubtful accuracy, the flying rumours, and the bits of gossip in general, gathered and retailed by the zealous surveyors of news, and serving but to confuse the brains of those who read them. Nevertheless, the fateful occurrences narrowed down to trustworthy sources of information present themselves as facts, and from these facts it is possible to draw inferences. There have been in all six murders committed in Whitechapel in as many months. The first victim was one Emma Elizabeth Smith, who was found badly injured on the early morning of Easter Tuesday, the 3rd of April in Osborne-street, and who, on being removed to the London Hospital, lived for some 24 hours. Before she expired she was able to state that she had been followed by several men, robbed, and mutilated. She was even capable of describing, in an imperfect way, one of her assailants. In the case of Emma Smith, the nature of her injuries favoured the conclusion that they had been inflicted by a blunt weapon, such as a walking stick. The second crime was discovered at three a.m. on Tuesday, the 7th of August. The slain woman Martha Tabram or Turner, as she also appears to have been called, was found on the first floor landing of George-yard buildings. She was quiet dead at the time, and the examination of her body disclosed that it had received 30 punctured wounds. Some such instrument as a dagger or bayonet was suspected in this instance; and the bayonet obtained in the first place the preferences, as there was some evidence to show that the deceased had been the associate of soldiers. The next victim was Mary Ann Nicholls, found on Friday, the 31st of August in Buck's-row. There were abdominal injuries of a fearful character in this case, and the woman's throat had also been cut. It was evident that a knife had been used. Following Mary Ann Nicholls, came Anne Chapman, found on the morning of Saturday, the 8th of September, in the back yard of 29, Hanbury-street. In this instance there was the same abdominal mutilation, accompanied by either the wilful abstraction or accidental disappearance of a particular organ of the body. As with the woman Nicholls, the throat had been cut. The remaining two murders were committed on the night of Saturday, the 29th of September. The first was discovered at about one o'clock in the yard of 40, Berner-street, Commercial-road; the other was detected in Mitre-square, Aldgate, a good sized yard with three entrances to it, shortly before two o'clock. The victims were both women, one of whom has been partially but not positively identified. The bodies were still warm, and in the case of the Berner-street crime there were no abdominal mutilations, though the throat had been cut. In respect of Mitre-square, however, the characteristics common to Nicholls and Chapman murders present themselves. Four victims were notoriously women who had sunk low in the social scale, and who were reduced to an irregular sort of prostitution, though at times they strove to maintain themselves by work. Of the other two, whose identity is doubtful, it is impossible to speak with certainty. The probability, however, is that they belonged to the same unhappy class. The crimes themselves were perpetrated all in the same locality, and in places not many hundred yards distant from each other. In something like an hour a man might very comfortably make a tour of inspection of the various spots collectively. From such facts there are deductions to be made. Emma Smith was assaulted by several men; Martha Tabram or Turner died riddled with punctured wounds. The other four were found with their throats cut, while three were disembowelled. The circumstances that the Berner-street victim did not receive abdominal injuries may, however, be very reasonably ascribed to the sudden appearance of Mr. Louis Diemschitz in the yard with his horse and trap. Assuming this, the irresistible inference is that the murderer cut the throats of his victims first, and mutilated them afterwards. This point is of some importance, as one at least of the medical men – Dr. Lewellys – deposed at the inquest held on Mary Ann Nicholls, that he w strongly of the opinion that the abdominal injuries were inflicted first, and caused instantaneous death. It is clear that the one man murder theory will not apply to the case of Emma Smith, the victim of a ruffian gang. Neither does the case of Martha Tabram, or Turner, riddled with 39 puncture wounds, warrant the assumption with any degree of certainty. The rest of the murders favour, however, very strikingly the suspicion that they have been committed by one person. Yet, who is he, and why has he been guilty of such hideously wanton outrage? That the slayer must have acquired skill as regards one deadly blow with the knife is evident. Mary Ann Nicholls was killed immediately beneath the window of the room in which Mrs. Green, an old woman and a light sleeper, reposed. The Berner-street victim was hurried to death in the yard close to the Social Club, while Mrs Diemschitz, the stewardess of that establishment, was in the kitchen on the ground floor, and quiet near the precise spot where the crime was achieved. Yet neither Mrs. Green nor Mrs. Diemschitz heard a single sound resembling a scream or groan. This betokens the sure hand with which the thrust was dealt, the knowledge of the exact place in which the knife would take prompt effect, and the extinct deliberation with which the set was done. The whole circumstances reviewed, the [illegible] is difficult to combat – in the mind at learnt of the present writes – that the murders of Emma Smith and Martha Tabram, or Turner, were not committed by the same hand steeped in the blood of the woman Nicholls, Chapman, and their two successors. Smith was murdered on April 3, Tabram on August 7. The latter revived the recollection of the former, and both were discovered simultaneously, and nowhere, perhaps, [illegible] interest as in Whitechapel, the locality of the crime. The facility with which murder could be committed without detection proved, we may be sure a prominent item of the [illegible] talk. Why not, then a reflex action, opening on the mind of some morbid subject, discarded by the incredible vanity which enters so largely in the composition of a certain class of criminals and of whom Percy Mapleton Lefroy, the [illegible] of Mr. Gold, may be cited as a fair example? But, it is not necessary at all to assume that this monstrosity in the shape of a man hails from America, or to identify him with any particular creed or race. He might well be no Englishman, a resident in Whitechapel, who, from sheer vanity, from a desire to posture before the world as remarkable, would engage even in such atrocities as have been perpetrated. BEAGLES AS DETECTIVES. An old sportsman writes as under to the Pall Mall Gazette:-

Your article of this evening has been read to me (being totally blind now, I cannot read myself), and as I have been for years advocating the use of dogs for the purpose of assisting the police in the detection of crime. Perhaps the public might be interested if I state in what way dogs would be useful. In the first place I was convinced that bloodhounds will not do, there being many objections to them, the first objection being that bloodhounds are savage, and if by accident they got onto the line of an innocent man they might when they [illegible] him do some serious mischief before the owner could come up: but to a sportsman there seems to be an undesirable objection- namely, they are too fast; and although it is true that you could keep up with them on horseback in the daytime, it must not be forgotten that the police require dogs as much in the night time as in the day, and it would be impossible to follow bloodhounds at night. It does not seem to be known that small beagles can be trained to hunt human beings quite as well, nay better than bloodhounds, for they will hunt a colder scent, being much keener in the nose. They are very good tempered, and I have never known them bite any person that I have hunted down with them, and they are very easily trained. In 1848 I had four couples of rabbit beagle puppies, and the idea struck me that I would try if I could train them to run human beings in the same way as I had trained my bloodhounds- thus: I placed two drops of the oil of aniseed on the sole of a boy's boot and made him run a short distance, then hide himself; the puppies in a very short time acknowledged the scent and ran it truly; I gradually decreased the quantity of oil, and at last sent off a boy without any on his boots, when I was delighted to find that they opened (with the aid of a bloodhound on the first occasion) and went away in full cry. I was always very particular to change boys every week. When these puppies were 12 months old I ran down a poacher with them after a hunt which lasted 40 minutes, and this man must have had a start of nearly 20 minutes. They ran him into town, and finally drew up at a public-house, in which the man was, with a rabbit in his pocket. It seemed to me that the scent was almost as good upon the pavement in the streets as in the fields. Surely the police would find them most useful in the country and the suburban districts, but I do not think they would be of much value in a town. If each rural police station had three well trained beagles kept there, all the police would have to do would be when they received information of an offence to take their hounds up to the spot as quickly as possible throw them across the garden and around the premises as if they were drawing for a hare; I am convinced that if a scent had not got too cold they would hit upon the line, and when they had well settled down they would run into the man wherever he was, the same as any bloodhound. They do not go too fast, so that they are easily followed on foot either by night or day, as their [illegible] will let you know where they are, let the night be ever so dark. I have no doubt that a class of the community will pooh pooh the idea without knowing anything at all on the subject, however, I know as a fact that they can be trained in the way I have already mentioned, and so can bloodhounds, so I have no doubt any owner of that class of dogs will agree if they have ever tried to train them in that way. I enclose you my card; and although it is many a long day since I viewed a fox, still I love the hounds, and would only be too happy to hear of their species becoming useful to the police and the public.

The Hull Daily Mail, October 5th 1888,

THE LONDON MURDERS. IMPORTANT EVIDENCE. ANOTHER LETTER. LATEST PARTICULARS. The Central News says: - The evidence given by the surgeon at the inquest on the body of the Mitre-square victim caused a profound sensation. It has been understood that, in this case, the murderer was so closely pressed for time that he had to content himself with putting his victim to death and then roughly mutilating the corpse, but the surgical evidence leaves no doubt that, notwithstanding the imminent danger of every moment's delay, the murderer went about his work with at least as much deliberation as he displayed in dealing with his Hanbury-street victim, for he removed two organs and then hacked the face of the dead woman – with the apparent object of increasing the difficulty of identification. Much importance is attached to this point. The murderer took no pains to mutilate the features of his previous victims; although, in most cases, he had time to do it. It is, therefore, believed that he met the woman Conway in the main thoroughfare some distance from Mitre-square. He would then have to walk along a well-lighted road in her company, when a good many people were about, and consequently he had some reason for supposing that he might have been noticed by policemen or passers-by. It was, therefore, good policy on his part to endeavour so to mutilate the woman's face as to render it impossible for any person to recognise it as that of the woman in whose company he was probably seen. Another piece of evidence which may prove of importance was confirmed at the inquest yesterday, namely, that the murderer cut off a portion of one of the dead woman's ears. It will be remembered that, in the letter addressed to the Central News by "Jack the Ripper," and purporting to come from the murderer, he expressed his intention of cutting off his next victim's ears and sending them by post to the police. It is not possible that the murderer did intend to secure the ear, but that when it became lost in the victim's clothing his attention was attracted to some other object, and that before he could recall his purpose he had to fly for his life. As far as can be ascertained, too, the special editions of the Sunday newspapers containing an account of the crime made no mention of the cutting off of the ear, but in the post card received by the Central News with the first post delivery on Monday morning, the writer stated he had not time to secure the ears for the police. The post card was apparently posted some time after midnight, and certainly long before the writer could have seen the Monday newspapers. These considerations operated with the authorities in their decision to publish the mysterious communications in fac similie. The announcement made by Dr Brown that the uterus was missing from the body of the Mitre-square victim revived temporarily the theory put forward by the coroner who held an inquest on the woman Chapman. But this theory is authoritatively disposed of by the British Medical Journal, which states that it is true inquiries were made at one

Mike Covell

or two medical schools early by a foreign physician who was spending some time in London as to the possibility of securing certain parts of the body for the purpose of scientific investigation, "but," continues the Journal, "no large sum was offered; the person in question was a physician of the highest respectability, and exceedingly well accredited to this country by the best authorities in his own, and he left London eighteen months ago. There was never any real foundation for the hypothesis, and the information communicated – which was not at all the nature which the public has been led to believe – was due to the erroneous interpretation by a minor official of a question which he had overheard, and to which a negative reply was given. This theory may be at once dismissed, and is, we believe, no longer entertained, even by its author." Up till nine o'clock last evening no further arrests had been made either the City or Metropolitan Police. The number of detectives on duty in the Whitechapel district last evening in as large as ever, and there were also about fifty workingmen on voluntary patrol duty, most of whom remained in the streets until daylight. The Local Vigilance Committee have charge of this movement, and they hope to arrange matters so that no man shall be required to give more than one night per week to the work. Bull, the "medical student," who was remanded on Wednesday on the charge brought against him in consequence of his own confession of having been concerned in the Mitre-square murder, will be brought up to-day at the Guildhall Police-court. It is probable that he will be at once discharged, as inquiries made since his apprehension by the City police show that he cannot be connected in any way with the recent crimes. It has been ascertained that Bull was formerly in the employment of Messrs Sylans and Co., warehousemen, of Wood-street, Cheapside. The Central Press received a letter, bearing the E.C. postmark, written in red ink in a round hand, apparently by a person indifferently educated. At the foot is a rude drawing of a sharp pointed knife blade measuring three inches and the handle one:- "3rd October. - Dear Boss, - Since last, splendid success. Two more and never a squeal. Oh, I am master of the art! I am going to be heavy on the guilded - now, we are. Some duchess will cut up nicely, and the lace will show nicely. You wonder how. Oh, we are masters. No education like a butcher's. No animal like a nice woman - the fat are best. On to Brighton for a holiday, but we shan't idle - splendid highclass women there. My mouth waters - good luck there. If not, you will hear from me in the West End. My pal will keep on at the East for a while yet. When I get a nobility - I will send it on to C. Warren, or perhaps to you for a keepsake. O it is jolly. - GEORGE OF THE HIGH-RIP GANG. - Red ink still, but a drop of the real in it." THE MITRE-SQUARE TRAGEDY. STORY TOLD BY THE VICTIM'S SISTER. A Central News reporter called on Wednesday on Eliza Gold (or Frost), the sister of the dead woman. Mrs. Gold, who lives on the second floor back of 6, Thrawl-street, Spitalfields, is suffering from a serious attack of illness from the sudden knowledge of her sister's shocking end, for till this morning she had not recognised Catherine Eddowes in the "Mrs. Kelly" of the pawn tickets. It has so greatly affected her that only with much difficulty, and with the help of a kindly neighbour, could any facts as to the dead woman he obtained from her. "It was this morning," she said, "when I was called to the mortuary to identify her, poor girl. I never dreamed she would come to such an end as this, and I can't get over it. No, I really don't know how old she was, but I am 52, and she was considerably younger. Perhaps she was about 42. She was born at Wolverhampton. All of us were born there." "Was she married to Conway there, Mrs Gold?" "No, she never was married at all, but she went to live with him while in London. She has lived here almost all her life." "Then her name is not Conway, as the police have it?" "No, her name is Catherine Eddowes. Conway was in the army, but I don't know what regiment. She had two or three children by him. It's rather strange, one of 'em, the girl that's married, came to me last week and asked me if I had seen anything of her mother. She said it was a very long time since she had seen her, but it was a long time since I had, too, and I told her so; in fact, I have not seen her much oftener than once or twice since she has been with Kelly, though we lived so close together. The fact is we were not on the best of terms." "How long ago is it since Conway left your sister?" "I think it is only five or six years since. Then she got on with Kelly, and, I believe, she has stuck to him all along. No, I certainly don't think she ever went out with other men, though I have told you that I didn't see much of her. She was always a regular jolly sort, but she would never do anything wrong." "What do you think she could not have been doing in Mitre-square at that time in the morning?" "That's a question I cannot answer. I cannot imagine what she was doing there." "Perhaps," put in the neighbour, "she had a drop of drink, and had a few words with Kelly." "Can you remember when you last saw your sister?" the reporter asked. "It is a long time ago; five or six months since, and she came then because Emma told her I was ill. She had been in a better position once, you know, than she was in lately. She was educated at the Dowgate Charity School in the City. No, I don't think there is anything else I can tell you about her, only that she was always a good girl, poor thing." THE INQUEST. IMPORTANT MEDICAL EVIDENCE. Dr Langham yesterday morning opened an inquest at the City Mortuary, Golden-lane. Mr. McWilliam (Chief of the City Detective Department), Major Smith (Assistant Commissioner), Superintendent Foster, Inspector Collard, and others were present. The jury having been sworn, proceeded to view the body. Mr. Crawford, City Solicitor, appeared to watch the proceedings on behalf of the City Authorities. The first witness called was Eliza Gold, of Thrawl-street, Spitalfields, widow. She recognized the deceased as her sister. Her name was Catherine Eddowes. She was a single woman, and her age was 43. She had been living with John Kelly for some years, and before that lived with a man named Conway. She lived some years with Conway, and had two children by him. Witness could not say for how many years. She did not know whether Conway was still living. Conway had been in the army, and was a pensioner. She did not know whether deceased and Conway parted on good or bad terms. By Mr. Crawford: She last saw deceased with Kelly about three or four weeks ago. They were on good terms. They were living at a lodging house in Flower and Dean-street. From that time until witness identified deceased in the mortuary she had not seen her sister. John Kelly said he lived at 55, Flower and Dean-street, Smithfields. He was a labourer, working in the markets. He recognised the body as that of Eliza Conway, the name by which she went. He had been living with her for seven years. Deceased used to hawk things about the streets for a living. They lived together at the address he had given. It was a common lodging house. Witness was last in deceased's company at two o'clock on Saturday afternoon in Houndsditch. They parted on good terms. She said she was going over to Bermondsey to see if she could find her daughter. He believed Conway was the father of the daughter. Deceased promised to be back by four, but did not return. He heard she had been locked up at Bishopsgate-street Police-station. He was told that by a woman, who said she saw her being taken to the station by two constables. He did not make any inquiries, because he thought she would be released on Sunday morning. He was told that she had had a drop too much to drink. He never suffered her to go out for an immoral purpose. She was in the habit of slightly drinking to excess. When witness left deceased she had no money about her. She went over to see her daughter with the view of getting some money. Neither of them had any money with which to pay for their lodgings. Witness did not know of anyone who was likely to injure her, or with whom she was at variance. Witness had never seen Conway, and did not know whether deceased had seen him lately. He could not say whether Conway was living. A juryman: What time was she in the habit of returning to her lodgings? Witness: She usually returned early, about eight or nine o'clock. By Mr. Crawford: He did not know with whom deceased had been drinking. Some months ago she left him through having a few words together about money on Saturday. He had heard that deceased's daughter lived in King-street, Bermondsey. Deceased had not been to her daughter for money for a year. Witness slept alone at the lodging house. On Friday night deceased did not walk the streets, but slept in the casual ward at Mile End. They did not sleep together in the lodging house during the whole of last week. Monday, Tuesday, and Wednesday they were in Kent, returning from hop picking. They arrived in London on Thursday, but had no money, and that night they slept at the casual ward, Shoe-lane. He earned sixpence on Friday afternoon. Deceased insisted on his taking fourpence and going to the lodging house while she went to the Mile End casual ward. He met her again on Saturday morning. The tea and sugar found in the tin box in deceased's possession was bought with half-a-crown, which witness got by pawning his boots. He pawned his boots on Friday or Saturday. They spent the half crown on drink and food. When they parted deceased was sober. He was not quite certain whether the boots were pawned on Friday or Saturday. Deceased pawned them witness standing outside in his bare feet. Mr Cawford here produced the pawn tickets, which bore the date of September 28th. Witness said he was so confused he could not remember days accurately. He had not been drinking. Frank William Wilkinson, deputy of the lodging house, said he had known deceased and Kelly for the last seven or eight years. They passed as man and wife, and lived in very good terms. They had a few words now and again, but never quarreled violently. He believed deceased got her living by hawking in the streets and cleaning amongst the Jews. Kelly was pretty regular in payment for the lodgings. Deceased was not often the worse for liquor. She was a very jolly woman, and fond of singing. He saw deceased last on Friday afternoon, when she returned from hop picking. He did not see Kelly. She went out on Friday night, and witness next saw her on Saturday morning, between ten and eleven. When Kelly came in between seven and eight, witness asked him "Where's Kate?" and he replied that he had heard she was locked up. They last slept at the house together five or six weeks ago, before they went hopping. He believed deceased was wearing an apron when he saw her on Saturday morning. By Mr. Crawford: He could not recollect whether any stranger came in between one and two on Sunday morning. At Mr. Crawford's request, the further examination of witness was postponed, so that he might refer to his books as to this point. P.C. Edward Watkin (881), City Police, said: I have been in the City Police Force 17 years. On Saturday night I went on duty at a quarter to ten on my regular beat, which extends from Duke-street, Aldgate, through Heneage-lane, a portion of Bury-street, through Creechurch-lane, into Leadenhall-street, along Leadenhall-street eastward into Mitre-street; and then into Mitre-square and King-street, along King-street and St. James's-place, round St. James's-place, and thence into Duke-street, the starting point. It took about twelve or fourteen minutes to patrol. From ten o'clock until one in the morning I had been continually patrolling that beat. Nothing excited my attention between those hours. I passed through Mitre-square at 1.30 on Sunday morning. I had my lantern fixed in my belt with the light turned on. I looked at different passages, corners, and warehouses. At 1.30 I did not see anybody about. No one could have been in any portion of the square at the hour without my seeing him. I entered Mitre-square about 1.44. I *turned to the right as I entered from the street. I saw the body of a woman lying on the ground; she was on her back with her feet facing the square. Her clothes were above her waist. I saw her throat was cut, and her bowels were protruding. The stomach had been ripped up. She was lying in a pool of blood. I did not touch the body, I ran across the road to Messrs Kearley and Tonge, wholesale provision merchants, and called the watchman. He came out, and I sent him for assistance. I remained by the side of the body until the arrival of P. C. Holland. He was followed by Dr Siqueria. Inspector Collard arrived about 2.0, together with Dr Gretton Brown, surgeon to the police force. When I entered the square I did not hear any footsteps of a man running away. Plans of the scene of the murder and the surrounding neighbourhood were here put in by Mr. Foster, surveyor, Old Jewry, who stated that it was about three-quarters of a mile from Berner-street to Mitre-square. The lodging house deputy, Wilkinson, now re-entered the witness box, with his book. He was unable to state, however, whether anybody came in about two on Sunday morning. The book showed that there were six strangers staying in the house on Saturday night. He could not say whether anybody went out about twelve o'clock at night. After a short adjournment for lunch, Inspector Collard, of the City of London Police, was called. He stated that he arrived on the scene of the murder shortly before two o'clock. The body was not touched until the arrival of Dr Gordon Brown a few minutes afterwards. No money was found upon deceased. The portion of the apron produced, which was found tied round deceased's waist, corresponded with the portion of an apron found in Goulstone-street. A large force of detectives were soon sent to the spot, and a house-to-house inquiry in the vicinity of the square was made. Nobody had heard any cries. There were no signs of a struggle. Dr Gordon Brown, surgeon to the City of London Police Force, gave evidence as to the state in which the body was found. There was a wound in the abdomen, from which a portion of the intestines had been drawn out and placed over the right shoulder. A piece of intestine about two feet long had been detached and placed between the left arm and the body. The throat was cut, the face disfigured, and the lobe of the right ear was cut obliquely. When the body was undressed at the mortuary several portions of the ear fell from the clothing. A post mortem examination was made on Sunday afternoon. In addition to the number of slashes across the face, the throat was cut, the wound extending from the left ear to about three inches below the lobe of the right ear. The larynx was severed, and all the deep structures cut to the bone, the knife touching the cartilage of the vertebral column. The cause of death was hemorrhage from the carotid artery. Death was immediate, and the other mutilations were inflicted after death. The front walls of the abdomen had been laid open, and the intestines detached to a large extent. The peritoneum lining and left kidney had been cut through, and the kidney carefully taken out. From the nature of the cuts it was evident that the kidney was taken by someone who knew its position, and how to take it out. The womb was cut horizontally, leaving a stump of three-quarters of an inch, and the rest of the womb had been taken away. By Mr. Crawford: The wounds were inflicted by a sharp pointed knife at least six inches long. The person who inflicted the wounds possessed a good deal of knowledge of the position of the organs in the abdominal cavity and the way of removing the parts. The parts removed would be of no use for surgical purposes. Such a knowledge would be likely to be possessed by one used to cutting up animals. The wounds might be inflicted in five minutes. As a professional man he could assign no reason for these parts being taken away. He thought the act was that of one person only. He would not expect to find much blood on the person inflicting the wounds. – The inquiry at this point was adjourned until Thursday next at half-past ten. THE BERNER-STREET TRAGEDY. The London Evening News published yesterday morning a story related by two private detectives, giving the result of their inquiries in connection with the East End murders. They claim thereby to have obtained an exact description of the Berner-street murderer from a fruit dealer who sold to him, when in company with the murdered woman, the grapes which it is believed were those afterwards found in her hand when dead. The fruit dealer also asserts having noticed a white flower in deceased's dress, petals of some kind of blossom being found on the ground near the corpse. The man is described as middle aged, stout, and square built, wearing a wideawake hat and dark clothes.*

October 6th 1888

The Hull Daily News, October 6th 1888,

TWO MORE WHITECHAPEL MURDERS. WOMAN HORRIBLY BUTCHERED. SHOCKING DISCOVERIES. MURDER IN BERNER STREET, COMMERCIAL-ROAD. It was sincerely hoped throughout the whole Kingdom that the murder and mutilation of the poor wretch Annie Chapman in Hanbury street, about three weeks ago would close the ghastly record of mysterious and diabolical atrocities which have been perpetrated on woman in the Whitechapel districts of London, but on Sunday we were confronted with two more horrible murders which as far as can be ascertained at present, leave little doubt as to it having been done by the same assassin or assassins who committed the others. One murder was discovered in Berner-street, Commercial-road, and the other in Mitre-square, Houndsditch. The scene of the first of these, the latest murders, is Berner-street, Commercial-road, on St. George's-in-the-East side and within about 200 yards of Buck's-row or Hanbury-street, where the last two murders took place.

Berner-street is a quite thoroughfare running from Commercial-road down to London, Tilbury, and Southend Railway. At the entrance to the court are a pair of large wooden gates, in one of which is a small wicket for use when the gates are closed. At the hour when the murderer accomplished his purpose these gates were open-indeed, according to the testimony of those living near, the entrance to the court is seldom closed. For a distance of 18 or 20 feet from the street there is a dead wall on each side of the court, the effect is to enshroud the intervening space in absolute darkness after sunset. Farther back some light is thrown into the court from the windows of a workingmen's club which occupies the whole length of the court on the right, and from a number of cottages occupied by mainly tailors and cigarette makers on the left. At the time when the murder was committed, however, the lights in all of the dwelling-houses in question had been extinguished, while such illumination as came from the club, being from the upper storey, would fall on the cottages opposite, and would only serve to intensify the gloom of the rest of the court. From the position in which the body was found it is believed that the moment the murderer had got his victim in the dark shadow near the entrance to the court he threw her to the ground, and with one gash severed her throat from ear to ear. The hypothesis that the wound was inflicted after and not before the woman fell is supported by the fact that there are severe bruises on her left temple and left cheek, this showing that force must have been used to prostrate her, which would not have been necessary had her throat already been cut. When discovered the body was lying as if the woman had fallen forward, her feet being a couple of yards from the street, and her head in a gutter which runs down the right side of the wall close to the wall. The woman lay on her left side, face downwards, her position being such that although the court at that point is only nine feet wide, a person walking up the middle might have passed the recumbent body without notice. The condition of the corpse, however, and several other circumstances which have come to light during the week, prove pretty conclusively that no considerable period elapsed between committal of the murder and discovery of the body- in fact, it is pretty general conjectured that the assassin was disturbed whilst at his ghastly work, and made off before he had completed his designs. All of the features of the case go to connect the tragedy with that which took place three-quarters of an hour later a few streets distant. The obvious poverty of the woman, her total lack of jewellery or ornaments and the soiled condition of her clothing, entirely oppose the theory that robbery could have been a motive, and the secrecy and despatch with which the crime was affected are equally good evidence that the murder was not the result of an ordinary street brawl. At the club before referred to the International Workmen's Educational Club, which is an off-shoot of the Socialist League and a rendezvous of a number of foreign residents chiefly Russians and Poles and continental Jews of various nationalities, it is customary on Saturday nights to have friendly discussions on topics of mutual interest, and to wind up the evening's entertainment with songs, &c. The proceedings commenced on Saturday about 8-20 with a discussion on the necessity for Socialism among Jews. This was kept up until about eleven o'clock when a considerable portion of the company left their respective homes. Between 20 and 30 remained behind, and the usual concert which followed was not concluded when the intelligence was brought in by the steward of the club that a woman had been done to death within a few yards of them and within earshot of the jovial songs. The people residing in the cottages on the other side of the court where all indoors, and most of them in bed by midnight. Several of these persons remember lying awake and listening to the singing, and they also remember the concert coming to an abrupt termination, but during the whole of the time from retiring to rest until the body was discovered no one heard anything in nature of a scream or woman's cry of distress. It was Lewis Diemstritz, the steward of the club, who found the body. Diemstritz, who is a traveller in cheap jewellery, had spent the day at Westby Hall, near Crystal Palace, in pursuance of his avocation, and had driven home at his usual hour, reaching Berner-street at one o'clock. On turning into the gateway he had some difficulty with his pony, the animal apparently determined to avoid the right hand wall. For the moment Diemstritz did not think too much of the occurrence because he knew the pony was given to shying, and he thought perhaps some mud or refuse was in the way. The pony, however, obstinately refused to go straight, so the driver pulled him up to see what was in the way. Failing to discern anything in the darkness, Diemstritz poked about with the handle of the whip and immediately discovered that some large obstacle was in his path. He at once jumped down a struck a match, and then it became at once apparent that something serious had taken place. Without waiting to see whether the dead woman, whose body he saw, was drunk or dead, Diemstritz entered the club by the side door, higher up the court, and informed those in the concert room upstairs that something had happened in the yard. A member of the club named Kozebrodski, but familiarly known as "Isaacs," returned with Diemstritz into the court, and the former struck a match while the latter lifted the body up. The body was still warm, and the clothes enveloping it were wet from the recent rain, but the heart had ceased to beat, and the stream of blood in the gutter, terminating in a hideous pool near the club door, showed but too plainly what had happened. Both men ran off without delay to find a policeman, and at the same time other members of the club, who had by this time found their way into the court went off with the same object in different directions. The search, was for some time fruitless. At last, however, after considerable delay, a constable was found in Commercial-road. With the aid of the policeman's whistle more constables were quickly on the spot, and the gates at the entrance to the court having been closed, and guard set at all exits of the club and the cottages, the superintendent of the district and divisional surgeon were sent for. In a few minutes Dr. Philips was at the scene of the murder, and a brief examination sufficed to show that life had been extinct for some minutes. Careful note having been taken of the position of the body, it was removed to the parish mortuary of St. George's, in East Cable Street, to await identification. A representative of the press, who saw the corpse, states that the woman appears to be about 30 years of age. Her hair is very dark, with a tendency to curl, her complexion is also dark. Her features are sharp and somewhat pinched, as though she had endured considerable privations recently, an impression confirmed by the entire absence of the kind of ornaments commonly affected by woman of her station. She wore a rusty black dress of a cheap kind of sateen with a velveteen bodice, over which a black diagonal worsted jacket with fur trimming. Her bonnet, which had fallen from her head when she was found in the yard, was of black crape, and inside, apparently with the object of making the article fit closer was folded a copy of The Star newspaper. In her right hand were tightly clasped some grapes, and in her left a small number of sweetmeats. Both the Jacket and the bodice are open towards the top, but in other respects the clothes were not disarranged. The linen was clean and in tolerably good repair, but some articles were missing. The cut in the woman's throat, which was the cause of death, was evidently effected with a very sharp instrument, and was made with one rapid incision. The weapon was apparently drawn across the throat rather obliquely from left to right, and in its passage it severed it severed the windpipe, the gash being about three inches long and nearly the same in depth. In the pocket of the woman's dress were discovered two pocket handkerchiefs- a gentleman's and a lady's- a brass thimble, and a skein of black darning worsted. In addition to Dr. Philips, the body was examined both before and after removal to the mortuary by Dr. Kaye and Dr. Blackwell, both of whom reside in the vicinity of Berner-street. On the arrival of the superintendent from Leman-street police-station, which took place almost simultaneously with that of the Divisional Surgeon, steps were immediately taken to ascertain whether the members of the club were in any way connected with the murder. The names and addresses of all the men present were taken, and a rigorous search of persons and premises was instigated, much to the annoyance of the members. The residents in the court had to submit to a similar scrutiny. In neither case, however, was any incriminating evidence discovered. The fact that another murder had been committed soon became known in the neighbourhood, and long before daybreak the usually quite thoroughfare was the scene of great excitement. Extra police had to be posted right along the street, and even with this precaution [illegible] from an early hour was a matter of extreme difficulty. A large crowd followed the body to the mortuary, and again it was found necessary to take unusual precautions to keep back the crowd. As the news circulated further afield immense numbers of people flocked to Whitechapel and before noon the neighbourhood of Aldgate and Commercial-road was literally invaded by persons curious to see the spots affected for this and the other murders of the series. Several matters have transpired which tend to fix precisely the time at which the unfortunate woman was murdered. Morris Eagle, one of the members of the club in Berner-street, says that about twelve o'clock, and after taking his sweetheart home, returned to the club at about twenty minutes to one with the intention of having supper. He walked up the yard and entered the club by the side entrance, but neither saw nor heard anything to make him suspect foul play was going on. Of course he might have passed the body in the darkness, but the probability is that he would have stumbled over it if the murder had been committed before that time. Another member of the club, a Russian named Joseph Lave, feeling oppressed by the smoke in the large room, went down into the court about twenty minutes before the body was discovered, and walked about in the open air for five minutes or more. He strolled into the street, which was very quiet at the time, and returned to the concert room without having encountered anything unusual. Charles Letchford, living at 30 Berner street, says:- "I passed through the street at half past 12, and everything seemed to me to be going on as usual, and my sister was standing at the door at ten minutes to one, but did not see anyone pass by. I heard the commotion when the body was found, and heard the policemen's whistles, but did not take any notice of the matter." In an interview with a representative of the Press, Dr. Blackwell made a statement in which he said that about ten minutes past one he was called by a policeman to 40 Berner street, where he found the body of the murdered woman. Her head had been almost severed from her body. The body was perfectly warm, and life could not have been extinct more than 20 minutes. The woman has been identified as Elizabeth Stride, who, it seems, had been leading an immoral life, and had resided latterly in Flower and Dean-streets. She was identified by her sister living in Holborn. Her husband, who resided at Bath, had lived apart from her for nearly five years. THE INQUEST. The inquest on the body of Elizabeth Stride was opened at eleven on Monday morning by Mr. Wynne Baxter, at the Vestry-hall, Cable-street, Commercial-road. The body on being viewed by the jury presented a dreadful sight, the head being almost severed from the body by one awful gash. William West was the first witness examined. He said he lived at the International Working Men's Institute and Club, Berner street, at the side of which a passage leading to the yard. Two large wooden gates protected the entrance to the yard, and they were sometimes open at night. In the yard there were two or three small tenements. The club was a Socialist Club, and persons of all nationalities were eligible. Witness was at the club on Saturday night from about half-past ten or eleven when members were discussing. The bulk of the members left the club by the front door before twelve. Witness's business was at 40, Berner street, but he lived at 2 William-street, Commercial-road, wither he went at 12-30. Before leaving he noticed that the gates were open, but there was nothing on the ground. Norris Eagle, travelling jeweller, and a member of the club, said he was at the club on Saturday, and left about a quarter to twelve. He returned about twenty minutes to one, and as the front door was closed he went in through the gateway and the side door. He saw nothing in the yard, but about twenty minutes later another member announced the discovery of the body.- Louis Diemstritz, steward of the club deposed that he returned to his home at the club at one o'clock, riding in a kind of barrow, drawn by a pony. He drove through the open gates of the yard when the pony shied at something on the ground. He felt with his whip handle and tried to move it, but failed and jumping down at once struck a light. He then saw it was a woman. He called his wife, and got a candle. When he saw blood he sent for the police, and just before they arrived a man, whom he did not know, took hold of the deceased's head and showed the wound in the throat. All the people in the club were searched before they left, and their names and addresses were taken. In reply to the coroner Inspector Reid said the body had not yet been identified. The Foreman of the Jury- But we have been told her name is Stride. How is that? The Coroner-Something is known of her, she has been partially been identified.- Inspector Reid said he would be prepared with better further evidence tomorrow, and the inquiry was accordingly adjourned. The inquest on the woman was resumed by Mr. Wynne Baxter on Tuesday afternoon at Whitechapel. Police Constable Lamb. 252H, said about one o'clock on Sunday morning he was in Commercial-street, when two men ran towards him and said there had been another murder. Witness, followed by another constable, ran in the direction indicated, and entering the gateway of No.40 found the body of a woman on the ground. Her throat was cut. Witness sent for a doctor and inspector. The woman's face and arms were still warm, and the right arm lay across the breast. Her face was about six inches from the wall. The clothes were not disturbed. Dr. Blackwell arrived about ten minutes afterwards, followed by Inspector Pinhorn. Witness then closed the gates. No one was allowed to leave the club after that. Edward Spooner, housekeeper for Messrs. Meredith biscuit makers, said just before one o'clock he followed two men who were running and calling out "Police." He went to the yard in Berner-street and saw the body inside the gate. About 15 people were standing around. Someone struck a light and witness lifted the chin. Blood was still flowing. A constable came five minutes afterwards. Mary Malcolm, Eagle-street, Holborn, wife of a tailor, said she recognised the deceased as her sister, Elizabeth Watts. She last saw her alive on Thursday evening at witness's house, and gave her a short jacket and 1s. The deceased never told her where she was living. Her husband was a son of Mr. Watts, wine merchant, bath. Witness believed he had gone to America because the deceased brought disgrace upon him eight years ago by her misconduct with a porter. She then had two children, one a girl, was now dead, and the boy was at school under care of his aunt. The deceased lived with a man who went to sea, and was drowned two or three years ago. Witness knew she was called "Long Liz," and used to meet her every Saturday afternoon at the corner of Chancery-lane. She had never missed a Saturday for three years till last Saturday. Witness felt a presentiment on reading the paper on Sunday morning, and went over to Whitechapel. On seeing her in the mortuary she did not at first recognise her by gaslight, but had done so since. Witness had a presentiment at twenty minutes past one on Sunday morning, when there came "a heavy fall on the bed," and she heard "three distinct kisses." Her husband heard the same. One proof of her identity was a mark on the leg caused by the bite of an adder when she was a child. Dr. Blackwell, of Commercial-road, deposed that when he first saw the body the neck and chest were quite warm. The silk neck scarf was tightly drawn, and the throat was cut about two inches below the angle of the jaw. The windpipe was completely severed. There was no blood on the clothing. The dress was undone at the top. The injuries were beyond the possibility of self-infliction. Witness had come to the conclusion that the silk scarf was pulled backwards, but only he could not say whether the throat was cut while she was lying on the ground or while she was standing. It night have been done while she in the act of falling. The inquiry was at this point adjourned till next day. Mr. Wynne E. Baxter resumed his inquiry on Wednesday at the Vestry-hall, Cable-street, on the body of the Berner-street victim, recognised up to the present as Elizabeth Watts. The interest in the proceedings had in no way abated, and on account of the discovery at Westminster on Tuesday public feeling had been greatly excited. Large crowds of people assembled outside Vestry-hall. The first witness was called Elizabeth Tanner, living at 32, Flower and dean-street, Whitechapel. She recognised deceased as Long Liz. Did not know her nationality. Deceased told witness that her husband and children were lost in the Princess Alice disaster. She last saw her alive on Saturday afternoon, in the Queen's Head public-house, Commercial-street. Did not see her again until that afternoon in the mortuary.

Witness was quite certain as to her identity. Deceased left a male acquaintance on Thursday, to live with witness. Never knew the deceased had relatives in Holborn, and never heard the name of Stride mentioned. Deceased, who was a Swede, worked among the Jews. Catherine Lane, living with the last witness, said she recognised the body as that of Long Liz. Deceased told witness on Saturday she had had a quarrel with the man she left on Thursday. Witness had heard deceased speak to people in her own language. Charles Preston, a barber, living at the same address, also identified the body as that of Long Liz and he last saw her alive on Saturday. He understood she was born at Stockholm, and came to England in a foreign gentleman's service. Deceased also gave witness to understand that her name was Elizabeth Stride, and that her mother was still alive in Sweden. Michael Kidney, living at 38, Dorset-street, Waterside, labourer, said deceased was Elizabeth Stride. He had lived with her for nearly three years. She was a Swede, and was born three miles from Stockholm. Her husband was a ship's carpenter at Sheerness, and once kept a coffee-house at Crisp-street, Poplar. He was drowned in the Princess Alice disaster. Did not see the deceased on Thursday. Saw her last Tuesday when they parted friendly. Never saw her again, and could not account for her disappearance. She had been away from witness five months since he had known her. He never neglected her, but treated her as a wife. Witness further stated voluntarily that he asked at Leman-street station for assistance of a young, strange detective, as he had important information. He could not get the assistance. The Coroner pressed witness to divulge his information, but witness only reiterated that he had the information.- Replying to Inspector Reid, he said if the police were under his own control he could catch the murderer red handed.- Witness admitted he was intoxicated when he applied at the police station. Edward Johnstone, assistant to Drs. Kay and Blackwell, deposed to being called to see the body. Thomas Coran, a lad of about eighteen, produced a knife which he found on the doorstep of No. 253 Whitechapel-road, twenty-four hours after the murder. The knife produced was about twelve inches long, and the handle was neatly folded in a silk handkerchief which had stains like blood on it.- Joseph Drage, H282 said he saw the boy find the knife. The handle and blade were covered in blood, which had dried on. The knife was not on the step a hour previously. Dr. Phillips having given the result of the post mortem examination, the inquiry was adjourned until Friday. CONSTABULARY IN HOUSE-TO-HOUSE VISITATION IN WHITECHAPEL. On Wednesday, plain clothes constables made a house-to-house visitation, leaving copies of a handbill requesting occupiers to give notice to the nearest police station of any suspicious matters which may come within their knowledge concerning the murders. THE VICTIMS ANTECEDENTS. The Press Association's Bath correspondent telegraphs corroborating the statement of Mrs Malcolm at the inquest, on Tuesday, as to the history and habits of the woman Elizabeth Watt's. She married, about twenty-seven or twenty-eight years ago, William Watts, son of a wine merchant in Bath, her husband being then only about twenty years of age. She was servant at his father's house. They only lived together two years, when deceased left her husband who went to America. He returned from that country four years ago. MURDER IN MITRE-SQUARE, ALDGATE. A HORRIBLE SCENE. The second murder discovered on Sunday morning exceeds in revolting details any of the series, and the more the facts become known the more ghastly does the deed appear. Mitre-square, where the body of the second woman was found, lies close to the orange market, the inhabitants of which are principally Germans and foreigners, who carry on a brisk trade on Sunday. This market is situated in St. James's-place and a narrow alley called Mitre-court leads into Mitre-square, in the corner of which the woman was found. In a corner of the square - one opening of which is from Mitre-street and the other from Duke-street by Church-street - Constable Watkins, who was on duty near the square, found the body about a quarter to two o'clock, the constable on duty in Mitre-street having passed only ten minutes previously, when he neither saw nor heard anything unusual. Constable Watkins, on discovering the body, immediately whistled for help, and Constable Harvey appeared on the scene. By the light of their lanterns they saw a horrible sight. The woman who appeared to be about forty years of age, was lying in a pool of blood. Her throat was cut open from ear to ear, the head had almost been severed from the body, the point of her nose had been taken off, a large gash was inflicted on the left cheek up to the eye, thus almost disfiguring the face beyond all recognition, and she was completely disembowelled. All the viscera were cut out and the lower part of the abdomen was lifted up bodily towards the breast. In fact, a more fearful case of mutilation could not be imagined. From various descriptions she is said to be a woman of fine physique, though undoubtedly debauched beyond all respectability. Dr. Brown, of Finsbury Circus was immediately summoned and ordered the body to be removed to the mortuary in Golden-lane. To show how mysteriously and quietly the murder must have been committed, it may be mentioned that a watchman was on duty in the square in a counting house all morning and saw nothing. Besides this, in St James's-place there is a fire station, where the fireman are on duty all night, and on being closely questioned they affirm that they heard no sound of a scuffle nor anything that such a diabolical deed was taking place. The general supposition is that the assassin, after cutting the woman's throat in Berner-street, was disturbed by some movement, and left his horrible work unfinished, but having determined to have that part of a woman's abdomen which he succeeded in acquiring in the case of Chapman, he proceeded to Houndsditch, which is about ten minutes' walk distant and committed the second murder. A number of doctors, including Dr. Phillips, visited the mortuary in Golden-lane, but acting on advice from Scotland Yard they declined to give any information whatsoever. Mitre-square is a small square in a densely populated district, and just the very place for a wretch to commit a murder. It is extremely quiet and most secluded, especially the south corner where the woman was found. The body lay against a small iron railing, which was boarded over. ANOTHER ACCOUNT. Another account of the second murder in Mitre-square- Aldgate, says:- Shortly before two o'clock on Sunday morning, or about three-quarters of an hour after the Berner-street crime was committed, it was discovered that a second woman had been horribly murdered, this being in Mitre-square, Aldgate, within the City boundaries, but on the confines of the now notorious district. It appears that Police-constable Watkins (No. 881), of the City police, was going round his beat when turning his lantern upon the darkest corner of Mitre-square he saw the body of a woman in a pool of blood. He at once blew his whistle, and several persons being attracted to the spot, he despatched messengers for medical men and police. Inspector Collard, who was in command at the time of Bishopsgate Police Station, only a short distance off, quickly arrived, followed a few moments after by Mr. G.W. Sequeira, surgeon, of 34, Jewry-street, and Dr. Gordon Brown, the divisional police doctor, of Finsbury Circus. The scene then disclosed was a most horrible one. The woman, who was apparently about 40 years of age, was lying on her back quite dead, although her body was still warm. Her head was inclined to the left side. Both arms were extended. The throat was cut half way round, revealing a dreadful wound, from which blood had flowed in great quantities, staining the pavement for some distance. Round across the right cheek to the nose was another gash, and a part of the right ear had been cut off. Following the plan in the Whitechapel murders, the miscreant was not content with merely killing his victim. The poor woman's clothes had been pulled up over her chest, the abdomen ripped completely open, and part of the intestines laid on her neck. After careful notice had been taken of the position of the body when found it was conveyed to the City Mortuary, in Golden-Lane. Here a more extended examination was made. The murdered woman was apparently about 40 years of age, about five feet in height and evidently belonged to that unfortunate class of which the woman done to death in Whitechapel were members. Indeed, one of the policemen who saw the body expressed his confident opinion that he had seen the woman several times walking in the neighbourhood of Aldgate High-street. She was dark complexioned, with auburn hair and hazel eyes, and was dressed in shabby dark clothes. She wore a black cloth jacket with imitation fur collar and three large metal buttons. Her dress was made of green chintz, the pattern consisting of Michaelmas daisies. In addition she had on a thin white vest, a light drab Lindsay skirt, a very old dark green alpaca petticoat, white chemise, brown ribbed stockings (mended at the feet with white material), black straw bonnet trimmed with black beads and green and black velvet, and a large white handkerchief round the neck. In the pockets of the dress a peculiar collection of articles was found. Besides a small packet containing tea and other articles which people who frequent the common lodging houses are accustomed to carry, the police found upon the lady a white pocket handkerchief, a blunt bone-handled table knife, a short clay pipe, and a red cigarette case, with white metal fittings. The knife bore no traces of blood, so could have no connection to the crime. INTENSE EXCITEMENT. When the news of this additional murder became known the excitement in the crowded district of Aldgate was intense. Usually a busy place on Sunday morning, Houndsditch and the connecting thoroughfares presented a particularly animated appearance. Crowds flocked to the entrances to the square where the body had been discovered, but the police refused admittance to all but a privileged few. Sir Charles Warren visited the spot at a particularly early hour, and made himself thoroughly conversant with the neighbourhood and the details of the affair. The police theory is that the man and woman had met in Aldgate, watched the policeman pass round the square, and then they entered it together. There her throat was cut as described above, causing instant death. The murderer then hurriedly proceeded to mutilate the body, for the wounds, though ghastly, do not appear to have been caused so skilfully and deliberately as in the case of the murder of Annie Chapman in Hanbury-street. Five minutes, some of the doctors think, would have sufficed for the completion of the murderer's work, and he was thus enabled to leave the ground before the return of the policeman on duty. A man who passed through Church-lane, Aldgate, at half past one on Sunday morning, says he saw a man seated on a doorstep, wiping his hands. The man who is described as wearing a short jacket and sailor's hat, tried to conceal his face. Early on Monday a police-constable found in Whitechapel-road, a black handled knife, sharp and pointed like a carving knife. The blade was ten inches long. OPENING OF THE INQUEST-SESNATIONAL REVELATIONS. On Thursday, Mr. Langham, the city coroner, opened the inquest upon the body of the woman murdered in Mitre-square, on Sunday morning, and whose name has been variously given as Eddowes, Conway, and Kelly. Mr. Crawford, the city solicitor, represented the police; Major Smith, acting commissioner, and Mr. Superintendent Foster, also being present. Eliza Gold, first witness, living at 6, Thrawl-street, identified the body as that of her sister Catherine Eddowes, who was a single woman who had lived with John Kelly for some years. Witness last saw her sister alive about four or five months ago. Deceased was a hawker, of sober habits, and before living with Kelly, deceased lived with a man named Conway for some years and had children by him. Witness did not know whether Conway, who was an army pensioner, was still alive. In reply to Mr. Crawford, witness said she had not seen Conway for some years. John Kelly, living at a lodging house in Flower and Dean-street, a market labourer, said deceased had lived with him for seven years. Her name was Conway, and he last saw her on Saturday last at two o'clock in the afternoon. They parted on very good terms in Houndsditch, deceased saying she was going to Bermondsey to find her daughter. She promised to return by four o'clock. He heard she had been locked up in Bishopsgate for drunkenness, but made no enquiries, believing she would return on Sunday. Deceased never went out for immoral purpose. When they parted deceased had no money and she left with the intention of getting some from her daughter. She was on bad terms with nobody, and usually returned home about eight o'clock at night. Witness did not know where deceased had got drink, considering she had no money. Deceased last year got money from her daughter. On Friday last the deceased went to Mile-end, and stopped in the casual ward. Early in the week witness and deceased were in Kent together, and on Thursday arrived in London, spending the night together at Shoe-lane casual ward, as they had no money. On Friday they arranged that deceased should go to Mile-end Workhouse, and witness stay at lodging house. They pawned a pair of boots on Saturday, and spent the great portions of the half a crown in food and drink. Witness stood outside with bare feet whilst deceased pawned the boots. It might have been Friday, and not Saturday. Frederick Wilkinson, deputy of the lodging house in Flower and Dean-street, corroborated the last witness as to Kelly and deceased living there on good terms. Deceased did not walk the streets. She said the name of Conway was bought and paid for, meaning that she was married. Deceased on Saturday was wearing an apron. Police Constable Watkins deposed to finding the murdered woman in Mitre-square on Sunday morning, as already reported, her throat was cut, body ripped open, and in a pool of blood. Witness had not heard any footsteps or cry whilst near the square. Mr. Frederick Foster produced plans and maps of the locality. Wilkinson, lodging house deputy, recalled, said he could not tell whether any stranger came there between two and three on Sunday morning. Over one hundred lodged in the house. After luncheon Inspector Collitt was examined and deposed to being called to the scene of the murder immediately after the discovery. Three black buttons, generally used for woman's boots, small metal buttons, a metal thimble, and mustard tin, containing two pawn tickets, were picked up near the body. There was also a piece of apron on the body, corresponding with another piece picked up in Goulston-street, some little way off. Witness detailed the steps taken by the police with the object of tracking the murderer. A house to house inquiry has been made in the vicinity with practically no result. Dr. Gordon Brown, surgeon to the City Police, described the position of the body when he saw it a few minutes after two o'clock on Sunday morning. The way in which the body was mutilated was horrible in the extreme. There was no blood on the front of the clothes. A piece of ear cut off dropped from her clothes when the body was stripped at the mortuary. In describing the injuries to the abdomen, witness said the left kidney was carefully taken out, and in his opinion must have been done by someone who knew where to find it. The uterus was cut through, leaving a stump of about three quarters of an inch. The rest of it was missing. The wounds were inflicted with a sharp knife, which must have been pointed. The wounds in the face were about six inches long. Judging by the cuts in the abdomen a good deal of knowledge of position of the organs in the abdominal cavity was displayed. The parts removed would be no use for professional purposes. The removal of the left kidney was especially difficult. Would not such a knowledge be likely to be possessed by one accustomed to cutting up animals?- Yes. Have you been able to form any opinion as to whether the perpetrator of this act had been disturbed during the performance of it?- I think he had sufficient time. The whole of the injuries could not be done under five minutes and would probably take longer. As a professional I cannot imagine any reason for the removal of the missing parts. I think it was the act of one man. Can you account for the fact that no sounds were heard?- The throat might be so suddenly cut that there would be no time for an alarm. Would you expect to find much blood on the person who inflicted these wounds?- No. With regard to the apron, are the blood spots on it of recent origin?- They are. Dr. Phillips brought a piece of apron found in Gouldstone-street, and that exactly fit's the piece of apron found on the deceased. It is an impossibility to say whether it is human blood upon it, but it is blood. The piece found is smeared with blood, as if hands had been wiped on it. The mutilation of the face I should think was done to disfigure the corpse. The inquiry was adjourned for a week. The Press Association Wolverhampton correspondent says that Eddowes was a native of that town, and several of her relatives state that her father was a tinplate worker. She ran away to London, when twenty years of age. MYSTERIOUS LETTER AND POSTCARDS. One of the most extraordinary things in connection with the mysterious outrages in London lately was the receipt of several letters signed Jack the Ripper, purporting to have been written by the murderer. The Central News says:- On Thursday week the following letter, bearing the E.C. postmark, and directed in red ink, was delivered to this agency:-

Dear Boss, I keep on hearing the police have caught me but they won't fix me just yet. I have laughed when they look so clever and talk about being on the right track. That joke about Leather Apron gave me real fits. I am down on ------ and I shan't quit ripping them till I do get buckled. Grand work the last job was. I gave the lady no time to squeal. How can they catch me now. I love my work and want to start again. You will soon hear of me with my funny little games. I saved some of the proper red stuff in a ginger beer bottle over the last job to write with but it went thick like glue and I can't use it. Red ink is fit enough I hope ha. ha. The next job I do I shall clip the lady's ears off and send to the police officers just for jolly wouldn't you. Keep this letter back till I do a bit more work, then give it out straight. My knife's so nice and sharp I want to get to work right away if I get a chance. Good Luck. Yours truly, Jack the Ripper

Don't mind me giving the trade name, PS Wasn't good enough to post this before I got all the red ink off my hands curse it No luck yet. They say I'm a doctor now. Ha! Ha!

The whole of this extraordinary epistle is written in red ink, in a free, bold, clerkly hand. It was, of course, treated as the work of practical joker, but it is singular to note that the latest murders have been committed within a few days of the receipt of the letter, and that apparently in the case of his last victim the murderer made an attempt to cut off the ears, and that he actually did mutilate the face in a manner which he has never before attempted. The letter is now in the hands of the Scotland Yard authorities.

The Central News says:- A postcard, bearing the stamp "London E., October 1" was received on Monday morning, addressed to the Central News office; the address and subject matter being written in red; and undoubtedly by the same person from whom the sensational letter already published was received on Thursday week. Like the previous missive, this also has reference to the horrible tragedies in East London, forming, indeed, a sequel to the same letter. It runs as follows:-

I was not codding dear old Boss when I gave you the tip, you'll hear about Saucy Jacky's work tomorrow double event this time number one squealed a bit couldn't finish straight off. ha not the time to get ears for police. thanks for keeping last letter back till I got to work again.

Jack the Ripper

The card is smeared on both sides with blood, which has evidently been impressed thereon by the thumb or finger of the writer, the corrugated surface of *the skin being plainly shown upon the back of the card. Some words are nearly obliterated by a bloody smear. It is not necessarily assumed that this has been the work of the murderer, the idea that naturally occurs being that the whole thing is a practical joke. At the same time the writing of the previous letter immediately before the commission of the murders on Sunday was so singular a coincidence that it does not seem unreasonable to suppose that the cool calculating villain who is responsible for the crimes has chosen to make the post a medium through which to convey to the press his grimly diabolical humour. The Central News has received the following letter, bearing the E.C. postmark, written in red ink, in a round hand, apparently by a person indifferently educated. At the foot is a rude drawing of a sharp, pointed knife, measuring three inches and the handle one:-*

3rd October

Dear Boss - Since last splendid success, two more, and never a squeal. O, I am master of the art. I am going to be heavy on the gilded _____ now. We are. Some duchess will cut up nicely, and the lace will show nicely. You wonder how. O, we are masters; no education like a butcher's. No animal like a nice woman. The fat are best. On to Brighton for a holiday, but we shan't idle. Splendid high class women there. My mouth waters. Good luck there. If not, you will hear from me in the West End. My pal will keep on at the East a while yet. When I get a nobility _____ I will send it on to C Warren, or perhaps to you for a keepsake. It is jolly. George of the High Rip Gang. Red ink still, but a drop of real in it.

SINGULAR STATEMENTS. A man named Albert Barker has made the following statement:- "I was in the Three Nuns Hotel, Aldgate, on Saturday night, when a man got into conversation with me. He wanted to know whether I knew what sort of loose women used the public bar at that house, when they usually left the street outside, and where they were in the habit of going. He asked further questions and from hi manner seemed to be up to no good purpose. He appeared to be a shabby genteel sort of man, and was dressed in black clothes. He wore a black felt hat and carried a black bag. We came out together at closing time (twelve o'clock), and I left him outside Aldgate railway station." The young man Albert Bachert of 13, Newnham street, Whitechapel, made a further statement on Monday to a representative of the press. It will be noticed that the man who spoke to him in the Three Nuns Hotel on Saturday night carried a black shiny bag, and it is remarkable that the only man, Mrs. Mortimer observed in Berner street two hours afterwards also carried a black shiny bag. Mrs. Mortimer said:- "The only man whom I had seen pass through the street previously was a young man carrying a black shiny bag who walked very fast down the street from the Commercial road. He looked up at the club, and then went round the corner by the board school." Albert Bachert says:- "On Saturday night at about seven minutes to 12 I entered the Three Nuns Hotel, Aldgate. While in there an elderly woman, very shabbily dressed, came in and asked me to buy some matches. I refused, and she went out. A man who had been standing by me remarked that those persons were a nuisance, to which I responded "Yes." He then asked me to have a glass with him, but I refused, as I had just called for one myself. He then asked me if I knew how old some of the women were who were in the habit of soliciting outside. I replied that I knew or thought that some of them who looked about 25 were over 35, the reason they looked younger being on account of the powder and paint. Having asked other questions about their habits, he went outside and spoke to the woman who was selling matches, and gave her something, I believe. He returned to me and I bid him good-night at about 10 minutes past 12. I believe the woman was waiting for him. I do not think I could identify the woman, as I did not take particular notice of her, but I should know the man again. He was a dark man, height about 5ft. 6in. or 7in. He wore a black felt hat, dark clothes, (morning coat), black tie, and carried a black shiny bag." MEETING OF THE DISTRICT BOARD OF WORKS. A meeting of the Whitechapel District Board of Works was held last evening, Mr. Robert Gladding presiding.- Mr. Cotmur said he thought that the Board as the local authority, should express their horror and abhorrence at the crimes which had been perpetrated in the district. The result of these tragedies had been loss of trade to the district, and the stoppage of certain trades by reason of woman being afraid to pass through the streets without an escort. The inefficiency of the police was shown by the fact that an hour or two later than the tragedies in Berner street and Mitre square the post office in the vicinity had been broken into and much property stolen. The Rev. Daniel Greatorex said emigrants "houses of call" were feeding the panic to such an extent as emigrants refused to locate themselves in Whitechapel, even temporarily. He ascribed the inefficiency of the police to the frequent changes of the police from one district to another, whereby the men kept ignorant of their beats.- Mr. Teller said he hoped that these recent crimes might result in reversion to the old system by which constables were acquainted with every corner of their beats.- Mr. G. T. Brown suggested that the government should be communicated with rather than the Home Secretary or the Chief Commissioner of Police, who were themselves really only on their trial. A REPORTER ARRESTED. The Dublin Evening Mail's London correspondent telegraphs that among the persons arrested on suspicion *of being concerned in the murders, is a reporter who imagined that he might confront the murderer if he walked about at night dressed as a woman. He donned female attire and shaved. The experiment, however, failed, for his eccentric appearance caused his sex to be discovered, and he was arrested.* LIST OF THE EAST END MURDERS. *Six woman have now been murdered in the East End under mysterious circumstances, five of them within a period of eight weeks. The following are the dates of the crimes and names of the victims so far as known:-*

1, Last Christmas week,- an unknown woman found murdered near Osborne and Wentworth Streets, Whitechapel.

2, August 7th,- Martha Turner found stabbed in thirty nine places on a landing in model dwellings known as George Yard Buildings, Commercial Street, Spitalfields.

3, August 31st,- Mrs Nicholls, murdered and mutilated in Bucks Row, Whitechapel.

4, September 7th,- Mrs Chapman, murdered and mutilated, Hanbury Street, Whitechapel.

5, September 30th,- Elizabeth Stride, found with throat cut in Berner Street, Whitechapel.

6, September 30th,- Woman unknown, murdered and mutilated in Mitre Square, Aldgate.

A SINGULAR THEORY. *The Times Vienna correspondent, in referring to the Whitechapel murders, recalls the case of a Jew named Riller, who was accused in 1884 of having murdered and mutilated a Christian woman near Cracow. He was undoubtedly innocent, but was three times condemned, and in the Court of Appeal eventually quashed the sentence/ It was proved that among certain fanatical Jews there existed a superstition that if a Jew became intimate with a Christian woman he would atone for his offence by killing and mutilating the object of his passion. Passages of the Talmud were quoted in support of this view.* REWARDS OFFERED. *The Public indignation at the inability of the police by their existing methods to bring to justice the murderer or murderers of the six unfortunate women who have been so foully done to death in the East End of London found a practical shape yesterday in the spontaneous offers of* substantial rewards by public bodies and private individuals towards the detection of these desperate crimes. A meeting of the Vigilance Committee which has for some time been formed in Whitechapel was held yesterday at Mile End, and a resolution was passed calling upon the Home Office to issue a substantial Government reward for the capture and conviction of the murderer, and a letter embodying this was at once sent to the Home Secretary. One of the murders of Sunday morning took place within the precincts of the City of London, and this fact led one of the Common Councilmen yesterday to give notice that at the next meeting he would move that a reward of £250 should be offered by the Corporation for the detection of the Mitre Square murderer; but the necessity for this step was removed when, later in the day, the Lord Mayor, Mr. Polydore de Keyser, after consulting with Colonel Sir James Fraser, K.C.B, Chief Commissioner of Police of the City of London, announced that a reward of £500 would be given by the Corporation for the detection of the miscreant. The proprietors of the Financial News, a monetary organ, also came forward on behalf of several readers of that journal with a cheque for £300, which was forwarded by their request to the Home Secretary, who was asked to offer that sum for the same purpose in the name of the Government. The proprietors of the Evening Post, which is also chiefly devoted to the interests of the financial world, has commenced a subscription list with a sum of 50 guineas, and has invited other contributions towards a rewards fund. The Vigilance Committee, formed in Whitechapel after the murder of Annie Chapman in Hanbury street, have also raised £300 to stimulate the search for the murderers. Mr. S, Montagu, M.P., it will be remembered offered £100 reward for the detection of the Whitechapel murderer after the Hanbury street crime. The excitement which was created in London on Sunday by the news of the atrocious crimes of Berner street and Mitre square was doubly intensified yesterday morning, when the daily newspapers carried the startling news into every household, and there was but one subject of conversation everywhere. Thousands of people visited the localities of the crimes, but there was nothing then to see. The police had removed all traces of the murder from the yard in Berner street, where the unfortunate Elizabeth Stride was found with a terrible gash in her throat, while at Mitre square there was nothing which could recall the horrible spectacle which met the eyes of Constable Watkins at a quarter to two o'clock on Sunday morning. The remains of the disembowelled victim had been removed to the City mortuary, and the pavement had been cleansed. In connection with the latter place, however, a startling discovery was made during the afternoon. Sergeant Dudman had his attention drawn to, 36, Mitre street, a house a short distance from the spot where the murdered woman was found and there he found what appeared to be bloodstains upon the doorway and underneath the window, as if *a person had wiped his fingers on the window ledge and drawn a blood stained knife down part of the doorway. Mr. Hurtig, who lives on the premises, said he had only just before noticed the stains, and then quite by accident. Almost immediately afterwards the same police officer had his attention drawn to similar marks on the plate glass window of Mr. William Smith, at the corner of Mitre square, but Mr. Smith scouted the idea that they could have anything to do with the murders, as the windows were covered at night by shutters. The discovery, notwithstanding, caused increased excitement for a time in the locality. The only other trace left by the murderer was the portion of an apron picked up in Goldston street, which corresponded with a piece left on the body of the victim. A SELF ACCUSED MEDICAL STUDENT EXTRAORDINARY STATEMENT. At Guildhall, London on Wednesday, William Bull, describing himself as a medical student at a London hospital, and living at Stannard road, Dalston, was charged on his own confession, with having committed the murder at Mitre Square. Inspector Izzard said that at 20 minutes to 11 on Tuesday, the accused came to his room at Bishopsgate-street station, and made the following statement:- "My name is William Bull and I live at Dalston. I am a medical student at the London Hospital. I wish to give myself up for the murder in Aldgate, on Saturday night or Sunday morning about two o'clock. I think I met the woman in Aldgate. I went with her up a narrow street not far from the main road for an immoral purpose. I promised to give her half-a-crown, which I did. While walking along together there was a second man, who came up and took the half-a-crown from her. I cannot endure this any longer. My poor head-(here he put his hand to his head, and cried or pretended to cry)- I shall go mad. I have done it and I must put up with it." The Inspector asked what had become of the clothing he had on when the murder was committed. The accused said, "If you wish to know they are in the Lea, and the knife I threw away." At this point the prisoner declined to say any more. He was drunk. Part if the statement was made in the presence of Major Smith. Prisoner gave correct address, but is not known at the London Hospital. His parents were respectable. The Inspector asked for a remand to make enquiries, and this was granted. Prisoner now said he was drunk when he made the statement. He was remanded. DESCRIPTION OF A SUSPECT. A description has been issued by the police of the man said to have been in the company of Elizabeth Stride on Saturday night. He is described as of 28 years of age about 5ft. 7in. High, dark complexioned: he had no whiskers, and wore dark clothes and black felt hat which was stained. THREATENING TO STAB A WOMAN. At the Thames Police-court on Tuesday, Charles Ludwig, was again brought up on a charge of threatening to stab Elizabeth Burns, an unfortunate, of 55, Flower and Dean-street, Spitalfields, and with threatening to stab a coffee-stall keeper. The woman said she accompanied him up Butchers-row a fortnight ago, and that when they reached a gateway Ludwig pulled out a long bladed knife. She screamed and the police came up. Ludwig walked off, but from her statement he was afterwards arrested. The coffee-stall keeper said the prisoner came to him the following morning and threatened to stab him. Accused, who seemed of excitable disposition, was discharged. ALMOST ANOTHER VICTIM. An alarming story was told to a detective on Tuesday and it is understood (The Daily Telegraph says) that the Metropolitan Police have for some time been cognisant of its details. If this statement be true- and there appears to be no reason to question it- then sometime between the date of the Hanbury street murder and last Sunday the bloodthirsty maniac who is now terrifying Whitechapel unsuccessfully attempted another outrage. The woman who so narrowly escaped death is married; but she admits having entered into conversation with a strange man for an immoral purpose. She alleges that he tripped her up , so that she fell on the pavement. He made an effort to cut her throat; but she shielded herself with her arm, and in doing so received a cut upon it. Alarmed by his failure, and fearing her shrieks, the would be murderer ran off, and the woman, when discovered, was removed to the hospital. She has since been discharged, and the wound upon the arm is still to be seen. The occurrence is alleged to have taken place ten days ago, in a by-turning off Commercial-street. Unfortunately, the woman was so much in liquor when she was assaulted that she cannot recollect the man's face or dress, and has been unable to give a description of him, which may account for the secrecy which has been maintained in regard to the attack. A SENSATIONAL RUMOUR-EXCITING CHASE. Late last night reports came to hand again and again that the murder had been captured. Shortly before midnight a story was circulating that an unknown murderer had been surprised in the act of attempting another outrage on a woman in Union Street, Whitechapel. The story went that the woman was lured by the "Monster" into a side street, but the gleam of a steel blade at once roused her to a sense of her danger, and her screams brought to the spot a man and two women, who were said to have been watching the movements of the couple. The would be murderer, it was stated, was pursued by a man who knocked the knife out of his hand. The unknown one, however, jumped into a passing cab, bidding the cabman drive wherever he liked. A howling mob swarmed after the fugitive and the police soon captured the vehicle and took the occupant to Leman Street police station. Investigation, however, soon proved that the romantic story had but a slight foundation. It was ascertained that about ten o'clock a well-dressed man rushed out of the Three Nuns public house, in Aldgate, followed by a woman , who had declared he had "been molesting" her. To escape the crowd, the stranger jumped into a cab, and was pursued and captured as above stated. When he was formally charged, the woman stated positively that the prisoner had accosted her first in Whitechapel High Street, and that when she refused his proposals, he threatened her with violence. The woman nevertheless declined to prefer any charge, and left the station. The man was detained, pending inquiries. He is an athletic, determined fellow, about 40 years of age, no weapons were found on him. He gave a name but declined to state his address. When removed to the cell his attitude became defiant, and he kept up a conversation with a slightly American accent. He is stated to have been slightly under the influence of drink. He remains in custody. A Maltese sailor arrested at a late hour was released this morning, as was also a third man arrested near Cable street. ANOTHER DESCRIPTION OF THE SUPPOSED MURDERER. The Evening news (London), this evening states that a greengrocer named Mathew Packer, has been found, who states that at a quarter to twelve on Saturday night a man, aged 35, stout, and wearing a wide awake hat, and dark clothes. He was accompanied by a woman with a white flower in her bosom, came to his stall, two doors from the scene of the Berner Street murder, and purchased some grapes. They left in the direction of the club, about a quarter past twelve o'clock. PUBLIC FEELING. A correspondent telegraphing on Thursday night says: The excitement and indignation which are apparent in East London, have been increased to-day by the startling announcement by Dr. Brown at the inquest that the similar organ missing from the body of Annie Chapman had been cut away from the body of Kate Eddowes, found in Mitre-square. There had been a suspicion of this fact, which now renders the murderer's object the more mysterious since the doctor is so emphatic in his assertion that the obtaining of these portions of a woman's body could be no use to medical research. Dr. Browne stated that the clever manner in which the left kidney and the other organ were removed betokened that the murderer was well versed in anatomy, but not necessarily human anatomy, for he could have gained a certain amount of skill by reason of his being a slaughterer of animals. These remarks conclusively show that the same hand which caused the death of the previous victims is also responsible for killing Kate Eddowes, and in all probability Elizabeth Stride in Berner-street, although in the latter case he may have been disturbed before he had time to complete the mutilation in the peculiarly horrible manner which characterized his fiendish work. The three men who were arrested late on Wednesday night have been liberated, they having satisfactorily established their identity. The man apprehended under suspicious circumstances when leaving the Three Nuns Tavern in Aldgate was very violent throughout the night, and refused to satisfy the police as to his antecedents until Thursday morning, when he was discharged. Since the release of these men on Thursday morning the police have made no apprehensions in connection with the crimes, but the most*

> *extraordinary rumours were flying about throughout the locality on Thursday of the capture of the much sought for criminal, and the effect upon the public, already well-high goaded into exasperation at the continued non-success of the police to hunt down the murderer, was indescribable. Another correspondent writes:- The announcement of Dr. Browne of the disappearance of the portion of the body revived for a time the theory put forward by Mr. Wynne Baxter, the coroner in the Hanbury-street case. The British Medical Journal, however, states that the foreign physician who sought to purchase specimens was a gentleman of the highest respectability, that he did not offer a large price, and that he left London eighteen months ago.*

The Hull and East Yorkshire and Lincolnshire Times, October 6th 1888,

> *DISCOVERY OF HUMAN REMAINS AT GUILDFORD. The Press Association says that Detective Inspector Marshall, of the Whitechapel police, yesterday proceeded to Guildford to obtain some human remains, consisting principally of the legs of a woman, which were picked up on the railway there some time ago. Dr Bond will then compare them with the trunk lying at the Westminster Mortuary. A later telegram from the Press Association's Guildford correspondent says that some sensation was caused in Guildford yesterday by a report that the remains, which were discovered on August 21st in a brown paper parcel lying on the railway near the station, were supposed to part of the body of the woman, the trunk of which was found in the new police barracks at Whitehall. It is remembered that the remains found at Guildford consisted of a right foot and a portion of the [illegible] leg, from the knee down to the ankle, where it was severed. The police surgeon examined the remains and certified them to be human, whilst he also considered them to be those of a woman; but the flesh had either been roasted or boiled. No clue had been found to solve the mystery, but after the discovery at Whitehall, Superintendent Barry, of the Guildford Borough Police, wrote to the Scotland Yard authorities with the result that Detective Inspector Marshall, who has the Whitehall mystery in hand, proceeded yesterday to Guildford, and had the remains, which had been buried in the cemetery, disinterred, and in the evening he conveyed them to the police in London.- Mr Marshall, in reply to the correspondent stated that he could form no opinion as to whether the remains were part of the trunk referred to above, but on his arrival in London he would immediately take them to Drs Bond and W Hibbard, by whom they would be carefully examined.*

The Hull Daily News, October 6th 1888,

ANOTHER LONDON HORROR. MURDER AND DISMEMBERMENT. DISCOVERY OF A WOMAN'S MUTILATED BODY. Another ghastly discovery was made in London on Tuesday afternoon. About five o'clock a carpenter named Frederick Wildborn, employed by Messrs J. Grover and Sons, builders, of Pimlico, who are contractors for the new Metropolitan Police Head-quarters on the Thames Embankment, was working on the foundation, when he came across a neatly done up parcel which was secreted in one of the cellars. Wildborn was in search of timber when he found the parcel, which was tied up in paper and measured about two and half feet long by about two feet in width. It was opened, and the body of a woman, very much decomposed, was found carefully wrapped in a piece of cloth, which is supposed to be a black petticoat. The trunk was minus the head, both arms, and both legs, and presented a ghastly spectacle. The officials of the works were immediately apprised of the discovery and the police were fetched. Dr. Bond, the divisional surgeon to A Division, and several other medical gentlemen were communicated with, and subsequently examined the remains, which were handed over to the care of some police officers, who were told of to see that the trunk was not disturbed. From what can be ascertained the conclusion has been arrived at by the medical men that these remains are those of the woman whose arms have recently been discovered in different parts of London- one in Pimlico and the other in Lambeth, on the opposite side of the other of the River Thames. Dr. Neville, who examined the arms of the female found a few weeks ago in the Thames, off Ebury Bridge, Pimlico, said, on that occasion that he did not think it had been skilfully been taken from the body, and this fact would appear to favour the theory that the arm, together with the one found in the grounds of the Blind Asylum in the Lambeth-road last week, belong to the trunk discovered today, for it is stated that the limbs appear to have been taken from the body found this afternoon in anything but a skilful manner. The building which is in course of erection is the new police depot for London, the present scattered head-quarters of the Metropolitan police force and Criminal Investigation Department in Great Scotland Yard and Whitehall-place having been found too small for the requirements of the London police system. The builders have been working on the site for some considerable time now, but have only just completed the foundation. It was originally the site for the National Opera House, and extends from the Thames Embankment, through to Cannon-row, Parliament-street, at the back of St Stephen's Club and the Westminster Bridge Station on the District Railway. The prevailing opinion is that to place the body where it was found the person conveying it must have scaled the 8ft, boarding which encloses the works, and carefully avoiding the watchmen who do duty by night, must have dropped it where it was found. There appears to be little doubt that the parcel had been in the cellar for some considerable time. A workman who has a thorough knowledge of the facts connected with the finding of the ghastly remains has made the following statement:- "As one of our carpenters was putting away his tools at about five on Tuesday night in one of the vaults which are to form the foundation of the main building of the new offices which are to accommodate the police, he saw what seemed to be a heap of paper. As it is very dark in this particular spot, even during the day, the matter somehow did not appear to strike him as curious or out of the way, his passing thought being that it was merely a bundle of canvas which was being used on the works. He consequently mentioned the matter to no one, and, having left his tools, came away and went home, thinking no more about the mysterious parcel which was to reveal another dreadful crime, probably perpetrated within 100 yards of King-street police station, about 200 or 300 yards from the present offices of the Criminal Investigations Department, and within 50 yards of the Houses of Parliament. Next morning, when he went to fetch his tools, he became aware of a very peculiar smell proceeding from the dark corner, but at the time made no attempt to ascertain the cause. The matter however, had taken possession of his mind, and later on in the day he mentioned the circumstances to one of two of his fellow workmen. They at once decided to tell the foreman, This was done, and the foreman, accompanied by some of the men, proceeded to the spot. One of the labourers was called to shift the parcel. It was then opened, and the onlookers were horrified to find that it contained a human body. The legs, arms and head were missing, and the body presented a most sickening spectacle. The woman had evidently been dead for many days, as decomposition was far advanced. I never saw such a dreadful sight in my life, and the smell was dreadful. After we had got over the first surprise and nausea we sent for the police, and a doctor was also sent for. We could see that the body was that of a full grown woman and when the doctor came he said the same thing. Almost immediately after that, Dr. Bond, of the Middlesex Hospital, came and saw the body. He found that it was very brown, and I believe he said it was the body from which the arms found in the Thames a few days ago had been cut. The body was wrapped in what looked like part of an old black dress of very common material, and it is a very strange thing that the other parts of the same dress have been found in other parts of the yard. The police took possession of the remains, and gave orders that no stranger was to be admitted to the enclosure. How long do I think it possible the body could have been lying there? Well, it could not have been where we found it above two or three days, because men are continually passing the spot. The place is very dark and it is possible that it might have escaped notice [illegible] but now I come to think of it. I know for a fact that it was not there last Friday, because we had occasion to do something at that very spot. Asked for his opinion as to how the parcel got into such a curious place, our informant seemed to be taken aback at the simplicity of the question, but he said that the person who put the bundle there could have very well have got into the enclosure from the embankment side and not only would the risk of detection be very great, but it would stand a good chance of breaking his neck. EXAMINATION OF THE REMAINS. A later account says that there is no doubt now that the discovery is connected with a terrible murder from the way in which the body had been treated. From the way in which the body has been treated it is impossible that it could have been spirited away from a dissecting room after having answered the purpose of lawful operations. Persons who have seen the trunk describe it as being in a particularly advanced stage of decomposition, so much so that it was pronounced dangerous by the medical gentlemen present for anyone to touch it with the naked hand. One end was quite black, and upon it being taken to the mortuary disinfectants were freely used, and it was placed in spirit to await the post-mortem examination. When the parcel was found and opened there was not a scrap of clothing on the trunk, and it was tied with rope lengthways and crossways, just as one would tie up a parcel. The vault is about 24 feet by 30 in size, and 12 or 13 feet deep, and it is nearly covered over with lose planks on the ground showing only a small space at each end of the place.

The Hull Daily News, October 6th 1888,

AN OLD WOMAN BURNT TO DEATH. An elderly woman named Mary Foley, who occupied rooms at 18, Booth-street, Spitalfields, was on Thursday found by a neighbour lying in her room burned to death. Her clothing had evidently been ignited from her fire place.

Mary Foley:

The story of Mary Foley appeared in the following publications, The North Eastern Daily Gazette, October 5th 1888, The Belfast News Letter, October 6th 1888, The Birmingham Daily Post, October 6th 1888, The Cheshire Observer, October 6th 1888, The York Herald, October 6th 1888, and The Lancaster Gazette and General Advertiser for Lancashire, Westmorland and Yorkshire, October 10th 1888

Mary Foley's death is registered thus,

Mike Covell

> Name: Mary Foley, Estimated Birth Year: abt 1797, Date of Registration: Jul- Aug- Sep- 1888, Age at Death: 91, Registration District: Poplar, Inferred County: London, Vol: 1c, Page: 399

The Hull and East Yorkshire and Lincolnshire Times, October 6th 1888,

> *THE WHITECHAPEL CRAZE IN HULL. The excitement which has been caused throughout the country by the horrible atrocities committed in Whitechapel, London, has been equally great in Hull, and it appears a repetition of those incidents which have been frequent in the Metropolis of late has to some extent taken place in Hull. At Hull Police Court this afternoon, before the Mayor (Alderman Toozes) and Mr. T Stratton, a poorly clad woman, named Jane Feeney, was charged on warrant with having used threats towards a woman named Minnie Kirlew.- The Prosecutrix stated that the prisoner threatened her in Manor Street yesterday and said she would "Whitechapel Murder her". Witness stated that she was afraid of the prisoner. A man who was called as a witness said he heard the prisoner when acting very violently, threaten to Whitechapel murder the Prosecutrix.- The Bench ordered the accused to find one surety in £10 to keep the peace for six months, and also sent her to prison or seven days for having been disorderly.*

> **Jane Feeney and Minnie Kirlew:**
>
> Jane Feeney was constantly in trouble with the Hull police and there are numerous articles about her criminal escapades. These included,
>
> The York Herald, July 30th 1878, Stealing £3 10s with her husband Thomas
>
> The Hull Packet and East Riding Times, August 2nd 1878, Same charge as above
>
> The Hull Packet and East Riding Times, January 31st 1879, Drunk and disorderly prostitutes, three months in prison
>
> The Leeds Mercury, October 23rd 1880, Jane Feeney went to Leeds, from Hull, and robbed her own mother taking £1 12s 6d. Feeney was left to pay costs

The York Herald, October 23rd 1880, Features a similar report but also claims that Feeney assaulted her mother.

The Hull Packet and East Riding Times, October 29th 1880, Features the same case

The Hull Packet and East Riding Times, August 11th 1882, Features Feeney being charged with being drunk and ordered to pay 10s

The Yorkshire Herald and The York Herald, December 10th 1890, Feeney is sent to prison for 21 days for stealing a clothes brush for 2d to buy drink. It was also claimed that Feeney had also sold her boots and the boots of her child to buy drink!

The 1881 Census shows Jane Feeney and her husband Thomas thus, 1 Caroline Place,

Thomas Feeney	32	Head	Dock Side Labourer
Jane Feeney	31	Wife	B. abt 1850 Leeds
John Feeney		14	Son
Margaret Feeney			

[RG11, P4767, F59, P13, GSU1342151]

The 1891 Census is problematic, there is only one Jane Feeney, born in Leeds, residing in Hull, but the date of birth is incorrect. The children and their date of birth do, however, fit in with the earlier entry. The 1891 entry reads,

Jane Feeney	50	Head	B. abt 1841 Leeds
John Feeney	24	Son	Dock Labourer
Margaret Feeney	11	Dau	Scholar

[RG12, P3933, F124, P9, GSU6099043]

Minnie Kirlew is something of an enigma, with only one entry in the 1881 Census for her, it reads,

Mike Covell

29 Bishop Lane, Hull			
George Kirlew	28	Head	Dock Side Labourer
Bella Kirlew	24	Wife	
Minnie Kirlew	2	Dau	B. abt 1879
George A Kirlew	3	mo Son	

[RG11, P4767, F4, P1, GSU1342151]

If this is the Minnie Kirlew in the article she would have been approx. 9 years old at the time and hardly a "woman" as claimed in the article. There are no other mentions of Minnie Kirlew in the Census leading me to believe that Minnie Kirlew was perhaps a false name or that the newspaper misreported the incident and got the name wrong.

The Hull Daily News, October 6th 1888,

LATEST NEWS. THE TRAGEDIES IN LONDON. YESTERDAYS TELEGRAM. THE CONFESSION BY AN ALLEGED MEDICAL STUDENT. Wm. Bull, calling himself a medical student, who was remanded on Tuesday, at the Guildhall, Police-court, London, on his confession of having committed the Aldgate murder, was brought up again yesterday. Inspector Izzard now informed Ald. Stone that inquiries had proved that the prisoner could not have been connected with the murder in any way. The Alderman, after expressing regret that he could not punish the prisoner for the trouble he had given, discharged him from custody. THE RESUMED INQUEST ON THE BERNER STREET VICTIM. THE QUESTION OF IDENTIFICATION. The inquest on Elizabeth Stride, victim of the recent street murder, was resumed yesterday afternoon by Mr. Wynne E. Baxter. Notwithstanding the positive statement of Mrs. Malcolm that the deceased was her sister, Elizabeth West, it became known yesterday before the commencement of the proceedings that the deceased was named Gustafsdotter. She was born Nov 1843, at Forslander in Gothenburg, Sweden, and married Thomas Stride, a carpenter. The inquest in the proceedings is still maintained. At a quarter past two all present were surprised to hear the coroner's clerk inform the jury that they were to resume the inquiry into the death of a person unknown, and immediately after Dr. Phillips was re-called and stated that he had again examined the body, and could not find any injury to the palate. He had not been able to find any blood on the handkerchief, the stains being those of fruit. He was convinced that the deceased had not swallowed either the skin or seeds of grapes within many hours of her death. The knife found could have produced the injuries which might have been done in two seconds. In cases of suicide the carotid artery was not generally cut as in the present case, and the murderer displayed knowledge of where to cut the throat. Dr Blackwell corroborated the last witness. Sven Ollson, clerk to the Swedish Church, Prince's-square, said that he had known the deceased seventeen years. He bore out the facts above, and produced a register which showed that she was married to Stride-- he thought in '69. The register did not give the date. He gave deceased the hymn book found in her lodgings. William Marshall, living at 64 Bernes-street, said he saw the deceased and a man standing about twenty feet from him at a quarter to 12 on Saturday night. They were talking, and the man seemed like a middle-aged clerk. James Brown, living near the scene of the murder, said he saw the deceased with a man in Berners-street at a quarter to one on Sunday morning. The man was young, and wore a long overcoat. WM Smith, constable on the Berners-street beat, said it took twenty-five minutes to complete his round, and he was at the scene of the murder twenty minutes before the body was found, but saw nothing and heard no cries. Kidney, who lived with the deceased, identified the hymnbook produced. The inquest was then adjourned till October 23rd. THE WHITEHALL MYSTERY. The Press Association says that Detective Inspector Marshall, of the Whitechapel Police, yesterday proceeded to Guildford to obtain some human remains, consisting principally of the leg of a woman which was picked up on the railway there some time ago. Dr. Bond will compare them with the trunk lying at Westminster mortuary. It is currently stated that among the police that some important evidence has been attained that may lead to the identification of the body and the probably an arrest. ARREST OF AN ARMED VOLUNTEER. The Press Association says a man was arrested in the Whitechapel district early yesterday for disorderly conduct. He carried a rifle and bayonet, and this fact gave rise to widespread rumours that the [illegible] Whitechapel murderer had been caught. The owner of the rifle, who was presumably a volunteer, was subsequently liberated. STILL NO CLUE. Telegraphing last night the Press Association says,- Practically nothing of any moment transpired yesterday in connection with the recent murders. Early in the morning the police posted up at all the stations facsimile copies of the post card and letter which pretend to be written by the murderer, and these bills were eagerly read and discussed by large crowds. At the time of telegraphing, the police admit they have practically no clue, but the activity at the headquarters betoken that the authorities are fully alive to the responsibility resting on them. THE CANONBURY MURDER Henry Glennie, aged 34, was charged on remand at Clerkenwell Police-court yesterday, with the

Mike Covell

> *murder of Mrs. Wright, at Canonbury. Mr Fulland (?) prosecuted. He said that prisoner had been in the country for a considerable time, and since his return had been living with a woman named [illegible] who would give evidence. [The rest of the report is unreadable]*

The Eastern Morning News, October 6th 1888,

> *THE LONDON MURDERS. A NEW "MYSTERY OF A HANSOM CAB." AN INSENSIBLE WOMAN FOUND. A woman was found lying insensible in Back-lane shortly after midnight. A crowd quickly collected, and great excitement prevailed. It seems that about half past eleven o'clock three men noticed a hansom cab, containing two men and a woman, turn down Air-street. Having reached a dark railway arch, the men in the cab got out and deposited upon the ground the woman, who was apparently insensible. The three men who were watching, having their suspicions aroused, raised an alarm. The two mysterious men jumped into the cab and the cabman drove hurriedly off. One of the men, however, returned to the spot where the woman was deposited and was pointed out to a constable, who took him to Commercial-road Police Station. He gave the name of Johnson; but, as he was unable to dispel the suspicions of the police, he was detained. SUPPOSED CLUE TO THE MURDERER. A MALAY "WANTED." (FROM OUR CORRESPONDENT.) NEW YORK. FRIDAY. An English sailor named Dodge, who has arrived here, states that he met a Malay named Alaska at Poplar last August, who said that Whitechapel woman had robbed him two years' savings, and unless he recovered the money he would murder and mutilate every Whitechapel woman he met. – The City police authorities, says the Central News, attach much importance to this telegram. Dodge belonged to the steamer Glenorchy. He met the Malay in London on August 13th, and heard him threaten to murder prostitutes. Immediately on the receipt of a copy of the cablegram, detectives were sent to make inquiries at the Glen Line Steamship Company, the Sailors' Home, the Home for Asiatics, and other places in the East End where it was likely the information respecting the Malay could be obtained. At the same time a special representative of the Central News was despatched to the East End to investigate the matter. Amongst other places, our representative called at the Home for Asiatics, and was most courteously received by Mr Freeman, the esteemed manager and superintendent of that institution. Mr Freeman stated that he had been at the Home for 30 years, and had never known a Malay of the name of "Alaska." Malays, he said, are Mahomedans, and do not use European names, but "Alaska" is the Mahomedan name for "Seaman," and Dodge might have been misled. While our representative was conversing with Mr Freeman, Detective-Sergeants Lythel*

and Coston, of the City Police, called and asked for an interview, which was readily accorded. Mr Freeman, it appears, is much respected by Asiatics, who, indeed, look upon him as a friend and brother. Mr Freeman's long connection with the Home has made his name well-known in the "Far East," and such is the confidence which he inspires that Asiatics are in the habit of depositing their money with him. Most of the men who have lodged at the Home lately have used it for years whenever their ships are in London, but recently a crew of Japanese sailors had lodged there, and Mr Freeman admitted that one of these men was a desperate character, for, upon one occasion, he stabbed three of his comrades who were staying in the house. He was arrested; but when his trial came on the injured men had taken ship and gone away. Again, about September 12th, a riot occurred opposite the Home, and a Japanese named Suji Waxim stabbed a woman in a shocking manner, and was subsequently sentenced to six months hard labour. On the day after this man was arrested the hall-keeper of the Asiatic Home found a small but very sharp knife behind the stove in the hall, "But," continued Mr Freeman, "It is a well-known fact that these Asiatics rarely, if ever, travel even a short distance from the West India Docks. After they are discharged and are waiting for another ship, they do not go far from the Home, but spend their time in the public-houses, gambling dens, and other houses which abound in the neighbourhood." Continuing his inquiries, our representative visited the Queen's Music Hall, where Dodge states he met "Alaska." The hall is most luxuriously fitted up in a style equal to many of the West End music halls. Mr Wood, the manager, said he heard nothing of the alleged robbery of the Malay, and referred his inquirer to two attendants – Alexander Nowlan and Henry Pierce – who look after the boxes, in which sailors returned from a voyage usually disport themselves. Both men declared that no such robbery could have taken place on the premises without their hearing of it, and, as far as they were aware, no such thing had happened. At the Exchange Tavern, which is a kind of East End "Criterion," where people congregate after the Music Halls are closed, the Central News' representative was shown over the premises by Mr Charles Harrison, the proprietor. Neither he nor his assistants had heard of the robbery referred to by Dodge. Mr Axel Welin, secretary of the Scandinavian Sailors' House, West India Docks, was next applied to. This gentleman, who is extremely popular with British and foreign sailors, ransacked his boxes, but could find no trace of either of Dodge or the Malay. Messrs McGregor Gow, and Co., owners of the Glen Line of steamers trading to Singapore, China &c., informed the representative that the Glenorchy sailed in April from London to China, and returned on August 14th; after taking cargo at Antwerp, she again sailed for China on September 8th, and was last reported on the 23rd September at Suez. They have no one named

Mike Covell

Alaska on board. The chief cook of the Glenorchy is a thoroughly respectable Chinaman, who has been in the service of the firm for many years, and they have no Malays on the ship. When the Glenorchy passed Gravesend on the last voyage the captain telegraphed that all the crew were on board. The police were on Thursday night successful in finding Mrs Phillips, the daughter of the murdered woman Eddowes. Mrs Phillips had not seen her mother for about two years, and had no idea that the woman killed in Mitre-square was she until a neighbour, who had seen some the facts stated in the newspapers, called her attention to the statements made by Kelly and Mrs Gold. Then she at once went to Seething-lane Police-station, and afterwards to Bishopsgate-street, where she learned definitely that it was her mother who was lying dead in the mortuary in Golden-lane. She did not, however, view the body, as it was thought that the evidence of identification was already sufficiently conclusive. The difficulty experienced by the police in finding Mrs Phillips arose from the fact that about two years ago her husband – who is a gunmaker – left King-street, Bermondsey, New-road, and since then the various members of the family had practically no communication with each other. The funeral of Eddowes will take place on Monday next; the remains will leave the City Mortuary between two and three o'clock, and will be interred in the Cemetery at Ilford. The relatives have accepted the offer of Mr Hawkes, of Banner-street, St. Luke's, to bear the expenses of the funeral. The Central News continues to receive a large number of communications (signed and anonymous) in reference to the Whitechapel murderer. Letters purporting to come from "Jack the Ripper" average about thirty daily, but not a single additional communication has been received in the same hand writing as the previous letter and post-card. In connection with the bloodstains on the post-card, the medical evidence given at the inquest, on the Berner-street victim yesterday (and which will be found below) has furnished another strange coincidence – or, as some would think, another proof – of the writer's identity with the murderer. All the known facts of the Berner-street tragedy had, up till yesterday afternoon, justified the belief that the victim – as in the other murders – had been despatched in such a complete manner that she could not possibly have given or attempted to give an alarm, but the writer of the post-card which was posted on Sunday evening stated that "Number one" (the Berner-street victim) "squealed a bit." This statement has been corroborated by the evidence given by Dr Phillips before the coroner. The police are now engaged, amongst other things in looking over all unoccupied warehouses, and making inquiries wherever premises are not left in charge of caretakers. THE BERNER-STREET TRAGEDY. The Evening News stated yesterday that Matthew Packer, the fruiterer, at 44, Berners-street, at, whose shop a man and a woman purchased some grapes on Saturday last, has seen the body of Elizabeth Stride in the mortuary, and has identified the woman as the one for whom the grapes were bought. Packer says the police have not made any inquiries whatsoever at his shop in reference to the grapes. He says the deceased came with the man to his shop between half past eleven and twelve o'clock, walking from the direction of Ellen-street. The man was from 30 to 35 years of age, of medium height, and with rather a dark complexion. He wore a black coat, and black soft felt hat. He looked like a clerk. RESUMED INQUEST. IMPORTANT EVIDENCE. The inquest on the body of Elizabeth Stride, alias Watts, who was found dead in Berner-street on Sunday morning, with her throat cut, was resumed by Mr Baxter, coroner, at St. George's Vestry Hall, Shadwell, yesterday afternoon. Dr Phillips, re-called, stated that since the last inquiry, in accordance with the coroner's request, he had carefully re-examined the body of deceased, particularly with regard to her mouth. He could not find any injury to, or absence of, any part of the hard or soft palate. He had also been requested to examine some handkerchiefs, and had done so. He could not find any blood upon them, and he believed the stains upon the larger handkerchief were fruit stains. He was convinced that deceased had not swallowed the skin or the seed of a grape for many hours before her death. He had examined the knife which was picked up in the street by a boy. The knife had recently been blunted, and its edge turned apparently by being rubbed on a kerbstone. It was evidently a sharp knife before. The injuries on deceased's neck could have been inflicted by such a weapon, but in his opinion the knife in question was not the one used. From the position of the body he thought that deceased was seized by the shoulder and placed on the ground, and the perpetrator of the deed was on her right side when he inflicted the cut. He seemed to have possessed some knowledge as to where to inflict a deadly wound in the throat. There was great dissimilarity between Chapman's case and this. In the former the neck was severed all round to the vertebral column. The perpetrator of the deed, assuming that he was to the right of the deceased, might have kept clear of bloodstains. The chief injury to the neck was away from him, and the stream of the blood would not flow in his direction. The deed would only take a few seconds to commit. He could not find any traces of anaesthetic. If deceased did not utter any cry, he could not account for it. Sven Olsson said he was clerk to the Swedish Church in Princess-square. He had known deceased for about 17 years. She was Swede, and her maiden name was Gustafsdotter, and she was born neat Gothenburg in 1843. She was the wife of a carpenter named John Thomas Stride. He got these particulars from the church register. He thought deceased married Stride in 1869. She told him that her husband was drowned in the Princess Alice disaster. William Marshall, labourer, 64, Berner-street, said he saw the deceased in Berner-street about a quarter to twelve on Saturday night. She was standing on the pavement

Mike Covell

talking quietly to a man. Witness did not see the face distinctly. He wore a short black coat, dark trousers, and a peaked cap. He should say he was a middle aged man, about five feet six inches in height, and inclined to be stout. He looked like a clerk. He heard the man say to the deceased, "You would say anything but your prayers." The woman laughed at the man's remark, and they then went away together. A young man named James Brown stated that he saw the deceased in company with a man standing near the Board School in Berner-street at a quarter to one on Sunday morning. The man was wearing a long overcoat which reached almost down to his heels. He heard the woman say "No; not to-night; some other night." The deceased's companion was about five feet seven inches in height and of average build. P.C. William Smith, the constable on the beat, deposed that he passed by the deceased in Berner-street at 12.30 on Saturday night. She was talking to a man, and standing a few yards away from where her body was found. Her companion was carrying a parcel wrapped in a newspaper. It was about 18 inches long, and five or six inches broad. He was about 5ft 7in in height, and wore dark clothes and a low felt hat. Other evidence was of a formal nature was given, and the inquiry adjourned until Tuesday fortnight, the 23rd inst. THE WESTMINSTER MYSTERY. Police-Inspector Marshall went to Guildford yesterday to bring to London the leg of a woman, which was recently found near the railway line there, and which was stated to have been boiled. The limb will be compared by Dr Bond with the trunk lately found at Whitehall. It is believed that some very important information has been obtained, which will shortly lead to the identification of the murdered woman, and to an arrest. It is a singular coincidence – and one that may prove a link in the chain of evidence in the elucidation of the mystery – that the newspaper found with the trunk had been found to be part of an issue of the date – viz, Aug. 24 – when these remains were discovered. -- The Central News is authorised to state that Sir Charles Warren has been making inquiries as to the practicability of employing trained bloodhounds for use in special cases in the streets of London, and having ascertained that dogs which have been accustomed to work in a town can be procured he is making immediate arrangements for their use in London. -- The mania of the Whitechapel murderer is evidently spreading its evil influence to this part of the country. A middle aged woman named Jane Henley was charged at the Hull Police-court yesterday with using threats to a married woman named Minnie Kirlew. In the evidence adduced, it was stated that the specific threat was that prisoner had said she'd "Whitechapel" her. Prisoner was ordered to find one surety in £5, and, on another charge of being drunk and disorderly, was sent to prison for seven days.

The Hull and East Yorkshire and Lincolnshire Times, October 6th 1888

ANOTHER CHAPTER OF HORRORS. MORE ATROCITIES IN LONDON. TWO WOMEN MURDERED. HORRIBLE MUTILATION. The Metropolis was yesterday (Sunday) morning thrown into a state of renewed consternation by the announcement that the bodies of two more murdered women had been discovered in the East End. The first of the series of murders was committed so far back as last Christmas, when a woman, whose identity was never discovered, was found murdered in, or consiguous to, the district known as Whitechapel. There were circumstances of peculiar barbarity about the mode in which the body was treated. This fact did not attract so much notice at the time as it did when, on August 7 last, a woman, named Martha Turner, aged 35, was found dead on the first floor landing of some model dwellings in Spitalfields, with 39 bayonet or dagger wounds on the body. On the 31st of the same month the woman Nichols, an unfortunate, was found dead in Buck's-row, Whitechapel. With this probably begins the series of crimes which have lately horrified and terrified the public, for the mutilation of the body was done with so much technical skill and audacity as to suggest a definite but extraordinary, and at that time unexplained, purpose. What that object was the Coroner recently suggested in the summing up at the inquest of the woman Chapman, who was murdered in the same district, and under similar circumstances, on September 8th. That crime created almost a panic, which had scarcely died away when it became known yesterday that two more murders of apparently the same kind had been committed under circumstances detailed hereunder. THE BERNER STREET MURDER. The scene of the first of the present outrages is a narrow court in Berner-street, a quite thoroughfare running from Commercial-road down to the London, Tilbury, and Southend Railway. At the entrance to the court are a pair of large wooden gates, in one of which is a small wicket for use when the gates are closed. At the hour when the murderer accomplished his purpose these gates were open. Indeed, according to the testimony of those living near the entrance, the court is seldom closed. For a distance of 18 or 20 feet from the street there is a dead wall on each side of the court the effect of which is to enshroud the intervening space in absolute darkness after sunset. Further back some light is thrown into the court from the windows of a Workingmen's Club, which occupies the whole length of the court on the right, and from a number of cottages occupied mainly by tailors and cigarette makers on the left. At the time when the murder was committed, however the lights in all of the dwelling houses in question had been extinguished, whilst other illumination as came from the club, being from the upper storey, would fall on the cottages opposite, and would only serve to intensify the gloom in the rest of the court. From the position in which the body was found it is believed that the moment the murderer has got his victim in the dark shadow near the entrance to the court he threw her to the *ground and with one gash cut her throat from ear to ear. The hypothesis that the wound was inflicted after, and not before the woman fell, is supported by the fact that there are severe bruises on her left temple and left cheek, thus showing that force must have been used to prostrate her, which would not have been necessary had her throat been already cut. When discovered, the body was lying as if the woman had fallen forward, her feet being about a couple of yards from the street, and her head in the gutter, which runs down the right hand side of the court. The woman lay on her left side face downwards, her position being such that although the court at that part is only nine feet wide a person walking up the middle might have passed the recumbent body without notice. The condition of the corpse, however, and several other circumstances which have come to light during the day, prove pretty conclusively that no considerable period elapsed between the committal of the murder and discovery of the body. In fact, it is pretty generally conjectured that the assassin was disturbed at his ghastly work, and made off before he had completed his designs. All the features of the case go to connect the tragedy with that which took place three-quarters of an hour later, a few streets distant. The obvious poverty of the woman, her total lack of jewellery or ornaments, and the soiled condition of her clothing, are entirely opposed to the theory that robbery could have been the motive. The secrecy and despatch of which the crime was effected are equally good evidence that the murder was not the result of an ordinary street brawl. At the club referred to above- the International Workmen's Club- which is an offshoot of the Socialist League, and a rendezvous of a number of foreign residents, Poles, and Continental Jews of various nationalities, it is customary on Saturday nights to have friendly discussion on topics of mutual interests, and to wind the up the evening's entertainment with songs, &c. The proceedings commenced on Saturday about 8.30 with a discussion on the necessity for Socialism amongst Jews. This was kept up until about eleven o'clock, when a considerable portion of the company left for their respective homes. Between 20 and 30 remained behind, and the usual concert which followed was not concluded when the intelligence was brought in by the steward of the club that a woman had been done to death. Within a few yards of them, and within earshot of their jovial songs. The people residing in the cottages on the other side of the court were all indoors and most of them in bed by midnight. Several of these persons remember laying awake and listening to the singing, and they also remember the concert coming to an abrupt termination. But during the whole of the time, from retiring to rest until the body was discovered, no one heard anything in the nature of a scream or woman's cry of distress. It was Louis Diemshitz, the steward of the club, who found the body. Diemshitz, who is a traveller in cheap jewellery, had spent the day at Westow Hill market, near the Crystal Palace, in pursuance of his avocation, and had driven home at this unusual hour, reaching Berner-street at one o'clock. On turning into the gateway he had some difficulty with his pony, the animal being apparently determined to avoid the right hand wall. For the moment Diemshitz did not think much of this occurrence, because he knew the pony was given to shying. He thought perhaps some mud or refuse was in the way. Failing to discern anything in the darkness, Diemshitz poked about with the handle of the whip, and immediately discovered that some large obstacle was in the path. To jump down and strike a match. Was the work of a second, and then it became at once apparent that something serious had taken place. Without waiting to see whether the woman, whose body he saw was drunk or dead, Diemshitz entered the club by the side door higher up the court, and informed those in the concert room upstairs that something had happened in the yard. A member of the club named Kozebrodski, but familiarly known as "Isaacs," returned with Diemshitz into the court, and the former struck a match while the latter lifted the body up. It was at once apparent that the woman was dead. The body was still warm, and the clothes wet from the recent rain. But the heart had ceased to beat, and the stream of blood in the gutter, terminating in a hideous pool near the club door, showed but too plainly what had happened. Both men ran off without delay to find a policeman, and about the same time other members of the club, who had by this time found their way into the court, went off with the same object, in different directions. The search was for some time fruitless. At last, however, after considerable delay, a constable was found in Commercial-road. With the aid of the policeman's whistle more constables were quickly on the spot, and the gates at the entrance to the court having been closed, and a guard set on all the exits of the club and the cottages, the superintendent of the district, and divisional surgeon were sent for. In a few minutes Dr Phillips was at once at the scene of the murder, and a brief examination sufficed to show that life had been extinct some minutes. Careful notes having being taken of the body, it was removed to the parish mortuary of St Georges in the East, Cable-street, to await identification. A representative of the Press Association, who has seen the corpse, states that the woman appears to be about 30 years of age. Her hair is very dark, with a tendency to curl, and her complexion is also dark. Her features are sharp and somewhat pinched, as though she has endured considerable privations recently, an impression confirmed by the entire absence of the kind of ornaments commonly affected by women of her station. She wore a rusty black dress of a cheap kind, of sateen, with a velveteen bodice, over which was a black diagonal [illegible] jacket, with fur trimming. Her bonnet, which had fallen from her head when she was found in the yard, was of black crape, and inside, apparently with the object of making the article fit closer to the head, was folded a copy of the Star newspaper. In her right hand were tightly clasped some grapes, and in her left she held a number of sweetmeats. Both the jacket and the bodice were open towards the top. But in other respects the clothes were not disarranged. The linen was clean and is tolerably good repair. But some articles were missing. The cut in the woman's throat, which was the cause of death, was evidently affected with a very sharp instrument, and was made with one rapid incision. The weapon was apparently drawn across the throat rather obliquely from left to right, the gash being about three inches long and nearly the same depth. In the pocket of the woman's dress were discovered two pocket handkerchiefs (a gentleman's and a lady's), a brass thimble, and a skein of black darning worsted. In addition to Dr Phillips the body was examined both before and after removal to the mortuary, by Dr Kaye and Dr Blackwell, both of whom reside in the vicinity of Berner-street. On the arrival of the Superintendent from leman-street Police Station, which took place almost simultaneously with that of the divisional surgeon, steps were immediately taken to ascertain whether the members of the club were in any way connected with the murder. The names and addresses of all the men present were taken, and a vigorous search of persons and premises was instituted, much to the annoyance of the members. The residents in the court had to submit to a similar scrutiny. In neither case, however, was any incriminating evidence discovered. It was five o'clock before the police had finished the investigations at the club, for, in addition to the search referred to above, inquiries were made which resulted in a number of written statements which had to be signed by members. The body of the woman murdered in Berners-street has been identified as that of Elizabeth Stride, better known as Lizzie Long, lately living at 32, Flower and Dean-street. THE INQUEST. The inquest on the body of Elizabeth Stride was opened at eleven o'clock this morning by Mr Wynne Baxter at the Vestry Hall, Cable Street, Commercial road. The body was being viewed by the jury presented a dreadful night, the head being almost severed from the body by one awful gash.- William West was the first witness examined. He said that he lived at the International Working Men's Institute and Club, Berner Street, at the side of which is a passage leading to the yard. Two large wooden gates protected the entrance to the yard, and they were sometimes open at night. In the yard there were two or three small tenements. The club was a Socialist Club, and persons of all nationalities were eligible. Witness was at the club on Saturday night from half past ten or eleven when the members were discussing. The bulk of the members left the club by the front door before twelve. Witness's business was at 40, Berner Street; but he lived at 2 William Street, Commercial Road, wither he went past at half past twelve. Before leaving he noticed the gates were open, but there was nothing on the ground.- Norris Eagle, travelling jeweller, and member of the club, said he was at the club on Saturday, and left about quarter to 12. He returned about 20 minutes to one, and as the front door was closed he went through the gateway and side door. He saw nothing in the yard, but about 20 minutes later another member announced the discovery of the body.- Louis Diemschitz, steward of the club, deposed that he returned to his home at the club at one o'clock, riding in a kind of barrow drawn by a pony. He drove through the open gates of the yard, when his pony shied at something on the ground. He felt it with his whip handle, and tried to move it but failed, and jumping down at once he struck a light. He then saw it was a woman. He called his wife, and got a candle. When he saw blood he sent for the police, and just before they arrived a man who he did not know took hold of the deceased's head and showed the wound in the throat. All people in the club were searched before they left, and their names and addresses taken.- In reply to the coroner, Inspector Reid said the body had not yet been identified,- The Foreman of the jury: But we have been told her name is Stride, How is that? The Coroner: Something is known of her. She has been partially identified,- Inspector Reid said he would be prepared with further evidence tomorrow, and the inquiry was accordingly adjourned. The inquest was resumed on Wednesday, and after evidence of identification had been given, Thomas Coram, a lad of about eighteen, produced a knife which he found on the doorstep of No 253 Whitechapel road twenty four hours after the murder. The knife produced was twelve inches long, and the handle was neatly folded in a silk handkerchief, which had stains like blood upon it. Joseph Drage, 282, said he saw the boy find the knife. The handle and blade were covered with blood, which had dried on the knife, which was not on the step an hour previously. The inquiry was again adjourned. The inquest on Elizabeth Stride, the victim of the Berner-street murder, was resumed yesterday by Mr. Wynne E. Baxter. Notwithstanding the positive statement of Mrs. Malcolm that the deceased was her sister, Elizabeth Watt, it became known this morning before the commencement of the proceedings, that deceased was named Gustafsdotter. She was born in November, 1843, at Forslander, in Gothenburg, Sweden, and married Thomas Stride, a carpenter. The interest in the proceedings is still maintained. At a quarter past two all present were surprised to hear the coroner's clerk inform the jury that they were to resume the inquiry into the death of a person unknown, and immediately after Dr Phillips was recalled and stated that he had again examined the body and could not find any injury to the palate. This is in direct contradiction to the statements by the man Kidney and others, that deceased had in her life lost the roof of her mouth. He had not been able to find any blood on the handkerchief, the stains being those of fruit. He was convinced that the deceased had not swallowed either the skin or the seeds of grapes within many hours of her death. The knife found could have produced the injuries, which*

Mike Covell

might have been done in two seconds. In cases of suicide the carotid artery was not generally cut as in the present case, and the murderer displayed a knowledge where to cut the throat. – Dr Blackwell corroborated the last witness. The case was not one of suicide, as no instrument was found near the body. – Sven Olsson, clerk to the Swedish Church, Prince's-square, said he had known the deceased 17 years. He bore out the facts stated above, and produced a register whish shows that she was married to Stride. He thought this was in 1869. The register did not give the date. He gave the deceased the hymn book found in her lodgings. ANTECEDENTS OF THE MURDERED WOMAN. The Press Association's Bath correspondent telegraphs corroborating the statement of Mrs. Malcolm at the inquest, yesterday, as to the history and habits of the woman Elizabeth Watts. She married, about twenty seven or twenty eight years ago, William Watts, son of a wine merchant in Bath. Her husband being then only about twenty years of age. They only lived together two years, when deceased left her husband who went to America. He returned from the country four years ago. THE MITRE SQUARE TRAGEDY. Shortly before two o'clock yesterday morning, or three quarters of an hour after the crime described above was discovered, a second woman was horribly murdered and mutilated, this being in Mitre-square, Aldgate, within the city boundaries, but on the confines of the now notorious district. It appears that Police constable Watkins (No. 881) of the City Police was going round his beat, when turning his lantern upon the darkest corner of Mitre-square he saw the body of a woman, apparently lifeless, in a pool of blood. He at once blew his whistle, and several persons being attracted to the spot, he despatched messengers for medical and police aid. Inspector Collard, who was in Command of Bishopsgate Police Station, but a short distance off, quickly arrived, followed a few moments after by Mr G. W. Sequeira, surgeon, of 34, Jewry-street, and Dr Gordon Brown, the divisional police doctor, of Finsbury Circus. The scene then disclosed was a most horrible one. The woman, who was apparently about 40 years of age, was lying on her back, quite dead, although still warm. Her head was inclined to the left side, her left leg being extended, whilst the right was flexible. Both arms were extended. The throat was cut half way round, revealing a dreadful wound, from which blood flowed in [illegible] quantity, staining the pavement for some distance round. Across the right cheek to the nose was another gash, and a part of the right ear had been cut off. Following the plan in the Whitechapel murders, the miscreant was not content with merely killing his victims. The poor woman's clothes had been pulled over her chest, the abdomen ripped completely open, and part of the intestines laid on her neck. After careful notice had been taken of the position of the body when found, it was conveyed to the City Mortuary in Golden-lane. Here a more extended examination was made. The murdered woman was apparently about forty years of age, about 5ft in height, and evidently belonged to the unfortunate class of which the woman done to death in Whitechapel were members. Indeed, one of the policemen who saw the body expressed his confident opinion that he had seen the woman several times walking in the neighbourhood of Aldgate High-street. She was of dark complexion, with auburn hair, and hazel eyes, and was dressed in shabby dark clothes. She wore a black cloth jacket with imitation fur collar, and three large metal buttons. Her dress was made of green chintz the pattern consisting of Michaelmas daisies. In addition she had on a thin white vest, light drab linsey skirt, a very old dark green alpaca petticoat, white chemise, brown ribbed stockings (mended at the feet with white material), black straw bonnet (trimmed with black beads and green and black velvet), and a large white handkerchief round her neck. In the pockets of the dress a peculiar collection of articles was found, besides a small packet containing tea and other articles, which people who frequent the common lodging houses are accustomed to carry. The police found upon the body a white pocket handkerchief, a blunt bone handled tableknife, a short clay pipe, and a red cigarette case with white metal fittings. The knife bore no traces of blood, so could have no connection with the crime. When the news of this additional murder became known the excitement in the crowded district of Aldgate was intense. Usually a busy place for a Sunday morning, Houndsditch and connecting thoroughfares presented a particularly animated appearance. Men with barrows vending fruit and eatables were doing a brisk trade. Crowds flocked to the entrances of the square where the body had been discovered. But the police refused admittance to all but a privileged few. Sir Charles Warren visited the spot at a particularly early hour, and made himself thoroughly conversant with the neighbourhood and the details of the affair, Major Smith (acting superintendent of the City police), Superintendent Foster, Detective Inspector McWilliams (chief of the City detective department), Detective Sergeants Bownes and Outram, also attended during the morning. A little while after finding of the body all traces of blood had been washed away by the directions of the authorities, and there was little to indicate the terrible crime which had taken place. The police have made an important discovery throwing light on the direction in which the murderer made his escape. A portion of an apron was found in Goldston-street, and when the body of the woman found in Mitre-square was examined it was found that she was wearing a portion of the same apron. It was, therefore, inferred that the murderer escaped through Whitechapel. A man who passed through Church-lane, Aldgate, at half past one on Sunday morning, says he saw a man sitting on a doorstep wiping his hands. The man, who is described as wearing a short jacket and sailor's hat, tried to conceal his face. THE INQUEST. IMPORTANT MEDICAL EVIDENCE.

This morning Mr. Langham, the City Coroner, opened the inquest upon the body of the woman murdered in Mitre-square on Sunday morning, and whose name has been variously given as Eddowes, Conway, and Kelly. Mr. Crawford, City Solicitor, represented the police, Major Smith, Acting Commissioner, and Mr. Superintendent Forster also being present. Eliza Gold, the first witness, living at 6 Thrawl-street, identified the body as that of her sister, Catherine Eddowes, who was a single woman, who lived with John Kelly for some years. Witness last saw her alive about four or five months ago. The deceased was a hawker, of sober habits, and before living with Kelly deceased lived with the man Conway for some years, and had children by him. Witness did not know whether Conway, who was an army pensioner, was still alive. In reply to Mr. Crawford, witness said she had not seen Conway for some years. John Kelly, living at a lodging house in Flower and Dean-street, a market labourer, said deceased had lived with him for seven years. Her name was Conway, and he last saw her on Saturday last at two o'clock in the afternoon. They parted on very good terms in Houndsditch, the deceased saying she was going to Bermondsey to find her daughter. She promised to return by four o'clock. He heard she had been locked up in Bishopsgate for drunkenness, but made no inquiries, believing she would return on Sunday. Deceased never went out for an immoral purpose. When they parted deceased had no money, and she left with the intention of getting some from her daughter. Witness did not know where deceased had got drink on Saturday, considering she had no money. The deceased last year got money from her daughter. On Friday last deceased went to the Mile-end, and stopped in the casual ward. Early in the week witness and deceased were in Kent together, and on Thursday arrived in London, spending the night together at Shoe-lane Casual Ward, as they had no money. On Friday they arranged that deceased would go to the Mile-end Workhouse, and witness stay at a lodging house. They pawned a pair of boots on Saturday, and spent the greater portion of half-crown in food and drink. Witness stood outside with bare feet whilst the deceased pawned the boots. It might have been Friday and not Saturday. Frederick Wilkinson, deputy of the lodging house in Flower and Dean street, corroborated the last witness as to Kelly and the deceased living there on good terms. Deceased did not walk the streets. She said the name of Conway was bought and paid for, meaning that she was married. Police-Constable Watkins deposed to finding the murdered woman in Mitre-square on Sunday morning, as already reported, with her throat cut, body ripped open, and in a pool of blood. Witness had not heard any footsteps or a cry whilst near the square. Mr. Frederick Foster produced plans and maps of the locality. Wilkinson, the lodging house deputy, recalled, said he could not tell whether any stranger came there between two and three o'clock that morning. Over one hundred people lodged in the house. After luncheon, Inspector Collett was examined, and deposed to being called to the scene of the murder immediately after the discovery of the body. Three black buttons generally used for women's boots, a small metal button, a metal thimble, and a mustard tin containing two pawn tickets were picked up near the body. There was a piece of apron on the body corresponding with another piece picked up in Goulston street, some little way off. Witness detailed the steps taken by the police, with the object of tracking the murderer. A house to house inquiry had been made in the vicinity with practically no result. Dr Gordon Brown, surgeon to the city police, described the position of the body when he saw it a few minutes after two o'clock on Sunday morning. The way in which the body was mutilated was horrible in the extreme. There was no blood on the front of the clothes. A piece of the ear, cut off, dropped from the body. In describing the injuries to the abdomen, witness said the left kidney was carefully taken out, and in his opinion this must have been done by someone who knew where to find it. The womb was cut through, leaving a lump of about three quarters of an inch. The rest of it was missing. The wounds were inflicted with a sharp knife, which must have been pointed. Judging by the cuts in the abdomen, a good deal of knowledge of the position of organs in the abdominal cavity was displayed. The parts removed would be of no use for professional purposes. The removal of the left kidney was especially difficult. Such knowledge would be likely to be possessed by a slaughterer of animals. Witness thought the infliction of all the injuries could be done in five minutes. Witness could assign no reason for the parts being taken away. He felt sure there was no struggle. He believed the act was that of one man only. He should not expect much blood on the person inflicting the wounds described. The inquiry was then adjourned. TOUCHING SCENE AT THE MORTUARY. The Press Association states that it was between ten and eleven o'clock on Wednesday night that the identification of the victim of the Mitre-square tragedy took place. During the day the man John Kelly, who is a poorly clad labourer, thick set, dark, and of medium height, had been in communication with the City police authorities at Jewry-street, and the information imparted by him resulted in his going in the evening, in company with a detective officer, to the mortuary in Golden-lane, where the remains of the unfortunate woman lay. As is now well known, he had not the slightest difficulty, despite the mutilated condition of the face, in recognising the body as that of Kate Conway, a woman with whom he had been living for some seven years, latterly at 55 Flower and Dean-street. Although Kelly was most positive as to the identity of the body, the police deemed it prudent to obtain corroborative evidence on the point, and the man was accordingly closely questioned as to the relatives of the dead woman. DISCOVERY OF DECEASED'S SISTER. He at once informed them that, to his knowledge, a sister of "Kate's" was living at 6, Thrawl-street, a thoroughfare *adjacent to Flower and Dean-street. Inquiries were made early on Wednesday morning established the accuracy of this statement, for Kelly, accompanied by a detective and a little girl went straight to the house, and no difficulty was experienced in finding the sister of the deceased. Mrs Frost to use the name which she first gave to the police, lives on the top floor of the house, and the girl was sent upstairs to see her, found the old lady in bed, from which at first she refused to rise. The lass returned to the detective and Kelly with this message, but was requested by the former again to go upstairs, and this time to tell Mrs Frost that her sister was dead, and that it was necessary she should see the police. Thus appealed to, the woman rose, dressed and was soon ready to accompany Detective Abbott on the mission of identification at Golden-lane. Mrs Frost was accompanied by her son, George Gold, and also a young married woman named Lizzie Griffiths. The mortuary was reached at one o'clock, and the sister on beholding the body of her mutilated relative had no difficulty recognising the features. The poor woman, as might be naturally expected, gave way to a paroxysm of grief after gazing on the dreadful sight, and had to be led from the mortuary. Her son George, who is a woodchopper in Thrawl-street, made the question of identity still more certain at once declaring the body to be that of aunt Kate. STATEMENT OF MRS. FROST. Mrs Frost, on recovering composure, made a brief statement to the police. It was to the effect that she had not previously seen her sister for some two years; that the deceased had at one time lived with a man named Conway, and subsequently with John Kelly; and that there were two children whom she had had by Conway still living, one daughter and the other a son. She further mentioned that the daughter was married to a man named Phillips, who is a gunmaker in the neighbourhood of Bermondsey, but that she did not know her address. As to the whereabouts the boy, she declared that she had not the slightest knowledge. The police, it is understood, are anxious to obtain the address of the daughter, though so far they have been unable to obtain any definite information. News is supposed to spread with amazing rapidity in Flower and Dean-street and that immediate neighbourhood, but strange to relate, the intelligence of the identification of the body by Kelly and the sister of the deceased was not generally known there till the morning. This is all the more singular when the fact is remembered that both Kelly and "Kate," the latter in particular, are both well known in Flower and Dean-street. A representative of the Press Association was in the street as late as half past three in the morning making enquiries, but no one with whom he then came in contact- and they were not a few in number- knew that "Kate" had been identified. MRS. FROST INTERVIEWED. A STRANGE STORY. On Wednesday evening a representative of the Press Association interviewed Mrs Frost at her residence in Thrawl-street, Whitechapel. She is a middle sized, stout* and somewhat elderly lady, with a face which, though now clouded with sorrow, still retained a pleasant and agreeable appearance. On being ushered into the dimly-lighted room at the top of the house the reporter was received with the utmost courtesy, and the conversation opened by Mrs. Frost explaining that although she had described herself as Mrs. Frost to the police, yet she was known as Mrs. Gold, which was the name of her first husband. She stated, in reply to questions, that her present husband worked at the waterside in unloading cargoes of fruit. She had lived in that street for seventeen years, but although so near she seldom saw her deceased sister. Although on friendly terms, yet they did not associate much together. The last occasion on which they met was, so far as she could remember, some four or five months ago, and then the dead woman called upon her. The real name of her sister was Catherine Eddowes, for she had never been married. For many years "Kate" as they called her, went by the name of Conway, an army pensioner with whom she lived, and by whom she had children. Years ago they separated, and after that and down to the time of her death the deceased lived with the man Kelly. She (Mrs. Frost) was on speaking terms with Kelly, but did not mix with him. Mrs. Frost proceeded to state that she did not know anything of the murder of her sister until that morning, until Kelly came round to the house accompanied by a police officer and a little girl. The latter was sent upstairs to see her, but she was in bed at the time, and told the child she was too ill to get up. Shortly afterwards the girl returned and told her her sister Kate was dead, and that her body was lying at the Golden-lane mortuary. That was between eleven and twelve, and she then got up, and shortly afterwards accompanied the detective to the mortuary. Her son George and a young married woman named Lizzie Griffiths went with her. Disfigured though the face was, yet she had no difficulty in recognising the features and forms of her sister. Here Mrs. Frost commenced to sob violently, and exclaimed twice, with a broken voice, "Oh, my poor sister! That she should come to such and end as this." Somewhat recovering her composure, the old lady went on to say that she did not see the tattoo marks on the arm, nor was she even aware of their existence. To see the face was quite sufficient to convince her of the identity of the dead woman. Although she could not read, she had of course heard about the Whitechapel murders, but she little thought until that morning that her sister was one of Sunday's victims. So far as she could tell the deceased was about 42 years of age. [Section illegible] As to the son, she knew nothing about him, and should not know him even if she saw him. The daughter was about 18 years of age, but the boy was older. Her sister was very well known in the neighbourhood, and had never, to her knowledge, led the life of a prostitute. Here the poor old lady burst forth once more into tears, and gave way to the most violent grief, mourning again and again, "Oh my poor sister! The

Mike Covell

Lord save us!" It was with the utmost difficulty that those present were able to console Mrs Frost and to induce her to cease crying. CONFESSION BY A MEDICAL STUDENT. EXTRAORDINARY STATEMENT. At Guildhall, London on Wednesday, William Bull, describing himself as a medical student at a London hospital, and living at Stannard road, Dalston, was charged on his own confession, with having committed the murder at Mitre-square. Inspector Izzard said that at 20 minutes to 11 on Tuesday, the accused came to his room at Bishopsgate-street station, and made the following statement:- "My name is William Bull and I live at Dalston. I am a medical student at the London Hospital. I wish to give myself up for the murder in Aldgate, on Saturday night or Sunday morning about two o'clock. I think I met the woman in Aldgate. I went with her up a narrow street not far from the main road for an immoral purpose. I promised to give her half-a-crown, which I did. While walking along together there was a second man, who came up and took the half-a-crown from her. I cannot endure this any longer. My poor head-(here he put his hand to his head, and cried or pretended to cry)- I shall go mad. I have done it and I must put up with it." The Inspector asked what had become of the clothing he had on when the murder was committed. The accused said, "If you wish to know they are in the Lea, and the knife I threw away." At this point the prisoner declined to say any more. He was drunk. Part if the statement was made in the presence of Major Smith. Prisoner gave correct address, but is not known at the London Hospital. His parents were respectable. The Inspector asked for a remand to make enquiries, and this was granted. Prisoner now said he was drunk when he made the statement. He was remanded. Bull was brought up again yesterday. Inspector Izzard now informed Alderman Stone that inquiries had proved that prisoner could not have been connected with the murder in any way. – The Alderman, after expressing regret that he could not punish the prisoner for trouble he had given, discharged him from custody. It may be mentioned in connection with the murder that the foreman of the sewer hands who are engaged in Aldgate in sweeping the streets and clearing away the refuse, &c., in the early hours of the morning, has stated most positively that at the time when the murder is supposed to have been perpetrated he was standing not more than 20 yards away from the spot where the body was subsequently found by the constable and himself. He states emphatically that he never heard any woman's cries for help, nor did any sounds of a struggle reach his ear. ANOTHER ALLEGED OUTRAGE IN WHITECHAPEL. EXCITING CHASE AND CAPTURE. Shortly before midnight a story was circulating that the unknown murderer had been surprised in the act of attempting another outrage on a woman in Union-street, Whitechapel. The story went that the woman was lured by the "Monster" into a side street, but the gleam of a steel blade at once roused her to a sense of her danger, and her screams brought to the spot a man and two women, who were said to have been watching the movements of the couple. The would be murderer, it was stated, was pursued by a man who knocked the knife out of his hand. The unknown one, however, jumped into a passing cab, bidding the cabman drive wherever he liked. A howling mob swarmed after the fugitive and the police soon captured the vehicle and took the occupant to Leman Street police station. Investigation, however, soon proved that the romantic story had but a slight foundation. It was ascertained that about ten o'clock a well-dressed man rushed out of the Three Nuns public house, in Aldgate, followed by a woman, who had declared he had "been molesting" her. To escape the crowd, the stranger jumped into a cab, and was pursued and captured as above stated. When he was formally charged, the woman stated positively that the prisoner had accosted her first in Whitechapel High Street, and that when she refused his proposals, he threatened her with violence. The woman nevertheless declined to prefer any charge, and left the station. The man was detained, pending inquiries. He is an athletic, determined fellow, about 40 years of age, no weapons were found on him. He gave a name but declined to state his address. When removed to the cell his attitude became defiant, and he kept up a conversation with a slightly American accent. He is stated to have been slightly under the influence of drink. A FALSE RUMOUR. The Evening News (London) in a third edition to-day, states that a man was seen to go behind a hoarding in High Street, Shadwell, with a woman at half past four this morning. The watchman on duty followed them and called the police. The man killed the watchman with his knife, but was secured by several constables who had hurried up. The Evening News adds that it is believed the man is the Whitechapel murder. A later telegraph from The Press Association says that upon an inquiry at the chief police station for the Shadwell district, in which it was stated that a watchman had been killed this morning, that no information had been received by the police of the alleged murder, and that certainly no arrest had been made in connection with such occurrence. The rumour created much excitement both in the City and Whitechapel when first circulated. HOUSE TO HOUSE VISITATION. Plain clothes constables made a house-to-house visitation, leaving copies of a handbill requesting occupiers to give notice to the nearest police station of any suspicious matters which may come within their knowledge concerning the murders. AN ARREST AT TIPTREE. The Press Association's Bishop Stortford correspondent telegraph is that a man has been arrested at Tiptree Heath, near here, on suspicion of being concerned in the Whitechapel murders. He asked alms of Sergeant Creswell, who arrested him. He objected to be searched, and was taken to Kelvedon, where he was detained for inquiries. He answered the description circulated by the Metropolitan police. ARREST OF AN IRISH

"LEATHER APRON." On Thursday a tramp, whose name is unknown, but who describes himself as "Leather Apron," was arrested by the police here on a charge of drunkenness and disorderly conduct. When taken into the police barrack, he violently assaulted the constable. In his possession were found three halfpence, a knife covered with blood, and a letter, also stained with blood, addressed to the Roman Catholic Primate. "JACK THE RIPPER." Great consternation has been caused locally by a report that "Jack the Ripper" has sent a post card to Barrett's confectionery factory at Wood green saying that he should visit the neighbourhood and "do for six of the girls employed at the factory." It is further said that a man answering the published description of the supposed murderer has been seen in Wood green. People speak of their intentions to carry arms to be prepared for a sudden attack. ANOTHER LETTER FROM THE SELF ALLEGED MURDERER. The Central News has received the following letter, bearing the E.C. post-mark, written in red ink, in a round hand. Apparently by a person indifferently educated. At the foot is a rude drawing of a sharp pointed knife, the blade measuring three inches and the handle one: - "3rd October. - Dear Boss, - Since last, splendid success. Two more and never a squeal. Oh, I am master of the art! I am going to be heavy on the guilded - now, we are. Some duchess will cut up nicely, and the lace will show nicely. You wonder how. Oh, we are masters. No education like a butcher's. No animal like a nice woman - the fat are best. On to Brighton for a holiday, but we shan't idle - splendid high-class women there. My mouth waters - good luck there. If not, you will hear from me in the West End. My pal will keep on at the East for a while yet. When I get a nobility - I will send it on to C. Warren, or perhaps to you for a keepsake. O it is jolly. - GEORGE OF THE HIGH-RIP GANG. - Red ink still, but a drop of the real in it." WHO IS "THE RIPPER"? IS THERE A GANG? Several correspondents, says the Daily Telegraph, refer to the calligraphy of the "Ripper." "F.C." says "the writing is a decided Civil Service hand." "M.S." has no doubt "the writer is an American." H.E. Ball sets forth many reasons for thinking that "the man is a fish cleaner in one of the markets or elsewhere." Henry Harrison, on the other hand, thinks the expression "squealed" points to a pig sticker, and "Amateur Detective" emphasises the fact that "there are slaughter houses near the scene of the tragedies, and one is a place where the decayed and "played out" horses are butchered." Among the various "hints to the police" are many which have already been acted upon. "F.T.," however thinks "that of the empty warehouses and factories of the district have not been sufficiently searched"; and Alfred C. Calmour (Arundel Club) "ventures to suggest that the sewers in the neighbourhood of the late murders should be searched, as there is just the possibility of the murderer having escaped by them." "M.H." says, "A man could escape through the sewers to more than one

place of safety, and could hide his change of clothing on his way to and from the scenes of his dreadful "work," as the "Ripper" calls it." "Bloodhound," combating the idea that the murderer is a madman says: "I have had a larger practical acquaintance with homicidal maniacs than Dr Forbes Winslow ever had, for I have lived with them, and I emphatically assert that this series of crimes is the work of no lunatic, homicidal or otherwise. There is too much coherence of idea, too much fixity of purpose, too much self-control displayed. Insanity has its saving clauses, and this is one of them. These atrocities are the handiwork of no individual but a confederacy. This explains everything: the amazing audacity, the ease with which detection has been evaded, and the commission of two consecutive murders in one night, obviously by the same agency, but not, possibly by the same hand." LETTER FROM THE HOME SECRETARY. The following letter was received last evening by the editor of the Financial News:- "Oct 1, 1888, "My dear sir,- I am directed by Mr Matthews to acknowledge the receipt of your letter of this date containing a cheque for £300, which you say has been contributed on behalf of several readers of the Financial News, and which you are desirous should be offered as a reward for the discovery of the recent murders in the East End of London. If Mr Matthews had been of the opinion that the offer of a reward in these cases would have been attended by any useful result, he would himself have at once made such an offer, but he is not of that opinion. Under these circumstances I am directed to return your cheques (which I enclose), and to thank you and the gentlemen whose names you have forwarded, for the liberality of their offer, which Mr Matthews much regrets he is unable to accept,- I am sir, your very obedient servant, "E. Leigh Pemberton, "Harry H, Marks, Esq." LETTER FROM SIR CHARLES WARREN. Sir Charles Warren, replying to a letter from the Whitechapel District Board of Works, complaining of the inefficiency of the police, writes that the police force cannot possibly do more than guard or take precautions against any repetition of recent atrocities, so long as the victims actually, but unwillingly connive at their own destruction. In this particular class of murderer to some retired spot and place themselves in such a position that they can be slaughtered without a sound being heard. Sir Charles requests the board to do all in their power to dissuade the unfortunate women about Whitechapel from going into lonely places in the dark with any persons, whether acquaintances or strangers. He assures the board that every nerve is being strained to detect the criminal, and to render more difficult further atrocities, and he emphatically denied that any changes affecting the efficiency of the police had been made. DR. WINSLOW'S OPINION. Dr Forbes Winslow, the eminent specialist in lunacy cases, states:- "I am more certain than ever that these murders are committed by a homicidal maniac, and there is no moral doubt in my mind that the assassin in each case is the same man. I have carefully read the reports in the morning papers, and they confirm me in the opinion which I had previously formed. While I am clearly of the opinion that the murderer is an homicidal lunatic, I also believe him to be a monomaniac, and I see no reason why he should not, excepting at periods when he the fit is upon him, exhibit a cool and rational exterior. I have here in my book- a work on Psychology- a case in which a man had a lust for blood as of in this case, and he was generally a person of bland and pleasant exterior. In all probability the whole of the murders have been committed by the same hand, but I may point out that the imitative faculty is very strong in persons of unsound mind, and that is the reason why there has been a sort of epidemic of knives. We shall probably find that a good many knives will be displayed to people within the next few weeks. Still all the evidence that is forthcoming up to the present moment shows clearly enough that the Whitechapel crimes have been perpetrated by the same hand. My idea is that under the circumstances the police ought to employ, for the protection of the neighbourhood and with the view of selecting the criminal, a number of officers who have been in the habit of guarding lunatics- that is to say, warders from asylums and other persons who have had charge of the insane. These men, if properly disposed in the neighbourhood, would assuredly note any person who was of unsound mind. I have sent a letter embodying this suggestion to Sir Charles Warren, but I have received only a formal communication, acknowledging its receipt. It is not easy to prevail upon the police to accept a suggestion for outside service. This I discovered the other day, when a man in emulation of the Whitechapel murderer, drew a knife and sharpened it in the presence of a relative of mine at Brighton, under circumstances which have been published in the newspapers. When I made a statement to the police on the occasion, they thought very little of it indeed. I attach not the least importance to the American physiologist story. It is a theory which is utterly untenable, and I should think there are very few medical men who ever entertained it seriously. All that has recently happened appears to me as strong confirmation of the views which I have previously given expression to upon this subject. The murderer is a homicidal maniac of infinite cunning, and I fear he will not be brought to justice unless he be caught while engaged in the commission of one of his crimes. INFERENCES TO BE DRAWN. [From the "Newcastle Chronicle"] A dense fog still hangs over the atrocious crimes committed at the East End of London. Nor is the thickness of theories in the least diminished by the amplified details of doubtful accuracy, the flying rumours, and the bits of gossip in general, gathered and retailed by the zealous surveyors of news, and serving but to confuse the brains of those who read them. Nevertheless, the fateful occurrences narrowed down to trustworthy sources of information present themselves as facts, and from these facts it is possible to draw inferences. There have been in all six murders committed in Whitechapel in as many months. The first victim was one Emma Elizabeth Smith, who was found badly injured on the early morning of Easter Tuesday, the 3rd of April in Osborne-street, and who, on being removed to the London Hospital, lived for some 24 hours. Before she expired she was able to state that she had been followed by several men, robbed, and mutilated. She was even capable of describing, in an imperfect way, one of her assailants. In the case of Emma Smith, the nature of her injuries favoured the conclusion that they had been inflicted by a blunt weapon, such as a walking stick. The second crime was discovered at three a.m. on Tuesday, the 7th of August. The slain woman Martha Tabram or Turner, as she also appears to have been called, was found on the first floor landing of George-yard buildings. She was quiet dead at the time, and the examination of her body disclosed that it had received 30 punctured wounds. Some such instrument as a dagger or bayonet was suspected in this instance; and the bayonet obtained in the first place the preferences, as there was some evidence to show that the deceased had been the associate of soldiers. The next victim was Mary Ann Nicholls, found on Friday, the 31st of August in Buck's-row. There were abdominal injuries of a fearful character in this case, and the woman's throat had also been cut. It was evident that a knife had been used. Following Mary Ann Nicholls, came Anne Chapman, found on the morning of Saturday, the 8th of September, in the back yard of 29, Hanbury-street. In this instance there was the same abdominal mutilation, accompanied by either the wilful abstraction or accidental disappearance of a particular organ of the body. As with the woman Nicholls, the throat had been cut. The remaining two murders were committed on the night of Saturday, the 29th of September. The first was discovered at about one o'clock in the yard of 40, Berner-street, Commercial-road; the other was detected in Mitre-square, Aldgate, a good sized yard with three entrances to it, shortly before two o'clock. The victims were both women, one of whom has been partially but not positively identified. The bodies were still warm, and in the case of the Berner-street crime there were no abdominal mutilations, though the throat had been cut. In respect of Mitre-square, however, the characteristics common to Nicholls and Chapman murders present themselves. Four victims were notoriously women who had sunk low in the social scale, and who were reduced to an irregular sort of prostitution, though at times they strove to maintain themselves by work. Of the other two, whose identity is doubtful, it is impossible to speak with certainty. The probability, however, is that they belonged to the same unhappy class. The crimes themselves were perpetrated all in the same locality, and in places not many hundred yards distant from each other. In something like an hour a man might very comfortably make a tour of inspection of the various spots *collectively. From such facts there are deductions to be made. Emma Smith was assaulted by several men; Martha Tabram or Turner died riddled with punctured wounds. The other four were found with their throats cut, while three were disembowelled. The circumstances that the Berner-street victim did not receive abdominal injuries may, however, be very reasonably ascribed to the sudden appearance of Mr. Louis Diemschitz in the yard with his horse and trap. Assuming this, the irresistible inference is that the murderer cut the throats of his victims first, and mutilated them afterwards. This point is of some importance, as one at least of the medical men – Dr. Lewellys – deposed at the inquest held on Mary Ann Nicholls, that he w strongly of the opinion that the abdominal injuries were inflicted first, and caused instantaneous death. It is clear that the one man murder theory will not apply to the case of Emma Smith, the victim of a ruffian gang. Neither does the case of Martha Tabram, or Turner, riddled with 39 puncture wounds, warrant the assumption with any degree of certainty. The rest of the murders favour, however, very strikingly the suspicion that they have been committed by one person. Yet, who is he, and why has he been guilty of such hideously wanton outrage? That the slayer must have acquired skill as regards one deadly blow with the knife is evident. Mary Ann Nicholls was killed immediately beneath the window of the room in which Mrs. Green, an old woman and a light sleeper, reposed. The Berner-street victim was hurried to death in the yard close to the Social Club, while Mrs Diemschitz, the stewardess of that establishment, was in the kitchen on the ground floor, and quiet near the precise spot where the crime was achieved. Yet neither Mrs. Green nor Mrs. Diemschitz heard a single sound resembling a scream or groan. This betokens the sure hand with which the thrust was dealt, the knowledge of the exact place in which the knife would take prompt effect, and the extinct deliberation with which the set was done. The whole circumstances reviewed, the [illegible] is difficult to combat – in the mind at learnt of the present writes – that the murders of Emma Smith and Martha Tabram, or Turner, were not committed by the same hand steeped in the blood of the woman Nicholls, Chapman, and their two successors. Smith was murdered on April 3, Tabram on August 7. The latter revived the recollection of the former, and both were discovered simultaneously, and nowhere, perhaps, [illegible] interest as in Whitechapel, the locality of the crime. The facility with which murder could be committed without detection proved, we may be sure a prominent item of the [illegible] talk. Why not, then a reflex action, opening on the mind of some morbid subject, discarded by the incredible vanity which enters so largely in the composition of a certain class of criminals and of whom Percy Mapleton Lefroy, the [illegible] of Mr. Gold, may be cited as a fair example? But, it is not necessary at all to assume that this monstrosity in the shape of a man hails from*

America, or to identify him with any particular creed or race. He might well be no Englishman, a resident in Whitechapel, who, from sheer vanity, from a desire to posture before the world as remarkable, would engage even in such atrocities as have been perpetrated. AMATEUR DETECTIVES AT WORK. Should the murderer again attempt to give effect to his infamous designs in the Whitechapel district he will require, in the interests of his own personal security, not only to avoid the uniformed and plain-clothed members of the Metropolitan Police Force, but to reckon with a small, enthusiastic body of amateur detectives. Convinced that the regular force affords inadequate protection of life and property in this densely populated neighbourhood, a number of local tradesmen decided a few weeks ago to appoint a Vigilance Committee. The duties of the newly-formed band were twofold. In the first place, they were to publish far and wide their disagreement with the Home Secretary by offering a substantial reward to "anyone - citizen or otherwise," who should give information as would bring the murderer or murderers to justice: and, in the second place, they were themselves to patrol the most secluded parts of the district in the dead of night with a view to running the criminal to earth. So worthy a motive they felt confident would at once command the sympathy and support of "the tradesmen, ratepayers, and inhabitants generally." Unfortunately, however, for the realisation of their hopes, experience had proved that those to whom they appealed were more ready to commend than to co-operate. Excluding one or two subscriptions of considerable amounts they have been compelled to admit that funds have not "rolled" in. Nor has the suggestion to hold a large public meeting in furtherance of the objects of the Vigilantes been responded to with alacrity. Yet, undaunted by these disappointments, the committee have worked persistently on. Night after night, at 9 o'clock, meetings have been held in the upper room of a public-house in the Mile End-road, placed at the disposal of the committee by the landlord, who occupies the post of treasurer. The leaders of the movement are drawn principally from the trading class, and include a builder, a cigar manufacturer, a tailor, and a picture-frame maker, a licensed victualler, and "an actor." Inexperienced in practical police duty, the committee decided to call in professional assistance rather than rely solely upon their own resources. For this purpose they engaged the services of two private detectives - men who, though unattached to either metropolitan or city police forces, hold themselves out as experts in the unravelling of mysteries. At the disposal of these executive officers are placed about a dozen stalwart men possessing an intimate acquaintance with the highways and by-ways of Whitechapel. Only those have been selected who are "physically and morally" equal to the task they may any night be called upon to perform. As they were previously numbered among the unemployed, it became unnecessary to fix a high scale of remuneration. Shortly before 12 o'clock these assassin-hunters are dispatched upon their mission. Their foot-fall is silenced by the use of galoshes, and their own safety is assured by the carrying of police-whistles and stout sticks. The area over which this additional protection is afforded is divided into beats, each man being assigned his respective round. Nor is this all. At half an hour after midnight the committee-rooms close by an Act of Parliament, and thence emerge those members of the committee who happen to be on duty for the night. Like sergeants of police they make their tours of inspection, and while seeing that their men are faithfully performing their onerous duties, themselves visit the most sequestered and ill-lighted spots. The volunteer policemen leave their beats between 4 and 5 o'clock in the morning. It should be added that supervision in this way by members of the committee is not forthcoming every night. The fact that most of them are engaged from early in the morning until late at night in the transaction of their own businesses obviously renders such constant effort physically impossible. If it were practicable there are several who would undoubtedly devote night after night with the utmost willingness to ferreting out the being who has caused terror to prevail in the hearts of thousands of residents in the back streets of the district. Although the work of the committee has not yet been crowned with success, it is claimed on their behalf that they have gained much information that may be of service hereafter. By the regular police, it is satisfactory to add, they have not been thwarted in their endeavour to bring the criminal to justice. Suspicions, surmises, and possible clues are notified to the nearest police-stations from time to time, and one member of the committee at least honestly believes that he is on the right track. Whether his private opinion is justified by fact, time alone can reveal. Meanwhile, he and his colleagues are determined to leave no stone unturned, and firmly continue to maintain that the dark places of Whitechapel demand a more thorough watchfulness on the part of the police than is at present devoted to them. They further report that the number of women of the class to which the victims have belonged has appreciably diminished in the district within the past week. LIST OF THE EAST END MURDERS. Six women have now been murdered in the East End under mysterious circumstances, five of them within a period of eight weeks. The following are the dates of the crimes and names of the victims so far as known:-

1. Last Christmas week. - An unknown woman found murdered near Osborne and Wentworth-streets, Whitechapel.

2. August 7. - Martha Turner, found stabbed in 39 places, on a landing in model dwellings, known as George-yard Buildings, Commercial-street, Spitalfields.

3. August 31. - Mrs. Nicholls, murdered and mutilated in Bucks-row, Whitechapel.

4. September 7. - Mrs. Chapman, murdered and mutilated in Hanbury-street, Whitechapel.

5. September 30. - Elizabeth Stride, found with her throat cut in Berners-street, Whitechapel.

6. September 30. - Woman unknown, murdered and mutilated in Mitre-square, Aldgate. THE WHITECHAPEL CRAZE IN HULL. The excitement which has been caused throughout the country by the horrible atrocities committed in Whitechapel, London, has been equally great in Hull, and it appears a repetition of those incidents which have been frequent in the Metropolis of late has to some extent taken place in Hull. At Hull Police Court this afternoon, before the Mayor (Alderman Toozes) and Mr. T Stratton, a poorly clad woman, named Jane Feeney, was charged on warrant with having used threats towards a woman named Minnie Kirlew.- The Prosecutrix stated that the prisoner threatened her in Manor Street yesterday and said she would "Whitechapel Murder her". Witness stated that she was afraid of the prisoner. A man who was called as a witness said he heard the prisoner when acting very violently, threaten to Whitechapel murder the Prosecutrix.- The Bench ordered the accused to find one surety in £10 to keep the peace for six months, and also sent her to prison or seven days for having been disorderly.

The Lord Mayor of London, acting on the advice of the City Commissioner of Police, has in the name of the Corporation, offered a reward of £500 for the detection of the Whitechapel murderer. The proprietors of the Financial News have written to the Home Secretary, offering, as instigation of several subscribers to offer through the Government a reward of £500 for the detection of the Whitechapel murderer.

Another meeting of the Whitechapel Vigilance Committee was held at 74, Mile End Road, this morning, when a resolution was passed that a further letter should be sent to the Home Secretary insisting upon the offer of a large Government reward immediately. A letter was despatched.

Mike Covell

> About six o'clock on Wednesday, a man whose name was subsequently ascertained to be John Lock, a seaman, was rescued by the police from an excited crowd in the neighbourhood of Ratcliffe Highway, who were following him and shouting "Leather Apron" and "Jack the Ripper." The cause was not readily explained. When, however, he was examined at the police station his light tweed suit was found to bear stains which were found to be paint, but which the crowd had mistaken for blood. His explanation was perfectly satisfactory, but it was some considerable time before the crowd dispersed and the man able to depart. Colonel Sir Alfred Kirby, J.P., the officer commanding the Tower Hamlets Battalion Royal Engineers has offered, on behalf of his officers, a reward of £100, to anyone who will give information that will lead to the discovery and conviction of the perpetrator of the recent murders committed in the district in which his regiment is situated. Sir Alfred Kirby is also willing to place the services of not more than fifty members of his corps at the disposal of the authorities, to be utilized in assisting them in any way they may consider desirable at this juncture, either for the protection of the public or finding out the criminals. Of course the Volunteers will have to be made use of as citizens, and not in a quasi-military capacity.
>
> SHOCKING DISCOVERY AT WESTMINSTER. A WOMAN'S MUTILATED BODY. Another ghastly discovery was made in London on Tuesday afternoon. About five o'clock a carpenter named Frederick Wildborn, employed by Messrs J. Grover and Sons, builders, of Pimlico, who are contractors for the new Metropolitan Police Head-quarters on the Thames Embankment, was working on the foundation, when he came across a neatly done up parcel which was secreted in one of the cellars. Wildborn was in search of timber when he found the parcel, which was tied up in paper and measured about two and half feet long by about two feet in width. It was opened, and the body of a woman, very much decomposed, was found carefully wrapped in a piece of cloth, which is supposed to be a black petticoat. The trunk was minus the head, both arms, and both legs, and presented a ghastly spectacle. The officials of the works were immediately apprised of the discovery and the police were fetched. Dr. Bond, the divisional surgeon to A Division, and several other medical gentlemen were communicated with, and subsequently examined the remains, which were handed over to the care of some police officers, who were told of to see that the trunk was not disturbed. From what can be ascertained the conclusion has been arrived at by the medical men that these remains are those of the woman whose arms have recently been discovered in different parts of London- one in Pimlico and the other in Lambeth, on the opposite side of the other of the River Thames. Dr. Neville, who examined the arms of the female found a few weeks ago in the

Thames, off Ebury Bridge, Pimlico, said, on that occasion that he did not think it had been skilfully been taken from the body, and this fact would appear to favour the theory that the arm, together with the one found in the grounds of the Blind Asylum in the Lambeth-road last week, belong to the trunk discovered today, for it is stated that the limbs appear to have been taken from the body found this afternoon in anything but a skilful manner. The building which is in course of erection is the new police depot for London, the present scattered head-quarters of the Metropolitan police force and Criminal Investigation Department in Great Scotland Yard and Whitehall-place having been found too small for the requirements of the London police system. The builders have been working on the site for some considerable time now, but have only just completed the foundation. It was originally the site for the National Opera House, and extends from the Thames Embankment, through to Cannon-row, Parliament-street, at the back of St Stephen's Club and the Westminster Bridge Station on the District Railway. The prevailing opinion is that to place the body where it was found the person conveying it must have scaled the 8ft, boarding which encloses the works, and carefully avoiding the watchmen who do duty by night, must have dropped it where it was found. There appears to be little doubt that the parcel had been in the cellar for some considerable time.

A man employed upon the works, who was one of the first to see the remains, has made the following statement to a newspaper representative:- "I went down into one of the cellars, which is about 20ft. by 15ft. in size to look round, when I saw a parcel lying in a corner as though it had been thrown there carelessly. I might say that the cellar is really part of the half-finished basement of what are to be the new police officers. The parcel was a paper one, which could easily be carried under the arm. When the parcel was opened I saw that it contained the trunk of a woman wrapped up in a coarse cloth. In cutting off the legs a portion of the abdomen had been cut away. The head and arms were also cut off close to the trunk. The police have been digging up the rubbish and any place where it seems likely any more remains could be hidden but I don't think they have found anything more. The contents of the parcel were very much decomposed, and looked to have been in the place where they found for three weeks or a month. My opinion is that the person putting the parcel where it was found must have got over the hoarding in Cannon-row, and then thrown the bundle down." Another workman says that the parcel was discovered by a man whom he only knows as "George" who went down to get some timber. In his opinion the parcel had been there quite three weeks, as the contents were terribly decomposed. Another workman who has a thorough knowledge of the facts connected with the finding of the ghastly remains has made the following statements:- "As one of our carpenters was putting away his tools at about five o'clock last night in one of the vaults which are to form the foundation of the main building of the new offices which are to accommodate the police, he saw what seemed to be a heap of paper. As it is very dark in this particular spot, even during the day, the matter somehow did not appear to strike him as curious or out of the way, his passing thoughts being that it was merely a bundle of canvas which was being used on the works. He consequently mentioned the matter to no one, and having left his tools, came away and went home, thinking no more about the mysterious parcel which was to reveal another dreadful crime, probably perpetrated within 100 yards of the King street police station, about 200 or 300 yards from the present offices of the Criminal Investigation Department, and within 50 yards of the Houses of Parliament. This morning, when he went to fetch his tools, he became aware of a peculiar smell proceeding from the dark corner, but at the time made no attempt ascertain the cause. The matter, however, had taken possession of his mind, and later on in the day he mentioned the circumstances to one or two of his fellow workmen. They at once decided to tell the foreman. This was one and the foreman, accompanied by some of the men, proceeded to the spot. One of the labourers was called to shift the parcel. It was then opened and the onlookers were horrified to find that it contained a human body. The legs, arms, and head were missing, and the body presented a most sickening spectacle. The woman had evidently been dead for many days, as decomposition was far advanced. I never saw such a dreadful sight in my life, and the smell was dreadful. After we had got over the first surprise and nausea we sent for the police, and a doctor was also sent for. We could see that the body was that of a full grown woman, and when the doctor came he said the same thing. Almost immediately after that Dr. Bond, of the Middlesex Hospital, came and saw the body. He found that it was very brown, and I believe he said that it was the body from which the arms found in the Thames a few days ago had been cut. The body was wrapped in what looked like part of an old black dress of very common material, and it is a very strange thing that other parts of the same dress have been found in other parts of the yard. The police took possession of the remains, and gave orders that no stranger was to be admitted to the enclosure. How long do I think it possible the body could have been lying there? Well, it could not have been where we found it above two or three days, because men are continually passing the spot. The place is very dark, and it is possible that it might have escaped notice on that account; but, now I come to think of it, I know for a fact that it was not there last Friday because we had occasion to do something at that very spot." Another report remarks that it is simply astonishing that any man could have carried such an offensive burden through the public street without attracting attention, and it is still more extraordinary how it could have been taken into the vault without discovery. The route from Cannon row to the vault is a difficult one. A hoarding some seven or eight feet high would have to be climbed, and the ground is of a very broken character. From the Embankment side the hoarding is about the same height and to reach the vault one must actually pass through the building in course of construction and round it, about which several policemen are constantly patrolling. It is more reasonable to assume that the vault was gained from Cannon row and so that it seems pretty certain that more than one person was concerned in the disposal of the ghastly parcel. One man probably climbed to the top of the hoarding with the assistance of his accomplice from whom he then received the parcel, dropped it on the inner side and then let himself down after it. The other man presumably kept watch while his confederate disposed of the remains. How the man could have known of the existence of the vault is not clear, for strangers are not admitted to the works except on business. Possibly the original intention was to place the remains in some out of the way corner in the works and they were only taken to the vault after the obviously desirable place of concealment had been accidentally discovered. MEDICAL EXAMINATION. We understand that the surgeons who conducted the autopsy yesterday on the remains found at Westminster came to the conclusion that the arm which was washed up by the Thames near Pimlico, and which had been conveyed to Westminster mortuary from Ebury-street, where it had been preserved, fitted into the trunk found at Whitehall. It is also stated that the cord tied around the limb found in the river and a portion of that which was used to tie up the parcel were similar. At the conclusion of the examination the clothing was disinfected and thoroughly inspected by the police, who state that it was covered with maggots and vermin. Adhering to one portion was found a piece of newspaper saturated with blood. It bore no date, but the date when the paper was published can easily be ascertained. The dress stuff was found to be a rich flowered silk underskirt, which proves that the unfortunate victim was not one of the poorer class of society. Nothing was discovered to indicate the cause of death, but the doctors are of the opinion that the woman had been murdered about three weeks, and the advanced state of decomposition was due to exposure. The doctors are preparing an elaborate report of the whole case, which will be submitted at the inquest to be held at the sessions house, Westminster, on Monday next. THE ALLEGED MURDER WITH A HAMMER. At the Thames Police Court yesterday, Richard Bartlett was committed for trial for murdering his wife with a hammer at Poplar. ANOTHER TRAGEDY IN LONDON. ATTEMPTED MURDER OF A SON. – SUICIDE OF THE MOTHER. Elizabeth Bloxham, aged 24, wife of a mechanic living at 46, Georgian-street, Camden Town, London, on Thursday took Oxalic acid, and also administered some to her four year old boy.

Mike Covell

> She died, but the boy survived. The cause of the act is unknown. WIFE MURDER IN LONDON. John Brown, 45, was charged at Westminster Police Court on Monday with the willful murder of his wife at Regent Gardens, Westminster. It appears that prisoner returned home on Saturday night, quarreled with his wife, and cut her throat with a knife, almost severing her head from her body. He then gave himself up to the police. It was stated that the woman had previously sought police protection, the prisoner having been strange in his behavior. – Prisoner made no remark, and was remanded.

The Hull and East Yorkshire and Lincolnshire Times, October 6th 1888,

> THE LONDON TRAGEDIES. MORE THREATENING LETTERS. The following postal telegram was received by the Metropolitan police, at five minutes to 12 last night. It was handed in at an office in the Eastern District at eight p.m.:- "Chas, Warner, head of the Police News, Central Office: Dear Boss, - If you are willing enough to catch me I am now in the City-road, longing, but near. You will have to find out, and I mean to do another murder to-night in Whitechapel. – Yours, Jack the Ripper."
>
> A letter was also received at the Commercial-street Police Station by the first post this morning, addressed "Commercial-street Police Station," in black lead pencil, and the contents, which were also written in pencil, were crouched in ridiculous language. The police believe that it is the work of a lunatic. It was signed "Jack the Ripper," and said he was "going to work" in Whitechapel last night. He added that he was going to commit a murder in Goswell-road to night, and spoke of having "several bottled of blood underground in Epping Forest." And frequently referred to "Jack the Ripper" underground. The letter has been handed in to Inspector Abberline, who has communicated it to the G Division, in whose district Goswell-road is. Similar ridiculous letters have been received by the police. ANOTHER FALSE ALARM. A false alarm was raised that a man had been arrested in Brick-lane under very suspicious circumstances, but the affair proved to be a drunken squabble, having no connection with the murders. EXTRA POLICE PRECAUTIONS. It was noticed that in Aldgate, the immediate vicinity, the city police patrol had been doubled, but for obvious reasons no detective officer was anywhere to be seen. There have been no further arrests up to one o'clock to-day in connection with the London murders. The telegram received by the Metropolitan Police has been proved to have been banded in at the chief office of the Eastern District, in Commercial-road, but no information is forthcoming as to how it came to be accepted by the telegraphic authorities, or by whom it was handed in. The police are inquiring into the matter.

BLOODHOUNDS TO BE USED. *The Central News is authorised to state that Sir Charles Warren has been making inquiries as to the practicability of employing trained bloodhounds for use in special cases in the streets of London, and having ascertained that dogs which have been accustomed to work in a town can be procured, he is making immediate arrangements for their use in London.* THE WESTMINSTER MYSTERY. *Respecting the Westminster mystery, it is to-day stated that the police have discovered that the flowered skirt round the corpse was obtained from a London West end draper, and that the piece of newspaper wrapped up with the body belongs to one bearing date August 24th, which is further said to be the date on which the remains were found at Guildford.* ANOTHER CONFESSION. ARREST AT BIRMINGHAM. *At the Birmingham Police Court to-day, a man giving the name of Alfred Napier Blanchard, canvasser, from London, was charged on his own confession with the Whitechapel murder. The prisoner was arrested on the strength of a statement he had making in a public house containing a circumstantial account of proceedings. He now denies any connection, and explains his confession by pleading mental excitement, caused by reading about the affair. He was remanded till Monday, but the police do not consider the arrest important. A* NEW "MYSTERY OF A HANSOM CAB." AN INSENSIBLE WOMAN FOUND. *A woman was found lying insensible in Back-lane shortly after midnight. A crowd quickly collected, and great excitement prevailed. It seems that about half past eleven o'clock three men noticed a hansom cab, containing two men and a woman, turn down Air-street. Having reached a dark railway arch, the men in the cab got out and deposited upon the ground the woman, who was apparently insensible. The three men who were watching, having their suspicions aroused, raised an alarm. The two mysterious men jumped into the cab and the cabman drove hurriedly off. One of the men, however, returned to the spot where the woman was deposited and was pointed out to a constable, who took him to Commercial-road Police Station. He gave the name of Johnson; but, as he was unable to dispel the suspicions of the police, he was detained. Johnson was subsequently released, it having been soon established that he had no connection with the murders. The woman who was with him was his wife, and as they were both intoxicated when they alighted from the hansom under the archway, which is a very dark spot, and failed to give any explanation, they were taken to Commercial-street Station. A relative, named Mills, residing in the vicinity, to whom it seems they were going, called at the station, and on his statement they were released. The incident, happening as it did in a very dark and suspicious neighbourhood, naturally attracted the attention of passers-by, and no end of excitement prevailed, as the affair was speedily connected with the murders.* IMPORTANT STATEMENT BY A SAILOR. *A telegram from New York*

Mike Covell

states: "The atrocious crimes committed in Whitechapel have aroused intense interest here. The following statement has been made by an English sailor named Dodge. He says he arrived in London form China on Aug. 13 by the steamship Glenorchy. He met at the Queen's Music-hall, Poplar, a Malay cook, named Alaska. The Malay said he had been robbed by women of bad character, and swore that unless he found them and recovered his money he would murder and mutilate every Whitechapel woman he met. He showed Dodge a double-edged knife which he always carried with him. He was about 5ft. 7in. in height, 180lb in weight, and apparently 36 years of age. Of course he was very dark. The City Police authorities at first, it is said, attached considerable importance to this telegram. Immediately on receipt of a copy of the cablegram detectives were sent to make inquiries at the Glen Line Steamship Company, the Sailors' Home, the Home for Asiatics, and other places in the East end where it was likely information respecting the Malay could be obtained. A short while later a reporter called at the Home for asiatics, and was courteously received by Mr. Freeman, the manager and superintendent of that institution. Mr. Freeman stated that he had been at the Home for thirty years, and had never known a Malay of the name of Alaska. Malays, he said, are Mahomedans, and do not use European names. But a "Lascar" is the Mahomedan name for "seaman," and Dodge might have been misled. Most of the men who have lodged at the Home lately have used it for years whenever their ships are in London, but recently a crew of Japanese sailors had lodged there, and Mr. Freeman admitted that one of these men was a desperate character, for upon one occasion he stabbed three of his comrades, who were staying in the Home. He was arrested, but when the trial came on the injured men had taken ship and gone away. Again, about September 12, a riot occurred opposite the Home and a Japanese, named Suji Waxim, stabbed an "unfortunate" in a shocking manner, and was subsequently sentenced to six months' hard labour. On the day after this man was arrested the hall keeper of the Asiatic Home found a small but very sharp knife behind the stove in the hall. But, continued Mr. Freeman, it is a well-known fact that these Asiatics rarely if ever travel even a short distance from the West India Docks. After they are discharged, and are waiting for another ship, they do not go far from the Home, but spend their time in the public houses, gambling dens, and immoral houses which abound in the neighbourhood. The Queen's Music hall, where Dodge states he met "Alaska," is most luxuriously fitted up, in a style equal to many of the West end music halls. Mr. Wood, the manager, states that he had heard nothing of the alleged robbery of the Malay, and referred his inquirer to two attendants - Alexander Nowlan and Henry Pierce - who look after the boxes in which sailors returned from a voyage usually disport themselves. Both men declared that no such robbery could have taken place on *the premises without their hearing of it, and, as far as they were aware, no such thing had happened. The Queen's Music hall accommodates about three thousand persons, and it is usually well filled. At the Exchange Tavern, where people congregate after the music halls are closed, nothing had been heard of the robbery referred to by Dodge. Mr. Axel Welin, secretary of the Scandinavian Sailors' Temperance House, West India Docks, was next applied to. This gentleman ransacked his books, but could find no trace either of Dodge or the Malay. Messrs. M'Gregor, Son and Company, owners of the Glen Line of steamers trading to Singapore, China, &c., stated that the Glenorchy sailed in April from London to China, and returned on August 14. After taking in cargo at Antwerp she again sailed for China on September 8, and was last reported on Sept. 23 at Suez. They have no one named Alaska on board. The chief cook of the Glenorchy is a thoroughly respectable Chinaman, who has been in the service of the firm for many years, and they have no Malays on the ship. When the Glenorchy passed Gravesend on the last voyage the captain telegraphed that all the crew were on board.*

The Hull News, October 6th 1888,

ANOTHER LONDON HORROR. MURDER AND DISMEMBERMENT. DISCOVERY OF A WOMAN'S MUTILATED BODY. Another ghastly discovery was made in London yesterday afternoon. About five o'clock a carpenter named Frederick Wildborn, employed by Messrs J. Grover and Sons, builders, of Pimlico, who are contractors for the new Metropolitan Police Head-quarters on the Thames Embankment, was working on the foundation, when he came across a neatly done up parcel which was secreted in one of the cellars. Wildborn was in search of timber when he found the parcel, which was tied up in paper and measured about two-and-a-half feet long by about two feet in width. It was opened, and the body of a woman, very much decomposed, was found carefully wrapped in a piece of cloth, which is supposed to be a black petticoat. The trunk was minus the head, both arms, and both legs, and presented a ghastly spectacle. The officials of the works were immediately apprised of the discovery and the police were fetched. Dr. Bond, the divisional surgeon to the A. Division, and several other medical gentlemen were communicated with, and subsequently examined the remains, which were handed over to the care of some police-officers, who were told off to see that the trunk was not disturbed. From what can be ascertained the conclusion has been arrived at by the medical men that these remains are those of the woman whose arms have recently been discovered in different parts of London- one in Pimlico and the other in Lambeth, on the opposite side of the River Thames. Dr. Neville, who examined the arms of a female found a few weeks ago in the Thames, off Ebury Bridge, Pimlico, said on that occasion that he did not think it had been skilfully taken from the body, and this fact would appear to favour the theory that the arm. Together with the one found in the grounds of the Blind Asylum in the Lambeth road last week, belong to the trunk discovered today, for it is stated that the limbs appear to have been taken from the body found this afternoon in anything but a skilful manner. The building, which is in course of erection is the new police depot for London, the present scattered headquarters of the Metropolitan police force and the Criminal Investigation Department in Great Scotland Yard and Whitehall Place have been found too small for the requirements of the London police system. The builders have been working on the site for some considerable time now, but have only just completed the foundation. It was originally the site for the National Opera House, and extends from the Thames Embankment, through to Cannon row, Parliament street, at the back of St Stephen's Club, and the Westminster Bridge Station on the District Railway. The prevailing onion is that to place the body where it was found the person conveying it must have scaled the 8ft. hoarding which encloses the works, and carefully avoided the watchmen who do duty by night, must have dropped it where it was found. There appears to be little doubt that the parcel had been in the cellar for some considerable time. A workman employed upon the works, who was one of the first to see the remains, has made the following statement to a newspaper representative:- "I went down into one of the cellars, which is about 20ft. by 15ft. in size to look round, when I saw a parcel lying in a corner as though it had been thrown there carelessly. I might say that the cellar is really part of the half-finished basement of what are to be the new police officers. The parcel was a paper one, which could easily be carried under the arm. When the parcel was opened I saw that it contained the trunk of a woman wrapped up in a coarse cloth. In cutting off the legs a portion of the abdomen had been cut away. The head and arms were also cut off close to the trunk. The police have been digging up the rubbish and any place where it seems likely any more remains could be hidden but I don't think they have found anything more. The contents of the parcel were very much decomposed, and looked to have been in the place where they found for three weeks or a month. My opinion is that the person putting the parcel where it was found must have got over the hoarding in Cannon-row, and then thrown the bundle down." Another workman says that the parcel was discovered by a man whom he only knows as "George" who went down to get some timber. In his opinion the parcel had been there quite three weeks, as the contents were terribly decomposed. Another workman who has a thorough knowledge of the facts connected with the finding of the ghastly remains has made the following statements:- "As one of our carpenters was putting away his tools at about five o'clock last night in one of the vaults which are to form the foundation of the main building of the new offices which are to accommodate the police, he saw what seemed to be a heap of paper. As it is very dark in this particular spot, even during the day, the matter somehow did not appear to strike him as curious or out of the way, his passing thoughts being that it was merely a bundle of canvas which was being used on the works. He consequently mentioned the matter to no one, and having left his tools, came away and went home, thinking no more about the mysterious parcel which was to reveal another dreadful crime, probably perpetrated within 100 yards of the King street police station, about 200 or 300 yards from the present offices of the Criminal Investigation Department, and within 50 yards of the Houses of Parliament. This morning, when he went to fetch his tools, he became aware of a peculiar smell proceeding from the dark corner, but at the time made no attempt ascertain the cause. The matter, however, had taken possession of his mind, and later on in the day he mentioned the circumstances to one or two of his fellow workmen. They at once decided to tell the foreman. This was one and the foreman, accompanied by some of the men, proceeded to the spot. One of the labourers was called to shift the parcel. It was then opened and the onlookers were horrified to find that it contained a human body. The legs, arms, and head were missing, and the body presented a most sickening spectacle. The woman had evidently been dead for many days, as decomposition was far advanced. I never saw such a dreadful sight in my life, and the smell was dreadful. After we had got over the first surprise and nausea we sent for the police, and a doctor was also sent for. We could see that the body was that of a full grown woman, and when the doctor came he said the same thing. Almost immediately after that Dr. Bond, of the Middlesex Hospital, came and saw the body. He found that it was very brown, and I believe he said that it was the body from which the arms found in the Thames a few days ago had been cut. The body was wrapped in what looked like part of an old black dress of very common material, and it is a very strange thing that other parts of the same dress have been found in other parts of the yard. The police took possession of the remains, and gave orders that no stranger was to be admitted to the enclosure. How long do I think it possible the body could have been lying there? Well, it could not have been where we found it above two or three days, because men are continually passing the spot. The place is very dark, and it is possible that it might have escaped notice on that account; but, now I come to think of it, I know for a fact that it was not there last Friday because we had occasion to do something at that very spot." Asked for his opinion as to how the parcel got into such a curious place, our informant seemed quite taken aback at the simplicity of the question, but said that the person who put the bundle there could not very well have got into the enclosure from the embankment side, as not only would *the risk of detection be very great, but he would stand a good chance of breaking his neck. EXAMINATION OF THE REMAINS. A later account says that there is no doubt now that the discovery is connected with a terrible murder from the way in which the body has been treated, it is impossible that it could have been spirited away from a dissecting room after having answered the purpose of lawful operations. Persons who have seen the trunk have described it as being in a very advanced state of decomposition- so much that it was pronounced dangerous by the medical gentleman present for anyone to touch it with the naked hand. One end was quite black, and upon it being taken to the mortuary disinfectants were freely used, and it was placed in spirit to await the post mortem examination. When the parcel was found and opened there was not a scrap of clothing on the trunk, and it was tied with rope lengthways and crossways, just as one would tie up a parcel. The vault is about 24 feet by 30 in size, and 12 or 13 feet deep, and it is nearly covered over with loose planks, the ground showing only a small space at each end of the place. The trunk must have been carried either from the embankment or from Cannon-row. It certainly could not have been thrown over to where it lay from either roadway. It's general appearance, indeed, indicated rather that it had been carefully placed. It is simply astounding that any man could have carried such an offensive burden through the public street without attracting attention, and it is still more extraordinary how it could have been taken to the vault without discovery. The route from Cannon-row to the vault is a difficult one. To reach the vault one must actually pass through the building in course of erection, about which several policemen are constantly patrolling. It is more reasonable to assume that the vault was gained from Cannon-row, and in that case it seems pretty certain that more than one person was concerned in the disposal of the ghastly parcel. One man probably climbed to the top of the hoarding with the assistance of his accomplice, from whom he received the parcel, dropped it on the inner side and then let himself down after it. The other man presumably kept watch while confederate disposed of the remains. How the men could have known of the existence of the vault is not clear, for strangers are not admitted to the works except on business. Possibly the original intention was to place the remains in some out of the way corner in the works in some out-of-the-way corner in the works, and that they were only taken to the vault after that obviously desirable place of concealment had been accidentally discovered. It is satisfactory to state that in view of the possibility of discovery such as that made last night, the arms found at Westminster and Lambeth a short time ago, of which mention is made below, were not buried , as had been supposed. They have been preserved in the usual way and will be taken to the mortuary, in which the trunk now lies. One of the first things which the surgeons will have to do will be to test by actual experiment whether the discovered severed limbs belong to the trunk, and the result will be awaited with profound interest, and anxiety, for if they do not fit the trunk, we shall be driven to the conclusion that not one, but two more mysterious, and horrible crimes have been committed in London. For the present the police and surgical experts are hopeful that the various ligaments will be found to be part of the same body. The head, the most important part for purposes of identification, and legs, are still missing. As to the remaining limbs, the only thing certain is that two arms have been found. The first arm was found on the afternoon of September the 11th by a man named Moore, who works in a timber yard in Grosvenor roar, Westminster. The arm when seen by Moore was lying on the mud on the foreshore of the Thames near Grosvenor road railway bridge. The arm had been cleanly severed from the shoulder, and it evidently belonged to a well-proportioned young woman. Although it had been in the water for several days it presented a white and shapely appearance. The woman must have been between 25 and 30 years of age. In the opinions of the surgeons who examined the limb, although a knife had been adroitly used, it was not wielded by a surgical expert, and it had certainly never been inside a dissecting room. Everything, in fact, seemed to point to murder, and with this view, it is understood, the police reluctantly agreed, and orders were issued for the river to be dragged, and every arrangement was made for the detection of the murderer, should he endeavour, as it was reasonable to suppose, to dispose of the other parts of the victims body. Nothing occurred, however, until the 19th ult., when a second arm was found in Southwark. A boy was walking along the Lambeth-road about half past seven o'clock on the morning of that date, when he noticed just within the Blind School Garden a parcel, which curiosity prompted him to inspect more closely. He reached it, opened it, and saw to his horror that it enclosed a human arm. The limb was somewhat decomposed, and lime had been thrown over it, but it was recognisable as that of a woman. It was handed over to the police of L Division, and after that it came into their possession little more was heard of it, the police maintaining the utmost reserve regarding the discovery. The Press Association says an Inspector and a number of plain clothes police were again searching the basement of the new police offices in Whitehall, on Thursday, in search of the remaining members of the body found there on Tuesday. It is believed the person who deposited the remains was familiar with the ground passages leading to the spot, which is dark and full of pitfalls. A later report from Westminster states that the police have been informed that on Saturday afternoon, a respectable looking man, aged about 35, was seen to get over the hoarding in Canon-row, and walk quietly away. A description of the man has been circulated.*

Mike Covell

October 8th 1888

The Eastern Morning News, October 8th 1888,

> MURDEROUS ASSAULT. A man named Donald is in custody at Newcastle upon Tyne on a charge of murderous assault upon a woman named Cooper, with whom he lived. He left her last Monday but returned on Saturday, and upon finding a man in the house, he turned him out then attacked the woman with a table knife, seriously wounding her throat. He escaped through a window whilst the woman's screams attracted neighbours. She was removed to the infirmary. Her depositions have been taken. Donald was arrested in a public house.

The Eastern Morning News, October 8th 1888,

> THE LONDON MURDERS. VIGILANCE IN THE EAST END. NUMEROUS ARRESTS. The Central News Agency says that, up to a late hour last night, all was quiet in the Whitechapel district, and the excitement had somewhat subsided. Nevertheless the police and the Local Vigilance Committee by no means relaxed their watchfulness, and the inhabitants of the district, disregarding the improbability of the murderer risking his freedom under these circumstance, still appear to expect the early commission of a new crime. During Saturday night and the early hours of Sunday morning several persons were arrested, and detained at the local police stations until all the circumstances in connection with their apprehension were thoroughly sifted. Several of these were given into custody on grounds which proved an inquiry to be flimsy and even foolish, the police being in consequence put to a good deal of trouble without any corresponding result. It seemed at times as if every person in the streets were suspicious of everyone else he met, and as if it were a race between them who should first inform against his neighbour. Last evening a passing sensation was caused in Commercial-street by a very ordinary incident, which well illustrates the existence of this suspicion. Amateur East-end athletes, whom circumstances prevent from practicing in the country, are in the habit of organizing running – matches through the less frequented thoroughfares on Sunday evenings. They dress in some kind of athletic costume – sometimes divesting themselves of all clothing except such as is necessary for decency. In one of these competitions last night a young man, who was far in advance of his competitors, was nearing the Shoreditch end of Commercial-street, running at high speed. Almost instantly the rumour spread that a man half-clad was running for his life from the police. People hurried to their doors and rain in the direction indicated, only to find that an ordinary footrace was in progress. The

announced intention of the authorities to employ bloodhounds in the hunt for the murderer has attracted keen attention in the East End, and a rumour – readily seized upon, but not substantiated – was passed from mouth to mouth last night that the police had been practicing dogs in trial scents through the streets yesterday. The Working – Men's Vigilance and Patrol Committee have been augmented by some thirty able-bodies men, well acquainted with the locality. These were selected by a special meeting of representative working men connected with the dock industries, who assembled at Bow Common-lane on Saturday night. The new patrols will join in assisting the police to capture, if possible, the assassin, who, in the words of the chairman of the meeting, "has disgraced the name of civilization." Various incidents more or less suspicious were reported last night. In one instance a man stopped a woman in Hanbury-street. The latter naturally became frightened, and in order to get rid of the man, she promised to meet him at half-past eleven o'clock to-night. The intruder then went away, and he has not since been traced. A respectably-dressed young man was taken to Commercial-street Police Station by one of the Vigilance Committee's detectives as bearing a resemblance to one of the sketches printed by the Daily Telegraph on Saturday – that representing a man with a hard felt hat. The prisoner carried an umbrella and a black bag, in which was a razor. He said he lived at Chelsea, and had been attending a place of worship close by. He complained bitterly of his detention, but the police felt compelled to keep him until inquiries had been completed. Some curious mistakes arose yesterday through the Vigilance Committee's detectives not being known to the City and Metropolitan detectives. The amateurs and the professionals frequently watched one another with mutual suspicion. The East End murders last night afforded a means of revenge to a woman who had become incensed against a man. Accosting her enemy near a coffee-stall in Lambeth, she loudly accused him of having threatened to "rip her up." The policeman on duty in the neighbourhood was constrained to take the man to Kennington-road Police-station, for examination, but the woman's false charge was rapidly exploded, and her victim was liberated after a few minutes' detention. The following postal telegram was received by the Metropolitan police, at five minutes to 12 last night. It was handed in at an office in the Eastern District at eight p.m.:- "Chas, Warner, head of the Police News, Central Office: Dear Boss, - If you are willing enough to catch me I am now in the City-road, longing, but near. You will have to find out, and I mean to do another murder to-night in Whitechapel. – Yours, Jack the Ripper."

A letter was also received at the Commercial-street Police Station by the first post this morning, addressed "Commercial-street Police Station," in black lead pencil, and the contents, which were also written in pencil, were crouched in

Mike Covell

> *ridiculous language. The police believe that it is the work of a lunatic. It was signed "Jack the Ripper," and said he was "going to work" in Whitechapel last night. He added that he was going to commit a murder in Goswell-road to night, and spoke of having "several bottled of blood underground in Epping Forest." And frequently referred to "Jack the Ripper" underground. The letter has been handed in to Inspector Abberline, who has communicated it to the G Division, in whose district Goswell-road is. Similar ridiculous letters have been received by the police. A handsome polished oak coffin has been provided for Eddowes, the Mitre-square victim. THE WESTMINSTER MYSTERY. Respecting the Westminster mystery, it is to-day stated that the police have discovered that the flowered skirt round the corpse was obtained from a London West end draper, and that the piece of newspaper wrapped up with the body belongs to one bearing date August 24th, which is further said to be the date on which the remains were found at Guildford. ANOTHER CONFESSION. At the Birmingham Police Court on Saturday, Alfred Napier Blanchard was charged on his own confession with having committed the murders in Whitechapel. Prisoner entered a Birmingham public house about noon on Friday, and sat drinking beer for some hours. He led the conversation of the company to the recent murders, and, avowing himself the murderer, explained his method of procedure with much circumstance and detail. The excited company at length gave him into custody. Prisoner now declared that he was innocent, and said that he could bring witnesses to prove him a book canvasser of perfect responsibility, travelling for a London firm. BODY FOUND IN THE THAMES. The body of a woman named Mrs. Judson was picked up in the Thames, off Pimlico Pier, on Saturday, and conveyed to the mortuary. How she came into the river is unknown. It is believed to be a drowning case.*

The Hull Daily Mail, October 8th 1888,

> THE EAST END HORRORS. ANOTHER ARREST TO-DAY. DESPERATE STRUGGLE. The Press Association says:- A man was arrested at Baker's-row, Whitechapel, this afternoon, after a desperate resistance. He was at once conveyed to Bethnal Green Police Station, and there charged on suspicion of being concerned in the recent murders. FUNERAL OF THE MITRE-SQUARE VICTIM. The funeral of Catherine Eddowes, victim of the Mitre-square murder, took place this afternoon at Ilford, Essex, where the City of London Cemetery is situated. The expenses of the funeral were borne entirely by a private citizen. The corpse was decently laid in a plain [illegible] coffin, with the name and age of the deceased engraved thereon, and was removed at half-past one from the golden Lane Mortuary. Thousands of people lined the streets in the vicinity of

the mortuary, evincing much sympathy. The remains were borne an open hearse, followed by two carriages. Several wreaths were on the coffin. The crowds in the streets of the East End were so dense that a force of police had to direct the traffic. THE WHITEHALL MURDERS. OPENING OF THE INQUEST. *This afternoon John Troutbeck, the coroner for Westminster, opened an inquest on the remains found a week ago under the New Police Offices, on the Thames Embankment. The greatest interest was manifested in the proceedings, and large numbers of people gathered outside of the mortuary at Mill Bank and the Sessions House, Westminster.- The Jury were summoned to meet at the mortuary at two o'clock, and they did not return to the Sessions House until three. The body in the mortuary presented an awful spectacle. It was locked in a room, and was viewed by the jury through a window for fear of contagion. It was on a table propped up, and the arm recently found was placed in the socket. The body was of a dark brown colour.- At twenty past three the first witness called was Frederick Wildoorn, carpenter, employed on the works. He said he first saw what he thought was an old coat on Monday morning. He took no notice of the matter then, and saw the parcel again the same evening. On the following day he called the assistant-foreman's attention to the parcel. It was then found to contain the body of the woman. He did not notice any smell. Witness pointed out where the body was found, on a maze like plan of the vaults, and he said it would be very difficult anyone unacquainted with the place to find his way there. The workman's tools had been placed there for ten weeks, up to two weeks before the body was found.- George Budgen, brick-layers labourer, engaged in the works, said he was told by another workman to go and see what the parcel was. He untied the parcel, and produced the cord which had served that purpose. The body was then seen, and the police were sent for.- Detective Thomas Hawkins, A-Division, deposed to being called and seeing the body. It was wrapped in a dress material (produced). The wall was very black, and the body was in an advanced state of decomposition. The vaults were very dark, and no stranger could have found his way without a light. The person would have to cross a trench which could not be seen in the dark.- Frederick Moore and Charles William Brown, assistant foreman to Messrs Grover, the contractor for the works, having given evidence, the Courts adjourned.* A "JACK THE RIPPER" SCARE. *At Brierley Hill Police Court this morning, Alfred-Pearson, moulder, was charged with stopping Thomas Plant and his sweetheart in a dark lane and threatening them as "Jack the Ripper," and with brandishing a long knife. The lady was driven into hysterics. Pearson was bound over to keep the peace. At Glovan, Glasgow, this morning, Michael Devine, who described himself has "Jack the Ripper II," was fined three guineas for knocking down a married woman and brandishing a knife over her.* THREATENING MORE WOMEN.

Mike Covell

> Thomas Johnson, travelling sailor, was sent to gaol for a month, in default of finding sureties, at Croydon, this morning, for violently threatening two married woman in a public house. The affair caused much excitement following upon the recent London outrages. ANOTHER WOMAN'S BODY FOUND IN THE THAMES. Another body of a woman, unknown was found in the Thames this afternoon near Waterloo Bridge. The deceased, who appeared about 30 years of age, had met her death by drowning about ten days ago.

The Hull Daily Mail, October 8th 1888,

> THE LONDON ATROCITIES. SATURDAY NIGHT'S PRECAUTIONS. FEVERISH EXCITEMENT AT WHITECHAPEL. Throughout Saturday the inhabitants of Whitechapel were kept in a state of feverish excitement by the knowledge that threatening letters were constantly being received by the police authorities at the various stations intimating that the assassin would shortly recommence his ghastly work. Towards the evening the dismay became remarkably intensified, as reports of further threats were circulated, many of them appearing to be the pure inventions of cruel tritlers. But whether true or false, they at least served as an incentive not only to the police to adopt extra precautions, but even stimulated the residents to, if possible, prevent a repetition of the horrible murders. Soon after ten o'clock the streets of Whitechapel and Spitalfields assumed an almost deserted appearance as far as women were concerned, and those who ventured abroad did not do so singly, but moved about in twos and threes. Even the unfortunate class were not an exception to this rule. This plan seems to have been adopted by women of this character, and doubtless will prove a great obstacle to the movements of the murderer, who, knowing that a third party haunts his actions, will not find another opportunity so easily of carrying out his designs. The police were nervously apprehensive that the night would not pass without some startling occurrence. The most extraordinary precautions were taken in consequence, and so complete were the measures adopted, both by the City and Metropolitan Police authorities, that it seemed impossible for the murderer to make his appearance in the East End without detection. Large bodies of plain-clothes men were drafted by Sir Charles Warren to the Whitechapel district from other parts of London, and these, together with the detectives, were so numerous that in the more deserted thoroughfares almost every man met with a police-officer. The city police, far from being outdone in their exertions to ensure the protection of the public, more than doubled the patrols, so that almost every nook and corner of the various beats came under police supervision every five minutes. In addition to this measure men were stationed at fixed distances to watch for any suspicious

looking persons, and when thought at all necessary to follow them. These arrangements to ensure safety and to reassure the public of the efforts taken on their behalf applied equally to other parts of the metropolis, it being thought that the murderer finding Whitechapel rather too warm for him might transfer his operations to another district. The parks, where the fiend would have no difficulty in finding victims, were especially well patrolled, and the police in the most outlying districts were keenly alive to the anxieties of the situation. Most of the men were on duty all Friday night in the East End; the extra work, therefore, was particularly harassing. But every man entered heartily into the work, and not a murmur was heard. All wore upon their mettle, and if collective and individual zeal were all that was required, the murderer would soon be hunted down. Supplementing the energy displayed by the police, hundreds of people living in the back streets sat up all night, whilst dozens of sturdy householders paid occasional visits to yards and other secluded spots in their immediate vicinity. The volunteer patrols organised by the Whitechapel Vigilance Committee lent marked assistance to the police. Their patrols were told off to well-planned beats, many of these amateur policemen being furnished with noiseless boots, a measure which has lately been strongly urged upon the Metropolitan police. It is supposed that the murderer is armed with a revolver, and, if detected, will shoot at the first person who attempted to capture him: in any case his knife, in such skillful hands, would, if he had the slightest chance of dealing a blow, prove mortal. The large reward offered has, however, afforded sufficient stimulus to as large a number of strong, able-bodied men as are required for the dangerous duty of tracking down the murderer. THE WHITECHAPEL MYSTERY. THE SUPPOSED MURDERER'S PORTRAIT RECOGNISED. THE POLICE ON HIS TRACK. There has been a startling development in the mysterious tragedies in Whitechapel. The police have now a tangible clue - a distinct, definite clue. This clue they even hope will actually lead to the capture of the murderer. They have now something like evidence of his identity - or, at least, of a man who is believed to be him. As news of this fact comes to hand, we also learn that the authorities, having satisfied themselves of the practicability of using bloodhounds in special cases in the streets of London, have made arrangements for their future use in the Metropolis. A man has been identified - or, rather, the sketch portrait of a man has been. This man is believed to be the fellow who was talking to the murdered woman in Berner street within a quarter of an hour of the time when she was killed. He has been identified by the man Packer, who declares that he saw him two doors from the scene of the murder late on Saturday night. It was noticed that Packer, as also another important witness, at once rejected the faces of men of a purely sensuous type, and that they thus threw aside the portraits of several noted

American criminals. Both witnesses inclined to the belief that the man's age was not more than 30, in which estimate they were supported by the police constable, who guessed him to be 28. If the impressions of two men, who, it may be supposed, have actually conversed with the alleged murderer, be correct, then an important piece of evidence has been discovered. THE FRUITERER'S STORY. This is how Packer describes the incident which brought the man to his notice:- On Saturday night, about half past eleven o'clock, this man and the woman he has identified as the deceased, came to the fruiterer's shop which he keeps. It was not necessary for them to enter it, as customers usually stand upon the pavement, and make their purchases through the window, which is not a shop front of the ordinary kind. Packer is certain that a woman, who wore dark jacket and a bonnet with some crepe stuff in it, was playing with a white flower which she carried. The man was square built, about 5ft 7in in height, thirty years of age, full in the face, dark complexioned, without moustache, and alert looking. His hair was black. He wore a long black coat and soft felt hat. It seemed to Packer that he was a clerk, and not a working man. He spoke in a quick, sharp manner, and stood in front of the window. The man purchased half a pound of black grapes, which were given to him in a paper bag, and he paid threepence in coppers. The couple then stood near the gateway of the club for a minute or so, and afterwards crossed the road and remained talking by the Board school for some time. They were still then when Packer had had supper, and when he went to bed; and Mrs. packer remarked it as strange that they should remain, for rain was falling at the time. It is a remarkable circumstance - much more than an ordinary coincidence - that the description of the supposed murderer given by Packer was yesterday confirmed by another man who, without being aware of the fact, also chose from the sketches the one which had been already selected by Packer. THE DAIRYMAN'S INFORMATION. Search for an individual answering to the description, but having a small moustache and wearing a black deerstalker felt hat, instead of a soft one, has been made by the police in Whitechapel since Saturday, Sept. 1, the day following the Buck's row tragedy. Information was tendered at the King David's lane Police Station, at about that time, by a dairyman who has a place of business in Little Turner street, Commercial road. It will be recollected that on Saturday, Sept. 1, a desperate assault was reported to have been committed near to the music hall in Cambridge heath road, a man having seized a woman by the throat and dragged her down a court, where he was joined by a gang, one of whom laid a knife across the woman's throat, remarking, "We will serve you as we did the others." The particulars of this affair were subsequently stated to be untrue; but the milkman had reason to suppose that the outrage was actually perpetrated, and he suspects that the murderer of Mary Ann Nicholls in Buck's row had something to do with it. THE SUSPECT CHANGING HIS CLOTHES. *At any rate, upon that Saturday night, at a few minutes to eleven o'clock, a man, corresponding with the description given by Packer of the individual who purchased the grapes in Berner street, called at the shop, which is on the left of a covered yard, is daily occupied by barrows, which are let out on hire. He was in a hurry, and he asked for a pennyworth of milk, with which he was served, and he drank it down at a gulp. Asking permission to go into the yard or shed, he went there, but the dairyman caught a glimpse of something white, and, having suspicions, he followed the man in the shed, and was surprised to discover that he had covered up his trousers with a pair of white overalls, such as engineers wear. The man had a staring look, and appeared greatly agitated. He made a movement forward, and the brim of his hard felt hat struck the dairyman, who is, therefore, sure of the kind that he was wearing. In a hurried manner the stranger took out of a black, shiny bag, which was on the ground, a white jacket, and rapidly put it on, completely hiding his cutaway black coat, remarking meanwhile, "It's a dreadful murder, isn't it?" although the subject had not been previously mentioned. Without making a pause the suspicious person caught up his bag, which was still open, and rushed into the street, towards Shadwell, saying, "I think I've got a clue." The matter was reported to the police, and although strict watch has been maintained for the appearance of the man, he has not been seen in the street since. He is said to have had a dark complexion, such as a seafaring man acquires. The style of collar that he was then wearing was of the turndown pattern. He had no marked American accent, and his general appearance was that of a clerk or student whose beard had been allowed three days' growth. His hair was dark, and his eyes large and staring.* THE BLACK SHINY BAG. *This witness speaks of the man carrying a black shiny bag. It will be remembered that the man who called at the Three Nuns had a black shiny bag, and that the only man whom Mrs. Mortimer saw previously pass through Berner street had a black shiny bag. There are, of course, some divergences in the evidence of identity but the police are at last believed to have obtained a most important clue. They admit that one class of witness declares that the man had a beard, and that the other avers that he had not. But they point out that there was an hour between the two periods at which he was seen and that the man had ample time in that period to shave or get shaved. The features certainly bear a singular resemblance and that otherwise - the hat excepted - the second man answers the description of the first.* THE WHITEHALL MYSTERY. A MISSING YOUNG WOMAN. EXTRAORDINARY STORY. *An examination of the remains brought to London on Friday night from Guildford by Inspector Marshall, was made on Saturday, by Mr. Bond, the head surgeon at Westminster Hospital, and it has been ascertained that they do not belong to the trunk discovered in the vault at Whitehall. In fact the opinion of the medical man is that they are not human remains at all. In connection with the mystery the detective police are most assiduously investigating cases of missing young woman, and their attention has been specifically directed to the remarkable disappearance of a young woman named Lilly Vass, who left her home, 45 Tettcott road, Chelsea, on July 19th last, and has never been seen or heard of since. On September 27th Mrs. Vass, the mother of the young woman, applied to Mr. Biron, sitting Magistrate at the Westminster Police court, and some publicity was given to the extraordinary disappearance of her daughter, who was stated to be of rather prepossessing appearance. The detective police have several times called on Mrs. Vass to obtain additional particulars about the girl, and, at their request the mother accompanied an officer to the Millbank mortuary to view the remains there. She was, however, quite unequal to the ordeal of making an inspection, and only saw the black flowered skirt in which the trunk was found. She could not recognise this, and was the more disposed to discredit the supposition that the remains were those of her daughter from the fact that one of the police officers told her that they belonged to a woman at least six or seven years older. In an interview a person had with Mrs. Vass at her house she gave many additional particulars as to the disappearance of her daughter. She said that her daughter was in service with a lady in Sealcott road, Wandsworth common, and on July 19th she left home ostensibly to go back to her situation. "Although I had always found her a truthful girl, I am bound to say she deceived me in one respect," said Mrs. Vass. "She had left her situation, although she told me she had not. I think it was on the Monday she came home, and she left on the Thursday. She was then wearing a black straw hat trimmed with crape, and a very dark ulster, with a velvet trimming front. She was a dark complexioned girl, fairly stout, quite of medium height, 5ft 5in certainly, and her dress was of black and white material - nothing like that I saw at the mortuary; but, of course, that goes for nothing. She had dark hair, fringed on the forehead, and her face was round and fresh coloured. We think she must have been enticed away. She was not a girl who kept a lot of company, and I believe the only person who ever wrote to her was a girl in service in Notting hill. Lilly has kept her places two or three years at a time, but she had only been with the lady at Wandsworth about six months. If she is alive, she must have been taken away right out of London, for we have looked and inquired everywhere for her, and can get no tidings." Questioned as to how the girl left home, the mother went on to say:- "She told me as I have already said, that she was going back to her place at Wandsworth, and that she thought she was going to travel with her mistress to the Isle of Wight. She left behind her mackintosh and bag, and went away with nothing but the clothes she stood upright in. I was not surprised at* this, because she explained that she had left her box with a charwoman of Chatham road, Wandsworth common. Everything pointed to the idea that she was going back to service, because she promised to send her brother a shilling to spend as a treat, and to repay me a very small sum I advanced her. She was a girl not devoid of sense, but rather abrupt in manner. I think that if she were alive she would write, even if she did not wish me to know where she was." Interrogated to the possible identity of her daughter with the victim of the mysterious crime now being investigated by the A division detectives, Mrs. Vass, somewhat distressed, said she hardly knew what to think - so many dreadful things were happening. Of course, recognition of the remains without the head was well nigh impossible, and so much depended on what the doctor said. Her daughter had fine arms, and her hand was rough from hard work. The only marks about the girl's body were on the neck, and they were the scars of old abscesses which had been lanced. A DISCOVERY. The police do not disguise the fact that they have obtained important information, which will lead to the identification of the murdered woman and possibly to the arrest of the perpetrator of the crime. One officer states that the maker of the silk shirt in which the body was found has been discovered. The maker is the proprietor of a West end establishment, having discovered so much, it is probable the person who ordered and received the skirt will be reached. Thus some sensational development of the case is anticipated. The date of the committal of the crime was fixed under rather peculiar circumstances. The piece of a London paper adhering to the remains was only about six inches long and four broad. Upon searching the files at the office of the paper, however, it was found that it was a portion of an edition published on the 24th of August. The doctors and the police thereupon came to the conclusion, comparing this with post mortem indications, that the deed must have been committed either on that date or shortly anterior thereto. A POSSIBLE CLUE. Mr. Edward Deuchar has communicated some information to the police which may afford a clue to the discovery of the man who deposited the body of the woman in Whitehall and the arm in the Thames. Mr. Deuchar is a commercial traveller, and a little over three weeks ago he went on a tram car from Vauxhall Station to London bridge. According to the Morning Advertiser, he noticed a man on the car carrying a parcel. He would not have taken particular notice of the parcel but for the fact that there was a terrible smell emanating from it. The olfactory organs of most of the passengers were affected by the extraordinary stench which pervaded all the car. A lady gave her husband, who was sitting next to the man, some lavender to hold to his nose. The parcel seemed to be heavy. the man carried it with extreme care under his arm. It was tied up in brown paper. The top of it was under his arm while he held the corner end in his hand. Mr. Deuchar says the man looked ill at ease and

Mike Covell

> *agitated. He described him as a powerfully built man, of rough appearance, with a goatee beard, and rather shabbily dressed. Mr. Deuchar is confident that he could recognise him again. The car went on, and when at the Obelisk, St. George's circus, several persons alighted. Mr. Deuchar still remained on the car, but when about thirty yards past the Obelisk, said, "This stink is awful; I can't stand it any longer," and proceeded to go out. Just at that moment the suspicious looking individual with the parcel asked the conductor, "Have we passed the Obelisk yet?" and then jumped out. Mr. Deuchar, when he had descended and walked some distance towards London bridge, called a policeman's attention to the retreating form of the "man with the stinking parcel," and told him to "keep an eye on him." ANOTHER "SPIRIT RAISING" JOKE. An extraordinary statement bearing upon the Whitechapel tragedies was made to the Cardiff police yesterday by a respectable looking elderly woman, who stated that she was a "Spiritualist," and in company with five other persons, held a séance on Saturday night. They summoned the spirit of Elizabeth Stride, and after some delay it came, and, in answer to questions, stated that her murderer was a middle aged man, whose name she mentioned, and who resided at a given number in Commercial road or street, Whitechapel, and who belonged to a gang of twelve. ANOTHER FOOLISH JOURNALIST. A journalist on Saturday night attempted to play the role of amateur detective by donning women's clothes. He succeeded in evading suspicion for some time, but eventually was surrounded by some women who declared that he was a man, and as a crowd soon gathered and continued to increase he found it desirable to proceed to Southwark police station, where the people called upon the police to take him into custody, but as he was professionally well known there, he was ultimately able to return to his home without further molestation. THE SAILOR'S STORY FROM NEW YORK. REFUSAL TO GIVE INFORMATION. New York, Saturday. – The New York Herald declares that the seaman named Dodge, who recently stated that a Malay whom he met in London threatened to murder a number of Whitechapel women for robbing him, said that he knew the street where the Malay stayed, but that he would not divulge the name until he learned what chance there was of a reward. He stated, however, the street was not far from the East India Dock Road, but he was not certain about the house where the man lived. Another seaman said he thought the Malay was now on a vessel plying in the North Sea.*

October 9th 1888

The Eastern Morning News, October 9th 1888,

THE LORD MAYOR OF LONDON AND THE MURDERS. (FROM OUR OWN CORRESPONDENT)

BRUSSELS, Monday. The Independence Belge publishes an interview with one of its representatives with Mr De Keyser, Lord Mayor of London, concerning the recent Whitechapel tragedies. His Lordship expresses the belief that the assassin is undoubtedly mad. Should he recommence his atrocious crimes he will be assuredly taken in the act, though it would not be surprising if he should soon commit suicide. The Lord Mayor states that neither has nor had any belief that the offer of a reward would prove efficacious in bringing the murderer to justice, and he only consented to adopt the course which he has done in this respect to calm the public excitement. He has written, he says to Mr Matthews to explain this, and to disavow all idea of opposition to the Government's decision. His Lordship attributes the Anti-Ministerial attacks which have been made to ambitious persons who are seeking by these means to secure election to the new County Council. He is sure that the police force for the City of London is sufficiently large.

EXTRAORDINARY AFFAIR AT CARDIFF. GIRL STABBED BY A TRAMP. A HOUSE PILLAGED.

Last evening a tramp knocked at the door of a house on Adam Street, Cardiff, and asked the girl who answered it, and who was alone, for bread. She refused. He struck her in the face, followed her into the house, and having closed the door, dragged her to the stairs. Tying her to the bannisters, he stabbed her in three places with a knife. He then searched the house from top to bottom, securing all the portable property of value. When he had descended the stairs he again stabbed the girl, and quickly walked away. Up to the present time, he remains at large. ANOTHER LONDON MYSTERY. A WOMAN'S BODY FOUND IN THE THAMES. The dead body of a woman apparently about 29 years of age, was found floating in the Thames near Waterloo Bridge yesterday. It was rescued by the river police and taken to Lambeth mortuary, where it awaits identification. No evidence is yet forthcoming as to whether the deceased met with her death by violence, accident, or suicide. The discovery occasioned great excitement amongst the riverside population.

The Eastern Morning News, October 9th 1888,

THE EAST END TRAGEDIES. EXTRAORDINARY DISCOVERY. The Central News Agency says:--"A startling fact has just come to light. After killing

Mike Covell

Katherine Eddowes in Mitre-square, the murderer, it is now known, walked to Goulston-street, where he threw away the piece of the deceased woman's apron upon which he had wiped his hands and knife. Within a few feet of this spot he had written upon the wall, "The Jews shall not be blamed for nothing." Most unfortunately one of the police officers gave orders for this writing to be immediately sponged out, probably with a view of stifling the morbid curiosity which it would certainly have aroused. But in so doing a very important link was destroyed, for had the writing been photographed a certain clue would have been in the hands of the authorities. The witnesses who saw the writing, however, state that it was similar in character to the letters sent to the Central News and signed 'Jack the Ripper,' and though it would have been far better to have clearly demonstrated this by photography, there is now every reason to believe that the writer of the letter and postcard sent to the Central News (facsimiles of which are now to be seen outside every police-station) is the actual murderer. The police, consequently, are very anxious that any citizen who can identify the handwriting should without delay communicate with the authorities. Another communication has been received from the writer of the original 'Jack the Ripper' letter, which, acting upon official advice, it has been deemed prudent to withhold for the present. It may be stated, however, that although the miscreant avows his intention of committing further crimes shortly it is only against prostitutes that his threats are directed, his desire being to respect and protect honest women." The Metropolitan police last night made an arrest, which was thought likely to lead to important results. The arrest was made through the instrumentality of Mr Richard S Parkes, manager of the Central Branch of the London Clothing Repairing Company, 69, Gray's Inn-road. This firm carry on their business of cleaners as well as repairers, at nine different establishments in the Metropolis, and last Wednesday afternoon a man called at the central shop between twelve and two o'clock in the afternoon, with two garments, an overcoat, and a pair of trousers, to be cleaned. They were both blood stained. The coat was especially smeared near one of the pockets, and there were large spots of blood on various parts of the trousers. Mr Parkes was away at the time, and his wife took charge of the garments. The man said he would call them on Friday or Saturday. Mrs Parkes naturally called her husband's attention to the blood stains on his return, and he communicated with the Metropolitan Police, who examined the clothes, and took them to Scotland Yard. Ever since then two detectives were secreted on the premises awaiting the stranger's return. Last evening he stepped into the shop a few minutes before closing time. Detective-sergeant George Godley and a companion seized him without much ceremony, and he was taken straight to the Leman-street Police-station. Meanwhile the prisoner accounted for the presence of the blood marks by the assertation that he had cut his hand. His explanation was not considered altogether consistent, as he first said that he had cut himself last Saturday, and then that he had also cut his hand previously. The prisoner further stated that he had had the garments by him in his lodgings for two or three weeks, but he refused to give his address. He was, however, liberated after the police had satisfied themselves of his innocence. The apparent inconsistency of his explanations was doubtless due to his embarrassment. The police had yesterday searched all the lodging houses in Limehouse, Shadwell, St. George's in the East, Spitalfields, and the Borough, as well as others at Hoxton and Islington, but nothing which will afford them a clue, has been discovered. Inquiries, too, have been made amongst local butchers, and at all slaughterhouses, to find out whether any one, recently employed in this capacity, has lately become deranged. These inquiries, too, have been fruitless. A remarkable feature in the case of the discovery of the mutilated body at Whitehall is the number of missing women brought to the notice of the authorities by persons making inquiries respecting the remains. It is thus shown that very many women leave their friends without communicating with them, and pass out of sight of those nearest to them. No trustworthy clue to the murder has yet been obtained from these inquiries, though each piece of information is closely sifted. This afternoon Mr Troutbeck opened the inquest on the remains. The inquiry was held at the Westminster Sessions House. The first witness was a carpenter, who first discovered the parcel, this was on Monday last, but it was not till the next day that he and one of his mates opened the parcel and discovered what were the contents. There was nothing new in his evidence, but the witness went on to say that it would be difficult to get at the vault without knowing something of the place. Another labourer who gave evidence said he thought the parcel "was a lot of old bacon," so he dragged it out into the light, cut the string, and opened it. He had not been in the vault, which was quite dark, for some time before this. Then a detective deposed to going to the pace when information had been given to the police, and taking charge of the remains, which were wrapped up in a piece of dress material and tied loosely with string. Near the spot where the parcel was found he saw some more dress material. Witness thought it impossible for any stranger to find his way into the vault. Frederick Moore, a porter, gave evidence of the finding of an arm in the mud of the river off Grosvenor road, Pimlico. It was not wrapped in anything, but a string was tied round the upper part of the arm. Charles Brown, assistant foreman at Messrs Grover's works in Cannon row, said that the site was shut off from the surrounding streets by a hoarding 17 feet high. There were three entrances to the street, two were in Cannon row. All the gates were as high as the hoarding. The vaults had been completed three months. No one was admitted to the works

Mike Covell

> *but the workmen and those who had business with the clerk of the works. The gates were all locked on the Saturday before the body was found, but one of the doors was only fastened by a piece of string. It would not be easy for anybody unacquainted with the place to unlock the gate. From your knowledge of the works do you think it would require previous knowledge of the building to get at these vaults. Yes, I certainly do, because nobody would think of going to such a place without having looked for it. Ernest Hedge, another labourer, said that he had occasion to go into the vault on Saturday before the discovery, but there was no parcel there then. Dr. Bond deposed that on October 2nd he was called to the new Police Buildings. It seemed to him that the remains had been there for several days. He had since made an examination, assisted by Mr Hibberd. The trunk was that of a woman of considerable stature, and well nourished. The head had been severed and the lower limbs removed by a series of long, sweeping cuts. The circumference of the chest was 35½ inches and waist 28½ inches. The skin was light and some parts not much decomposed. The arms had been removed at the shoulder joint by several incisions from above downwards. The arm had been then disarticulated through the joint. The body appeared to be wrapped up in a very skilful manner. The woman was about 25 years of age, but there was no evidence of her having nourished a child. The date of death he judged to be between six weeks and two months ago. The arm brought to the mortuary corresponded with the trunk of the body. The hands indicated that the woman had not been used to manual labour. The wounds were made after death. There was nothing to indicate the cause of death, but in his opinion it was not due to drowning or suffocation. The height of the woman would be about 5ft 8in. The parts missing from the victims of the recent Whitechapel murders were also absent from the trunk. Dr. Hibberd, assistant to the last witness, said he had examined the arm referred to. It had been separated from the body after death. The cut in the skin and bone exactly corresponded to those on the trunk. A certain amount of skill was shown in severing the limbs and in tying up the parcel, but not the skill of the dissecting room. Inspector Marshal, Criminal Investigation Department, said the dress material in which the trunk was found was cheap and an old pattern. The inquest was adjourned for a fortnight.*

The Hull Daily Mail, October 9th 1888,

> THE LONDON ATROCITIES. ANOTHER RUMOURED OUTRAGE ON A WOMAN IN LONDON. A POLICE CONSTABLE STABBED. The Press Association says that on Monday evening the police at Eyre-street Hill, Clerkenwell, were informed early this morning that a man had assaulted a woman in the neighbourhood.- Detective Sergeant Robinson of the G Division,

having been informed that the man had entered a cab-yard in Phoenix-place, borrowed a cloak and hat and secreted himself behind some cabs. Some Italians afterwards entered the yard to see if he had been successful in capturing the man, when some men employed in the yard went up to the sergeant and demanded to know what he wanted. Then he told them he was a police officer and they went away; but afterwards two other men came up and told the officer to clear out as they were going to protect their masters property. One of them struck him a violent blow on the face, and taking from his pocket a knife stabbed the officer in the face, while the other man kicked him. The officer called out that he was stabbed, and a young man named Henry Doncaster came to his assistance. Doncaster also was assaulted and stabbed. Police assistance arriving, two men were arrested and taken to King's [illegible] road Police Station, were the injuries of Robinson and Doncaster were dressed by the police surgeon. PRISONERS BEFORE THE MAGISTRATES. At the Clerkenwell Police Court this morning, James Phillips, aged 37, and William Jarvis, aged 40 cab washers, were charged with being concerned in cutting and wounding Henry Doncaster at the same time and place. Both prisoners had blood stained bandages on their head, and Robinson had cuts on the nose and forehead. Robinson detailed the circumstances under which he followed a suspected man into a cab-yard in Phoenix place. Witness was dressed in a woman's hat and mantle. Prisoners came into the yard, and he explained his presence there, whereupon Jarvis drew a pocket knife and stabbed him in the face, and the other prisoner kicked him. He had used his staff in self-defence, - Henry Doncaster, who had his hand bandaged, said he was also watching a suspected person in a cab yard. Both prisoners said they were protected their masters property. Dr Maller described the wounds received, and said those on Robinson and Doncaster could not have been caused by a sharp instrument.- They might have been caused by a blunt handle of a knife. The prisoners were remanded for a week. Bail was asked for, but the magistrate declined to grant it. MORE ARRESTS. Another arrest on suspicion was made in Clerkenwell on Monday night in connection with the Whitechapel murder, but the man was afterwards liberated. This morning a well-dressed man was seen walking about Covent Garden Market carrying a small black bag. He was taken to Bow-street, and after explaining his business was discharged. THE DISCOVERY OF KNIVES. The Press Association says that the man who left three knives at the Bull's Head Tavern, Oxford-street called for them last night, and a detective being in waiting, he was arrested. He was taken to Bow-street but after satisfactorily accounting for himself, he was discharged. TRYING BLOODHOUNDS IN HYDE PARK. Mr George Krehl has communicated to the Evening News, London, some interesting details of a trial of bloodhounds made at the direction

Mike Covell

> *of Sir Charles Warren in Hyde Park this morning. Two hounds belonging to Mr Edwin Brough, were obtained, and at 7 a.m. Sir Charles Warren met them and their keeper at the Albert Gate. Sir Charles offered to act as the hunted man, and set off towards Bayswater. After he went out of sight the dogs were released, and after making one or two faults where the track had been crossed they [illegible] their man. Another of the party next gave a run of 700 yards, and the hounds successfully found it. These hounds will be kept ready where they can be summoned instantly, and reach Whitechapel in less than half an hour.*

The Hull Daily Mail, October 9th 1888,

> *THE THIEVES "CANDLES" THEORY. The Standard's Vienna correspondent, telegraphing on Monday night, states that Dr. Bloch, a member of the Austrian Reicherath or the Galician constituency of Kokomea, has called his attention to certain facts which may throw a new light on the Whitechapel murders, and perhaps afford some assistance in tracing the murderer. In various German criminal codes of the seventeenth and eighteenth centuries, as also in Statutes of a more recent date, punishments are prescribed for the mutilation of female corpses, with the object of making from the uterus and other organs the so called Diebslichler or Schlafslichter, respectively "thieves' candles" or "soporific candles." According to an old superstition, still rife in various parts of Germany, the light from such candles will throw those upon whom it falls into the deepest slumbers, and they may, consequently, become a valuable instrument to the thieving profession. Hence their name. In regard to these "schlafslichter," quite a literature might be cited. They are referred to by Ave Lallement in his "Das Deutsche Gaunerthum" published in Leipzig in 1858; by Loffler, in "Die Mangelhafte Justiz" by Thiele, and numerous others. They also played an important part in the trials of robber bands at Odenwald and in Westphalia, in the years 1812 and 1841 respectively. The "schlafslichter" were heard of, too, at the trial of the notorious German robber, Theodor Unger, surnamed "the handsome Charley," who was executed at Magdeburg in 1810. It was on that occasion discovered that a regular manufactory had been established by gangs of thieves for the production of such candles. That this superstition has survived among German thieves to the present day was proved by a case tried at Biala, in Galicia, as recently as 1875. In this the body of a woman had been found mutilated in precisely the same way as were the victims of the Whitechapel murderer. At that trial, as at one which took place subsequently at Zeszow, which is also in Galicia, and in which the accused were a certain Ritter and his wife, the prevalence among thieves of superstition was alluded to by the Public Prosecutor. In the Ritter case, however, the Court preferred harping on another*

alleged superstition of a ritual character among the Jews of Galicia, which, however, was shown to be a pure invention of the Judenhettzer. Dr. Bloch, who for ten years was a rabbi in Galicia and has made the superstitions of that province his special study, affirms that the "thieves' candle" superstition still exists among robbers of every confession and, as he believes, also of every nationality. He considers, however, that it prevails most among German thieves. Among other German laws where the crime in question is dealt with, the "Code Theresiana," chap. xxii., clause 59, may be referred to.

The York Herald, October 9th 1888,

HULL POLICE REPORTS. MONDAY(Before Mr. T. W. Palmer and Mr. E. Lambert). EMULATING "JACK THE RIPPER" Samuel Noble, a mulatto, was charged with being disorderly on in Adelaide Street, on Saturday night. P.C. Leonard said he saw prisoner behaving in a strange manner, and on going up to him he ascertained that he had been annoying some woman by calling out he was "Jack the Ripper." He had thrown one woman's clothes over her head, after which he had molested another woman, who fell fainting to the ground. He was, therefore, arrested, and he became so violent a waggonette was obtained to convey him. To the police station. The magistrates considered the case a bad one, and imposed a penalty of 40s, and costs. – A young man named Patrick McDermott was charged with being drunk and disorderly on Saturday night. Prisoner had been flourishing a short thick stick and frightening pedestrians by declaring he was "Jack the Ripper." He approached a constable, who took him into custody. Prisoner stated that he had been in Prestwich Asylum. Fined 5s and costs.

October 10th 1888

The Eastern Morning News, October 10th 1888

THE WHITECHAPEL MYSTERIES. TWO MORE TRAGEDIES. HORRIBLE MUTILATIONS. The Central News says: The sensations of horror and fear inspired by the awful crime committed in Hanbury-street on the morning of the 8th of September had begun to subside; people had ceased suspecting their neighbours, and the seething population of the East of London was fast settling down to its normal condition of dogged industry and apathetic misery, when popular dismay and terror were revived and intensified by the discovery of two more murders committed in one night, and to all appearances the work of one fiendish hand. For a while people would not credit the appalling news, but ample confirmation was quickly forthcoming. The wretched and abandoned frequenters of the streets fled in terror to their miserable shelters, and by half-past two not a woman was to be seen throughout the densely populated district. Unhappily, the circumstances connected with the murders committed on Saturday night (or early Sunday morning) do not differ materially from those which marked their predecessors, except perhaps that the Mitre-square crime was perpetrated with a bestial ferocity, a reckless daring, and a rapidity exceeding that exhibited by the fiend who despatched and mutilated poor Annie Chapman in the gloomy backyard in Hanbury-street on the 8th of September. THE MITRE-SQUARE MURDER. MITRE-SQUARE is a sort of yard about 120 feet square. There are three entrances to it, the principal being from Mitre-street, which is broad enough to accommodate two vehicles abreast. There is also a short covered court, about 30 yards long, leading into St. James's-place, another square popularly known as the Orange Market, in the centre of which is a urinal, a street fire-station (consisting simply of a waggon on wheels), and also a permanent street fire-station in course of erection. There is also a fire-escape there at night, and three men of the Metropolitan Brigade are always on duty until daylight. Another passage, 30 or 40 yards long, open to the sky, and known as Church-passage, leads into Duke-street. Two sides of Mitre-square are occupied by warehouses of Messrs Kearley and Tonges, tea and coffee merchants, and a private house occupied by a City constable named Pearce. The third side is occupied by the warehouse of Messrs Horner and Sons, drug merchants. On the fourth side – where the roadway leads into Mitre-street – one corner is occupied by Messrs Walter Williams and Co., and the opposite corner is used as a workshop, and is locked up at night. Next to it are three empty houses, the backs of which look into the square. During business hours the square is extensively used; but after six o'clock it is comparatively deserted, and, according to people in the vicinity, it is about as quiet a place as could be found in the City of London. It may be added that the square is well lighted, there being one standard lamp in the square itself, another fixed to the wall at the left-hand entrance from Mitre-street, a third at the corner of the court at St. James's-place end, and two more fixed in the wall in Church-passage, one being placed at each end, so that altogether there are five lamps throwing their light into the square. DISCOVERY OF THE VICTIM. At a quarter to two o'clock yesterday (Sunday) morning, City Constable Watkins (881), was on his beat, and, as he passed through Mitre-square, he saw a body lying on the south-west corner. He had passed through the square about fifteen minutes previously, and he is certain that then there was no body there. The corpse was that of a woman, and it was lying on its back in the corner on the footway, with the head towards a hoarding and the feet to the carriage way. The head was inclined on the left side, and both the arms were extended outwards; the left leg was extended straight out, and the right leg was bent away from the body. After the first shock of discovery, the constable bent down and felt the body, which he found to be quiet warm. Blood was all around the body, but it was not congealed. Watkins immediately ran across to George James Norris, a night-watchman, in the employ of Messrs Kearley, and sent him to Dr Signeira's, at 34, Jewry-street, and then proceeded to call up Constable Pearce, who, as before mentioned, lives in one of the houses in the square itself. AN AWFUL SPECTACLE. The constables then returned to the south west corner, and, throwing the light of their lanterns fully upon it, found to their horror that the woman's throat was cut from ear to ear, and half-way round the head. The clothes had been raised up to the chest, and – more horrible still – the body had been completely ripped from the pelvis right up to the chest, the flaps of flesh being turned back and revealing intestines. In addition to these fearful injuries, a portion of the right ear was cut off, and the nose was slashed half-way through; the face was also slashed and cut about in the most dreadful fashion, and a portion of the intestines was also placed on the neck. MEDICAL AND OFFICIAL EXAMINATION. Dr Signeira arrived at five minutes to two o'clock, and shortly after that time Major Smith (Assistant Chief Commissioner of the City Police), Detective Inspector McWilliam (Chief of the City Detective Department), Superintendent Forster, and Inspector Collard, of the Bishopsgate-street Station, were on the spot. They had been preceded, however, by Dr Brown, surgeon to the City Police Force, while Dr Phillips, of Spital-square, surgeon to the "H" Division of the Metropolitan Police, who had previously examined the body of the woman found in Berners-street (concerning which particulars follow) was also present. The doctors proceeded at once to make an examination of the body. It was lying in a pool of blood which had flowed from the terrible wound in the throat, and there was also a considerable quantity round the abdomen. The ground around was eagerly examined by the police, but it soon became clear that the murderer had carefully avoided treading in the blood, and consequently no footmarks could be seen. At the conclusion of this preliminary examination, the body was removed to the City Mortuary in Golden-lane, where in the course of the afternoon an exhaustive post-mortem examination was made. As soon as the corpse had been removed from Mitre-square, the south-west corner was carefully washed down, in order to disappoint morbid sightseers, and it was not long before all traces of the awful crime had been removed. A sketch of the place was also made under the direction of the police in charge of the case. The following is the official description of the body and clothing: - "Age about 40, length five feet, dark auburn hair, hazel eyes, black jacket with imitation fur collar, three large metal buttons, brown bodice, dark green chintz (with Michaelmas daisy and garden lily pattern), skirt (three flounces), think white vest, light drab linsey underskirt, dark green alpaca petticoat, white chemise, brown ribbed stockings (mended at feet with piece of white stocking), black straw bonnet trimmed with black beads and green and black velvet, large white handkerchief round neck, a pair of men's old lace boots and piece of coarse white apron. The deceased had "T.C." on the left fore-arm, tattooed in blue ink." TRAGEDY IN BERNERS-STREET. The second of these tragedies of Sunday morning was committed in Berners-street, and this, the Central News says, as far as can be ascertained at present, leaves little doubt as to its having been done by the same assassin or assassins who committed the others. The scene of this murder is Berners-street, Commercial-road, on the St. George's in-the-East side, and within about 200 yards of Buck's-row or Hanbury-street, where the two previous murders took place. THE DISCOVERY. About five minutes to one o'clock yesterday morning, a youth about 20 years of age named Joseph Koster was met by a little boy who came running up to him as he was passing on the opposite side of 40 Berner-street (used by the International Socialist Club), and was told by him that a woman was lying in the gateway next to the club with her throat cut. Koster immediately ran across the road, and saw a woman lying on her side in the gateway leading into Dutfield's stabling and van premises. The gate, which is a large wooden one, was partly opened, and partly opened, and partly in the street. He immediately roused the neighbours, and, by the aid of a candle it was seen that the woman's throat was cut open very nearly from one ear to another, and her lips were drawn up as if she had suffered sharp pain. She was dressed in black, and appeared to be in mourning. She wore a black bonnet, elastic sided boots, and dark stockings; in her breast was a small bouquet of flowers, and in her left hand she held a small packet of scented cachous. Constable Lamb (252), East Division, soon afterwards appeared, and with the assistance of two other constables, had the body (which was quiet warm when found) removed to 40, Berners-street, where it was placed in a back room. To all appearances, the woman seems to have been taken into this stabling yard for an immoral purpose, and, after having been treated like the former victims, carried out and laid openly in the street. The case, in fact, resembles in many points the Bucks-row tragedy. She appears to have been about 28 years of age, and it is not thought that she belonged to the locality in which she was found. The wound must have been inflicted with a very sharp instrument – no trace of which has yet been found – as it was very deep, and she was lying in a pool of blood, with which her clothes were saturated. EXAMINATION BY DETECTIVES AND DOCTORS. The news of the tragedy fled with great rapidity, and a large number of detectives from Scotland-yard, together with superintendents and inspectors of police, were soon on the spot. All those who were near the place at the time were detained, taken in the house, and closely examined as to the discovery, but nothing has yet been obtained which can afford a clue to the murder, and the police have nothing whatever to go on. None of the woman in the district who saw the body knew the woman, and it was some time before she was identified. Dr Blackhall and his assistant examined the corpse and pronounced that the woman must have been murdered, as she could not have taken her own life. Dr Phillips (who, it will be remembered, examined the woman found in Hanbury-street) was also called in, and made an examination of the woman, but he was ordered to keep the result secret at present. A THEORY. The affair naturally created a great sensation throughout London, and the only surmise which can be given at present is that the woman was taken from a respectable district to Whitechapel, and there murdered by the author of the former atrocities. Her name was Elizabeth Stride, and she, it seems, had been living a "gay life," and had lodged latterly in Flower and Dean-street. She was identified by a sister living in Holborn. NARRATIVES. Lewis Diemshitz, the steward of the International Working-men's Club, in the yard of which the murder was committed made the following statement to a Central News reporter:- "I am a traveller in the common jewellery trade, working for myself alone. I have been steward of this club for some six or seven years, and I live on the premises. It has been my habit for some time past to go on Saturdays to Westow Hill, Crystal Palace, where there is a market, at which I sell my wares. This (Sunday) morning I got back from Westow Hill as the usual about one o'clock. I drove up to the gate of the club house in my little cart, drawn by a pony. After being all day at the market my pony inclined to shy a little, and it struck me when I was passing through the double gates into the yard that he wanted to keep too much to the left side against the wall. I couldn't make out what was the matter, so I bent my head to see if there was anything to frighten him. Then I noticed that there was something unusual about the ground, but I could not tell what it was except that it was not level. I mean that there was something like a little heap, but I thought it was only mud or something of the kind, and did not take much notice of it. However, I touched it with my whip handle, and then I was able to tell that it was not mud. I wanted to see what it was, so jumped out of the trap and struck a match. Then I saw that there was a woman lying there. At that time I took no further notice, and did not know whether she was drunk or dead. All I did was to run indoors and ask where my misses was, because she is of weak constitution, and I did not want to frighten her. I found that my wife was sitting downstairs, and I then told some of the members in the club, that something had happened in the yard, but I did not say whether the woman was murdered or only drunk. One of the members, who is known as Isaacs, went out with me. We struck a match and saw blood running from the gate all the way down to the side *door of the club. We had the police sent for at once, but I believe it was several minutes before a constable could be found. There was another member of the club named Eagle, who also ran out to get a policeman. He went in a different direction to the other, and managed to find two officers somewhere in Commercial-road. One of them was 252H. An officer blew his whistle and several more policemen came. One of them was sent for a doctor, Dr Phillips the police surgeon, of Spital-square, and Dr Kaye, of Blackwall, both came. The police afterwards took names of all the members of the club, and they say that all of us have to give evidence about it. Having been asked to describe the body as well as he could, Diemshitz said: I should think the woman was about 27 or 28 years old. I fancy she was of a light complexion. (This turns out to be incorrect description but the man was too frightened to make a careful examination) It seemed to me that her clothes were in perfect order. I could see that her throat was fearfully cut. There was a great gash in it over two inches wide. She had dark clothes on, and wore a black crape bonnet. Her hands were clenched, and when the doctor opened them I saw that she had been holding grapes in one hand and sweetmeats in the other. I could not say whether or not she was an unfortunate, but if she was I should judge her to be of a rather better class than the woman we usually see about this neighbourhood. I don't think anybody in this district, and certainly none of our members, had ever seen her before. The police removed the body to Cable-street Mortuary. When I first saw the woman she was lying on her left side. Her left hand was on the ground, and the right was crossed over her breast. Her head was down the yard, her feet towards the entrance, and more than about a yard or so inside the gates, I keep my pony and trap inside the gates. But I went down to the club first to deposit my goods there. The man Diemshitz is a Russian Jew, but he is an intelligent person, and speaks English fairly well. A man named Morris Eagle, also a Russian Jew, says "I frequent this club, and I was passing into it so late as twenty minutes to one on Sunday morning, which was just 20 minutes before the body was discovered. I had been there early on the evening, but left about 12 o'clock in order to take home my young lady. When I returned, I came along the small streets in the district, but noticed nothing unusual. There were a number of men and women about, as there are about that time, but the streets were more lively than usual, and I saw nothing suspicious when I got back to the club in Berner-street, the front door was closed, and so I passed through the gate on the left hand side of the house to get in by the side door. I went over the same ground as Diemshitz did later on, but I saw nothing on the ground. The gates were thrown wide back. In fact, it is very seldom that they are closed. It is customary for members of the club to go in by the side door to prevent knocking at the front. There is no light in the yard, but of course there are lamps in the streets. After I* got into the club there was some singing, and after I had been in some 20 minutes a man came in, and said something about a woman being in the yard. I went and struck a match, and then I could see there was blood on the ground. I heard someone calling for the police, and I ran into Commercial-road. I found two officers at the corner of Christian-street, and told them what was the matter. When one of the policemen saw the blood, he sent his companion for a doctor. In the meantime I went straight to Leman-street, and called out an inspector. I did not notice the appearance of the woman because the sight of the blood upset me, and I could not look at it. A young Russian Pole, named Isaac M. Kozebrodski, born in Warsaw, and who spoke the English language imperfectly, gave the following information:- I was in the club last night, I came in about half past six in the evening, and I had not been away since about twenty minutes to one on Sunday morning. Mr Diemshitz called me out into the yard, and told me to come and see what it was. When we got outside he struck a match, and when we looked down on the ground we could see a long stream of blood. It was running down the gutter from the direction of the gate, and reached to the back door of the club, I should think there was blood in the gutter for a distance of five or six yards. I went to look for a policeman at the request of Diemshitz, or some member of the club, but I took the direction towards the Grove-street, and could not find one. I afterwards went into the Commercial-road, and there, along with Eagle, found two officers. The officers did not touch the body, but sent for a doctor. A doctor came, and an inspector arrived just afterwards. While the doctor was examining the body, I noticed she had some grapes in her right hand and some sweets in her left. I think she wore a dark and black dress. I saw a little bunch of flowers stuck above her right bosom. Joseph Lave, a man just arrived in England from the United States, and who was living temporarily at the club until he could find lodgings, says: "I was in the club card this morning about 20 minutes to one. I came out first at half past 12 to get a breath of fresh air. I passed out into the street, but did not see anything unusual. The district appeared to me to be quite. I remained out until 20 minutes to one, and during that time no one came into the yard. I should have seen anybody moving about there. THE LOCALITY. The yard in which the body was found is about 10 feet wide. This width is continued for a distance of eight or ten yards, at which point there occurs on the left hand side a small row of houses, which are set back a little, so that the width is increased by two feet or more. The extreme length of the court is 30 yards, and it terminates in a workshop, which is at present being used as a dwelling house. The spot where the murder was committed, therefore, is overlooked on three sides, and insomuch as the gates were open last night, any casual pedestrian might easily have seen the commission of the crime. The windows of the club room are within 10 feet of the spot, while the cottages stand *almost opposite and command a complete view of it. None of the occupants of these houses, however, heard the faintest noise in the course of Saturday night or Sunday morning. The residents in the yard are tailors and cigarette makers, and they are not in the habit of retiring very early. A reporter who made inquiry amongst them, however, was unable to find any person who had either seen or heard anything suspicious. The club spoken of is occupied by what is known as the National Workmen's Educational Society, and is affiliated to the Socialist League, of which it is a foreign league. Its members seem to be largely composed of Russian Jews, and Jews of other nationalities also find a welcome there. Many of them live on the premises, which, however, are not extensive. At the back there is a fair sized hall, made by demolishing partition between two rooms, and here on Saturday night the numbers gather for the purpose of debate and amusement. On Saturday night the debate was largely attended by Germans, nearly a hundred being at one time in the room. The subject of discussion was- "Is it necessary that a Jew should be a Socialist?" It is proved so interesting that it was carried on to a late hour. After it had terminated there was a concert, at which 60 persons remained. There was considerable singing, and there is no doubt that the noise would have drowned any outcry which might have been made by the wretched creature who was being murdered in the yard beneath. Berner-street is in a very notorious part of Whitechapel. It is close to a district which was formerly known as Tigers Bay, because of the ferocious character of the desperados who frequented it. A few yards distant is the house wherein Lipsky murdered Miriam Angel, and the neighbourhood generally has an evil repute. During the course of yesterday thousands of persons congregated in the vicinity of the scene of the crime, and it was with the greatest of difficulty that the police could keep the street clear. The bulk of the residents are Jews. At the back of the Workingmen's Club there is a Jewish paper published called the Workmen's Friend, which is printed in Hebrew. Shops and lodging homes kept by Jews are very frequently met with. THEORIES. The body of the murdered woman, which now lies in St George's mortuary, close to St George's Parish Church, presents a dreadful spectacle, it is the corpse of a woman about 40 years of age, and lies on a slab, exhibits prominently a fearful wound on the throat. The head is slightly thrown to the right, and the gaping orifice is so clearly scooped out that the divisions of the jugular vein and the windpipe can be easily seen. The knife or other implement with which the deed was committed must have been of large size, and very keen. The wound is so wide that there is room for supposition that after the blade was inserted it was partially turned, then drawn with great force from the left to the right. The vertebrae of the neck was scraped, owing to the great force with which the weapon was wielded, and it is obvious that if the murderer had not been interrupted the poor creature* would have been hideously mangled, for the savagery of her assailant is evidenced not alone by the terrible wound in the throat, but also by two severe contusions on the head, one on the temple, the other cheek, which seems to point to the conclusion that he was proceeding to further outrage when some chance incident alarmed him and caused him to desist from his infamous work. With the exception of the injuries mentioned, the body bore no sign of ill usage. The woman has the appearance of an unfortunate, but not one of the worst class. Her black curly hair had been well combed, and tied up. Her underclothing was clean, and her two petticoats and black frock were good, although old. She had a black alpacca frock, a black jacket, trimmed with fur, an old velveteen body, once black, but now brown, and a crape bonnet, with some rare space which had been filled up by a current copy of a London evening newspaper, white stockings, white stays, and side spring boots. The bodice of the woman was open, exposing her chest, and the theory built upon this circumstance is the assassin was intending to HACK HER STOMACH but could not carry out his purpose. In the pockets were found two handkerchiefs- one a man's, the other a woman's- and a thimble and a skein of black worsted. There were no rings on the fingers. In her jacket was pinned a small bunch of roses and ferns. Her hair was matted with wet dirt, showing that a struggle had taken place on the ground. It is not believed, however, that the woman was in a recumbent position when attacked, the theory being that her murderer was standing with his left arm around her neck, and that while so placed he drew a knife and inflicted a mortal wound. The position of the body, when found, favours this view, insomuch as no attempt had been made to disarrange the clothing. The woman was lying in an almost natural attitude. ACTION OF THE POLICE. After the police authorities had been notified of the murder the case was given into the hands of Chief Inspector Swanson and Inspector Abberline, of Scotland yard. In the first instance the police turned their attention to the Working Men's Club. The doors were guarded and no person was allowed egress. After the body had been removed to St George's Mortuary the detectives entered the club, and made careful examination of the inmates. Their pockets were searched, their hands and clothing particularly scrutinized. Some of them allege that they were made to take off their boots. All knives had to be produced, and each man had to give an account of himself before he was allowed to depart. Some of the members say that the detective treated them badly, swearing at them, and shouting "You're no foreigners, or else where's your knives." As a matter of fact, however, the police found nothing suspicious in the club or upon its members, and in the late morning surveillance was withdrawn. Some of the neighbours were also subjected to investigation, but no clue was found. It may be mentioned here that the police discovered no blood splashes upon the wall in the yard. They caused *the blood which had flown down the gutter to be removed at an early hour. The information of the crime reached Leman-street Police Station at 10 minutes past one o'clock, and Dr Philips, of 2, Spital-grove, the divisional police surgeon, was immediately communicated with. After he had made an external examination of the body it was removed to St, George's Mortuary, where the post mortem will be made to-day. In the course of yesterday Sir Charles Warren, the Chief Commissioner of Police visited the scene of the murder. The police have no clue to the murderer, nor do they profess any hope of discovering one. He has disappeared without leaving a trace of the faintest kind, and there is nothing whatever upon which the detectives can work. A woman' apron was found in Goulston street, which is believed to have belonged to the deceased woman. It is suggested therefore that the murderer travelled to Mitre square, the scene of the second murder, by way of Goulston street, and took away the apron for the purpose of cleansing his weapon upon it. In consequence of the many murders in the locality the police force at Leman street and Commercial street Stations, as well as the adjacent stations, has recently been augmented from King street, Scotland Yard, and other centres. This has been done as a matter of precaution, as in some quarters a disposition is manifested to cast upon the Jewish population of the neighbourhood the responsibility for the murders. The following is a description of a man stated to have been seen in company with the woman murdered in Berner street, and for whom the police are looking:- "Age 28, height 5ft 8in., complexion dark, no whiskers, black diagonal coat, hard felt hat, collar and tie, carried a newspaper parcel, was of respectable appearance." In the case of both of the murders committed yesterday morning the assassin had a very narrow escape from detection. The evidence that is forthcoming establishes the fact that the murderer commenced operations first in Berner street. Here the murder was committed as near as possible at 1 o'clock, and it is very probable that the man was proceeding to the commission of further outrages when he was disturbed by the arrival of Diemshitz, the steward of the club, who drove into the yard under the circumstances related elsewhere. Having failed in his purpose, which as in other cases appears to have been to secure certain portions of the body, he betook himself towards the city, and in Mitre court his second victim was done to death. Police beats in the city are considerably shorter than in the Metropolitan district, every beat being patrolled each ten minutes or quarter of an hour. None of the men on duty in the neighbourhood noticed anything suspicious in the course of the night, the neighbourhood being a particularly quiet one. Had Watkins, the policeman on the beat, been five minutes earlier, eh must inevitably have caught the murderer red-handed, as the deed had not been done more than a few minutes before he discovered it. Watkins has been in the city police a number of years, and is looked upon as a thoroughly reliable and trustworthy officer. There is a police constable actually residing in Mitre square - a man named Pearce, who says that he went to bed before 12 o'clock, and was only aroused when Constable Watkins called him up. He heard nothing whatever of the occurrence. Inquiries were made in the publichouses in the neighbourhood with a view of ascertaining whether any suspicious characters had been seen there drinking with a woman, but no clue could be obtained. Some of the inhabitants of the district have started the theory that in the case of the murder in Mitre court the woman was first chloroformed. The supposition is not sustained by any evidence, and probably promulgated merely as an explanation of the silence in which the deed was perpetrated. The scenes of both murders were guarded throughout the day by a number of policemen, who allowed no one to pass through the barriers. Curious crowds colleted at various points of interest, and they were followed in turn by scores of hawkers and fruit vendors, who drove a thriving trade. Mr Wynne Baxter, the Coroner for East Middlesex, has fixed the inquest on the woman murdered in Berner street for to-morrow (Monday), at 11 a.m., at the Vestry Hall, St. George's. Although up to this time the police are without a clue, it is hoped that now the city police have the matter in hand as well as the metropolitan that the murderer may be arrested. Mitre square is a thoroughfare leading out of Aldgate, and so comes under the surveillance of the city authorities, who are now for the first time actively interested in the East End murders. Berner street is within a stone's throw of Hanbury street where the woman Annie Chapman was recently murdered, and adjacent also to Buck's row, where Mary Anne Nichols met her death, and to Osborne street, wherein still another of the unfortunates was shamefully mutilated. It lies to the right of Commercial road going east, and is about eight minutes' walk from Mitre square. Therefore it is seen that the murderer has confined his operations to a radius of about a quarter of a mile, and it is within that area that the police expect to find him, if, indeed, he be ever found. The city police adopt the view that the miscreant for whom they are searching is a man of a different class to that which he has hitherto been supposed to have been a member. They point to a fact that women of the street obviously yield readily to his solicitation, and draw the inference that he is a person of respectable appearance, and by no means the rough uncouth creature which the popular imagination has depicted him.*

Up to half-past 7 last evening the police had no clue except the discovery of the woman's apron mentioned elsewhere, which apron, by the way, has turned out to belong to the woman murdered in Mitre square, nor had either of the dead persons been identified. A strong opinion was expressed in the neighbourhood that the Government should be appealed to on the question of offering a substantial reward for the discovery of the murderer. This, it is thought, would put the whole of the residents on the alert, and lead them to keep a sharp look out each upon the doings of his neighbour, and to report to the police any suspicious proceedings. In view of the identification of the apron belonging to the woman murdered in Mitre square, it appears that the murderer must have gone to his home by way of Goulston street, and so lives in all probability in the district between Houndsditch and Commercial street. This neighbourhood is being closely watched as well as other portions of the district, and a large number of extra police and detectives have been placed on duty. The post-mortem examination of the woman found in Mitre-square was made this afternoon at the City Mortuary, Golden lane. The proceedings lasted from 2.30 until 6 o'clock. Dr. Brown, of 17 Finsbury Circus, surgeon to the city police force, conducted the operations, and was assisted by Dr. Sequeiras, of 34 Jewry street, and Dr. G. B. Phillips, of 2 Spital square. Dr. Sedgwick Saunders was also present. The doctors decline to say whether any portion of the body is missing or to give any information as to the autopsy until the inquest is held. This will probably be on Tuesday at the mortuary in Golden lane. During the day the police thoroughly searched the empty houses in Mitre street, and also the yard where the body was found, and took up a grating near the spot where the woman was discovered. Nothing, however, in the shape of a weapon was found, nor did the investigations lead to anything likely to throw light upon the matter. The public were not admitted to the square until late in the afternoon, after an official plan of the square had been made for production at the inquest. Up to a late hour in the evening the woman had not been identified, although several people have been to the Bishopsgate street police station and have seen the clothing. Two women who inspected this and also saw the corpse were certain that it was the body of a woman named Jane Kelly, but subsequently on inquiries being made, it was found that this individual was alive. A man who saw the body said he was sure it was that of a woman known as "Phoebe the Jewess," but the inquiries in this case are not yet complete. A representative of the Central News last night visited Elizabeth Stride's last residence, No. 32, Flower and Dean-street, Spitalfields, a common lodging-house inhabited by men and women of the poorest kind. The female occupants were afraid to venture into the streets after sunset; but they were listening with eagerness to the information afforded them from time to time by male occupants arriving from the streets. Inquiries made among these people elicit the fact that the deceased, who was commonly known as "Long Liz," left Flower and Dean-street between six and seven o'clock on Saturday night. She then said that she was not going to meet anyone in particular. Stride is believed to be a Swedish woman, from

Stockholm. According to her associates she rarely quarrelled with anyone, ad was so good natured that she would "do a good turn for anyone." Her occupation was that of a charwoman. She lost her husband in the Princess Alice disaster on the Thames some years ago. She had lost her teeth, and suffered from a throat affection.

The Central News says:- On Thursday last the following letter bearing the E.C. postmark, and directed in red ink, was directed to this agency: 25th September 1888. Dear Boss, - I keep on hearing that the police have caught me, but they won't fix me just yet. I have laughed when they look so clever, and talk about being on the right track. The joke about Leather Apron gave me real fits. I am down on ------, and I shan't quit ripping them till I do get buckled. Grand work the last job. I gave the lady no time to squeal. How can they catch me now? I love my work and want to start again. You will soon hear of me and my funny little games. I saved some of the proper red stuff in a ginger beer bottle over the last job to write with, but it went thick, and I can't use it. Red ink is fit enough, I hope, ha, ha! The next job I do I shall clip the ladies' ears off and send them to the police officers, just for folly, wouldn't you? Keep this letter back till I do a bit more work, then give it out straight. My knife's so nice and sharp. I want to get to get a chance. Good luck. - Yours truly, JACK THE RIPPER. Don't mind me giving the trade name. Wasn't good enough to post this before I got all the red ink off my hands, curse it. No luck yet. They say I am a doctor. Ha! ha!

The whole of this extraordinary epistle is written in red ink in a free bold clerky hand. It was of course treated as the work of a practical joker, but it is singular to note that the latest murders have been committed within a few days of the receipt of the letter, that apparently in the case of his last victim the murderer made an attempt to cut off the ears, and that he did actually mutilate the face in a manner which he had never before attempted. The letter is now in the hands of the Scotland Yard authorities.

The Eastern Morning News, October 10th 1888,

THE LONDON TRAGEDIES. THE BERNER-STREET VICTIM. AN EXTRAORDINARY STORY. *The Central News says: - Notwithstanding the apparently conclusive evidence given at the inquest by Michael Kidney as to the identity of the Berner-street victim, many people believed that the poor creature was really Elizabeth Watts, formerly of Bath. It will be remembered that Mrs. Mary Malcolm, of Red Lion-square, swore positively that the deceased was her sister, Elizabeth Watts, and that she had last seen her on the Thursday preceding*

Mike Covell

> the murder. The Central News state that, as a result of inquiries prosecuted by them they have succeeded in finding Elizabeth Watts alive and well in the person of Mrs. Stokes, the hard-working respectable wife of a brickyard labourer, living at Tottenham. Mrs. Stokes says:- "My father was a publican in the village of Colerne, near Chippenham, Wiltshire. There were eight children in our family, four girls and four boys. I have one sister in New Zealand, and a brother still lives in Wiltshire, but I have no idea where the rest of the family are. My maiden name was Elizabeth Perrin. I have been married three times. My first husband was Mr. Watts, a wine merchant at Bath, to whom I was married at Bristol. My second husband's name was Speller, whom I married at Deal; and my third and present husband's name is Stokes, to whom I was married at St. Andrew's Church, New Kent-road, on December 15th, 1884. He has been employed lately at Plowman's Brickfield, Tottenham. Mrs. Malcolm, who gave evidence at the inquest, is my sister, but I have not seen her for years, and I do not expect to see her until I attend the adjourned inquest on the 23rd inst. My sister, Mary Malcolm, has never, as she swore, given me any money. It is untrue that I saw her on the Thursday preceding the murder. I was out washing that day at Mrs. Peterkin's laundry, near White Hart-lane. I never used to meet her, as she said, in Red Lion-street, to receive a shilling from her. I am not short of clothes, and I never lived in Commercial-road, nor kept a coffee house in Poplar. I may take a little drink now and then, but my sister never saw me in drink. My two children by my first husband, Watts, were taken from me, and that preys on my mind at times. I never quarrelled with my first husband. Watts's friends did not approve of our marriage on account of my being a poor girl. He was sent abroad, and died in America, leaving me with the two children, a boy and a girl. Where they are I do not know. Their father's friends took the children from me, and I was placed in the lunatic asylum of Fisherton House, near Salisbury. The relieving officer of Bath got me out and I then went to live as a domestic servant at Walmer. There I made the acquaintance of Speller, whom I afterwards married at Deal Church. He was engaged on a vessel in the Royal Navy, which was stranded on St. Paul's Island, and there he died. His half-pay was then stopped, and I was left destitute. Subsequently I was put in the Peckham Lunatic Asylum, under Dr. Stocker and Dr. Brown, because I endeavoured to gain possession of my two children, whom I have never seen or heard of since they were taken from me. The Lunacy Commissioners afterwards pronounced me to be sane, and I was again discharged, perfectly destitute. Owing to my troubles my memory is somewhat impaired. I married my present husband, Stokes, four years ago

The Hull Daily Mail, September 10th 1888,

THE HORRIBLE TRAGEDY IN WHITECHAPEL. LATEST PARTICULARS. A Press Association telegram, despatched at 9:45 this morning, states that there is practically nothing new up to this hour in regard to the shocking crime of Saturday morning. Although two or three men have been apprehended on suspicion, they have given satisfactory accounts and have been liberated. Inspector chandler, at Commercial-road Police Station, received information after midnight on Sunday that a person was detained at Deptford on suspicion. He proved to be a young man apprehended in the Old Kent Road, and his answers to interrogations being considered satisfactory, he was shortly afterwards released. At the time of this dispatch a number of people were standing around the police station in Commercial-street in expectation of anything transpiring in connection with the enquiries of the police. Although the police have made most diligent inquiry after the murderer of the woman, whose real name is Chapman, they had up to last night failed to find the slightest clue to his whereabouts. As a matter of fact, they are in the dark as to the personal appearance of the man for whom they are looking. It is true that they possess the description of a man who is known as "Leather Apron," and will arrest him if he can be found, but their theory is that "Leather Apron" is more or less a mythical personage, and that he is not responsible for the terrible crimes with which his name has been associated. All the same the details of his appearance have been widely circulated, with a view to his early apprehension. All the police in the vicinity are on the look-out for him. On Saturday night a large force of police constables and detectives closely watched the neighbourhood. Men were posted at all the entrances and exits of the numerous alleys and passages in the neighbourhood, who every few minutes made a thorough examination of the places under their surveillance, and from time to time these were visited by the Inspectors on duty, with a view to ascertaining whether any suspicious character had been observed. From ten o'clock at night until late in the morning a large crowd occupied Hanbury street, in the vicinity of the notorious house, No. 29. When the publichouses emptied the occupants swarmed into the street, causing a good deal of trouble to the police by their behaviour. The people living in the adjoining houses obtained no rest until between four and five o'clock, when the crowd gradually melted away, only, however, to reassemble again in greater force as soon as daylight appeared. In the course of Saturday night and Sunday morning the police arrested two men on suspicion of being concerned in the crime. One man, whose appearance left little doubt in the minds of his captors that he was the Hanbury street murder, was found by an officer in Buck's row shortly after 1 o'clock on Sunday morning. A murder was, it will be remembered, committed in the neighbourhood but a short time since, and the police have since been constantly pursuing their investigation in that quarter. The man upon whom suspicion rested presented a most forbidding appearance. He appeared to be hiding in the street, and when accosted by the officer, rushed off at the top of his speed. An alarm was raised, and after a short race he was arrested. He was a villainous-looking fellow with long hair and shaggy beard, dressed only in a pair of ragged blue serge trousers and an old dirty shirt. He resisted his captors, but was eventually secured and conveyed to Bethnal Green Police Station. It was said at the time that he was carrying a long knife concealed in the sleeve of his shirt, but on examination no weapon was found upon him. He gave an account of himself which was, in the first instance, considered unsatisfactory, but inquiries were immediately set on foot, and in the result the man, who appears to be a common vagrant, was released from custody. The second arrest was effected in Gloucester street, where a man aged about 40, having the look of a seafarer, was arrested. It was pretty obvious, however, from the replies which he gave, and his general appearance that he was not the man sought for, and after he had spent some time in Commercial street Station he was also set at liberty. It is suggested that the first mentioned man is the person who has been spoken of by Mrs Fiddymont, wife of the proprietor of the Prince Albert public-house, situate at the corner of Brushfield street and Stewart street. Mrs Fiddymont has stated to the police that at seven o'clock on Saturday morning a rough-looking man came into the place and got some ale. He presented an excited appearance, and some blood-spots were said to have been observed on his right hand. This man, however, had a coat and hat on. The police, however, who gave information very unwillingly, and who do not accept the theory that the crime has been committed by the man designated "Leather Apron," are indisposed to believe that the person seen by Mrs Fiddymont has any connection with the crime. They are unwilling, indeed, to accept assistance or suggestion from any private source and work upon a plan of their own, which consists of frequent visits to the common lodging-houses of the neighbourhood and a strict watch at night on all the streets in the vicinity. All day to-day five policemen have guarded the scene of the crime in Hanbury street. No one was admitted unless he lived in the house. In the street half a dozen costermongers took up their stand and did brisk business in fruit and refreshments. Thousands of respectably dressed persons visited the scene, and occasionally the road became so crowded that the constables had to clear it by making a series of raids upon the spectators. The windows of the adjoining houses were full of persons watching the crowd below. A number of people also visited the house in Dorset street where the murdered woman lodged. It may be mentioned here that the soldier who had frequently visited the woman at this place did not return to the house on Saturday night. The police, however, attach no importance to this circumstance. Inquiries have been made at Vauxhall and at Windsor where Chapman or

"Sievy," as she was more generally called, is said to have relatives, but so far without any fresh information obtained as to her antecedents. The deceased has been identified by persons who have known her since she has lived in London, but her relatives, if she possesses any, have not yet communicated with the police. The small portion of writing on the envelope found upon the body, bearing the stamp of the Sussex Regiment, has not yet been identified or traced. The authorities of St Bartholemew's Hospital, where the woman spent some time, have been communicated with, but they have not been able to afford any information of a useful character. The usually lively condition of Whitechapel and Spitalfields on a Sunday was considerably augmented to-day by reason of the excitement aroused by the murder. In the course of the day nearly a dozen persons were arrested, and conveyed to the Commercial street Police Station. In the afternoon a vast crowd had collected about the streets. As each apprehension was made they rushed pell mell towards the station, obviously under the idea that the murderer of the woman had been caught. Shortly before five o'clock a man was arrested in Dal street after a long chase on a charge of assault. The officer who arrested him proceeded with his prisoner by way of Hanbury street to the police station and so was obliged to make his way through the crowd. Outside the house his prisoner stood in some danger of being mobbed, but the crowd eventually gave way, and the prisoner was safely lodged in the station. A few minutes later two men were arrested in Wentworth street. As soon as the crowd saw them in the hands of the police there were loud cries of "Leather Apron," and thereupon hundreds of persons turned out from the side streets and followed the officers in a tumultuous throng to the station. Not five minutes afterwards a woman was apprehended on some small charge, and the excitement became so intense that a posse of officers was sent out from the building to preserve order. These marched three and four abreast up and down the pavement, and while they were so engaged yet another prisoner was brought in. There was a good deal of shouting in the mob, which surged about in a dangerous fashion, but by-and-bye a diversion was caused by the rapid passage along Banbury street of three men who were supposed to be two detectives and their prisoner. The centre man bore a striking resemblance to "Leather Apron," and the cry of "That's him," having been raised, a rush was made at him, but the little party immediately turned down a side street, and the police prevented the crowd from proceeding further. In the neighbourhood of the mortuary, which is situated in Eagle place, at the Whitechapel end of Hanbury street, all was quiet during the day. The green doors opened now and again to admit some inspectors of police and several medical gentlemen, but all others were rigidly excluded. The inquest on the body will be held to-morrow (Monday) by Dr MacDonald, the coroner for the district. Dr Phillips, the surgeon, and the witnesses who first

Mike Covell

> *discovered the body, will be called, and the police will also give certain evidence. Dr Phillips believes that the woman had been dead for two hours or more when she was discovered. It is a remarkable fact, however, that the man Richardson, who first went into the yard where the corpse was discovered says that he actually sat down on the step of the passage to cut a piece of leather off his shoe and yet did not see the body. This, however, may be explained by the circumstances that the passage door opens outward and toward the left, and so would conceal the body behind it. It is the custom to leave both of the passage doors open at night, and although they were found shut on the morning of the murder no suspicion was excited on that account. The advisability of employing bloodhounds to trace the perpetrator of the crime has been eagerly discussed by the inhabitants of the district. It is considered by experts that the time has gone by for such an experiment, and it is pointed out also that in the case of the Blackburn murderer, who was discovered by this means, the circumstances were different, and that the present case does not admit of that. To-night the police are posted in strong force throughout the neighbourhood. Their precautions are such that they consider it impossible that any further outrage can be perpetrated. The inhabitants of the place, however, although by day regarding the matter as one for discussion and excitement rather than serious regard, profess to fear that the miscreant will soon be at his dark work again, and that if he be captured at all he will be taken red handed in the commission of another horrible crime. A correspondent supplies the following: - Last night the Scotland yard authorities had come to a definite conclusion as to the description of the murderer of two of the women found dead at the East end, and the following is the official intimation sent to every Station throughout the Metropolis and suburbs:- "Commercial street, 8.20 p.m. - Description of a man wanted, who entered a passage of the house at which the murder was committed, with a prostitute, at 2.0 a.m., on the 8th. Age 37, height 5ft 7in, rather dark beard and moustache. Dress - Short, dark jacket, dark vest and trousers, black scarf, and black felt hat. Spoke with a foreign accent."*

October 11th 1888

The Hull Daily News, October 11th 1888,

> *THE WHITECHAPEL MURDERS. LATEST PARTICULARS. Upon inquiry at the principal police stations in the East End yesterday morning a reporter was informed that no further arrests had been made in connection with the murders in the district, and that there is now no one in custody on that charge. At all the stations matters were reported unusually quite- a state of affairs due in great*

measure, doubtless, to the elaborate system of patrols recently instituted by the police in the neighbourhood , and the disappearance of many of the most disorderly characters from the streets at a comparatively early hour, owing to the prevailing terror. Members of the vigilance committees lately instituted were also freely met with, while policeman and detectives in plain clothes were posted at various points within easy hail of each other in the event of an alarm being raised. The opinion generally expressed by the police and others on the watch for the murderer is that he will find the district too closely watched to allow him to repeat his terrible crime without detection, and that if heard of again it will be in some other part of the metropolis. A Liverpool correspondent states that the police there have no knowledge of the report which has been circulated that they were cognisant of the movements of a man suspected of being concerned in the Whitechapel murders. The head constable has, however, given instructions for the railway stations and departing steamers to be closely watched, but up to now there is no trace of the murderer so far as Liverpool is concerned. Notices of the rewards offered have been posted at Liverpool police courts. THE MURDERER ALLEGED TO BE KNOWN. A correspondent of the Central News in company with Dr Saunders, the medical superintendent, visited some of the wards of St Georges-in-the-East on Tuesday. He found the unfortunate women inmates in a state of great excitement over the Whitechapel murders. Not one of them would entertain fanciful theories respecting the identity and object of the murderer. They were positive the recent crimes have been the work of one man, who, by the descriptions given and anecdotes related, appears to be a street bully of a somewhat superior type. One woman, named Jenny, stated to Dr. Saunders that if she were well enough to get about she would soon find the identity of the man whom she is certain is the murderer. He frequently maltreated the women of the streets, and extorted money from them under threats of "Ripping 'em up." They had sometimes appealed to the police, with the only result of a terrible beating from the scoundrel the very next night. Jenny averred that every woman in the ward would be able to pick the man out of a thousand. She described him as a foreigner, about 40 years of age. She believed he had been a doctor. He dressed fairly well , and generally carried a big heavy stick. We believe the police have received more than one statement of this character from women of the street, and inquiries have been made with the view of testing their accuracy. But in each case the information obtained went to show that female fears had exaggerated the facts. The police, of course, have been careful to obtain the fullest information of the movements of the man suspected. ANOTHER OUTRAGE ON A WOMAN. Considerable excitement was caused in the neighbourhood of Blackfriars road, London, last evening by a report that another outrage had been committed on a woman in a narrow passage leading

> out of that thoroughfare. It appears that a woman's screams attracted the attention of passers-by, and two men were seen to run away and were pursued, but not captured. The woman had been thrown down and cuts inflicted on her face, but it is believed the injuries are not serious. The object of the attack was apparently robbery, for the woman's purse, containing about 18s. Was picked up near the spot. CLUES TO THE WHITEHALL MYSTERY. The medical evidence given at the inquest held on Monday on the headless and limbless body found at Whitehall has placed the police in possession of a description of a woman who was the subject of the horrible crime thus committed. A great many cases of missing women have been brought before the police, and the number has caused some embarrassment. Now, however, the police have before them the fact that the deceased woman was a plump woman of about 5ft, 8in, or 5ft, 9in, high; that she had suffered from pleurisy; that she was from 24 years of age upwards; that she had fair skin and dark hair; and that her hand, found with the arm at Pimlico, showed that she had not been used to hard work. Moreover, the police have the fact that the death may have been from six weeks to two months prior to the 2nd of October, which would bring the end of her life to about the 20th of August, and her death is defined as having been one which drained the body of blood. This last point means that wherever the woman met her death - and it was not in the water- the place would be marked with blood. Anxious search is being made for the missing head.

The Eastern Morning News, October 11th 1888,

> THE LONDON TRAGEDIES. THE MURDERER KNOWN. The Central News states that up to eleven o'clock to-night no further arrests were made in connection with the Whitechapel murders. A reporter who patrolled the East End districts this evening states that the popular excitement has already entirely subsided. More women have been on the streets than have been seen for weeks past, and there were no signs of special police precautions. It is understood, however, that the police have in no degree relaxed their vigilance and that the number of plain-clothes men and amateur patrols has not been reduced. A correspondent of the Central News, in company with Dr Saunders, the medical superintendent, visited some of the wards of the infirmary of St. George's-in-the-East yesterday, found the unfortunate women inmates in a state of great excitement over the Whitechapel murders. Not one of them would entertain fanciful theories respecting the identity and objects of the murderer. They were positive the recent crimes have been the work of one man, who, by the descriptions given and anecdotes related, appears to be a street bully of a somewhat superior type. One woman named Jenny stated to Dr. Saunders that if

she were well enough to get about she would soon find and identify the man who she is certain is the murderer. He frequently maltreated the women of the streets, and extorted money from them under threats of "ripping them up." They had sometimes appealed to the police, with the only result of a terrible beating from the scoundrel the very next night. Jenny said every woman in the ward would be able to pick the man out of a thousand. She described him as a foreigner about 40 years of age. She believed he had been a doctor. He dressed fairly well and generally carried a big heavy stick. The police have received more than one statement of this character from women of the street, and inquiries have been made with the view of testing their accuracy. But in each case the information obtained went to sow that female fears had exaggerated the facts. The police, of course, have been careful to obtain the fullest information of the movements of the man suspected. THE "JACK THE RIPPER" MANIA. A respectably dressed young man named Stephen Rorke was charged at Manchester yesterday with annoying and threatening a woman on the previous night. The woman was accosted by the prisoner on her road home, and on refusing to comply with his wishes, he said he was "Jack the Ripper," and threatened her. A man approached, and prisoner was then given into custody. The police stated that great terror existed among the woman, and that the streets were almost clear at night. Prisoner was remanded. THE GATESHEAD MURDER. William Waddel, suspected of murdering his sweetheart at Birtley, near Gateshead, was brought before the magistrates at Chester-le-street yesterday. An application to remand the prisoner till the conclusion of the adjourned inquest was granted. The examination will probably be resumed on the 25th inst.

October 12th 1888

The Hull Daily Mail, October 12th 1888,

THE LONDON HORRORS. THE MITRE SQUARE TRAGEDY. SUPPOSED DISCOVERY OF THE VICTIM'S HUSBAND. The Press Association says this morning a constable was called to the Duke of York public house, Clerkenwell Road, London, by the barman, who said a pensioner from the [illegible], named Conway, had entered the bar and asked the barman to sign some document to the effect that he had lost his pension papers. The barman, having noticed from the newspaper reports of the inquest on the victim of the Mitre Square murder that the police were looking for a pensioner of that name, who was believed to be the husband of the murdered woman, thought this might be the man. The constable took the man to Kings Cross Road Police station, and after being questioned he was removed to Bishopgate street police station, where he will be confronted with the relatives of the murdered woman. He is not, strictly speaking, under arrest; but it is thought that if he is the woman's former husband or paramour he may be able to throw light on her recent movements. The police, on examination found that the murdered woman's husband, was a much older man than the individual now detained, and without sending for Catherine Eddowes' sister they let the man go. ANOTHER SUSPECT AT THE EAST END. The police have under close observation in connection with the Whitechapel murders, a man now an inmate of the East End Infirmary, who was admitted since the murders began under suspicious circumstances. STRANGE ARREST IN BELFAST. EXTRAORDINARY EVIDENCE. Shortly before twelve o'clock on Thursday night a man, who gives his name as John Foster, was arrested in Belfast, on suspicions of being the Whitechapel murderer, and refusing to give account of himself. The prisoner, who was found lodging at the house of Samuel Beatty, Memel Street, had in his possession a bag containing a large knife and three razors. One of the latter bears marks of blood. The man is 30 years of age, 5ft, 8in, or 9in high, of slight build, and fair complexion, and is shabbily dressed. He also had close upon £20. He stated to the police that he has been in Belfast since last Sunday, Previously he was two days in Glasgow, and before that two days in Edinburgh; but he declines to give further information regarding himself. At Belfast Police court this morning John Foster, who was arrested on being suspicious of being concerned in the Whitechapel murders was brought up.- Constable Carrand deposed that from information received he went to Memel Street, and there found the prisoner, who gave the name of William John Foster, and said he had no place of residence. In reply to a question, he said he arrived in Belfast on Sunday evening, having previously been for two days at Greenock, and for four days previous to that at Glasgow, and still earlier at Edinburgh. A clasp knife was found on him, and in a bag were three razors, two knives and a number of watchmakers appliances. He said he was a watchmaker. He had £19 in money, a watch with the monogram "A.M.R.," a locket, and a piece of a necklet. He wore boots similar to those worn by soldiers. The magistrates remanded him for a week for enquiries. THE ELTHAM ARREST. The police, having satisfied themselves that the casual arrested at Eltham Union, Kent, could have nothing to do with the Whitechapel murders, he will be set at liberty. AN OLD WOMANS TALE. A strange story is transmitted from Liverpool. On Wednesday evening a young lady was walking along Shiel Road, not far from Shiel Park, when she was stopped by an elderly woman, who, in an excited manner, urged her not to go into the park. She explained that a few minutes previously she had been resting on one of the seats in the park, when she was accosted by a respectable looking man, dressed in a black coat, light trousers, and a soft felt hat, who enquired if she knew if there

> were any loose woman about the neighbourhood, and immediately afterwards he produced a knife with a long thin blade, and stated that he intended to kill as many loose woman in Liverpool, as in London, adding that he would send the ears of the first victim to the editor of the Liverpool paper. The old woman stated that she was terribly frightened that she hardly knew how she got away from the man.

The Eastern Morning News, October 12th 1888,

> THE LONDON TRAGEDIES. THE MITRE SQUARE MURDER. INQUEST. – VERDICT. The inquest on the body of Catherine Eddowes, the victim of the Mitre-square murder, was resumed this morning before Mr. Langham, the city coroner, at the mortuary in Golden-lane. Colonel Sir James Fraser and Chief Superintendent Foster represented the police, and Mr. Crawford, City Solicitor, watched the case on behalf of the City authorities. There was again a great amount of interest taken in the proceedings, and a considerable number of persons assembled outside the mortuary. - Dr. G. W. Sequeira, of Dewry-street [sic], Aldgate, deposed that he was the first medical man to reach the body in Mitre-square on the morning of the 30th ult. He entirely agreed with the evidence given on the last occasion by Dr. Gordon Brown, but supplemented it by stating in answer to Mr. Crawford, that though the body was lying in the darkest corner of the square, the lamps would give light enough to enable the murderer to inflict the injuries. He did not regard it as probable that the murderer had designs on any particular organ, and did not consider that he performed the mutilations with any anatomical skill. Life could not have been extinct for more than a quarter of an hour when he first saw the corpse. The person who committed the deed need not necessarily have been bespotted with blood. - Dr. Sedgwick Saunders, city analyst, stated that he made a careful examination of the deceased woman's stomach, without, however, finding any trace of narcotic or other poisons. He supported the other doctors in the theory that anatomical skill was not shown by the murderer. - Annie Phillips, wife of a lamp black packer, living at 12, Dilston-park, Southwark Park-road, stated that she was the daughter of the deceased by Thomas Conway, to whom, her mother had always told her, she was married. He and her mother used to get on badly together because the latter used to drink, whereas he was a teetotaler. It was seven or eight years since Conway left her mother, whom she herself had not met for over two years. - Dr. Brown at this point took occasion to add to his previous evidence a refutation of the suggestion that the body had been conveyed to Mitre-square after the murder. - Evidence was then taken showing the movements of the murdered woman on the night of the 29th. At half-past eight

Mike Covell

> P.C. Robinson saw her lying very drunk on the pavement in Aldgate High-street, and someone in the crowd which had gathered knew her. As she was unable to stand he took her to Bishopsgate-street station. She was wearing an apron, now identified as that subsequently picked up marked with bloodstains near the body. Deceased was locked up till one o'clock, when, as she had got sober, she was discharged on giving her name and address. These, she said, were Mary Ann Kelly, of 6, Fashion-street. On leaving the station she was seen by the gaoler to turn towards Houndsditch, which would lead her in the direction of Mitre-square. Before going, however, she remarked on learning the time, that she would get a "fine hiding" when she got home. - Joseph Lewindale [sic] stated that as he and some friends were leaving the Imperial Club, Duke-street, about half-past one, they saw a man and a woman talking together in Church Passage. He did not see the woman's face, but deceased's clothes looked like those she was wearing. The man had on a peaked cloth cap. - Mr. Crawford, interposing, asked that unless the jury particularly wished it, the man's appearance should not be further described. - The jury agreed, and witness only added that he doubted whether he should recognise the man again. - Police-constable Alfred Lock [sic] proved the finding of the blood-stained apron in Goulston-street just before three o'clock on Sunday morning, and stated that on the wall just above the place where it was discovered were written in chalk the words, "The Jews are the men, and will not be blamed for nothing." He had previously passed the spot at 2:20, when the apron was not there. After searching the neighbourhood he reported the matter at Commercial-street. - Mr. Burrows: Was not this the sentence: "The Jews are not the men and will be blamed for nothing?" Witness replied that he thought he had copied the writing verbatim, but admitted that the first copy was in his pocket book, which he had not got with him. He would not swear that the word "Jews" was not written "Juess." At the request of the jury, the constable went for his pocket book. During his absence, Detective-Inspector Halse, one of the city police, proved that when the writing on the wall was reported to him he sent off an officer to make arrangements for having it photographed. Definite directions to this effect were given, but before a photographer could arrive, the Metropolitan Police Authorities, fearing that the words might lead to an outbreak against the Jews, had rubbed them out. - Mr. Burrows: Did no one suggest that it would be possible to rub out the word "Jews" only? - Witness: I suggested that the top line alone need be rubbed out, and the rest photographed. The words seemed to have been recently written in white chalk on the bricks, and were:- "The Juees (sic) are not the men that would be blamed for nothing." - The Foreman: Why did you allow the metropolitan police to rub the writing off? - Mr. Crawford: Did you not protest against its being rubbed out? - Witness: I did. - By the jury: The writing was like

a schoolboy's writing. Good round hand. - A juror regarded it as singular that the police did not make further inquiries at the lodging-house in the passage of which the apron was found - Mr. Crawford replied that a most vigilant search was made as soon as the matter came to the knowledge of the city police, but that, unfortunately, the apron was found by a member of the metropolitan force, and that some delay occurred. - Lock, on his return, adhered to his former reading of the sentence. - Mr. Crawford intimated that he could not carry the case any further, and the Coroner having briefly summed up, the jury returned a verdict of "Wilful murder against some person or persons unknown." THE WRITING ON THE WALL. The Pall Mall Gazette asserts that Sir Charles Warren himself gave orders for the erasure of the words "Jews shall not be blamed for nothing," which the Whitechapel murderer wrote upon the wall after slaughtering the Mitre-square victim, by which the City police were thus prevented from photographing the hand-writing. A SEQUEL TO THE MURDERS. Mrs Sodeaux, wife of a Spitalfields weaver, living in Hanbury-street, near the scene of the murder of Annie Chapman, was found yesterday to have hanged herself to the banisters of her house. She had been much excited and affected by the circumstances attending the murder. CLUES TO THE WESTMINSTER MYSTERY. The medical evidence given at the inquest held on Monday on the headless and limbless body found at Whitehall, has placed the police in possession of a description of the woman who was the subject of the horrible crime thus committed. A great many cases of missing women have been brought before the police, and the number has caused some embarrassment. Now, however, the police have before them the fact that the deceased woman was a plump woman, of about 5ft. 8in. or 5ft. 9in. high; that she had suffered from pleurisy; that she was from 24 years of age upwards; that she had fair skin and dark hair; and that her hand, found with the arm at Pimlico, showed that she had not been used to hard work. Moreover, the police have the fact that the death may have been from six weeks to two months prior to October 2, which would bring the end of her life to about August 20, and the death, moreover, is defined as having been one which drained the body of blood. This last point means that wherever the woman met her death- and it was not in the water- the place would be marked with blood. Anxious search is being made for the missing head.

October 13th 1888

The Hull Daily News, October 13th 1888,

Mike Covell

> *THE "JACK THE RIPPER" MANIA. A LETTER TO THE "HULL NEWS." The following letter was brought to-day, about noon to the office of this paper. It was enclosed in an envelope and left surreptitiously on the office counter, it is believed by a lad, who immediately ran away. Of course no importance is attached to the effusion, it being only an attempted hoax:- Hull Oct 5th'I arrived in Hull last night from Manchester, and may as well inform you that I have a job or two to do here.*
>
> *London's got two hot for me.*
> *'It's all that I want is blood, blood, blood.*
> *For why, you will know when I'm (copped?)*
> *I'll sharpen my knifes and I'll take their lives,*
> *and enjoy myself till I stopped.*
>
> *The letter is written in pencil on a leaf torn from a pocket-book, and at the bottom is the drawing of a knife represented to be dripping with blood.*

The Hull Daily News, October 13th 1888,

> *HULL POLICE REPORTS. MONDAY(Before Mr. T. W. Palmer and Mr. E. Lambert). EMULATING "JACK THE RIPPER" Samuel Noble, a mulatto, was charged with being disorderly on Saturday night in Adelaide Street. P.C. Leonard (111) saw prisoner behaving in a manner likely to cause a disturbance, and afterwards ascertained he had ripped one woman's clothes above her head, and on molesting another female she had fallen in a dead faint. A baguette had to be procured to take the prisoner to the station.- The magistrates imposed a fine of 40s. And costs, considering the case a very bad one.*
>
> *A young man named Patrick McDermott, charged with being drunk and disorderly on Saturday night, was fined 5s. And costs. Prisoner had been flourishing a short thick stick, half a broom handle and frightening pedestrians by declaring he was "Jack the Ripper" He approached the constable, who took him into custody, and in a menacing manner threatened to "Jack the Ripper" him.- Prisoner now admitted he had been in Prestwich Asylum.*

> **Samuel Noble and Patrick McDermott:**

Newspapers from Hull Volume 1

The 1881 Census of Hull shows just one entry for a Samuel Noble, the entry reads,
8 Air-street, Sculcoates, Hull

Samuel Noble	28	Head	General Labourer
Margaret Noble	24	Wife	
James Noble	3	Son	
Mary Jane Noble	10 mo	Dau	
Margaret Jackson	Grandmother		
Mary Torpey	26	Sister	

[RG11, P4758, F149, P7, GSU1342149]

The 1891 Census shows the family
21 Air-street, Sculcoates, Hull

Samuel Noble	39	Head	General Labourer
Margaret Noble	35	Wife	
James Noble	12	Son	Scholar
Mary Jane Noble	10	Dau	Scholar
Thomas Noble	8	Son	Scholar
Harry Noble	6	Son	Scholar
Maggie Noble	3	Dau	
Julia Noble	12 mo	Dau	

[RG12, P3927, F114, P6, GSU609937]

Patrick McDermott is registered in the 1881 Census thus,
17 Anns Place,

Patrick McDermott	42	Head	Iron Worker B. abt 1839

Mike Covell

Ceclia McDermott	41	Wife
Alice McDermott	16	Dau
John McDermott	15	Son
Sarah McDermott	13	Dau
Mary McDermott	11	Dau
Ellen McDermott	9	Dau
Jane McDermott	9	Dau
Margaret McDermott	6	Dau
Patrick McDermott	4	Son

[RG11, P4746, F134, P28, GSU1342146]

Hearing that Patrick Dermott had been admitted to the Prestwich Asylum, in Lancashire, I decided to check their admissions and sure enough I discovered the following entry featuring Patrick McDermott, admitted to the asylum in 1888,

Patrick McDermott, Admitted: April 20th 1888, Male Patient Number: 7016, Birthplace: Unknown, Age 29, Single, Occupation: Labourer, Discharged: September 21st 1888, {LRO: QAM6/6/29]

This entry is at odds with the 1881 Census and 1891 Census as it gives the age of 29 for Patrick Dermott, thus giving a birth date of 1859.

The 1891 Census
4 Granville Terrace, Sculcoates, Hull

Patrick McDermott	48	Head	Boilermakers Assistant b. abt 1843
Ceclia McDermott	48	Wife	
Sarah McDermott	23	Dau	Employee

401

Marry McDermott	22	Dau	Packer
Jane McDermott	20	Dau	Packer
Margaret McDermott	17	Dau	Dressmakers Apprentice
Patrick McDermott	14	Son	Saw Mill Employee

[RG12, P3924, F41, P5, GSU6099034]

The York Herald, October 13th 1888,

> HULL POLICE REPORTS. MONDAY(Before Mr. T. W. Palmer and Mr. E. Lambert). EMULATING "JACK THE RIPPER" Samuel Noble, a mulatto, was charged with being disorderly on in Adelaide Street, on Saturday night. P.C. Leonard said he saw prisoner behaving in a strange manner, and on going up to him he ascertained that he had been annoying some woman by calling out he was "Jack the Ripper." He had thrown one woman's clothes over her head, after which he had molested another woman, who fell fainting to the ground. He was, therefore, arrested, and he became so violent a waggonette was obtained to convey him. To the police station. The magistrates considered the case a bad one, and imposed a penalty of 40s, and costs. – A young man named Patrick McDermott was charged with being drunk and disorderly on Saturday night. Prisoner had been flourishing a short thick stick and frightening pedestrians by declaring he was "Jack the Ripper." He approached a constable, who took him into custody. Prisoner stated that he had been in Prestwich Asylum. Fined 5s and costs.

The Eastern Morning News, October 13th 1888,

> THE LONDON TRAGEDIES. AN IMPORTANT ARREST AT BELFAST. A man was arrested in Belfast on Thursday, suspected of connection with the Whitechapel murders, and was charged at the Belfast Police Court yesterday. Constable Edward Cartaud, who made the arrest, said that the accused would give no further account of himself than that he was the son of a London brewer, that he had an income, and that he had been in Edinburgh, Glasgow, and Greencock. Among the articles found upon him were a large clasp knife, a chisel, three razors and a table knife. Further evidence went to show that the accused, who first gave the name of William John Foster, but afterwards said it was John Foster, had informed the police that he was a watchmaker, but did not work at his trade. The prisoner, who is about 30 years of age, wears a slight

Mike Covell

> *sandy moustache, and speaks with a Cockney accent, was remanded for a week. He wore a white turned down collar, marked with bloodstains. The deputy of the Bee Hive Lodging-house, Brick-lane, on Thursday informed the police of the peculiar behaviour of a lodger named Andrew, known about Spitalfields as Parnell. Inquiries were instituted and Parnell was requested to give account of himself. If his statements be proved correct he will probably be soon released. People at the lodging-house state he did not sleep there on the night of Hanbury-street and Mitre-square murders. The Central News learns that the police authorities attach a great deal of importance to the spelling of the word "Jews" in the writing on the wall at the spot where the Mitre-square murderer threw away a portion of the murdered woman's apron. The language of the Jews in the East-end is a hybrid dialect, known as Yiddish, and their mode of spelling the word "Jews" would be "Juwes." This, the police consider a strong indication that the crime was committed by one of the numerous foreigners by whom the East-end is infested. A correspondent states that the police have grave reason to suspect as the Whitechapel murderer a man now a patient in an East-End infirmary, who was admitted since the commission of the last murder. He is under surveillance.*

The case of Stephen Rorke was featured in The Western Mail, dated October 11th 1888. The article stated,

> *TERROR IN MANCHESTER STREETS. A respectably dressed young man, named Stephen Rorke, was charged at Manchester on Wednesday with annoying and threatening a woman at twelve o'clock the previous night. The woman was accosted by the prisoner on the road home, and on refusing to comply with his wishes he said he was "Jack the Ripper," and threatened her. The police stated that great terror existed among the women, and the streets were almost clear at nine. The prisoner was remanded.*

The Hull and East Yorkshire and Lincolnshire Times, October 13th 1888,

> *THE EAST END HORRORS. THE MITRE SQUARE TRAGEDY. ADJOURNED INQUEST. The inquest into the circumstances attending the death of Catherine Eddowes, aged 43, the Mitre-square victim, was resumed on Thursday at the City Mortuary, Golden-lane, by Mr. Langham, City Coroner. The interest in the proceedings is in no way abated, and the usual crowds congregated round the doors of the buildings. Colonel Sir James Fraser and Superintendent Foster represented the City Police, and Mr. Crawford was the solicitor on behalf of the Corporation of the City of London. Dr. Sequeira, who was the first medical man*

to arrive at the scene of the murder, corroborated the previous medical testimony. Replying to the City Solicitor, witness said there was sufficient light in the square to enable the murderer to do his work, without extra light. He was of the opinion that the murderer had no design on any particular organ of the body and further that no anatomical skill was displayed. He accounted for the absence of noise by death being instantaneous. Dr. Saunders, medical officer of health of the city of London, said he examined the stomach of deceased more particularly for poisons of a narcotic class, with a negative result. He agreed with the other doctors that the murderer had no design on any particular organ, and that the murderer had no great anatomical skill. Annie Phillips said she identified the deceased as her mother. Witness's father, whose name was Thos. Eddowes, was a hawker. Did not know where he was. Her father was in the 18th Royal Irish, and subsequently a pensioner. He left his wife eight or nine years ago because she took to drink. By the City Solicitor: Her father might have been a pensioner of the Connaught Rangers. She was not certain. She knew her father lived with her two brothers, but she could not say where. Her father never threatened her mother, but they were not on good terms. The Coroner said it would be desirable to show that every effort was being made to clear the matter up. Detective Sergeant Mitchell stated that he had endeavoured to trace the deceased's husband and sons, but without success. He had ascertained that a man named Conway, which was the name of the deceased's husband, and not Eddowes, belonged to the 18th Royal Irish, but he was satisfied that the man was not the person who lived with the deceased. Detective Baxter Hunter said he had confronted the man Conway with two of the deceased's sisters, but they did not recognise him. A Juror asked why the daughter had not seen Conway? The City Solicitor replied that the daughter had not then been found, but she should see Conway. Dr. Brown was re-called to abolish the theory that the deceased was taken to Mitre-square after death. He was certain that the murder was committed on the spot as the blood showed the deceased did not more. Constable Roberts said he took the deceased into custody on the day of her death for being drunk. Police Sergeant Byfield said he kept the deceased in the cell until one o'clock in the morning, and then discharged her. She gave the name of Sarah Ann Kelly, and said she had been hopping. By the Jury: The acting inspector was responsible for discharging the prisoners. It was the custom to discharge the prisoners at all hours of the night. Deceased was sober when she left. George Morris, watchman to Messrs Tierney and Tonge, tea merchants, Mitre-square, deposed to being called by a constable to fetch assistance. He did not see any suspicious persons about, and heard no noise or cry of distress. The Court then adjourned for lunch. After the adjournment Constable Harvey explained his beat, and deposed to being called to the *deceased. George Clapp, caretaker, said he lived on the second floor of the building overlooking Mitre-square. He heard no noise during the night, and was not aware of the murder until the morning. Constable Pearce, living in the square, also said he heard no noise. Mr. Lawende, a foreigner, said he saw a man and woman near the scene of the murder, and was about to describe the dress of the deceased, when the City Solicitor suggested that unless the jury desired it he would rather that the evidence should not be given, for particular reasons. The description of the man was accordingly withheld from the public, although the police have full details. Joseph Levey, butcher, said he saw a man and woman talking just before the discovery of the murder. The man was about three inches taller than the woman. Constable Lock deposed to finding the portion of the apron worn by the woman in the passage of No. 118, Gouldstone-street, near the scene of the murder. He saw the following writing on a wall written in chalk: Jews are the men that will not be blamed for nothing." Detective Halse said he also saw the writing, and instructions were given for it to be photographed. Fearing a riot among the Jews if that were done, the writing was rubbed off. By the City Solicitor: The fear of a riot was suggested by the Metropolitan Police, and that was the only reason why the writing was not photographed. He protested against the writing being rubbed out; but as it was on Metropolitan ground he had no authority. This closed the evidence offered at the present on behalf of the police. A Juror complained that no search was made in the house outside which the apron was found. The clue up to the present had consequently been lost. The Coroner then briefly summed up the evidence, stating that there could be no doubt that the woman was fiendishly murdered. It would be better to leave the police to trace the clues in their possession, and to return a verdict of murder against some person or persons unknown. This was accordingly done. FUNERAL OF THE VICTIM. The funeral of Catherine Eddowes, victim of the Mitre-square murder, took place on Monday at Ilford, Essex, where the City of London Cemetery is situated. The expenses of the funeral were borne entirely by a private citizen. The corpse was decently laid in a plain deal coffin, with the name and age of the deceased engraved thereon, and was removed at half past one from the Golden-lane Mortuary. Thousands of people lined the streets in the vicinity of the mortuary, evincing much sympathy. The remains were borne an open hearse, followed by two carriages. Several wreaths were on the coffin. The crowds in the streets of the East End were so dense that a force of police had to direct the traffic. SUPPOSED DISCOVERY OF THE VICTIM'S HUSBAND. The Press Association yesterday says a constable was called to the Duke of York public house, Clerkenwell-road, London, by the barman, who said a pensioner from the Hussars, named Conway, had entered the bar and asked the barman to sign some document to the effect* that he had lost his pension papers. The barman having noticed from the newspaper reports of the inquest on the victim of the Mitre-square murder that the police were looking for a pensioner of that name, who was believed to be the husband of the murdered woman thought this might be the man. The constable took the man to King's Cross-road Police Station, and after being questioned he was removed to Bishopgate-street Police Station, where he will be confronted with the relatives of the murdered woman. He is not, strictly speaking, under arrest; but it is thought that if he is the woman's former husband or paramour he may be able to throw light on her recent movements. The police, on examination, found that the murdered woman's husband was a much older man than the individual now detained, and without sending for Catherine Eddowes sister they let the man go. SUICIDE THROUGH THE LONDON HORRORS. Mrs. Sodeaux, wife of a Spitalfield weaver, living in Hanbury-street, near the scene of the murder of Annie Chapman, was found on Thursday to have hanged herself to the banister of her home. She had been much excited and affected by the circumstances attending the murder. THE MILITARY AS POLICE. Sir Alfred Kirkby, Colonel of the Tower Hamlets Fusiliers, recently made an offer to provide thirty or fifty men belonging to that regiment for service in connection with tracking the perpetrator of the Whitechapel and Aldgate murders. The Home Secretary has written to Sir Alfred, saying that having consulted Sir Charles Warren, he had come to the conclusion that it would not be advisable to put the men on for service. A TRAMP DETAINED AT ELTHAM. SUSPICIOUS APPEARANCES. An individual who sought admission to the casual ward at Eltham Union, Kent, has been detained by the master as answering one of the descriptions of the suspected Whitechapel murderer. Blood was found on his trousers and shirt. He wore a black cloth coat and a hard felt hat. The local police have communicated with the London police. OUTRAGE ON WIMBLEDON COMMON. J. H. writes from Putney on 5th October: - "This afternoon being fine, my wife, and lady friend, went out to walk as far as the Windmill on the Common, when, on passing a clump of trees and bushes half way between the latter and the large red brick house, she was pounced upon by a man lying there in concealment, who, seizing her from behind by the shoulder and skirt, tried to pull her to the ground. She got away from his grasp. He made the second attempt, but with the loud screaming and terror of the ladies took to his heels across the Common in the direction of Wimbledon. No help was near. Time 2.45 pm. Short man, rather thick set, about 40, close shaven, round felt hat, shabby greenish coat. MORE ARRESTS. Another arrest was made in Clerkenwell on Monday night in connection with the Whitechapel murder, but the man was afterwards liberated. On Tuesday a well-dressed man was seen walking about Covent Garden Market carrying a small black bag. He was taken to Bow-street, and after explaining his business was discharged. Considerable excitement was caused on Monday afternoon by a report that a man had been arrested at Baker's-row, Whitechapel, after a desperate struggle, and that he had been at once conveyed to Bethnal Green Police station, and there charged on suspicion of being concerned in the recent murders. It was ascertained on inquiry, however, that the man was arrested, simply charged with stealing an oil cask, and that the struggle which ensued gave rise to a report in the locality that he was suspected of complicity in the murders. THE DISCOVERY OF KNIVES. The Press Association says that the man who left three knives at the Bull's Head Tavern, Oxford-street, called for them on Tuesday and a detective being in waiting, he was arrested. He was taken to Bow-street, but after satisfactorily accounting for himself, he was discharged. ANOTHER SUSPECT AT THE EAST END. The police have under close observation in connection with the Whitechapel murders, a man now an inmate of the East End Infirmary, who was admitted since the murders under suspicious circumstances. STRANGE ARREST IN BELFAST. EXTRAORDINARY EVIDENCE. Shortly before twelve o'clock on Thursday night a man, who gives his name as John Foster, was arrested in Belfast, on suspicions of being the Whitechapel murderer, and refusing to give account of himself. The prisoner, who was found lodging at the house of Samuel Beatty, Memel Street, had in his possession a bag containing a large knife and three razors. One of the latter bears marks of blood. The man is 30 years of age, 5ft, 8in, or 9in high, of slight build, and fair complexion, and is shabbily dressed. He also had close upon £20. He stated to the police that he has been in Belfast since last Sunday, Previously he was two days in Glasgow, and before that two days in Edinburgh; but he declines to give further information regarding himself. At Belfast Police court this morning John Foster, who was arrested on being suspicious of being concerned in the Whitechapel murders was brought up.- Constable Carrand deposed that from information received he went to Memel Street, and there found the prisoner, who gave the name of William John Foster, and said he had no place of residence. In reply to a question, he said he arrived in Belfast on Sunday evening, having previously been for two days at Greenock, and for four days previous to that at Glasgow, and still earlier at Edinburgh. A clasp knife was found on him, and in a bag were three razors, two knives and a number of watchmakers appliances. He said he was a watchmaker. He had £19 in money, a watch with the monogram "A.M.R," a locket, and a piece of a necklet. He wore boots similar to those worn by soldiers. The magistrates remanded him for a week for enquiries. TRYING BLOODHOUNDS IN HYDE PARK. Mr George Krehl has communicated to the Evening News, London, some interesting details of a trial of bloodhounds made at the direction of Sir Charles Warren in Hyde Park this morning. Two hounds *belonging to Mr Edwin Brough, were obtained, and at 7 a.m. Sir Charles Warren met them and their keeper at the Albert Gate. Sir Charles offered to act as the hunted man, and set off towards Bayswater. After he went out of sight the dogs were released, and after making one or two faults where the track had been crossed they [illegible] their man. Another of the party next gave a run of 700 yards, and the hounds successfully found it. These hounds will be kept ready where they can be summoned instantly, and reach Whitechapel in less than half an hour. THE LORD MAYOR OF LONDON AND THE MURDERS. BRUSSELS, Monday. The Independence Belge publishes an interview with one of its representatives with Mr De Keyser, Lord Mayor of London, concerning the recent Whitechapel tragedies. His Lordship expresses the belief that the assassin is undoubtedly mad. Should he recommence his atrocious crimes he will be assuredly taken in the act, though it would not be surprising if he should soon commit suicide. The Lord Mayor states that neither has nor had any belief that the offer of a reward would prove efficacious in bringing the murderer to justice, and he only consented to adopt the course which he has done in this respect to calm the public excitement. He has written, he says to Mr Matthews to explain this, and to disavow all idea of opposition to the Government's decision. His Lordship attributes the Anti-Ministerial attacks which have been made to ambitious persons who are seeking by these means to secure election to the new County Council. He is sure that the police force for the City of London is sufficiently large. A POLICE CONSTABLE STABBED. At the Clerkenwell Police Court this morning, James Phillips, aged 37, and William Jarvis, aged 40 cab washers, were charged with being concerned in cutting and wounding Henry Doncaster at the same time and place. Both prisoners had blood stained bandages on their head, and Robinson had cuts on the nose and forehead. Robinson detailed the circumstances under which he followed a suspected man into a cab-yard in Phoenix place. Witness was dressed in a woman's hat and mantle. Prisoners came into the yard, and he explained his presence there, whereupon Jarvis drew a pocket knife and stabbed him in the face, and the other prisoner kicked him. He had used his staff in self-defence, - Henry Doncaster, who had his hand bandaged, said he was also watching a suspected person in a cab yard. Both prisoners said they were protected their masters property. Dr Maller described the wounds received, and said those on Robinson and Doncaster could not have been caused by a sharp instrument.- They might have been caused by a blunt handle of a knife. The prisoners were remanded for a week. Bail was asked for, but the magistrate declined to grant it. ANOTHER FEROCIOUS ATTACK ON A WOMAN. IMITATING THE WHITECHAPEL MONSTER. Considerable excitement was caused at Maryport yesterday by the report that a young woman had been savagely attacked by "Jack the Ripper." It appears that a young woman named Margaret Dixon, living in Eaglefield-terrace, Maryport, arrived at her work at Watergate Colliery, about five o'clock, in a most exhausted condition, with hair dishevelled and garments torn. She was understood to say she had been chased and attacked by a man, but before she could give any details she fainted, and lay semi-conscious for several hours. She was conveyed home, and, on examination, it was found that her corset had been almost torn from her body. Dr. Spurgeon was soon in attendance, and he found that the girl was unable to speak. In answer to questions put to her, however, she made signs that she had been attacked in a wood near the pit by a man, who endeavoured to take liberties with her. She succeeded in freeing herself, and ran to the colliery. The man wore a hard felt hat, and had whiskers. It is also stated that another young woman was chased by a man near the same place. THE WHITEHALL MYSTERY. OPENING OF THE INQUEST. On Monday Mr. John Troutbeck, the coroner of Westminster, opened an inquest on the remains found a week ago under the new Police Offices, on the Thames Embankment. The greatest interest was manifested in the proceedings, and large numbers of people gathered outside the mortuary at two o'clock, and they did not return to the Sessions House until three. The body in the mortuary presented an awful spectacle. It was locked in a room, and was viewed by the jury through a window through fear of contagion. It was on a table propped up, and the arm recently found was placed in the socket. The body was of a dark brown colour. At twenty past three the first witness called was Frederick Wildborn, carpenter, employed on the works. He said he first saw what he thought was an old coat on Monday morning. He took no notice of the matter then, and saw the parcel again the same evening. On the following day he called the assistant foreman's attention to the parcel. It was then found to contain the body of a woman. He did not notice the smell. Witness pointed out where the body was found, on a maze like plan of the vaults, and he said it would be very difficult for anyone unacquainted with the place to find his way there. The workmen's tools had been placed there for ten weeks, up to two weeks before the body was found. – George Bugden, brick layers labourer, engaged in the works, said he was told by another workman to go and see what the parcel was. He untied the parcel, and produced the cord which had served that purpose. The body was then seen, and the police were sent for. – Detective Thomas Hawkins, A Division, deposed to being called and seeing the body. It was wrapped in a dress material (produced). The wall was very black, and the body was in a very advanced state of decomposition. The vaults were very dark, and no stranger could have found his way without a light. The person would have to cross a trench which could not be seen in the dark. – Frederick Moore and Charles William Brown, assistant foreman to Messrs. Grover, the contractor for the works, having given evidence, the Court adjourned. AN OLD WOMAN'S TALE. A strange story is transmitted from Liverpool. On Wednesday evening a young lady was walking along Shiel-road, not far from Shiel Park, when she was stopped by an elderly woman, who, in an excited manner, urged her not to go into the park. She explained that a few minutes previously she had been resting on one of the seats in the park, when she was accosted by a respectable looking man, dressed in a black coat, light trousers, and a soft felt hat, who inquired if she knew if there were any loose women about the neighbourhood, and immediately afterwards he produced a knife with a long thin blade, and stated that he intended to kill as many women in Liverpool as in London, adding that he would send the ears of the first victim to the editor of the Liverpool paper. The old woman stated that she was so terribly frightened that she hardly knew how she got away from the man. 14,000 CRIMINALS IN LONDON. There are in London 14,000 suspected criminals and offenders against the law. In addition to these we have in the Metropolis 120,000 children destitute of proper guardianship and left to the training of beggars or thieves. The evil is terrifying and monstrous. I hear that a movement is on foot, initiated by a number of philanthropists, for the purpose of promoting the co-operation of official and private charitable agencies, and to adopt measures for the employment of the destitute and vagrant, for the industrial training and education of the homeless and uncared for children, and the supervision and employment of the criminal classes. It we could only secure the rising generation, and bring them up to honest and healthy labour, we should have made a great advance towards extinction, as far as extinction is possible, both of pauperism and of crime. There are children running about the streets whom we might predict with certainty that they will by and bye swell the ranks of the criminal classes, if they do not belong to them already. To place them in an industrial school is to give them opportunity of becoming honest and industrious men and women.*

Mrs. Sodeaux:

The case of Mrs. Sodeaux was featured in the following publications,

The Echo, October 11th 1888, The Evening News, October 11th 1888, The Belfast News Letter, October 12th 1888, The Daily News, October 12th 1888, The Evening News, October 12th 1888, Freeman's Journal and Daily Commercial Advertiser, October 12th 1888, The Liverpool Mercury Etc, October 12th 1888, The York Herald, October 12th 1888, The Morning

Mike Covell

Advertiser, October 12th 1888, The Hull and East Yorkshire and Lincolnshire Times, October 13th 1888, The Huddersfield Chronicle and West Yorkshire Advertiser, October 13th 1888, The York Herald, October 13th 1888, The Eastern Post, October 13th 1888, The People, October 14th 1888

In Early January Mr. Sordeaux committed suicide using the same method as his wife, the death was reported in the Trewman's Exeter Flying Post or Plymouth and Cornish Advertiser, January 7th 1889, which stated,

THE WHITECHAPEL TRAGEDIES. A SAD SUICIDE. Information was conveyed to the coroner for North East Middlesex, to-day, that a weaver, named Joseph Sodeaux, living in Hanbury-street, Spitalfields, had hanged himself. He had been very despondent since the suicide of his wife, who hanged herself in the same way. The revolting murders and mutilations in the neighbourhood prayed on her mind, and she was afraid to go out, and when the woman Chapman was murdered a few doors away, Mrs. Sodeaux took her own life.

The suicide of Joseph Sodeaux was featured in the following publications,

The North Eastern Daily Gazette, January 8th 1889, The Huddersfield Daily Chronicle, January 8th 1889, The Northern Echo, January 8th 1889, The York Herald, January 8th 1889, The Aberdeen Weekly Journal, January 9th 1889, The Derby Mercury, January 9th 1889, The Morning Post, January 10th 1889, The Aberdeen Weekly Journal, January 12th 1889, The Huddersfield Daily Chronicle and West Yorkshire Advertiser, January 12th 1889, The Newcastle Weekly Courant, January 12th 1889, The York Herald, January 12th 1889,

With the main gist of the story being thus,

The particulars of a sad case of suicide which took place at No. 65, Hanbury-street, Spitalfields, a house few doors away from the spot the unfortunate woman Annie Chapman was murdered, reached Dr. Macdonald, the coroner for North-east Middlesex, this morning. It appeared that the top floor of that address is occupied by a silk weaver named Sodeaux, his wife, and a child aged eight years. For some time past Mrs. Sodeaux has been depressed, and since the perpetration of the horrible murders which have taken place in the district during the past few weeks she has been greatly agitated. On Sunday she was found to have a razor in possession, and it was taken from her, as it was thought she meditated suicide. The following day she appeared to be more cheerful, and was left alone with her child. Yesterday, however, she left her room, saying she was going on an errand, but when some time elapsed, and she did not return, her daughter went in search of her, and was horrified to find her hanging with a rope round her neck to the stair banisters. The child ran for assistance, but no one would go up to the body, and eventually the police were called in and the body cut down. Life was then extinct, but as the body was quite warm, it is believed that had assistance been rendered immediately on the discovery being made the woman's life might have been saved. The inquest on the remains will be held on Saturday morning, at 11 o'clock.

It has been suggested that the surname of the family was actually Sodo, and not Sodeaux, as previously published, the name of Joseph was also problematic as we shall see. To learn more about the family we must start at the beginning:

London, England, Births and Baptisms, 1813-1906 lists,

Name: Elizabeth Jessy Harrington, Record Type: Baptism, Baptism Date: December 10th 1837, Father's Name: Charles Harrington, Mother's Name: Elizabeth Harrington, Parish or Poor Law Union: Bethnal Green, St Matthew, Borough: Tower Hamlets, Register Type: Parish Registers.

1851 Census, 2 Little [illegible] Street, Bethnal Green, [Class HO107, P1542, F428, P33, GSU174772]

Charles Harrington	Head	40	Weaver
Elizabeth Harrington	Wife	38	
Charles Harrington	Son	16	Pupil
Elizabeth Harrington	Dau	13	Pupil
Louisa Harrington	Dau	8	Pupil
Thomas Harrington	Son	6	Pupil
William Harrington	Son	4	Pupil

London, England, Marriages and Banns, 1754-1921 features the following,

Mike Covell

Name: John Sodo, Estimated Birth Year: abt 1836, Age: 21, Spouse: Elizabeth Harrington, Spouse Age: 20, Record Type: Marriage, Event Date: December 13th 1857, Parish: Bethnal Green, St Judes, Borough: Tower Hamlets, Father's Name: John Sodo, Spouse's Father's Name: Charles Harrington, Register Type: Parish Register.

1861 Census, Bethnal Green, [Class RG9, P262, F128, P12, GSU542602]

Charles Harrington	Head	53	Cabinet Maker
Elizabeth Harrington	Wife	50	Laundress
Charles Harrington	Son	26	Tailor
Elizabeth Soda	Dau	23	Silk Weaver
Louisa Harrington	Dau	19	
Henry Harrington	Son	16	
William Harrington	Son	12	
Thomas Harrington	Son	9	Scholar
Kate Harrington	Dau	5	Scholar
Lizzie Lude	G.son	3	Scholar

1871 Census, Bethnal Green, [Class RG10, P495, F87, P40, GSU823376]

John Sada	Head	33	Weaver
Eliza Sada	Wife	32	Weaver
Elizbaeth Sada	Dau	13	Scholar
Emma Sada	Dau	2	
Charles Sada	Son	3mo	

The 1881 Census, 65 Hanbury-street, Spitalfields, London, [Class RG11, P439, F21, P36, GSU1341095]

John Sodo	Head	44	Silk Maker
Elizabeth Sodo	Wife	43	Silk Maker
Emma Sodo	Dau	13	Scholar
Charles Sodo	Son	10	Scholar
John Sodo	Son	7	Scholar
Walter Sodo	Son	5	Scholar
Arthur Sodo	Son	4	Scholar
Ada Sodo	Dau	1	

The England and Wales Death Index 1837 – 1915 features the following,

Name: Elizabeth Jessie Sodo, Estimated Birth Year: abt 1838, Date of Registration: Oct- Nov- Dec- 1888, Age at Death: 50, Registration District: Whitechapel, Inferred County: London, Vol: 1c, Page: 217.

The England and Wales Death Index 1837 – 1915 features the following,

Name: John Sodo, Estimated Birth Year: abt 1837, Date of Registration: Jan- Feb- Mar- 1889, Age at Death: 52, Registration District: Whitechapel, Inferred County: London, Vol: 1c, Page: 199.

October 15th 1888

The Eastern Morning News, October 15th 1888,

THE LONDON TRAGEDIES. A PATHETIC INCIDENT. A curious instance, writes a correspondent, was afforded at the inquest on Thursday on the Mitre Square victim of how little the poor of London knew each other even when related by ties of blood. I happened to be in the Coroner's Court, and when the woman's blood stained apron was produced a respectable young woman in

Mike Covell

> *mourning commenced to cry bitterly. A sister of the deceased, on asking me who was weeping, was surprised to find it was her own dead sister's child. She had grown up to be a young married woman without her aunt having ever known of her existence. According to the evidence on Thursday, a man was seen talking to the deceased fifteen minutes before her mutilated body was found in Mitre Square. The police withhold the description of him, but I have the best authority for stating that he exactly corresponds with the description given by three or four witnesses of the man observed with the woman who was murdered up a court in Berner Street on the same night. Mitre Square, although a quiet place, is criminally historic. Apart from the recent tragedy, it was the scene of the capture of the dynamiters who blew up a portion of the Tower of London. Then, not more than twenty years ago, two men blew up a house in the Square - and themselves at the same time - with gunpowder. ANOTHER LETTER FROM "JACK THE RIPPER"*
>
> *"Jack the Ripper" writes to a Welsh newspaper the following letter, bearing a London postmark:-*
>
> *London October 9th, 1888*
>
> *Dear Old Boss,*
>
> *What do you think of my little games here? Ha! Ha! Next Saturday I am going to give the St Mary Street girls a turn. I shall be fairly on their track, you bet. Keep this back until I have done some work, ha! ha! Shall down Friday.- Yours &c,*
>
> *Jack the Ripper (trade mark)*
>
> *To the Editor of the Western Mail*
>
> *The communication is written across a half sheet of note paper, and the hand writing and phraseology indicate that the missive has issued from the same source as the previous letters.*

The Hull Daily News, October 15th 1888,

> *THE WHITECHAPEL ATROCITIES. ANOTHER LETTER FROM THE HOME OFFICE. Though the police are still without any definite clue to the perpetrator, arrests upon suspicion are continuing to be made, and all cases where there is the slightest feasibility of truth being carefully sifted. At the Leman Street police*

station two men were detained on Saturday upon information given, but little importance was attached to the arrests, the particulars bearing a great resemblance to the many already affected. Altogether upwards of 780 letters giving information have been inquired into by the police, with a vast amount of trouble and with no success. The difficulties the police have to contend with are much greater than the public are aware of. These have been enhanced by so many man wandering about the East End who by their strange behaviour, unaccountable movements, and apparent resemblance to the vague description of the man who is wanted, have given rise to suspicions which have necessarily terminated in police investigation. The murder scare has spread to other parts of the metropolis, as an instance of which about noon on Saturday a sensation was occasioned in the locality of High Holborn. A gentleman was proceeding along Holborn, in the direction of the City, when he was suddenly pounced upon by a strange man of the labour class, who exclaimed in an excited manner, "This is Jack the Ripper." A struggle ensue, and the two fell heavily to the ground. The scene soon attracted a very large crowd of people who quickly collected, thinking that the Whitechapel murderer had been arrested. Much excitement prevailed, and the man was conveyed to the police station. Such incidents are traceable to the effect of the threatening letters which have been circulated purporting to have been written by "Jack the Ripper." Another letter, and most recent, was written to Mr George Lusk, of the Whitechapel Vigilance Committee, as follows:-

"I write you a letter in black ink, as I have no more of the right stuff. I think you are all asleep in Scotland Yard with your bloodhounds, as I will show you tomorrow night (Saturday.) I am going to do a double event, but not in Whitechapel. Got rather too warm there; had to shift. No more till you hear from me again-

JACK THE RIPPER"

This letter was shown to the police. It bears a Kilburn postmark, and the handwriting is very similar to that of the post card sent to the Central News, which had been copied and posted on the hoardings throughout the East End by the police. It is believed that the letter to Mr. Lusk will furnish a clue to the originator of most of the letters which have lately disturbed the public mind and created widespread consternation.

The following communication has been received by Mr. Lusk, of 1 Alderney Road, Mile End, from the Home Office, Whitehall, in answer to a request that a

Mike Covell

> *free pardon might be proclaimed to an accomplice or accomplices of the murderer:-*
>
> *"October 12.*
>
> *Sir, - I am desired by the Secretary of State to thank you for the suggestions in your letter of the 7th inst. on the subject of the recent Whitechapel murders, and to say in reply that, from the first, the Secretary of State has had under consideration the question of granting a pardon to accomplices. It is obvious that not only must such grant be limited to persons who have not been concerned in contriving or in actually committing the murders, but the expediency and propriety of making the offer must largely depend on the nature of the information received from day to day, which is being carefully watched, with a view to determining that question.*
>
> *"With regard to the offer of a reward, Mr. Matthews has, under the existing circumstances, nothing to add to his former letter. "I am, Sir, your obedient servant, "GODFREY LUSHINGTON."*

October 16th 1888

The Hull Daily Mail, October 16th 1888,

> *THE LONDON MURDERS. THE WHITEHALL TRAGEDY. The police are in possession of a piece of evidence in connection with the discovery of the mutilated body in the vault of the new police buildings at Westminster. It has been supplied by an inhabitant of Llanelly, South Wales. He happened to be in Cannon Row on the Saturday before the body was found, and at an hour when the place was practically deserted. His attention was directed to a man who climbed over a hoarding into the ground whereon the new police office is being erected, and where afterwards the body was discovered. Two other men were with him, who had a barrow, on which was a bundle. When the remains were found the man gave information to the police. The statement made by the individual at Llanelly that he saw a man climb the palings surrounding the building where the trunk of a woman was recently found, in Westminster, has been found to have no bearing on the crime, the men being workman. THE MITRE SQUARE TRAGEDY. Thomas Conway, who some years ago lived with Catherine Eddowes, the woman murdered in Mitre Square, yesterday afternoon went with his two sons to the detective office of the City police, in Old Jewry, and was at once taken to see Mrs Annie Phillips, Eddowes Daughter, who*

recognised him as her father. He states that he left Eddowes in 1880, in consequence of her intemperate habits, which prevented them from living comfortably together. He knew that she had since been living with Kelly, and has once or twice seen her in the streets, but he has, as far as possible, kept out of her way, as he did not wish to have any further communication with her. THE TYNE SUSPECT. The description furnished to the Metropolitan Police of the suspected man who sailed from the Tyne has resulted in a satisfactory explanation of his identity.

October 18th 1888

The Hull Daily News, October 18th 1888,

ANOTHER LONDON TRAGEDY. THE WHITECHAPEL MURDERS. A man arrested on Tuesday, is under detention at Leman Street Police station for enquiries. THE ARREST CONSIDERED OF GREAT IMPORTANCE. The Press Association says- Much importance is attached by the police to the arrest made at King Street Police Station, Whitehall, on Tuesday morning. The man entered the above named station about nine o'clock and complained of having lost a black bag. While the officials were taking note of his case, he commenced talking about the Whitechapel murders, and offered to cut off the sergeant's head and other rambling nonsense. It will be remembered that several people have testified to seeing a man with a black bag in the region of the murders, and who has not since been traced. This fact was at once remembered by the police, and the man was further questioned. In answer to an inquiry as to his business, he said he studied for some years for the medical profession, but gave it up for engineering, and that he had been stopping for some nights in coffee houses. His manner then became so strange that Dr. Bond divisional surgeon was sent for to examine the man. The doctor subsequently gave it as his opinion that the man was a very dangerous lunatic of homicidal tendencies, and as his appearance tallied with that published of the man who was seen with the murdered woman, he was removed to Bow Street, but before being taken thither, photos of his person were taken. He was also asked to write his name and it is stated the writing is somewhat similar to that of the letters received by the police and others. He gave his age as 67, but said he looks fully twenty years younger. The police are endeavouring to trace his antecedents and movements for the past two weeks. THE WHITEHALL MYSTERY. FURTHER REMAINS FOUND. The place where the trunk of a woman was found in the new police buildings at Whitehall, was further examined on Wednesday, when a Spitzbergen dog, belonging to Mr Jasper T.C Waring, was employed. The dog began to sniff at a mound of earth

Mike Covell

> which was dug over, and when much of the soil had been removed the animal seized a strange looking object, which on being examined by candle light was found to be portions of a human leg, which had been severed at the knee joint. Upon the leg was a portion of a stocking of some woollen substance. It is remarkable that the leg was found only a yard and a half distant from the spot where the body was found, and the police were supposed to have searched the whole of the ground. A medical man was summoned, and he at once took charge of the limb, with the view of making a detailed examination of it. THE GATESHEAD TRAGEDY. William Waddell was again brought before the magistrates at Durham on Wednesday, charged with the murder of Jane Beetmoore, near Gateshead, and was further remanded for a week.

The Hull Daily News, October 18th 1888,

> THE WESTMINSTER MURDER. The Press Association says that contrary to expectations, the search at the new police office buildings in Whitehall, was resumed late last night, by means of candles. A bloodhound, one of those which had been used in the Hyde Park experiment, was brought from King Street police station, and a staff of constables with Inspectors Peters and Marshall, were engaged for an hour and half in turning over the earth, but on the work being suspended at 10 p.m., no new discovery had been made. The search will be resumed this afternoon, when the hound will again be taken to the spot. Sir Charles Warren is expected to attend the experiment. Dr. Bond, divisional surgeon, made an examination this morning of the portion of the leg found yesterday, and on comparing it with the trunk already in the mortuary, is of the opinion that it is a portion of the same body, but much better preserved, the reason for this being that it was sufficiently buried to exclude the air. Dr. Bond also believes both portions found have been lying in the place for over 6 weeks.

The Eastern Morning News, October 18th 1888,

> THE LONDON MURDERS. THE WHITEHALL MYSTERY. DISCOVERY OF FURTHER REMAINS.
>
> STATEMENT BY SIR C. WARREN. Sir Charles Warren wishes to say that the marked desire evinced by the Whitechapel district to aid the police in the pursuit of the author of the recent crimes, has enabled him to direct that, subject to the consent of the occupiers, a thorough home search should be made within a defined area. With few exceptions, the inhabitants of all classes and creeds have freely fallen in with the proposal, and have materially assisted the officers

engaged in carrying it out. Sir Charles Warren feels that some acknowledgement is due on all sides for the cordial co-operation of the inhabitants, and he is much gratified that the police officers have carried out so delicate a duty with the marked good will of all those with whom they have come in contact. Sir Charles Warren takes this opportunity of acknowledging the receipt of an immense volume of correspondence of a semi-private character on the subject of the Whitechapel murders, which he has been quite unable to respond to in a great number of instances, and he trusts that the writers will accept this acknowledgement in lieu of individual replies. They may be assured that their letters have received every consideration. With regard to the statements current as to finding a blood-stained shirt at a lodging-house in Whitechapel, it appears the story is founded on some matters which occurred more than a fortnight ago. A man, apparently a foreigner, visited the house of a German laundress, at 22, Batty-street, and left four shirts, tied in a bundle, to be washed. The bundle was not opened at the time, but when the shirts were afterwards taken out one was found considerably blood-stained. The woman communicated with the police, who placed the house under observation, detectives at the same time being lodged there to arrest the man should he return. This he did last Saturday, and was taken to the Leman-street Police-station, where he was questioned, and within an hour or two released, his statement being proved correct. The man recently arrested at Limavady, Co. Donegal, on suspicion of being concerned in the London murders, has been discharged, inquiries respecting him having been satisfactory.

October 19th 1888

The Eastern Morning News, October 19th 1888,

THE LONDON TRAGEDIES. THE MITRE-SQUARE MURDER. ANOTHER PRACTICAL JOKE? The Central News says a portion of a kidney, alleged to be human, and said to have been received by post by a gentleman in the East End, was taken to Scotland-yard yesterday afternoon, and a statement was made by the recipient. The object was handed to the City police authorities, in whose jurisdiction the Mitre-square murder took place. It will be formally examined by the City police force to-day, but, as at present advised, the authorities treat the whole matter as the work of a practical joker. The Central News says: -

The Central News says another man has just been arrested in Whitechapel by the police on information received, on suspicion of being concerned in the East-end murders. He is about 35 years of age, and has recently been living in

Mike Covell

> *Whitechapel. He is somewhat confused as to his whereabouts lately, and will be detained pending inquiries. he force of police in private clothes specially selected to make the house-to-house search in the neighbourhoods of Hanbury-street, Commercial-street, Dorset-street, Goulston-street, Buck's-row, Brick-lane, Osborne-street, &c., completed their labours to-day. They have distributed many thousands of handbills, leaving them in every room in the lodging-houses. The greatest good feeling prevails toward the police, and noticeably in the most squalid dwellings the police had no difficulty in getting information, but not the slightest clue to the murderer has been obtained. Several Whitechapel tradesmen have forwarded to the Home Secretary a memorial stating that the police force in the district is insufficient, and praying that it may be largely increased. THE WHITEHALL MYSTERY. EXAMINATION OF THE REMAINS. Yesterday morning Dr. Bond, in conjunction with Dr. Hibberd, made a further examination, at the mortuary, Millbank-street, of the leg and foot found on Wednesday. The examination lasted for some time, but no marks which might lead to identification were discernible. The foot and leg are well moulded, and the foot has been well cared for, the nails being well trimmed, while corns or bunions, which would probably distinguish the foot of a poor woman, are absent. There is no doubt these remains belong to the trunk and arm previously found, although of course, it is impossible to fit them to the trunk, as the upper portion of the leg has not been found. All the parts which have been found are now at the mortuary. Bloodhounds have been used, and, wherever they showed a desire to linger, the soil was dug up with spades and minutely examined. It has transpired that some time ago a carman saw two men and a boy with a cart, conveying a large bundle, stop outside the works. The boy scaled the hoarding and opened the wicket gate, through which the men carried the bundle. The well at the new police buildings where it was thought some more remains might be found, has been pumped out, but nothing further has been discovered.*

October 20th 1888

The Hull and Lincolnshire Times, October 20th 1888,

> *THE WHITECHAPEL MURDERS. No person was in custody or under detention at either of the police stations in the East End at six o'clock last evening in connection with the recent murders. The house to house inspection is all but complete, and has not led to any discovery of importance. The police at Commercial Street station have learned that this afternoon a strange man at Islington was observed to write on a wall, "I am Jack the Ripper," he was pursued, but was lost sight of.*

The Hull and Lincolnshire Times, October 20th 1888,

ANOTHER LONDON MYSTERY. *A man giving the name of William Russell, and stating that he was discharged a week ago from an American ship, the National Eagle, at the Victoria Docks, Liverpool, has given himself up to the police at Maidenhead, accusing himself of having committed a murder in London on Tuesday night last. He says that on the night in question he had been drinking with a prostitute, whom he calls "Annie." They subsequently quarrelled, and he threw the woman over the parapet of Westminster Bridge into the Thames. He then ran away, and has since been hiding at Kew and Windsor. Haunted, however by the belief that he was being hunted down, he became so uneasy that he could get no rest, and consequently surrendered himself to the police. He describes the woman as rather good looking, of dark complexion, and rather stout - "the type," he says, "of a London girl." Russell was detained by the police, and late last night the attention of Sergeant Meade was attracted by a strange gurgling sound, as of someone suffocating. The officer went to the room where the prisoner was confined, and found him black in the face from an attempt to strangle himself. He had tied a silk handkerchief tightly round his throat, the sergeant arriving just in time to remove it and save the man's life. He was charged before the magistrates, to-day, with attempting suicide, and remanded for a week for inquiries to be made.*

The Hull and Lincolnshire Times, October 20th 1888,

THE LONDON MURDERS. A WOMANS KIDNEY SENT BY POST. A HORRIBLE STORY. *From enquiries made in Mile End we are enabled to give the following additional particulars of communications made to the members of the Whitechapel Vigilance Committee:- Mr Lusk, builder, of Alderney-road, has received several letters purporting to be from the perpetrator of the Whitechapel murders, but believing them to be the product of some practical joker he has regarded them as of no consequence. On Tuesday evening he received the following letter in a cardboard box containing some fleshy substance:- From hell.*

Mr Lusk, Sir,-I send you half the Kidney I took from one woman and preserved it for you t'other piece I fried and ate it was very nice. I may send you the bloody knife that took it out if you only wait a while longer. (signed) Catch me when you can Mishter Lusk." Receiver was at first disposed to think another hoax had been perpetrated but eventually, but eventually decided to take the opinion of the Vigilance Committee on Thursday morning. That body decided to take the contents of the cardboard box to a medical man, whose surgery was near. Mr. F.

Mike Covell

S. Reed, assistant to Dr. Wiles, examined the contents of the box, and declared the substance to be half a human kidney, divided longitudinally, but in order to remove any reason any reason for doubt he conveyed it to Dr. Openshaw, who is pathological curator to the London Hospital Museum, who examined it, and also pronounced it to be a portion of a human kidney, a "ginny" kidney -that is to say, it belonged to a person who had drunk heavily. He was further of the opinion that it was the organ of a woman about 45 years of age, and that it had been taken from the body within three weeks. It will be within recollection of the public that the left kidney was missing from the body of the woman Eddowes who was murdered and mutilated in Mitre-square. Mr. Lusk and another member of the Vigilance Committee took the parcel on Thursday to Scotland Yard; but the police authorities there referred them to the detectives at Leman-street. At the latter place the officer who is directing inquiries took down Mr. Lusk's statement, which he considered to be of great importance, and the box and its contents were left in the care of the police pending further investigation. Mr. Lusk states that a day of two before receiving the box he had sent to him a post-card, which he now considers of sufficient importance to make public. It is in the following words:-- "Say Boss, you seem rare frightened. Guess I'd like to give you fits, but can't stop. Time enough to let you have box of toys. Play copper games with me. But hope to see you when I don't hurry too much. Good bye, Boss." The Press Association says the London police believe the Whitechapel kidney story to be a hoax.- Dr. Sedgwick Saunders, medical officer to the City of London, yesterday was questioned by a representative of the press as to the report that a medical man had declared the half a kidney belonged to a female. He said, "It is a pity some people have not the courage to say they don't know. You may take it there is no difference whatever between the male and female kidney. As for those in animals, they are similar. The cortical substance is the same, and the structure differs in shape. I think it would be quite possible to mistake it for a pig's. You may take it that the right kidney of the woman Eddowes was perfectly normal in its structure and healthy, and, by parity of reasoning, you would not get much disease in the left. The liver was healthy, and gave no indications that the woman drank. Taking the discovery of the half of the kidney, and supposing it to be human, my opinion is that it was a student's hoax. It is quite possible for any student to obtain a kidney for the purpose."

THE BLOOD STAINED SHIRT. The startling story published on Monday with reference to the finding of a blood-stained shirt and the disappearance of a man from a lodging-house in the East-end proves upon investigation to be of some importance. On Monday afternoon the truth of the statement was given an unqualified denial by the detective officers immediately after its publication and *this presumably because they were anxious to avoid a premature disclosure of facts of which they had been for some time cognisant. From the very morning of the murders, the police, it is stated, have had in their possession a shirt saturated with blood. Though they say nothing they are evidently convinced that it was left in a house in Batty-street by the assassin after he had finished his work. Having regard to the position of this particular house, its close proximity to the yard in Berner-street, where the crime was committed, and to the many intricate passages and alleys adjacent, the police theory has, in all probability, a basis of fact. An examination of the surroundings leads to the conclusion that probably in the whole of Whitechapel there is no quarter in which a criminal would be more likely to evade police detection, or observation of any kind, than he would be in this particular one. At the inquest on Mrs. Stride one of the witnesses deposed to having seen a man and a woman standing at the junction of Fairclough and Berner-streets early on the morning of the murder. Assuming that the man now sought was the murderer, he would have gained instant access to the house in Batty-street by rapidly crossing over from the yard and traversing a passage, the entrance of which is almost immediately opposite to the spot where the victim was subsequently discovered. The statement has been made that the landlady of the lodging-house, 22, Batty-street - the house in which the shirt was left - was at an early hour disturbed by the movements of the lodger who changed some of his apparel and went away; first, however, instructing her to wash the cast-off shirt by the time he returned. But in relation to this latter theory, the question is how far the result of the inquiries made yesterday is affected by a recent arrest. Although, for reasons known to themselves, the police during Saturday, Sunday, and Monday answered negatively all questions as to whether any person had been arrested or was then in their charge, there is no doubt that a man was taken into custody on suspicion of being the missing lodger from 22, Batty-street, and that he was afterwards set at liberty. The German lodging house keeper could clear up the point as to the existence of any other lodger absent from her house under the suspicious circumstances referred to, but she is not accessible, and it is easy to understand that the police should endeavour to prevent her making a statement. IMPORTANT STATEMENT BY A SUSPECT. The Press Association says, much importance is attached by the police to the arrest made at King-street Police Station, Whitehall. On Tuesday morning the man entered the above named station about nine o'clock, and complained of having lost a black bag. While the officials were taking notes of his case, he commenced talking about the Whitechapel Murders, and offered to cut off the sergeant's head, and other rambling nonsense. It will be remembered that several people have testified to seeing a man with a black bag in the region of the murders, and who has not been traced. The fact was at once remembered by the police, and the man was further questioned. In answer to the inquiry as to his business, he said he studied for some years for the medical profession, but gave it up for engineering, and that he had been stopping for some nights in a coffee house. His manner then became so strange that Dr. Bond, divisional surgeon, was sent for to examine the man. The doctor subsequently gave it as his opinion that the man was a very dangerous lunatic of homicidal tendency, and as his appearance somewhat tallied with that published of the man who was seen with the murdered woman, he was removed to Bow-street. But before being taken thither photographs of his person were taken. He was also asked to write his name, and it is stated his writing is somewhat similar to that of the letters received by the police and others. He gave his age as 67, but it is said he looks a full twenty years younger. The police are endeavouring to trace his antecedents and movements for the past few weeks. THE BELFAST SUSPECT. At the Belfast Police Court yesterday John Foster was charged on remand with having being connected with the Whitechapel murders.- The police gave evidence to the effect that a locket and chain found in the prisoners possession had been identified as having been stolen from a house in Bootle.- The prisoner is wanted at Bootle on a charge of housebreaking.- The Magistrates remanded him for a week, in order that further inquiries may be made regarding him. THE WHITEHALL MYSTERY. FURTHER REMAINS FOUND. The place where the trunk of the woman was found in the new police buildings, at Whitehall, was further examined on Wednesday, when a Spitzbergen belonging to Mr Jasper T.C. Waring was employed. The dog began to sniff at a mound of earth, which was dug over, and when much of the soil had been removed the dog seized a strange looking object, which on being examined by a candle was found to be a portion of a human leg, which had been severed at the knee joint. Upon the leg which had been severed at the knee joint. Upon the leg was a portion of stocking of some woollen substance. It is remarkable that the leg was found only a yard and half from the spot where the body was found, and the police have supposed to have searched the whole of the ground. A medical man was summoned, and he at once took charge of the limb with a view of making a detailed examination of it. THE BLOODHOUNDS LOST. The Press Association's Woolwich correspondent says the bloodhounds hired by Sir Charles Warren were out of practice at Tooting on Thursday and were lost. Telegrams have on Thursday been sent to all the Metropolitan Police Stations that if they are seen anywhere intimation is to immediately sent to Scotland Yard. Sir Charles Warren states that the marked desire evinced by the Whitechapel district to aid the police in the pursuit of the author of the recent crimes has enabled him to direct that, subject to the consent of the occupiers a thorough house to house search should be made within a defined area. With few expectations the inhabitants, of all classes and creeds, have freely fallen in with the proposal , and have materially assisted the officers engaged in carrying it out. Sir Charles Warren feels that some acknowledgement is due on all sides for the cordial co-operation of the inhabitants, and he is much gratified that police officers have carried out so delicate a duty with the marked goodwill of all those with whom they have to come in contact. Sir Charles Warren takes this opportunity of acknowledging the immense volume of correspondence of a semi private character. On the subject of the Whitechapel murders, which he has been quite unable to respond to it in a great number of instances, and he trusted that the writers will accept this acknowledgment in lieu of individual replies. They may be assured that their letters have received every consideration.*

The Hull and Lincolnshire Times, October 20th 1888,

LOCAL AND NATIONAL NOTES. William Waddell was again brought before the magistrates at Durham on Wednesday, charged with the murder of Jane Beetmore near Gateshead, and was further remanded for a week. An American Clergyman has made the discovery that in just 32 years the electricity stored on the earth will come in contact with the heat inside and blow the world up. Unfortunately, most of us will not be here to see; but if Mr. Johnson is still in the flesh in 1921, it is to be hoped that someone will make him show where his calculations were at fault- Echo. The Press Association says a fog of extraordinary density spread over the City of London shortly before 10 a.m. on Wednesday, and at the later hour all street and railway traffic was brought to an almost sudden stoppage. The sky was obscured by a dense black vapour, which even artificial lights in the street failed to penetrate. After hanging over the City for a couple of hours the fog gradually lifted, and traffic resumed its ordinary course.

The Hull and Lincolnshire Times, October 20th 1888,

GREAT FIRE IN WHITECHAPEL. EXCITING SCENES. A fire broke out on Thursday at a few minutes to ten on the premises occupied by Messrs H. Koenberg, Harris, and Son, furriers, 25, Commercial-street, Whitechapel. The building is a three storied one, and at the time of the outbreak about 50 work people were on the premises. The work people were warned by the smell of smoke, and some of them on running downstairs into the shop saw that the place was on fire. The only means of egress was by a small door in an iron shutter- which was drawn down over the front of the shop. This was quickly opened by

Mike Covell

> *those who were first to reach the ground floor, who rushed [illegible] into the street, crying "Fire." One or two returned and assisted the female operatives to escape by the doorway. Only those who made for the staircase on the first alarm were able to escape by this means, the blinding smoke driving back about 15 or 20. These clustered at the first floor windows and uttered piteous cries. Aid was soon at hand. The Commercial-road Fire Station is but a few hundred yards away, and within a brief time an engine and fire escape were upon the spot. The people in the street called out to them to wait for the escape but just as the ladder appeared at the top of the street, being rapidly wheeled along by firemen, policemen and others, a young girl named Grace Newson climbed out onto the coping, which is at a height of about twenty feet, and jumped to the ground. She was caught by the crowd, and escaped uninjured. A boy next risked the leap, but he sufficient presence of mind to let himself hang down from the coping by his hands and then drop. He too was safely caught by the people standing on the pavement. The escape and a detached ladder were quickly put into position and the fireman rescued the people with great rapidity, amidst hearty cheers. One fireman walked along the coping carrying a girl and a lad in his arms. Both were nearly unconscious, and as he passed his living burden on to a comrade on the escape the daring feat called forth loud expressions of praise from the onlookers. Another girl, evidently half crazed with terror, would not wait to be rescued by the escape, but following the example of Grace Newson, jumped onto the street and escaped with a severe shaking, her fall being broken by the arms of the people who were standing below.*

The Hull and Lincolnshire Times, October 20th 1888,

> *ANOTHER LONDON MYSTERY. A man giving the name of William Russell, and stating that he was discharged a week ago from an American ship, the National Eagle, at the Victoria Docks, Liverpool, had given himself up to the police at Maidenhead, accusing himself of having committed a murder in London on the night of the 12th inst. He says that on the night in question he had been drinking with a woman, whom he calls "Annie." They subsequently quarrelled, and he threw the woman over the parapet of Westminster Bridge into the Thames. He then ran way, and has since been hiding at Kew and Windsor. Haunted, however, by the belief that he was being hunted down, he became so uneasy that he could get no rest, and consequently surrendered himself to the police. He described the woman as rather good looking, of dark complexion, and rather stout - "the type," he says, "of a London girl." Russell was detained by the police, and late on Sunday night the attention of Sergeant Mead was attracted by a strange gurgling sound, as of someone suffocating. The officer went to the*

> room where the prisoner was confined, and found him black in the face from an attempt to strangle itself. He had tied a silk handkerchief tightly round his throat, the sergeant arriving just in time to remove it and save the man's life. He was charged before the magistrates on Monday with attempting to commit suicide, and remanded for a week for inquiries to be made.

The Eastern Morning News, October 20th 1888,

> THE LONDON MURDERS. HUMAN REMAINS SENT BY POST. From inquiries made in Mile End on Thursday we are enabled to give particulars of communications made to members of the Whitechapel Vigilance Committee. Mr Lusk, builder, of Alderney road, has received several letters purporting to be from the perpetrator of the Whitechapel murders, but believing them to be the product of some practical joker he has regarded them as of no consequence. On Tuesday evening, however, he received the following letter in a cardboard box, containing some fleshy substance :- "From Hell. Mr Lusk, - Sir, I send you half the kidney I took from one woman, preserved it for you; 'tother piece I fried and ate. It was very nice. I may send you the bloody knife that took it out if you will only wait a while longer. Signed, CATCH ME WHEN YOU CAN, MR LUSK." The receiver was at first disposed to think that another hoax had been perpetrated, but eventually decided to take the opinion of the Vigilance Committee. This morning that body decided to take the contents of the cardboard box to a medical man whose surgery was near. Mr F.S. Reed, assistant to Dr. Miles, examined the contents of the box and declared the substance to be half a human kidney divided longitudinally, but in order to remove any reason for doubt, he conveyed it to Dr. Openshaw, who is pathological curator to the London Hospital Museum, who examined it, and also pronounced it to be a portion of a human kidney, a ginny kidney - that is to say, it had belonged to a person who had drunk heavily. He was further of opinion that it was the organ of a woman about 45 years of age, and that it had been taken from the body within the last three weeks. It will be within the recollection of the public that the left kidney was missing from the body of the woman Eddowes, who was murdered and mutilated in Mitre square. Mr Lusk and another member of the Vigilance Committee took the parcel to-day to Scotland Yard, but the police authorities there referred them to Leman street. At the latter place the officer who is directing the inquiries took down Mr Lusk's statement, which he considered to be of great importance, and the box and contents were left in care of the police pending further investigation. Mr Lusk states that a day or two before receiving the box he had sent to him a postcard which he now considers of sufficient importance to make public. It is in the following words:-

Mike Covell

> "Say, boss, you seem rare frightened. Guess I'd like to give you fits, but can't stop. Time enough to let your box of toys play copper games with me; but hope to see when I don't hurry too much. Good bye, boys." The Vigilance Committee held another meeting to-night, when this new feature in the case was considered. A later message says that only a cursory examination of the kidney has yet been made. A small portion only of the renal artery adheres to the kidney, and it will be remembered that in the Mitre-square victim a large portion of the renal artery adhered to the body. This leads the police to attach more importance to the matter than they otherwise would. The organ has been preserved in spirits for some time. At the Belfast Police Court yesterday, John Foster was charged on remand with having been concerned in the Whitechapel atrocities. The Bootle authorities telegraphed that the accused was wanted there on a charge of housebreaking, and a remand was granted. Nothing further has transpired in connection with the Whitehall mystery. The police yesterday overturned all the soil in the immediate neighbourhood of the spot where remains were found, but their search was fruitless. They will resume their investigations to-day. LOSS OF SIR C. WARRENS BLOODHOUNDS. It is stated that Sir Charles Warren's bloodhounds were out for practice at Tooting on Thursday morning and were lost. Telegrams have been despatched to all the metropolitan police stations stating that, if seen anywhere, information is to be immediately sent to Scotland-yard.

The Hull and East Yorkshire and Lincolnshire Times, October 20th 1888,

> THE LONDON MURDERS. A WOMAN WOMAN'S KIDNEY SENT BY POST. A HORRIBLE STORY. From enquiries since made in Mile End we are enabled to give the following additional particulars of communications made to the members of the Whitechapel Vigilance Committee:- Mr. Lusk, builder of Alderney-road, has received several letters purporting to be from the perpetrator of the Whitechapel murders, but believing them to be the product of some practical joker he has regarded them as of no consequence. On Tuesday evening he received the following letter in a cardboard box containing some fleshy substance: - "From hell, Mr. Lusk. Sir, - I send you half the kidney I took from one woman. Preserved it for you. T'other piece I fried and ate. It was very nice. I may send you the bloody knife that took it out if you wait a while longer. (Signed) Catch me if you can. Mr. Lusk." Receiver was at first disposed to think another hoax had been perpetrated, but eventually decided to take the opinion of the Vigilance Committee on Thursday morning. That body decided to take the contents of the cardboard box to a medical man, whose surgery was near. Mr. F. S. Reed, assistant to Dr. Wiles, examined the contents of the box, and declared

the substance to be half a human kidney, divided longitudinally, but in order to remove any doubt he conveyed it to Dr. Openshaw, who is pathological curator to the London Hospital Museum, who examined it, and also pronounced it to be a portion of a human kidney, a "ginny" kidney – that is to say, it had belonged to a person who had drunk heavily. He was further of the opinion that it was the organ of a woman about 45 years of age, and that it been taken from the body within three weeks. It will be within recollection of the pubic that the left kidney was missing from the body of the woman Eddowes who was murdered and mutilated in Mitre-square. Mr. Lusk and another member of the Vigilance Committee took the parcel on Thursday to Scotland Yard, but there police authorities there referred them to the detectives at Leman-street. At the latter place the officer who is directing inquiries took down Mr. Lusk's statement, which he considered to be of great importance, and the box and contents were left in the care of the police pending further investigation. Mr. Lusk states that a day or two before receiving the box he had sent to him a postcard which he now considers of sufficient importance to make public. It is in the following words: - "Say, boss, you seem rather frightened. Guess I'd like to give you fits, but can't stop. Time enough to let you. Box of toys, play copper games with me, but hope to see you when I don't hurry too much. Good bye boss." The Press Association says the London police believe the Whitechapel kidney story to be a hoax. – Dr. Sedgwick Saunders, medical officer to the City of London, yesterday was questioned by a representative of the press as to the report that a medical man had declared the half kidney belonged to a female. He said, "It is a pity some people have not the courage to say they don't know. You may take it that there is no difference whatever between the male and female kidney. As for those in animals, they are similar. The cortical substance is the same, and the structure only differs in shape. It would be quiet possible to mistake it for a pig's. You may take it that the right kidney of the woman Eddowes was perfectly normal in structure, and healthy, and by parity of reasoning you would not get much disease in the left. The liver was healthy, and gave no indication that the woman drank. Taking the discovery of half a kidney, and supposing it to be a human, my opinion it that it was a student's antic. It is quite possible for any student to obtain a kidney for the purpose. THE BLOOD STAINED SHIRT. The startling story published yesterday on Monday to the finding of a blood-stained shirt and the disappearance of a man from a lodging-house in the East-end proves upon investigation to be of some importance. On Monday afternoon the truth of the statement was given an unqualified denial by the detective officers immediately after its publication and this presumably because they were anxious to avoid a premature disclosure of facts of which they had been for some time cognisant. From the very morning of the murders, the police, it is stated, have had in their possession a shirt saturated with blood. Though they say nothing they are evidently convinced that it was left in a house in Batty-street by the assassin after he had finished his work. Having regard to the position of this particular house, its close proximity to the yard in Berner-street, where the crime was committed, and to the many intricate passages and alleys adjacent, the police theory has, in all probability, a basis of fact. An examination of the surroundings leads to the conclusion that probably in the whole of Whitechapel there is no quarter in which a criminal would be more likely to evade police detection, or observation of any kind, than he would be in this particular one. At the inquest on Mrs. Stride one of the witnesses deposed to having seen a man and a woman standing at the junction of Fairclough and Berner-streets early on the morning of the murder. Assuming that the man now sought was the murderer, he would have gained instant access to the house in Batty-street by rapidly crossing over from the yard and traversing a passage, the entrance of which is almost immediately opposite to the spot where the victim was subsequently discovered. The statement has been made that the landlady of the lodging-house, 22, Batty-street - the house in which the shirt was left - was at an early hour disturbed by the movements of the lodger who changed some of his apparel and went away; first, however, instructing her to wash the cast-off shirt by the time he returned. But in relation to this latter theory, the question is how far the result of the inquiries made yesterday is affected by a recent arrest. Although, for reasons known to themselves, the police during Saturday, Sunday, and Monday answered negatively all questions as to whether any person had been arrested or was then in their charge, there is no doubt that a man was taken into custody on suspicion of being the missing lodger from 22, Batty-street, and that he was afterwards set at liberty. The German lodging-house keeper could clear up the point as to the existence of any other lodger supposed to be absent from her house under the suspicious circumstances referred to, but she is not accessible; and it is easy of understanding that the police should endeavor to prevent her making any statement. IMPORTANT STATEMENT BY A SUSPECT. The Press Association says much importance is attached by the police to the arrest made at King-street Police station, Whitehall. On Tuesday morning the man entered the above named station about nine o'clock, and complained of having lost a black bag. While the officials were taking note of his case, he commenced talking about the Whitechapel murders, and offered to cut off the sergeant's head, and other rambling nonsense. It will be remembered that several people have testified to seeing a man with a black bag in the region of the murders, and who has not since been traced. The Fact was at once remembered by the police, and the man was further questioned. In answer to the inquiry as to his business, he said he had studied for some years for the medical profession but gave it up for engineering, and that he had been stopping for some nights in the coffee houses. His manner then became so strange that Dr. Bond, divisional surgeon, was sent for to examine the man. The doctor subsequently gave it as his opinion that the man was a very dangerous lunatic of homicidal tendency, and as his appearance somewhat tallied with that published of the man who was seen with the murdered woman, he was removed to Bow-street. But before being taken thither photographs of his person were taken. He was also asked to write his name, and it is stated the writing is somewhat similar to that of the letters received by the police and others. He gave his age as 67, but it is said he looks fully twenty years younger. The police are endeavouring to trace his antecedents and movements for the past few weeks. THE BELFAST SUSPECT. At the Belfast Police Court yesterday John Foster was charged on remand with having been connected with the Whitechapel Murders. – The police gave evidence to the to the effect that a locket and chain found in the prisoner's possession had been identified as having been stolen from a house in Bootle. – The prisoner is wanted at Bootle on a charge of housebreaking. – The Magistrates remanded him for a week, in order that further inquiries may be made regarding him. THE WHITEHALL MYSTERY. FURTHER REMAINS FOUND. The place where the trunk of the woman was found in the new police buildings, at Whitehall, was further examined on Wednesday, when a Spitzbergen belonging to Mr. Jasper T.C. Waring was employed. The dog began to sniff at the mound of earth, which was dug over, and when much of the soil had been removed the dog seized a strange looking object, which on being examined by a candle was found to be a portion of a human leg which had been severed at the knee joint. Upon the leg was a portion of a stocking of some woollen substance. It is remarkable that the leg was found only a yard and a half from the spot where the body was found only a yard and a half from the spot where the body was found, and the police were supposed to have searched the whole of the ground. A medical man was summoned, and he at one took charge of the limb with a view of making a detailed examination of it. THE BLOODHOUNDS LOST. The Press Association's Woolwich correspondent says the bloodhounds hired by Sir Charles Warren were out for practice at Tooting on Thursday and were lost. Telegrams have on Thursday been sent to all the Metropolitan police stations that if they are seen anywhere intimation is to be immediately sent to Scotland Yard. Sir Charles Warren states that the mark desire evinced by the Whitechapel district to aid the police in the pursuit of the author of the recent crimes has enabled him to direct that, subject to the consent of the occupiers a thorough house to house search should be made within a defined area. With few exceptions the inhabitants, of all classes and creeds, have freely fallen in with the proposal, and have materially assisted the officers engaged in carrying it

Mike Covell

> out. Sir Charles Warren feels that some acknowledgement is due on all sides for the cordial co-operation of the inhabitants, and he is much gratified that police officers have carried out so delicate a duty with the marked goodwill of all those with whom they have come in contact. Sir Charles Warren takes this opportunity of acknowledging the receipt of an immense volume of correspondence of a semi private character, on the subject of the Whitechapel murders which he has been quiet unable to respond to in a great number of instances, and he trusts that the writers will accept this acknowledgement in lieu of individual replies. They may be assured that their letters have received every consideration.

October 25th 1888

The Hull Daily Mail, October 25th 1888,

> *THE QUEEN AND THE EAST-END MURDERS. During the three days of the week following the Sunday on which the two murders were committed the following petition to the Queen was freely circulated among the women of the labouring classes of East London through some of the religious agencies and educational centres: - "To our Most Gracious Sovereign Lady Queen Victoria." "Madam, - We, the women of East London, feel horror at the dreadful sins that have been lately committed in our midst, and grief because of the shame that has fallen on our neighbourhood. "By the facts which have come out in the inquests, we have learnt much of the lives of those of our sisters who have lost a firm hold on goodness and who are living sad and degraded lives. "While each woman of us will do all she can to make men feel with horror the sins of impurity which cause such wicked lives to be led, we would also beg that your Majesty will call on your servants in authority and bid them put the law which already exists in motion to close bad houses within whose walls such wickedness is done and men and women ruined in body and soul. "We are, Madam, your loyal and humble servants." The petition, which received between 4,000 and 5,000 signatures, was presented in due form and the following reply has been received: -*
>
> *"Whitehall. "Madam, - I am directed by the Secretary of State to inform you that he has had the honour to lay before the Queen the petition of women inhabitants of Whitechapel praying that steps may be taken with a view to suppress the moral disorders in that neighbourhood, and that Her Majesty has been graciously pleased to receive the same. "I am to add that the Secretary of State looks with hope to the influence for good that the petitioners can exercise, each in her own neighbourhood, and he is in communication with the Commissioners*

of Police with a view to taking such action as may be desirable in order to assist the efforts of the petitioners and to mitigate the evils of which they complain.

"I am, Madam, your obedient servant, "GODFREY LUSHINGTON. "Mrs. Barnett, St Jude's Vicarage, Commercial-street, E".

November 9th 1888

9th November 1888 Mary Jane Kelly

Name: Marie Jeanette Kelly, Estimated Birth Year: abt 1863, Date of Registration: Oct- Nov- Dec- 1888, Age at Death: 25, Registration District: Whitechapel, Inferred County, London, Vol: 1c, Page: 211

November 10th 1888

The Hull News, November 10th 1888,

LATEST NEWS. ANOTHER TERRIBLE TRAGEDY IN WHITECHAPEL. A WOMAN BRUTALLY MURDERED. HEAD ALMOST SEVERED FROM THE BODY. FIENDISH MUTILATION. About half past ten o'clock yesterday morning a horrible discovery was made in Miller-court, Dorset-street, Spitalfields, in the immediate neighbourhood of Hanbury-street, a locality rendered notorious by the crimes of the past few months. The body of a woman shockingly mutilated, was found by a man named John Bowyer, in a room of a house at the end of the Court, Bowyer had been sent by Mr. McCarthy, the landlord, to collect the rent of the room No. 13, which was occupied by the murdered woman Mary Jane Kelly who was in arrears. Upon knocking at the door Bowyer received no answer, and looking through a broken window he saw the woman lying on her back quiet naked, while there were marks of blood about the place. Finding the door locked and the key having been removed, Bowyer informed McCarthy of the discovery and he having looked through the broken pane sent Bowyer to Commercial-street police station. Inspector Buck was the first officer on the spot and before anything was done to disturb the body or its surroundings information was sent to Scotland Yard. Inspector Abberline afterwards arrived, and was followed by Superintendent Arnold. The door was then forced, and on entering the room it was seen that the body of the unfortunate woman had been terribly mutilated. The nose was cut off, the face lacerated beyond recognition, the breasts were both cut off and placed on the table, the heart and liver were beside the body, and the uterus was missing.

Mike Covell

Portions of flesh had been cut from the thighs, and other barbarities were committed by the murderer. The deceased was known as a prostitute, and was about five and twenty years of age. She lived with a man who was a salesman in Billingsgate market, but who is said to have been away from the deceased for eight or ten days past. The last seen or heard of the murdered woman was about one o'clock yesterday morning, when she was under the influence of liquor, and was heard singing in her room. Whether the murderer was then in her company is uncertain, but there seems to be no doubt that she took a man to her lodgings for an immoral purpose. On Thursday night she was in the streets as usual, and complained to some of her acquaintances that she was unable to obtain some money for her rent. None of the neighbours appear to have heard any unusual noise during the night. The court in which the deceased lived is situate near No. 25, Dorset-street, and terminates in a square yard. The room occupied by deceased is on the ground floor. Dr. Duke was the first medical man to reach the spot. Dr. Phillips and Dr. Bond, of Westminster, are making the post-mortem examination. It is stated that bloodhounds will be employed in the case. NO BLOODHOUNDS AVAILABLE. A later telegram states that bloodhounds were not employed as expected, it being understood there were none available. LATEST PARTICULARS. The remains of the victim were removed at four o'clock in a rough coffin to the Mortuary in Shoreditch, to await the inquest. The police up to ten o'clock last night had no clue to the murderer, but there is a belief among some of them that he is employed on one of the continental cattle boats which come to London on Thursdays or Fridays, and leave again on Sundays or Mondays. There was intense excitement in Spitalfields last night, and the streets were thronged with people discussing the details of the crime. FURTHER DETAILS. The following telegrams have also been received respecting the tragedy: -

London, Friday afternoon. The streets in the vicinity of the crime are crowded with people eagerly discussing the latest horror. The women of a certain class being particularly excited at the fact that another of their number had been so brutally murdered. It is confidently stated that deceased was seen after ten o'clock this morning in company with a paramour, when they were both drinking at a public house at the corner of Dorset-street. Her name is Mary Jane Kelly, and the man she lived with sells oranges in the streets. After speaking to her in the public house he left there to sell oranges, and he states that he did not see her again until her corpse was discovered. The mutilations of the body revealed such a state of things as has probably never been equalled in the annals of crime. The head was not lying apart from the body, but was hanging by a mere thread. Both ears and the nose were cut off, all the flesh was stripped completely off the thighs, and the woman was not only disembowelled, but the womb and other parts are missing, similar to the previous murders in this locality. Dr. Bond, of the Westminster Hospital, was in the room with the other doctors when the examination was being held. The body was this afternoon photographed. Dr. J. R. Gabe, of the Mecklenburg-square has seen the body, but in reply to questions put to him by a Press Association representative, he declined to give any details. He merely says he has seen a great deal in dissecting rooms, but never in his life saw such a horrible sight as the murdered woman presented. LATEST DETAILS. In addition to the mutilations previously described, the woman's forehead and cheeks were flayed, and one hand had been pushed into the stomach. Most contradictory statements are met with as to the last hour at which the woman was last seen alive, but it is believed the murder must have taken place shortly before ten o'clock. Up to three o'clock no bloodhounds had arrived, but they were expected. The police have drawn a cordon round the streets in the vicinity. A SUSPICIOUS INCIDENT. A young woman who sells roasted chestnuts at the corner near the scene of the murder, has told a Press Association reporter that about 12 o'clock a gentlemanly dressed man came up and asked if she had heard of the murder? She said she had, and the man grinned, and said, "I know more about it than you." He then stared and walked off. He wore a black coat, black silk hat, and speckled trousers and carried a black bag. The woman further states that the same man accosted three young unfortunates in Dorset-street last night, and they chased him and asked him what he had in the bag, he said, "Something the ladies don't like."

QUESTIONS IN THE HOUSE OF COMMONS. Mr. Conybeare asked the Home Secretary whether he had seen in to-night's evening papers the report of another terrible murder at Whitechapel: and whether he did not think the time had arrived for Sir Charles Warren to be replaced by an efficient officer? The Speaker – The hon. Gentleman must give notice of the question in the ordinary way. Mr. Cunningham Graham – Is it true that Sir Charles Warren is in St. Petersburg at the moment? Mr. w. H. Smith – No, it is not true. ANOTHER ACCOUNT. Last night's Echo says: - Whitechapel is panic stricken. A murder as horrible in its details as any yet committed in the East-end, and resembling the recent atrocities perpetrated there, was discovered this morning shortly before eleven o'clock in a room at a place known as Miller's-court, a turning out of Dorset-street, Commercial-street. So reticent are the police in the matter, and such are the extraordinary precautions taken by the police to preserve whatever clue may be left, that the roads adjacent are blocked by the authorities, and only persons having any business in the immediate vicinity are allowed to enter the purlieus of the spot where the tragedy has occurred. The court where the murder has taken place is an alley the house where the body was found being overlooked by a mews – No. 25, Dorset-street. Inspector Abberline, Inspector Beck, Detective Sergeants Thicke and White, together with other officers sent specially over from Scotland-yard, are now searching all the houses within a stone's throw of No. 25, Dorset-street. At every street corner excited groups of people conversing about this, the latest East-End mystery. Mrs. Hewitt, who lives at the Mews at No. 23 Dorset-street, said the first she heard of the murder at eleven o'clock this morning, when upon looking out of her window, she saw the place surrounded by about fifty police. Mrs. Hewitt heard no screams last night. The woman is not yet defiantly identified. The detectives engaged in the case assert that they believe it is only the work of a few hours before the miscreant will be brought to justice. Dr. G. B. Phillips, the divisional surgeon of police, was quickly summoned when the discovery was made. At his direction no one has been allowed to interfere with the position in which the body was found. The question is being asked in the neighbourhood as to why the bloodhounds have not been made use of on the present occasion. The opportunity was surely a good one to prove their utility or otherwise. In spite of the extraordinary precautions taken by the police authorities to keep secret the facts connected with the crime are oozing out, and from special inquires made at Whitechapel by an Echo reporter this afternoon, it appears that the poor girl had rented one room at the house for about 15 months. The premises are not used strictly as a lodging house – for it was unregistered, it is believed – but were let to separate tenants, who paid small weekly sums for each room. The house belongs to Mr. McCarthy, who keeps a chandler's shop in Dorset-street, and also owns some common lodging-houses in the district, notably one in which "Pearly Poll," Mog Sullivan, and other women – incidentally mentioned in the inquiries relating to the atrocities – were accustomed to live. The young woman found murdered this morning was about 23 years of age, and was only known to Mr. McCarthy as Mary Jane. In this wretched locality, where the common ages – even the ordinary decencies – of life are unrecognised in the "moral" code of the wretched woman who lead a life of shame, their very surnames are often unknown t their associates, and even their Christian names are not known to them. The murder is one of the most horrible character, worse than any of the preceding. The woman was found lying on a bed, the one arm extended, and the other across her breast, which was ripped open, and the breasts cut off. The flesh on her legs was cut down in strips, the thighs being almost bare to the bone. Her face was also mutilated beyond recognition, and her nose was cut off. Lately the deceased woman had been living with the man supposed by Mr. McCarthy to her husband. He recently left her. It is conjectured that [illegible] murderer last night, he [illegible] her to the [illegible] then perpetrated the crime in the stillness of the night. No sound was heard, or any cries of distress. AN ARREST. A man was arrested last night in Whitechapel on suspicion of having committed the Dorset-street murder. He was pointed out to the police by some woman as a man who had accosted them on the previous night, and the movement's excited suspicion. He was taken to Commercial-street police station, followed by an [illegible] crowd.

The Hull and East Yorkshire and Lincolnshire Times, November 10th 1888,

ANOTHER OUTRAGE IN WHITECHAPEL. MURDER OF A WOMAN. THE BODY FOUND IN AN EMPTY HOUSE. THE VICTIM DISEMBOWELLED. EARS AND NOSE CUT OFF. EXCITEMENT IN THE STREETS. The Press Association says a report from Spitalfields at noon, states that a woman was murdered this morning in Dorset-court, Dorset-street, Whitechapel. The particulars have not yet transpired. The Press Association says at half past ten this morning the dead body of a woman, with her head almost severed from her body, was found in an untenanted outhouse or shed in Dorset-court, Dorset-street, Commercial-street, Spitalfields. It had evidently laid there for some hours, but several scavengers, who were in the court at nine o'clock this morning declare that the body was not there then. They might, however, have been mistaken, as the place is very dark. An alarm was immediately raised, and an inspector of police and a number of constables were soon on the spot. It is remarkable that Dorset-court is exactly opposite the house in Dorset-street in which the unfortunate woman Annie Chapman used to lodge. The discovery created the greatest excitement in the neighbourhood and crowds quickly gathered at the scene. Lewis, a tailor, states that he was playing pitch and toss in the court at nine o'clock this morning, and an hour before that he had seen the woman leave the house and return with some milk. There is evidence as to who was in the house with her, and up to two o'clock there was no clue to the perpetrator of the murder. The court is in the lowers part of Spitalfields. The street in the vicinity of the crime are crowded with people eagerly discussing the latest "horror," the woman of a certain class being particularly excited at the fact that another of their number had been brutally murdered. It is confidently stated the deceased was seen after 10 o'clock this morning in the company with a paramour, when they were both drinking at a public house on the corner of Dorset-street. Her name is Mary Jane Kelly. The man she lived with sells oranges, and he states that he did not see her again until her corpse was discovered. The mutilations of the body reveal such a shocking state of things as

Mike Covell

has probably never been equalled in the annals of crime. The head was not lying apart from the body, but was hanging by a mere thread. Both ears and the nose was cut off. All the flesh was stripped completely off the thighs, and the woman was not only disembowelled, but the womb and other parts are still missing, similar to the previous murders in this locality. Dr. Bond, of Westminster Hospital, was in the room with the other doctors when the examination was being held. The body was this afternoon photographed. – dr. J. R. Gabe, of Mecklenburgh-square, has seen the body, but in reply to questions put to him by the Press Association's representative he declined to give any details. He merely says he has seen a great deal in dissecting rooms, but never in his life saw such a horrible sight as the murdered woman presented. In addition to the mutilations previously described, the woman's forehead and cheeks were flayed, and one hand had been pushed into the stomach. Most contradictory statements are met with as to the last hour at which the woman was last seen alive, but it is believed the murder must have taken place shortly before 10 o'clock. Up to three o'clock no bloodhounds arrived, but they were expected. The police have drawn a cordon round the streets in the vicinity. THE BLOODHOUNDS. The bloodhounds were not employed as expected, it being understood there were none available. REMOVAL OF THE VICTIM'S REMAINS. The remains of the victim were removed at four o'clock in a rough coffin to the mortuary in Shoreditch, to await the inquest. EXTRAORDINARY RUMOUR. The police up to ten o'clock last night had no clue to the murderer, but there is a belief among some of them that he is employed on one of the Continental cattle boats which come to London on Thursdays or Fridays, and leave again on Sundays and Mondays. There was intense excitement in Spitalfields last night, and the streets were thronged with people discussing the details of the crime. AN ARREST. A man was arrested last night in Whitechapel on suspicion of having committed the Dorset-street crime. He was pointed out to the police by some women as a man who had accosted them on Thursday night, and whose movements excited suspicion. He was taken to Commercial-street Police Station, followed by an intense crowd. HOW THE MURDER WAS DISCOVERED. The crime was first discovered by a young man named McCarthy, who went to the house this morning with his mother to collect the rent. On opening the front door he saw the body lying in the passage, and he immediately closed the door again, and drew his mother away crying, "Mother there's another murder." An alarm was soon raised, and the police at once took possession of the house, and refused admission to all except officials. THE MURDERER SPOKEN WITH. A young woman who sells roasted chestnuts at the corner near the scene of the murder has told the Press Association reporter that about 12 o'clock a gentlemanly dressed man came up and asked if she had heard of the murder. She said she had, and the man grinned and said, "I know more about it than you." He then stared, and walked off. He wore a black coat, black silk hat, and speckled trousers, and carried a black bag. The woman further states that the same man accosted three young unfortunates in Dorset-street, on Thursday night, and they chased him and asked him what he had in the bag, and said, "Something the ladies don't like." ANOTHER ACCOUNT. The Press Association, in another account says: - About half past 10 yesterday morning a horrible discovery was made in Miller-court, Dorset-street, Spitalfields, in the immediate neighbourhood of Hanbury-street, a locality rendered notorious by the crimes of the past few months. The body of a woman, shockingly mutilated, was found by a man named John Bower in a room of a house at the end of the court. Bowyer had been sent my Mr. McCarthy, the landlord, to collect the rent of the room No. 13, which was occupied by the murdered woman, Mary Jane Kelly, who was in arrears. Upon knocking at the door, Bowyer received no answer, and on looking through a broken window he saw the woman lying on her back quiet naked, while there were marks of blood about the place. Finding the door locked, and the key having been removed, Bowyer informed McCarthy of the discovery, and he having looked through the broken pane, sent Bowyer to Commercial-street Police Station. Inspector Buck was the first officer on the spot, and before anything was done to disturb the body or its surroundings information was sent to Scotland Yard. Inspector Abberline afterwards arrived, and was followed by Superintendent Arnold. The door was then forced. On entering the room it was seen that the body of the unfortunate woman had been terribly mutilated. The nose was cut off, the face lacerated beyond recognition, the breasts were both cut off, and placed on the table, the heart and liver were beside the body, and the uterus was missing. Portions of flesh had been cut from the thighs, and other barbarities committed by the murderer. The deceased was known as a prostitute, and was about five and twenty years of age. She lived with a man who was a salesman in Billingsgate Market, but who is said to have been away from deceased for eight or ten days past. The last seen or heard of the murdered woman was about one o'clock yesterday morning, when she was under the influence of liquor and was heard singing in her room. Whether the murderer was then in her company is uncertain, but there seems to be no doubt that she took a man to her lodging for immoral purpose. On Thursday night she was in the streets as usual, and complained to some of her acquaintances that she was unable to obtain money for her rent. None of the neighbours appeared to have heard any unusual noise during the night. The court in which the deceased lived is situate near No. 25, Dorset-street, and terminates in a square yard. The room occupied by the deceased is on the ground floor, - Dr. Duke was the first

Mike Covell

> *medical man to reach the spot. – Dr. Phillips and Dr. Bond, of Westminster, are making the post mortem examination.*

November 12th 1888

The Hull Daily News, November 12th 1888,

> *THE BLOOD CURDLING CRIMES IN WHITECHAPEL. THE LATEST ATROCITY. AN IMPORTANT STATEMENT. DESCRIPTION OF THE SUPPOSED MURDERER. London, Saturday. A representative of the Press Association, who has since last night been investigating the circumstances of the murder of Mary Jane Kelly, in Dorset-street, Spitalfields, states that the excitement has in some degree subsided. Between one and four this morning numbers of unfortunate woman frequented the thoroughfares in the neighbourhood with an unconcern which must deemed remarkable. The strong detachment of additional detectives who have been requisitioned, as well as the volunteer watchers, performed their unenviable duties in the regular manner; but otherwise there was nothing in the aspect of affairs to excite the attention of a passer-by. Many persons state that the unfortunate woman never left the house, 26, Dorset-street, after she entered it at midnight on Thursday. Others who were companions of the deceased, state that she came out of her house at eight o'clock on Friday morning for provisions, and that they were drinking at with her in the Britannia Tavern at ten o'clock, an hour before her mutilated body was found. The hour at which the murder was committed is thus a matter of the first importance. A woman named Kennedy, who was staying with her parents at a house in the court immediately opposite the room in which the body was found, makes a statement which, if trustworthy, which there seems little reason to doubt, fixes conclusively the time of the murder. She says that about three o'clock on Friday morning she entered her parents' house, which is just opposite, and noticed three persons at the corner of the street near the Britannia Public-house. There was a young man, respectably dressed, with a dark moustache, talking to a woman whom she did not know. There was also another woman, poorly clad without any headgear. The man and woman appeared to be the worse for liquor, and she heard the man ask "Are you coming?" whereupon the woman turned in an opposite direction from that in which the man wished her to go. Kennedy, at her parent's house, sometime about half past three states she heard a cry of "Murder," from the direction of Kelly's room. That cry was not repeated, and she took no further notice until she heard of the murder. She has since stated as follows:- On Wednesday evening I and my sister were in the neighbourhood of Bethnal Green-road, when we were accosted by a suspicious*

man, about forty years old, 5ft, 8in. high, and wore a short jacket, over which he had a long top coat and billycock hat. He had a black moustache. He asked us to accompany him to a lonely spot, as he was known about here, and there was a policeman looking at him. She asserts that no policeman was in sight. He made several strange remarks and he was very white in the face, which he endeavoured to conceal. He carried a black bag. He led the way to a very dark thoroughfare at the back of the workhouse, and they followed him. He pushed open a small door in a pair of iron gates, and he asked one of them to follow him, saying, "I only want one." They became alarmed, and escaped, raising the cry of "Jack the Ripper." A gentleman who was passing is stated to have intercepted the man whilst the woman made their escape. The man, Mrs Kennedy states, whom she saw on Friday closely resembles the one who alarmed her on Thursday evening, and she would recognise him again. Her description tallies with that already in the possession of the police as that of the supposed murderer. There is every probability therefore that the murderer entered the unhappy woman's house early on Friday morning. A second man was arrested early this morning and is still in custody. He is a foreigner, but the case against him is not known. FURTHER PARTICULARS. The two men arrested during the night were afterwards liberated, and this morning there is no one in custody. The date of the inquest has not yet been fixed. A crowd of loiterers assembled during the forenoon in Dorset-street, and hung about the house where the crime was committed, but no one was allowed to enter Millers-court, the entrance to which was guarded by three constables. No fresh clue has been discovered. LATEST DETAILS. The inquiries for the man Barnett, at Buller's lodging-house, New-street, Bishopsgate-street, have been so numerous that the landlord states he has turned Barnett out of the house, his presence there having become a nuisance. The inquest has been fixed for Monday next at Eleven o'clock, at Shoreditch town-hall, before Dr. McDonald, M.P. Further inquiries show that the boy who stayed with Kelly was not her child, but that of a woman who had stayed with her on several occasions. POST-MORTEN EXAMINATION HELD. A post-mortem examination was made at the district mortuary in Shoreditch, this morning of the murdered woman's remains by Dr. Bond, of Westminster Hospital, Dr. Gordon Brown, Surgeon to the City Police, and Dr. Phillips, divisional surgeon. The police intend examining the ashes in the grate in Kelly's room in search of remains of the organs, which it is suspected may have been burnt. Portions of a coat and hat where found amongst the rubbish underneath the grate. OFFICIAL COMMUNICATION-OFFER OF PARDON TO ACCOMPLICE. The Press Association has received the following official communication from Sir Charles Warren:-

Mike Covell

> *"Murder. Pardon. "Whereas, on Nov. 8th or 9th, in Miller's-court, Dorset-street, Spitalfields, Mary Janette Kelly was murdered by some person or persons unknown, the Secretary of State will advise the grant of Her Majesty's gracious pardon to any accomplice, not being a person who contrived or actually committed the murder, who shall give such information and evidence as shall lead to the discovery and conviction of the person or persons who committed the murder. - "Charles Warren," "The Commissioner of Police of the Metropolis, "Metropolitan Police, 4, Whitehall-place, "10th November, 1888."*

The Hull Daily Mail, November 12th 1888,

> *REPORTED RESIGNATION OF SIR CHARLES WARREN. The Press Association is informed that Sir Charles Warren sent in his resignation on Saturday, after the statement made by Mr Matthews in the House of Commons regarding the publication of the article in Murray's Magazine that Sir Charles Warren had been requested to observe the rules of the Home Office as to the publication of works on matters relating to the service. Sir Charles took counsel with his friends, on Saturday and the result was that, on the same evening he sent his resignation, couched in the briefest language to the Home Secretary, stating as his grounds for doing so that he could not accept the reproof administered to him. This morning all his books and papers were removed from the Chief Commissioners office at Scotland Yard, and this was the first intimation at Scotland Yard that he had relinquished the position. The Press Association is a later telegram says the fact of Sir Charles Warren's resignation is officially confirmed this afternoon.*

The Hull Daily Mail, November 12th 1888,

> *THE WHITECHAPEL MURDER. OPENING OF THE INQUEST. This morning Dr. McDonald, M.P., coroner for North-East Middlesex, opened an inquest at Shoreditch Town Hall, on the body of Mary Jeanette Kelly, murdered in Miller's-court, Dorset-street, Spitalfields, during Thursday night or Friday morning. The jury having been sworn, proceeded to view the body, and afterwards visited the scene of the murder. On their return evidence was taken. The crowd was much smaller than at the inquest of the previous victims. Mr. Vanderhart, represented the Whitechapel Vigilance Committee, and Inspector Abberline was present on behalf of the police. AN UNFOUNDED STATEMENT. The Coroner complained of unfounded statements in the Press as to alleged communications between himself and Mr. Wynn Baxter with regard to jurisdiction. EXAMINATION OF THE WITNESSES. IDENTIFICATION OF*

THE BODY. Joseph Barnett, labourer, deposed: I identify the body of the deceased as that of a young woman with whom I have lived with for eight months. I separated from her on the 30th of last month. I left her because she brought a prostitute to live in our room. I saw deceased last between half past seven and a quarter to eight on Thursday night. We were on friendly terms. Before leaving I said I had no money. Deceased was sober, and told me her father's name was John Kelly, gaffer at an ironworks in Carnarvonshire. She was born in Limerick. Was married in Wales to a man named Davis, killed in a colliery explosion. After leading an immoral life in Cardiff deceased came to a house in the West End of London. A gentleman induced her to go to France. She returned and lived at Ratcliffe-highway, then at Pennington-street. I met her in Commercial-street, and arranged to live with her. At deceased's request I read to her newspaper reports of the previous Whitechapel murders. Did not hear her express fear of any person. The jury expressed a wish that Dr. Phillips, police surgeon, who was not present, should attend, so that some medical evidence might be taken. Thomas Bowyer, Dorset-street, Spitalfields, said: On Friday morning I went to the house of the deceased to collect rent for Mr. McCarthy. I knocked, but got no answer. I found the window broken. Inspector Ledger now put in a plan of the premises. Bowyer resumed: I put the curtain aside, and, looking in, saw two lumps of flesh on the table. Looking a second time, I saw the body on the bed and a pool of blood on the floor. I reported the discovery to the police. John McCarthy, grocer, lodging house keeper, Dorset-street, deposed: Within five minutes he came back saying he had seen blood in No. 13 room of Miller's-court. I went and saw the body. I could say nothing for a little time, but when I recovered I accompanied my man to the police. An inspector came with me to the house. I do not know that Barnett and deceased had any serious quarrel. I let the room at 4s 6d a week. Deceased was 29s in arrears. I often saw the deceased the worse for drink. When drunk, she became noisy and sang. Mary Ann Cook deposed: I live at 5 Miller's-court, opposite deceased. About midnight on Thursday I saw deceased in Dorset-street. She was very much the worse for drink. I saw her go up the court with a short stout man, shabbily dressed. He carried a pot of ale, and wore a black coat and hat. He had a clean shaven chin, sandy whiskers and moustache. Deceased wished me "good night," and went into her room. I heard her singing the song, "A violet I plucked from my mother's grave." I afterwards went out of my room, coming back at one o'clock she was still singing. I again went out. Coming back, I saw the light in deceased's room had been put out and all was silent. I did not sleep after going to bed. If there had been a cry of murder during the night I must have heard it. *WHAT ANOTHER WITNESS OBSERVED.* Elizabeth Prater, Miller's-court, said: I live in the same house. I went into my own room at one o'clock on Friday morning. I then saw no glimmer in the deceased's room. I woke about four, and heard a suppressed cry of "Murder" appearing to come from the court. Did not take particular notice, as I frequently hear such cries. Caroline Maxwell, wife of a lodging house "deputy" in Dorset-street, was next sworn. Mrs Maxwell then deposed: I saw deceased at the corner of Miller's-court shortly after eight o'clock on Friday morning. The deceased told me she felt ill, and vomited. I went with my husband's breakfast. On my return I saw the deceased speaking with a man outside Britannia public house. I cannot give a particular description of the man. He wore a dark clothes, and a sort of plaid coat. Deceased wore a dark skirt, with a velvet body, a shawl but no hat. The man was short and stout. A MAN OBSERVED IN MILLER'S COURT. Sarah Lewis, great Powell-street, stated: I visited a friend at Miller's-court on Friday morning at half-past two o'clock. I saw a man standing on the pavement. He was short and stout, and wore a wide awake hat. I stopped with a friend, Mrs Keyler. I fell asleep in the chair, and awoke at half-past three. I sat awake till a little before four. I heard a female voice scream "Murder!" loudly. I thought the sound came from the direction of the deceased's house. I did not take much notice. Such cries are often heard. THE GENTLEMAN WITH THE BLACK BAG AGAIN! HOW HE WAS DRESSED. At eight o'clock on Wednesday night, when with a female friend, witness was accosted in Bethnal Green-road by a gentleman who carried a bag. He invited one of us to accompany him. Disliking his appearance we left him. The bag was about 9 inches long. The man had a pale face and dark moustache. He wore dark clothes, overcoat, and a high felt hat. On Friday morning, when coming to Miller's-court about half-past two, I met that man with a female in Commercial-street. As I went into Miller's-court they stood at the corner of Dorset-street. THE POLICE SURGEON'S EVIDENCE. Dr. George Baxter Phillips deposed: I am surgeon to the H Division Metropolitan Police. I cannot give the whole of my evidence to day. On Friday morning about eleven o'clock I proceeded to Miller's-court. In a room there I found the mutilated remains of a woman lying two thirds over towards the edge of the bed nearest the door. Subsequent to the injury that caused death the body had been removed from the opposite side of the bed which was nearest the wooden partition. The presence of a quantity of blood on and under the bed leads me to the conclusion that the severance of the carotid artery which was the immediate cause of death, was inflicted while the deceased was lying on the right side of the bedstead, and her head and neck in the right corner. That is as far as I propose to carry my evidence to-day. The Coroner said he proposed to continue taking evidence for another hour. The jury expressed a wish to adjourn for some time. The Coroner replied he would resume in a quarter of an hour. On resuming, Julia Venturney said: I am a charwoman, and live at Miller's-court. Deceased told me she liked *another man, other than Joe Barnett, and he often came to see her. I was at home during Thursday night. Had there been any noises, witness would have heard them. Maria Harvey, a laundress, said: I have slept with deceased on several occasions. Never heard her express fear of anyone. Inspector Beck (H Division) said: I accompanied Dr Phillips to house. Do not know that deceased was known to police. INSPECTOR ABERLINE'S EVIDENCE. Inspector Abberline, Scotland Yard, deposed: I went to Miller's-court at 11.30 a.m. on Friday. When there I received the intimation that the bloodhounds were on the way. I waited until 1.30 p.m., when Superintendent Arnold arrived and said the order for the bloodhounds had been countermanded. The door was then forced. In the grate were traces of woman's clothing having been burnt to give sufficient light for the murderer to do his work. THE VERDICT. The Coroner said this concluded the evidence offered to-day. The question was whether the jury had not already heard sufficient testimony to enable them to determine the cause of death. His own opinion was they might conclude and leave the case to the police. The jury, after a moment's consultation, returned a verdict of "Wilful murder against some person or persons unknown." THE QUESTION OF A REWARD. In the House of Commons this afternoon, replying to Mr. Cunninghome Graham and Mr. Hunter, the Home Secretary said that in declining to offer a reward for the discovery of the Whitechapel murderer, he was following a precedent set by his predecessors. THE REPORTED THREATENING LETTER. The Press Association's reporter on inquiring at Commercial-street Police Station subsequently was informed that no such letter had been received there. The Press Association says that later inquiries show that such a letter was received by Mrs McCarthy. The text was as follows:- "Don't alarm yourself. I am going to do another, but this time it will be a mother and daughter." The letter, which was signed "Jack the Ripper," was at once handed to the police authorities. A MAN IN WOMAN'S DRESS. A man dressed in woman's clothes was arrested on Saturday night in Clerkenwell. He said he only did it for a freak. STATEMENT BY AN AQUINTANCE OF THE VICTIM. Elizabeth Foster, who lives in a lodging house in Dorset-street, has made the following statement to a Press Association reporter:- I have known Mary Jane Kelly for the last 18 months, and we were always good friends. She used to tell me she came from Limerick. She was as nice a woman as one could find, and, although an unfortunate, I don't think she went out on the streets whilst she lived with Barnett. On Wednesday night I was in her lodgings with her, and the next evening I met her in the Ten Bells public house, near Spitalfields Church. We were drinking together, and she went out about five minutes past seven o'clock. I never saw her after that. LIST OF THE WHITECHAPEL MURDERS. Seven woman have now been murdered in the*

Mike Covell

> East End under mysterious circumstances. The following are the dates of the crimes and names of the victims so far as known:-
>
> 1, Last Christmas week,- an unknown woman found murdered near Osborne and Wentworth Streets, Whitechapel.
>
> 2, August 7th,- Martha Turner found stabbed in thirty nine places on a landing in model dwellings known as George Yard Buildings, Commercial Street, Spitalfields.
>
> 3, August 31st,- Mrs Nicholls, murdered and mutilated in Bucks Row, Whitechapel.
>
> 4, September 7th,- Mrs Chapman, murdered and mutilated, Hanbury Street, Whitechapel.
>
> 5, September 30th,- Elizabeth Stride, found with throat cut in Berner Street, Whitechapel.
>
> 6, September 30th,- Woman unknown, murdered and mutilated in Mitre Square, Aldgate.
>
> 7, November 9th ,- Woman murdered in Miller's-court, Dorset-street, Whitechapel.

The Hull Daily Mail, November 12th 1888,

> THE WHITECHAPEL HORROR. The public statement created by the latest tragedy has not abated to any extent, and Dorset-street was this afternoon and this evening in a crowded condition, and the throng, which extended even into Commercial-street, rendered locomotion all but impossible. Jostling the ensembled people were vendors of pamphlets, fresh from the press, describing the Whitechapel crimes, and other itinerant vendors were doing a thriving trade. Two police constables guarded the entrance to Miller's-court, and the adjacent shop of the landlord of the house where the body of the murdered woman was found was besieged. A short distance away a street preacher sought to "improve" the occasion. The onlookers within and about Dorset-street comprised men and woman of every class, and now and again a vehicle would be driven up containing a load of persons impelled by curiosity to visit this locality. Public excitement was for the time intensified by the report, which

spread like lightening that another woman had been murdered in Jubilee-street. The rumours were at once accepted as true, thus demoting that the public entertain little doubt that, if so disposed, the murderer might almost with impunity add to the catalogue of his crimes. Jubilee-street is off Commercial-road, and thither the people at once proceeded from various directions, but inquiries elicited that the rumour had arisen from an accident to a woman necessitating her removal to the hospital. The further post mortem examination on the body of the deceased woman Kelly, led the medical men to the conclusion that she had been murdered some hours before the discovery of the crime. This conclusion, however, conflicts with a statement made to-day to a reporter by people in the neighbourhood. It is asserted that Kelly was seen alive as late as eight o'clock on Friday morning. She was observed about that time standing at the entrance to Miller's-court, and one informant stated that the woman was seen to purchase milk for breakfast. A young woman, who goes by the name of Margaret says: I saw Kelly on Thursday night in Dorset-street. She told me she had no money, and intended to make away with herself. She would only be too pleased if she could get a "friend" to go home with her. Shortly after that a man of shabby appearance came up, and Kelly walked away with him. This was the first occasion, it is said, deceased was to take the strange man to her room. Some statements have appeared respecting the deceased's antecedents, and as to her having formerly lived for some time in a "fashionable" house of resort in the West End. There is reason to believe that not only are these statements well founded, but that she maintained some sort of connection with the companions of her more prosperous days. Seeing that it was contrary to Kelly's custom to take strangers to her room, it is believed that her destroyer offered some exceptional inducement. While the police have been working zealously in the hope of making some discovery of value, the public themselves appear to feel the responsibility was shared by them. "IMPORTANT CAPTURE" Considerable importance is attached to an arrest which was [illegible] at an early hour this morning, through the [illegible] of two men living in Dorset-street. Like many others in the neighbourhood, they appear to have transformed themselves into amateur detectives, and have been perambulating the streets on the lookout for a suspicious person. About three this morning the attention was drawn to two men in Dorset-street who were loitering about. The two men separated and one of them was followed by the two youths into Houndsditch. They carefully observed his appearance, which was that of a foreigner about 5ft, 8in in height, and having a long pointed moustache. He was dressed in a long black overcoat and deerstalker hat. When near Bishopgate-street the young man spoke to a policeman, who at once stopped the stranger and took him to Bishopgate-street Police Station. Here he was searched, and it was found he was carrying a sort of pocket medical chest containing several small bottles of chloroform. In rather imperfect English, he explained he lived in Pimlico. Where he was well known. After this preliminary examination he was taken to Commercial-street Police Station, in which district the murder was committed. He was detained on suspicion, but subsequently was taken to Marlborough-street Police Station for the purpose of facilitating his identification. Another man is detained at Commercial-street on account of his suspicious movements. A man named Peter Maguire says that about eleven o'clock on Saturday night he was drinking at a public house kept by Mrs Feddymont, in Brushfield-street, when he noticed a man talking very earnestly to a young woman. He asked her to accompany him up the neighbouring court, but she refused, and afterwards left the bar. Maguire followed the man who, noticing this, commenced running. He ran into Spitalfields market, Maguire following. The man then stopped, went up a court, took off a pair of gloves he was wearing, and put on another pair. By a roundabout route, he arrived at Shoreditch and got into a bus which Maguire also followed. A policeman was asked by Maguire to stop this bus, but it is said he refused, and Maguire continued in pursuit until he met another constable, who at once stopped the vehicle. The man was visibly huddled up in a corner. Maguire explained his suspicions and the man was taken to Commercial-street Police Station, where he was detained pending enquiries. THE PRISONER DISCHARGED. A later despatch says:- The man Compton has since been discharged. The police telegraphed to the authorities at Kind David-lane, Shadwell, and finding the main statements to be true he was detained no longer. Still later information from the East End states that all the men who were in custody to-day have given satisfactory explanations of their movements, and have been released. ANOTHER ARREST: EXCITING SCENE. Telegraphing at eleven o'clock a correspondent says: Great excitement was caused shortly before ten o'clock last night in the East End by the arrest of a man with a blackened face who publicly proclaimed himself to be "Jack the Ripper." This was at the corner of Wentworth-street, Commercial-street, near the scene of the latest crime. Two young men, one a discharged soldier, immediately seized him, and the great crowd, [illegible] always on Sunday night parade this neighbourhood, raised a cry of "lynch him." Sticks were raised, and the man was furiously attacked, and but for the timely arrival of the police, he would have been seriously injured. The police took him to Leman-street station, when the prisoner proved to be a very remarkable person. He refused to give any name, but stated that he was a doctor at St George's Hospital. He is about 35, height 5ft, 7in, complexion dark, dark moustache, and he was wearing spectacles. He wore no waistcoat, but an ordinary jersey vest beneath his coat. In his pocket he had a double peaked light check cap, and at the time of the arrest he was bareheaded. It took four constables and four civilians to take him to the station to protect him from the infuriated crowd. He is detained in custody, and it seems the police attach much importance to the arrest, as the man's appearance answers the police description of the man wanted. LATEST PARTICULARS. WHO THE VICTIM WAS. ANOTHER ACCOUNT. PRESS ASSOCIATION TELEGRAMS THIS MORNING. London, Monday. Further inquiries during the night have thrown little fresh light on the circumstances of the Whitechapel murder. There is good reason to believe that the unhappy woman Kelly was a native of Cardiff, where her family, according to her statement, were well-to-do people. She is stated to have been very well educated, and an artist of some pretensions. HOW KELLY WAS LED ASTRAY. On her arrival in London she made the acquaintance of a French lady residing at Knightsbridge, who initiated her into the course which has led to so tragic an end. At this time she drove in a carriage, and made several visits to Paris. It is not known precisely how she drifted from this position to the life she led at the East End, but she appears to have lived with a woman named Buki. The two women shortly afterwards went to the house of the lady at Knightsbridge, and demanded her trunk, containing dresses of a costly description. At this time Kelly is stated to have indulged very freely in intoxicants. She next resided with Mrs McCarthy, Pennington-street, which place she left about eighteen months ago to her last residence in Dorset-square. Mrs McCarthy believes that Kelly, when she left her, went to live with a man in the building trade, who Mrs McCarthy believed would have married her. Some short time ago she was aroused about two o'clock one morning by Mrs Kelly who came with a strange man, and asked Mrs McCarthy to give her a bed, which she did, receiving 2s payment. Since then, Mrs McCarthy has never seen her. AN ARREST ON SUNDAY.- A DANGEROUS POSITION. The only arrest yesterday which promised any useful results terminated in as lame a conclusion as the rest. At about ten o'clock a medical gentleman, who was in the vicinity of Wentworth-street suddenly found himself pursued by an excited crowd. Cries of "Jack the Ripper" and "Lynch him" were heard, and he was pinned from behind. With great difficulty he was conveyed to Leman-street Station. He at first refused his name, and his appearance was remarkable, for his face was blackened with soot. He had a dark moustache and some hair on his face, but his chin was close shaven. He had on a black morning coat and under vest, but no waist coat or shirt, nor was he wearing a hat, but a cap was found in his pocket. He announced that he was a Doctor at St Georges Hospital, and gave an address at Willesden, and the name of Holt. He was detained for three hours and a half while enquiries were being made, the result of which justified the police in releasing him. He stated that he had passed several nights in the East End in

Mike Covell

> *various disguises, and complained of the severity with which his arms had been pinioned when arrested, this having been affected by a well-known pugilist, Bendoff, who assisted to get him to the station. THE BLOODHOUNDS-WHERE ARE THEY? The non-appearance of the bloodhounds has been much remarked upon, in view of a recent order by Sir Charles Warren. One explanation is that Sir Charles being out of town at the time, no one else knew where the animals were to be found. It is stated, moreover, that as Government has not decided to employ this means of detection, the cost must have fallen upon private individuals. The scent was kept warm for five hours, and experiment would have been valuable. ANOTHER ARREST THIS MORNING. The Press Association says the police at Commercial-street Station made another arrest at three o'clock this morning in Dorset-street, at the scene of the murder. The man, who does not answer the published description of the murderer, was acting very suspicious, and refused to satisfy the officers as to his recent whereabouts. Inquiries are being [illegible], but up to nine o'clock this morning the man was still in custody. ANOTHER LETTER FROM "JACK THE RIPPER" TWO MORE MURDERS THREATENED. It is reported that Mrs McCarthy, wife of the landlord of No. 26 Dorset-street, this morning received in the post a letter signed "Jack the Ripper," saying they were not to worry themselves, because he planned to do two more in the neighbourhood; a mother and a daughter this time." The letter was immediately sent to Commercial-street Police Station and handed to the inspector on duty.*

The Hull Daily News, November 12th 1888,

> *LATEST NEWS. THE WHITECHAPEL TRAGEDIES. CHEQUERED CAREER OF THE LATEST VICTIM. INTERESTING NARRATIVE. Further inquiries during the night have thrown little fresh light on the circumstances of the Whitechapel murder. There is good reason to believe that the unhappy woman Kelly was a native of Cardiff, where her family, according to her statement, were well-to-do people. She is stated to have been very well educated, and an artist of some pretensions. On her arrival in London she made the acquaintance of a French lady residing at Knightsbridge, who initiated her into the course which has led to so tragic an end. At this time she drove in a carriage, and made several visits to Paris. It is not known precisely how she drifted from this position to the life she led at the East End, but she appears to have lived with a woman named Buki. The two women shortly afterwards went to the house of the lady at Knightsbridge, and demanded her trunk, containing dresses of a costly description. At this time Kelly is stated to have indulged very freely in intoxicants. She next resided with Mrs McCarthy, Pennington-street, which*

place she left about eighteen months ago to her last residence in Dorset-square. Mrs McCarthy believes that Kelly, when she left her, went to live with a man in the building trade, who Mrs McCarthy believed would have married her. Some short time ago she was aroused about two o'clock one morning by Mrs Kelly who came with a strange man, and asked Mrs McCarthy to give her a bed, which she did, receiving 2s payment. Since then, Mrs McCarthy has never seen her. ARREST OF MAN WITH BLACKENED FACE. ANOTHER ACCOUNT. The only arrest yesterday which promised any useful results terminated in as lame a conclusion as the rest. At about ten o'clock a medical gentleman, who was in the vicinity of Wentworth-street suddenly found himself pursued by an excited crowd. Cries of "Jack the Ripper" and "Lynch him" were heard, and he was pinned from behind. With great difficulty he was conveyed to Leman-street Station. He at first refused his name, and his appearance was remarkable, for his face was blackened with soot. He had a dark moustache and some hair on his face, but his chin was close shaven. He had on a black morning coat and under vest, but no waist coat or shirt, nor was he wearing a hat, but a cap was found in his pocket. He announced that he was a Doctor at St Georges Hospital, and gave an address at Willesden, and the name of Holt. He was detained for three hours and a half while enquiries were being made, the result of which justified the police in releasing him. He stated that he had passed several nights in the East End in various disguises, and complained of the severity with which his arms had been pinioned when arrested, this having been affected by a well-known pugilist, Bendoff, who assisted to get him to the station. THE NON-APPEARANCE OF THE BLOODHOUNDS. The non-appearance of the bloodhounds has been much remarked upon, in view of a recent order by Sir Charles Warren. One explanation is that Sir Charles being out of town at the time, no one else knew where the animals were to be found. It is stated, moreover, that as Government has not decided to employ this means of detection, the cost must have fallen upon private individuals. The scent was kept warm for five hours, and experiment would have been valuable. ANOTHER ARREST THIS MORNING. The Press Association says the police at Commercial-street Station made another arrest at three o'clock this morning in Dorset-street, at the scene of the murder. The man, who does not answer the published description of the murderer, was acting very suspicious, and refused to satisfy the officers as to his recent whereabouts. Inquiries are being [illegible], but up to nine o'clock this morning the man was still in custody. MORE MURDERS THREATENED. A MOTHER AND DAUGHTER TO BE SACRIFICED. It is reported that Mrs McCarthy, wife of the landlord of No. 26 Dorset-street, this morning received in the post a letter signed "Jack the Ripper," saying they were not to worry themselves, because he planned to do

Mike Covell

> *two more in the neighbourhood; a mother and a daughter this time." The letter was immediately sent to Commercial-street Police Station and handed to the inspector on duty.*

The Eastern Morning News, November 10th 1888,

> *ANOTHER ATROCITY IN WHITECHAPEL. MYSTERIOUS MURDER. HORRIBLE MUTILATIONS. DESCRIPTION BY A DISCOVERER. This morning, in the midst of the popular demonstration connected with the Lord Mayor's Show, the tens of thousands of persons who had assembled along the line of route from the City to the West End to watch the civic pageant pass were startled and horrified by the hoarse cries of the street newspaper hawkers announcing the perpetration of another terrible murder in Whitechapel. The news received speedy confirmation, and even the meagre particulars immediately obtainable left no doubt that this, the latest of the series of crimes which has for months past kept the East of London in a state of fear almost amounting to panic, exceeded in its cold-blooded fiendish atrocity any that have preceded it. In the details of the murder itself there is unhappily little that can be described as novel - the same mournful story of want, immorality, and inhuman crime, but in one most important circumstance the murder differs in a startling manner from all that have gone before it. It was committed not in the open air, but in a house, into which the murderer had been taken by his too willing victim. The scene of the murder is Miller court, Dorset-street, Commercial-street, a district composed of big warehouses, squalid streets, and in a striking degree of registered lodging-houses. Dorset street is a fairly wide thoroughfare, and at night, owing to the lamps in the windows and over the doors of the numerous lodging-houses, it may be described as well-lighted. Miller court is approached by an arched passage not more than three feet wide, which is unlighted, and from this passage open two doors leading into the houses on each side. The house on the left hand side is kept as a chandler's shop by a respectable man named M'Carthy, to whom also belongs the house in the court in which the crime was committed. The court is a very small one, about 30 feet long by 10 broad. On both sides are three or four small houses, cleanly whitewashed up to the first floor windows. The ground floor of the house to the right of this court is used as a store, with a gate entrance, and the upper floors are let off in tenements, as is the case also with M'Carthy's house. Opposite the court is a very large lodging-house, of a somewhat inferior character. This house is well lighted and people hang about it nearly all night. There is another well frequented lodging-house next door to M'Carthy's, and within a yard or two to the entrance to the court is a wall lamp, the light from which is thrown nearly on*

to the passage. But perhaps the most curious item in the entire surrounding is a large placard posted on the wall of the next house but one from the right hand side, offering, in the name of an illustrated weekly paper, a reward of one hundred pounds for the discovery of the man who murdered the woman Nicholls in Hanbury-street. The murder was committed at No 2 Miller court, sometime after midnight. The murdered woman is not particularly well known even to her neighbours. As is customary among people of her class, she had several nicknames, including "Mary Jane," and "Fair Emma," but the name by which she was known to her landlord, and which has proved to be correct, was Mary Jane Kelly. She had been married for some years, or at any rate had lived regularly with a man named Kelly. But it is known that she went on the streets irregularly at first; but after separating from her husband, chiefly on account of her drunken habits and quarrelsome disposition, she took to prostitution as a regular means of living. Almost the only friend she is known to have had was a woman named Harvey, who used to sleep with her occasionally. Kelly went out as usual last evening, and was seen in the neighbourhood about 10 o'clock, in company with a man, of whom, however, no description can be obtained. She was last seen, as far as can be ascertained, in Commercial street about half-past 11. She was then alone and was probably making her way home. It is supposed that she met the murderer in Commercial street, and he probably induced her to take him home without indulging in more drink; at any rate, nothing was seen of the couple in the neighbouring public-houses, nor in the beerhouse at the corner of Dorset street. The pair reached Miller court about midnight, but they were not seen to enter the house. The street door was closed, but the woman had a latchkey, and as she must have been fairly sober, she and her companion would have been obliged to enter the house and reach the woman's room without making a noise. A light was seen shining through the window of the room for some time after the couple must have entered it, and one person asserts positively that the woman was heard singing the refrain of a popular song as late as one o'clock this morning. But here again there is a conflict of testimony which the police are even now engaged in endeavouring to reconcile. That which follows is beyond doubt. At about 10 o'clock this morning Mr M'Carthy set a man who works for him to the house with orders to see Kelly and obtain from her some money on account of the rent of which she was largely in arrears. The man went and knocked at the door, but received no answer. He had assumed the woman would be up, because not infrequently she would make purchases in M'Carthy's shop before that hour. He listened, but heard no sound, and then becoming alarmed, tried the door. It was quite fast, and seemed to have been locked from the outside. Determined to find out what was wrong, the man went to the window commanding a view of the whole room, with the intention of *entering if necessary. One glance in the room, however, was sufficient. He saw on the bed the body of a woman dead, and mutilated in such a ghastly manner that the observer nearly fainted from horror. He rushed affrighted out of the court and into M'Carthy's shop, begging him for God's sake to come and look. M'Carthy, hardly less horrified, returned to the house with his man, and both looked into the room. The place looked like a shambles. Blood was everywhere, and pieces of flesh were scattered about the floor, while on the little table, in full view of the window, was a hideous lump. M'Carthy sent his man for the police, and Inspector Buck, of Commercial road Station, and Inspector Abberline, of the Criminal Investigation Department, stationed at Leman street, arrived within ten minutes. A strong squad of police were also despatched from Commercial street Station to assist the regular patrol men in maintaining order. A large crowd had already assembled, and Inspector Buck's first care was to clear Dorset street of idlers, to close the entrance to the court with two policemen, and then to draw a cordon across each end of Dorset street. From that time forward only authorised persons were permitted in Dorset street. The constables in charge of the entrance to Miller court allowed no one to pass in or out, not even the inhabitants of the place. Meanwhile no attempt had been made to force an entrance to the room. The two inspectors had looked through the window, and had seen sufficient to prove that a most murderous crime had been committed, but neither officer seemed to care to undertake responsibility, and it was not until some twenty minutes after the first alarm had been given that Superintendent Arnold, the officer in charge of the division, arrived on the scene, and at once took over charge. By his direction M'Carthy obtained a pickaxe, and the door was forced open, and the police officers entered the room. They did not care to remain longer than was necessary to note accurately the position of the body, the general appearance of the apartment, and the character of the principal mutilations. The sight was enough to unnerve strong men, even so experienced an officer as Inspector Abberline, who had immediate charge of the inquiries connected with most of the recent murders. The throat had been cut with such ferocious and appalling thoroughness that the head was almost severed from the trunk. The body, which was almost naked, had been ripped up and literally disembowelled. The chief organs had been entirely removed. Some were thrown upon the floor, and others placed on the table. Dr. Duke, the police surgeon of the H Division, was the first medical man to arrive on the spot, and he at once undertook a preliminary examination. Half an hour later he was joined by Dr. Bond, the chief surgeon of the metropolitan police, and together they commenced a post-mortem examination on the spot as soon as the requisite authority had been obtained. Sir Charles Warren arrived at Miller court at a quarter to 2 o'clock, having driven from Scotland Yard in a hansom. He viewed the room, and received from Superintendent Arnold a report of what had been done. The Commissioner remained on the spot until the completion of the post-mortem examination at a quarter to 4, and then returned to Scotland Yard, taking Dr Bond with him. Previous to the post-mortem examination, a photographer, who was brought on the scene only after considerable difficulty and delay, was set to work, with a view to obtaining permanent evidence as to the state of the room, the condition of the body, and other points, trivial perhaps, but possibly important, which have heretofore been too much neglected in the investigation of the series of crimes of which to-day's horror is surely the climax. The state of the atmosphere was unfortunately not favourable to good results. A slight drizzling rain was falling, the air was dusky, even in the open thoroughfare, and in the little court it was at times almost dark, especially inside the miserable houses. The photographer, however, did his best, and succeeded in securing several negatives, which he hopes will be useful. The post-mortem examination lasted just two hours, and was of the most thorough character. Every indication as to the manner in which the murderer conducted his awful work was carefully noted, as well as the position of every organ and the larger pieces of flesh. The surgeon's report will, in consequence, be of an unusually exhaustive character, but it will not be made public until the surgeons give their evidence at the coroner's inquest. Sufficient is known to place the crime beyond doubt in the same category as those perpetrated in George Yard, Buck's-row, Berner-street, Hanbury-street and Mitre-square. At ten minutes to four o'clock a one-horse carrier's cart, with the ordinary tarpaulin cover, was driven into Dorset-street, and stopped opposite Miller court. From the cart was taken a long shell or coffin, dirty and scratched, with constant use. This was taken into the chamber, and there the remains were temporarily coffined. The news that the body was about to be removed caused a great rush of people from the courts running out of Dorset-street, and there was a determined effort to break the police cordon at the Commercial street end. The crowd which pressed round the van was of the very humblest class, but the demeanour of the poor people was all that could be desired. Ragged caps were doffed, and slatternly-looking women shed tears as the shell covered with a ragged-looking cloth was placed in the van. The remains were taken to the Shoreditch Mortuary, where they will remain till they have been viewed by the coroner's jury. The inquest will open on Monday morning. In an interview with a representative of the Central News, John M'Carthy, the owner of the houses in Miller's Court, who keeps a chandler's shop in Dorset street, made the following statement as to the murdered woman:- "The victim of this terrible murder was about 23 or 24 years of age, and lived with a coal porter named Kelly, passing as his wife. They, however, quarrelled sometime back and separated. A woman named Harvey slept with her several nights since Kelly separated from her, and she was not with her last night. The deceased's Christian named was Mary Jane, and since her murder I have discovered that she was an "unfortunate," and walked the streets in the neighbourhood of Aldgate. Her habits were irregular, and she often came home at night the worse for drink. Her mother lives in Ireland, but in what county I do not know. Deceased used to receive letters from her occasionally. The unfortunate woman had not paid her rent for several weeks; in fact she owed me 30s altogether, so this morning about 11 o'clock I sent my man to ask her If she could pay the money. He knocked at the door, but received no answer. Thinking this very strange, he looked in at the window, and, to his horror, he saw the body of Kelly lying on the bed covered with blood. He immediately came back to me and told me what he had seen. I was, of course, as horrified as he was, and I went with him to the house and looked in at the window. The sight I saw was more ghastly even than I had prepared myself for. On the bed lay the body as my man had told me, while the table was covered with what seemed to me to be lumps of flesh. I said to my man "Harry go at once to the police station and fetch someone here." He went off at once and brought back Inspector Buck, who looked through the window as we had done. He then despatched a telegram to Superintendent Arnold, but before Superintendent Arnold arrived Inspector Abberline came and gave orders that no one should be allowed to enter or leave the court. The Inspector waited a little while and then sent a telegram to Sir Charles Warren to bring the bloodhounds, so as to trace the murderer if possible. As soon as Superintendent Arnold arrived he gave instructions for the door to be burst open. I at once forced the door with a pickaxe, and we entered the room. The sight we saw I cannot drive away from my mind. It looked more like the work of a devil than of a man. The poor woman's body was lying on the bed undressed. She had been completely disembowelled, and her entrails had been taken out and placed on the table. It was those that I had seen when I looked through the window. The woman's nose had been cut off and her face gashed and mutilated, so that she was quite beyond recognition. Both her breasts too had been cut clean away and placed by the side of the intestines on the table. The body was, of course, covered with blood, and so was the bed. The whole scene is more than I can describe. It is most extraordinary that nothing should have been heard by the neighbours, as there are people passing backwards and forwards at all hours of the night, but no one heard as much as a scream. A woman heard Kelly singing "Sweet Violets" at 1 o'clock this morning, so up to that time, at all events, she was alive and well. So far as I can ascertain no one saw her take a an into the house wither her last night." Mr M'Carthy is spoken of by the police as a most respectable man, and was recently awarded a prize for collecting money for the* hospitals. He is naturally much distressed at the terrible tragedy which has occurred literally at his door. Dr. Forbes Winslow has favoured the Central News with the following opinion on this latest murder:- "That it is the work of the same homicidal lunatic who has committed the other crimes in Whitechapel. The whole harrowing details point to this conclusion. The way in which the murder was done and the strange state in which the body was left is not consistent with sanity. The theory I stated some days ago has come true to the letter. This was to the effect that the murderer was in a 'lucid interval,' and would recommence directly this state had passed away. It appears that the authorities were forgetting this theory, and that someone had been persuading them that from the fact of so long a time intervening between the murders, therefore it could not be a homicidal maniac. I desire as being originally responsible for this theory, to flatly deny this, and to state more emphatically than ever that the murderer is one and the same person, and he is a lunatic suffering from homicidal monomania, who during the lucid intervals is calm and forgetful of what he has been doing in the madness of his attack. I also say that unless those in authority take the proper steps as advised and drop the red-tapism surrounding a Government office, such crimes will continue to be perpetrated in our metropolis to the terror of London. It appears to me it is the burning question of the hour, and of much more vital importance than some now attracting the attention of our community." A reporter who to-night saw the room in which the murder was committed says it was a tenement by itself, having formerly been the back parlour of No 26 Dorset street. A partition had been erected cutting it off from the house, and the entrance door opened into Miller's court. The two windows also faced the court; and as the body could be seen from the court his morning, it is evident that unless the murderer perpetrated his crime with the light turned out, any person passing by could have witnessed the deed. The lock of the door was a spring one, and the murderer apparently took the key away with him when he left, as it cannot be found. The more the facts are investigated the more apparent becomes the cool daring of the murderer. There are six houses in the court besides the tenement occupied by the deceased. The door of Kelly's room is the first on the right-hand side on entering from the street, and the other houses, three on either side, are higher up the passage. Mrs Prater, who occupies a room in 26 Dorset street above that of the deceased, stated to-night that she had a chat with Kelly yesterday morning. Kelly, who was doing some crochet work at the time, said, "I hope it will be a fine day to-morrow as I want to go to the Lord Mayor's Show." "She was a very pleasant girl," added Mrs Prater, "and seemed to be on good terms with everybody. She dressed poorly as she was, of course, badly off." The young woman Harvey who had slept with the deceased on several occasions also made a statement. She *said she had been on good terms with the deceased, whose education was much superior to that of most persons in her position. Harvey, however, took a room in New court, off the same street, but remained friendly with the unfortunate woman, who visited her in New court last night. After drinking together they parted at half-past 7 o'clock, Kelly going off in the direction of Leman-street, which she was in the habit of frequenting. She was perfectly sober at the time. Harvey never saw her alive afterwards. This morning, hearing that a murder had been committed, she said "I'll go and see if it's anyone I know," and to her horror found that it was her friend. Joseph Barnett, an Irishman, at present residing in a common lodging-house in New-street, Bishopsgate, informed a reporter this evening that he had occupied his present lodgings since Tuesday week. Previous to that he had lived in Miller's court, Dorset-street, for eight or nine months with the murdered woman, Mary Jane Kelly. They were comfortable together until an unfortunate came to sleep in their room to which he strongly objected. Finally, after the woman had been there two or three nights, they quarrelled and he left her. The next day, however, he returned and gave Kelly money. He called several other days, and gave her money when he had it. Last night he visited her between half-past 7 and 8, and told her he was sorry he had no money to give her. He saw nothing more of her. He was indoors this morning when he heard that a woman had been murdered in Dorset street, but he did not know at first who the victim was. He voluntarily went to the police, who, after questioning him, satisfied themselves that his statements were correct, and therefore released him. Barnett believed Kelly, who was an Irishwoman, was an unfortunate before he made her acquaintance. She used occasionally to go to the Elephant and Castle district to visit a friend. Telegraphing later, the Central News states, upon indisputable authority, that no portion of the murdered woman's body was taken away by the murderer. As already stated, the post-mortem examination was of the most exhaustive character, and the surgeons did not quit their work until every organ had been accounted for. The most unaccountable feature of the case is the manner in which the murderer mutilated the face of the victim, as if to make identification difficult or perhaps impossible. In the case of his Mitre-square victim, as a woman picked up in the street and murdered in the open air, the murderer's motives in endeavouring to render the features unrecognisable can readily be understood, but he could scarcely suppose that the identity of a woman renting her room as a regular lodger, and well known in the immediate locality of the crime would fail to be capable of comparatively easy proof. It is therefore assumed that the mutilation of the face was done in a transport of mad ferocity. There is reason to believe that the injuries to the face were inflicted after the more elaborate mutilations of the remainder of the body, as though the murderer, on taking a final look round previous to taking to flight, became exasperated at the tranquil appearance of his victims features. Up till a late hour last night the police were still in charge of Miller's-court, and refused entrance to all save residents. Dorset-street was thronged with people, who, however, were kept constantly on the move. Very few fresh facts transpired respecting the murdered woman's movements. A woman living at No. 5, Miller's-court, informed the Central News reporter that the victim and her murderer spent some time together in the room upon the most friendly terms, so that there could have been nothing in the appearance of the man to create alarm of suspicion. Other residents in the court declared that, about a quarter to two, they heard a faint cry of "Murder," which would seem to fix with tolerable exactitude at the time at which the crime was committed, but against this must be set the statement of a woman living at 26. Dorset-square – a house, the back rooms of which abut upon the court – according to whom a cry of "Murder" was heard at three o'clock. It is characteristic of the locality that no one thought anything of the incident, which, indeed, is of too common occurrence to cause interest or alarm. A man engaged as a market porter, who lives at 3, Miller's-court, states that, although his rooms face the scene of the murder, he heard nothing of it until he went out in the morning at half past ten to get some milk, and was stopped by the police. A man's pilot coat has been found in the murdered woman's room, but whose it is has not been ascertained. Last evening, a man was arrested near Dorset-street on suspicion of being concerned in the murder. He was taken to Commercial-street Police Station, followed by a howling mob, and is still detained there. Another man, respectably dressed, wearing a slouch hat and carrying a black bag, was arrested and taken to Leman-street Station. The bag was examined, but its contents were perfectly harmless, and the man was at once released. Such is the excitable feeling in Whitechapel that any stranger carrying a black bag runs considerable risk of being mobbed. The door of the room in which the body was found has been padlocked, and the window boarded up.*

November 13th 1888

The Hull and Lincolnshire Times, November 13th 1888,

THE WHITECHAPEL MURDERS. THE ASSASSIN SEEN IN LONDON. The Press Association says a that fresh interest has been aroused in Whitechapel in reference to the recent murders by the statement of Matthew Packers, who keeps a fruit stall near the scene of the Berner-street murder, and from whom the murderer is believed to have bought some grapes for the unfortunate woman, Elizabeth Stride, shortly before the murder. He says that he saw the man last

Mike Covell

> *Saturday night standing near his fruit stall and looking at him in a menacing manner. Packer states that being alarmed, he asked a shoeblack standing near to watch the man, who, however, then ran off and jumped on a passing tramcar, and Packer could not leave his stall to follow him. There have been renewed complaints to the police recently from woman who have been accosted by a man resembling the description of the assassin.*

The Hull Daily News, November 13th 1888,

> *THE WHITECHAPEL TRAGEDIES. STATEMENT BY AN AQUAINTANCE. Elizabeth Foster, who lives in a lodging house in Dorset street, has made the following statement to a Press Association's reporter: I have known Mary Jane Kelly for the last eighteen months, and we were always good friends. She used to tell me she came from Limerick. She was as nice a woman as one could find, and although an unfortunate, I don't think she went on the streets whilst she lived with Barnett. On Wednesday night I was in her lodgings with her, and the next evening I met her in the Ten Bells public house, near Spitalfields Church. We were drinking together, and she went out about five minutes past seven o'clock. I never saw her after that. A MAN IN FEMALE ATTIRE. A man dressed in woman's clothes was arrested on Saturday night in Clerkenwell. He said he only did it for a freak. RESIGNATION OF SIR CHARLES WARREN. The Press Association says the report is current at Scotland yard that Sir Charles Warren has sent in his resignation. No official confirmation or denial can be obtained. The Press Association is informed that Sir Charles Warren sent in his resignation on Saturday after the statement by Mr. Matthews in the House of Commons on Thursday last. Regarding the publication of the article in Murray's Magazine that Sir Charles Warren had been requested to observe the rule of the Home Office as to the publication of works on matters relating to the service. Sir Charles too counsel with his friends, on Saturday, and the result was that on the same evening he sent in his resignation, couched in the briefest language, to the Home Secretary, stating his grounds for doing so that he could not accept the reproof administered to him. This morning, all his books and papers were removed from the Chief Commissioner's office, at Scotland yard, and this was the first intimation at Scotland yard that he had relinquished his position. The Press Association, in a later telegram, says the fact of Sir Charles Warren's resignation is officially confirmed. OPENING OF THE INQUEST. On Monday, Dr. MacDonald, M.P., coroner for North East Middlesex, opened an inquest at Shoreditch Town hall, on the body of Mary Jeanette Kelly, murdered in Millers court, Dorset street, Spitalfields, during Thursday night, or Friday morning. The jury having been sworn, proceeded to view the body, and afterwards visited the*

scene of the murder. On return their evidence was taken. The crowd was much smaller than at inquest on previous victims. Mr. Vander Hant representing the Whitechapel Vigilance Committee. Inspector Abberline was present on behalf of the police. The Coroner complained of the unfounded statements in the Press as to alleged communications between himself and Mr. Wynn Baxter with regard to jurisdiction. Joseph Barnett, labourer, deposed:- I identify the body of the deceased as that of a young woman with whom I have lived for eight months. I separated from her on the 30th of last month. I left her because she brought a prostitute to live in our room. I saw deceased last between half past seven and a quarter to eight on Thursday night. We were on friendly terms. Before leaving, I said I had no money. Deceased was sober. Deceased told me her father's name was John Kelly, gaffer of ironworks in Carnarvonshire. She was born in Limerick, and was married in Wales to a man named Davis, killed in a colliery explosion. After leading an immoral life in Cardiff. Deceased came to a house in West-end of London, and a gentleman induced her to go to France. She returned, and lived at Radcliffe Highway, then Pennington street. I first met her in Commercial street, and arranged to live with her. At deceased's request I read her the newspaper reports of previous Whitechapel murders. Did not hear her express fear of any person. The jury expressed a wish that Dr. Phillips, police surgeon, who was not present should attend, so that some of the medical evidence might be taken.- Thomas Bowyer, Dorset street, Spitalfields, said- On Friday morning I went to the house of deceased to collect the rent for Mr. McCarthy. I knocked, but got no answer. I found a window broken.- Inspector Ledger now put in a plan of the premises.- Bowyer resumed- I put the curtain aside, and looking in, I saw two lumps of flesh on the table. Looking a second time, I saw the body on the bed, and a pool of blood on the floor. I reported the discovery to the police. John McCarthy, grocer and lodging-house-keeper, Dorset street, deposed: I sent the last witness to Miller's-court for the rent. Within five minutes he came back, and said he had seen blood in No. 13 room of Miller's-court. I went and saw the body. I could say nothing for a little time, but when I recovered I accompanied my man to the police. An inspector came with me to the house. I do not know that Barnett and deceased had any serious quarrel. I let the room at 4s. 6d. A week. Deceased was 29s in arrear. Often saw deceased worse for drink. When drunk she became noisy and sang. Mary Ann Cook deposed:- I live at 5, Miller's-court, opposite deceased. About midnight (Thursday), I saw deceased in Dorset-street. She was very much the worse for drink. Saw her go up the court with a short, stout man, shabbily dressed. He carried a pot of ale, and wore a black coat and hat; had a clean shaven chin, sandy whiskers, and moustache. Deceased wished me "good night" and went to her room. I heard her singing the song- "A violet I plucked from my mother's grave." I afterwards went out of my room. Coming back at one o'clock she was still singing. I again went out, coming back, I saw that the light in deceased's room had been put out. All was silent. Heard footsteps in the court about six o'clock. I did not sleep after to bed. If there had been a cry of murder during the night I must have heard it.- Elizabeth Prater, Miller's-court, said I live in the same house. Went into my own room at one o'clock on Friday morning. Saw no glimmer of the deceased's room. Woke about four. Heard a suppressed cry of "Oh Murder," appearing to come from the court. Did not take much notice as frequently we hear such cries.- Caroline Maxwell, wife of the lodging house deputy in Dorset-street, was next sworn.- The Coroner cautioned her to be careful, as her evidence differed from other statements made.- Mrs Maxwell then deposed. I saw deceased at the corner of Miller's-court shortly after eight o'clock on Friday morning. Deceased told me she felt ill. Went with my husband's breakfast, on my return I saw deceased speaking with a man outside Britannia Public House. Cannot give a particular description of the man. He wore dark clothes and sort of a plaid coat. Deceased wore a dark skirt, with velvet body shawl, no hat. Man was short and stout. Sarah Lewis, Great Powell street, stated, I visited a friend at Miller's Court, on Friday morning at half past two o'clock. Saw a man standing on pavement. Was short, stout, and wore a wide awake hat. I stopped with a friend- Mrs Keyler. I fell asleep in a chair, but woke at half past three. I sat awake till a little before four. I heard a female voice scream murder loudly. Thought the sound came from the direction of the deceased's house. Did not take much notice. Such cries are often heard. At eight o'clock on Wednesday night, when with a female friend, I was accosted in Bethnal Green road by a gentleman who carried a bag. He invited one of us to accompany him. Disliking his appearance we left him. The bag was about nine inches long. The man had pale face, dark moustache, work a dark cloth, overcoat, and high felt hat. On Friday morning when I was coming to Millers Court, about half past two, I met that man with a female in Commercial street. As I went into Miller's Court, they stood at the corner of Dorset street. Dr. George Baxter Phillips, Surgeon to the H. Division, also gave evidence. Further evidence was also taken, and the coroner summed up. The jury after a moments consultation, returned a verdict of "Wilful murder" against some person or persons unknown.

November 17th 1888

The Hull and East Yorkshire and Lincolnshire Times, November 17th 1888,

THE WHITECHAPEL MURDERS. INQUEST AND VERDICT. *On Monday Dr. Macdonald, M.P., coroner for North East Middlesex, opened an inquest at Shoreditch Town Hall, on the body of Mary Jeanette Kelly, murdered in Miller's-court, Dorset-street, Spitalfields, during Thursday night or Friday morning. The jury having been sworn, proceeded to view the body and afterwards visited the scene of the murder. On their return evidence was taken. The crowd was much smaller than at the inquests on the previous victims. Mr. Vander Hart represented the Whitechapel Vigilance Committee, and Inspector Abberline was present on behalf of the police. EXAMINATION OF THE WITNESSES. Joseph Barnett, labourer, deposed - I identify the body of deceased woman as that of a young woman with whom I have lived for eight months. I separated from her on the 18th of last month. I left her because she brought another woman to live in our room. I saw deceased last between half-past 7 and a quarter to 8 on Thursday night. We were on friendly terms before leaving. I said I had no money. Deceased was sober. She told me her father's name was John Kelly, and he was gaffer of ironworks in Carnarvonshire. She was born in Limerick, and was married in Wales to a man named Davis, who was killed in a colliery explosion. After leading an immoral life in Cardiff deceased came to the house in the West End of London. A gentleman induced her to go to France. She returned and lived at Ratcliffe Highway, then at Pennington street. I first met her in Commercial street, and arranged to live with her. At deceased's request I read to her newspaper reports of previous Whitechapel murders. Did not hear her express fear of any person. Thomas Bowyer, Dorset street, Spitalfields, said - On Friday morning I went to the house of the deceased to collect rent for Mr M'Carthy. I knocked but I got no answer. I found a window broken. Inspector Ledger now put in the plan of the premises. Bowyer resumed - I put the curtain aside, and on looking in I saw two lumps of flesh on the table. Looking a second time I saw a body on the bed and a pool of blood on the floor. I reported discovery to the police. John M'Carthy, grocer, lodging house keeper, Dorset Street, deposed - I sent last witness to Miller's court for rent. Within five minutes he came back saying he had seen blood in No. 13 room of Miller's court. I went and saw the body. I could say nothing for a little time, but when I recovered I accompanied my man to the police. An inspector came with me to the house. I do not known that Barnett and deceased had any serious quarrel. I let the room at 4s 6d a week. Deceased was 29s in arrear. I often saw deceased the worse for drink. When drunk she became noisy, and sang. Mary Anne Cox deposed - I live at 5 Miller's court, opposite the deceased. About midnight on Thursday I saw deceased in Dorset street. She was very much the worse for drink. I saw her go up the court with a short, stout man, shabbily dressed. He carried a pot of ail, and wore a black coat and hat, had clean shaven chin, sandy whiskers and moustache. Deceased wished me good-night, and went into her room. I heard her singing the song - "A violet I plucked from mother's grave." I afterwards went out of my room. Coming back at one o'clock she was still singing. I again went out, and on coming back I saw the light in deceased's room had been put out. All was silent. I heard footsteps in the court about 6 o'clock. I did not sleep after going to bed. If there had been a cry of murder during the night I must have heard it. Elizabeth Prater, Miller's court, said - I live in the same house. I went into my own room at 1 o'clock on Friday morning. I then saw no glimmer in deceased's room. I awoke about 7 o'clock and heard a suppressed cry, "Oh, murder!" appearing to come from the court. Did not take particular notice, as frequently I hear such cries. Caroline Maxwell, wife of the lodging-house deputy in Dorset street, was next sworn. The Coroner cautioned her to be careful, as her evidence differed from other statements made. Mrs Maxwell then deposed - I saw deceased at the corner of Miller's court shortly after 8 o'clock on Friday morning. Deceased told me she felt ill and had vomited. I went with my husband's breakfast, and on my return saw the deceased speaking with a man outside the Britannia public-house. I cannot give a particular description of the man. He wore dark clothes and a sort of plaid coat. Deceased wore a dark skirt with a velvet body shawl, and no hat. The man was short and stout. Sarah Lewis, Great Powell street, stated - I visited a friend at Miller's court on Friday morning at half-past 2 o'clock. I saw a man standing on the pavement. He was short, stout, and wore a wideawake hat. I stopped with a friend, Mrs Keyler. I fell asleep in a chair, and woke at half-past 3. I saw awake till a little before 4. I heard a female voice scream "Murder" loudly. I thought the sound came from the direction of deceased's house. I did not take much notice. Such cries are often heard. At 8 o'clock on Wednesday night when with a female friend I was accosted in Bethnal green by a gentleman who carried a bag. He invited one of us to accompany him. Disliking his appearance we left him. The bag was about nine inches long. The man had a pale face, dark moustache and wore dark clothes, an overcoat, and a high felt hat. On Friday morning when coming to Miller's court about half-past 2, I met that man with a female in Commercial street. As I went into Miller's court they stood at the corner of Dorset street. Dr George Baxter Phillips, deposed - I am surgeon to H Division Metropolitan Police. I cannot give the whole of my evidence to-day. On Friday morning, about 11 o'clock, I proceeded to Miller's court, and in a room there found the mutilated remains of a woman lying two thirds over towards the edge of the bed nearest the door. Subsequent to the injury which caused death the body had been removed from the opposite side of the bed which was nearest the wooden partition. The presence of a quantity of blood on and under the bed leads me to the conclusion that the severance of the carotid artery, which was the immediate cause of death, was inflicted while the deceased was lying at the right side of the bedstead, and her head and neck on the right hand corner. That is as far as I propose to carry my evidence to-day. The Coroner said he proposed to continue taking evidence for another hour. The Jury expressed a wish to adjourn for some time, The Coroner replied he would resume in a quarter of an hour. On resuming, Julia Venturney deposed - I occupy a room in Miller's Court, and the man I am now living with is named Harry Owen. I knew the deceased. It was sometime before I became acquainted with her, but when I knew her she told me her name was Kelly, and she was a married woman. I knew the young man, Joe Barnett, with whom she lived. They lived happily together. He objected to her walking the streets. I have frequently seen the deceased the worse for drink, but when she was cross Joe Barnett would go out and leave her to quarrel with herself. She told me that she was fond of another man, that she could not bear the man Joe she was living with. Strangely, the other man, she said, was named Joe. She went to bed on Thursday night in Miller's court about 8 p.m. She did not sleep. She could not tell why, but she did not sleep at all. Perhaps she dozed a bit. She heard a strange sound with some door which was not like the way in which the deceased used to shut the door. There was no nose in the court that night, and she heard no singing. If there had been any singing she must have heard it. The deceased used to sing Irish songs. Inspector Walter Beckett, H Division, stationed at Commercial street, said information was brought to the stationhouse at five minutes to 11 on Friday morning. He went at one and gave directions to prevent anyone leaving the court, and he directed other constables to make a search. Inspector G. Abberline, of Scotland Yard, said he was in charge of the case on behalf of the police. He reached the court about 11.30 on Friday last. When he reached the place he was informed by Inspector Beach that the bloodhounds had been sent for, and were on their way, and Dr. Phillips said it would be better not to force the door until the dogs arrived. At 1.30 Superintendent Arnold arrived, and stated that the order for the dogs had been countermanded, and gave directions for the door to be forced. I looked through the window and saw how matters really were before we entered. I subsequently took an inventory of the things in the room. There were traces of a large fire having been kept in the grate, and the spout of the kettle had been melted off. We have since gone through the ashes of the grate and have found portions of the brim of a hat and portions of a shirt. I consider that the articles were burnt to enable the murderer to see what he was about. There was a small piece of candle standing in a broken wine glass. The key of the lock had been missing for some time, and the door could be opened by putting a hand through the broken window and pushing the latch back. A man's clay pip was found in the room belonging to Barnett. The Coroner said that was all the evidence they were prepared to lay before the jury to-day. It was for them to say whether they were satisfied with it or whether they would adjourn and hear the further evidence on a future occasion. If the coroner's jury came to the conclusion as to the cause of death, that was all they had to do. The police would take charge of the case, and it was for the jury to say whether they had sufficient evidence to enable them to come to a conclusion as to the cause of the death. His own opinion was they might conclude and leave the case to the police. The Jury, after a moments consultation, returned a verdict of "Wilful murder against some person or persons unknown." IMPORTANT INFORMATION BY A GROOM. On Tuesday, a man named George Hutchinson, a groom, who is now working as a labourer, made the following statement to the reporter of a news agency:- On Thursday I had been to Romford, in Essex, and I returned from there about two o'clock on Friday morning, having walked all the way. I came down Whitechapel road into Commercial street. As I passed Thrawl street I passed a man standing at the corner of the street, and as I went towards Flower and Dean street I met the woman Kelly, whom I knew very well, having been in her company a number of times. She said, "Mr. Hutchinson, can you lend me sixpence?" I said, "I cannot, as I am spent out, going down to Romford." She then walked on towards Thrawl street, saying, "I must go and look for some money." The man who was standing at the corner of Thrawl street then came towards her, put his hand on her shoulder, and said something to her which I did not hear; they both burst out laughing. He put his hand again on her shoulder, and they both walked slowly towards me. I walked on to the corner of Fashion street, near the public house. As they came by me his arm was still on her shoulder. He had a soft felt hat on, and this was drawn down somewhat over his eyes. I put down my head to look him in the face, and he turned and looked at me very sternly. They walked across the road to Dorset street. I followed them across and stood at the corner of Dorset street. They stood at the corner of Miller's court for about three minutes. Kelly spoke to the man in a loud voice, saying, "I have lost my handkerchief." He pulled a red handkerchief out of his pocket and gave it to Kelly, and they went up the court together. I went to look up the court to see if I could see them, but could not. I stood there for three quarters of an hour to see if they came down again, but they did not, and so I went away. My suspicions were aroused by seeing the man so well dressed, but I had no suspicion that he was the murderer. The man was about 5ft 6in in height and about thirty four or thirty five years of age, with dark complexion, and dark moustache turned up at the ends. He was wearing a long dark coat trimmed with astrachan, a white collar, with black necktie in which was affixed a horseshoe pin. He wore a pair of dark "spats" with light buttons over button boots, and displayed from his waistcoat a massive gold chain. His watch chain had a big seal with a red stone hanging from it. He had a heavy moustache, curled up, dark eyes, and bushy eyebrows. He had no side whiskers, and his chin was clean shaven. He looked like a foreigner. I went up the court, and stayed there a couple of minutes, but did not see any light in the house or hear any noise. I was out on Monday night until three o'clock looking for him. I could swear to the man anywhere. I told one policeman on Sunday morning what I had seen, but did not go to the police station. I told one of the lodgers here about it on Monday, and he advised me to go to the police station, which I did at night. The man I saw did not look as though he would attack another one. He carried small parcel in his hand about eight inches long, and it had a strap round it. He had it tightly grasped in his left hand. It looked as though it was covered with dark American cloth. He carried in his right hand which he laid upon the woman's shoulder a pair of brown kid gloves. One thing I noticed, and that was that he walked very softly. I believe he lives in the neighbourhood, and I fancied that I saw him in Petticoat lane on Sunday morning, but I was not certain. I have been to the Shoreditch mortuary and recognised the body as that of the woman Kelly whom I saw at two o'clock on Friday morning. Kelly did not seem to me to be drunk, but was a little bit "spreeish". I was quite sober, not having had anything to drink all day. After I left the court I walked about all night, as the place where I usually sleep was closed. I came in as soon as it opened in the morning. I am able to fix the time, as it was between ten and five minutes to two o'clock as I came by Whitechapel Church. When I left the corner of Miller's court the clock struck three. One policeman went by the Commercial street end of Dorset street while I was standing there, but not one came down Dorset street. I saw one man go into a lodging house in Dorset street, and no one else. I have been looking for the man all day. MUNIFICENT OFFER BY BARONESS BURDETT COUFTIS. Baroness Burdett Couftis will give a £1 a week, or its equivalent, to any person, including the police, giving evidence leading to the conviction. SEARCH FOR "JACK THE RIPPER" AND ITS RESULT. At Clerkenwell Police Court, on Thursday, John Brinkly was charged with being drunk and causing a crowd to assemble in Goswell-road, on Monday, by wearing a woman's skirt, shawl, and hat over his ordinary clothes. He was drunk, and said he was going to find "Jack the Ripper." The magistrates sentenced him to 14 days had labour. "SHOWING HOW THE MURDER WAS DONE." – THE EFFECT. At Clerkenwell Police Court on Tuesday, John Avery was also charged with being drunk. He [illegible] a [illegible] in York-road on Monday night, and saying he was "Jack the Ripper" and would show him how he committed the murders, scratched his neck. – Prisoner said he was respectably connected, but the magistrate inflicted a similar sentence. LIST OF THE WHITECHAPEL VICTIMS. The Press Association says that inquiries show that a letter has been received by Mrs.*

Mike Covell

> McCarthy. The text was as follows: - "Don't alarm yourself. I am going to do another, but this time it will be a mother and daughter." The letter, which was signed "Jack the Ripper," was at once handed to the police authorities. Elizabeth Foster, who lives in a lodging house in Dorset-street, has made the following statement to a Press Association reporter: - I have known Mary Jane Kelly for the last 18 months, and we were always good friends. She used to tell me she came from Limerick. She was as nice a woman as one could find, and, although an unfortunate, I don't think she went on the streets whilst she lived with Barnett. On Wednesday night I was in her lodgings with her, and the next evening I met her in the Ten Bells public house, near Spitalfields Church. We were drinking together, and she went out about five minutes past seven o'clock. I never saw her after that. The St. Stephen's Review says: - Apropos of "Jack the Ripper" the following story is going the rounds: - One day lately two ladies, well known in London society, were walking down the street discussing the murders, and happened to express a desire that should the murderer be discovered he should be delivered up to the woman of London to be lynched. The next day they both received a communication signed "Jack the Ripper," informing them that they had been overheard and traced to their respective homes, and warning them of a speedy visit from their anonymous correspondent. Having taken these missives to Scotland Yard, it was found that they were both in the same handwriting as the more important of those received by the authorities previous to the Mitre-square and Berner-street tragedies, and the two ladies have since then been under the special protection of the police. The Press Association says the agitation in regard to the alleged insufficient police protection of Spitalfields is taking a definite form, and it is expected that within a few days the Home Secretary will be waited upon by a deputation representing the district. No fresh arrests have been made, and although the police are investigating the statements made by the fruiterer Packer, they have not yet discovered the man who were talking to him as stated.

November 19th 1888

The Hull Daily Mail, November 19th 1888,

> THE WHITECHAPEL MURDERS. ARREST AND RELEASE OF A MEDICAL MAN. On Saturday afternoon a communication from the Birmingham detectives to the effect that a man suspected of being concerned in the Whitechapel murders had left Birmingham by train for London was at once acted upon by Scotland Yard authorities. Detectives Leach and White, of the Criminal Investigation Department, proceeded to Willesden Junction and Euston

respectively, and at the latter station, Inspector White, on the arrival of the Birmingham train, detained the suspected individual and conveyed him to Scotland Yard. It was stated that the man had been staying at a common lodging house in Birmingham since Monday last, and the theory was that if, as was supposed by the police he was connected to the East End crimes, he left the Metropolis by an early train on the morning of the tragedies. The suspected man was a medical man who was some years ago practising in London with another gentleman of some repute. He was of gentlemanly appearance and manners, and somewhat resembled the description of witnesses at the inquest as having been seen in company with Kelly early on the morning that she was murdered. Upon being minutely questioned as to his whereabouts at the time of the murders, the suspect was able to furnish a satisfactory account of himself, and was accordingly liberated. The statement made by a man to Packer, the fruit seller of Berner Street, that he was of opinion that his cousin had committed the foul deeds, is still being investigated by the detectives, who are inclined to doubt the veracity of a greater portion of the details. They, however, believe they have found the cousin referred to, and attach little importance to what was at first supposed to be a substantial clue. The funeral of the murdered woman Kelly has once more being postponed. It seems that the deceased was a Catholic, and the man Barnett, with whom she lived, and her landlord, Mr M'Carthy, desired to see her remains interred with the ritual of her church. The funeral will then take place on Tuesday in the Roman Catholic Cemetery at Leytonstone. The hearse will leave the Shoreditch Mortuary at half past 12. The Press Association believes that the police authorities have received some information to the affect that the Whitechapel murderer is supposed to travel up from Manchester, Birmingham, or some other town in the Midlands for the purpose of committing the crimes. Detectives have been engaged at Willesden and Euston watching the arrival of trains from the Midlands and the North, and are looking for any suspicious passengers, but their efforts up to the present have not met with success. 7th

November 21st 1888

The Hull Daily Mail, November 21st 1888,

ANOTHER TRAGEDY IN WHITECHAPEL. DETERMINED ATTEMPT TO MURDER A WOMAN. EXCITING CHASE FATER AND ESCAPE OF THE ASSAILANT. DESRIPTION OF THE CRIMINAL. In our first edition we published the following telegrams purporting to show that another atrocious murder had been committed in Whitechapel. Subsequent messages, however, state that the victim is still living, although a determined attempt seems to have been made to carry a murderous intention into effect:- A telegram says that another woman has been brutally murdered in Whitechapel. The tragedy took place in a lodging house. The victim, as in previous cases, had her throat cut and was otherwise shockingly mutilated. The murderer has escaped. The house in which the tragedy occurred is a small two storied building, fronting George street, and right opposite the Lolesworth Model Dwellings, and is within a few hundred yards of Miller's Court, Dorset Street, where the last murder occurred. The houses in George street are mostly let out as lodging houses, some of them being used by the women of the streets. The Star gives the following particulars:- This morning, in a lodging house in George street, Spitalfields, within a short distance of Dorset street, a man cut a woman's throat. The pair had been in in a room all night. About half past nine this morning it is alleged that the man attacked the woman with a knife, she managed to raise an alarm, and the man ran out of the place. He was pursued by three other men at the lodging house through three or four streets, but was lost at Heneage Street, nearby. [LATER SPECIAL TELEGRAMS] The Press Association, in a later despatch, says the first report received by the police stated that a woman named Farmer was murdered in George street, but on inquiry that was found not to be the case. It appears that about eight o'clock a man and Farmer engaged a bed at a common lodging house, 19, George street, Spitalfields, and at about 9.30 screams were heard and a man rushed out, Farmer was seen to be bleeding profusely from a wound in the throat. She was taken to Commercial street station, and after the wound was dressed gave a description of her assailant as follows:- Height 5 feet 6 inches, fair moustache and wore a black diagonal coat and hard felt hat. He is known, and his capture is confidently anticipated. Superintendent Arnold, Inspector Ferrett, and Detective Officers Thicke, Dew and Pearce, Record, and McQuire have the case in hand. The Press Association, telegraphing later, says: The following telegraphic communication has been circulated amongst the police this morning:- "Wanted, for attempted murder on the 21st instant, a man aged 36 years, height 5ft, 6in, complexion dark, no whiskers, dark moustache. Dress: Black jacket, vest and trousers; round black felt hat; respectable appearance, can be identified." A Press Association representative had an interview with a woman who professed to have a knowledge of the circumstances. The informant stated the injured woman is called Matilda, and she lodges in various common lodging houses in the locality. She is, so far as personal appearances go, very good looking, and appears to have been brought up in far better surroundings than she now occupies. I believe she has known the man who has attacked her for about 12 months. From what I hear, it is not true the couple slept in Dorset street on

Tuesday night. It was about seven o'clock in the morning when the woman met the man, near Spitalfields Church. He asked her what she was doing at such an early hour, and she said she had not been able to pay for a bed, as the charge was 8d. He gave the woman 6d, and they went to a house in Dorset street together. They had not been long in the room when the woman shouted out, "He's cut my throat," and she followed the man downstairs. He made off, but some men in the lodging house, hearing the cry of a woman, pursued the man, but they lost sight of him, and he got away. In the neighbourhood of the outrage the general opinion seems to be that "Jack the Ripper" is not the man who has done the deed. It is stated that the woman had a severe struggle with her assailant, and his face was torn and scratched severely. It has further ascertained a man stood opposite the lodging house door at the moment when the fugitive was escaping, but he made no effort to arrest him, thinking it was petty theft of some kind that he had committed. The injured woman told the police she was willing to walk to the station, but the police insisted on taking her there on a stretcher, which naturally aroused much excitement, especially as a cover was thrown over the woman. The Superintendent of the Commercial street Police Station informed the Press Association's reporter that Farmer's wound is quite superficial. She is detained at the station this afternoon. Her name is Annie Farmer. Esther Hall, who lives at 19, George street, said on hearing the alarm this morning that a woman had been murdered, she ran upstairs and saw Farmer covered with blood, half dressed, and asked her if she knew the man, Farmer replied that she knew him twelve months ago, and he had ill-used her then. He made her drunk this morning before he took her to the house. The scene of the outrage is within three minutes' walk of Dorset street, and it is singular the victim of the George yard murder lodged at the same house, and the woman murdered in Osborne street lived next door. ANOTHER ACCOUNT. The Press Association, telegraphing at noon, says another murder was attempted to-day in broad daylight in a common lodging house, no 19, George street, Flower and Dean street, Spitalfields. It appears that at about four o'clock this morning a woman, aged about 28 years, went to the lodging house with a plan and took a double bed in a room partitioned off into a number of compartments. It is said the woman was intoxicated, and commenced singing, which continued until eight o'clock when, according to Phillip Harris, who lodges at the home, the singing ceased. About half past nine Harris was sitting in the kitchen eating his breakfast when he saw a man come from the room and hurriedly leave the house. About the same time the woman, who is known as "Dark Sarah," came downstairs in her petticoat. Her throat was cut and she was bleeding profusely, the blood streaming all over her breast underclothing. Harris further stated to the Press Association representative:- I saw what was the matter, and several of

> us rushed out of the house and pursued the man, who we were told had gone up Thrawl Street. We saw him running before us but when we got to the corner of Brick Lane we lost sight of him. He was about 5 feet 6 inches in height, and wore a thick black moustache. I noticed that he had an overcoat with a cape on it, but did not see anything in his hand. John Arundell, a coal heaver, living at 15 Wood-street, Spitalfields, said that he went to no. 19, George street this morning and saw a woman sitting on a bed. Dr. Phillips, divisional surgeon, was dressing her throat. After she had been attended to she got up, and walked downstairs, was placed in an ambulance, and taken to Commercial street police station. The woman's injuries are not likely to terminate fatally, but there is a strong belief that the man who attempted the murder is the individual now known as "Jack the Ripper." The streets are crowded with people eagerly discussing the latest outrage.

November 24th 1888

The Hull and Lincolnshire Times, November 24th 1888,

> *ANOTHER TRAGEDY IN WHITECHAPEL. On Wednesday another murder was attempted in broad daylight in a common lodging house, 13 George-street, Flower and Dean-street, Spitalfields. It appears that at about four a.m. on Wednesday a woman aged about 28 years, went to the lodging house with a plan and took a double bed in a room partitioned off into a number of compartments. It is said the woman was intoxicated, and commenced singing, which continued until eight o'clock when, according to Phillip Harris, who lodges at the home, the singing ceased. About half past nine Harris was sitting in the kitchen eating his breakfast when he saw a man come from the room and hurriedly leave the house. About the same time the woman, who is known as "Dark Sarah," came downstairs in her petticoat. Her throat was cut and she was bleeding profusely, the blood streaming all over her breast underclothing. Harris further stated to the Press Association representative:- I saw what was the matter, and several of us rushed out of the house and pursued the man, who we were told had gone up Thrawl-street. We saw him running before us but when we got to the corner of Brick Lane we lost sight of him. He was about 5 feet 6 inches in height, and wore a thick black moustache. I noticed that he had an overcoat with a cape on it, but did not see anything in his hand. The Press Association says that the arrest in Spitalfields on Wednesday night is not so important as, as first thought. The arrest seems to have arisen out of an ordinary drunken quarrel. In the present state of excitement in the neighbourhood every such incident is magnified. The man was removed to Commercial Street Police Station, pending the usual police*

enquiries. *The man was still in custody on Thursday, and the police will not state whether there is an importance attached to the arrest. The locality of the supposed outrage is quiet now. Other arrests were made in Whitechapel and neighbourhood during the night, but the individuals were not detained for long.*

December 5th 1888

The Hull Daily Mail, December 5th 1888,

THE MURDER OF A SWEETHEART NEAR DURHAM. DATE OF THE EXECUTION. The Press Association's Durham correspondent, telegraphing on the authority of the High Sheriff, states the convict William Waddle will be hanged at Durham Gaol on Tuesday, December 18th. The executioner will be Berry, to suit whose engagements a delay of one day will be made. Waddle received the news with the reticence which he never altered since being sentenced. Not the slightest hope is entertained of a reprieve. Four press representatives will be admitted to the execution. THE EAST END OUTRAGES. TEXT OF THE "JACK THE RIPPER" LETTER. On Tuesday Mr Saunders, the presiding magistrate at the Thames Police Court, received a letter, addressed "Mr Saunders, Chief Magistrate, Police Court, Whitechapel". The contents were as follow:- "Dear Pal- I am still at liberty. The last job in Whitechapel was not bad, but I mean to surprise them on the next. Shall joint is. Ha! Ha! Ha! After that shall try on the lazy lurchers who live on unfortunates. We have just enrolled several pals for the job. I am in the country now, for the benefit of my health. I met the super here (Wellingborough) the other day, and like him immense. He looks like a yard of pump water starched. Shall try a job here next time. So look out for news from "JACK THE RIPPER"

December 7th 1888

The Hull Daily Mail, December 7th 1888,

THE WHITECHAPEL MURDERS. ARREST OF A POLISH JEW. The Metropolitan police yesterday made a singular arrest which was reported to be in connection with the Whitechapel murders.- It appears that during the afternoon a man described as a Polish Jew was arrested near Drury-lane, but for what offence is not quite clear. This individual, who is of a short stature, with black moustache, was taken to Bow-street station, where he was detained for a time. A telegraphic communication was forwarded, thence to Leman-street police station, the headquarters of the Whitechapel division, requesting the attendance of one of the inspectors. Detective Inspector Abberline immediately proceeded to Bow-street, and subsequently brought away the prisoner in a cab, which was strongly escorted. While on the one hand he is reputed to have stolen a watch, there is reason to believe that the circumstances other than that of the corresponds with the description of the supposed Whitechapel murderer. He is detained by the police. The detectives of the East End are making every inquiry in the neighbourhood concerning the suspect, who is well known in the locality, although he is said to have been absent lately. Great reticence is observed regarding the affair, and at Commercial-street Station the officials deny knowledge of the arrest, although the man is understood to be detained there. It was subsequently ascertained that the man was apprehended for stealing a watch, with which offence he has been charged. The police however, were led to believe that he was connected, not with the mutilations, but with the recent attempt to murder a woman in George-street, Spitalfields. Exhaustive inquiries were made, but, as far can be ascertained, the man could in no way be connected to the outrage.

December 8th 1888

The Hull and East Yorkshire and Lincolnshire Times, December 8th 1888,

THE WHITECHAPEL MURDER. ARREST OF A POLISH JEW. ACCUSED BEFORE THE MAGISTRATES. *The Metropolitan police on Thursday made a singular arrest which was reported to be in connection with the Whitechapel murders. It appears that during the afternoon a man described as a Polish Jew was arrested near Drury-lane, but for what offence is not quite clear. This individual, who is of short stature, with black moustache, was taken to Bow-street station, where he was detained for a time. A telegraphic communication was forwarded thence to Leman-street police-station, the head-quarters of the Whitechapel division, requesting the attendance of one of the inspectors. Detective-Inspector Abberline immediately proceeded to Bow-street, and subsequently brought away the prisoner in a cab, which was strongly escorted. While on the one hand he is reputed to have stolen a watch, there is reason to believe that for circumstances other than that he corresponds with the description of the supposed Whitechapel murderer. He is detained by the police. The detectives at the East End are making every inquiry in the neighbourhood concerning the suspect, who is well known in the locality, although he is said to have been absent lately. Great reticence is observed regarding the affair, and at Commercial-street Station the officials deny knowledge of the arrest, although the man is understood to be detained there. It was subsequently ascertained that the man was apprehended for stealing a watch, with which offence he has been charged. The police, however, were led to believe that he was connected, not with the mutilations, but with the recent attempt to murder a woman in George-street, Spitalfields. Exhaustive inquiries were made, but, as far as can be ascertained, the man could in no way be connected with that outrage. Joseph Isaacs (30), described as a cigar maker, with no fixed abode, was charged at Worship-street Police Court yesterday with stealing a watch. Prisoner is the man arrested on Thursday afternoon in Drury-lane on suspicion of being concerned in the Whitechapel murders. – It transpired that while he was being watched as a person "wanted," he stole the watch. Prisoner is the man arrested. The prosecutor, Levenson, stated that the prisoner entered his shop on Wednesday, and asked him to repair a violin bow. While discussing the matter prisoner suddenly bolted out with a watch belonging to a customer. The watch was afterwards recovered from a pawn-broker. – Mary Cusins, deputy of a lodging house in Paternoster-row, Spitalfields, said the prisoner lodged at her house for three or four nights before the Dorset-street murder. He disappeared after the murder, leaving the violin bow behind him. Witness gave information to the police during the house-to-house inspection in Whitechapel, and a look-out was kept for the man. On Wednesday last he called for the violin bow, and witness followed him. She saw him enter Levinson's shop. – Detective Record asked for a remand, which was granted.*

December 15th 1888

The Hull Daily News, December 15th 1888,

ANOTHER OUTRAGE IN LONDON. At Southwark Police Court on Tuesday, William Atkins, 21, Labourer, was charged with wounding Lucretia Pembroke, with intent to inflict grievous bodily harm, by cutting her throat.- Detective Bradford said that in consequence of information received he arrested the prisoner at Limasole Street, Bermondsey and told him the charge. Prisoner asked whether the girl was dead, and handed witness a pocket knife, witness to the prisoner to the station, and then went to Guy's Hospital, where he saw Lucretia Pembroke, who said that Bill Atkins, known as "Silly Billy," entered the coffee house at Spa-Road, Bermondsey, on Tuesday and cut her throat. She served him with some tea when he came in and was walking away when he took out a pocket knife, and attacked her in the manner described. In answer to Mr Shiel, the magistrate, the witness said there was no blood on the knife. The girl's wounds are very serious. Remanded for a week.

Mike Covell

The Hull Daily News, December 15th 1888,

THE WHITECHAPEL MURDERS. INCREASED POLICE PRECAUTIONS. The discovery which has come to light in connection with the Whitechapel murders applies only to the last of the series. It shows that the assassin was even more barbarous in his treatment of the woman Kelly then was at first supposed and increases the supposition that the man is a foreigner. Beyond this, it is impossible to go into details, as the facts adduced by the medical men are unfit for publication. Unfortunately the discovery sheds no light that seem calculated to [illegible] in [illegible] the mystery of the murders. Mr. Moore, the new Police Commissioner has drafted a number of special detectives into Whitechapel, the idea being that more crimes will be committed, being still entertained.

December 22nd 1888

The Hull Times, December 22nd 1888,

DISGRACEFUL AFFAIR IN LONDON. THE "JACK THE RIPPER" CRAZE. At Dalston Police Court, London, on Wednesday, a poor woman, giving the name of Sarah Dellicar, aged 40 was charged with being drunk under the following circumstances:- A constable at one o'clock this morning heard terrible screams proceeding from a stable yard and running to the spot, found the accused lying in a costermonger's barrow, quite nude, and bearing traces of blows on the face. An inhabitant of the house overlooking the mews said she was alarmed by the screams, and looking out saw a woman lying on the barrow with two men near her. Thinking it was "Jack the Ripper" at work, she aroused a lodger, who shouted from the window, and the men ran off.- Prisoner said she was a poor widow, and her late husband held a respectable position. She could not remember how she got into the mews; but she was badly treated, and two rings were stolen. She was remanded.

The Hull Daily Mail, December 22nd 1888,

THE BIRTLEY MURDER. EXECUTION OF WADDELL. William Waddell was executed at Durham gaol at eight o'clock on Monday morning for the murder of Jane Beardmore, at Birtley, near Gateshead. The culprit is stated to have slept well during the night, and to have awakened at half past five, when he partook of a little breakfast. The officials of the prison soon afterwards assembled, and under the Sheriff, Mr. Hutchinson, of Darlington, formally demanded the body of the culprit from the custody of the governor (Lieut. Col. Armstrong) Meanwhile Waddell had been removed from his cell, escorted by two warders and Berry the executioner, and taken to the press room, where he was pinioned. He showed decided signs of mental anguish , but he walked firmly to the scaffold, and submitted to the final office of the executioner without exhibiting any feeling. The customary procession accompanied the culprit, there being, in addition to the prison officials, four reporters. Waddell once only placed his hand on the arm of a warder as if needing support, but quickly steadied himself and walked to the drop without again faltering. The chaplain offered up a final extempore prayer, Berry drew the bolt, and the culprit died apparently without struggle.

Mike Covell

Stop the Press – Editors Comments

The creation of this book has been a long and often difficult road, but I hope you appreciate and enjoy the end result. Here, in one volume, is a collection of newspaper reports that you can read from start to finish, putting yourself into the terrible shoes of those in Hull, Whitechapel, and other locales during the "Autumn of Terror," or you can refer to over and over again as a point of reference for future research. Whilst researching and transcribing the articles I have learnt of many new letters to the police and the press, and names of witnesses and suspects that have often been overlooked, as well as crimes and criminals who have fell by the wayside in favour of what many refer to as "Celebrity Suspects," such as Lewis Carroll, Queen Victoria, and Walter Sickert.

In 19th Century Britain the press was a powerful tool and a way of keeping everyone informed whether the reports were truthful or elaborations, and informing them on local, national and even international events. Big bold headlines would scream at the reader, and in the 19th century it was common place for newspaper vendors to walk the streets screaming at the top of their lungs informing potential readers of "another horrible murder," or "The Ripper claims another victim" and their impact was so much that letters to the editor often features calls from readers, mostly female, to stop the horrible and ghastly vendors disturbing the peace. Nowadays we see less and less newspaper vendors, and walking through both Hull and London recently I could count street sellers on one hand.

Theories have also arisen that the press was responsible for the Jack the Ripper craze, fuelling the fire with a series of unrelated murders linked to form an East End serial killer.

In 1996 Peter Turnbull's book The Killer Who Never Was, [Lawrence, 1996] put forward the idea that more than one, unnamed hand was responsible for the murders, and that the press linked them to sell more editions.

Andrew Cook's book, Jack the Ripper, [Amberley Books, 2009] was released back to back with a Channel 5 documentary, entitled Jack the Ripper: Tabloid Killer, [Jack the Ripper: Tabloid Killer, Channel 5, Broadcast June 24th 2009] which was presented by former editor of The Sun, Kelvin McKenzie. Both the book and the documentary put forward the theory that the Ripper scare of 1888 was created by T.P. O'Connor, who was the editor of The Star. It is claimed that O'Connor linked both the murder of Martha Tabram and Mary Ann Nichols and created a lone killer which would help boost circulation.

Sadly as well as the press informing the people, it also made them aware of the killer at large in Whitechapel, and helped create numerous copycat cases across Hull, Yorkshire, Britain, and even further afield. Wannabe Jack the Ripper's cropped up in Germany, France, America, and Australia, and the press were ever eager to draw comparisons, and for a short while even ask "Is this Jack the Ripper?" Of course most of the crimes seemed to be nothing more than misrepresentation, and in one particular case on which I gained access to the original court transcripts, the official documentation made no remark regarding Jack the Ripper like conduct, but instead recorded a verdict unrelated to the Whitechapel Murders, thus proving that the case was misrepresented in the press and leading one to question how many other cases were victim to the press and their ongoing desire to create a sordid story to sell more copies.

What we tend to forget when reading the press reports and hearing about the police, authorities and suspects, is that there where real victims. Whether it is the canonical five claimed to be at the hand of Jack the Ripper, or the Thames Torso Murders. Whether it is the Whitechapel Murders, The Gateshead Murder, the Hull Ripper Scares, or the murder of John Gill, people were dying up and down Britain and even further afield, and the press were reporting them as Ripper related.

Mike Covell

Appendix I - Currency

Farthing	4 to the penny	960 to the pound.	
Halfpenny	2 to the penny	480 to the pound.	
Penny		240 to the pound.	
Threepence		80 to the pound.	
Sixpence		80 to the pound.	Also known as a Tanner.
Shilling		20 in a pound.	12 Pennies in a Shilling.
Florin		10 to the pound.	2 Shillings, also known as Two Bob.
Half a Crown		8 to the pound.	Worth 2 Shillings and Sixpence. Worth 30 Pennies.

| Crown | | | |

Mike Covell

Appendix II - Police Districts – London

The Metropolitan Police area was defined by an act in 1829, this covered just a seven mile radius from Charing Cross.

In the beginning there were just 17 divisions,

A= Westminster

B= Chelsea

C= Mayfair and Soho

D= Marlybone

E= Holborn

F= Kensington

G= King's Cross

H= Stepney

K= West Ham

L= Lambeth

M= Southwark

N= Islington

P= Peckham

R= Greenwich

T= Hammersmith

V= Wandsworth

The following divisions were added in 1865

W= Clapham

X= Willesden

Y= Holloway

The following division was added in 1886

J = Bethnal Green

Mike Covell

Appendix III - Hull Ripper Craze's 1888 - 1988

In 2008 I was approached to write for Ripperologist Magazine about my research into material that I had discovered locally. Not wanting to give too much away, but to create a little bit of a buzz, I wrote the following article. The article appeared in the April 2008 edition of Ripperologist Magazine and is presented here, albeit slightly edited, to give an idea of how I created awareness of the cases in and around Hull. This article would also open up other doors and avenues of research. I was invited to lecture on this topic at various venues including the 2010 Jack the Ripper Conference in London, Hull's Central Library, The Carnegie Heritage Centre, and the Hull History Centre. Curiously, on the day I lectured at the Hull History Centre the 10,000th visitor walked through the doors and into my lecture. I was warned that it might happen as pre awareness and interest was extremely high, but it was only after the day that the Hull press published the fact that the visitor, who was awarded a prize and certificate, came to the centre to visit my lecture!

Hull Ripper Craze's

A look at Hull based Ripper Crazes 1888-1988

Mike Covell

Kingston upon Hull during the late 1800's was similar to London in many respects, it was a thriving City, one of the busiest ports in Europe but it also had its problems. Bodies were often found in many of the docks that surrounded the City, prostitution was rife and drunken attacks were common place. Infanticide, theft and murder were daily occurrences. Influx of sailors, foreigners and families all looking for work forced the population to breaking point. They resided in lower class habitation which backed on to wealthy merchants houses. Dark alleys and crowded courts were common place and the city's police force was stretched to the limit.

Then in the Autumn of 1888 the vicious crimes attributed to "Jack the Ripper" became known through the vast coverage in the press, and many local newspapers were keen to report the atrocities. Many of the Hull newspapers obtained their stories from the Central News Agency, or The Star, but some local newspapers did manage to have their own reporters already in the nation's capital on other business. (1)

My aim was to collect articles related to the atrocities committed in the East End of London, a task which took several months, lots of money and the reading and cataloguing of 4 newspapers over the last quarter of 1888!

It was my intention to see if I could find any information on the previously named Ripper Suspects with links to Hull,

Robert D'Onston Stephenson, Frederick Bailey Deeming, Albert Edward Prince of Wales, Albert Victor Duke of Clarence, Lewis Carroll, Thomas Sadler, Queen Victoria, Walter Sickert.

The Newspapers in question were,

The Hull Daily Mail,

The Eastern Morning News,

The Hull and East Yorkshire and Lincolnshire Times,

The Evening and Daily News,

It was the smaller local stories which drew my attention, the stories pertaining to the Ripper but with a local slant. I was also drawn to look further forward to the events surrounding the capture and trial of Frederick Bailey Deeming who was eventually imprisoned in Hull for his attempts to defraud a Hull jewellery store. (2)

Then again during his trial in Melbourne the Hull Newspapers were quick and keen to cover the story looking at the murderer's links to the city and alleged links to the East End Murders of 1888.

It was then that I decided that 1888, although a very important year to start looking at Ripper related articles, the following years were just as important.

Mike Covell

Friday 5th October 1888 The Hull Daily Mail, featured the following report,

> "JACK THE RIPPER" CRAZE IN HULL. EXTRAORDINARY CONDUCT OF A DARKEY. OUTRAGE ON A WOMAN. At the Hull Police Court this forenoon before Mr. T. W. Palmer and Mr. E. Lambert, a man of colour, named Samuel Nobb, was charged by Police Constable Leonard (111) 3 with having been disorderly in Adelaide Street on Saturday night.- The officer stated that the prisoner was about the street shouting he was "Jack the Ripper." He saw Noble get hold of one lady and lift her clothes above her head, after which he took hold of another woman, who fell on the street in a dead faint.- Deputy Chief Constable Jones said it took five constables to get the accused into a waggonnette and conduct him into a Police Station.- Mr. Palmer said the Bench considered this to be a very bad case, and imposed a fine of 40s, and costs with alternative of 30 days imprisonment with hard labour.

Friday 5th October 1888 The Hull Daily Mail carried The Whitechapel Craze in Hull,

> THE WHITECHAPEL CRAZE IN HULL. The excitement which has been caused throughout the country by the horrible atrocities committed in Whitechapel, London, has been equally great in Hull, and it appears a repetition of those incidents which have been frequent in the Metropolis of late has to some extent taken place in Hull. At Hull Police Court this afternoon, before the Mayor (Alderman Toozes) and Mr. T Stratton, a poorly clad woman, named Jane Feeney, was charged on warrant with having used threats towards a woman named Minnie Kirlew.- The Prosecutrix stated that the prisoner threatened her in Manor Street yesterday and said she would "Whitechapel Murder her". Witness stated that she was afraid of the prisoner. A man who was called as a witness said he heard the prisoner when acting very violently, threaten to Whitechapel murder the Prosecutrix.- The Bench ordered the accused to find one surety in £10 to keep the peace for six months, and also sent her to prison or seven days for having been disorderly.

Saturday 6th October 1888 Hull and East Yorkshire and Lincolnshire Times carried the same article The Whitechapel Craze in Hull,

> THE WHITECHAPEL CRAZE IN HULL. The excitement which has been caused throughout the country by the horrible atrocities committed in Whitechapel, London, has been equally great in Hull, and it appears a repetition of those

> incidents which have been frequent in the Metropolis of late has to some extent taken place in Hull. At Hull Police Court this afternoon, before the Mayor (Alderman Toozes) and Mr. T Stratton, a poorly clad woman, named Jane Feeney, was charged on warrant with having used threats towards a woman named Minnie Kirlew.- The Prosecutrix stated that the prisoner threatened her in Manor Street yesterday and said she would "Whitechapel Murder her". Witness stated that she was afraid of the prisoner. A man who was called as a witness said he heard the prisoner when acting very violently, threaten to Whitechapel murder the Prosecutrix.- The Bench ordered the accused to find one surety in £10 to keep the peace for six months, and also sent her to prison or seven days for having been disorderly.

Saturday October 13th 1888 Hull News carried the article, The Jack the Ripper Mania,

> THE "JACK THE RIPPER" MANIA. A LETTER TO THE "HULL NEWS". The following letter was brought to-day, about noon to the office of this paper. It was enclosed in an envelope and left surreptitiously on the office counter, it is believed by a lad, who immediately ran away. Of course no importance is attached to the effusion, it being only an attempted hoax:-
>
> Hull Oct 5th
>
> "I arrived in Hull last night from Manchester, and may as well inform you that I have a job or two to do here. London's got two hot for me. "It's all that I want is blood, blood, blood. For why, you will know when I'm (copped?) I'll sharpen my knifes and I'll take their lives, and enjoy myself till I stopped.
>
> The letter is written in pencil on a leaf torn from a pocket-book, and at the bottom is the drawing of a knife represented to be dripping with blood.

Upon finding this article I was quite excited, I quickly scanned it and sent it to several members of the community to gain their views, and was quick to receive several replies. The general consensus surrounding this letter is that is, in all probability a hoax.

I decided to pursue the matter and see if any of the local depositories held any further information, boxes of correspondence or anything from the period that might shed more light on the letter in question. Hull's Local

Mike Covell

Studies Library had only the basic dates and locations regarding the newspaper along with the initial film rolls containing the articles.

My next step was to contact Hull City Archives, who were quick to respond and inform me that there were no Hull News files kept in the archives. It seemed like the trail had gone cold until I noticed a small article at the bottom of one of the pages of the Hull News dated Saturday October 13th 1888,

> *NOTICE: The London offices of the HULL NEWS are at 13a Salisbury Square, (Dorset Street), Fleet Street, E.C, where advertisements are received, and copies of the Daily and Weekly Papers can be obtained.*

I quickly contacted the National Archives, who listed several collections pertaining to the Hull News, they in turn pointed me towards the East Riding Archives out at Beverley, I checked their website and sure enough they list several boxes regarding the newspaper. I have made contact and was informed,

> *"I have checked our database and although we hold various editions of the paper we do not anything else connected with the paper."*

I also visited the Local Studies Library again, to ascertain which Hull Newspapers had Offices in London and their locations, and the locations of their offices in Hull.

Hull News, 58 Whitefriargate, Hull, James Alfred Cooke, 47 Fleet Street, London,

Eastern Morning News, 42 Whitefriargate, William Hunt, 47 Fleet Street, London,

Hull Express, 42 Whitefriargate, William Hunt, 47 Fleet Street, London,

Hull Daily Mail, 22 Whitefriargate, Richard Simmons,

Hull Times, 22 Whitefriargate, Richard Simmons, (4)

So what is the provenance of the letter?

I believe the letter to be one of the following possibilities,

1, Genuine,

2, A Hoax perpetrated by someone at the Newspaper,

3, A Hoax perpetrated by the Newspaper,

4, A Hoax by a reader or resident of Hull.

1, Genuine

It is always difficult in Ripperology to sort the wheat from the chaff, with strong debates raging over which letters, if any are authentic, and which are of course fake. The "Pencil" used also differs from the rest of the known Ripper Letters with most written in Black or Red ink, and only a few written in pencil.(5)

2, A Hoax perpetrated by someone at the Newspaper,

It has been written by several of the top ranking officials who served either during or just after the events of 1888 that the letters are hoaxes, set in motion by the works of an "Enterprising Journalist",

If this is the case, could the letter here be the work of someone within the Hull News? It is certainly possible, but one minor point crops up to argue against this.

During the period the Hull News boasted of having a higher readership than any other Hull based Newspaper, it was obviously well thought of among the local population.

3, A Hoax perpetrated by the Newspaper,

I doubt that the newspaper would jeopardise its standing and reputation, especially when news of the letter was posted several columns in, a quarter of the way down on page 6! If it was a hoax perpetrated by the newspaper, I would have expect more column inches devoted to it, and it being positioned in a more prominent place.

4, A Hoax by a reader or resident of Hull,

Mike Covell

This in my eyes is possibly the best explanation for the letter, as we know from history that when something such as this arrives people are quick and keen to jump on the bandwagon. After all three top serving officials Anderson (6), Macnaghten (7), Littlechild (8) all believed the Ripper letters to be fakes!

This was not, of course the only letter with Hull links,

Letter sent 1888 October 19th From Brierley Hill, to Sir Charles Warren Chief Commissioner of Police Scotland Yard London (9)

> *Wouster*
>
> *Oct. 19) 1888*
>
> *Dear boss iff you are the boss you have not got the right man 100 miles off scent bloodhounds no use will not catch me have been in Wouster a week have spotted 3 out will visit them again shortly dont know much about this part off to Brum to-day/*
>
> *Post this on me way, hope I shall have luck there The atmosphere was to hot at Whitechapel had to clear off smelt a rat saw last victim buried and I felt rather down hearted over my knife which I lost coming here must get one to night. I shall kill 15 at Brum call and settle 3 I have spotted at Wouster I shall then finish/ up at Hull before going to Poland. Silly looking in low lodging houses for me do not visit them description posted at ploice station nothing like me. look out for Octer. 27th at Brum will give them a ripper.*
>
> *Jack a Poland Jew*
>
> *Better Known as Jack the ripper*
>
> *[On the fourth page there appears to be a drop of blood with the postscript]*
>
> *A drop of Strides Blood*

Letter sent 1888 November 11th from Hull to the Press Association (10)

> *Nov 11th*

> *[Crude drawings of skull and crossbones]*
>
> *Sirs- this time*
>
> *I am not afraid of letting you know the whereabouts I am I can't help but laugh at the idea of Sir C. Warren & his bloodhounds It is of no use the police to be so reticent in the matter next time head clean off I have my eye on the next on the list there is plenty in Hull all good blood/ I have lost the real stuff. Take warning next time I carrie the head away with me in my bag the blood [illegible]? I take good care of the uterus. I will give next one gip [?] no mersey*
>
> *Jack the R-*

Unfortunately due to the lack of the Saturday October 13th Hull letter, there can be no comparison, between the other Hull based letters. Could it be that the writers of the letters simply knew of Hull because of its importance in the shipping industry during the period?

Saturday October 13th 1888 The Hull News carried two articles in its Police reports,

> HULL POLICE REPORTS. MONDAY. *(Before Mr. T. W. Palmer and Mr. E. Lambert).* EMULATING "JACK THE RIPPER" *Samuel Noble, a mulatto (11), was charged with being disorderly on Saturday night in Adelaide Street. P.C. Leonard (111) (12) saw prisoner behaving in a manner likely to cause a disturbance, and afterwards ascertained he had ripped one woman's clothes above her head, and on molesting another female she had fallen in a dead faint. A baguette had to be procured to take the prisoner to the station.- The magistrates imposed a fine of 40s. And costs, considering the case a very bad one. A young man named Patrick McDermott, charged with being drunk and disorderly on Saturday night, was fined 5s. And costs. Prisoner had been flourishing a short thick stick, half a broom handle and frightening pedestrians by declaring he was "Jack the Ripper" He approached the constable, who took him into custody, and in a menacing manner threatened to "Jack the Ripper" him.- Prisoner now admitted he had been in Prestwich Asylum. (13)*

Adelaide Street is still in existence today, although the passage of time and aftermath of the blitz left little standing. The Street stretches from East to

Mike Covell

West parallel to Anlaby Road, and Hessle Road, in an area plagued by drugs, crime and prostitution.

Saturday February 7th 1891 The Hull News featured in the weekly rundown of Police Reports, this little snippet appeared on the Thursday,

> THURSDAY. "JACK THE RIPPER" CONDUCT. *John Rouse, labourer, was charged with being drunk and disorderly on the day previous.- From the evidence it appeared that the prisoner was seen following children about and seizing hold of them. He had two knives in his possession and was threatening people with them. He was also using disgusting language to females, and a gentleman Mr. R. Elder took several children from him, and eventually gave him into the custody of P.C. Wardell (171) (14) .- Mr Twiss imposed a fine of 20s and costs, in default 30 days. His Worship commended Mr. Elder for his prompt action in the matter.*

I don't for one second believe this to be a phenomena to hit just Hull, I believed there are little snippets and articles like this the World over awaiting discovery. It is certainly easy to see why people got carried away, as the press were covering all aspects of the horrible atrocities, and like Chinese Whispers the facts and the fallacies were quick to spread. I can also understand why Hull residents would be afraid, seeing that it was the closest and busiest port to London. One can only imagine the terror that these people must have gone through during this awful yet intriguing period in history.

The latest Hull Ripper craze swept the city on the centenary of the murders,

The first report is from The Hull Daily Mail, July 1st 1988, regarding a possible tourist boom,

> TV SPECIAL ON "JACK" MAY SPARK BOOM. RIPPER TOURS SET FOR HULL. HULL IS SET FOR A MACABRE BOOST....THANKS TO JACK THE RIPPER. *By Jonathon Carr-Brown. For the centenary of London's Whitechapel murders this August will be heralded by a prime time American TV show centering on new claims that the fiendish killer was the son of a Hull mill owner. An expert Melvyn Harris believes this will lead to hundreds of trans-Atlantic Ripper hunters swarming into the city. Hull City Council's tourism marketing officer, Val Woof says that, if necessary, she will put on coach tours for the*

> *enthusiasts seeking out the roots of prime suspect Robert Stephenson. CONCENTRATING The major US TV network NBC plans to screen a two hour "special" on the murderer this October, concentrating on the theory that the Ripper came from Hull. The programme "The Secret Identity of Jack the Ripper" will be seen by millions across the United States and Canada. It will be in two parts and will feature lurid scenes of Hull born doctor Robert Stephenson practising black magic. FEATURES Scenes from the lives of other suspects in the gruesome murders of seven prostitutes will also be featured. In the second part of the programme criminal specialists and computer experts will try to evaluate who the most likely culprit was. But Melvyn Harris, has no doubts. He is now writing his second book which he believes will conclusively prove rich mill-owner's son Robert Stephenson was the slaughterer. He will be explaining his theory on the show, live via satellite from his home in Essex. There is some suggestion that some of the programme might be filmed in the back streets of Hull's Old Town. ADDICT Born Robert Donston Stephenson, in Hull, in 1841, the bright doctor and journalist became the black sheep of his respectable family, when he became a drug addict and became obsessed with black magic, Mr Harris says. For some time he was a Customs officer, but after an argument with a smuggler in which he was shot in the thigh, he moved to London.*

So what went wrong?

It is my belief that the tours never took place because of the lack of locations mentioned in Harris books, by this point not enough research had been done, and only a couple of locations had been mentioned in writing. The areas that were mentioned and associated with Stephenson have long gone, mainly due to The Corporation of Hull Slum Clearance, World War Two and the expansion of the City.

For those who have seriously studied Stephenson, they will note that the descriptions of the man, are highly dubious.

By August 18th 1988 The Hull Daily Mail wrote a follow up article again mentioning the imminent tourist boom.

> *NEW RIPPER FILE TO SPARK TOURIST BOOM? By MATTHEW LIMB NEW EVIDENCE from the Jack the Ripper case could shed light on speculation that Britain's most chilling mass murderer came from Hull. Original documents and*

Mike Covell

> photographs of the killer's victims, which went missing from official records many years ago were put on show at Scotland Yard today. They could illuminate the mystery as to whether the murderer of prostitutes in Victorian London's East End was Hull born Dr Robert Donston Stephenson. And they are likely to fuel the City's predicted tourist boom for the centenary of the notorious crimes. The Ripper slaughtered seven women in Whitechapel between August and November 1888. It was first thought the complete file on the case was passed to the Public Records Office in 1951 and the public was given access in the early Seventies. DOCUMENTS But last November a large brown envelope was sent anonymously from the Croydon area to Scotland Yard. Its contents have been established as genuine Ripper documents which disappeared from Yard records many years ago. A Scotland Yard spokesman said "Within the last few months an album of photographs was found among the effects of a deceased senior officer." "His family forwarded them to the Yard, who discovered three photographs of Ripper victims which have never been published" A spokesman for the Metropolitan Police Museums Trusts aid "I am enormously pleased the documents and photographs have been restored to us, They are of great historical interest." BONANZA Author and Ripper expert Melvin Harris wrote a book claiming the murderer was the son of a Hull mill owner. He believes a planned American TV series highlighting the Hull claims will spark a macabre tourist bonanza in the City.

120 years have passed since "Jack the Ripper's" reign of terror, 20 years since the Hull Daily Mail informed the residents of Hull they would see an influx of tourists on "Ripper tours" yet so far nothing has happened, in my research into several suspects in the case with Hull links I have documented over 100 locations associated with them, some of which visited the same places!!

We have seen just how the press covered the incidents in Hull over 120 years ago, and the reaction by the local police, and the effect on the local population.

Reports that spread fear and terror into the hearts of Victorian Hull, a tactic still employed today.

References:

| 1 | Several of the Hull based Newspapers had offices in London, and |

	had reporters residing there covering Politics. All the newspapers had sections detailing "Life in the Capitol"
2	Deeming's Trial was covered extensively in The Hull and East Yorkshire and Lincolnshire Times, 19th March, 1892. Deeming spent time in Hull Jail after defrauding Reynoldson and Son Jewellery store in 1890.
3	P.C. Abraham Thomas Leonard was assigned the number 111 on February 9th 1888, The Policemen of Hull, A.A. Clarke, Hutton Press 1992.
4	Jack the Ripper, letters From Hell, Stewart P. Evans and Keith Skinner, Sutton Publishing 2001.
5	Atkinson's Trade Directory of Hull, 1888, P. 35,
6	Sir Robert Anderson in The Lighter Side of My Official Life, Blackwoods Magazine, 1910, "I will only add here that the 'Jack-the-Ripper' letter which is preserved in the Police Museum at Scotland Yard is the creation of an enterprising London journalist"
7	Sir Melville Macnaghten, Days of My Years, 1914, "I have always thought I could discern the stained forefinger of the journalist - indeed, a year later, I had shrewd suspicions as to the actual author!"
8	Chief Inspector John Littlechild, "The Littlechild Letter", 1913, "With regard to the term 'Jack the Ripper' it was generally

	believed at the Yard that Tom Bullen of the Central News was the originator, but it is probable Moore, who was his chief, was the inventor. It was a smart piece of journalistic work."
9	Letter sent 1888 October 19th From Brierley Hill, to Sir Charles Warren Chief Commissioner of Police Scotland Yard London, "Jack the Ripper, Letters From Hell", Stewart P Evans and Keith Skinner, Sutton Publishing, 2001.
10	Letter sent 1888 November 11th from Hull to the Press Association, "Jack the Ripper, Letters From Hell", Stewart P Evans and Keith Skinner, Sutton Publishing, 2001.
11	A Mulatto is a person of mixed race. http://en.wikipedia.org/wiki/Mulatto
12	P.C. Abraham Thomas Leonard was assigned the number 111 on February 9th 1888, The Policemen of Hull, A.A. Clarke, Hutton Press 1992.
13	Prestwich Asylum was established in 1851 and was still very much in use as a specialist hospital until 1994, http://www.gmcro.co.uk/education/education4.htm, http://www.institutions.org.uk/asylums/england/LAN/prestwich_asylum.htm
14	P.C. John W. Wardell was assigned his number 171 on May 31st 1881, The Policemen of Hull, A.A. Clarke, Hutton Press 1992.

Appendix IV - Newspaper Reports featured

Newspaper reports,

Pre – 1888

The Hull Packet and East Riding Times, September 12th 1873

The Hull Packet and East Riding Times, September 12th 1873

The Hull Packet and East Riding Times, September 12th 1873

The Hull Packet and East Riding Times, September 19th 1873

The Hull and North Lincolnshire Times, September 20th 1873

The Hull and North Lincolnshire Times, September 20th 1873

The Hull and North Lincolnshire Times, September 30th 1873

The Hull Times, September 30th 1873

The Hull Packet and East Riding Times, October 24th 1873

The Hull Packet and East Riding Times, November 7th 1873

1888

The Hull Daily Mail, April 6th 1888

The Hull Daily Mail, April 9th 1888

The Hull Daily News, April 9th 1888

The Hull Daily News, August 10th 1888

The Hull Daily Mail, August 15th 1888

Mike Covell

The Eastern Morning News, September 1st 1888

The Hull Daily Mail, September 3rd 1888

The Eastern Morning News, September 4th 1888

The Eastern Morning News, September 6th 1888

The Hull Daily News, September 8th 1888

The Hull and East Yorkshire and Lincolnshire Times, September 8th 1888

The Hull News, September 10th 1888

The Hull Daily News, September 10th 1888

The Hull Daily News, September 10th 1888

The Hull Daily News, September 10th 1888

The Hull Daily Mail, September 10th 1888

The Hull Daily News, September 10th 1888

The Hull Daily Mail, September 10th 1888

The Eastern Morning News, September 10th 1888

The Hull News, September 10th 1888

The Hull Daily Mail, September 10th 1888

The Hull Daily News, September 11th 1888

The Hull Daily News, September 11th 1888

The Hull Daily Mail, September 11th 1888

The Eastern Morning News, September 11th 1888

The Hull Daily News, September 11th 1888

The Hull Daily Mail, September 12th 1888

Newspapers from Hull Volume 1

The Hull Daily Mail, September 12th 1888

The Hull Daily Mail, September 12th 1888

The Hull Daily Mail, September 12th 1888

The Hull Daily Mail, September 12th 1888

The Hull Daily News, September 12th 1888

The Hull Daily News, September 12th 1888

The Eastern Morning News, September 12th 1888

The Hull Daily News, September 13th 1888

The Hull Daily News, September 13th 1888

The Eastern Morning News, September 13th 1888

The Hull Daily News, September 13th 1888

The Hull Daily News, September 13th 1888

The Eastern Morning News, September 13th 1888

The Hull Daily News, September 13th 1888

The Eastern Morning News, September 13th 1888

The Hull Daily News, September 13th 1888

The Hull Daily Mail, September 14th 1888

The Eastern Morning News, September 14th 1888

The Eastern Morning News, September 15th 1888

The Hull and East Yorkshire and Lincolnshire Times, September 15th 1888

The Hull Daily News, September 15th 1888

The Hull and East Yorkshire and Lincolnshire Times, September 15th 1888

Mike Covell

The Hull Daily Mail, September 17th 1888

The Eastern Morning News, September 17th 1888

The Hull Daily News, September 17th 1888

The Hull Daily Mail, September 18th 1888

The Eastern Morning News, September 19th 1888

The Hull Daily News, September 20th 1888

The Eastern Morning News, September 20th 1888

The Eastern Morning News, September 22nd 1888

The Hull and East Yorkshire and Lincolnshire Times, September 22nd 1888

The Hull Daily Mail, September 24th 1888

The Hull Daily Mail, September 25th 1888

The Eastern Morning News, September 25th 1888

The Eastern Morning News, September 26th 1888

The Hull Daily Mail, September 27th 1888

The Hull Daily Mail, September 27th 1888

The Eastern Morning News, September 27th 1888

The Hull Daily Mail, September 28th 1888

The Hull and East Yorkshire and Lincolnshire Times, September 28th 1888

The Eastern Morning News, September 28th 1888

The Hull Daily News, September 29th 1888

The Hull Daily News, September 29th 1888

The Hull Daily News, September 29th 1888

The Hull Daily News, September 29th 1888

The Hull and East Yorkshire and Lincolnshire Times, September 29th 1888

The Hull and East Yorkshire and Lincolnshire Times, September 29th 1888

The Hull News, September 29th 1888

The Hull Daily Mail, September 29th 1888

The Hull Daily Mail, October 1st 1888

The Hull Daily News, October 1st 1888

The Hull Daily Mail, October 1st 1888

The Hull Daily Mail, October 1st 1888

The Hull Daily Mail, October 1st 1888

The Hull Daily News, October 1st 1888

The Eastern Morning News, October 1st 1888

The Hull Daily Mail, October 2nd 1888

The Hull Daily Mail, October 2nd 1888

The Hull Daily Mail, October 2nd 1888

The Hull Daily Mail, October 2nd 1888

The Eastern Morning News, October 3rd 1888

The Hull Daily News, October 3rd 1888

The Hull Daily News, October 3rd 1888

The Hull Daily News, October 3rd 1888

The Hull Daily Mail, October 3rd 1888

The Hull Daily Mail, October 3rd 1888

Mike Covell

The Hull Daily Mail, October 3rd 1888
The Hull Daily News, October 4th 1888
The Hull Daily Mail, October 4th 1888
The Hull Daily Mail, October 4th 1888
The Hull Daily Mail, October 4th 1888
The Hull Daily Mail, October 4th 1888
The Hull Daily Mail, October 4th 1888
The Hull Daily News, October 4th 1888
The Hull Daily Mail, October 4th 1888
The Hull Daily Mail, October 5th 1888
The Hull Daily Mail, October 5th 1888
The Hull Daily News, October 5th 1888
The Hull Daily Mail, October 5th 1888
The Hull Daily Mail, October 5th 1888
The Hull Daily Mail, October 5th 1888
The Hull Daily News, October 6th 1888
The Hull and East Yorkshire and Lincolnshire Times, October 6th 1888
The Hull Daily News, October 6th 1888
The Hull Daily News, October 6th 1888
The Hull and East Yorkshire and Lincolnshire Times, October 6th 1888
The Hull Daily News, October 6th 1888
The Eastern Morning News, October 6th 1888

The Hull and East Yorkshire and Lincolnshire Times, October 6th 1888

The Hull and East Yorkshire and Lincolnshire Times, October 6th 1888

The Hull News, October 6th 1888

The Eastern Morning News, October 8th 1888

The Eastern Morning News, October 8th 1888

The Hull Daily Mail, October 8th 1888

The Hull Daily Mail, October 8th 1888

The Eastern Morning News, October 9th 1888

The Eastern Morning News, October 9th 1888

The Hull Daily Mail, October 9th 1888

The Hull Daily Mail, October 9th 1888

The York Herald, October 9th 1888

The Eastern Morning News, October 9th 1888

The Eastern Morning News, October 10th 1888

The Eastern Morning News, October 10th 1888

The Hull Daily News, October 11th 1888

The Eastern Morning News, October 11th 1888

The Hull Daily Mail, October 12th 1888

The Eastern Morning News, October 12th 1888

The Hull Daily News, October 13th 1888

The Hull Daily News, October 13th 1888

The York Herald, October 13th 1888

Mike Covell

The Hull and East Yorkshire and Lincolnshire Times, October 13th 1888

The Eastern Morning News, October 15th 1888

The Hull Daily News, October 15th 1888

The Hull Daily Mail, October 16th 1888

The Hull Daily News, October 18th 1888

The Hull Daily News, October 18th 1888

The Eastern Morning News, October 18th 1888

The Eastern Morning News, October 19th 1888

The Hull and Lincolnshire Times, October 20th 1888

The Hull and Lincolnshire Times, October 20th 1888

The Hull and Lincolnshire Times, October 20th 1888

The Hull and Lincolnshire Times, October 20th 1888

The Hull and Lincolnshire Times, October 20th 1888

The Hull and Lincolnshire Times, October 20th 1888

The Eastern Morning News, October 20th 1888

The Hull and East Yorkshire and Lincolnshire Times, October 20th 1888

The Hull Daily Mail, October 25th 1888

The Hull News, November 10th 1888

The Eastern Morning News, November 10th 1888

The Hull and East Yorkshire and Lincolnshire Times, November 10th 1888

The Hull Daily News, November 12th 1888

The Hull Daily Mail, November 12th 1888

The Hull Daily Mail, November 12th 1888

The Hull Daily Mail, November 12th 1888

The Hull Daily Mail, November 12th 1888

The Hull Daily News, November 12th 1888

The Hull and Lincolnshire Times, November 13th 1888

The Hull Daily News, November 13th 1888

The Hull and East Yorkshire and Lincolnshire Times, November 17th 1888

The Hull Daily Mail, November 19th 1888

The Hull Daily Mail, November 21st 1888

The Hull and Lincolnshire Times, November 24th 1888

The Hull Daily Mail, December 5th 1888

The Hull Daily Mail, December 7th 1888

The Hull and East Yorkshire and Lincolnshire Times, December 8th 1888

The Hull Daily News, December 15th 1888

The Hull Daily News, December 15th 1888

The Hull Times, December 22nd 1888

The Hull Daily Mail, December 22nd 1888

Hull Ripper Crazes 1888 – 1988

The Hull Daily Mail, October 5th 1888

The Hull Daily Mail, October 5th 1888

The Hull and East Yorkshire and Lincolnshire Times, October 6th 1888

Mike Covell

The Hull News, October 13th 1888

The Hull News, October 13th 1888

The Hull News, February 7th 1891

The Hull Daily Mail, July 1st 1988

The Hull Daily Mail, August 18th 1988

Bibliography, References and Further Reading

There are hundreds of books on the market that give varying details of the case, many of which are suspect based. Whilst I have many of these in my library, I have chosen to refer to the books which use primary sources and give a better overview of the case.

References:

Introduction – A brief History of Kingston upon Hull

1	Several books worth reading include, The Jack The Ripper A-Z, by Paul Begg, Martin Fido, and Keith Skinner, Headline Publishing, 1991. Jack the Ripper An Encyclopedia, John J. Eddleston, Metro Publishing, 2002. Both include detailed biographical information on the many suspects proposed over the years. It is also worth checking both Ripper Casebook and JTR Forums for regular updates on research.
2	Jack the Ripper, Letters From Hell, Stewart P. Evans and Keith Skinner, Sutton Publishing, 2001, page 49-50. The Jack The Ripper A-Z, by Paul Begg, Martin Fido, and Keith Skinner, Headline Publishing, 1991, P. 209.
3	Jack the Ripper, Letters From Hell, Stewart P. Evans and Keith Skinner, Sutton Publishing, 2001, PP. 49-50. For brief biographical details see, Jack the Ripper An Encyclopedia, John J. Eddleston, Metro Publishing, 2002, pages 136, and 141 respectively.

4	Jack the Ripper, Letters From Hell, Stewart P. Evans and Keith Skinner, Sutton Publishing, 2001, P. 72.
5	Book of Hull, The, John Markham, Barracuda Books Limited, 1989, P. 50.
6	Ibid, p. 51
7	Ibid, p. 50
8	Ibid, p. 83
9	Ibid, p. 46
10	Ibid, p. 83
11	Ibid, p. 83
12	Ibid, p. 83
13	Policeman of Hull, The, A. A. Clarke, Hutton Press, 1992, p. 48 1855 Report for Chief Constable showing, 423 known to the police, 79 of which are under 20 years old, 175 are between 20 and 25, 78 between 25 and 30, and 91 are above 30 years of age. There are 244 known brothels, 196 of which keep prostitutes, 48 of which are frequented by prostitutes.
14	Trains, Shelters and Ships, an unpublished papers by A. Newman,

	N. Evans, Presented to the Jewish Genealogical Society of Great Britain, 1999
15	Atkinson's Trade Directory of Hull, 1888, P. 32 gives this number.
16	Ibid, P.32.
17	Ibid, P. 1
18	Report for the Health of the Borough of Kingston upon Hull for the year 1888, John W. Mason, M.B., C.M., D.P.H. (Aberd.), M.R.C.S.E., Harland and Son, 1889, Ref: Reference L352.04
19	Ibid, P. 9
20	Ibid, P. 59
21	Ibid, P. 68

Notes on the Hull Police

References:

1	Atkinson's Trade Directory of Hull 1888, P.48
2	Policeman of Hull, The, A. A. Clarke, Hutton Press, 1992, P.153

Mike Covell

3	Atkinson's Trade Directory of Hull 1888, P.48
4	Country Coppers – The Story of the East Riding Police, A. A. Clarke, Arton Books, 1993, P. 37
5	Atkinson's Trade Directory of Hull 1888

Hull Newspapers

References:

1	The Fourth Estate in Hull - The Life and Times of the Daily Press, Geoffrey Boland, Hull Local Studies, 2005
2	Atkinson's Trade Directory of Hull 1888
3	Kelly's Trade Directory of Hull 1889
4	The Fourth Estate in Hull - The Life and Times of the Daily Press, Geoffrey Boland, Hull Local Studies, 2005
5	Atkinson's Trade Directory of Hull 1888
6	Kelly's Trade Directory of Hull 1889

7	The Fourth Estate in Hull - The Life and Times of the Daily Press, Geoffrey Boland, Hull Local Studies, 2005
8	Atkinson's Trade Directory of Hull 1888
9	The Fourth Estate in Hull - The Life and Times of the Daily Press, Geoffrey Boland, Hull Local Studies, 2005
10	Atkinson's Trade Directory of Hull 1888
11	Kelly's Trade Directory of Hull 1889
12	The Fourth Estate in Hull - The Life and Times of the Daily Press, Geoffrey Boland, Hull Local Studies, 2005
13	Atkinson's Trade Directory of Hull 1888
14	Ibid
15	Ibid
16	The Street of Ink, by H. Simonis, London, Cassell, 1917
17	Wikipedia.
18	Kingston Communications, A History in Words 1904-2004

Mike Covell

19	Implementing Reforms in the Telecommunications Sector: Lessons from experience, Bjorn Wellenius and Peter A. Stern, World Bank Publications, 1994, P. 532
20	Atkinson's Trade Directory of Hull 1888
21	A History of Hull's Railways, G.G. MacTurk, Revised by Ken Hoole, Nidd Narrow Gauge Railways Ltd, 1970, Page 4
22	Ibid Page 4
23	Ibid Page 25
24	Ibid Page 37
25	Ibid Page 42
26	Ibid Page 48

Introduction to the Newspaper reports
References:

1	Britain in the Nineteenth Century- 1815-1914, Chris Cook, Pearson Education, 1999, P. 133
2	Ibid, P. 133

3	Ibid, P. 133
4	Ibid, P. 133
5	Ibid, P. 133
6	Nineteenth Century Britain, A Very Short Introduction, Christopher Harvie and H. C. G. Matthew, Oxford Press, 2000, P. 69
6	Ibid, P. 69
8	Ibid, P. 69
9	Get Me A Murder A Day! Kevin Williams, Oxford University Press, 1998, P. 49

Brief notes on the London Press
References:

1	Jack the Ripper and the London Press, L. Perry Curtis, Yale University Press, 2001. P. 59
2	Ibid, P. 113

Mike Covell

3	Ibid, P. 113
4	The Jack the Ripper A-Z, Paul Begg, Martin Fido, and Keith Skinner, Headline Publishing, 1994, P. 328
5	Jack the Ripper and the London Press, L. Perry Curtis, Yale University Press, 2001. Page 59
6	Ibid, P. 62

Jack the Ripper - General Reference

American Murders of Jack the Ripper, R. Michael Gordon, Lyons Press, 2005

Autobiography of Jack the Ripper, The, James Carnac, Bantam Press, 2012

Beaver Book of Horror, The, Daniel Farson, Beaver Books, 2007

Bell Tower, The, Robert Graysmith, Regnery, 1999

By Ear and Eyes, Karyo Magellan, Longshot Publishing, 2005

Carroty Nell – The Last Victim of Jack the Ripper, John E. Keefe, Menotomy Publishing, 2010

Carroty Nell – The Last Victim of Jack the Ripper, John E. Keefe, Menotomy Publishing, 2012

Complete History of Jack the Ripper, The, Philip Sugden, Robinson Publishing, 2002

Complete Jack the Ripper, The, Donald Rumbelow, W. H. Allen, 1976

Complete Jack the Ripper, The, Donald Rumbelow, Penguin Books, 1988

Complete Jack the Ripper, The, Donald Rumbelow, Penguin Books, 2004

Crimes and Times of Jack the Ripper, The, Tom Cullen, Fontana, 1973

Crimes, Detection and Death of Jack the Ripper, Martin Fido, George Weidenfield and Nicholson Ltd,

1987

Crimes, Detection and Death of Jack the Ripper, Martin Fido, Orion Books, 1993

Crimes of Jack the Ripper, The, Paul Roland, Arcturus Publishing, 2006

Diary of Jack the Ripper, The, Shirley Harrison, Hyperion Publishing, 1993

Diary of Jack the Ripper, The, Shirley Harrison, Blake Publishing, 1998

Diary of Jack the Ripper, The, - Another Chapter, James Stettler, Area Nine Publishing, 2009

Dracula Secrets, The, Jack the Ripper and the Darkest Sources of Bram Stoker, Neil R. Storey, History

Press, 2012

E1- A Journey Through Whitechapel and Spitalfields, John G. Bennett, Five Leaves Publishing, 2009

Enigma of Jack the Ripper, The, John de Locksley, 1994

Epiphany of the Whitechapel Murders, Karen Trenouth, Author House, 2006

First Jack the Ripper Victim Photographs, The, Robert J. McLaughlin, Zwerghaus Books, 2005

Fox and the Flies, The, Charles Van Onselen, Vintage, 2008

From Hell- The Jack the Ripper Mystery, Bob Hinton, Old Bakehouse Publications, 1998

Identity of Jack the Ripper, The, Donald McCormick, Arrow Books, 1970

Illustrated Guide to Jack the Ripper, An, Peter Fisher, P. and D. Riley, 1996

Mike Covell

In the Footsteps of the Whitechapel Murders, John F. Plimmer, The Book Guild, 1998

Jack the Ripper, Andrew Cook, Amberley, 2009

Jack the Ripper, Daniel Farson, Sphere, 1973

Jack the Ripper, John McIlwain, Pitkin Guides, Jarrold Publishing

Jack the Ripper, Mark Whitehead and Miriam Rivett, Pocket Essentials, 2001

Jack the Ripper, Mark Whitehead and Miriam Rivett, Pocket Essentials, 2006

Jack the Ripper, Susan McNicoll, Altitude Publishing, 2005

Jack the Ripper- A Bibliography and Review of the Literature, Andrew Kelly, Association of Assistant

Librarians, 1973

Jack the Ripper- A Bibliography and Review of the Literature, Andrew Kelly, Association of Assistant

Librarians, 1984

Jack the Ripper- A Bibliography and Review of the Literature, Andrew Kelly, Association of Assistant

Librarians, 1994

Jack the Ripper- A Bibliography and Review of the Literature, Andrew Kelly, Association of Assistant

Librarians, 1995

Jack the Ripper- A to Z, Paul Begg, Martin Fido, and Keith Skinner, Headline Book Publishing, 1991

Jack the Ripper- A to Z, Paul Begg, Martin Fido, and Keith Skinner, Headline Book Publishing, 1992

Jack the Ripper- A to Z, Paul Begg, Martin Fido, and Keith Skinner, Headline Book Publishing, 1994

Jack the Ripper- A to Z, Paul Begg, Martin Fido, and Keith Skinner, Headline Book Publishing, 1996

Jack the Ripper- A to Z, Paul Begg, Martin Fido, and Keith Skinner, John Blake, 2010

Jack the Ripper- American Hero, Jacob Corbett, Amazon, 2012

Jack the Ripper- An Encyclopaedia, John J. Eddleston, Metro Publishing, 2002

Jack the Ripper- An Encyclopaedia, John J. Eddleston, Metro Publishing, 2010

Jack the Ripper- Anatomy of a Myth, William Beadle, Wat Tyler Books, 1995

Jack the Ripper- And Black Magic, Spiro Dimolianis, McFarland, 2011

Jack the Ripper- And the East End, Alex Werner, Chatto and Windus, 2008

Jack the Ripper- And the Irish Press, Alan Sharp, Ashfield Press, 2005

Jack the Ripper- And the London Press, Lewis Perry Curtis, Yale University, 2001

Jack the Ripper- Black Magic Rituals, Ivor Edwards, John Blake Publishing, 2003

Jack the Ripper- Casebook, Richard Jones, Andre Deutsch, 2008

Jack the Ripper- Crime Archive, Val Horsler, National Archives, 2007

Jack the Ripper- End of a Legend, Calum Reuben Knight, Athena Press, 2005

Jack the Ripper- His Life and Crimes in Popular Entertainment, Gary Colville and Patrick Lucanio,

McFarland, 2009

Jack the Ripper- Infamous Serial Killer, Filiquarian Publications, 2008

Jack the Ripper- In Fact and Fiction, Robin Odell, Mandrake Publishing, 2009

Jack the Ripper- Letters from Hell, Stewart P. Evans and Keith Skinner, Sutton Publishing, 2004

Jack the Ripper- Light Hearted Friend, Richard Wallace, Gemini Press, 1997

Jack the Ripper- Location Photographs, The, Philip Hutchinson, Amberley

Mike Covell

Publishing, 2009

Jack the Ripper- Media, Culture, History, Alexandra Warwick and Martin Willis, Manchester University

Press, 2007

Jack the Ripper- One Hundred Years of Mystery, Peter Underwood, Blandford Press, 1987

Jack the Ripper- Opposing Viewpoints, Katie Colby-Newton, Greenhaven, 1990

Jack the Ripper- Quest for a Killer, M. J. Trow, Wharncliffe True Crime, 2009

Jack the Ripper- Revealed and Revisited, John Wilding, Express Newspapers, 2006

Jack the Ripper- Scotland Yard Investigates, Stewart P. Evans and Donald Rumbelow, Sutton Publishing,

2006

Jack the Ripper- Summing up and Verdict, Colin Wilson and Robin Odell, Corgi Books, 1992

Jack the Ripper- The 21st Century Investigation, Trevor Marriott, John Blake Publishing, 2005

Jack the Ripper- The 21st Century Investigation, Trevor Marriott, John Blake Publishing, 2007

Jack the Ripper- The American Connection, Shirley Harrison, Blake Publishing, 2003

Jack the Ripper- The Bloody Truth, Melvin Harris, Columbus Books, 1987

Jack the Ripper- The Celebrity Suspects, Mike Holgate, History Press, 2008

Jack the Ripper- The Definitive History, Paul Begg, Pearson Education Limited, 2004

Jack the Ripper- The Facts, Paul Begg, Robson Books, 2006

Jack the Ripper- The Final Chapter, Paul H. Feldman, Virgin Books, 2002

Jack the Ripper- The Final Chapter, Paul H. Feldman, Virgin Books, 2007

Jack the Ripper- The Final Solution, Stephen Knight, Harrap, 1976

Jack the Ripper- The Final Solution, Stephen Knight, Panther, 1981

Jack the Ripper- The Final Solution, Stephen Knight, Harper Collins, 1994

Jack the Ripper- The Hand of a Woman, John Morris, Seren Books, 2012

Jack the Ripper- The Murders and the Movies, Denis Meikle, Reynolds and Hearn Ltd, 2002

Jack the Ripper- The Mystery Solved, Paul Harrison, Robert Hale, 1993

Jack the Ripper- The Satanic Team, Karen Trenouth, Author House, 2007

Jack the Ripper- The Simple Truth, Bruce Paley, Headline Publishing, 1996

Jack the Ripper- The Uncensored Facts, Paul Begg, Robson Books, 1989

Jack the Ripper, The Whitechapel Murderer, Terry Lynch, Wordsworth Editions, 2008

Jack the Ripper- Unmasked, William Beadle, John Blake Publishing, 2009

Jack the Ripper- Unveiled, John de Locksley, 1994

Jack the Ripper- Walk, The, Paul Garner, Louis London Walks, 2002

Jack the Ripper- Whitechapel Murders, The, Kevin O'Donnell, Andy and Sue Parlour, Ten Bells

Publishing, 1997

Jimmy Kelly's Year of the Ripper Murders, 1888, John Morrison, 1983

Last Victim, The, Anne E. Graham and Carol Emmas, Headline Publishing, 1998

Lodger- Arrest and Escape of Jack the Ripper, The, Stewart P. Evans and Paul Gainey, Century Publishing,

1995

London of Jack the Ripper Then and Now, The, Robert Clack and Philip

Mike Covell

Hutchinson, Breedon Books, 2007

London of Jack the Ripper Then and Now, The, 2nd Edition, Robert Clack and Philip Hutchinson, Breedon

Books, 2009

Mammoth Book of Jack the Ripper, The, Maxim Jakubowski and Nathan Braund, Constable and Robinson,

1999

Mammoth Book of Jack the Ripper, The, Maxim Jakubowski and Nathan Braund, Castle Books, 2005

Mammoth Book of Jack the Ripper, The, Maxim Jakubowski and Nathan Braund, Constable and Robinson,

2008

Man that Hunted Jack the Ripper, The, Nicholas Connell and Stewart P. Evans, Amberley, 2009

Many Faces of Jack the Ripper, The, M. J. Trow, Summersdale Publishing, 1997

Murder and Madness- The Secret Life of Jack the Ripper, David Abrahamsen M.D., F.A.C.Pn., Avon

Books, 1993

Mystery of Jack the Ripper, The, Leonard Matters, Arrow Books, 1964

News from Whitechapel, The, Alexander Chisholm, Christopher Michael DiGrazia, Dave Yost, McFarland

And Co, 2002

Portrait of a Serial Killer-Jack the Ripper-Case Closed, Patricia Cornwell, Little Brown, 2002

Portrait of a Serial Killer-Jack the Ripper-Case Closed, Patricia Cornwell, Time Warner, 2003

Prince Jack- The True Story of Jack the Ripper, Frank Spiering, Jove Books, 1980

Public Reactions to Jack the Ripper, Stephen P. Ryder (Ed) Inklings Press, 2006

Ramble with Jack the Ripper, A, John de Locksley, 1996

Ripper and the Royals, The, Melvyn Fairclough, Duckbacks, 2002

Ripper Code, The, Thomas Toughill, Sutton Publishing, 2008

Ripper File, The, Elwyn Jones and John Lloyd, Futura Publications, 1975

Ripper File, The, Melvin Harris, W. H. Allen and Co., 1989

Ripper in Ramsgate, The, Christopher Scott, Michaels Bookshop, 2008

Ripper Legacy, The, Martin Howells and Keith Skinner, Sphere Books Ltd, 1988

Ripper Suspect, D. J. Leighton, Sutton Publishing, 2006

Ripperology, Paul Begg (Ed) Barnes and Noble, 2007

Ripperology, Robin Odell, Kent State University Press, 2006

Saucy Jack- The Elusive Ripper, Paul Woods and Gavin Baddeley, Ian Allan Publishing, 2009

Sickert and the Ripper Crimes, Jean Overton Fuller, Mandrake Publishing, 2003

Search For Jack the Ripper- A Psychic Investigation, Pamela Ball, Midpoint Press, 2006

Secret of Prisoner 1167- Was this man Jack the Ripper?, James Tully, Robinson Publishing, 1998

The Harlot Killer- The story of Jack the Ripper in Fact and Fiction, Alan Barnard, Dodd Mead, 1953

The Man who would be Jack – The Hunt for the real Ripper, David Bullock, Robson Press, 2012

The Prince, His Tutor, and the Ripper, Deborah McDonald, McFarland and Company Inc. 2007

The Trial of Jack the Ripper, Euan Macpherson, Mainstream Publishing, 2005

Mike Covell

Thames Torso Murders, The, M. J. Trow, Wharncliffe Books, 2011

Ultimate Jack the Ripper Sourcebook, The, Stewart P. Evans and Keith Skinner, Robinson Publishing, 2001

Uncle Jack, Tony Williams and Humphrey Price, Orion Books, 2006

Uncovering Jack the Ripper's London, Richard Jones, New Holland, 2007

Victims of Jack the Ripper, The, Neal Stubbings Sheldon, Inklings Press, 2007

Whitechapel Murders Solved, The, John Plimmer, House of Stratus, 2003

Who was Jack the Ripper? Winston Forbes-Jones, Pipeline Promotions, 1988

Will the Real jack the Ripper, Arthur Douglas, Countryside Publications, 1979

Jack the Ripper – Press Associated

Illustrated Police News, Steve Jones, Wicked Publications, 2002

Jack the Ripper, Andrew Cook

Jack the Ripper and the London Press, L. Perry Curtis, Jnr, Yale University, 2001

London Correspondence: Jack the Ripper and the Irish Press, Alan Sharp, Ashfield Press, 2005

News From Whitechapel-Jack the Ripper in the Daily Telegraph, Alexander Chisholm, Christopher Michael DiGrazia, and Dave Yost, McFarland and Company Inc, Publishers, 2002

Public Reactions to Jack the Ripper, Stephen P. Ryder, Inklings Press, 2006

Ripper Notes-How the Newspapers Covered the Jack the Ripper Murders, Issue 21, Edited by Dan Norder, Inklings Press, January 2005

Hull History

Architecture of the Victorian era of Kingston upon Hull 1830-1914, Highgate

Press, Ian N Goldthorpe, 2005.

Aspects of Hull, David Goodman, (Ed,) Wharncliffe Books,

Aspects of the Yorkshire Coast, Alan Whitworth, (Ed,) Wharncliffe Books,

Aspects of the Yorkshire Coast 2, Alan Whitworth, (Ed,) Wharncliffe Books, 2000

Atkinson's Trade Directory of Hull 1888

The Book of Hull, John Markham, Barracuda Books Limited, 1989

Breath of Sculcoates, A, Hull and District Local History Research Group, Heitage Lottery Fund, Developing our Communities, 2007

East Riding Chapels and Meeting Houses, East Yorkshire Local History Society, David Neave and Susan Neave, 1990

Forgotten Hull Kingston Press, Graham Wilkinson

Forgotten Hull 2, Kingston Press, Graham Wilkinson, 2000

Fourth Estate in Hull - The Life and Times of the Daily Press, The, Geoffrey Boland, Hull Local Studies, 2005

Georgian Hull, Ivan and Elisabeth Hall, William Sessions Ltd, 1978

Historical Atlas of East Yorkshire, An, Susan Neave and Stephen Ellis, (Ed,) University of Hull Press, 1996

History of the Yorkshire Coast Fishing Industry 1780-1914, Roy Robinson, Hull University Press, 1987

History of Seed Crushing in Great Britain, Harold W. Brace, Land Books, 1960

Hull and Scarborough Railway, C. T. Goode, Burstwick Publicity Services, 2000

Hull Schools in Victorian Times, Pete Railton, 1995

Illustrated History of Hull's Railways, Irwell Press, M Nicholson and W.B.Yeadon, 1993

Images of Victorian Hull - F.S. Smith's drawings of the Old Town, Text by Caroline Aldridge, Hutton Press, 1989

Innes Heritage Collection of Hull, The, Michael Thompson, Hutton Press, 1994

Mike Covell

Kelly's Trade Directory of Hull 1889

Lost Churches and Chapels of Hull, Hutton Press, David Neave, 1991

Lost Pubs of Hull, Kingston Press, Paul Gibson and Graham Wilkinson, 1999

Lost Railways of Holderness, the Hull-Hornsea lines, the Hull-Withernsea lines, Hutton Press, Peter Price, 1989

More Illustrated History of Hull's Railways, Challenger Publications, W.B.Yeadon, 1995

Old and New Hull, T. Tindall Willdridge, M. C. Peck and Son, 1884

Railways of Hull, C. T. Goode, Burstwick Publicity Services, 1992

Sculcoates- Ancient and Modern, Christine Gould and David Knappett, Oriel Printing Company, 1991

Maps

Jack the Ripper, Whitechapel Map 1888, Geoff Cooper and Gordon Punter, 2003

Whitechapel, Spitalfields and the Bank 1873, Alan Godfrey Maps, 2006

Whitechapel, Spitalfields and the Bank 1894, Alan Godfrey Maps, 2006

Highbury and Islington 1871, Alan Godfrey Maps, 2006

Highbury and Islington 1894, Alan Godfrey Maps, 2006

Highbury and Islington 1914, Alan Godfrey Maps, 2006

Upper Holloway 1869, Alan Godfrey Maps, 1999

Upper Holloway 1894, Alan Godfrey Maps, 2005

Upper Holloway 1914, Alan Godfrey Maps, 1997

Hull Old Town 1853, Alan Godfrey Maps, 1988

Hull Railway Dock and Paragon Stn 1853, Alan Godfrey Maps, 2008

Hull Alexandra Dock 1908, Alan Godfrey Maps, 2007

Hull Hessle Road 1928, Alan Godfrey Maps, 1987

Hull East 1908, Alan Godfrey Maps, 2007

Hull East 1928, Alan Godfrey Maps, 1987

Hull North East 1980, Alan Godfrey Maps, 2007

Hull West 1908, Alan Godfrey Maps, 2006

Hull West 1928, Alan Godfrey Maps, 1987

I also consulted numerous maps held on file at Hull Local Studies Library.

Miscellaneous Files

CQB436 Michaelmas Quarter Sessions 1900

CQB437 Epiphany Quarter Sessions 1901

CQN/1 Calendar of Prisoners 1893-1904

CDPM/2/6 Minute Book January – April 1891

Acknowledgments

First and foremost I would like to acknowledge the support of my family, who have stood by my crazy ideas and decisions and sat quietly whilst I tried to type this up! My wife Susan has been a rock and I wish to take this opportunity to thank her for her love and support, my children Bradley, Alyssa, and William, for their cuddles and smiles. My Mother and Father, for their constant support, inspiration and technical help. During the time of writing my Father passed away but his ongoing support and encouragement helped me along this path. We have seen some dark times, and hopefully this is the start of something positive. No book on Hull Newspapers would be complete without the invaluable help of all the staff at Hull Local Studies Library. Each and every question was asked and each and every need catered for. Every time the staff went above and beyond the call of duty, and for that I truly thank them. I also offer my deepest thanks to Hull City Council's Archives Department, who again helped me in every step I took. Their hard work and dedication did not go unnoticed. At the time of writing the Hull Local History unit and the Hull City Council's Archives have amalgamated with the Hull University Archives to form the Hull History Centre. I have had the pleasure of lecturing at the Hull History Centre on several occasions and they building, staff and crowd are always fantastic. My thanks also go to the hardworking staff at The Carnegie Heritage Centre, whose warm and knowledgeable staff make every visit one to remember. Special thanks must go to Liz Shepard and Paul Gibson of the Carnegie Heritage Action Group for their help and advice. I have had the pleasure of lecturing on the Ripper and my research at Carnegie and it is always a warm welcome and great atmosphere with a cracking cuppa! Special thanks and acknowledgements to Howard and Nina Brown of the JTR Forums, http://www.jtrforums.com/ Howard and Nina have helped shape and mould my many theories and helped provide a sound stage for my research. Not only that, but they have become close friends, and for that alone I thank them. Thank you to Stephen P Ryder of the Ripper Casebook http://www.casebook.org/intro.html, who provided me with a stage for my research and a casebook blog for my work to be presented. Stephen is a major force in the community and an inspiration to all Ripperologists. Thank you to all of the *Hull Daily Mail* "*Yourmail*" team who provided me with an excellent site to write about my passions! Whilst the site has since gone, the feedback that my work received inspired me to work on projects such as this. It also opened up several doors and avenues of research for me, and made me many friends and contacts for life. To Alan Brigham, Michael Lake, and Nicholas Evans, all have helped shape and inspire me to continue in this work. A special thank you must go to Richard Sutherland who was working at Waterstones in Hull when I began this book. Richard helped in the early stages, and is a very knowledgeable, friendly young man. To all the Ripperologists, whom I am lucky enough to call friends, who have helped along the way, I have put you all in alphabetical order to avoid you all arguing in the forums over who I mentioned first! Alan Sharp, Ali and Lee Bevan, Brian L. Porter, Bob Hinton, Chris George, Chris Scott, Chris Jones, Colin Cobb, Dave and Sandra Yost, Debra Arif, Gareth Williams, Jon Rees, John Savage, Martin Fido, Paul Begg, Philip Hutchinson, Ricky Cobb, Robert Clark, Robert J. McLaughlin, Richard Jones, Suzi Haney, and everyone else who has taken time out to discuss my research. To all the team at *Ripperologist Magazine*, including Adam Wood, Chris George, Chris Scott, and Paul Begg, who have helped me with my research, offered me a platform to talk about Ripper related blogs and all things connected to Hull. Thank you!! I would also like to thank everyone at the *Rippercast Podcast*, especially the main man Jonathan Menges for his help and support. I would also like to take this opportunity to thank the listeners who have contacted me from across the globe as far away as Australia, New Zealand, Japan, China, Canada, America and of course Kingston upon Hull. I would like to take this opportunity to thank everyone on the social media circuit that has supported my work, with fantastic help and advice from the gang on Facebook and Twitter, and of course all those who have visited my Jack the Ripper blog.

Mike Covell

Other works by Mike Covell

Jack the Ripper related:

Jack the Ripper, From Hell, From Hull? Volume I

Jack the Ripper, From Hell, From Hull? Volume II

Jack the Ripper, From Hell, From Hull? Volume III

Walking Jack the Ripper's Hull

Jack the Ripper, Newspaper's From Hull: Vol: II

True Crime:

The Marfleet Mystery

The Caughey Street Murder

Paranormal related:

Mike Covell's Paranormal Hull – The Paranormal Files

Mike Covell's Paranormal Hull – The Ghost Files

Mike Covell's Paranormal Hull – The UFO Files

Mike Covell's Paranormal Hull – The Cryptozoology Files

Mike Covell's Paranormal Hull – The Press Perspective

Walking Mike Covell's Paranormal Hull

Printed in Great Britain
by Amazon